Practical Yacht Joinery

Practical Yacht Joinery

Tools, Techniques, Tips

Fred P. Bingham

International Marine Publishing Company
Camden, Maine

© 1983 by International Marine Publishing Company

Typeset by Journal Publications, Camden, Maine
Printed by The Alpine Press, Stoughton, Massachusetts
Bound by Robert Burlen and Son, Inc., Hingham, Massachusetts

All rights reserved. Except for use in a review, no part of this book may be reproduced or utilized in any form or by any means, electronic or mechanical, including photocopying, recording, or by any information storage and retrieval system, without written permission from the publisher.

Published by International Marine Publishing Company
21 Elm Street, Camden, Maine 04843
(207) 236-4342

Library of Congress Cataloging in Publication Data

Bingham, Fred P., 1907-
   Practical yacht joinery.

   Includes index.
   1. Yacht-building.   I. Title.
VM331.B586   1983   623.8'223   81-81418
ISBN 0-87742-140-4

Dedication

A casual remark sparked this book.

When my son Bruce was still designing yachts back in 1974, I often peeked over his shoulder. Occasionally I offered a suggestion such as, "If you built it this way, it might be easier" — or stronger, or cheaper, or handsomer. Often he would make the little changes then and there. After accepting many of my ideas with good grace, he finally exploded, "If you know so much, why don't you write a book? To get you out of here, I'll do the . . . drawings!" That day I started jotting down little thoughts, and six years later I was ready for his incomparable illustrations (without which I would never have taken on the task). But by then Bruce had been cruising between Boston and the Bahamas for five years, up to his spreaders in illustration, rarely ashore. Communication was almost impossible. So with a lot of trepidation and some encouragement from Roger Taylor, I brushed up on my World War II training in perspective and plunged in.

During those years my wife, Vivian, was patient, pushed me when I faltered, put up with my messy desks and drawing boards and our considerable lack of income, and accepted it all with clenched teeth behind a serene facade.

So now I thank Bruce for his casual remark, Roger for his vision, Vivian for her support. I dedicate my work to these three; without any one of them, nothing would have happened.

Contents

	List of Illustrations	ix
	Preface	xv
	Acknowledgments	xvii

PART ONE

	Introduction	3
One	The Woodworker's Basic Hand Tools	10
Two	More Basic Hand Tools	30
Three	Electric Hand Tools	43
Four	Stationary Power Tools	54
Five	Tools, Jigs, and Accessories You Can Build	81
Six	Tips, Techniques, Facts, Opinions	106

PART TWO

Seven	Nineteen Useful Joints and How to Make Them	120
Eight	Tying It All Together	133
Nine	Decks	154
Ten	Cabin Trunk Construction	165
Eleven	Building the Yacht Interior	179
Twelve	Niceties and Necessities Below Decks	208
Thirteen	Things on Deck	220
Fourteen	Bulwarks, Log-rails, and Toerails	238
Fifteen	Spars	244
	Appendix	265
	Index	269

List of Illustrations

CHAPTER ONE

Fig. no.		Page no.
1- 1.	Author's tool box	11
1- 2.	Hammers	12
1- 3.	Finish nail and nail set	13
1- 4.	Pulling finish nail	13
1- 5.	Ringed nail	13
1- 6.	Hardwood try square	14
1- 7.	Squares	14
1- 8.	Checking accuracy with square	14
1- 9.	Aluminum level	14
1-10.	Torpedo level	15
1-11.	Bevel gauge	15
1-12.	Crosscut saw and ripsaw	15
1-13.	Starting saw cut	16
1-14.	Starting saw cuts	16
1-15.	Layout of miter box	16
1-16.	Miter box	17
1-17.	Precision miter box	17
1-18.	Direction of miter cut	17
1-19.	Position of moldings	17
1-20.	Sawing dado with blocks	17
1-21.	Keyhole sawing opening	17
1-22.	Planes	18
1-23.	Jointing an edge	18
1-24.	Planes	18
1-25.	80-year-old scrubbing plane	19
1-26.	Roughing iron	19
1-27.	Rail hollowed with plane	19
1-28.	Rabbets	19
1-29.	Rabbet planes	19
1-30.	Brush thumb against plane iron	20
1-31.	Planing direction	20
1-32.	Planing end grain	20
1-33.	Using grinding wheel	21
1-34.	Using grinding wheel	21
1-35.	Plane iron refinements	21
1-36.	Honing plane iron or chisel	22
1-37.	Plane blade with chisel honing guide	22
1-38.	Brookstone honing guide	22
1-39.	Stropping paddle	23
1-40.	Installation of irons	23
1-41.	Assembly of block plane	23
1-42.	Match screwdriver to screw	24
1-43.	"English pattern" screwdriver	24
1-44.	"Four-bit" magnetic screwdriver	24
1-45.	Eggbeater-style hand drill	24
1-46.	Breast drill	24
1-47.	Brace with powerful chuck	25
1-48.	Solid center bit	25
1-49.	Jennings double-twist bit	25
1-50.	Drill bits	25
1-51.	Ship's auger bits	26
1-52.	Expansion bits	26
1-53.	Twist drills	26
1-54.	Blacksmith's drill bit	27
1-55.	Spade bits	27
1-56.	Rasps	27
1-57.	Surform plane	28
1-58.	Device for fine sanding	28
1-59.	Square-shank wood countersink	28
1-60.	Stanley Screw-Mate	28
1-61.	Prick punch	28
1-62.	Brad awl	28

CHAPTER TWO

Fig. no.		Page no.
2- 1.	Clamps	31
2- 2.	C-clamps	31
2- 3.	C-clamps in use	31
2- 4.	Replacing C-clamp button	31
2- 5.	Fast-action bar clamp	32
2- 6.	Gluing up cabin trunk side	32
2- 7.	Machinist's vise	33
2- 8.	Vise liners	33

Fig. no.		Page no.
2- 9.	Woodworker's end vise	33
2-10.	Marples chisels	34
2-11.	Slick	34
2-12.	Chisels	34
2-13.	Chiseling techniques	35
2-14.	Cutting mortises	35
2-15.	Hacksaw	35
2-16.	Hacksaw blade for curves	35
2-17.	Yankee spiral screwdriver	36
2-18.	Can lid protects surface	36
2-19.	Spokeshave	36
2-20.	Drawknife	36
2-21.	Marking gauges	37
2-22.	High-speed plug cutter	37
2-23.	Stanley plug cutter	37
2-24.	Plugs match grain	37
2-25.	Trimming plugs	37
2-26.	Hand cabinet scrapers	38
2-27.	Blade cabinet scrapers	38
2-28.	Using a scraper	38
2-29.	Adjustable cabinet scraper	39
2-30.	Sharpening a scraper	39
2-31.	Scribing or spiling compass	40
2-32.	Tool box with slots	40
2-33.	Tool box compartments	40
2-34.	Tool box	41
2-35.	Saw rack	42
2-36.	Making tool box	42

CHAPTER THREE

Fig. no.		Page no.
3- 1.	Skilsaw	44
3- 2.	Seven-inch saw	44
3- 3.	Power saw blades	45
3- 4.	Sabersaw	45
3- 5.	Sabersaw plunge cut	45
3- 6.	Avoid sawing into grain	46
3- 7.	⅜-inch drill	47
3- 8.	Screwdriver attachment	47
3- 9.	Drill stand	47
3-10.	Sander patterns	47
3-11.	Breaking sandpaper sheet	48
3-12.	Belt sander	48
3-13.	Belt sander motion	48
3-14.	Sander	49
3-15.	Stanley jointer	49
3-16.	Honing plane or jointer knives	50
3-17.	Router	50
3-18.	Effects with router	51
3-19.	Dovetail fixture	51
3-20.	Craftsman router table	51
3-21.	Sears guide bushings	51
3-22.	Routed spar construction	52
3-23.	Routing out hollow mast	52
3-24.	Router feed direction	53
3-25.	Routing shelf dadoes	53
3-26.	Dado fittings	53
3-27.	Sequence of operations	53

CHAPTER FOUR

Fig. no.		Page no.
4- 1.	Grinder reservoir	55
4- 2.	Narrow grinding wheel	55
4- 3.	Panel edges	55
4- 4.	Four-inch belt sander	55
4- 5.	Sanding concave surfaces	56
4- 6.	Jointer	56
4- 7.	Jointer technique	57
4- 8.	Jointer technique	57
4- 9.	Jointing wide stock	57
4-10.	Jointer pusher	58
4-11.	Craftsman jointer	58
4-12.	Bench shaper	59
4-13.	Shaper split fence	59
4-14.	Shaper setups	59
4-15.	Drill bit guide	60
4-16.	15-inch drill press	60
4-17.	32-inch radial drill press	61
4-18.	Cone pulleys	61
4-19.	Spade bit	62
4-20.	Spur bit	62
4-21.	Shaper fence	62
4-22.	Rotary planer for drill press	62
4-23.	Spur or machine bit mortise	63
4-24.	Mortising chisel	63
4-25.	Rockwell 14-inch bandsaw	63
4-26.	Craftsman 12-inch bandsaw	64
4-27.	Adjusting bandsaw blade tracking	64
4-28.	Bandsaw tension adjustment	65
4-29.	Blade guides	65
4-30.	Bandsaw blade secret	66
4-31.	Relief cuts	66
4-32.	Resaw setup	66
4-33.	Faulty resawing	67
4-34.	Guide for concentric sawing	67
4-35.	Stack sawing	67
4-36.	Saving material on wide shapes	67
4-37.	Table saw with extensions	68
4-38.	10-inch homemade saw	69
4-39.	Inserts for table saw	69
4-40.	Splitter	69
4-41.	Alignment of blade with gauge	70
4-42.	Alignment of fence and blade	70
4-43.	Power tool blades	70
4-44.	Power tool blades	71
4-45.	Miter gauge fence	71
4-46.	Table saw extension stop bar	72
4-47.	Hold-down for saw or jointer	72
4-48.	Resawing	72
4-49.	Sawing molding	72
4-50.	Simple pusher	72
4-51.	Dado set	73
4-52.	Dadoing half lap	73
4-53.	Improper jointing	74
4-54.	Sawing groove with adjustable dado	74
4-55.	Rabbeting with saw blade	74
4-56.	Molding head	74
4-57.	Molding heads	75
4-58.	Molding tips	75
4-59.	Making table saw movable	75
4-60.	Radial-arm saw	76
4-61.	Safe crosscutting	76
4-62.	Safe ripping	76
4-63.	Radial-arm saw positions	77
4-64.	Sawing thick stock	78
4-65.	Ripping crooked plank	78
4-66.	Drum sander	79
4-67.	Disc sander	79

Fig. no.		Page no.
4-68.	Molder-planer	80
4-69.	Open-side molder-planer	80

CHAPTER FIVE

Fig. no.		Page no.
5- 1.	Gilliom 10-inch saw	82
5- 2.	Home-built bandsaw	82
5- 3.	Gilliom shaper	83
5- 4.	Sliding auxiliary table (SLAT)	84
5- 5.	SLAT set up for mitering	85
5- 6.	Ripping on SLAT	85
5- 7.	Converting router to shaper	86
5- 8.	Holding jig	86
5- 9.	Pilot follows edges	87
5-10.	Collar prevents burning	87
5-11.	Shaper guide pin	87
5-12.	Home-built disc sander	87
5-13.	Setup for "planing" strips	88
5-14.	Rounding a corner	88
5-15.	Inexpensive disc sander	89
5-16.	50-cent motor mount	90
5-17.	Mitering slide	90
5-18.	Mitering moldings	90
5-19.	Cut-off squares	91
5-20.	Panel ripping guide	91
5-21.	Boring jigs	92
5-22.	Adjustable shelf drill jig	93
5-23.	Drill depth stops	93
5-24.	$5 portable table saw	94
5-25.	Portable table saw top	94
5-26.	Mitering with portable table saw	95
5-27.	Jointer hold-down	95
5-28.	Belt sander hold-down	96
5-29.	Box or finger joint jig	97
5-30.	Bench hook	98
5-31.	Wedge and taper hooks	98
5-32.	Shooting board	98
5-33.	Jointer blade grinding fixtures	99
5-34.	Scarfing jig	100
5-35.	Scarfing jig	100
5-36.	"Instant" planking vise	101
5-37.	Radial-arm saw stop	101
5-38.	Stock pusher	101
5-39.	Hinge gain	102
5-40.	Gain routing fixture	102
5-41.	Half-lap joint jig	103
5-42.	Jig to scribe camber	104
5-43.	Geometric layout of camber	104
5-44.	Determining camber by arithmetic	104
5-45.	Planes	105
5-46.	Rabbet plane	105

CHAPTER SIX

Fig. no.		Page no.
6- 1.	Twisted belt on jointer	107
6- 2.	Flexible board for sanding	108
6- 3.	Tubing for sanding	108
6- 4.	Sanding ideas	108
6- 5.	Bending by kerfing	108
6- 6.	Flathead vs. panhead screw	109
6- 7.	Screw size table	109
6- 8.	Handmade wooden cleats	110
6- 9.	Stresses on adhesives	112
6-10.	"Sticking" lumber	113
6-11.	Lumber cuts	114
6-12.	Dorade vent	114
6-13.	Traditional pinrail	115

CHAPTER SEVEN

Fig. no.		Page no.
7- 1.	T butt	121
7- 2.	Dadoed butt	121
7- 3.	Dovetailed dado	122
7- 4.	Mortise and tenon	123
7- 5.	Doweled butt	124
7- 6.	Dowel groove jig	124
7- 7.	Mitered joint	125
7- 8.	Mitering moldings	125
7- 9.	Splined miter	125
7-10.	Miter spline groove	125
7-11.	Middle and end half lap	125
7-12.	Single dovetail	126
7-13.	Tongue and groove	126
7-14.	Jig for tongue and groove	126
7-15.	Base for saw	127
7-16.	Alternating grains	128
7-17.	Long pieces joined lengthwise	128
7-18.	Splined joint	129
7-19.	Blind groove	129
7-20.	Rabbeted corner	129
7-21.	Glue block corners	129
7-22.	Rabbet block corner	130
7-23.	Dovetailed corner	130
7-24.	"Blind" dovetail joint	130
7-25.	Box joint	130
7-26.	Half-lap corner	130
7-27.	Rail, covering board, flat scarfs	130

CHAPTER EIGHT

Fig. no.		Page no.
8- 1.	Cradle for fiberglass hull	134
8- 2.	In-hull scaffold	134
8- 3.	Bulkhead fitting with tick stick	136
8- 4.	Laminated bulkhead panel layout	137
8- 5.	Bulkhead bonding	139
8- 6.	Bulkhead bonding in wooden hulls	139
8- 7.	Bulkhead in rabbeted sill	140
8- 8.	Finding perimeter of cabin sole	140
8- 9.	Sole beam supports	141
8-10.	Beam-to-hull attachments	142
8-11.	Joints	143
8-12.	Sole aperture framing	144
8-13.	Decking with holly strips	145
8-14.	Built-up breasthook	145
8-15.	Sheer battens	146
8-16.	Clamps for sawed beams	147
8-17.	Laminated beam jig	148
8-18.	Beam treatments	149
8-19.	Form for laminating beams	149
8-20.	Springing carlings	150
8-21.	Beam attachments	151
8-22.	Side deck beam joints	152
8-23.	Deck blocking	153

CHAPTER NINE

Fig. no.		Page no.
9- 1.	Lodging and hanging knees	155
9- 2.	Joints in plywood decking	155
9- 3.	Deck-edge construction	156
9- 4.	Sprung and straight decking	157
9- 5.	Covering board joints	158
9- 6.	Scarfing with router/shaper patterns	159
9- 7.	Taffrail and quarter knees	160
9- 8.	Deck canvas layout	161
9- 9.	Hand clamp for pulling canvas	161
9-10.	Fabric inboard edges	162
9-11.	King plank and canvasing	163
9-12.	WEST System teak deck	164

CHAPTER TEN

Fig. no.		Page no.
10- 1.	Strongback for trunk sides	166
10- 2.	Trunk tumblehome form	167
10- 3.	Trunk corner post layout	167
10- 4.	Rabbeting corner block	168
10- 5.	Scribing to deck and beams	168
10- 6.	Completed corner post	168
10- 7.	Position of corner post	169
10- 8.	Two-piece corner posts	169
10- 9.	Cabin trunk side cleat	170
10-10.	Alternate facing pieces	171
10-11.	Upper reinforcements	171
10-12.	Clamp for laminating trunk side	171
10-13.	Strip-planked cabin trunk	172
10-14.	Strip alignment tool	173
10-15.	Hidden edge gauge	174
10-16.	Cabin beams in sharpie	174
10-17.	Portlight with scuppered spigot	176
10-18.	Plastic deadlights	177
10-19.	Rabbeted trunk side	177
10-20.	"Window" frame or deadlight	177
10-21.	Gougeon and Root portlights	177
10-22.	"Old-fashioned" cabin trunk	178

CHAPTER ELEVEN

Fig. no.		Page no.
11- 1.	Extension transom and sea berth	181
11- 2.	Extension transom upper berth	181
11- 3.	Extension berth construction	182
11- 4.	Extension berth construction	183
11- 5.	Bunkboards	183
11- 6.	Canvas pipe berth	184
11- 7.	Root-type stretcher berth	184
11- 8.	Framing berth top opening	185
11- 9.	Plywood frame	186
11-10.	Backrest as a table	187
11-11.	Galley frame	188
11-12.	Galley front and countertop	188
11-13.	Dresser front	189
11-14.	Dresser frame	189
11-15.	Built-up dresser front	190
11-16.	Drawer construction	191
11-17.	Single dovetail	192
11-18.	Drawer fronts	193
11-19.	Door and drawer trim	194
11-20.	Inside drawer fronts	194
11-21.	Vented door	195
11-22.	Ash plywood doors	196
11-23.	Woven door panel	196
11-24.	Simple frame for paneled door	197
11-25.	Built-up door frame	197
11-26.	Stiffening plywood door	198
11-27.	Door trim	198
11-28.	"Yacht style" passage	199
11-29.	Bulkhead trim and corner moldings	200
11-30.	Molding mitering jig	201
11-31.	Bending jig for laminating	201
11-32.	Bulkhead corner moldings	202
11-33.	Lightweight bookshelf	202
11-34.	Companionway ladders	203
11-35.	Companionway ladder and desk	203
11-36.	Ice chest	204
11-37.	Ice chest ideas	204
11-38.	Installing insulation	206
11-39.	Hull ceiling	206

CHAPTER TWELVE

Fig. no.		Page no.
12- 1.	"Cubicle"	209
12- 2.	Allegra's accommodations	210
12- 3.	Sam Rabl's hidden head	210
12- 4.	Sam Rabl's folding wash basin	212
12- 5.	Galley rack	212
12- 6.	Drop-leaf table	213
12- 7.	Folding table	214
12- 8.	Drop-leaf table	214
12- 9.	Gimbaled table	214
12-10.	Folding table	215
12-11.	Removable table leg	215
12-12.	Medicine chest	216
12-13.	Fiddle styles	217
12-14.	Boring and spacing jig	218
12-15.	Unfinished stove cover	218
12-16.	Magazine rack	218
12-17.	Bulkhead racks	219

CHAPTER THIRTEEN

Fig. no.		Page no.
13- 1.	Sliding hatches	221
13- 2.	Hatch cover	221
13- 3.	Hatch cover	222
13- 4.	Jig for splitting tubing	222
13- 5.	Sliding hatch	224
13- 6.	Hatch with contrasting plugs	224
13- 7.	Drop boards and louvered door	224
13- 8.	Louvered companionway doors	225
13- 9.	Four hatches	226
13-10.	Hatch cover hinges	227
13-11.	Dorade vent	228
13-12.	Dorade vent	228
13-13.	Propane tank box	228
13-14.	Generator cover	228
13-15.	Layout of grabrail	229
13-16.	Mahogany handrail	229
13-17.	Anchor brackets	230

Fig. no.		Page no.
13-18.	Running-light boards	230
13-19.	Cockpit coaming construction	231
13-20.	Fairing coaming to trunk	231
13-21.	Coaming block	231
13-22.	Rabbeted molded corner	231
13-23.	Cockpit hatch scuppers	232
13-24.	Teak hatch covers	233
13-25.	Cockpit hatch cover	233
13-26.	Skylight frame construction	234
13-27.	Skylight cover	234
13-28.	Gratings	235
13-29.	Dado setup for making gratings	235
13-30.	Teak cockpit grating	236
13-31.	Oval cockpit grating	236
13-32.	Rounded helmsman's seat	236

CHAPTER FOURTEEN

Fig. no.		Page no.
14- 1.	Bulwark construction	239
14- 2.	Lofting stanchions and bulwark cap	239
14- 3.	Joining caps	242
14- 4.	Rails and rail scarfs	242
14- 5.	Toerail at bow	243

CHAPTER FIFTEEN

Fig. no.		Page no.
15- 1.	Hollow spar sections	246
15- 2.	Mast taper layout	247
15- 3.	Spar stave	248
15- 4.	Spar bench styles	249
15- 5.	62-foot mainmast	250
15- 6.	Stave shifted to follow grain	250
15- 7.	Layout of joints	251
15- 8.	Matching staves on spar bench	252
15- 9.	"Make do" spar clamps	253
15-10.	Saw settings for spar radii	254
15-11.	Spar construction	254
15-12.	Masthead crane and tangs	255
15-13.	T-boom mainsheet bails	256
15-14.	Spar layout	258
15-15.	Devices for eight-siding spars	259
15-16.	Handmade spar calipers	260
15-17.	Sanding boards	260
15-18.	Hollow-core mast plan	261
15-19.	Hewing a solid spar	262

Preface

This is a book for doers and dreamers. I hope it helps doers in the task of building a satisfying watercraft. I also hope it helps the many who have never quite gotten around to building a boat. You are the ones who feed on hope year after year, always dreaming of the day your own boat will dip its keel into the water. You are the dreamers always looking ahead to next year. Bless you all, for I am one of you!

Although this book is primarily for the doers, I will try to give you dreamers some of the stuff that hopes are built on. I do this with a clear conscience, for it is your dream (and mine) that makes life bearable. Perhaps, however, there's more here for you than mere dreams. As you read along, you ought to be able to pick up information that can be turned into skills. Try your hand at first with simple things — a small storage cabinet, a bookcase, a picture frame, a cradle. Then try a small skiff. With success in these tasks, you will find it easy to move on to a pretty daysailer. Suddenly, the dreamer who once was convinced he had two thumbs per hand is saving to buy plans for a cruising yacht. If this happens, my effort in putting together this book will have been worth all the trouble and time involved.

For you doers, the book is a complete and comprehensive treatment of the tools and skills needed to produce a finely made wooden craft. I hope reading it will help you solve every problem you encounter as you build your own dream yacht.

Acknowledgments

A proper acknowledgment of the sources of the information in this book would have to include influences that date from my childhood. I was taught to sail as I was taught to walk. I cannot live away from water. I was fascinated by the working of wood, from whittling out wind propellers at the age of eight to building a 36-inch sailing model at 13. I began filing away articles from *The Rudder* and *Yachting* magazines in the early 1920s, lost them in 1940, began again in 1945, and gave these to my son in 1974.

I built, rigged, and sailed a couple of skiffs and finally a real sailboat, a Snipe, in 1931. Around that time I made a religion of L. Francis Herreshoff and compiled fat folders bearing the names of great designers — Olin Stephens, John Alden, Winthrop Warner, S.S. Crocker, Ralph Winslow, William Atkin, Fenwick C. Williams, Charles G. MacGregor, Ralph Wiley, Uffa Fox — too many to list them all. I still cherish (and use) the original series by Herreshoff, *The Common Sense of Yacht Design,* as well as his "How To" articles from *The Rudder,* designs such as *Nereia, Prudence, Marco Polo,* and *Rozinante.*

Howard I. Chapelle wrote a dozen or so intriguing articles for *Yachting* on our native working vessels — the No Man's Land boat, the pinky schooner, Chesapeake crabbing skiffs and bugeyes, and others. From these designs and those of the designers listed above, I acquired an appreciation and, yes, a knowledge of lines, rigs, and construction. Then in 1936 came Chapelle's *Yacht Designing and Planning,* which, added to my old *Skene's Elements of Yacht Design,* changed my life — I *had* to build boats — and in 1941 arrived the boatbuilder's Bible, *Boatbuilding,* followed in 1951 by *American Small Sailing Craft.*

Charles G. MacGregor was a *complete* naval architect and much more. He is little remembered for his almost anonymous contributions (under the names of more prestigious offices) to the designs of famous racing fishing schooners and large commercial craft and yachts. He also designed plywood aircraft (the Mosquito Bomber) in the 1930s, became a consultant to plywood manufacturers, and then was a regular contributor to *The Rudder.* He was the world's authority on the design and construction of plywood boats while still continuing his designing of lovely carvel-planked sailing yachts. In 1937, plywood was still a dirty word, but MacGregor was convincing because of his commitment to strong, practical, economical small boat and yacht construction. I built from four of his designs, (two of them created to my order) ranging from a 15-foot fin-keel daysailer to a 27-foot cruising sloop. One was a 23-foot carvel-planked cruising cutter with plywood decks and (horrors!) a mast stepped on deck. All were outstandingly successful (he called them expendable), low in cost, and the plywood hulls, decks, and bulkheads were still going strong 25 years later (the last I heard). MacGregor proved to me that there are always two or three ways to build, and low cost does not mean cheap.

During the four-year life of my little boatshop, I directed the work of a group of French, Scottish, Swedish, and German boatbuilding *crafts*men. My book learning and limited experience were sufficient to run the shop unprofitably, but I depended on the incredible skills of those wood artists. And I received from them a college education in boatbuilding and joinery techniques that I wish I could have continued. In 1940 I was exposed to all of the best at Fisher Boat Works, Inc. — experimental torpedo boats, a half-dozen yachtlike sub-chasers, fine yacht repair and construction. And it was there that I was privileged to spend much time looking over the shoulder of Nelson Zimmer, a talented naval architect and meticulous draftsman. Unfortunately, I had a little skill but less patience, so I absorbed only a small portion of his teaching. The approaching war forced me into aircraft production, technical writing, industrial advertising, and other matters far removed from my love. From that time on, I was an amateur boatbuilder.

In 1972, chafing for need of an activity, I began to build a few cabinets, bookcases, simple contemporary furniture. Having no background in this field, I went to the books for information. With my boatbuilding, joinery, and design experience, I gained a small income and much satisfaction from my one-man shop. The old urge was eased by a couple of sailing dinghies, a Delaware Ducker, a canoe, and the Allegra design (which appears in the Appendix to this book). My cabinetwork techniques and handy gimmicks were born of trial and error, the necessities of one-man operation. I had only the books to aid me. The following books were most helpful in the shop and later in this book: *New Complete Woodworking Handbook* by Jeannette T. Adams and Emanuele Stieri, *The Home Workshop* by William R. Wellman, *Complete Book of Home Workshops* by David X. Manners, *How to Build Your Own Workshop Equipment* by Arthur Wakeling, *Fun with a Saw* by R.J. de Cristoforo, *Complete Book of Woodworking* by Rosario Capotosto, *Cabinetmaking* by Paul Haynie, *Woodwork Joints* by Charles H. Hayward, *How to Work with Tools and Wood* by Robert Campbell and N.H. Mager.

These acknowledgments must also include the excellent book *Boatbuilding Manual,* originally a magazine series written by Robert M. Steward. Then there are the countless articles by Jim Emmett, published over many years as *The Skipper's Tool Chest* and *Jim Emmett's Boating Aids* in *The Rudder.* And last but not least, there are *National Fisherman*'s monthly "Comments From Here and There," written by the incomparable authority John Gardner.

I can only say in summary that I have learned something from every one of these sources in over 60 years of reading.

Practical Yacht Joinery

PART ONE

Introduction

You wouldn't be reading this book if you weren't interested in building something that floats. But what is it you see in your dreams? Is it a boat or is it a yacht? Any watercraft can be considered a boat. A yacht, however, is a watercraft designed, built, and fitted for racing or for pleasure.

A yacht is a vessel embodying beauty of line, excellent materials, careful workmanship, and fine finish. A yacht is designed to provide comfort, safety, satisfactory progress through the seas under all or most conditions, and pride of ownership. Given these attributes, a yacht also will be a sound long-term investment.

The crucial difference between a boat and a yacht of the same approximate dimensions may be their relative values. You have probably haunted yacht brokerage offices and are familiar with the wide variation in prices asked and received. A poorly built boat may sell for half the price or less of the similar yacht. Will yours be a boat or a yacht? The decision is yours to make because you can control quality to a large extent, even if you are not a skilled craftsman. Remember, too, when you make this decision, that the cost difference might be only a few hundreds or thousands of dollars, but that resale figures could be 10 or 20 thousands apart. Your decision could mean prompt and profitable resale, or complete indifference, perhaps even a flat refusal by brokers to handle your "home-built" or "backyard" vessel.

I don't have to point out that the well-constructed and well-designed yacht lasts years longer, performs better, and is far safer — as well as dry, warm, and comfortable. Best of all, such a vessel gives its builders a tremendous feeling of pride. No 50-footer you buy will ever give you the stirring exultation you feel when the 25-footer *you* built kisses the still water upon launching. That is, *if* you built it the best way you knew how.

It is the intention of this book to increase your knowledge of fine woodworking and to help develop your skills. Granted, some of you may feel that you have little natural ability with woodworking tools. This may be because you have never had an opportunity to work with one of the old craftsmen, to learn his ways. I can't put you in that position, but if you will read carefully, you will learn much that will increase your skill and productivity. And if you practice and experiment cautiously, your accomplishments will exceed your limited experience. Keep in mind that a large part of the fine craftsman's art is patience; patience and perseverance will enable you to produce creditable work, perhaps more slowly than your skilled friends, but with increasing precision as you acquire the touch.

This book was started on the assumption that there

are many who want to be told *how* to perform neat joinerwork rather than *what* to do. The plans of most yacht designers provide detailed construction, joiner sections, and other views that show what goes where in a yacht's interior and rig. But these plans rarely tell how to make and join the components to produce a complete and satisfying effect. Even the best boatbuilding books seem to assume that you have all the tools, that you know how to use and maintain them, and that you have the skills to perform all the steps in hull, interior joinery, deck, trunk cabin, hatch, and spar construction. "Rabbet the forward and after staves of spars as shown." Do you saw out that rabbet on a table saw or with a power handsaw, plane it out, rout it, or give up and haul it to a lumber mill?

In recent years there has been renewed interest in wooden boatbuilding. I don't know if this new interest is responsible for wonderful publications such as *WoodenBoat*, or if the publications have sparked the revival of interest. What I am sure of is that all of the editorial attention is fanning the flame. Magazines such as *Sail, Cruising World, Sea & Pacific Skipper*, and others are doing a great job telling readers *how* rather than *what*.

This book does not try to be all things to all people. You need not have a boatbuilding or carpenter's background to find it useful. Nor does the possession of such a background rule out the book as a source of valuable information. Take what you need from Part One on the selection, use, and maintenance of hand tools, power tools, and woodworking machines. The discovery of any shop tips new to you will make the time worth spending. Part Two describes alternate ways to construct cabin soles, bulkheads, doors, drawers, tables, cabin trunks, hatches, decks, rails, spars, and a score of other items; try some of the several methods illustrated. The chances are that some of these are not the traditional ways of doing things. Indeed, some may be more economical, some easier. All are described in detail, including the different tools able to do each job. All are illustrated with perspective drawings and photographs that anyone can understand.

YOUR DREAMS AND YOUR PLANS

About those plans. Your choice of the yacht to build is, of course, influenced by both your ability to construct it and your ability to pay the bill. It is my conviction that the pointers in these pages will bolster your courage. Aim high! You might find that your cabin interior, for example, can be improved by digressing slightly from the designer's plan. You might add a drawer here, a folding seat there, a decorative molded edge, or a clever fiddle. Perhaps your increased confidence will enable you to take on a larger job — a 42-schooner, say, instead of a 36-foot ketch. And you just might be able to complete the larger craft in nearly the same time, but in better fashion. That's why I hope you are reading this book before you fall irreversibly in love with a specific design. Even if you are highly skilled, and perhaps have already built a hull or purchased a kit, maybe — just maybe — this book will influence your style of workmanship and your plans from this point on.

I hope, too, that you are a reader of everything pertaining to the sea and boats. If you are new to this wet and fascinating world, I suggest as a starter that you plan to spend many hours at the library — they won't let you remove the best sources of information. At the library you will find files of boating magazines going back many years (the older the better, it seems to me). Dig into publications such as *Yachting, Rudder, Motor Boating & Sailing, Sail, Sailing, Sea & Pacific Skipper, Cruising World,* and others, including *National Fisherman* and *WoodenBoat* (excellent articles on construction). Take your notebook, for you'll find more information than you can possibly assimilate. Fortunately, a limited amount of photocopying is permitted.

On your bookshelf at home you must have *Boatbuilding* by Howard I. Chapelle, the unquestioned bible of builders all over the world for many decades. I recommend two of his other works, *Yacht Designing and Planning* and *American Small Sailing Craft,* too. Read all of Robert M. Steward's *Boatbuilding Manual, Second Edition.* Also get *Sensible Cruising Designs,* by L. Francis Herreshoff. You'll chuckle at his amusing philosophy and treasure the nuggets in the detailed plans of his famous Nereia, H-28, Marco Polo, and others. And you'll learn some of the fine points of wood construction from a master.

The sailing and yachting magazines frequently describe many other excellent books on design, construction, tools, sails, rigging, engines, and so on.

THE OLD HAT TRICK

You must do much more than merely read, however. If you are a beginner, or perhaps have limited sailing or boating experience, put on your hat and hang around marinas, boatyards, and boat shows. Take your camera along. If you are not yet able to distinguish a fine yacht from a fair or mediocre one (size alone is no criterion), ask around. Pick the brains of brokers. They're all nice guys and boat lovers, too. Just tell them outright that you want to see some examples of good construction. If these yachts are in slips, you are in luck, because you won't have to use a dinghy to inspect them. Do obey the rules of marine courtesy, and do not go aboard any vessel unless invited. Some owners will permit photographs, some will not.

If you can, take close-up photographs of hatches, cabin trunks, doghouses, rail caps and bulwarks, winch bases, pinrails, cockpit details, stemhead treatments, taffrails, and fittings — in short, everything you can get. Study the design of joints in the covering board and rail cap; notice how the decking is nibbed into the king plank; examine the construction of teak gratings; and check wherever one piece of wood joins another. If the pieces lock together, observe how the job was done and how snug the joints are. Such work may not show up on film. Make a simple sketch if you think a photograph won't do the job. You must gather and classify information of this kind because designers rarely show details this complete in their plans. They assume that their creations will be constructed by professionals who like to interpret designs according to their habit or the practice of the builder's yard. Thus, there is no need for extensive detail. If a designer did include such details, few could afford the cost. Most of the plans prepared today for amateur as well as professional construction include 15 to 20 large and remarkably detailed drawings. It hasn't always been this way. I remember building yachts up to 45 feet in length from designs by great names such as Winslow, Alden, MacGregor, Mower, and others, and the entire package consisted of six prints. All of the detail was left in the hands of the shop. Of course, that was back in the 1930s and 1940s, when life was much simpler.

THE REVIVAL OF WOOD CRAFTSMANSHIP

It is sad indeed that fewer and fewer real craftsmen are around today. They are dying off — or going into other fields that pay a lot better. In addition, the advent of fiberglass hulls and high-speed production has resulted in a need for quickly done joinery of lower quality. As a result, there are few apprentice programs. Fortunately, however, the last few years have seen the start-up of a small number of schools where one works and learns on traditional small craft such as pulling boats, peapods, wherries, and so on. We can only hope that this trend will continue and strengthen.

Fortunately, the spurt of construction of ferrocement vessels that started in the late 1960s and early 1970s has ended. However, a good many hulls are still being started, many of them quite large. I wish I could say that this movement was accompanied by an increase in the number of skilled craftsmen. Note that I do not mean that a ferrocement boat is, per se, a poor-quality boat. In one recent year, my son, Bruce, and I have seen as many as six that were competitive with better-than-average fiberglass one-off construction. In the same period, however, we inspected close to 50 jobs. Most of the poor work we saw was the result of impatience that led to sloppy workmanship. The best examples were built by men with little or no marine construction experience who adhered closely to three rules: They went strictly by the book; they kept at a task patiently until they got it right; they dashed down to the marina for a look-see whenever they ran into a problem beyond their experience. In all cases, these builders looked around until they found answers from qualified sources. Go thou and do likewise, and you too will achieve your quality goals.

YOUR DESIGN

Without a good design, no vessel is worth the material or the effort that goes into it. If you can afford the cost of a design geared to your specific needs, go to an established, recognized, thoroughly qualified naval architect or yacht designer. Or purchase a stock plan that fits your purposes. Be sure to take your designer into your confidence in as great a detail as possible. Developing a design that fully meets your needs is a complex and time-consuming process. The one exception in the choice of a design is this: Some yards and shops have over the years developed excellent workboats, fishing craft, yachts, and other vessels. You might not be able to purchase a design for one of these boats, but you should be able to contract for a boat in various stages of completion, from the bare hull up. This approach is more appropriate in the selection of a powerboat hull for conversion to a pleasure yacht. Very few shops build sailboats that were not designed by qualified and recognized designers.

Conversion of a workboat into a yacht requires major alterations in interior, cockpit, deck, equipment, power, and so on. Unless a boatyard has actually been successful producing such conversions, be wary. Any single alteration will affect displacement and/or the distribution of displacement. So if the boss says, "Oh, sure, she'll take a flying bridge," watch out! She might take it all right, but she might also roll like a destroyer. Find a designer who will at least check the alterations you require. Or, better yet, have the designer prepare drawings showing the required changes. This service will cost money, but it will be well spent. You may find that the yard or shop is qualified to perform these tasks. If so, by all means use their services.

(continued on page 9)

All of the beautiful workmanship shown in the photographs on the following pages was performed by an amateur boatbuilder, John Paul White. He purchased a Flicka hull, then built the decks, cockpit, cabin trunk, interior, and the spars for a gaff rig. His superb craftsmanship reflects his patience and his determination to achieve perfection. The photographs by Reg Hinnant demonstrate clearly that John reached his goal.

Top: *Traditional octagonal bowsprit. Note toerail clearance over deck. This is Bruce Bingham's 20-foot Flicka design.* **Center:** *Amateur-built spars and gallows frame are perfectly made and finished. This yacht stands out in any harbor.* **Bottom:** *Neat mast step on deck. Gaff jaws are replaced with efficient laminated, curved style.*

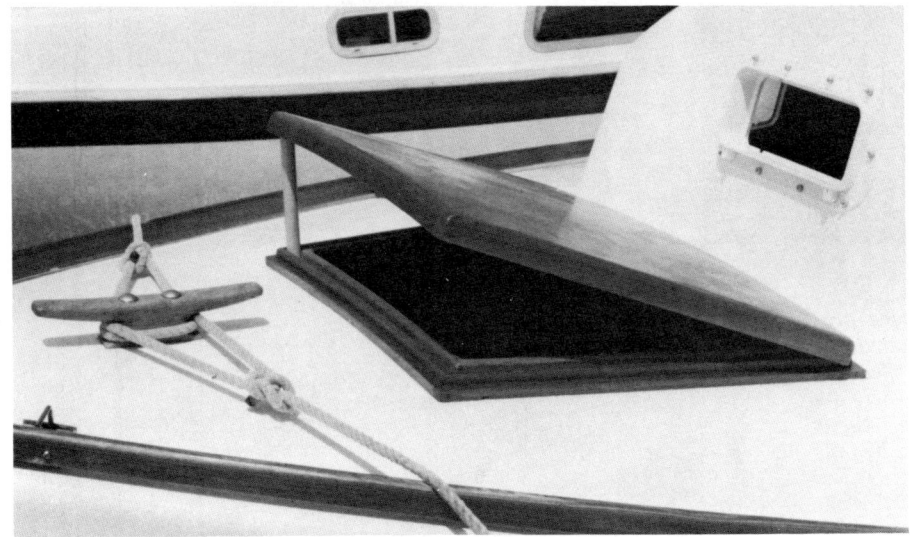

Top and Center: *Forward hatch fits into rabbet and over channel for double coaming. Excellent workmanship and design.* **Bottom:** *Companionway facing nicely scuppered. Strong handhold above ladder. Superb joinery by an amateur craftsman.*

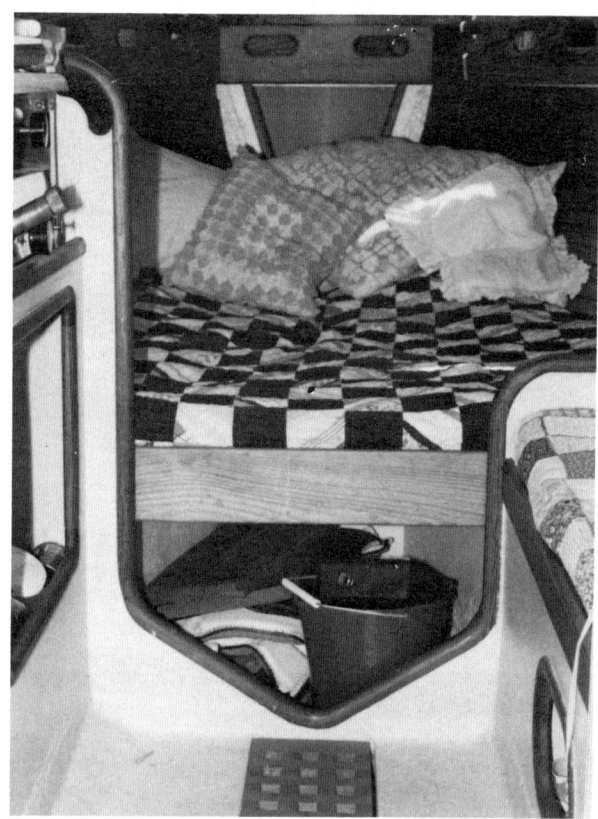

Above left: *Pine sliding hatch, double protected by scuppered channel covered by chromed brass trim.* **Above right:** *Perfect access opening trim. Hand grips everywhere are excellent. Note teak grating in sole.* **Right:** *Laminated mast-step beam supported by pine hanging knees and partial bulkhead.*

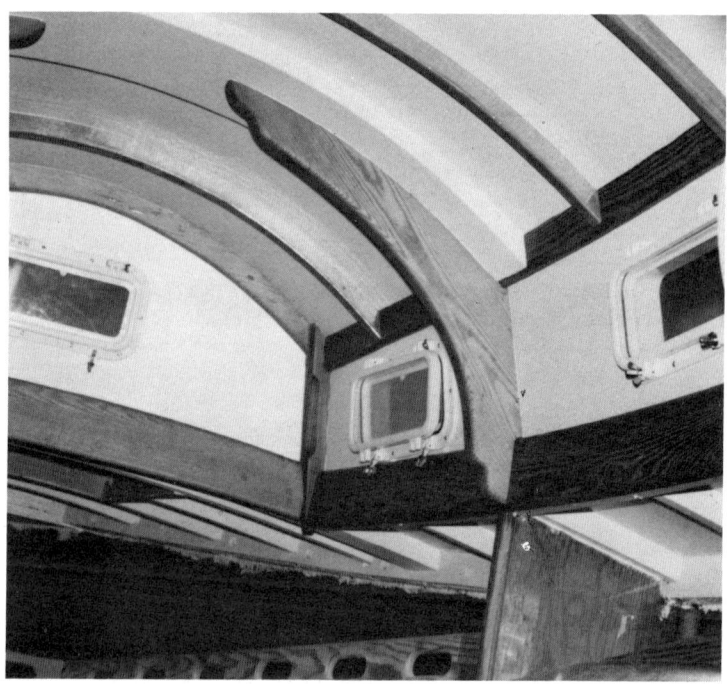

Galley fiddles and opening trim are 100-year-old pine from a barn. Design and execution equal top professional quality.

(continued from page 5)

The point is, you can't just buy a hull and then put a head here, a galley there, tanks under the berth, install 250 horsepower instead of 150, change to diesel, and so on. In sailing vessels, alterations of any kind are extremely critical, for they may affect stability, trim fore and aft, and speed. Moreover, stability affects a boat's ability to carry sail, its motion, and perhaps even the skipper's ability to work the vessel day after day under adverse conditions without killing fatigue. Don't assume that adding weights not called for in the design will increase the vessel's resistance to heavy weather by making it stiffer. On the contrary, excessive extra weight low in the hull produces motion not designed for. This in turn places excessive strain on the spars and rigging, and might be dangerous to crew members.

In short, do not make alterations without a designer's approval. Better yet, accept the original design as is — or obtain another design. If you must have a conversion, ask about the cost of the redesign work. Just remember, a designer is a professional. You are paying for his trained eye and years of experience. So be prepared for these alterations to cost money. But remember, too, what a small cost this is compared with the final value of the yacht. What is a few hundred dollars against many thousands? Or against years of satisfaction and peace of mind.

ONE

The Woodworker's Basic Hand Tools

The selection, use, and maintenance of woodworking tools and machinery require close scrutiny, good judgment, and careful work habits. Close scrutiny to ensure that you select tools that will stand you in good stead over a long period; good judgment to ensure that you don't go overboard and purchase more tools than you will need; and careful work habits for obvious reasons. The next four chapters will describe the selection, use, and maintenance of tools and machines suitable for yacht joinery.

Not all of the tools described are essential, for if time is not a problem, almost any job can be done with hand tools alone. If, on the other hand, you are going to invest a large sum in the yacht itself, plan also to set aside a substantial kitty for tools.

If you have already built your hull, you probably have much of what is needed to complete the job. If you plan to purchase a hull, however, and the proposed vessel's value would be about $50,000 if professionally built, then you probably should allocate as much as $2,500 for tools and equipment. If your yacht will be in the $5,000 class, you might benefit by investing as much as $1,000 on tools. Don't be alarmed by this high ratio of cost to final product. And remember that if you buy quality machines and tools, you almost certainly will recoup 90 percent or more if you decide to sell them. At the present rate of inflation, you might even make a profit.

As you read along, you'll be able to decide which tools you need and can finance right now, and which to build and add later as work progresses. Any tools you make from my instructions will sell for at least half the price of the average professionally manufactured item. Thus, you stand to save substantially by investing the time needed to make your own tools.

If you are looking for information on the traditional tools used by skilled boatbuilding craftsmen in the "good old days," you won't find much here. The methods I describe do not require those exotic tools, although if you have access to such tools and learn how to use them, more power to you. By all means pick up any handmade wooden planes you find, but be prepared to pay high prices.

With the hand tools listed in this chapter you'll be able to do almost anything in joinery that you want to do. I'm sure much good work has been done with far less. If you lay in a modest assortment of power tools, however, many of these hand tools will not be needed. Moreover, don't rush out and buy all these tools at once. When you anticipate the need for a tool you don't own, try to decide whether there will be additional uses for it. If it turns out to be a one-time use only, devise a

Figure 1-1. *The author's tool box. When every slot is full, the set of tools is complete.*

way to do the job with the tools you have, or borrow or rent the needed tool. For example, why buy a circle cutter for a drill press if you can do the job just as well with a keyhole saw or an electric sabersaw?

SOME USEFUL SOURCEBOOKS

For more complete information on tools, I recommend the many fine books on cabinetmaking and workshop procedures available. Several that I have found especially valuable are:

The Home Workshop, by William R. Wellman, Van Nostrand-Reinhold, 1953.

The Complete Woodworking Handbook, by J.T. Adams and Emanuele Stieri, Arco, 1969.

The Complete Book of Home Workshops, by David X. Manners, Popular Science Publishing Co., 1969.

All of these are now out of print. There are many others probably as good. Read as many as you can handle, as well as the boatbuilding references mentioned in the Introduction.

WHERE TO FIND TOOLS

Quality hand tools are available at local hardware stores, chains such as Sears and Ward's (obtain their fine special tool catalogs), industrial tool and equipment houses, building supply and home-improvement centers, lumberyards, and so on. Wherever you buy, play it safe and buy only well-known name brands. The higher quality is worth the small difference in price, and the guarantees are worth having.

Less obvious sources for tools are sometimes worthwhile. In California there is an institution called the "swap meet," although little is swapped. These gatherings of sellers and buyers on weekend mornings at drive-in theaters or fairgrounds are sometimes called flea markets. Often what people try to sell is junk; very frequently, however, you can pick up useful tools at very good prices. You may be able to bargain. He asks $2, you offer $1. Perhaps you get the tool for $1.75. Here are some of the items and their prices that I have found at "swap meets":

Three 36-inch bar clamps, $5 each
Dozens of C-clamps, $.75 to $2
Electric motors, $2 to $15, depending on horsepower
Small Stanley router, $22
A 24-inch jointer plane, $7.50
Antique drill press, $5
A 50-foot steel tape, $1.50

I've even found interesting things at rummage sales. Would you believe a Delta Homecraft jointer (somewhat rusted, but little used, with blades still sharp), minus fence, for $5? A heavy-duty Ward's reciprocating sander for $3? I have heard that you can "steal" tools at pawn shops if you are the first customer on Monday mornings. And don't forget the used-tool store, although I have rarely seen anything much more than 10 or 15 percent under new list price. I make a habit of reading the classified Miscellaneous For Sale and Machinery columns. Garage and yard sales, too, are often productive.

THE BASIC HAND TOOLS

Nail or claw hammer
6-inch try square or combination bevel square
Carpenter's square
12- to 16-foot pocket tape
Plane (9-10 inch), smooth or jack
Crosscut saw, 10 point
Backsaw, 12 inch, 14 point or more
Ripsaw, 5 to 7 point
Two straight screwdrivers
Two Phillips-head screwdrivers
Hand drill or breast drill
Wood bits, ¼ to 1 inch
Brace for wood bits
Set of twist drills, ¼ to ½ inch
Set of small twist drills, $\frac{1}{16}$ to ¼ inch
Wood countersink, squared shank
Rat-tail file
Rasp, flat/half-oval combination
Kit of nail sets
Fine oilstone
Brad awl or prick punch
Scribing compass

Portable woodworker's vise
Chisels, ¼ to 1 inch
Hacksaw
Keyhole saw
Marking gauge
Bevel gauge
Six 3- or 4-inch C-clamps
Six 6-inch C-clamps
Grinder

OTHER TOOLS YOU'LL WISH YOU HAD

Slick, a long chisel 1½ inches or wider
Yankee screwdriver
Spokeshave
Drawknife
Expansion bit
Counterbore bits, ⅜ and ½ inch
Ship's augers, 5⁄16, ⅜, ½ inch
Plug cutters, ⅜ and ½ inch
Bench vise
Dado plane or rabbet plane
Hand scraper
Cabinet scraper
Fore plane, 18 inch
Jointer plane, 22-24 inch
Block plane, low angle
Miter box
Three or four pipe clamps or bar clamps over 36 inches

SELECTING HAND TOOLS

Before offering some tips on the use of the basic hand tools, I'll comment on their selection. I'm now using many tools that are from 25 to 50 years old. I own and occasionally use a 24-inch wooden jointer plane over 100 years old. My Yankee screwdriver was purchased in 1937. Never reject a tool simply because it is old. A plane never wears out, although the blade may become quite short from years of grinding. Blades, of course, are easily replaced. Chisels can last for generations if the handles are renewed. The same may be said of many of the other tools listed.

First, look for a quality name. Finish per se means little. Some of the leading manufacturers produce tools that are not as nicely ground, polished, and/or enameled as their top-of-the-line products. In most cases the materials are the same, the tools perform just as well, and the prices are considerably lower. Always look for defects such as hairline cracks in a used tool. And never buy used tools that show evidence of welding or brazing.

If you are totally unfamiliar with tools, their features, and relative costs, write to manufacturers or pick up

Figure 1-2. *Hammers.* **Top to bottom:** *16-ounce nail or claw hammer, 16-ounce framing hammer, 12-ounce cabinetmaker's hammer.*

catalogs at tool supply houses. A few hours of study will give you much of what you need to know about quality tools. Send for the catalogs of Woodcraft (313 Montvale Ave., Woburn, MA 01888), Brookstone (127 Vose Farm Rd., Peterborough, NH 03458), and others offering good-quality and many rather hard-to-find tools. An excellent source of information is a carpenter, cabinetmaker, boatbuilder, or almost anyone else in the wood construction field. He'll tell you the names to look for, such as Stanley, Plumb, Millers Falls, Estwing, Vaughan, Chicago Pneumatic Tool, Black and Decker, Skil, Delta (now Rockwell), and others equally trustworthy.

USING HAND TOOLS

The use of many hand tools may seem quite obvious. If you already possess woodworking skills, you may consider some of my remarks superfluous. Remember, however, that other readers may not have your experience, skill, and dexterity. Note too that people with know-how and real skill using and maintaining tools sometimes use them in ways that can damage the work, the tools, or themselves. So please be tolerant, and look carefully for any information you can benefit from.

Hammers

Your hammer should be a claw hammer of the type shown in Figure 1-2. The curved claws are designed for pulling nails easily, but not for ripping apart old nailed work. The framing hammer with rather straight claws is usually a 20-ounce tool. This hammer is used for framing or general construction work and is useful for splitting, jamming between boards, and so on. Yours should be 16 ounces for general construction and joinery, and a much lighter one of about 12 ounces for much of the lighter cabinetry and trim work.

Look for a slightly convex hammer face. A face ground dead flat will bend finish nails and is more likely

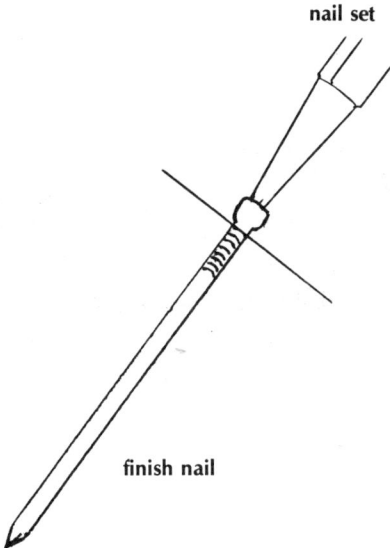

Figure 1-3. FINISH NAIL AND NAIL SET

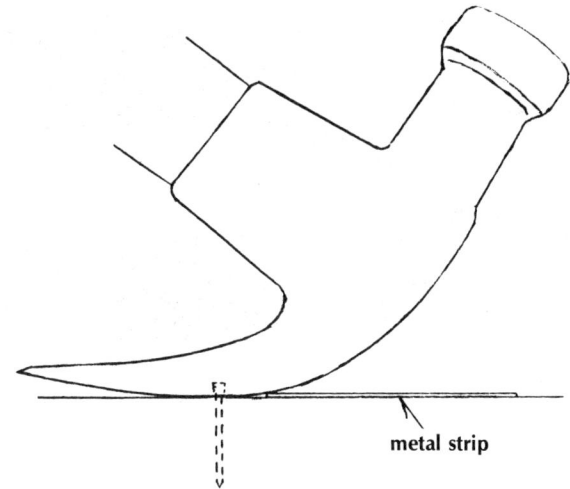

Figure 1-4. PULLING A FINISH NAIL

to mar your work. Of course, you should never drive a finish nail flush; you let it protrude $\frac{1}{16}$ to $\frac{1}{8}$ inch and then set it below the surface with a nail set. See Figure 1-3. No man breathes who has not let his hammer slip off the nail and dent the wood, so make sure you use a hammer with a convex face. Wooden handles are still preferred by many, but always replace a split or loose one immediately. Fit the new handle using any cutting tool — spokeshave, chisel, plane, rasp, and so on — and drive in two steel wedges, which you can pick up at any hardware store. The steel-shaft type of hammer is satisfactory, but I suggest that it be from a good U.S. manufacturer such as Plumb, Estwing, Stanley, Vaughan, or Craftsman. I happen to like the new fiberglass handle with a rubber grip. In any event, if the hammer balances well in your hand and feels good, that's it.

A word of warning. Never attempt to pull a nail without a block or pad under the claws to protect the work surface. Use a piece of ¼-inch plywood if the nail head is almost into the wood. Then use a piece of ¾-inch stuff up close to the nail as it is drawn out. To pull a finishing nail with just the head out, jam the tapered slot of the claw hard against the nail so the inner sharp edges cut into the shank, then insert a piece of $\frac{1}{16}$-inch metal between hammer and work. Figure 1-4 shows how this is done. It isn't good practice, but I've been guilty of using my try square blade when unable to get a piece of ¼-inch plywood under the hammer.

If you should get paint, glue, or grease on the face of your hammer, wipe or sand it off or you will surely bend nails you are hammering. If you are driving the serrated Anchorfast nails (Figure 1-5) so widely used in boat work, you have a problem. Unless the lead or pilot hole is correct, these soft nails bend easily, especially in oak. If you try to draw the nail, it will pull out all the surrounding wood with it or the head will come off. Don't

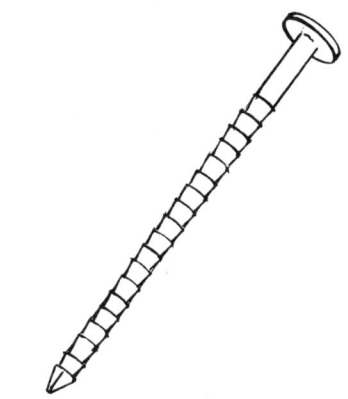

Figure 1-5. RINGED NAIL

try. Instead, grasp the head with pliers or Vise-Grips and bend the nail back and forth until it breaks off. If part still projects, set it below the wood surface with a large nail set and drive a new nail close by.

Squares

Many of the good try squares have hardwood heads. See Figure 1-6. If one shows signs of having been used as a tack hammer, reject it. This applies to the all-steel type, too. You will use this tool constantly, so keep it handy at all times. Keep it clean and rub a little oil into it occasionally. All of these suggestions apply to your carpenter's (or framing) square, too (Figure 1-7). If you find a good one, but it is somewhat rusted, sand it with emery cloth after soaking with Wrench. If you can't read the marks easily (this sometimes happens with new ones, too), wipe a contrasting paint into the indentations, then wipe the surface clean. The carpenter's

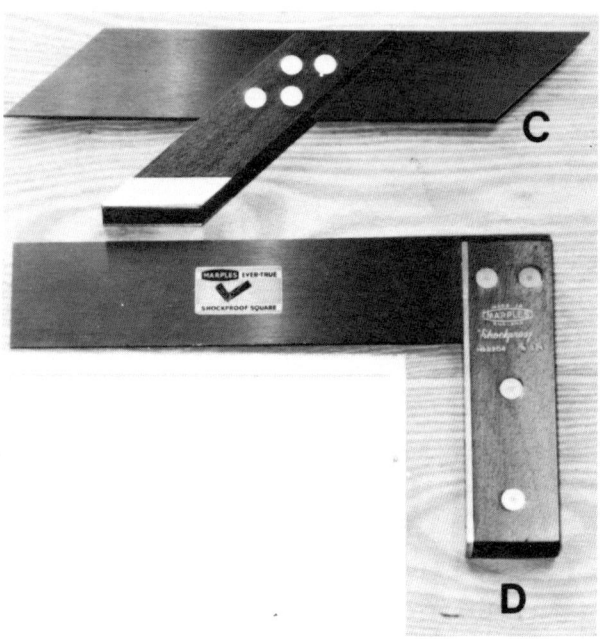

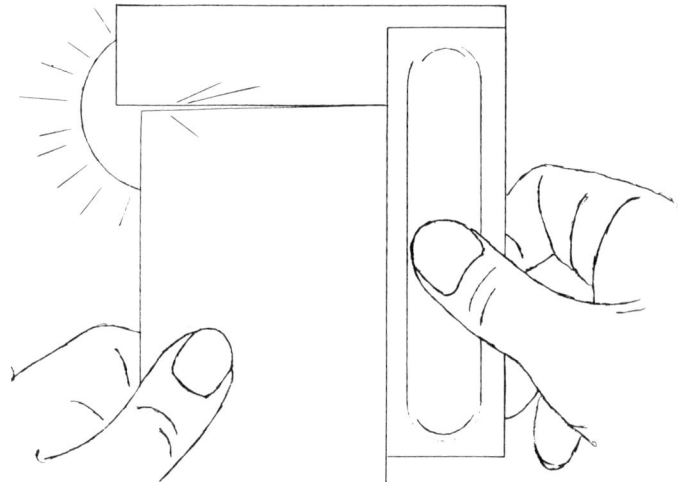

Above: Figure 1-6. *Hardwood try square with steel handle is inferior to those with rosewood handles but takes rough handling.* **Top right: Figure 1-7.** *Carpenter's or framing square is useful for laying out all kinds of angles, checking mitered joints, as a power-saw guide, and so on. The 12-inch sliding-T 45-degree bevel square is always useful.*

Figure 1-8. CHECKING ACCURACY WITH A SQUARE

square is needed for squaring larger parts such as cabinet doors, for drawer assembly, for checking table saw alignment, and for many other jobs. I make frequent use of a steel square as a guide for my Skilsaw when the work is too long or too heavy to cut on the table saw. Simply clamp the square accurately with two small C-clamps and run the sole or base of the saw along the square. For checking, use any square by holding the work piece and the square between you and the light, as shown in Figure 1-8.

Levels

I use an old wooden level with brass trim. The new aluminum ones, however, with 45-degree-angle features, adjustable bubbles, and so on, are quite versatile (Figure 1-9). A 24-inch level is usually adequate for inside work, but you should have a longer one. If you want to use an old one or the cheap wooden type you find on bargain tables, check it against building walls, columns, doorways, and floors. It must read the same with either face on the vertical or horizontal surface. If the bubble is always off to the same side of the mark, don't use the level. The little torpedo-type level (Figure 1-10) made of die-cast zinc or aluminum is a necessity in restricted areas. In a pinch, a 4-inch line

Figure 1-9. *The extra 6-inch length of this 30-inch aluminum level is handy. A 48-inch level is desirable. If you use an inexpensive wooden level, check it frequently.*

level will do for leveling shelves and for work where you can't get in with the 24-incher. Don't, however, count on these short levels for long surfaces such as cabin sole beams, bulkheads, and berths.

Speaking of levels, here is an important point. Do not plan to deck your hull or cover it over in some way and then complete the interior after launching. Your hull is not yet on its lines, so nothing is level or plumb. Moreover, the constant motion of the hull in water prohibits the use of instruments. Everything has to be taken from the waterline or the cabin sole and out from a centerline. All problems would be multiplied, wasting much good time.

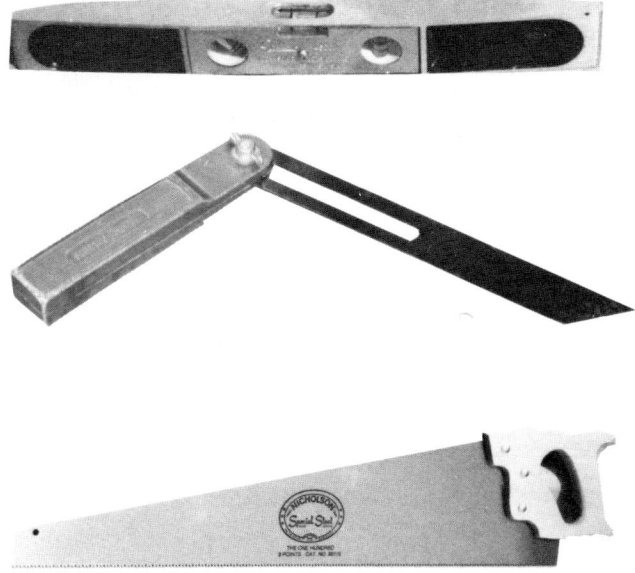

Top: Figure 1-10. *The little torpedo level is a must for working in close quarters. Laid on a straightedge, it takes the place of a long level.* **Center: Figure 1-11.** *A bevel gauge or square is used constantly in boat work.* **Bottom: Figure 1-12.** *The hand crosscut saw is used frequently, the ripsaw rarely. Ten or 12 points is best for clean work, 8 points for framing.*

Bevel Gauge

The bevel gauge (Figure 1-11) is a simple little tool that is indispensable for picking up angles in degrees from a protractor, setting saw blades for bevel cuts, marking for repeated angle cuts, and a myriad of other uses. You can make one out of hardwoods. The newer ones have plastic bodies, instead of the traditional hardwoods. They'll still last a hundred years.

Pocket Tape

A 12- or 16-foot tape measure is essential for taking inside measurements. If you are building scaffolds, molds, and spars, however, you must have a 50-foot steel tape.

Saws

Unless you have a hand power saw, or a bench or table saw, you will need four handsaws. The first is a 26-inch crosscut, with 10 points or more to the inch (Figure 1-12); then a ripsaw, usually 5 to 7 points; then a backsaw, 14 points, with a 12- to 14-inch blade; and, finally, a keyhole or compass saw. The crosscut and ripsaw may have either a straight back (stronger) or a skew back (curved and lighter). I think you might saw a straighter line with the straight back, but it's no big thing. The possibility of sawing a lot of plywood suggests the need for a really fine-toothed crosscut saw to reduce splintering. Otherwise, the backsaw is used for close cuts where a minimum of splintering is required.

To start a saw cut, place the side of your left thumb above the teeth to guide the saw safely on the waste side of the mark. See Figure 1-13. Never saw on the mark so that you lose it. You need some stock to plane off to square up the rough edge. You can split the line when you get to be expert. It is a good idea to pick up the habit of marking with the square, and then making another light mark an eighth of an inch or so from that line on the waste side. This will prevent accidental sawing on the wrong side of the mark — a real calamity. And don't think this is an error limited to greenhorns.

To get a really clean saw cut, mark with a knife. A score about $1/64$ inch deep is plenty to give you a nice dado edge, and it's much more accurate than the sharpest pencil.

Start a cross-grain cut with the saw at about a 45-degree angle above the work, with your head directly over the beginning point. See Figure 1-14. Rip at a higher angle, about 60 degrees. Always start with one or two upward strokes, dragging toward you with your thumb still guiding the saw. If your cut wanders from a straight line, twist the handle for the next few strokes to bring it back. Of course, the saw-blade side should be at right angles to the surface of the work.

A backsaw is often used in a miter box. In its simplest form, a miter box is an arrangement of three pieces of lumber (preferably hardwood) nailed together to form a U-shaped channel (Figure 1-15). Two 45-degree cuts and one of 90 degrees are carefully laid out and sawed with the backsaw perfectly square to the bottom of the box. These cuts must be absolutely true or the miter box will just waste hours of your time. You can buy a quite

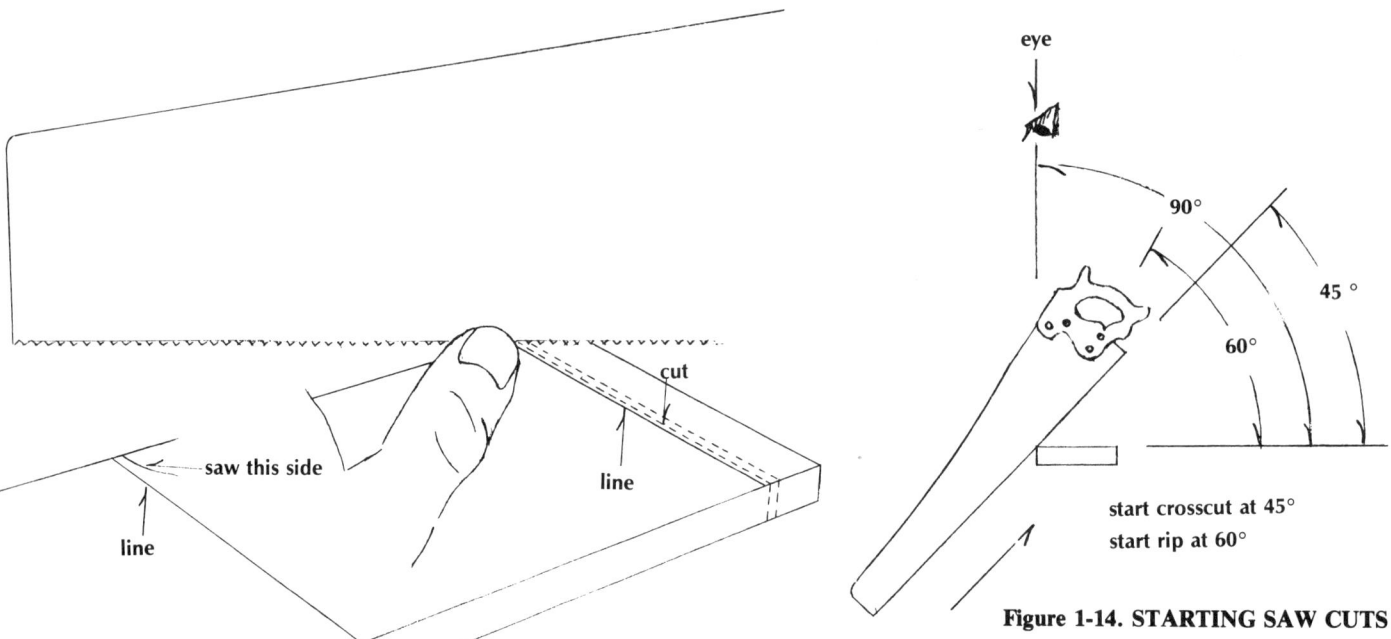

Figure 1-13. STARTING A SAW CUT

Figure 1-14. STARTING SAW CUTS

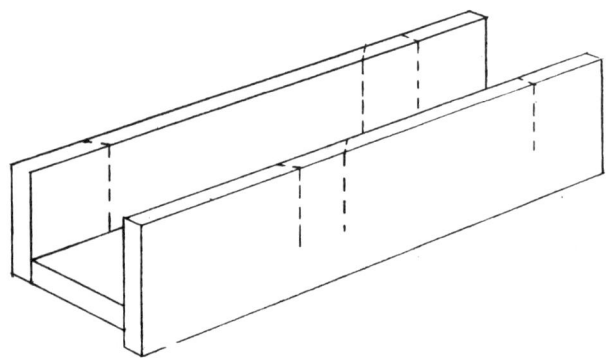

Figure 1-15. LAYOUT OF SIMPLE MITER BOX

satisfactory miter box in hardwood at any lumberyard or hardware store (Figure 1-16), so it's hardly worth your time to make one to save a couple of dollars. More elaborate affairs run from about $10 up to $100 (Figure 1-17). Most of these provide rapid setting of many angles. Even the wooden cheapie is fine for quick 90-degree cuts in small stuff, so keep one handy.

It's good practice to tack or clamp the miter box to a bench or a plank on sawhorses. When cutting, hold the piece hard against the back of the box, taking extreme care that the cut will be exactly where you want it. In measuring for mitering, always make a light pencil mark showing the direction of the miter (Figure 1-18). It's easy to become confused, especially with irregular moldings. Never set an irregularly shaped molding on the molded back (Figure 1-19); you won't get a true angle. The work will tend to creep sideways, so hold it tight or clamp it. Start cutting with a short pull or two, then lower the saw to the horizontal as the cut deepens. If you find that a miter has been cut just a bit too long, clamp another piece that has just been cut off against that end. The saw will cut through as if the union were not present.

It's a good idea to tack a piece of ¼-inch plywood to the bottom of the miter box to take the saw cuts, rather than saw up the box itself. Also, provide some kind of support for the ends of long pieces of molding, or you may get splitting at the cut end.

It is possible to dado (cut a groove across the grain) with a backsaw by clamping a block right on the line, placing the blade against this block, then clamping another block against the blade so there is no wobble. Repeat this for the other side of the dado. Watch your measurements carefully! Lastly, make another cut between these two cuts to make it easier to chisel out the dado. See Figure 1-20. Take care, too, to see that your saw does not rock, which will produce a dado shallower in the middle. There will be more on this later in the book.

A handy device for use with a backsaw or almost any crosscut saw is a bench hook. This can be an 8- to 12-inch-long 1 by 6 with a cleat screwed and glued across each end on opposite sides. You place one cleat in a vise or clamp, or tack the assembly to a bench or plank. Then you hold the work piece against the other cleat while you saw. A bench hook may be used with a crosscut saw by clamping it at the end of the workbench so you may stroke properly.

By the way, if your handsaw refuses to cut straight, even after lots of practice, take it to a saw sharpening shop. Even new saws sometimes have poor blade settings, or an amateur may have done a bad job trying to set and file your used saw. More set on one side will make even the best saw wander. I will say no more about sharpening saws because this is a matter for experts. If you are interested, some of the good woodworking texts give instructions.

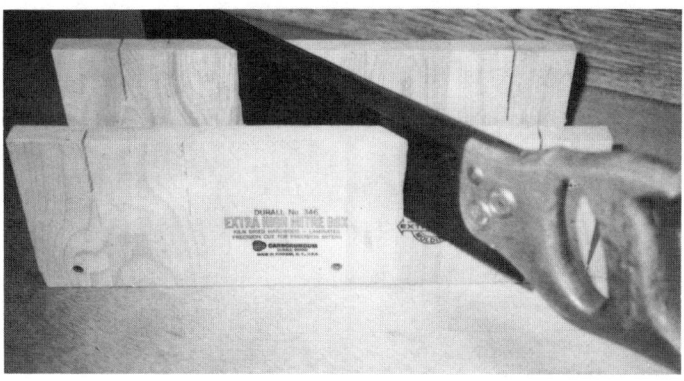

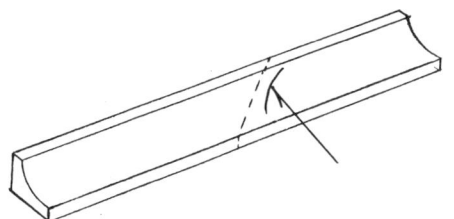

Figure 1-18. GENERAL DIRECTION OF MITER CUT

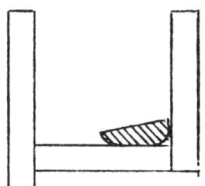

Figure 1-19. NEVER LAY MOLDINGS WITH IRREGULAR SIDE DOWN

Top: Figure 1-16. *This store-bought miter box has extra depth for large moldings. It is adequate for most work, but not for precise molding joints.* **Above: Figure 1-17.** *A precision miter box, one that cuts within .005 inch, is a necessity for fine handwork. Such boxes take 20-inch and longer blades.*

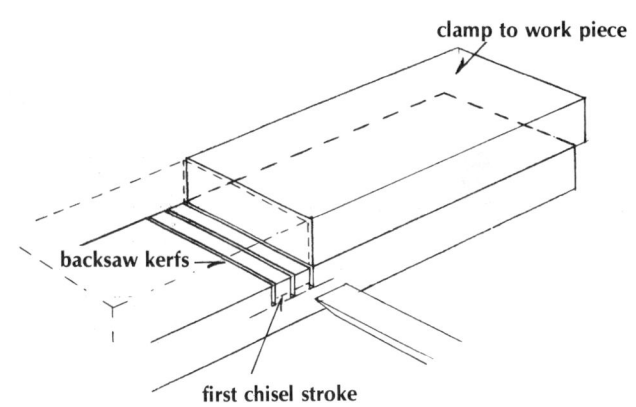

Figure 1-20. SAWING DADO WITH BLOCKS

The other saw you will require is a keyhole saw. This tool has a narrow tapered blade about 12 inches long. A keyhole saw is useful for cutting quite sharp curves of any kind, especially openings for portlights and other circular fittings. To make a circular cut, bore a hole ½ to ¾ inch in diameter near the mark and start the cut from this point (Figure 1-21). The blade of a keyhole saw is very coarse, so the resulting cut is rough. It's best to saw at least $\frac{1}{16}$ inch from the line so the rough surface can be dressed out with a spokeshave, rasp, chisel, or a coarse sanding block. Note that keyhole saw blades are very soft, there being little or no temper. As a result, they tend to bend easily. Just straighten a bent blade by hand and return to the job.

Planes

The plane is your most-used tool. See Figure 1-22. In boat carpentry and joinery, no sawed surface is left rough. At the beginning, you may get by with a smooth plane about 9 or 10 inches in length, especially if your sawing is accurate when ripping to a line. Such a plane

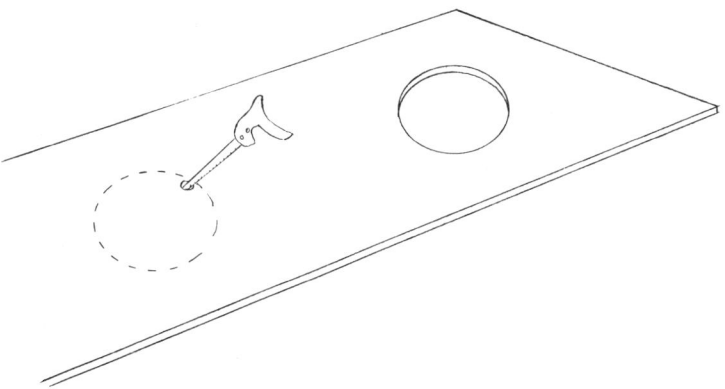

Figure 1-21. KEYHOLE SAWING OPERATION

Figure 1-22. *Planes. Clockwise from top: 24-inch jointer, 15-inch jack plane, 6-inch block plane, 9-inch smooth plane.*

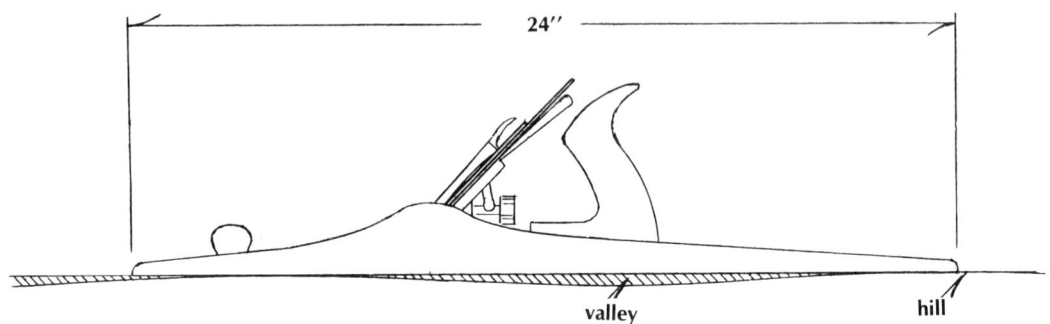

Figure 1-23. JOINTING AN EDGE

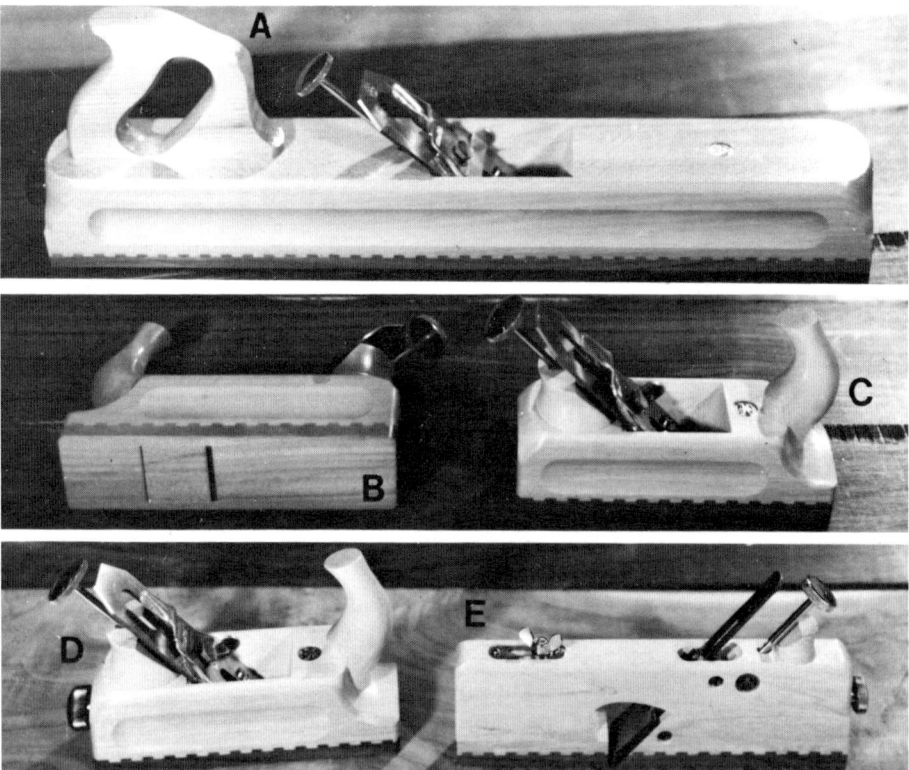

Figure 1-24. *Planes.* **(A)** *Primus 25⅝-inch jointer plane, 2⅜-inch blade.* **(B)** *Smooth plane, for fine cuts in wild grain; adjustable throat.* **(C)** *General smooth plane for finishing.* **(D)** *Jack plane. The low angle permits thick cuts; the workhorse of planes.* **(E)** *Shoulder rabbet plane. Adjustable front shoe provides great accuracy. All of these planes are European red beech; soles are lignum vitae. They have been made by Emmerich since 1852. (Courtesy Woodworker's Supply)*

will remove quite a lot of stock, but its relatively light weight is not the best for this task. The next size is the jack plane. This tool runs about 11 to 15 inches in length and is used for taking off material to a line. You then split the line with the smooth plane set fine. Check with the try square as the work progresses.

The next largest is the jointer plane, about 24 inches in length. This tool is best for long, straight work. It takes out high spots by spanning from one to the next more accurately than a jack plane will, as shown in Figure 1-23. The jointer is followed by a few strokes of the jack or the smooth plane. There is a size of plane between the jointer and the jack called the fore plane, but I doubt whether you will need quite this much variety. See Figure 1-24.

At the other end in size is the block plane, which runs from 5 to 6 inches in length. The blade of a block plane is set at a low angle desirable for planing across the grain and for plywood edges. This tool is great for all very fine work, such as dressing the surfaces of jointed

Figure 1-25. *An unusual 80-year-old scrub or roughing plane with 1¼-inch rounded blade. Used diagonally across the grain, also for hollowing planking. Also used as a rabbet plane with a square blade.*

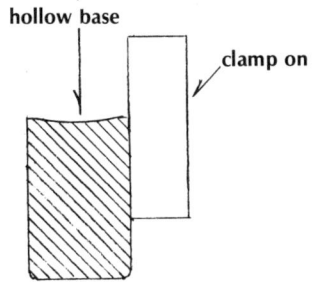

Figure 1-27. RAIL CAN BE HOLLOWED WITH PLANE

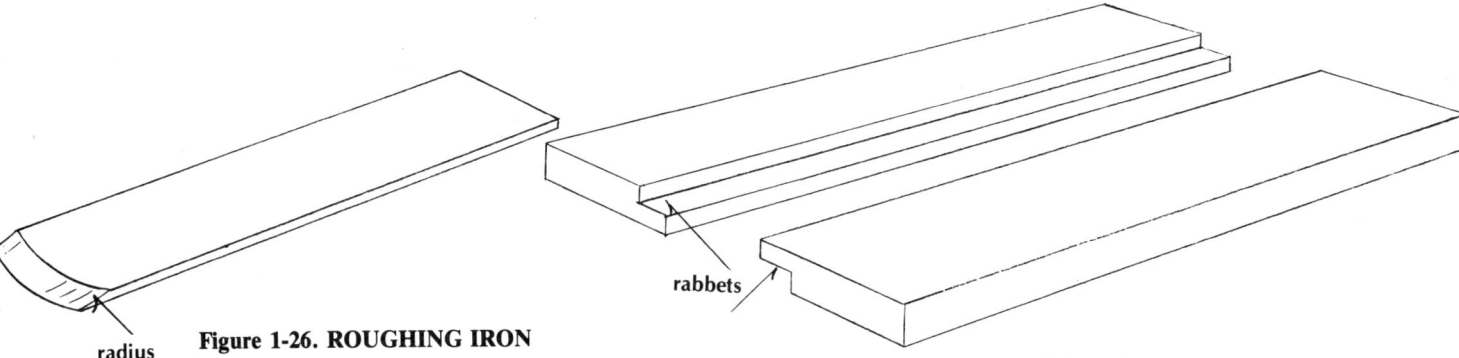

Figure 1-26. ROUGHING IRON

Figure 1-28. RABBETS

parts after assembly. If it is kept sharp, it will take off an almost transparent shaving. (It *must* be kept sharp to produce satisfactory results.)

Another special-purpose plane is the dado plane. (Remember, a dado is a groove cut *across* the grain, and a groove is a groove cut *with* the grain.) A dado set is a combination of blades used on a table saw to cut dadoes and grooves. If you don't have a table saw, you have to make these cuts with a backsaw and a chisel. The dado plane, which is very narrow, is run through the dado or groove to clean up the bottom, remove saw kerfs, and smooth out the cut. In Chapter Five, which discusses tools you can make, I will show you how to make a fine dado plane using a chisel as the iron.

On rare occasions, you may need a scrub or roughing plane (Figure 1-25). Usually quite narrow, perhaps 1¼ inches wide, the blade of a scrub plane is ground to an arc. See Figure 1-26. This plane can be used to remove material rapidly, either straight or diagonally across the grain (especially on oak). Then, after nearing the line with a jack or jointer to fair the surface, you finish up with a smooth plane. You can have an extra blade for your smooth plane ground to an arc for such roughing jobs. The scrub plane is similar to the planes (usually wooden — see Chapter Five) used for hollowing the backs of planking. Hollowing is good practice when a piece such as a handrail, toerail, hatchrail, and so on, must be bedded down securely, especially when being fastened to a curved surface like a cabintop. In such cases it is best to clamp a guide piece on the side of the work piece so the hollowing is centered accurately (Figure 1-27).

There will be many rabbet joints in your vessel. As shown in Figure 1-28, a rabbet is a recess running along the edge or end of a piece. Another matching piece is fitted into the first piece. You can power saw a rabbet out and then plane to the finished depth, as described above for the dado plane. Fine rabbet planes, however, come in sets with a guide rail or fence for planing parallel to an edge. The sole is slotted at the right side so the blade can cut right up to the side of the rabbet. Some planes have an additional seat in the forward end so the blade can plane up into or within ¼ inch of corners. This is called a bullnose. Several rabbet planes are shown in Figure 1-29.

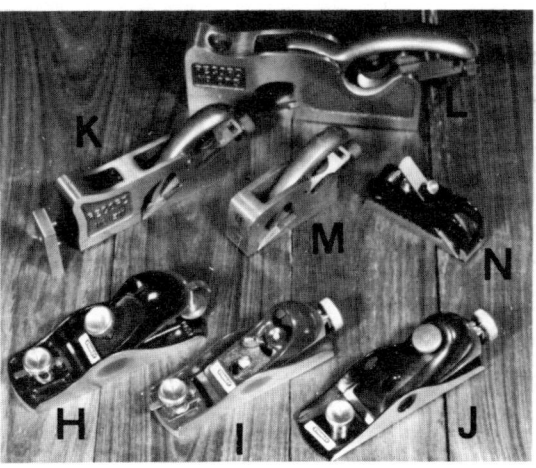

Figure 1-29. *Rabbet planes.* **(H)** *Fine 21-degree block plane.* **(I, J)** *12-degree planes.* **(K, L)** *Blades on these planes may be moved forward to bullnose position.* **(M)** *Four-inch adjustable-nose plane.* **(N)** *Plane that makes coarse to fine cuts. (Courtesy Woodworker's Supply)*

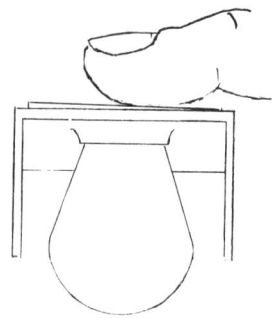

Figure 1-30. BRUSH THUMB AGAINST IRON AND/OR SIGHT TOWARD EDGE

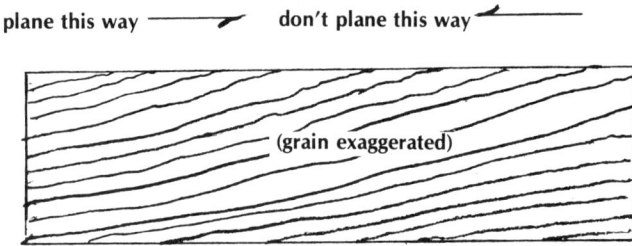

Figure 1-31. PLANING DIRECTION

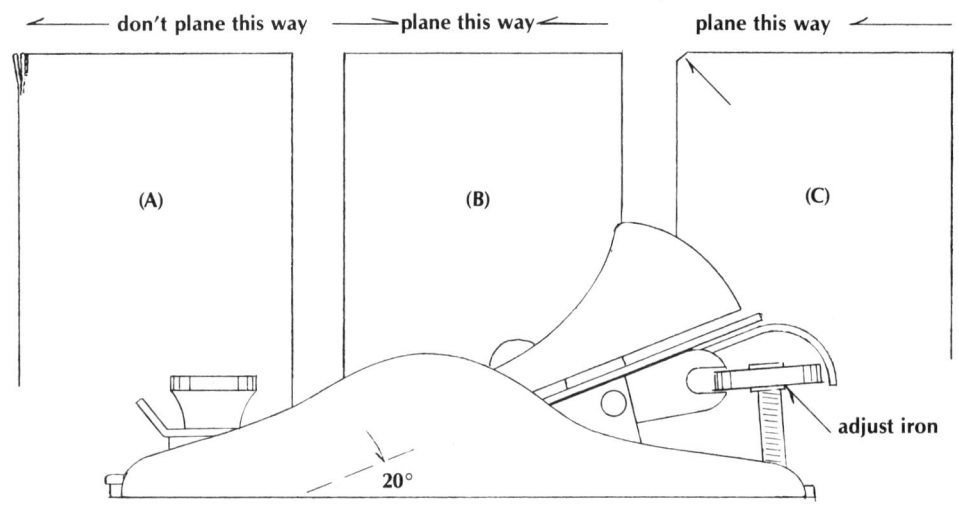

Figure 1-32. PLANE END GRAIN WITH LOW-ANGLE BLOCK PLANE

Wooden planes were once the mark of a real craftsman in boatbuilding. They were made of lignum vitae, beech, and other extremely hard, wear-resistant woods. These planes were generally much lighter than their cast-iron counterparts and were prized for planing hull planking, dressing spars, and other tedious jobs. Directions for making wooden planes can be found in books on making tools the old way. Or they can be purchased from such firms as Woodcraft Supply, Brookstone, and others. Be prepared for rather steep prices. Many, however, say they are worth it.

Setting a Plane

Always set a plane blade for the minimum cut for the first few strokes to find the direction of the grain. The depth of cut may then be increased slightly in terms of how much material has to be removed, but keep in mind that it is far better to take it off in many fine shavings than to try to hack it off in just a few strokes. Also, the finer cut allows you to check repeatedly for squareness of the edge. There are two ways to find the proper adjustment of the plane blade. One is to sight down the sole toward the cutting edge of the blade. You should be able to see whether either side is high or low and whether the squared blade will cut fine or coarse. The second way is to brush against the cutting edge with the ball of the thumb (never lengthwise on the cutting edge), as shown in Figure 1-30. This second method will come naturally with experience. To me, it is the only way.

To adjust the blade, hold the plane on its back, sole up, and grasp the knurled nut in your right hand. As you sight down the sole toward the cutting edge, turn the nut until the edge appears as a hairline. The edge probably won't be perfectly parallel to the sole, so adjust by moving the lever right or left as needed. Feel the blade with your thumb: does it drag about the same near both corners? Try the setting on a piece of scrap. Back the blade or advance it until you get a fine shaving. Now examine your work piece for grain direction. Never plane against the grain, for the surface will be very rough and large chips may tear out. See Figure 1-31. If the grain is in long waves (reversing direction), you may have to plane both ways by reversing the piece in the vise and finish by block sanding. Remember, you want sharp, fine shavings.

When you are through with a plane, even momentarily, lay it on its side, never on its sole. And when you're ready to store a plane, screw the blade back in so there is no chance of its being nicked or dulled.

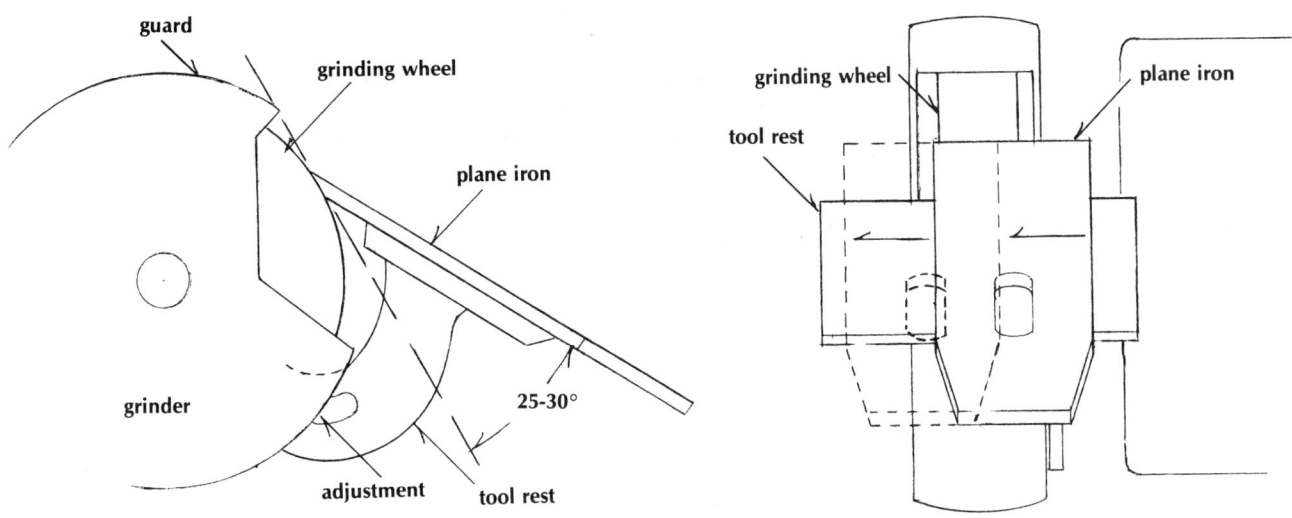

Figure 1-33. USING THE GRINDING WHEEL

Figure 1-34. USING THE GRINDING WHEEL

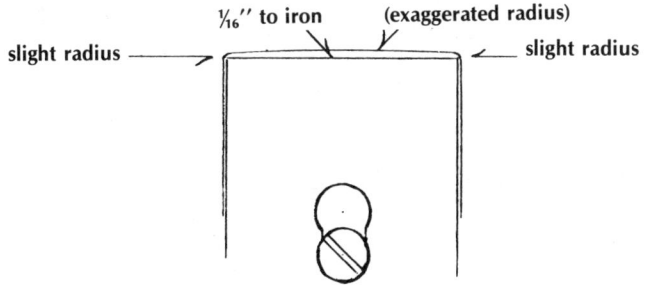

Figure 1-35. PLANE IRON REFINEMENTS

The Plane Stroke

Start a stroke with a bit of weight down on the forward knob, then apply equal pressure on knob and handle through the middle of the stroke. At the end, let up on the knob. Your shavings should have a fine feather edge at each end if your strokes are nice and long and you don't rush.

If you need to plane square across the grain at the end of a piece, do so before planing the edges along the grain. If you do not, you will surely split off the far edge (Figure 1-32(A)). This is not easy with a smooth plane, and it is even more difficult with a jack. The proper tool is the little block plane, generally used with one hand or with only slight pressure and control with the forward hand. The low angle of the blade has a slicing effect and produces a nice finish. To prevent splintering, plane toward the center or to a safe distance from the far edge, then reverse the piece in the vise and again plane to the center or somewhat beyond, watching the marks and checking for square both ways (Figure 1-32(B)). Another way, if there is ample stock, is to plane off a little corner of the far edge. Now you can stroke all the way across the end without danger of splitting (Figure 1-32(C)).

Sharpening a Plane Blade

If you keep in mind that a plane is actually a wide chisel held to a precisely controlled depth of cut, you will better understand its sharpening needs. The blade must be sharpened like a chisel, and hollow ground on an electric grinding wheel or your hand grinding wheel. The cutting edge must then be whetted on an oilstone. Your grinding wheel has some kind of flat tool rest that can be adjusted at all angles to the face of the wheel. To get started, find a chisel or plane blade with the proper bevel of 25 to 30 degrees. Lay this flat on the tool rest and move the rest up or down until the bevel is a close match to the cutting surface of the grinding wheel (Figure 1-33). Move the tool back slightly, and turn the wheel a few times while you touch the blade against it. Now examine the bevel. You'll see a bright spot on either the cutting edge or the back of the bevel. Adjust the tool rest so the grinding wheel touches at or near the center of the bevel. Now you're ready to grind.

With the wheel turning at full speed, slide the blade right and left repeatedly across the tool rest. See Figure 1-34. Do not rush, but always keep the blade moving. If you stop movement, the steel will become overheated. There should always be a can of water close at hand. Dip the blade in water after each five or six passes across the wheel. If the edge suddenly turns blue or black, plunge it instantly into the water. The burned area has lost temper and will not take an edge, being dead soft. It will have to be ground out. It is good practice to grind a bit of radius on each corner of the cutting edge so there is no sharp corner to mark the work (Figure 1-35). I think most craftsmen grind their plane blades so the edge has a slight, almost invisible curve; you should learn to do this, too.

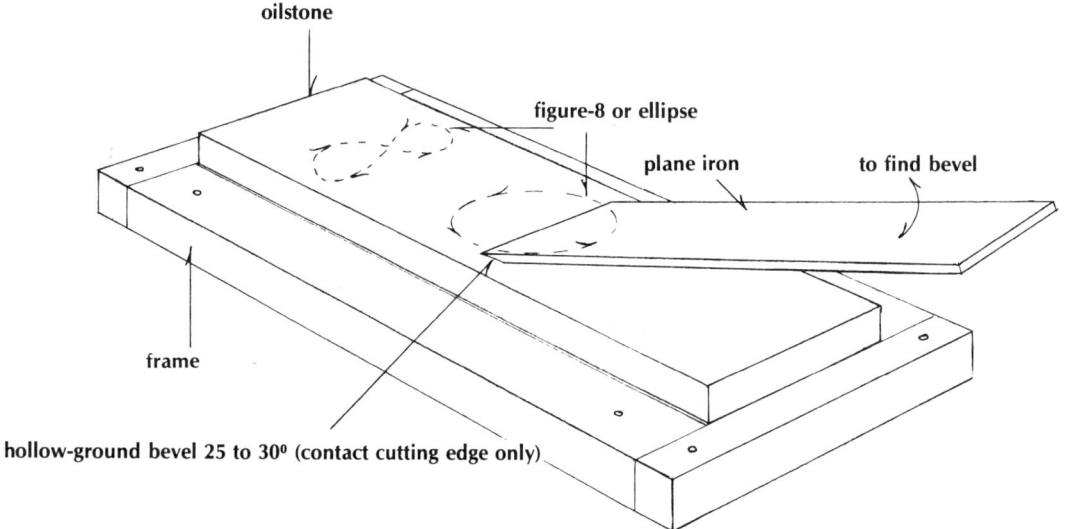

Figure 1-36. HONING OR WHETTING A PLANE IRON OR CHISEL

Whetting or Honing

Now you're ready to whet or hone the blade. Hold the oilstone firmly by tacking a frame around it on the bench, as shown in Figure 1-36. Spread three or four drops of machine oil thinned with kerosene on the fine surface of the stone. Now hold the blade in your right hand, and position it at an angle of about 25 to 30 degrees so just the cutting edge is in contact. I was taught as a boy to rock the bevel up and down slightly so its back edge also touched the stone lightly. Suit yourself, but keep the bevel as close to 25 degrees as you can. A greater angle produces an edge less likely to chip, but a finer edge cuts like a razor if you take care of it. An angle of less than 25 degrees will produce an edge too fragile for practicality.

The first two fingers of both hands are now used to apply a light pressure while you slide the blade about in a figure-eight or elliptical pattern. After half a dozen strokes, check the cutting edge. It should have a bright strip extending all the way across the blade, from corner to corner. The bright strip may not be more than $\frac{1}{32}$ inch wide. That's enough, for more than that simply reduces the life of the bevel between grindings. Do, however, whet your plane blades and chisels frequently. The honing devices shown in Figures 1-37 and 1-38 are excellent, as they control the bevel angle with precision.

At this point, there will be a burr or wire edge on the upper side of the blade. Carefully lay it flat on the stone, with the bevel side up, and slide it around in a figure-eight or circular motion, five or six times. Do not allow the blade to lift; it must remain flat. Lifting it would destroy the cutting edge, and it would have to be reground. Give another two or three strokes to the cutting edge, and another on the back. Then slice the sharp edge across the corner of a piece of scrap wood. This removes the last of the burr. Slicing with the grain should now take off a nice sliver without effort. If it doesn't, back to the oilstone! This hollow-ground edge can be whetted many times, but grind it before the bevel

Figure 1-37. *This plane blade with chisel honing guide rolls on the bench. Angle may be adjusted accurately.*

Figure 1-38. *An excellent honing guide from Brookstone. It rolls on the oilstone. (Courtesy Brookstone)*

becomes flat. Some old-timers strop the edge on a piece of leather tacked to a small paddle (Figure 1-39). Patternmakers use a neat trick. They touch the beveled edge for four or five seconds to a cotton polishing buff on the grinder arbor. And then briefly touch the back of the blade. The result? A razor-sharp edge.

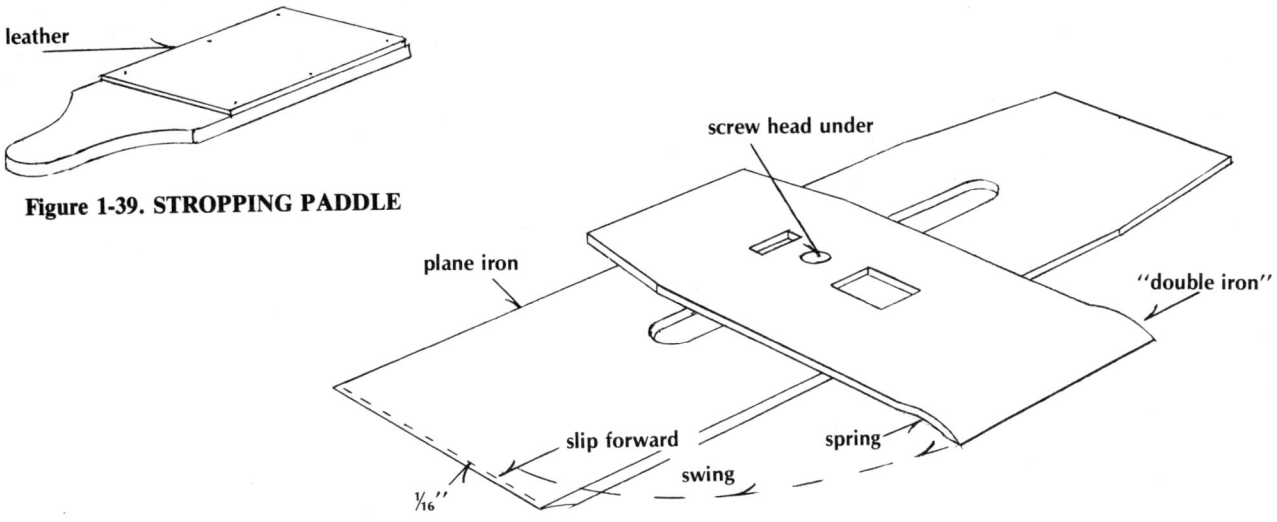

Figure 1-39. STROPPING PADDLE

Figure 1-40. INSTALLATION OF PLANE IRON AND DOUBLE IRON

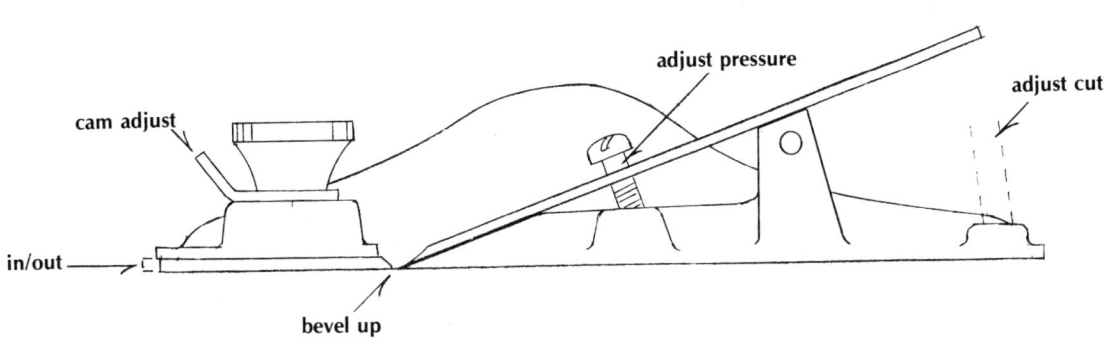

Figure 1-41. ASSEMBLY OF A BLOCK PLANE

Assembling the Plane

Now that you have a sharp blade, assemble the plane by placing the blade crosswise on the "double iron," with the large screw just covering the slot. See Figure 1-40. Rotate the blade with care until it is parallel to the double iron, but always extending well beyond the curved spring edge. Don't ever slide the blade so that the cutting edge contacts the hooked part of the double iron, for this will ruin your beautiful edge. Now bring the double iron forward slowly until it is about 1/16 inch from the edge of the blade. Tighten the screw. Set this assembly in its seat and place the heavy lever cap on top. Wiggle the assembly slightly to be sure it is properly seated, then lock it with the cam lever. The adjusting screw can be turned in or out so that the cam operates with considerable force. It should, however, be easy to unlock. Do not use a hammer. You might break the plane. Use your thumb instead.

Incidentally, the assembly of a block plane is different, for the low angle of the blade requires that it be placed with the bevel up. See Figure 1-41. There are several types of adjustment mechanisms. Some are cam levers, others are vertical and horizontal screws. All are simple. For dressing plywood edges, look for an extremely low blade angle.

Always start your work with the blade retracted, then bring it out gradually until you see fine shavings. Of course, a plane can be used with coarser settings for rapid removal of stock. In my opinion, however, it's best to saw close to the line or use a jointer.

Every now and then you will have to plane to a crooked line to get a close fit to an unfair surface. This can be done by using your little block plane diagonally or directly across the grain. A rasp or coarse production paper on a block will do the same job.

Screwdrivers

You will need both the straight slot type and the Phillips head (cross) style screwdrivers — two sizes of each. Do not use a tool tip that is too thick to reach the bottom of the slot or wider than the screw head. This will mar your

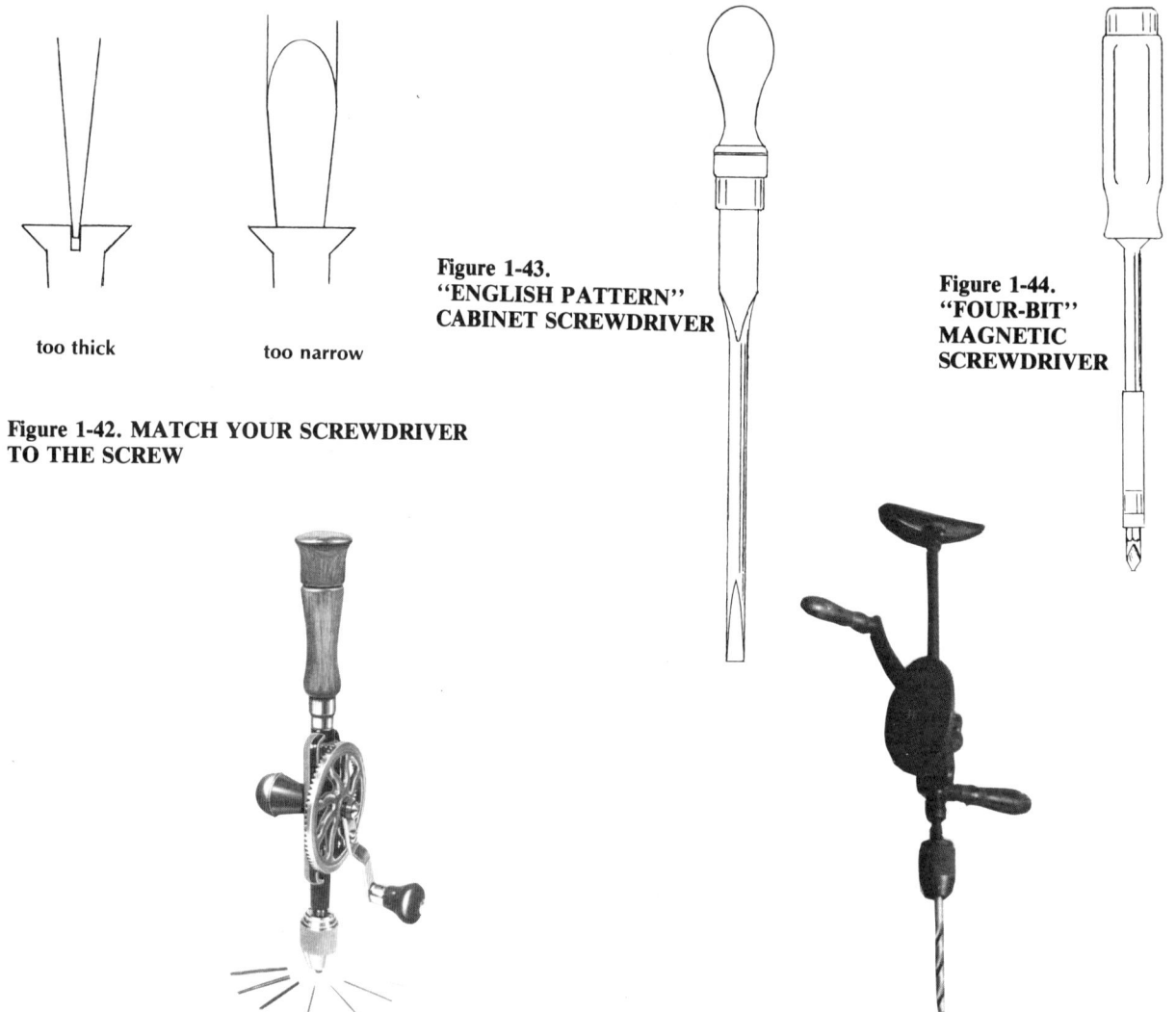

too thick   too narrow

Figure 1-42. MATCH YOUR SCREWDRIVER TO THE SCREW

Figure 1-43. "ENGLISH PATTERN" CABINET SCREWDRIVER

Figure 1-44. "FOUR-BIT" MAGNETIC SCREWDRIVER

Figure 1-45. *The eggbeater-style light-duty hand drill is excellent for pilot holes and for starting small screws. Bits are carried in the handle. (Courtesy Brookstone)*

Figure 1-46. *Pressing the chest against this breast drill develops lots of pressure. It is adequate for occasional metalwork, where time is not essential, and fine for wood.*

work. Too narrow a tip may jump out of the slot and chew it up. See Figure 1-42. A Phillips-head bit that is too small may spin around in the cross and possibly ruin both bit and screw. In general, the longer the screwdriver, the better. Screw and tool should always be aligned in the same axis; this is impossible with a stubby. The wide, flat portion just above the tip permits use of a small wrench for maximum torque. Square-shank tools also may be turned this way, a big help with large screws. The "English pattern" cabinet screwdriver does not have a wide flat, so you can drive screws into counterbores without tearing up the hole. See Figure 1-43. Note that the upper shank is flattened for using a wrench.

I have a little steel and plastic screwdriver set with a receptacle in the handle for storing four small octagonal bits — two Phillips, two straight (Figure 1-44). The chuck has a magnet built into the business end. Thus, the tip of a bit is magnetized when seated, and it holds screws while you are starting them in difficult spots.

This tool is useful for picking up lost screws, parts, spilled nails, and so on. Not designed for heavy production, this screwdriver is ideal for small hinges, latches, and other hardware.

Hand Drills

Two types of hand drills are useful in yacht joinery for limited drilling. The first is the lightweight egg-beater style of drill (Figure 1-45), quite adequate for drilling pilot holes in oak, or for screws in thin trim where heads are left exposed. I would not use this tool for counterboring or for plug cutting, as it has a tendency to wobble. Another tool useful for lead holes is the automatic push drill. These are rather costly, however. The heavier type is called a breast drill (Figure 1-46). This tool has a curved plate on the upper end of the shaft that provides a good strong grip, or you can lay

Figure 1-47. *Brace with a powerful chuck. It is ball-bearing throughout.*

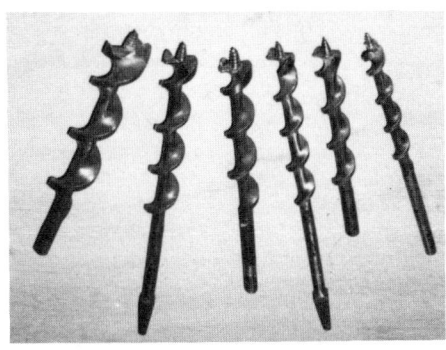

Figure 1-48. *Solid-center bit has double spurs and cutters with a medium-fast screw pitch. Available in sets ¼ to 1 inch, in 16ths. A must.*

Left: Figure 1-49. *The traditional Jennings double-twist bits clear chips easily. The tapered bodies prevent binding. Just about the best available.*

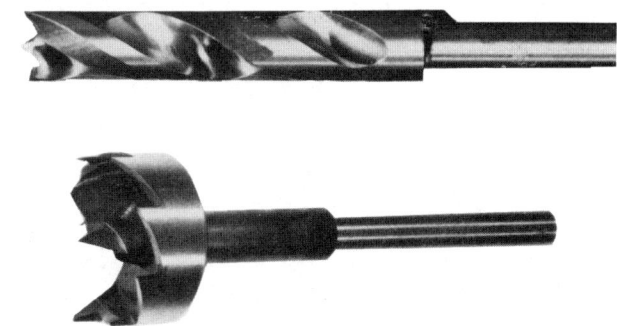

Figure 1-50. Top: *Machine brad point bores cleanly across or along grain.* **Above:** *Multi-spur does difficult jobs better — veneers, angles, overlapping, and so on. (Courtesy Woodworker's Supply)*

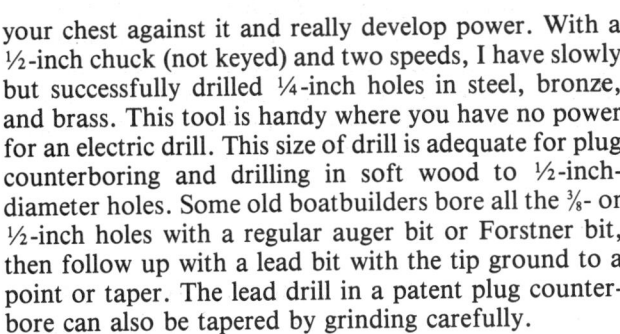

your chest against it and really develop power. With a ½-inch chuck (not keyed) and two speeds, I have slowly but successfully drilled ¼-inch holes in steel, bronze, and brass. This tool is handy where you have no power for an electric drill. This size of drill is adequate for plug counterboring and drilling in soft wood to ½-inch-diameter holes. Some old boatbuilders bore all the ⅜- or ½-inch holes with a regular auger bit or Forstner bit, then follow up with a lead bit with the tip ground to a point or taper. The lead drill in a patent plug counterbore can also be tapered by grinding carefully.

Brace and Bits

The brace holds the squared end of an auger bit (Figure 1-47). A brace will take a square-end screwdriver bit also, and is thus useful for driving large screws. For boring large holes and driving large screws, and in restricted spots, you may have to use the brace's built-in ratchet. Better braces have ball bearings in the head and turning grip. You can buy a cheapie for $5 or $6 or a good make for about $14.

There are several types of auger bit. The most frequently seen is the solid center or straight core with a single twist (Figure 1-48). This type cuts fast and clears chips easily, especially in wood full of gum. The double twist or fluted bit is not as fast, but it makes an accurate and clean hole and is good in softwoods (Figure 1-49). This type of bit is good for plug boring, for it does not chip around the hole, even at slow hand speeds. More rarely used is the Forstner bit. Forstner bits usually have no screw or lips, so they are hard to start accurately. Some, however, are provided with a spur or point for centering. These are often used in end grain, where the point can be pressed in slightly, then turned. Such a bit planes out the hole. Boring end grain with a standard auger bit, on the other hand, is difficult. The Forstner can also be used close to the end of a piece, where an ordinary bit would split the wood.

Bits come in sets of ¼, ⁵⁄₁₆, ⅜, and so on, in 16ths of an inch up to 1 inch, or in various combinations in smaller sets. Of course, you can buy any single bit you

Right: Figure 1-51. *Ship's auger bits for boring long, straight holes. There is no point to be deflected. Start in shallow hole drilled with a conventional bit. For cabin sides, centerboards, rudders, keels, and deadwood.* **Below: Figure 1-52.** *Expansion bits bore up to 4-inch diameters with hand brace. Do not use a drill press or electric drill. Cutter is adjustable for precision. Sharp spur cuts clean circle. (Courtesy Brookstone)*

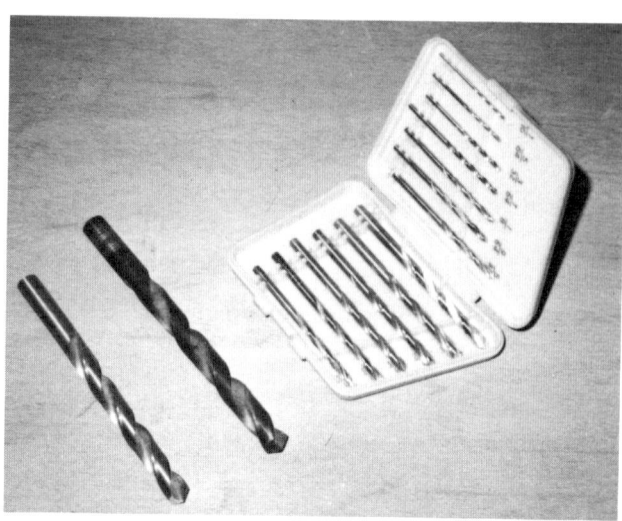

Figure 1-53. *Twist drills ground to about 60-degree angle for wood, 40-degree angle for metal. Weld shank extensions (of high-speed steel) for deep holes.*

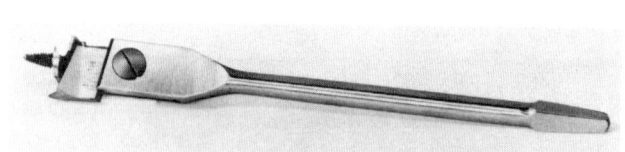

may need. The sizes are stamped into the square end; the figure means the number of 16ths of an inch in the diameter. One-quarter inch reads "4," $7/16$ inch reads "7," and so on. All the bits described here can be adapted for use in a slow-speed electric drill by sawing off the squared shank.

Ship's Auger Bits

Eventually you will need a couple of ship's auger bits (Figure 1-51). These are sometimes called barefoot bits because they have no screw or spur. They are used to bore deep, straight holes for drifts, long bolts, and dowels in such places as cabin trunk sides, in keel and deadwood, centerboard, rudder, or wherever else a long fastening is needed. Knots and hard grain have a tendency to deflect an ordinary screw auger bit and make it wander. The barefoot bit, however, has no point to be deflected.

To start, you first drill a shallow hole with an ordinary bit, then follow up with the ship's auger. Chips, especially if wet, green, or gummy, must be cleared frequently, or the bit will pack solidly and twist off. If you should have this problem, place a clench ring or washer over the bit and saw it off about one diameter above the ring. Then peen it over into a rivet. If it breaks off below the surface, fill the hole with hot tar or tallow and plug with wood. As Howard Chapelle says in *Boatbuilding,* "A good many boats have an auger bit serving as a drift in their keels." Drill another hole nearby, but a little to one side, so it's not in the same grain, to prevent a split from occurring.

Expansion Bits

You may have frequent use for an expansion bit (Figure 1-52). This type of bit has an adjustable cutter for boring diameters up to 3 inches. Always use an expansion bit in a hand brace, for they are very dangerous in a drill press or an electric drill. They are prone to grab the wood, and you and the drill suddenly rotate. Do not try to bore through with an expansion bit. When the point of the screw shows on the back side, reverse the piece in the vise and bore from that side. If you don't do it this way, you will create a badly chewed-up mess. If, after a few turns, the screw no longer pulls, you can make it bore by rocking it slightly from side to side as you turn the brace. You may have to chisel out the remaining plug. Better yet, when you start to bore, clamp a block of scrap to the work piece so the screw will continue to pull all the way through. This is advisable when you do any kind of boring with the back side accessible.

Twist Drill Bits

You can use twist drills, or machine bits (Figure 1-53), for much woodwork, but where a clean hole is mandatory, they are not always satisfactory. They are good for bolt and lead holes, of course. High-speed steel is best, although long bits known as electrician's bits are available in carbon steel. These should be turned at low speed to prevent heating and annealing (softening). High-speed steel takes the heat, and holds its edge 10 times longer than carbon steel, but it is brittle. If the chuck in your brace is not powerful enough to hold the round shanks when drilling deep holes, borrow a $3/8$- or $1/2$-inch electric drill. For drilling through deadwood, keels, cabin side, centerboards, and so on, it is common

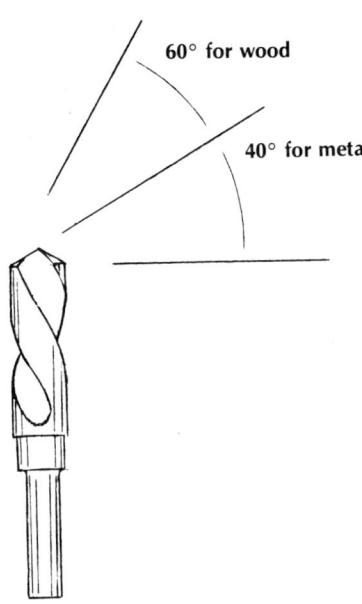

Figure 1-54. BLACKSMITH'S DRILL BIT

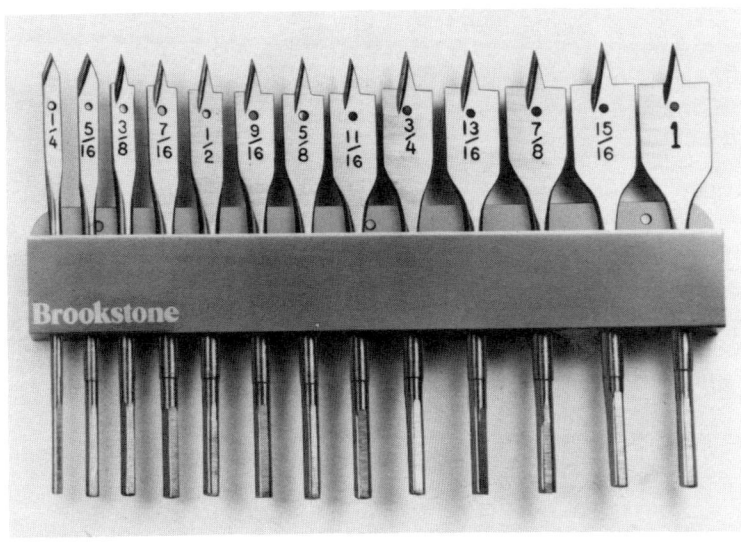

Figure 1-55. *A fine set of spade bits. These are fast and clean-cutting. They are filed sharp easily and are inexpensive. They cut best at fairly high speeds. (Courtesy Brookstone)*

to have the shanks on ordinary twist drills extended by welding or brazing on a foot or so of iron rod of 1/16 inch smaller diameter. This reduces friction. Be sure to back out the chips frequently, or you'll lose a good drill bit.

Occasionally, I have used a low-priced twist drill called a blacksmith's bit. Available in sets of three or four in carbon steel, from ¼ to ¾ inch in diameter, some have ¼-inch shanks for use in a small electric drill, breast drill, or even a brace. These bits are usually somewhat shorter than the average twist drill bit in tool steel. They won't handle much work in iron, so you'll be grinding often. See Figure 1-54.

Grinding Twist Drills

Twist drills used in wood are not ground the same as for use in metal. An angle of 40 degrees is supplied for metalwork. Wood requires about 60 degrees, as shown in Figure 1-54. While grinding drill bits is an art, it is one you can learn easily from the many good books available. If the idea appeals to you, there are many quite reasonable drill-grinding devices you can buy.

Spade Bits

Every hardware store has a very efficient bit called the spade bit (Figure 1-55). These bits employ a kind of scraping action, leave a clean hole, and are best if turned at moderately high speeds, ideal in an electric drill or a drill press. The bits can be sharpened with a small flat file, for their cutting edges work like a plane blade. Do not try to bore clear through with a spade bit. Always bore back to avoid serious splitting as the bit exits from the work.

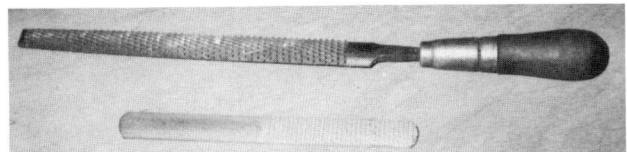

Figure 1-56. *Many types of rasps are available. Shoemaker's rasp has oval and flat, fine and coarse on one tool. Some fine boatbuilders frown on use of this tool.*

Rasps and Files

One useful rasp has a combination of coarse and fine — flat on one side, half oval on the other (Figure 1-56). Larger rasps have tangs for attaching handles and come with a variety of teeth. You'll have to keep cleaning compressed chips out of the cutting surfaces, so have a wire brush handy. Do not attempt to use a rasp on metal — it is not a file. Also, do not use a file on wood, for the teeth will fill up instantly. Rasps and Stanley Surform planes (Figure 1-57) can be used to round corners with the grain, but then sand with a hard block. For inside corners, use a rat-tail coarse file, but use it gently. You can follow up with a dowel of the appropriate size around which you wrap garnet or production paper (Figure 1-58). Never use white flint paper.

Nail Sets

A kit of nail sets is required, since all finishing nails (galvanized only) must be set below the surface and the holes filled with plastic wood or matching stuff. Never drive a finishing nail right down to the surface. Your hammer will leave a bad indentation. Leave the head

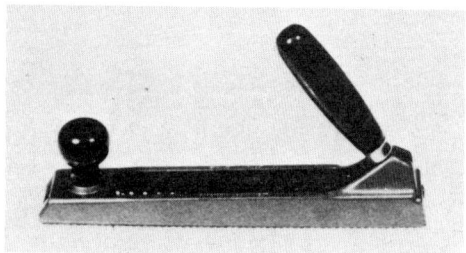

Figure 1-57. *Surform works like a plane for roughing off material. Cuts in any grain direction, even plywood. Flat and convex blades. Best on softwoods.*

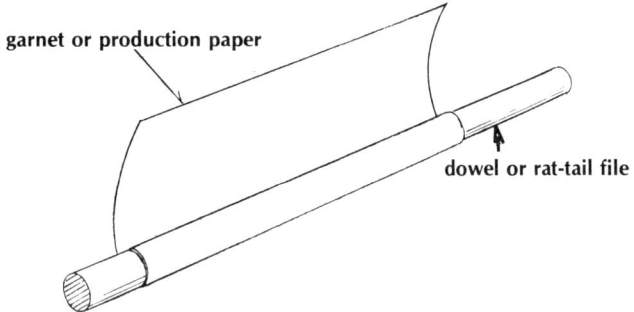

Figure 1-58. DEVICE FOR FINE SANDING

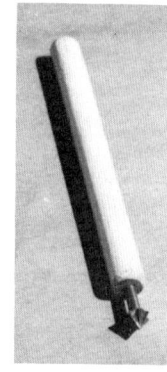

Figure 1-59. *Ordinary square-shank wood countersink driven into bore in broomstick. Long handle makes countersinking accurate, fast, and easy.*

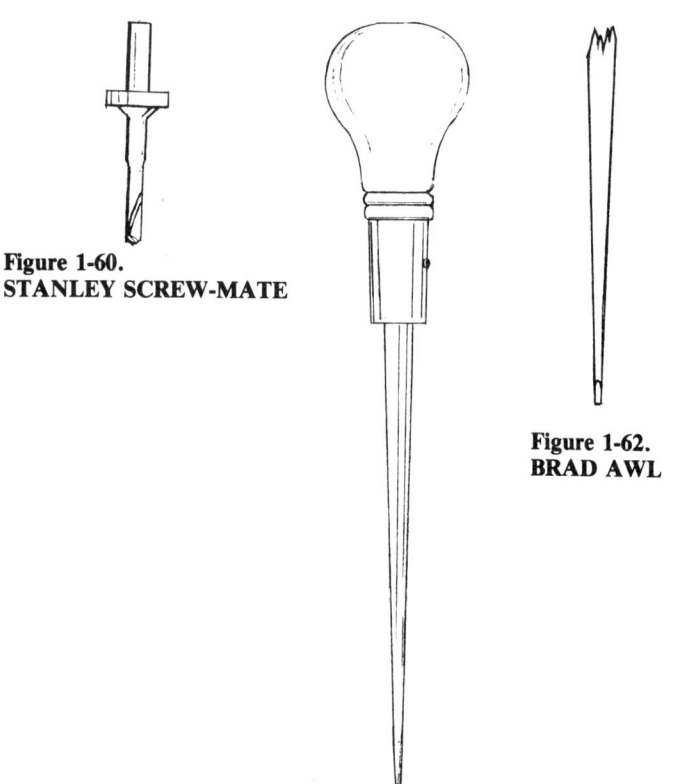

Figure 1-60. STANLEY SCREW-MATE

Figure 1-62. BRAD AWL

Figure 1-61. PRICK PUNCH

out about 1/16 inch, then sink it with a set slightly smaller than the head, as shown in Figure 1-3.

Here's a useful tip. If you mark a wood surface in any way, wet it two or three times with a drop or two of water. Yes, saliva works fine. If the dent is stubborn (such as, God forbid, from a C-clamp), place a damp cloth over it and press with a hot iron for a couple of seconds. These methods should expand the wood fibers to their original level. Let dry and then sand with a wood block.

Countersinks and Counterbores

I have found that the most useful countersink has a square shank for your brace. This must be sawed off to use the countersink with your hand drill. You can make a hand-operated countersinking tool, however, that will beat this for speed and convenience. Make or buy a long file handle, then drill a hole in the end slightly smaller than the square shank. Tap the handle onto the tool and it's done. See Figure 1-59. If you make your own handle, use a piece of broomstick. When you countersink, try to keep the tool nearly vertical to the work. Two or three twists is all it takes.

In addition, I recommend the inexpensive Stanley Screw-Mate bits that drill a pilot hole, shank diameter, countersink, and plug counterbore in one operation (Figure 1-60). Sears has a 12-piece set of similar tools. There is an adjustable type also in which the pilot and shank bits are movable, held by a set screw. These are suitable for up to a 2½-inch screw. They bore for plugs also. The patent counterbore is the cleanest cutting and has a stop for depth. This tool is rather costly, and usually is available only at marine hardware stores, for 3/8- and ½-inch plugs. When using any of the others in an electric drill, watch that you do not counterbore too deeply, for they cut very rapidly.

Brad Awl and Prick Punch

For starting small screws in softwoods, I use an old, sharp prick punch (Figure 1-61). For aligning hinges, this tool is great. You can move the hole as little or as much as you need to, even after the screw has entered, because the wood fibers are still there. They have not been removed, as they would have been if you had used a drill. The sharp point enables you to probe and move the fibers where you need them. Now, the experts recommend a brad awl, which has a flattened point (Figure 1-62). You start the brad awl with this flat across the grain. Thus, it chisels the fibers as it penetrates and prevents splitting. With either prick punch or brad awl, when attaching hinges to the edge of plywood, drill lead holes after you get one screw located exactly, then go back and drill that first hole. This prevents the plies from splitting or delaminating. If the end plies are already split slightly, pry them open a bit, dab in a few drops of glue, and let it set up before you install the hinges.

TWO

More Basic Hand Tools

CLAMPS

I know I could devote an entire chapter to the use of clamps in boat work. You can never have too many. That's true even if you are far past the type of work on a bent-frame hull that requires a half-dozen or so at a time. Just recently, for example, I laminated a small stem for a 16-foot duckboat, and I ended up with 12 C-clamps so close together it was a problem to turn the screws. Resolve right now to accumulate C-clamps of all sizes. Try garage sales, flea markets, used-tool shops, the classified columns, and so on. Borrow if you can't buy.

C-Clamps

I have found the 6-inch C-clamp (that's the maximum space between the button and the pad) to be the most useful (Figure 2-2), but all sizes are handy, right on down to the 1-inch miniatures. Of course, when you get into spar construction of any size and complexity, you'll need much larger capacities. A 40-foot mast of the usual hollow box type might easily require a total of 75 clamps.

The uses of C-clamps seem quite obvious, but let's just mention a few: to hold diagonals while you square up structures; to secure work pieces while you plane, chisel, bore, or whatever; to hold parts in position for accurate drilling, screwing, or nailing together; to clamp for gluing; to stand boards or plywood on edge while dressing with a plane (Figure 2-3); to position your straightedge for power sawing plywood sheets. The list goes on and on, especially if you work alone. That's when a clamped-on support for a long, heavy piece is as good as another man.

There are several types of clamps to look for. Even the light 3-inch and 4-inch sizes are useful when great pressure is not required (some of the modern glues don't require pressure). The deep-C style with a deeper throat, shown at the lower left in Figure 2-1(A), is excellent, and the cost is only pennies more. Even the cheapies of the sliding quick-acting bar design are handy, because they have the reach of a heavy 6-inch forged C-clamp at about one-third the cost. True, they are cheaply made, have poor buttons, and will loosen if there is any jarring or hammering. For gluing the average assembly, however, they will do the job if you use a bit of care.

Most of the newer C-clamps have a sliding bar handle. This is good because you can set the clamp close to a corner or another part, whereas the older wing types are impossible to turn when there is this kind of in-

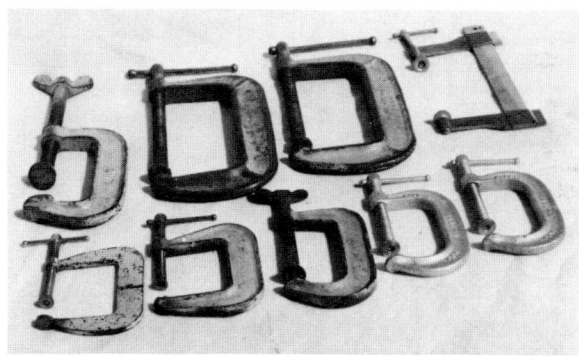

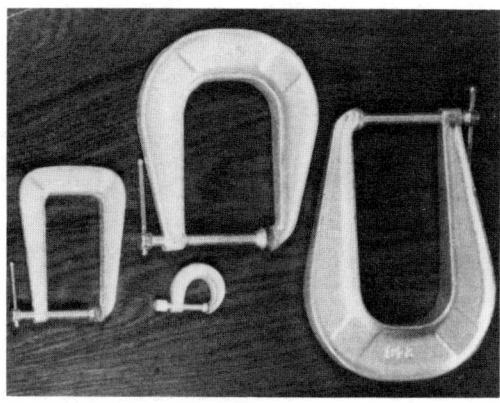

Figure 2-1. Top: (A) *Deep throat clamps in 3-inch and 4-inch sizes are desirable. The cheap 6-inch-capacity bar clamp at the upper right is good mainly for fast action and light pressure. (Courtesy Woodworker's Supply)* **Above: (B)** *Three deep-C clamps and a 1-inch miniature.*

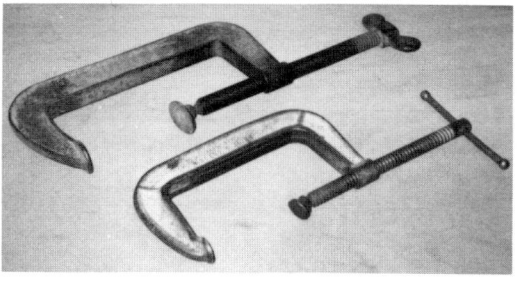

Figure 2-2. *The 6-inch C-clamp is the most versatile size. Use 8-inchers for heavy work.*

Figure 2-3. *C-clamps provide support for planks, doors, panels, and so on, on edge.*

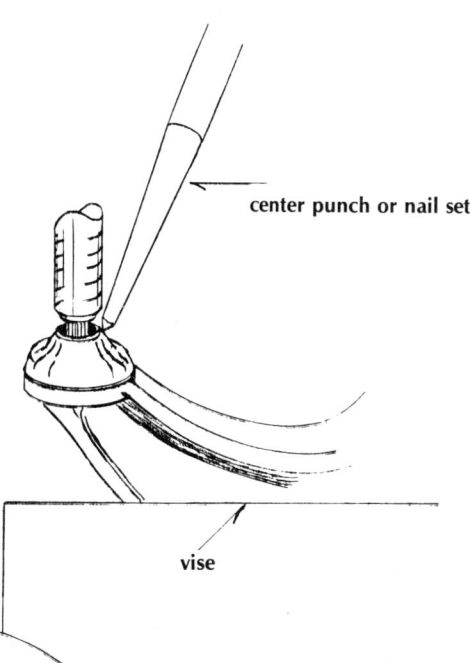

Figure 2-4. REPLACING C-CLAMP BUTTON

terference. This is a good place to point out that the bar or wing-type thumbscrew on your clamp was designed to be turned by hand only. Do not use wrenches or pipes. If you use some device to help turn the screw, you will in time spring the clamp. This will permanently deform it and make it useless. Also, you might generate so much pressure that you damage the pieces being clamped. The circular marks left by C-clamps have a way of expanding for years after they are sanded out. It's a shame so many so-called professionals do this regularly. Avoid such damage by always using 2-by-2-inch squares of plywood between the clamps and the work.

All C-clamps have one very bad drawback. They lose their buttons! A clamp without a button is highly destructive to wood surfaces. In some cases, the button can be replaced, at least temporarily. Slip it back on and fasten the clamp in a vise. See Figure 2-4. Then, using a nail set or a center punch, go all the way around the edge of the cup in the button. If the button is drop-forged, the punch will gradually reduce the inside diameter of the cup enough to close it over the ball end. There was a time when you could buy replacement buttons at good hardware and tool supply stores. It's becoming more and more difficult, however, to find little necessities like these. If you look, take your

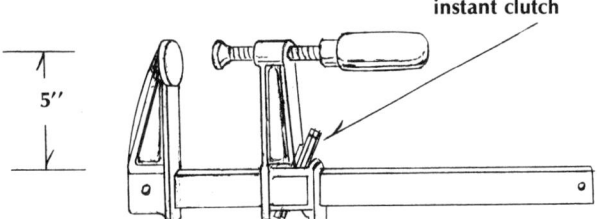

Figure 2-5. FAST-ACTION BAR CLAMP

C-clamp along to be sure you get the right size — they vary. The button should just slip on with a tap of a hammer. Keep the socket and the screw well oiled and your clamps will serve well for two or three generations.

Bar Clamps

Bar clamps are almost as indispensable as C-clamps. These quickly adjusted clamps (Figure 2-5) are used universally by cabinetmakers for drawing together cabinet joints for glue or fastenings. It is satisfying to see the glue ooze out of a dado joint when you put two or three bar clamps on it. Just be sure you have a diagonal or two on any box shape and check for square (measure corner to opposite corner), for the clamps can pull your structure far out of square. A common use of bar clamps is for edge-gluing, such as in a cabin side. First C-clamp the pieces to several cleats to hold the components flat. Then place bar clamps on each side of the C-clamp/cleat assembly to prevent buckling and damage. Remember, too, that glue will ooze out of the joints, so your cleats should have been covered with pieces of plastic such as Saran Wrap.

Bar clamps come in standard lengths, such as 24 inches, 36 inches, 42 inches, and so on. A 48-inch clamp, however, is pretty awkward for a 14-inch span, and if you need 50 inches, you are licked (although there are ways of hooking two clamps together). One answer to this problem is to acquire a number of pipe clamps. A set consists of the screw end and the adjustable lower jaw end. Two sizes are available, for ½- or ¾-inch pipe. The larger size is preferable, because the jaws are a bit deeper, so it generates more pressure. I have about six of each size and I find that the less costly one does a fine job in about 90 percent of the cases. If you collect an assortment of threaded used pipe in both sizes, you will have an endless choice. Any length of pipe can be used. I usually have pieces of black pipe from 4 feet up to 12 feet on hand at all times, for my cabinets sometimes run up to 10 feet end to end. Black pipe does not slip as galvanized pipe does, and it is sold very cheaply by the pound at scrap yards, so stock up. An edge-gluing job using pipe clamps is shown in Figure 2-6.

The Jorgensen clamp is a very nicely made bar clamp sold by hardware stores. These are usually limited to 24

Figure 2-6. *Gluing up a cabin trunk side is easy with inexpensive pipe clamps. (Bruce Bingham photo)*

inches and are rather costly by comparison with pipe clamps. Their jaws, however, are deeper, and they are instant-adjusting. The same type of quick-acting bar clamp comes in a short, heavier style, also with a deep throat. These are very expensive and hard to find on the used-tool market, but they are terrific for spar work. You might be able to rent some from a local cabinetmaker over a Saturday or Sunday when the shop is closed. Cheap 12-inch bar clamps of similar appearance but sorry foreign construction are worthless.

Spring Clamps

It would be hard to get along without a few spring or pinch clamps. These are great for holding parts during drilling of fastenings as well as for small gluing jobs. They generate an enormous amount of pressure and are positioned quickly.

PORTABLE VISE

For about $5 you can acquire an extremely useful little device that clamps to the end of a sawhorse, bench, or plank. This portable vise will hold a vertical piece such as a plywood panel on its edge on the floor, or a narrow part can be stood on end against the bench and clamped while you work on the upper edge. Some newer versions of this vise are aluminum, but I have a lot of faith in the old cast-iron ones.

BENCH VISES

There is always a certain amount of metalwork in a boat, so you may need a light- or medium-duty bench or

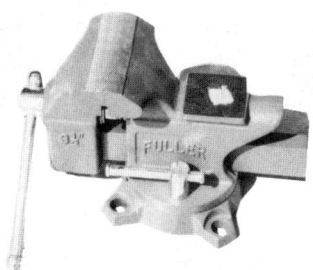

Figure 2-7. *A 4-inch machinist's vise is adequate for most small metalworking jobs, and fine, too, for woodwork with plywood inserts covering the vise's jaws.*

Figure 2-9. *Fine woodworker's end vise **(A) (above)** has quick release for positioning of the movable jaw, and **(B) (below)** is designed for face mounting on bench. (Courtesy Woodworker's Supply)*

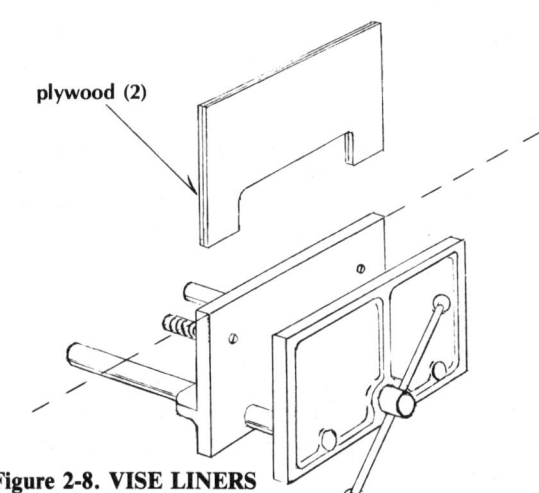

Figure 2-8. VISE LINERS

CHISELS

machinist's vise of the type shown in Figure 2-7. Any vise must be lined with plywood to cover the jaws if it is to be used for woodwork (Figure 2-8). I would not recommend a vise with a jaw width of less than 3½ inches. A medium-duty one runs about $20. Sears' best 4½-inch vise costs about $85, so if you find a used one for $20 or so, take it. Check for sloppy bearings, end play, beat-up anvil surface, bent screw and channel, cracks anywhere, and weakened welds. Such a vise must be bolted to a heavy bench near a corner so it can be swung for gripping vertically.

The fast-acting woodworker's bench vise is ideal. See Figure 2-9. Select one with jaws 6 to 8 inches wide. Maximum width is not mandatory, for you can let your wooden liners project an inch or so at each side. The best vises have a stop in the moving jaw that enables you to clamp side pieces on the flat between it and another stop on the bench. They also have a priceless feature — sliding jaws that open and close in a second with final pressure being applied with the screw. Some good ones open to 12 inches. These are quite costly, about $50. Without the quick-acting screw, they will cost about $25. Sears has one for a bit less.

In a later chapter I'll describe a split-second vise for holding planks and parts on edge. You can build one for the cost of five bolts and scrap 2-inch lumber.

Chisels come with three types of handles — tang, socket, and steel cap. The tang is a rectangular extension to be driven up into the handle. The handles, formerly wood, are now largely plastic. This is a light-duty chisel, intended to be used with hand pressure only, or driven by light taps of a small mallet or block of wood. But makes vary, as shown in Figure 2-10. The next heavier type is the socket chisel, so-called because the wood or plastic handle fits into a socket (see Figure 2-11). These handles are easily removed for storage or replacement; if made of wood, they should be capped with leather. It's better to use a mallet or block with any chisel. Hammer blows can damage the cap. The best chisel is the heavy-duty type in which the steel extends right up through the plastic handle and forms a cap.

Different chisel blades are used for different tasks. The tang or paring chisel, quite thin and short, allows for good control on fine work such as tenons. Butt chisels, usually socket types, are used most frequently for cutting gains, the recesses for butt hinges. They are useful for a wide variety of other work also. Long, narrow blades are best for mortising. You should have ¼-, ½-, ¾-, and 1-inch blades.

Another chisel widely used in boatbuilding and joinery is called the slick. One is shown in Figure 2-12. This type of chisel comes in many sizes, ranging from 2

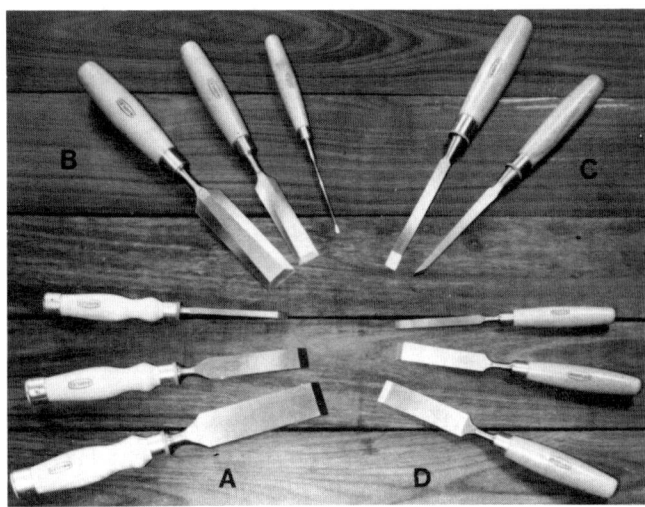

Figure 2-10. *Marples chisels:* **(A)** *Extra-thick, firmer chisels for mortising.* **(B)** *Sheffield steel cabinetmaker's chisels.* **(C)** *English mortise chisels with long blades.* **(D)** *Flat-ground, firmer chisels for general use and for hard, tough woods. (Courtesy Woodworker's Supply)*

Figure 2-11. *A worn-out slick. Slicks come in all sizes from 2 to 3 inches wide and up to 30 inches or more in length.*

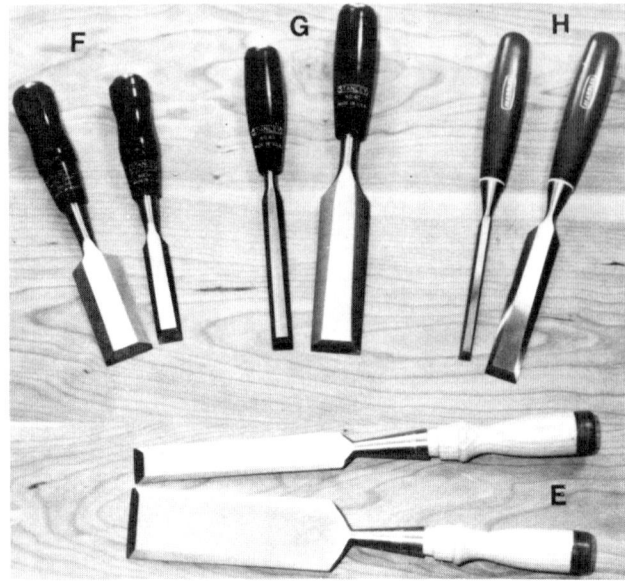

Figure 2-12. *Chisels.* **(E)** *Socket firmer chisels forged for holding edge under heavy work. These have hickory handles and leather rings. Two Stanley medium-duty* **(F)** *and heavy-duty* **(G)** *butt chisels, steel capped.* **(H)** *Two fine Marples heavy-duty socket butt chisels. (Courtesy Woodworker's Supply)*

to 4 inches wide with a blade length from 9 inches to well over a foot, plus a socket for a large wooden handle. One use is getting into corners you can't reach with a plane. You hold the flat side down on the work and slide it back and forth with some force. The blade cuts like a very low-angle plane. Sometimes the best results come from stroking diagonally across the grain, swinging from side to side and pressing down with the fingers of the left hand as you advance the blade into the work. The slick may have beveled or square sides. It is best if the upper or unbeveled side is straight for its full length, or nearly so.

Using a Chisel

The chisel should be ground just like a plane blade, and carefully whetted and honed. For rough cuts and concave shapes, work with the bevel down (Figure 2-13(A)). To cut a joint down to the line, rough out as much as you can with saw cuts, then chisel with bevel up (Figure 2-13(B)); slice in from one side to the middle across the grain, then do the same from the opposite side (Figure 2-13(C)). Clean the surface with a sort of paring motion until it makes a good flat surface. Do not press all the way across, as this will split out the opposite side. Always examine the direction of the grain, especially going with the grain, for the tool will try to bite too deeply if the grain is against you (Figure 2-13(D)). Do not try to cut to the line immediately. Work down to it in easy stages. When cutting a mortise, bore out first with a bit that is considerably smaller in size than the width of the mortise (Figure 2-14(A)). For ½ inch in width, use a ¼-inch chisel so you don't split the piece or go past the line (a knife mark). Work from end to middle from both sides, with the bevel down (Figure 2-14(B)). When you near the mark on both sides, you can start nearly perpendicular strokes, bevel up, paring.

Never use your chisels for prying, opening crates, or for splitting boards or firewood. Being hard steel, they are brittle. The cutting edge will chip or nick if you so much as touch a nail. Treat your chisels with care and they will last for several generations — if they were quality tools to begin with. You can buy quite a decent set of chisels for about $20. If your chisels are poor in quality, you will spend too much time sharpening — and you'll never get a good edge, anyway.

HACKSAW

You need a hacksaw for cutting drifts, threaded rods, bolt ends, and so on. It is important that the blade be kept in extreme tension; a heavy tubular frame is best for this. See Figure 2-15. I have seen hacksaw blades do a commendable job of cutting wood in restricted spots and on curves. Just wrap the blade with tape or paper to leave four or five inches for the stroke, as shown in Figure 2-16.

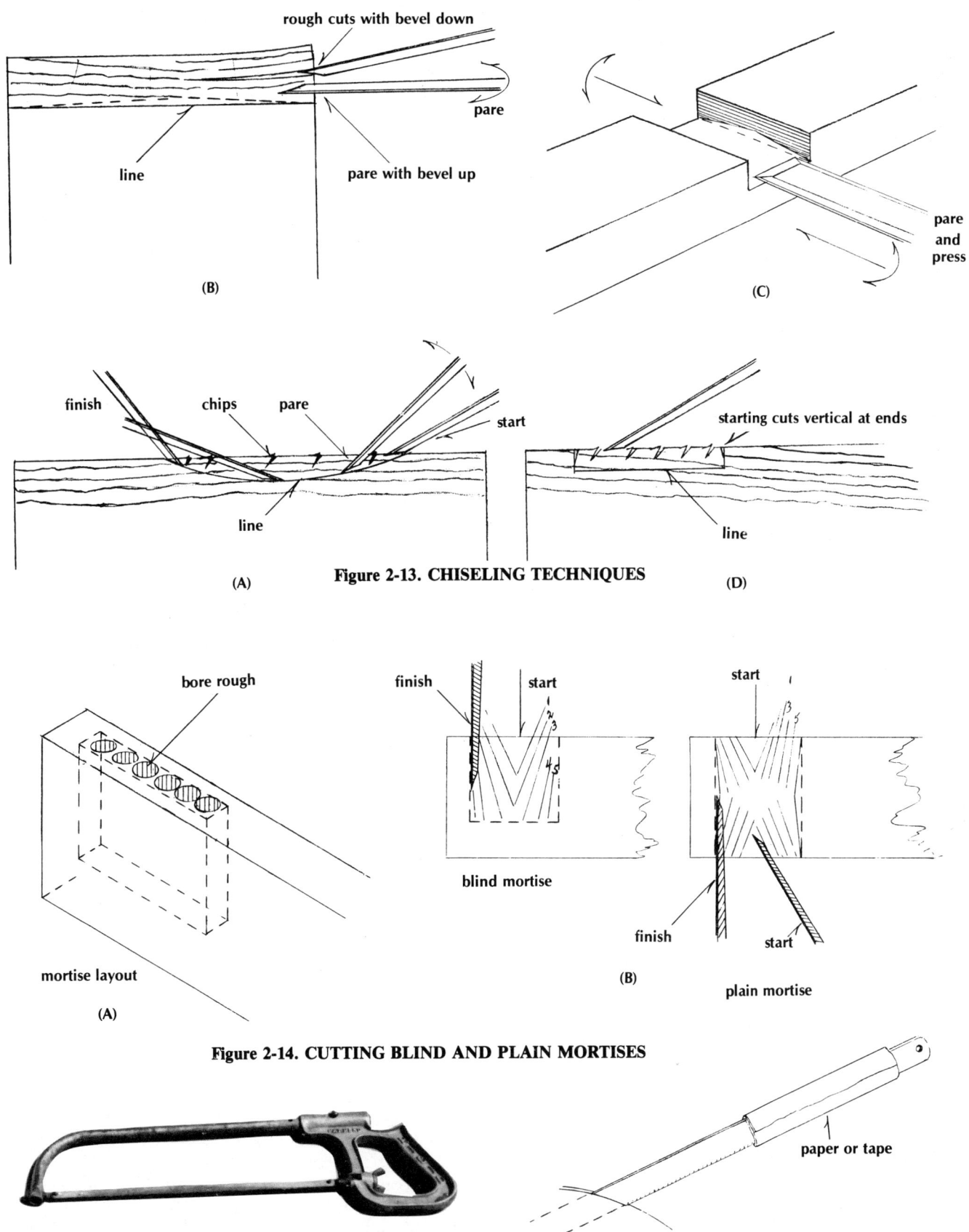

Figure 2-13. CHISELING TECHNIQUES

Figure 2-14. CUTTING BLIND AND PLAIN MORTISES

Figure 2-15. *This hacksaw has a rigid tubular frame. Blade must be set up as tightly as possible.*

Figure 2-16. HACKSAW BLADE CUTS CURVES

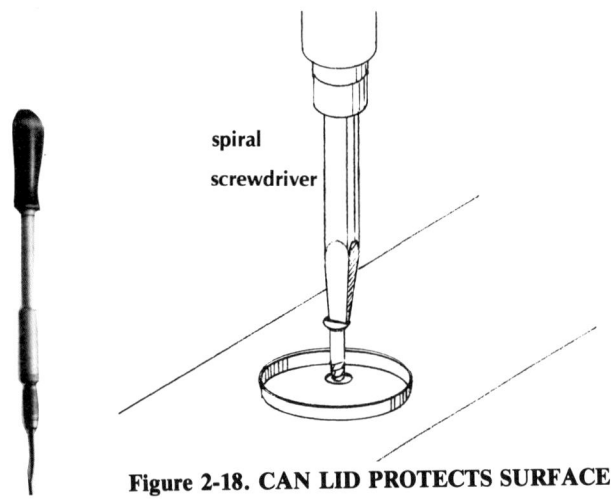

Figure 2-18. CAN LID PROTECTS SURFACE

Figure 2-17. *The indispensable original Yankee spiral screwdriver.*

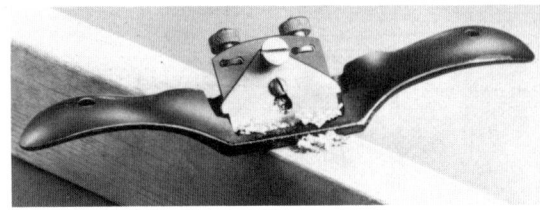

Figure 2-19. *Spokeshave with flat sole used for convex surfaces, for chamfering, and so on. A convex sole is used for shaping ogees and other concave edges. (Courtesy Brookstone)*

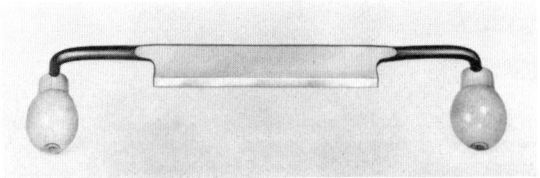

Figure 2-20. *A light drawknife. This tool is great for small spars before finishing with a plane. (Courtesy Brookstone)*

SPIRAL SCREWDRIVERS

The original and best-known spiral screwdriver is the Stanley Yankee, now also made by Millers Falls and others. This tool provides the fastest method for driving screws short of an electric screwdriver. The ideal size is 8 to 9 inches from handle to collet, with a 4-inch wood handle. See Figure 2-17. Newer models have longer plastic handles (for two hands, I suppose). The collet will take three bit sizes, both straight and Phillips heads.

To operate a spiral screwdriver, release the spiral carefully, and engage the tip of the bit and the screw head after starting the screw a turn or two with the fingers. Now press, keeping the driver in line with the direction of the screw. The spiral will run back into the barrel, rotating the screw six revolutions. Let up on the pressure and the spiral will return automatically for another stroke. Or you can use a series of short strokes. You get maximum power for sinking the head by turning with both hands with the spiral latched. The spiral is reversible for pulling out screws.

The Yankee presents just one hazard. It has a propensity for jumping out of the slot, usually because the tool is not kept in line with the axis of the screw. When this happens, the driver can bore a hole into the piece. To avoid this problem, punch a hole in a paint can lid and hang this on the screw. As shown in Figure 2-18, the work surface is protected by the paint can lid. Incidentally, every day I use a spiral screwdriver bought in the late 1930s. It has had no repairs and only a drop of oil now and then. What's more, I'm still using the original bits.

SPOKESHAVE AND DRAWKNIFE

The spokeshave is really a kind of plane. This tool (Figure 2-19) can be either pulled or pushed to make bevels or radii on either curved or straight corners. It also is good for dressing concave surfaces and shapes, such as the shaping on berth fronts, ogees in coamings and rails, and so on. The handles on each side of the spokeshave provide excellent control. The cutting edges must be ground and whetted just as you do with your plane blades and chisels. One I used for years had a block plane blade instead of the original. This blade was easier to grind and sharpen on the oilstone; its greater length made it a lot easier to manipulate.

The drawknife is related to the spokeshave, but it is used to remove large amounts of material, such as on solid spars. A drawknife has no sole, so there is nothing to restrict the depth of its cut (Figure 2-20). You draw toward you with the grain. Do not let the blade dig in, or you will rip off huge splinters. This blade, too, is hollow ground by drawing from end to end across the circumference of the grinding wheel. Then the blade is whetted by placing it vertically in a vise and stroking spirally with an oilstone. Some drawknives are made with adjustable handles for the most convenient grip.

MARKING GAUGE

The marking gauge is for scribing parallel to a straight or convex edge (Figure 2-21). Most of these tools have a sharpened pin near the outer end and an adjustable stop to be set to the required dimension. You mark by drawing the gauge toward you. The depth of the scribe mark can be controlled by rotating the gauge slightly until you produce just a slight scratch. Always set a marking gauge by measuring from the point to the stop. Do not rely on the graduated markings.

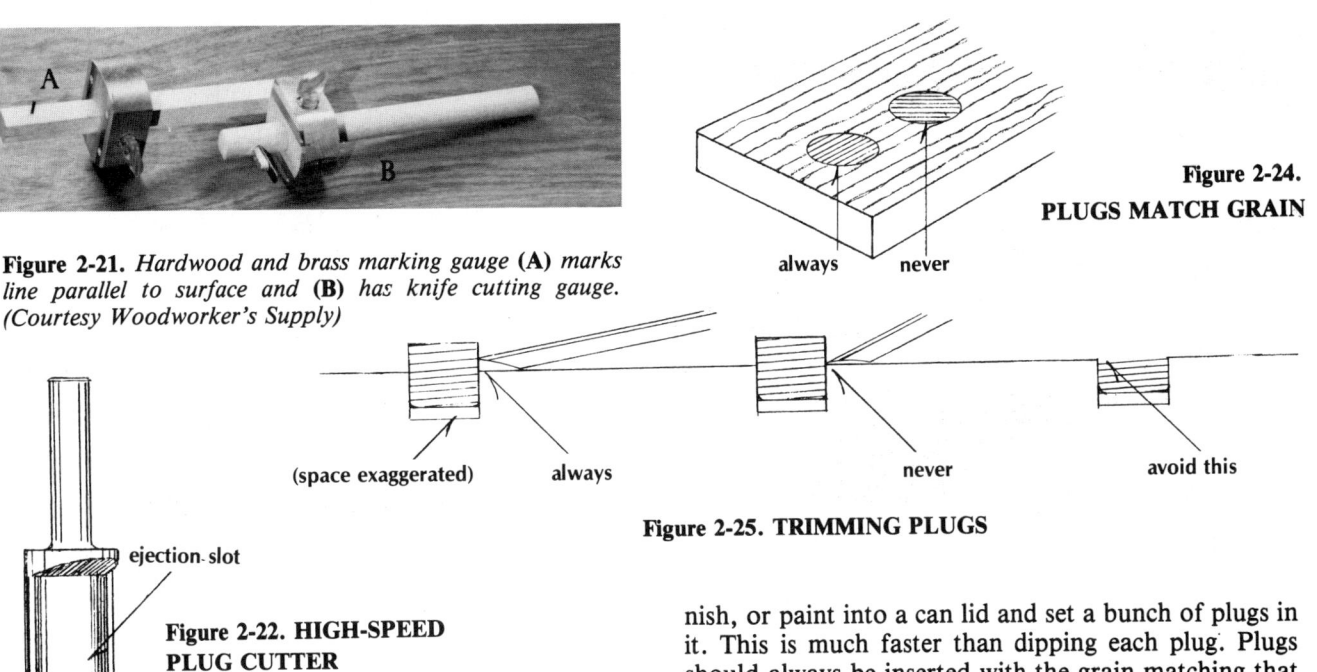

Figure 2-21. *Hardwood and brass marking gauge (**A**) marks line parallel to surface and (**B**) has knife cutting gauge. (Courtesy Woodworker's Supply)*

Figure 2-24. PLUGS MATCH GRAIN

Figure 2-22. HIGH-SPEED PLUG CUTTER

Figure 2-25. TRIMMING PLUGS

Figure 2-23. STANLEY PLUG CUTTER

PLUG CUTTERS AND BUNGING

If you have access to a drill press, you can save money by using a plug cutter (Figure 2-22) instead of buying plugs. The cutter shown ejects the plugs as they are cut, so you will need to place a carton on the drill press table to keep the plugs from flying all over the place. Set the stop on the press so the tip of the cutter just comes through into a piece of scrap. A lower-cost type of cutter does not bore all the way through ¾-inch stock, so the plugs remain seated, as shown in Figure 2-23. When you use up the piece of stock, resaw in a bandsaw or table saw and all the plugs will fall out as the saw cuts them loose. This cutter forms a radius that makes insertion into the hole easier. I usually pour a bit of glue, varnish, or paint into a can lid and set a bunch of plugs in it. This is much faster than dipping each plug. Plugs should always be inserted with the grain matching that of the work piece. See Figure 2-24.

After a plug has been tapped in lightly with a small mallet (never to the bottom of the hole, for it may expand and then protrude), it must be cut off carefully after the binder has set. Use a slick or a fairly heavy chisel. Hold the tool blade bevel down with the cutting edge $\frac{1}{16}$ to $\frac{1}{8}$ inch above the surface, as shown in Figure 2-25. Now slide the blade along or tap it with a block or small mallet. This will slice the plugs off at a safe distance above the work surface. Go back and notice which way the grain runs. Take one or two slices with the grain so it does not crack off below the surface and ruin the appearance of the job. I used to cut off plugs in planking by walking along the hull quite rapidly. Then they were just sanded off flush with coarse paper on a block. Inserting plugs does not have to be a painstaking or time-consuming chore if you use your noodle.

SCRAPERS

Throw away any hook scrapers you may have. Cabinet scrapers are used to remove planer corrugations, for dressing irregular, wavy, or curly grain in hardwood, and especially for finishing ribbon-grain Philippine mahogany and the flat grain of fir and many other woods. Scrapers are made of hard steel. They come in small rectangles and other shapes about 2½ by 4 inches in size and have no cutting edge when purchased. See Figures 2-26 and 2-27. They have to be worked carefully into a burred cutting edge. To use a scraper, hold it in both hands, inclined at an angle of about 75 degrees to the surface, and either push it or pull it. See Figure 2-28. It's easier to see the area being treated if you pull the scraper toward you. Try it both ways. Scraping pro-

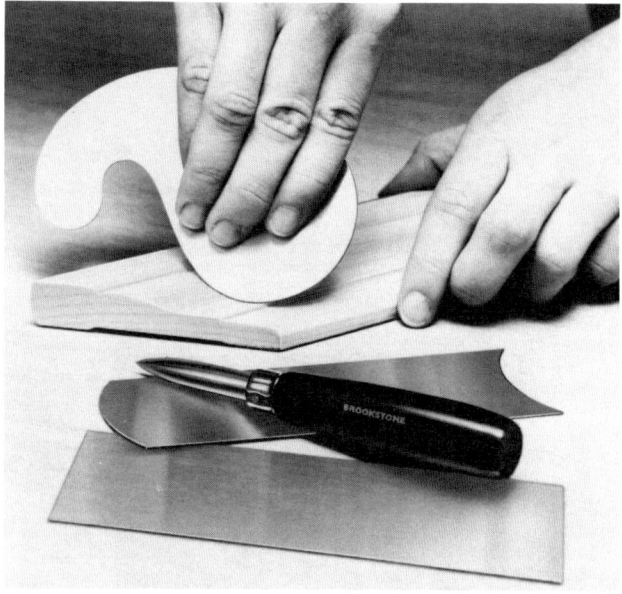

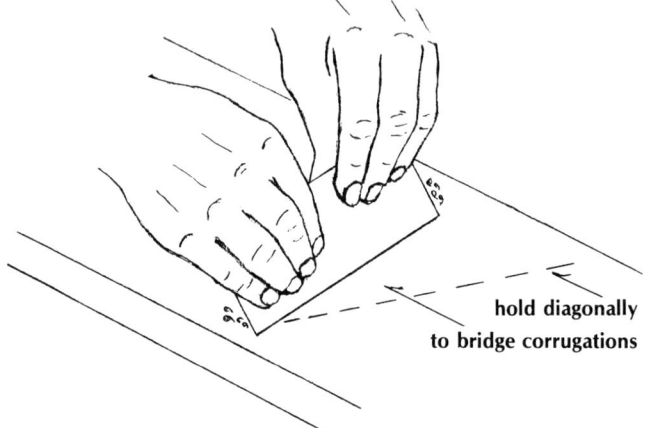

Figure 2-28. USING A SCRAPER

Figure 2-26. *Hand cabinet scrapers available in rectangles and concave and convex shapes. The hardened steel burnishing tool produces a fine burr on edges. (Courtesy Brookstone)*

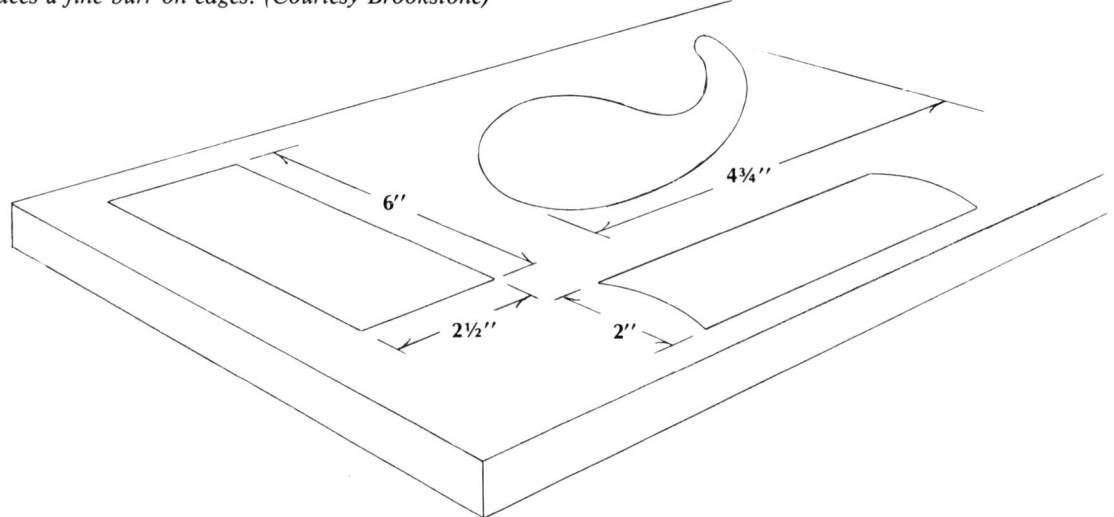

Figure 2-27. BLADE CABINET SCRAPERS, SIZES, SHAPES

duces very fine shavings and prepares the surface for fine sanding. It is a must for a superior varnish job.

A variation is the adjustable cabinet scraper (Figure 2-29). This tool has a frame or body with a flat sole and two handles. The blade is held by thumbscrews at an angle of about 75 degrees. It is usually pushed over the surface with some pressure — in long strokes and with the grain, of course. Incidentally, to remove planer corrugations, hold the scraper at an angle to the direction of the stroke so the blade bridges a number of the high spots at once. If you do not do this, the blade will simply ride up and down the hills and valleys.

As shown in Figures 2-26 and 2-27, shaped scrapers are available for fine convex and concave work. You may run into such needs occasionally. For convex surfaces such as round spars or box spars with a large radius, on the other hand, curved pieces of broken window glass do an adequate job at no cost. Just be sure to stick two or three thicknesses of masking tape on the edge you hold. You will find that very light pressure will take off a nice shaving until the sharp edge wears down. Then just throw away the piece of glass.

How to Sharpen Scraper Blades

Scraper blades generally are sharpened on their long sides, although there is no rule requiring this. Place the

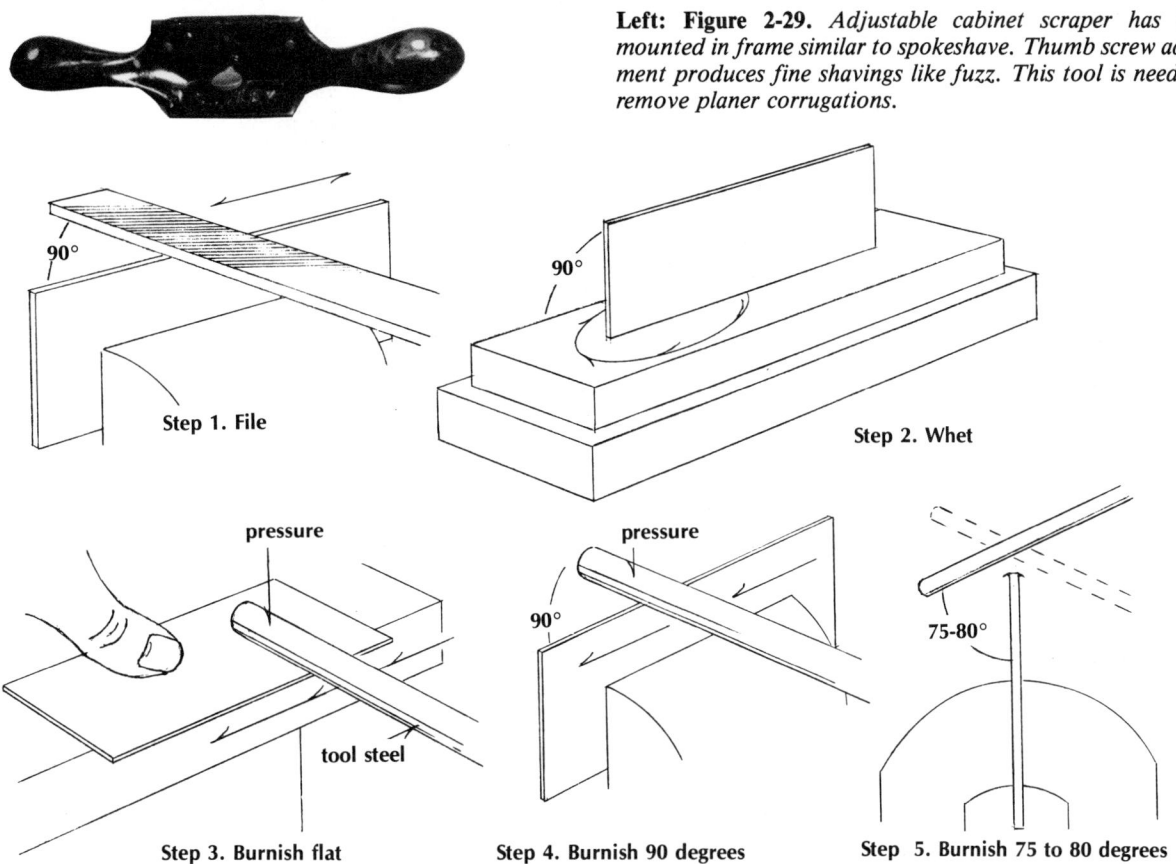

Left: Figure 2-29. *Adjustable cabinet scraper has blade mounted in frame similar to spokeshave. Thumb screw adjustment produces fine shavings like fuzz. This tool is needed to remove planer corrugations.*

Figure 2-30. SHARPENING A SCRAPER

blade in a vise and file the edge by holding a mill file crosswise on the blade and perpendicular to its side. Follow the steps in Figure 2-30.

Step one. Slide the file lengthwise on the blade, back and forth until the edge is bright and square. *Step two.* Whet the edge on an oilstone, holding the blade vertical. Remove any burrs by turning the blade flat on its side for several strokes. *Step three.* Now this edge must be burnished to form a hard, fine burr that is a microscopic hook. Use a burnishing tool made from a 6-inch length of drill rod or any hard, round tool. Or obtain a store-bought triangular burnisher. Lay the blade flat on the edge of a bench and stroke hard over its full length with the burnisher almost flat. Do this on both sides. *Step four.* Clamp the blade in a vise and draw the burnisher along the edge at 90 degrees to the face, using considerable pressure. Do this 10 or 15 times. *Step five.* End up with a final stroke or two at about 75 or 80 degrees. Feel the edge. Is there a sharp burr? Now repeat this last operation on the other side of that edge. This gives you two cutting edges. Tilting the blade to 75 degrees will make that burr cut. When you're sure you've got it, repeat all this on the other edges. This will give you eight working edges.

The blade for the two-handed cabinet scraper shown in Figure 2-29 is filed or ground to a 45-degree bevel, then burred over in stages with a burnisher at 50 degrees, then 60 degrees, and finally 75 degrees. This blade has just one cutting edge. It is clamped in the tool with the burr facing forward.

SCRIBING AND SPILING COMPASS

The scribing and spiling compass is a simple and inexpensive tool that should perhaps have been at or near the top of the list of basic tools, because you would simply be out of business without one (Figure 2-31). This tool differs from the ordinary compass in that instead of having a point on one leg, it has a rounded tip. The tip slides along a straight or curved surface while the pencil is marking the surface's shape. Always hold the scriber horizontal. Do not hold it so the mark is perpendicular (or concentric) to the surface you want fitted.

If you've been able to acquire most of the tools described so far, you are well on your way. And if you learn to handle them properly and to keep them sharp, clean, lubricated, and protected from moisture and rust, you are just about ready to turn that ordinary boat into a yacht.

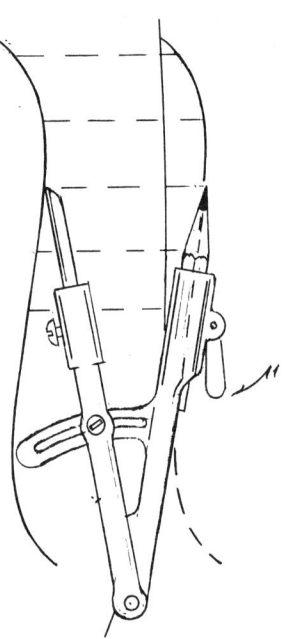

Figure 2-31. SCRIBING OR SPILING COMPASS

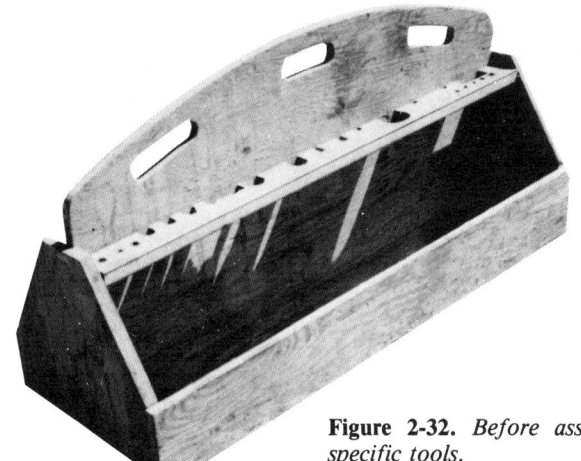

Figure 2-32. *Before assembly, saw the slots for specific tools.*

Figure 2-33. *Grooved strips seat backsaw and handsaw. The compartments hold planes, oilstone, drill bits, and so on.*

EVERYTHING IN ITS PLACE

While a carrying box might fit into the chapter on accessories that you can make, it seems to go well with the tools you'll be using. Of course, there are store-bought tool boxes. Any that are more than adequate, however, are very costly. And the modestly priced ones are simply wide-open trash containers. If you use your imagination and examine a few boxes used by carpenters and boatbuilders, you should be able to design and build a very satisfactory one for yourself. I have found the box described on the next few pages to be more than adequate. See Figure 2-32. Alter it as you please.

A criterion for my purposes was that the box had to be light enough, fully loaded, to be placed into and lifted out of the trunk of a car. Also, I like to see at a glance that my most-used tools and those small things that are easily misplaced are right where they belong and not down among the shavings somewhere. This carrier fulfills my requirements and still has some open space for such loose tools as a level, three planes, square, pliers, wrenches, auger bits, twist drills, and a few more. Figure 2-33 shows the box loaded.

To build a tool-carrying box, you'll need about one-fourth of a sheet of ½-inch plywood. This can be shop grade or the cheap utility exterior stuff with knots showing. You will also need a piece of ¼-inch plywood about 14 by 32 inches in size for the bottom and dividers. Add a bit of scrap ¾-inch lumber, glue, a few nails, and that's it. A plan you might find suitable is shown in Figure 2-34.

Rip out the tool retainer, a little shelf 2½ inches wide and just over 30 inches long. Using a pencil, lay out the spacing of your tool arrangement and the size of the notches. Go lightly. Tomorrow you may remember a tool that has to be there and you would have to respace everything. There may be several tools that can drop into slots in front of the tools lined up against the center panel — a try square, for example. Cut the notches deep enough to accommodate the entire tool. Chisels, for ex-

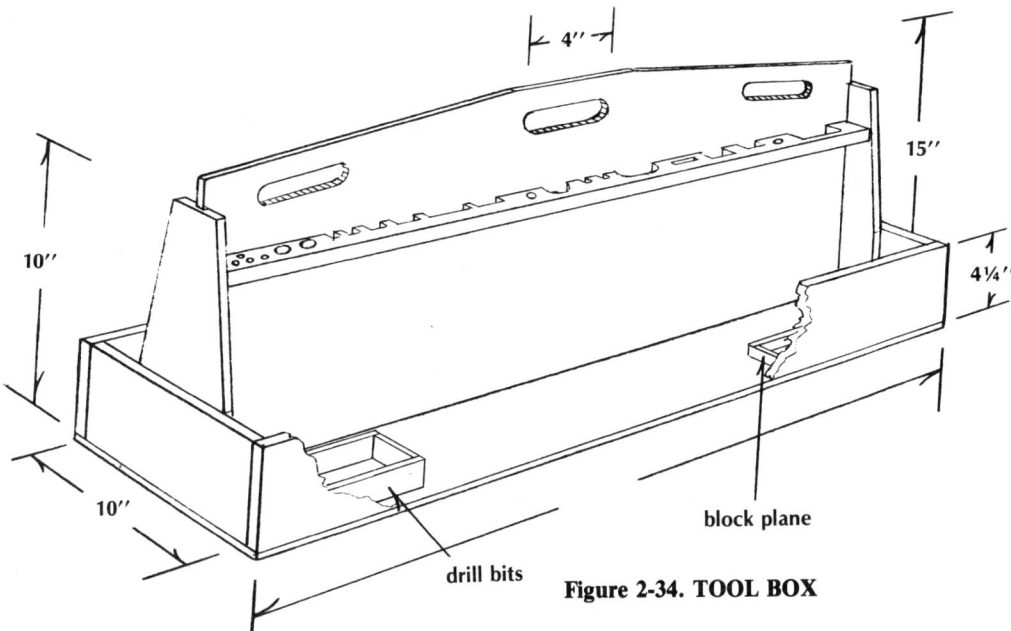

Figure 2-34. TOOL BOX

ample, must have slots much deeper than just for the blade itself so they will hang from the handles. Saw multiple cuts with your backsaw to make the notches, then chisel out the remainder, or use a sabersaw or keyhole saw.

Build the basic box as shown, but let the heads of the finish nails protrude for later gluing. This makes it easier to build the little rails that retain the planes, drill bits, and so on. The gable-shaped end pieces may be nailed or screwed and glued to the box ends. (I cut a groove ¼ by ½ inch in mine to strengthen the attachment of the center piece.) Eventually, the bottom will be nailed and glued to the box (or use 1-inch, No. 6 wood screws). Thus, this is a good time to cut the bottom to size and brad it temporarily in place.

The next step is to mark off on the bottom those fenced areas that will hold the planes, oilstone, and drill bits. The rails can be made from orange crate material ripped to about $\frac{5}{16}$ by ½ inch. Your crosscut saw will rip this thin stuff successfully. Smooth it up a bit with a block or smooth plane. If you use ¾-inch brads and set the strips on edge, the points won't come through the bottom. Another way is to use larger brads and clench them over underneath. Glue the strips down and they'll stay for a lifetime. The purist will miter the corners, but you're probably more interested in getting on with the boat!

To build the drill box, construct the 1½-inch sides and end, and nail and glue them together. Put this piece aside until the glue is set. To nail from the bottom into the sides of this little compartment, mark it on the bottom of the box inside and drive about four brads through. Pull out these brads and insert new brads from the opposite side of the bottom piece. This way you won't miss when you nail the drill box in. But you can't put this piece in to stay until everything is complete and the basic box is all glued and fastened.

Now let's do the center piece. Draw centerlines for the holes for the hand grips. Bore the holes 1 inch in diameter and saw out the material between holes with a sabersaw or keyhole saw. Rasp or sand all edges smooth. Knock off the sharp corners of the sloping edges with a plane and then sandpaper. Cut the length; it should be about 30 inches long and fit snugly between the gable ends. Before installing, rip a couple of strips approximately ¾ inch square and about the length of your backsaw and crosscut saw. Now comes a hitch: You need a groove in each of these strips in which your saws will sit. See Figure 2-35. I don't suggest that you try to saw this with a handsaw, although it's possible! If you do not yet have a table saw and can't borrow one, do you have access to a portable electric handsaw?

Place the power saw upside down in a vise — gently, don't crush it. Adjust the depth of cut to about ¼ inch. Clamp a small piece of scrap to the sole plate to act as a fence. See Figure 2-36. Tape or wire the switch to "on" or have someone hold it on for a minute. Just plug in and start. You now have a miniature table saw that will cut those slots in seconds. In Chapter Five, I'll show you how to build a great table saw using a portable electric handsaw as the power unit.

Now that the pieces are grooved, nail the longer one in the bottom of the other half of the box and against the center piece. Notice that the groove should not be centered. This is to provide for the thickness of a saw handle. Position the shorter piece so it clears the crosscut saw and is at the opposite end of the box. Don't let any nails enter the groove. To hold the saws in place, cut out small blocks ¾ inch thick to fit into the handles and fasten turnbuttons on top of these blocks.

Now make sure the notched tool shelf fits, and drill all holes for nail sets and other small items. Mark about five spots where screws can be driven from the opposite side. Drive 1¼- or 1½-inch flathead screws and set up

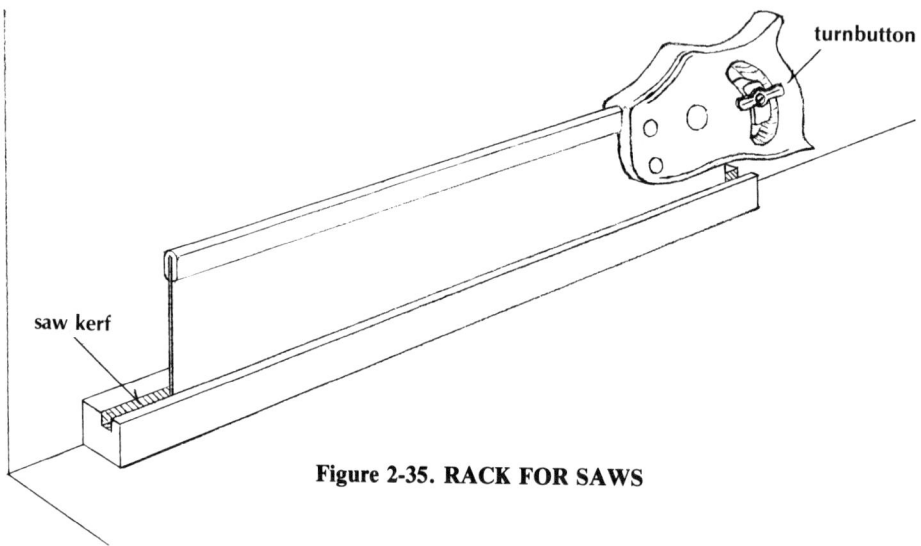

Figure 2-35. RACK FOR SAWS

Figure 2-36. *To make grooves in the tool box, a make-do table saw is used. A power saw is held in a wedge-action planking vise described in Chapter Five.*

with glue. Assemble the center piece between the gable ends, and nail and glue. Pull the temporary brads out of the box ends, glue the corners, and fasten with 1½-inch finish nails and/or screws. Now nail and glue the bottom in place. And, finally, place the drill box in position and brad up from the bottom to fasten it.

There's just one more job to do. Place the tools one by one in their slots and mark around them with a broad felt marker or crayon. Now you will see at a glance if a tool is missing or out of position.

Start thinking about this box even before you start collecting tools. Keeping your most-used tools organized will save you much time and give you great satisfaction.

Now let's move on to electric hand tools.

THREE

Electric Hand Tools

You may be one of the lucky amateur yachtbuilders who have few financial problems. If so, you are one in a hundred. Most amateurs are straining both their finances and their domestic tranquility to bring their dreams to life. I know what they are going through. In my many years of boatbuilding and boat ownership, I never quite had the funds to equip my shop or my boats with the best available. I always had to find ways to economize (I still do). As a consequence, you'll find that many of my suggestions follow a lower-cost approach to doing things.

It may seem a contradiction, but owning a few decent power tools is the economical thing to do. Sometimes the poorest-quality electric tool is overwhelmingly superior to the finest hand tool. Let's say you are renting space to build your boat. How many modestly priced new or used power tools could you buy with the rent money if you postponed renting for one month? Or, if you already have a location, how many months sooner would your vessel hit the water if you had some time-saving tools? Need I go on? Yes, I had better, for I've witnessed a grown man attempting to build a $35,000 to $50,000 yacht with just $75 worth of tools. His half-completed mold now sits abandoned while the rent bills pile up and court action threatens. I might mention also that he has never heard of Howard Chapelle's *Boatbuilding,* Robert Steward's *Boatbuilding Manual,* or Bruce Bingham's *Ferro-Cement Design, Techniques & Application.*

I know, of course, that none of you would exhibit such foolishness. So let's see what power hand tools are suitable, and how you use them in boatbuilding.

ELECTRIC HANDSAWS

I use the term *electric handsaw* rather than *power saw* to avoid any confusion with power tools or power machines such as table saws and radial-arm saws, which, incidentally, are also called circular saws. Your first acquisition must be an electric handsaw of the type called the Skilsaw. Skilsaw is the registered name for the products of the Skil Tool Company, Inc. See Figure 3-1.

Look for electric handsaws marketed by Skil, Stanley, Black & Decker, Sears, Ward's, and other companies. Unless you will be using a saw hour after hour cutting two inches or deeper, as some carpenters do, you don't have to buy a heavy-duty professional model. Any 7- or 7¼-inch-diameter blade is adequate. Saws this size develop 1½ to 1¾ h.p., are double insulated against short-circuits, and usually have bearings that do not require lubrication. The gears are usually spur gears

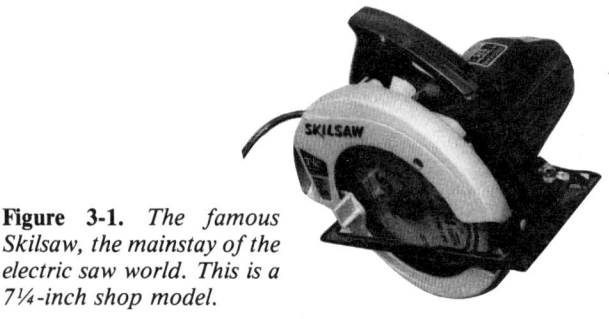

Figure 3-1. *The famous Skilsaw, the mainstay of the electric saw world. This is a 7¼-inch shop model.*

(you'll find them quite noisy), although some saws have helical gears. All should give you years of service for a reasonably modest investment. Avoid the low-priced bargain saws, although even these are much better than sawing by hand, especially on light work such as plywood. Moderation, of course, is the answer. So, if the case of your saw feels very hot, allow it to cool while you do something else.

Many advanced craftsmen will tell you that the type of saw I am advocating is cheap. Yes, it is, compared with the fine heavy-duty types at the top of the price range. On the other hand, such a saw is a low-cost tool that will do anything the costlier ones will do if you exercise reasonable care. They are backed by guarantees, but there are no warranties against stupidity. If you feel a saw running hot, stop cutting, then look for a scorch mark on the saw cut or kerf, as it is called. This tells you that your blade is dull, or that it has lost its set. Don't try to force a cut. If your project calls for extensive ripping of thick oak, or something similar, that's different. Take the job to someone with a 10- or 12-inch table saw, or borrow a heavy-duty saw.

Needed in any electric handsaw is a clear view of both sides of the saw blade, as shown in Figure 3-2. You'll be doing a lot of freehand sawing, following a line, and you must be able to see the teeth. If you are one of the lucky few who can afford two saws, consider a lightweight panel saw. This tool is useful for quick, light cutoffs and ripping with a guide. It also is terrific for long curves in plywood up to ⅝ inch thick, and it will handle a 3-foot radius with ease.

Saw Blades

Take a look at the drawings in Figure 3-3. These show most of the configurations of saw teeth. The combination blade, used for both ripping and crosscutting, is most useful. This blade is slightly slower than the blade designed for each purpose, but that is of little consequence. If you have a lot of ripping to do, spend a few dollars for a rip tooth just to make it easier on the tool and yourself. A table saw is best if you have a lot of ripping. The table saw will give you greater accuracy, too, although with practice you can get fairly good results with the rip guide on your electric handsaw.

Figure 3-2. *This 7-inch saw provides excellent visibility of the blade, necessary when starting a cut or for freehand work.*

Combination Blades for Fine Work

Another very valuable blade is the cabinet combination. This blade is sometimes called the cabinetmaker's or planer blade. Planer is the most accurate name, for these blades cut with or across the grain and leave a surface that feels as though it has been sanded. A planer blade is excellent for plywood up to ½ inch thick, or heavier for a short cut. Because these blades are taper ground and have no set, you cannot change direction at all once you have started. This is not a problem on a table saw because a rip fence or bevel gauge is used.

To use a planer blade on an electric handsaw, you must follow a straightedge. Clamp or tack to the work a piece of plywood or lumber that is 6 to 8 inches wide and rigid enough to guide your saw perfectly. Or use your carpenter's square clamped to the work piece. Better yet, make a square out of ¼-inch plywood. Cut it from the corner of a sheet to guarantee 90 degrees, then brad and glue straight strips along the lower edge. Cut out the center to lighten it. Both the carpenter's square and the plywood square are great time-savers. There's one thing to watch for, however. If the planer blade saw cut suddenly wavers, stop at once. Your blade has overheated and is temporarily warped. It is not capable of doing the job. You will have to use a plywood blade or a cut-off.

The plywood blade has fine teeth and a moderate set. The cut it produces is good, but not polished like the cut of a planer blade. Most plywood blades will not handle long cuts in ¾-inch plywood, such as an 8-foot rip, but they are adequate for up to about 4 feet. The best blade for this work is a so-called cut-off. The teeth of a cut-off are quite coarse compared with those of a plywood blade and have more set. As a result, the surface of the

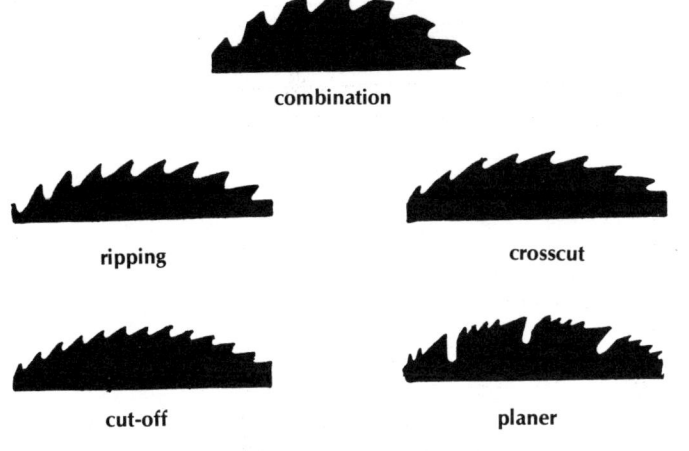

Figure 3-3. POWER SAW BLADES (From *How to Work with Tools and Wood.* © 1942, 1955, 1965 by Stanley Tools, New Britain, CT)

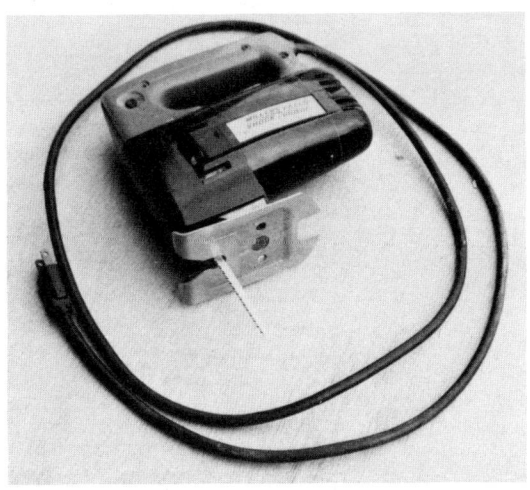

Figure 3-4. *A powerful sabersaw cuts curves as well as a bandsaw does, but more slowly. Also, material thickness is limited to ¾ inch. A sabersaw is easier on large plywood panels.*

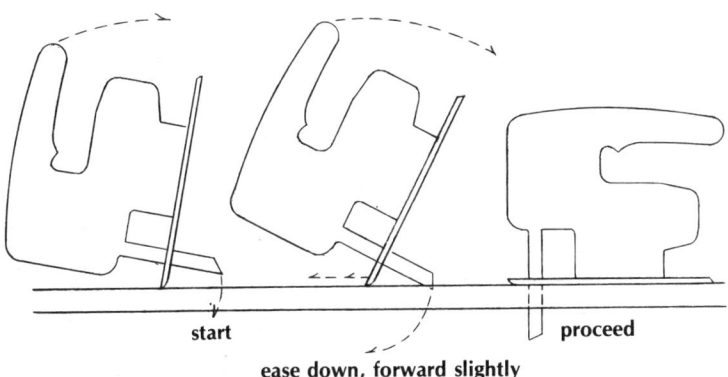

Figure 3-5. SABERSAW PLUNGE CUT

cut is not quite as fine. The cut-off, however, is fast, chips very little, and is an all-around good bet, whether for plywood or hardwood. For a perfect surface, invest in a carbide-tipped blade and get your purchase cost back in the low frequency of sharpenings required.

SABERSAWS

You will need a sabersaw, scroll saw, or jigsaw, as some call it, for cutting curves and for notching and completing power saw cuts. See Figure 3-4. Joinerwork curves, berth fronts, and other shapes normally handled on a bandsaw can be done with a sabersaw. Unfortunately, the thickness of material that can be cut is limited to about ¾ inch. In softwoods and lighter plywood, however, the sabersaw is great. This makes it the right tool for making patterns and templates from ¼- to ½-inch plywood.

The average light-duty sabersaw is reasonably inexpensive. I have seen one cut out all the mold sections for a 40-foot boat. It took two days with frequent rests, but it did the job. Variable-speed models are available, but I can see no advantage in this feature. Sears and Ward's both sell heavy-duty models at higher cost. The old reliables, however, are Stanley, Skil, Black & Decker, and Millers Falls.

Sabersaws are a bit tricky to use. First of all, the work must be well supported, especially if it's thin stock. Otherwise it will jump up and down violently with the saw blade. The sole of the tool must be kept flat on the work surface, and you must bear down slightly, or there will be an unholy clatter; you could snap the blade.

With practice, you can start a cut without first boring a hole (Figure 3-5). This is called a plunge cut. Begin by holding the base or sole almost perpendicular to the work surface, and keep the blade a safe distance from the line you wish to follow. Turn the tool on and slowly rock the blade down until its tip begins to jab into the wood. This will gradually produce a narrow groove that deepens as you lower the blade slowly into it. It helps to move the saw forward slightly to prevent the point from striking the end of the groove. In a few seconds, the point will penetrate the work stock and you will be able

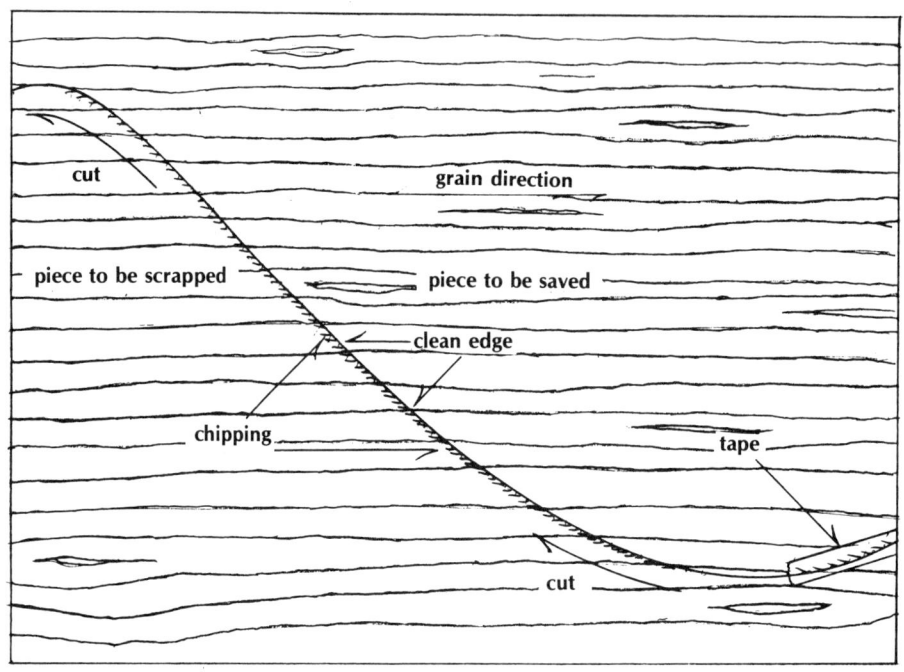

Figure 3-6. AVOID SAWING INTO GRAIN

to lower the sole flat on the work. Practice on scrap and you'll soon become adept, but don't try to plunge-cut hardwood. This method is faster than boring a starting hole and you could end up with a more usable remnant.

Always mark your line on the back side of the work, for the blades are quite coarse, and they pull upward. The splintering is unsightly, especially when cutting fir plywood. The direction of sawing also is important, as shown in Figure 3-6. When curves are cut across the grain or at an angle, the side of the blade going the hard way into the grain will chew it up badly, whereas the other side of the cut will be clean and sharp. You may have to reverse the sawing direction to save the piece from such damage. In many cases it may be practical to put masking tape on the work piece and mark on the tape. This will prevent 90 percent of the splintering. I suggest that you not try to saw too close to the line at any time, for sabersaws rarely saw square in heavy material. Plan to plane, rasp, or sand down to the line.

ELECTRIC DRILLS

Since most yacht joinery is plugged over screws, it is almost mandatory that you use a light pistol-grip electric drill, such as the one shown in Figure 3-7. This tool does a fast and neat job of boring for ⅜-inch and ½-inch bungs. You might make even better time if you have a hand or breast drill handy for drilling the lead holes. We have already covered the combination bits and counterbores available. All of these work well in a small electric drill.

Needless to say, there are scores of drilling jobs in any vessel. Many such jobs require quite deep holes. You will be way ahead using a power tool. For all-around service, choose a good ⅜-inch drill by Black & Decker, Stanley, Thor, Chicago Pneumatic, Skil, Craftsman, or Powercraft. Forget the ¼-inch models; they are too limited. Also, for woodwork, stay away from high speeds. Single-speed tools of 1,000 to 1,200 r.p.m. have worked out fine for me.

If you can afford a ½-inch drill, the variable-speed types are quite efficient, especially for use with a simple power screwdriver (Figure 3-8). This size is also very good for setting up in a drill press stand. See Figure 3-9.

Both the ⅜-inch and the ½-inch drills are suitable for cutting plugs, although the higher speed would be better. Reversible drills have some appeal for pulling screws and backing out long bits, but I doubt that the additional cost is justifiable for these reasons alone.

To sum up, you should be able to purchase all the capacity you'll ever need for a reasonable price. If you were going into keel, deadwood, floor timbers, big cabin sides, or similar work with long bits, you would need a heavy-duty ½-inch drill. It would be fine if this tool were reversible to clear chips, stuck drills, and the like.

The better electric drills have ball bearings for thrust, helical gears, double insulation, and high-impact plastic and/or aluminum housings. My preference, however, is for a more or less disposable drill that can be thrown away without much feeling of loss. That's why I bought a Black & Decker ⅜-inch drill in 1965, and I have used it to bore ½-inch holes in a cast-iron fin keel, plus hundreds of less sensational jobs. The thing is still going strong! If you used one to cut wood plugs only, you would save enough to pay for it several times over.

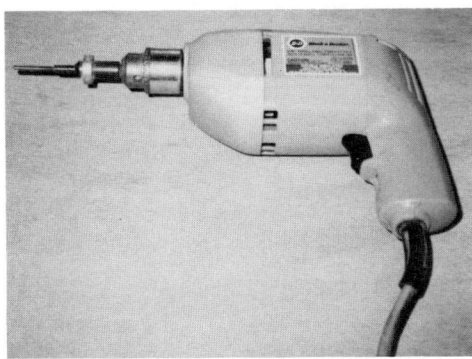

Figure 3-7. *A light ⅜-inch-capacity drill is indispensable. A speed of approximately 1,200 r.p.m. is recommended.*

Figure 3-9. *An inexpensive drill stand and a drill make a satisfactory press for most light work.*

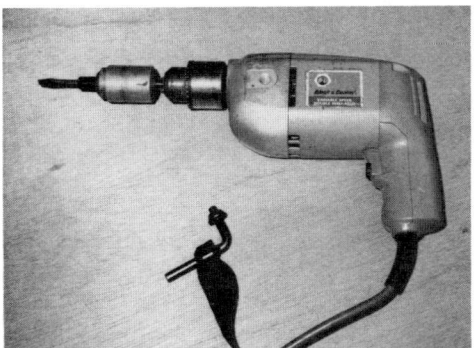

Figure 3-8. *This old screwdriver attachment in a ½-inch drill drives screws very well. Reversing variable-speed drills make satisfactory screwdrivers.*

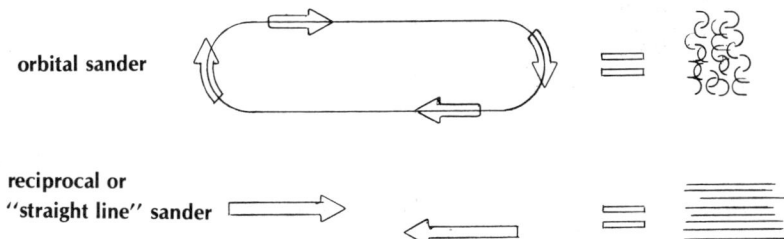

Figure 3-10. SANDER PATTERNS

SANDERS

Many boatbuilders advocate the use of portable electric sanders. I do not agree. I am still a believer in block sanding by hand, and especially in flexible long sanders for hulls. Let's discuss the types of electric sanders to help you make up your own mind. The reciprocating, or straight-line sander is a finish sander not intended for the removal of a lot of wood or old paint. On the other hand, you cannot do finish sanding with an orbital sander, except on work to be painted, not stained and varnished. See Figure 3-10 for a comparison of the cutting patterns of an orbital and a straight-line sander. The orbital sander leaves a pattern of tiny circular scratches that are almost impossible to see until you apply a stain or filler. Thus, this surface requires much hard sanding by hand block or by a straight-line sander. It's very difficult to remove these swirls. Granted, orbital sanding does remove material faster than a reciprocating sander. Orbital sanders are thus commonly used for preliminary sanding, to remove old flaking or powdery paint on wooden hulls, decks, and so on. Electric sanders are tiring, too. After you have swung either kind against a hull for three or four hours in the sun, you'll know it! Even a half-sheet block is a vacation by comparison. The only place an electric sander might get the nod is on a horizontal surface.

A good electric sander ranges in weight from 6 to 10 pounds and produces from ¼ to ½ h.p. These tools sell in a range from about $30 for orbital action only to $50 for dual action, ¼ h.p., and $65 for dual action, ½ h.p. Do not bother with anything lighter than this. The very light magnetic vibrator types especially are of no use around a boat. Years ago there was a professional straight-line sander called the Detroit E-Z. This tool had so much power you could sit on it and it would not stall. If you find one that still works, buy it, even though it may seem heavy to you.

The ¼ h.p. sanders usually take one-third of a standard sheet of garnet or aluminum oxide paper, open coat. Prepackaged sheets of this size are readily available, but I have found that those that contain an assortment of grits are never the ones I need. I use 60, 80, 100, and 120 grit. The finer grits will tear after a few strokes, but you should always finish up with fine paper on a block, about 220 grit or finer. Most of the ½ h.p. sanders use a half sheet. Never use the white flint paper. You will go broke in a hurry, as it has no life and removes very little.

The best way to cut sandpaper sheets is to use the toothed side of a hacksaw blade as a straightedge. Never use a knife, for the point will be ground away by the grit if it penetrates. It is necessary to break the glue backing

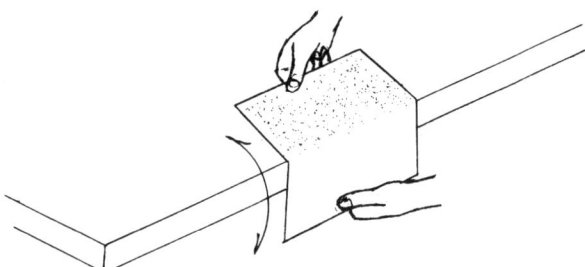

Figure 3-11. BREAKING THE SANDPAPER SHEET

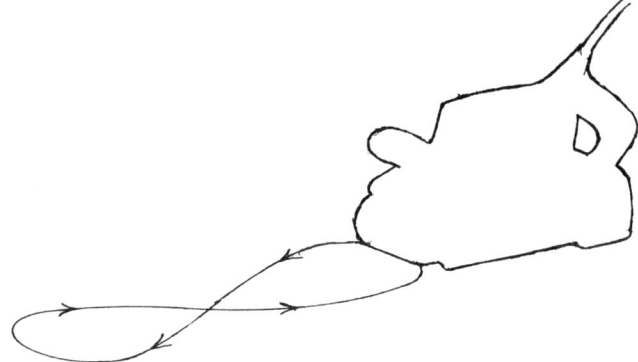

Figure 3-13. BELT SANDER FIGURE-8 MOTION

Figure 3-12. *A belt sander must be kept in constant motion and stroked in a figure-8 or orbital pattern.*

of the paper to prevent cracking and tearing. See Figure 3-11. Pull the paper back and forth over any corner, paper side down, right up to the ends. This makes it much easier to clamp the paper in the sander. Sometimes these clamping devices have a tendency to lose their grip. You can increase the holding power of the clamp by inserting a piece of wood about $\frac{1}{8}$ inch thick on the grit side along with the paper.

To use a portable electric sander, exert moderate pressure about as you would with a plane and stroke the same way, back and forth. Don't depend on the vibration alone to do the job. The weight is not adequate, either. Always work *with* the grain unless you must remove a lot of material. Beat the dust out of the grit every now and then with the palm of your hand. And when the paper begins to lose its cutting ability, change it. Don't struggle on; it's a waste of time. Some of those worn sheets of 60 or 80 grit are usable for hand sanding, but remember, the final sanding must be with a block of wood or hard foam and fine paper, as explained above.

Belt Sanders

The second most popular type of portable sander is the electric belt sander. See Figure 3-12. These tools start at about 10 pounds, so you would think twice about using one to sand vertical surfaces for any length of time. They are satisfactory for bench work or for horizontal work in general. The larger tools take off material quite rapidly. On lighter ones, a medium belt will produce a passable finish. Fine belts don't stand up very long; I find them a waste of time.

As with all tools, belt sanders require practice. Nothing is better for planking, deadwood, and so on. They have several characteristics, however, that can cause trouble. The sander must be in constant motion. If it is allowed to hesitate for a split second, it will leave a groove. If you stroke as with a plane, there is a momentary stop when you reverse direction. This causes the grooves. I use an oval or figure-eight motion, even at the expense of some scratches across the grain, as shown in Figure 3-13. The only other way is lots of experience with this type of sander.

Another unpleasant feature is that belt widths of 3 inches, the most popular size, mean the sole is only slightly larger. In addition, the tool is rather heavy, so it is possible to rock the machine slightly as you stroke. This results in disastrous grooves parallel to the stroke. The 4-inch models largely eliminate this hazard, but they are heavier still. Very probably the belt sander's most annoying characteristic is belt misalignment or tracking. The alignment adjustment, which is made while running, is extremely sensitive. You can find yourself wasting a lot of time on maddening adjustments every two or three minutes. Also, the belts are very expensive but quite long-lived if kept in line.

If you can find someone who knows all about belt sanders, he might show you how to avoid all this unpleasantness. Although I *sound* completely negative, I am not, because from time to time I use a Craftsman belt sander, which is sold in large numbers. One great advantage to this belt sander is that it is flat and thus will rest comfortably on its back (Figure 3-14). This means the tool can be used efficiently as a bench sander. Tack wood blocks around it to keep it from creeping off the bench. This allows you to pass work pieces lengthwise on the moving belt. Just be sure you have a firm hold on the work piece. Another good method is to place work pieces on the bench for sanding in the usual way. Tack pieces of ¼-inch plywood scraps to the

Figure 3-14. *Designed to rest solidly on its back, this model is good for sanding strips and small pieces.*

Figure 3-15. *A Stanley, the last word in jointing power planes. Shorter, lower-cost planers are excellent for removing material rapidly, roughing spars, and so on.*

bench as retainers, or use a C-clamp to clamp one end of a longer work piece. Avoid running the sander over an end or edge, for this will put a radius where you do not want one.

One final word on sanding: *Never* sand a piece of plywood, especially fir, until it has had several coats of sealer, varnish, or paint. And please note that flat-grained fir is never varnished. Sanding a fir plywood surface by hand or machine only cuts out the soft fibers, leaving the harder areas standing out worse than ever. Build up the surface with several coats, if it's rough, and then fine sand with a hard block. Concave surfaces and edges may be sanded efficiently with blocks shaped to conform to the curvature. In a later chapter, I'll go into some detail on this subject, for there are no satisfactory machines to do this work.

POWER PLANES

The electric plane is an extremely useful tool at all stages of boat construction. This is perhaps the most work-saving of all tools, because heavy planing is real labor, even though you are not likely to face it every day. Consider the power plane to be an upside-down jointer, especially the longer models. See Figure 3-15. A power plane is used for straightening plank edges rough from the mill (before ripping, for example), for removal of stock down close to the line, and occasionally for use as a thickness planer. Lengths of work pieces too unwieldy to handle on a jointer can be worked easily on a bench, unless you are surfacing wide planks. A power plane can be used for removing old paint and varnish, but you'll dull your knives (blades) in a hurry.

If you are building a conventional wooden boat, there are countless jobs for a power plane if you use it only for removal of stock: dressing down deadwood, centerboards, rudders, straight floor timbers, deck beams, and so on. Remember, however, that anything wider than the sole of the plane will show overlapping cuts rather clearly. If this happens, finish up with a jack or smooth plane. Power planes are intended for edging. I have used an elderly Wen plane on solid spars to shape up the square and the octagon. For the latter, the bevel fence set at 45 degrees is pretty handy.

Probably the greatest use for power planes is the fitting of doors. Some carpenters do dozens in a day. Some tools take off close to $\frac{1}{8}$ inch in a pass; these are heavy-duty planes designed for that type of work. If I had a lot of solid-spar work, I would find a good power plane somehow. Used ones, unfortunately, don't lie around long. On the other hand, if you have many other pressing needs, then a lighter and lower-cost plane will do the work. It might not be as fast, but the quality of your results should be as good as the condition of the knives and bearings in the tool permits. The models offered today are quite short compared with older heavy-duty types, so they are not as good for jointing edges. They cost less, too, and are quite noisy, since they are belt driven. These newer tools are principally aluminum and zinc die castings. The older heavy-duty models have a lot of steel throughout and ball bearings rather than sleeve bearings.

Most power planes have rotary heads that turn at about 15,000 r.p.m. The knives or blades (usually two) fit into slots and are locked in with special machine bolts. The cutting edges of the knives may be touched up with an oilstone while they are in the machine, but

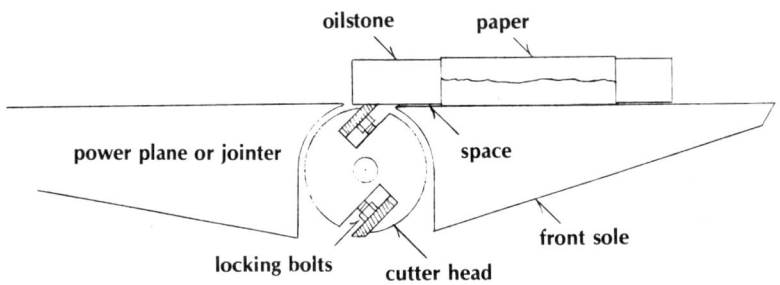

Figure 3-16. HONING PLANE OR JOINTER KNIVES

Figure 3-17. *A router is the most versatile power tool for molding edges, rabbeting, jointing, duplicating from a pattern, coving, and so on.*

they must be removed for grinding. As long as the knives show no nicks, you can maintain a satisfactory cutting edge by honing them in the head. Lower the front sole to about $\frac{1}{16}$ or $\frac{3}{32}$ inch. Wrap your oilstone in paper except for about 1 inch at one end, so the stone does not contact the surface of the sole. Rotate the head so the stone can be laid on the bevel at exactly the original ground angle. See Figure 3-16. Hold or wedge the head securely, and then slide the stone back and forth on the back sole lengthwise to the knife, counting the strokes until the blade feels sharp. This is to avoid realignment of the knives. Stroke the other blade the same number of times. Now turn the depth adjustment to $\frac{1}{16}$ inch or less and test. If the tool chatters or the surface of the work is rough, the knives are still dull and you'll have to try again. Dull knives will cause the motor to slow down and overheat. You will be able to tell by the high whine when the tool is turning at its best speed. Do not force cuts. Better 10 strokes to take off $\frac{1}{8}$ inch than three strokes to chew it off.

It will be necessary to grind the knives when whetting no longer produces a good edge. Most good saw-sharpening shops have the equipment and the skill. Note, however, that in Chapter Five you will find two knife-holding fixtures for grinding knives correctly. In addition, instructions are provided there for adjusting knives in the head.

ROUTERS

Many woodworkers feel that the router is the most versatile of all power tools. It is fundamentally a simple machine, consisting of a motor and a base, as shown in Figure 3-17. Yet you can create beautiful cabinetwork with a router by means of a variety of operations, such as dadoing, grooving, beading, fluting, coving, dovetailing, rabbeting, inlaying, carving, and, of course, jointing. I'm sure other operations are possible. These you'll discover if you study the router in depth. In yacht joinery, its ability to form molded edges easily, rapidly, and precisely, and work the finest of joints, makes it almost a must. It's also nice to have an assortment of cutters. By combining cuts — that is, by using one cutter and then following with another — you can achieve almost any conceivable edge effect. Admittedly, unusual shapes are used in furniture construction more often than in yacht work. A judicious display of molded trim, however, adds beauty and distinction to almost any interior (Figure 3-18).

Prices for routers vary considerably and are based on horsepower and engineering. The finer makes can cost more than $175. Stanley and Rockwell have a wide selection at this price and up. The Japanese-made Makita has been recommended highly to me by a number of cabinetmakers. Sears and Ward's offer more-than-adequate tools in the one-horsepower class from about $50. You can easily add $25 to $75 more for accessories and bits. Watch the classified ads for used routers. Good buys turn up frequently. Whatever tool you end up with, do not push it too hard. Overheating is fatal.

Accessories add to a router's usefulness. Craftsman dovetail fixtures turn out quite acceptable joints, a quality feature in drawer construction, and the device is almost foolproof. See Figure 3-19. Small steel tables are available to convert your router into a small shaper (a router really is just an inverted shaper). This is shown in Figure 3-20. The shaper table permits positioning and moving of the work piece, a desirable feature when shaping small parts. In Chapter Five, there's a design for a router-shaper table quite a bit larger than those you buy. I used this table with a $\frac{1}{3}$ h.p. router to make

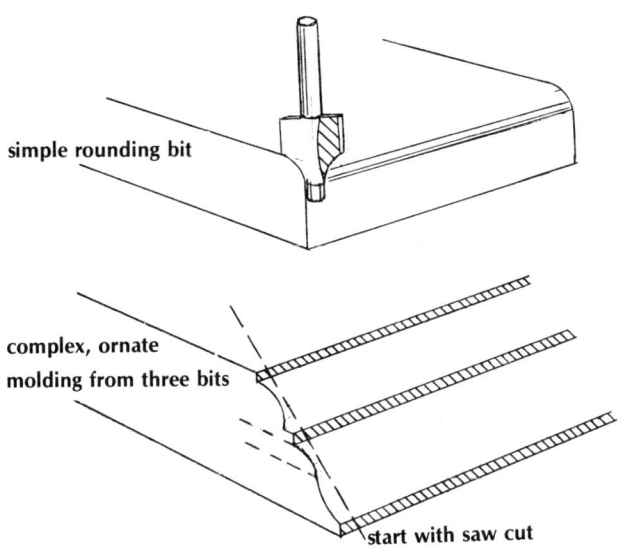

Figure 3-18. A ROUTER CREATES DECORATIVE EFFECTS

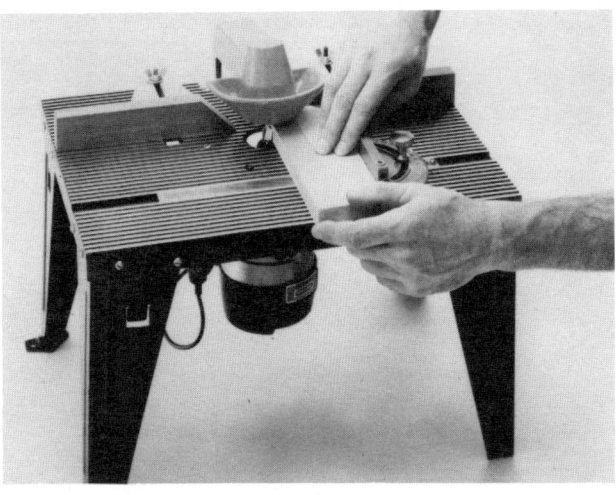

Figure 3-20. *This table is for a Craftsman router. It has a split fence, safety guard, and miter gauge. (Courtesy Sears, Roebuck)*

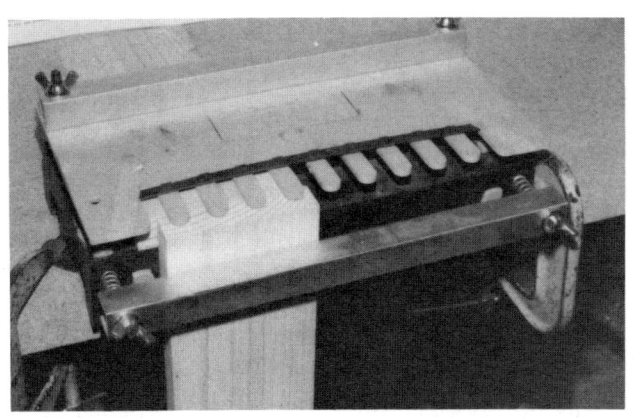

Figure 3-19. *This dovetail fixture produces accurate joints simultaneously in each part. It requires a dovetail bit and router guide bushing.*

Figure 3-21. *Sears guide bushings are screwed to the inside of the router base plate. These devices are used to follow any pattern, dovetail fixture, and so on. They are available in steel and plastic.*

lipped cabinet doors, cove and ogee edges, corner radii, and other items. With a more powerful machine, such as the 1½ to 1¾ h.p. Stanley, Rockwell, or Makita router, you should be able to do most of the operations normally done with a bench shaper.

One of the most interesting accessories for routers is a guide bushing (Figure 3-21). This device permits use of a straight bit and a pattern for producing repeated shapes — say, a dolphin vent in doors and locker fronts. You simply make a pattern of ¼- or ⅜-inch plywood, allowing a small tolerance for the wall thickness of the guide bushing. This technique also may be used to make a cutout or a carved design using a veining or V-shaped bit. I have made extremely complicated floral-design screens using this method.

A few years back I built several 36-foot rectangular masts. Each was made of two pieces glued together. See

Figure 3-22. I formed the two ends to the required tapers, with the joint running fore and aft. Then I clamped a short fence to the router sole and set this to leave a 1-inch wall thickness. I used a ¾-inch-diameter bit and cut down about 1¼ inches in three passes, leaving the solid areas as called for in the design. After the walls were finished, I went back and routed out the centers. I routed a groove through the solid areas for ventilation and wiring also. The next step was to plane the side tapers. This was easy, for I had to plane off just the side walls and the solid at the head. (Remember that this was done on the surfaces to be glued, not the outside of the spar.) This method produced pretty good spars, stronger than a glued-up box spar, but it did waste quite a bit of spruce. See Chapter Fifteen for details.

A router can be used for hollowing out streamlined

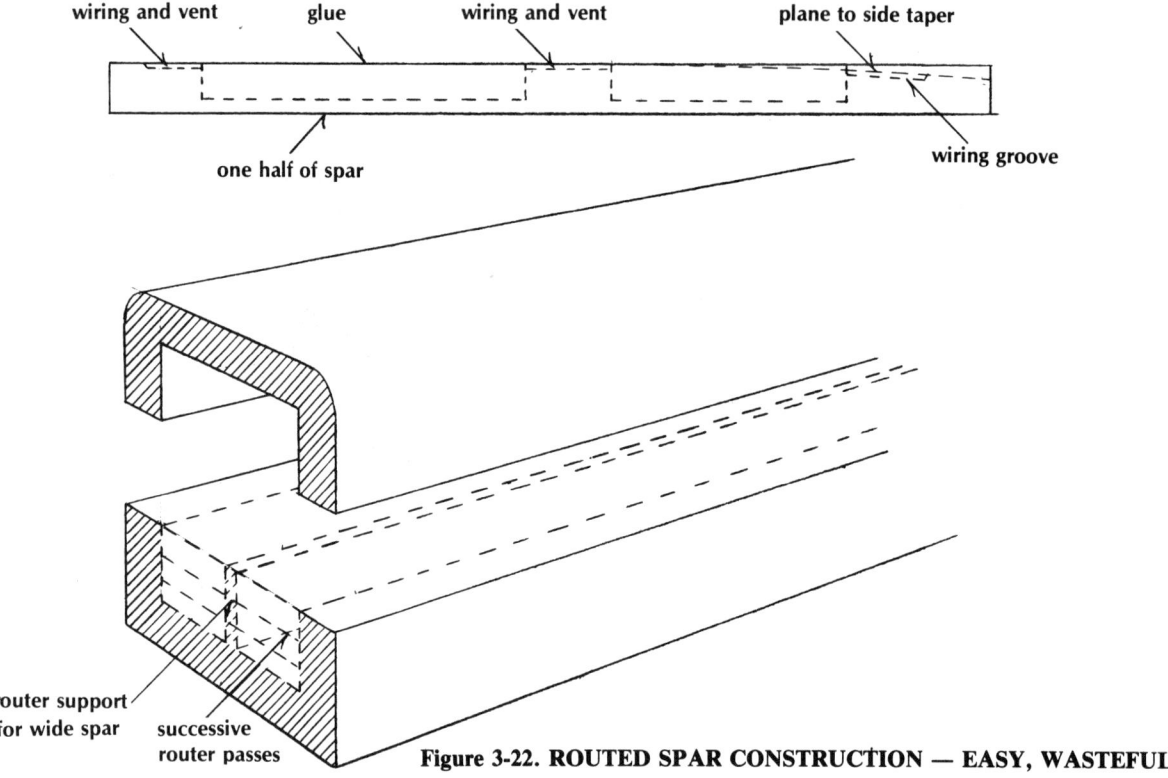

Figure 3-22. ROUTED SPAR CONSTRUCTION — EASY, WASTEFUL

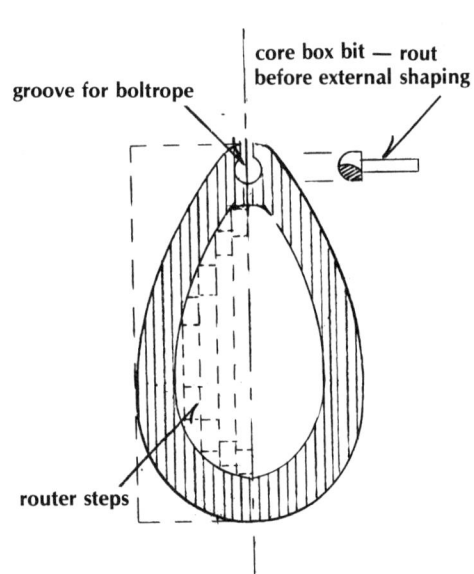

Figure 3-23. SOME STEPS IN ROUTING OUT A HOLLOW MAST

wooden spars and for cutting a groove for the bolt rope, as shown in Figure 3-23. There is nothing better than a router for cutting out the rabbets in the staves for box masts. With the shaper table, a router does a fine job of making tenons and lapped joints, too.

Some Router Tips

Never work on a router or make adjustments without disconnecting the cord. The router is a very dangerous machine. Once I picked one up and carelessly rested the sole for an instant against my side. At the same moment, I just happened to touch the switch. In a split-second, the bit chewed up and all but swallowed my belt, but I pulled away before it got to my skin!

The router bit shank is gripped by a ¼-inch-capacity collet (a chuck), usually set up with an open-ended wrench while the armature is locked. Be sure that *all* of the shank is in the collet and cinched up tight. At 25,000 r.p.m., a loose bit can do a lot of damage. The depth of the cut is set by adjusting the base plate up or down. Be sure to lock this adjusting device firmly. I have seen the results of vibration loosening the depth control. You don't want that.

Always move the router against the cutter rotation direction, never with the rotation, for the tool will suddenly try to take charge (Figure 3-24(A)). Once started, the bit must be kept moving. Do not stop or slow the movement of the bit while it is in contact with the wood, or it will burn a spot instantly, and possibly ruin the bit, too. Also, do not turn the router on or off while touching the work piece. This applies especially if you are using a bit with a pilot (an extension that runs along the edge of the work). See Figure 3-24(B). On the other hand, do not try to feed or push the tool too fast, for this will force the router to slow down and overheat. Keep that high whine sounding out! In most cases, you will have to make the cut in two or three passes to prevent overloading. Just set the cutter deeper each time. This is especially the case in hardwood. Always hold the router firmly against the work with both hands, but avoid pressing the pilot so hard that you burn the edge.

A router can do a decent job of dadoing (such as cutting the grooves for shelves). See Figure 3-25. I use a

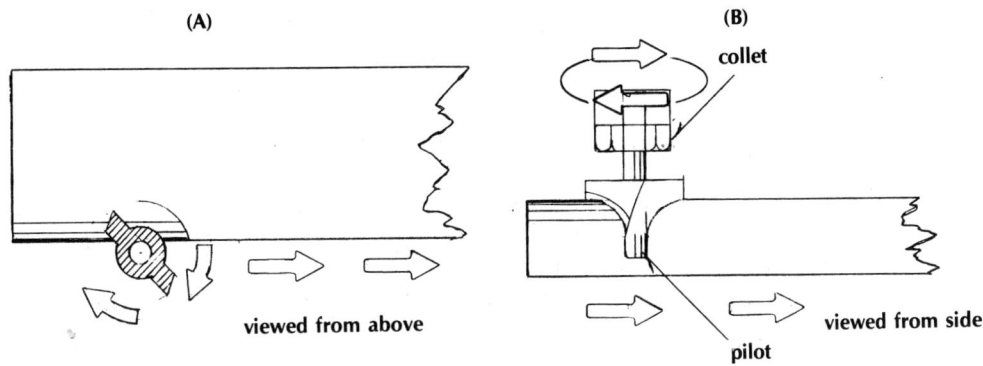

Figure 3-24. ROUTER FEED DIRECTION

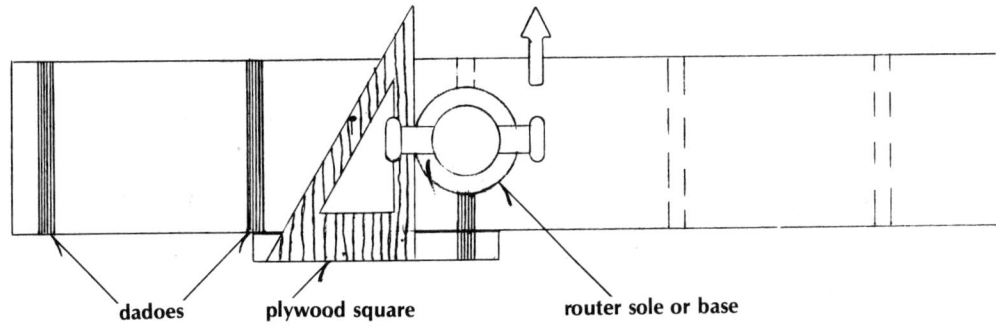

Figure 3-25. ROUTING SHELF DADOES

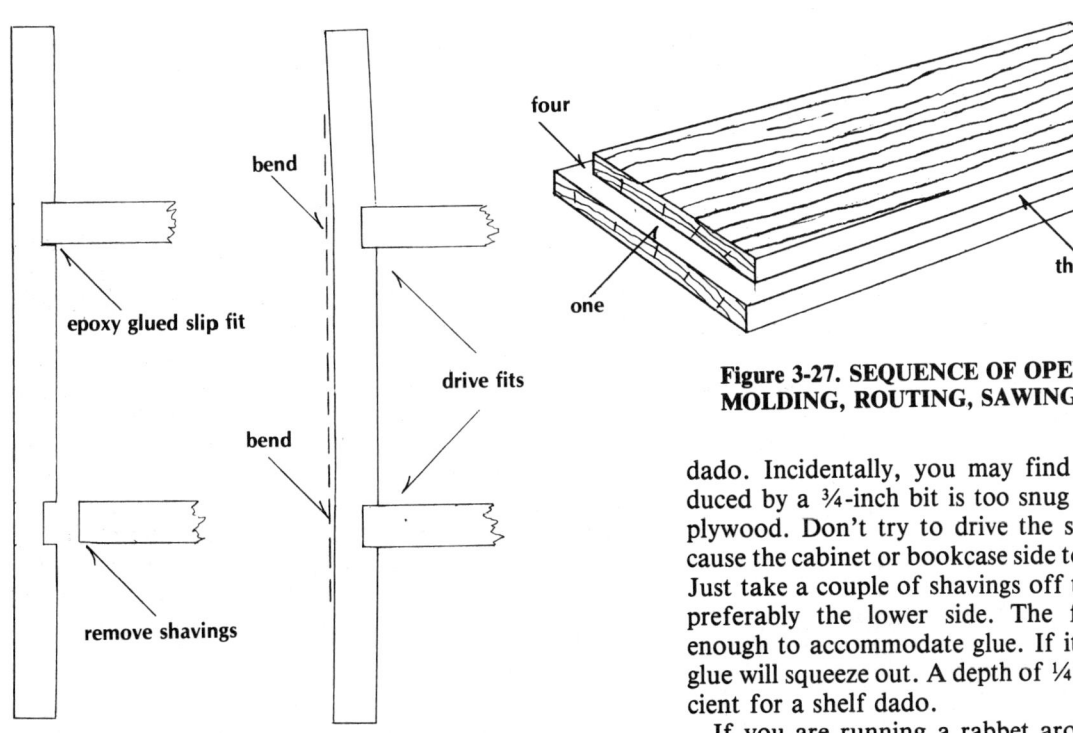

Figure 3-26. DADO FITTINGS

Figure 3-27. SEQUENCE OF OPERATIONS: MOLDING, ROUTING, SAWING

square made from ¼-inch plywood as a guide. The piece of 1 by 2 nailed and glued to the underside of the triangle may be dadoed by the router the first time you use it. Thereafter, this cut can be used to locate the next dado. Incidentally, you may find that the dado produced by a ¾-inch bit is too snug for some lumber or plywood. Don't try to drive the shelves in. This may cause the cabinet or bookcase side to bend (Figure 3-26). Just take a couple of shavings off the side of the shelf, preferably the lower side. The fit should be loose enough to accommodate glue. If it is too tight, all the glue will squeeze out. A depth of ¼ inch is usually sufficient for a shelf dado.

If you are running a rabbet around four sides of a piece, as shown in Figure 3-27, it is best to make the cuts across the end grain first so the side passes can remove any splintering at the corners.

These are but a few of the many facets of router operation. Sears offers a booklet that covers the subject quite well for the beginner. Check your library for more advanced information.

FOUR

Stationary Power Tools

In this chapter I shall discuss in some detail the types of stationary tools used in many professional boatbuilders' shops and in thousands of home shops as well. Do not be too concerned if your evaluation of a tool differs from mine. Quite aside from cost or capabilities, each tool has certain attributes that make it valuable if not absolutely essential to your kind of work. Some of the tools discussed may be eliminated if other tools perform the same functions.

GRINDERS

There's no way you can get by without a grinder for sharpening tools. I'm sure you could have someone turn a hand grinding wheel for you, but a hand grinder can't possibly do comparable work (with the exception of a wet grinder). The belt-driven wet grinder (offered by manufacturers such as Rockwell) is perfect for tool grinding but not for any other purpose. Industrial-rated grinders will handle grinding of metal parts as well as tools (using the proper wheel, of course). See Figure 4-1. These tools are powered by motors of ⅓ to ¾ h.p. Prices range up to $100 and more. These are double-arbor outfits for setups with two grinding wheels, or a buffing wheel, sanding drum, and so on. Well-known dependable names are Rockwell, Milwaukee, Thor, Black & Decker, and Skil. I would include Ward's and Sears in the lower price ranges.

If you're in my financial bracket, you'll find you can get along beautifully with a belt-driven double-end arbor powered by a ¼ to ⅓ h.p. used appliance motor (Figure 4-2). I recently ground a blade for a molding head to produce raised-panel doors and drawer fronts. The results were strictly professional, as you can see in Figure 4-3. I keep all of my planes and chisels in top shape with such a grinder. Mine is typical in that it takes a 6-inch grinding wheel, a buffing wheel, and a sanding drum — all at the same time. Mine has sleeve bearings. The ball-bearing type sells for $15 to $20. The reason for the buffing wheel is a patternmaker's trick: it's great for honing the cutting edges of plane blades, chisels, and so on, after whetting on the oilstone. Load the buff with Tripoli, polish the bevel edge a bit, then just a touch on the back, and you'll have an edge you can shave with. Another tip: Mount your grinder and motor on a plank about 3 feet long so you can move it around or carry it in your car.

In Chapter Five, I'll describe a number of homemade fixtures for holding tools so you can grind accurately.

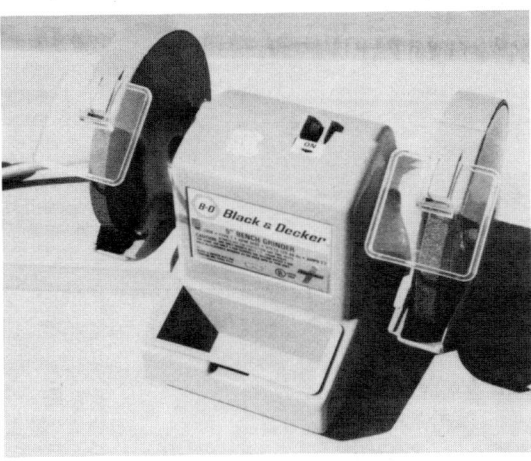

Figure 4-1. *The water reservoir in this tool grinder prevents overheating and annealing of cutting edges. Low-cost protection for your tools.*

Figure 4-3. *Panel edges produced by grinding cutter for single-knife molding head. The raised panel at the top requires a tilted table-saw arbor.*

Figure 4-2. *A narrow grinding wheel is not the best for grinding plane blades, but it can do a good job with solid tool support (see Chapter Five).*

Figure 4-4. *The author's low-cost 4-inch belt sander does a fine job of finish sanding on parts and strips, and removing saw marks from edges. Disc is small. The support helps handle long, flexible flat moldings and similar pieces. The motor is under the bench.*

BENCH DISC SANDERS

For many years, Delta (now Rockwell) manufactured a splendid 12-inch-diameter disc sander. Once in a blue moon, one turns up on the used-tool market. This sander turns at 3,450 r.p.m. and has one disadvantage: it will take off stock very rapidly, so be prepared. Rockwell now makes a smaller belt-driven sander of 8 to 8½ inches in diameter, but I have not used one.

With a miter gauge sliding in a groove parallel to the disc, you can use a sander to square up ends or fit miters. Just let the piece kiss the disc as you slide it across several times to bring it down to the mark. A disc is fine for rounding outside corners also. Plans for my homemade 8-inch disc sander are included in Chapter Five.

BENCH BELT SANDERS

The combination belt-and-disc sanders available in many makes are even more useful (provided that the disc is 8 inches or better). See Figure 4-4. The belt, 4 to 6 inches wide, runs over a platen up to about 15 inches long. The work piece is pulled over this platen against the direction of the belt. Thus, long pieces can be finished. Or the fence may be installed over the platen so very small pieces can be handled safely. A slight hand pressure is all that is required to remove planer corrugations and to do general surfacing of hard and soft woods. The piece, however, must be kept moving constantly. I often dress edges after ripping, skipping the jointer. Because I always use coarse belts, I must hand sand with fine papers for the final finish. Fine belts do not stand up satisfactorily, in my opinion.

As with a hand belt sander, tracking or alignment of the belt is tricky. The tension is adjustable on bench models, and I have found that belts will wander if belt tension is not adequate. The projecting end of the belt is fine for sanding inside curves and shapes (Figure 4-5). If installed at the end of a bench, this is better than a drum for inside sanding.

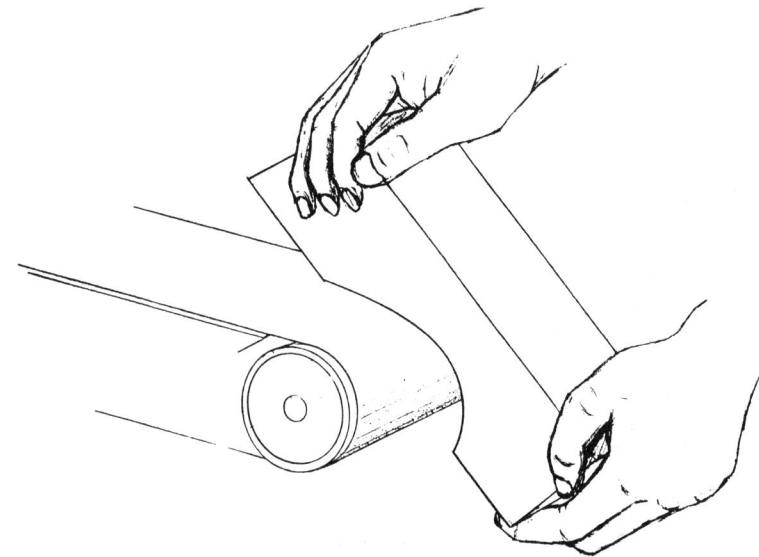

Figure 4-5. SANDING CONCAVE SURFACES ON A BELT SANDER

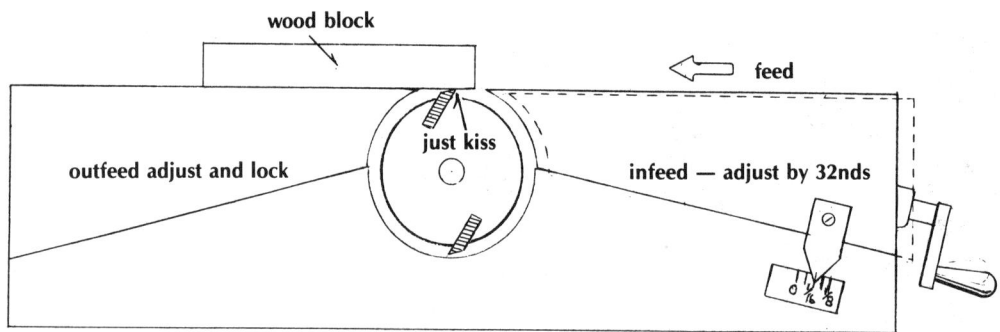

Figure 4-6. JOINTER ESSENTIALS

The bench sanders that take the 6-inch-by-48-inch belts sell for about $185 and up. They require at least a ½ h.p., 1,725 r.p.m. motor. The small 4-inch models are in the $40 to $75 range. Both are available with or without a disc. Some manufacturers are Atlas, American Machine & Tool, Rockwell, and others. They are marketed by Ward's, Sears, Western Auto, and other chains.

JOINTERS

If you have ever sweated over planing a straight edge on 2-inch oak, you'll agree that a jointer is indispensable. There isn't much oak in joinerwork, but there is a lot of mahogany, pine, fir, and plywood, and some teak. If you own a power plane, much of your problem has been solved. For straightening the sawed edges of pieces 2 feet or more in length, however, even the power plane comes out second best.

Here's how a jointer works. The outfeed or back table (on the end away from you) must be adjusted so that it is perfectly flush with the cutting edges of the knives or blades as the head rotates. See Figure 4-6. Check this with a smooth wood block or straightedge. Don't use metal. Now crank up the infeed or front table so that it, too, is even with the knives. The depth pointer should now read "0". If it does not, move it. Back the infeed table down a hair and try a piece of softwood. First, however, make sure the guard over the head is working freely, because this is a very dangerous tool. (A good friend has three beautifully tapered fingers because he was careless when pushing thin material through a jointer.)

If you back the table down $\frac{1}{32}$ inch, you should now take off just about that thickness. If you feed fast, you will see many little corrugations on the cut surface. You will notice also that the high-pitched hum of the machine drops to a much lower note. Both of these signs indicate that you are forcing the machine. This can produce a poor surface and possibly a burned-out motor. This is especially true when dressing a broad work surface, for the knives are working harder. If your outfeed is set correctly, the work will pass right over the table

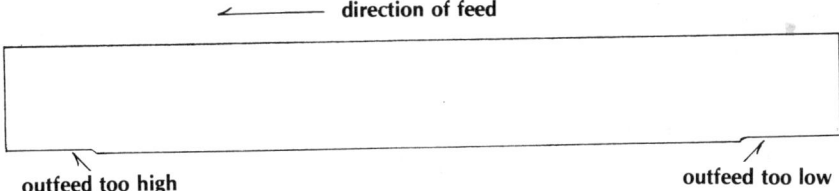

Figure 4-7. JOINTER TECHNIQUE

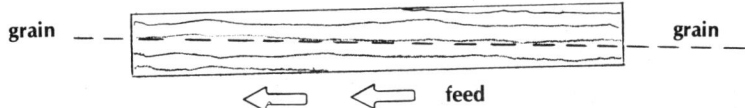

Figure 4-8. JOINTER TECHNIQUE

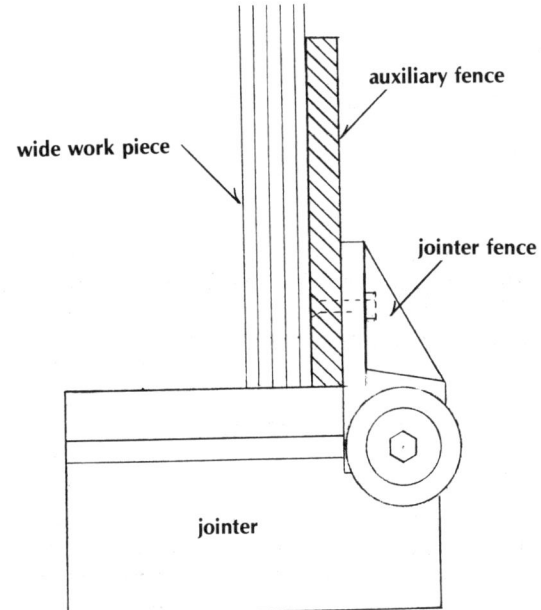

Figure 4-9. JOINTING WIDE STOCK

The jointer fence guides the work so the planed edge is true. Hence, it must be checked with a square or bevel gauge before you start to cut. Bear back against the fence. If you are edging a wide board or plywood (a door, for example), screw an extension 8 to 10 inches high to the fence so the work will be steady as you feed it. See Figure 4-9.

If it is necessary to plane thin stock ¾ inch or less in thickness, use a pusher block as shown in Figure 4-10(A). Handles for the pusher can be made from pieces of dowel or broomstick. Set them at about a 75-degree angle. A pusher block keeps the work from chattering (and your fingers attached to your hand also). A simple pusher is shown in Figure 4-10(B).

Always be sure that your fingers do not hold the edges or back end of a piece. The left palm should press a wide piece flat on the table while it is moved forward by a pusher stick in the right hand. For a perfect surface, long stock must be fed alternately with both hands. Do not stop. Have the pusher handy for the last few inches. Long and very thin stuff (say, ¼ inch thick) may be planed by placing a heavier piece on top of it. Glue a little stop across one end, as shown in Figure 4-10(A).

Material wider than the jointer knives may be dressed down adequately by removing the fence and guard and making several cuts. Overlaps may show, so be prepared to finish with a jointer, jack, or smooth plane.

Long pieces are hard to handle on a short jointer, for the slightest movement due to imbalance can spoil the surface. Attach extensions to eliminate the need for a helper. Incidentally, if you must have a helper, instruct him or her merely to *support* the piece. Never allow a helper to pull or push. This applies to a table saw or bandsaw as well. I have a split finger as evidence of my failure to instruct a young helper correctly. But then, I wasn't using a pusher, so who's to blame?

Jointers come in all sizes up to giants 36 inches wide. The best all-purpose size for the amateur yachtbuilder is 6 inches (the length of the knives). See Figure 4-11. The much lower-cost 4-inch jointer is a definite second best, but it should be considered carefully. I would hesitate if the overall length of the tool were under 24 inches. Most 6-inch jointers are 40 to 48 inches long; this is good. Lately, manufacturers have introduced built-in direct-

without hesitation and the planed surface will continue straight out to both ends, with no low spots at either end. If there is a low spot at the forward end of the piece, the outfeed table is too high. If the low spot is at the back end, the outfeed is too low. See Figure 4-7.

Whenever you are about to plane, examine the direction of the grain in the work piece. Do not cut into the grain if this can be avoided by turning the piece end for end. See Figure 4-8. If planing creates a crackling sound, you probably are cutting into the grain. This will produce a rough or pitted surface. If the grain is wavy or curly, as in ribbon-grained mahogany, taking fine cuts may help. It would be best, however, to leave a little stock for finishing with a bench sander. On a long crook, you may have to plane from one end and then the other, finishing up with a smooth plane. Remember that no jointed edge is acceptable for finish. Always sand. Remember, too, that you can use a portable power sander turned on its back if you don't have a bench sander.

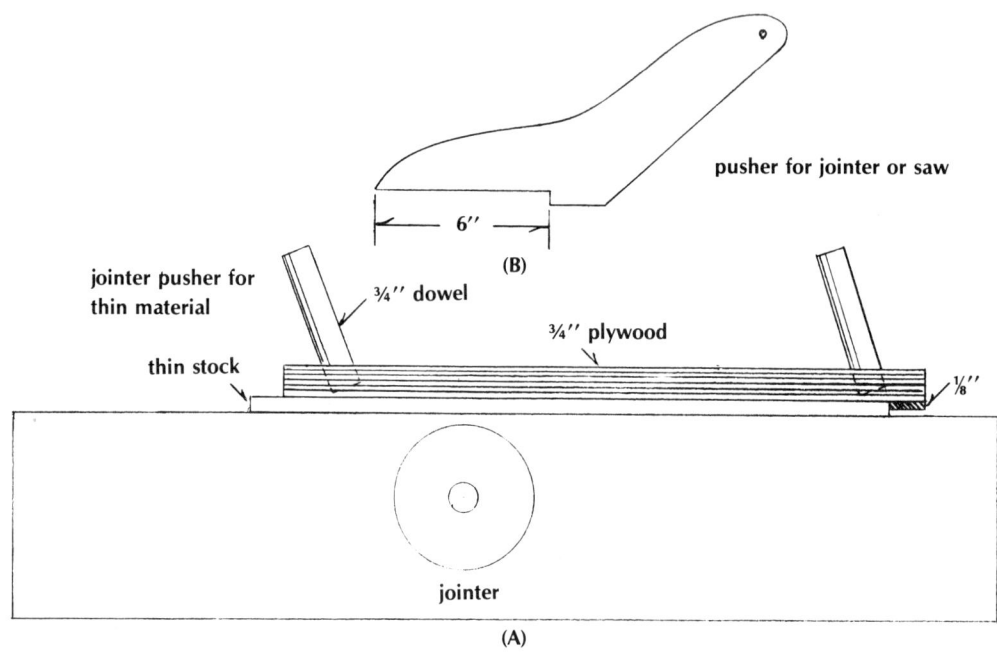

Figure 4-10. JOINTER PUSHERS

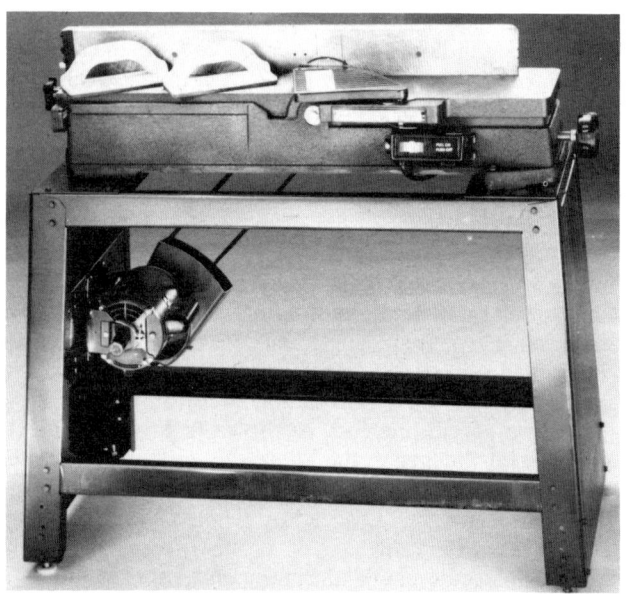

Figure 4-11. *This Craftsman 6-inch jointer is capable of the finest work required in any boatshop. It needs a ½ to ¾ h.p., 3,450 r.p.m. motor. (Courtesy Sears, Roebuck)*

drive motors that cost less than jointer-plus-motor, but I have no objection to belt drive. The better jointers have ball bearings. Sleeve bearings are common in the 4-inchers. The big chain stores have both 4-inch and 6-inch motor-drive and belt-drive jointers in a range from $250 to $350. The Sears 4-incher is $70 if belt-driven. A ⅓ h.p., 1,725 r.p.m. used appliance motor is sufficient to drive it. The 6-incher requires ½ h.p., and 3,450 r.p.m. is preferred. Rockwell, too, has a good line. Get all the catalogs or ask an experienced friend for advice, especially if you are looking at used tools. Don't sell this idea short, though. I found a somewhat rusty but relatively unused 4-inch Delta Homecraft jointer, minus fence, at a rummage sale for $5. The machine has performed to perfection for six years.

SHAPERS

As described in the section on routers, a shaper is basically just a large router turned upside down and mounted beneath a table. You will need a bench model for nonproduction boatbuilding. It's good to have your shaper and jointer on separate stands that may be moved about the shop or even into a boat's hull. The bench shaper base is of cast iron or semisteel; most have a provision for rapid adjustment of spindle or table height. See Figure 4-12. The surface should be ground and polished. If you find a used tool, your first job is to remove every vestige of rust from its surface. Follow up by sanding with a very fine emery cloth. Buffing with wax is not a bad idea, for the work piece must encounter no resistance as you move it into the cutters.

The shaper fence is divided into halves so that each section can be adjusted backward or forward. This corresponds to the infeed and outfeed on a jointer. See Figure 4-13. The fence or table should allow the installation of spring-steel hold-downs to prevent chatter. Small-shop bench shapers all have ½-inch-diameter spindles that take solid cutters from 1 inch to as much as 2 inches in height and up to 2½ inches in diameter. Many different cutters are available for each make, as are collars that enable you to mold curved pieces or to repeat shapes by riding a pattern against a collar (Figure 4-14). This is valuable for fitting scarfs and other joints, such as in covering boards and rail caps. There will be much more on this subject in Part Two.

Left: Figure 4-12. *A bench shaper is indispensable for reproducing from patterns, molding edges, rounding. It takes a high-speed ½ h.p. motor (see Chapter Five). (Courtesy Sears, Roebuck)* **Below: Figure 4-13.** *The author's shaper split fence could be used on the router-shaper table or shaper you can build. Both of these are described in Chapter Five.*

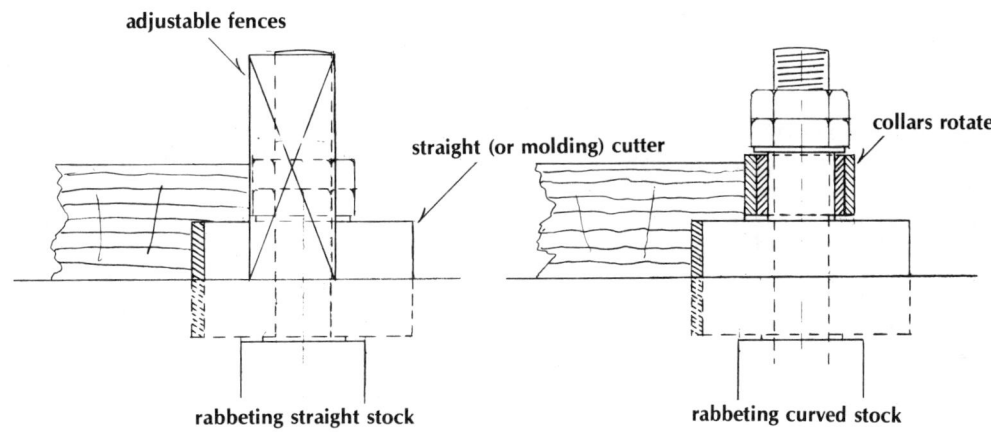

Figure 4-14. SHAPER SETUPS

Very likely the commonest use of a shaper is in forming rabbet joints. See Figure 4-14. A piece of work can be pushed through a decent shaper at a speed of one foot per second while making a ⅜- to ½-inch rabbet. The work must be supported properly so it does not spring up and down, causing a wavy cut. If the holddowns are not strong enough, you must build extensions on the table. On lighter tools, you will have to work more slowly. And if there is a lot of work (staves for spars, for example), it would be better to make two or even three passes to prevent overheating the cutters and armatures. If many shorter shapes are required, especially in hardwoods, three-lip cutters are available. These are useful for drawer joints, tongue-and-groove, coves, beads, ogees, glue joints, flutes, raised panels, drop leaves, and so on.

It is now next to impossible to buy hardwood moldings, even in Philippine mahogany. You can, however, make just about anything you want with a shaper and use up small scraps and rippings to boot. You may want decorative edges for your dresser and table tops, ladder treads, berth fronts and trim, drawer fronts, doors and door jambs, bulkhead corner trim, fiddles, and so on. These are the touches that make a vessel distinctive.

Toolcraft has an interesting shaper with a built-in 1 h.p. ball-bearing motor, a table size of 15¼ by 18 inches and a spindle speed of 18,000 r.p.m. Its price is around $185. The table size of this tool is minimal, so I would add permanent extensions. The Toolcraft appears to be similar to Ward's. Sears has a shaper with a good semisteel 19-inch-by-27-inch table at $210, but the spindle speed is only 9,000 r.p.m. This tool requires a belt drive and a ½ h.p., 3,450 r.p.m. capacitor-start

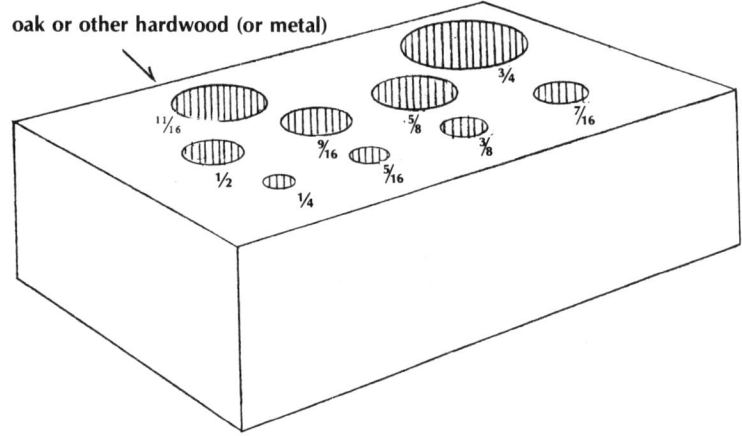

Figure 4-15. DRILL BIT GUIDE

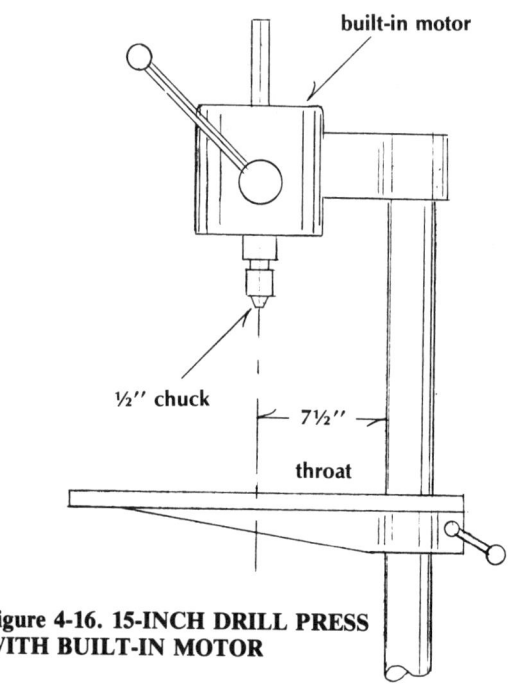

Figure 4-16. 15-INCH DRILL PRESS WITH BUILT-IN MOTOR

motor. Atlas has a heavier bench shaper equipped with an elevating table mounted on large-diameter pins. Although it looks like a real production machine, I have not seen it in use.

Most of these tools have threaded ½-inch spindles about 2½ to 3 inches under the nut. This is long enough to set up a two-part head that holds two knives about 1½ inches wide. Using straight knives, this arrangement would make a great edge planer or jointer for straight work against the fence or for square-edged shapes running a pattern against a collar. By grinding these straight knives identically to a desired shape, you can produce any reasonable molded effect. Remember, however, that these shaper heads swing a comparatively large radius, so it would be wise to set up for several passes and feed slowly. Raising or lowering the spindle can control the amount of material removed by each pass.

The versatility of the shaper cannot be described adequately in these few paragraphs. Check your library for additional information. Rockwell International, Power Tool Division, has a good booklet called *Getting the Most Out of Your Shaper*. If you prefer to go the router route, see the little conversion in Chapter Five, where I also describe a more efficient ½-inch spindle shaper you can build from a kit.

DRILL PRESSES

I can remember trying to get along without a drill press. There is one basic operation, however, that is next to impossible without one: boring a hole perpendicular to your work piece. I have gone so far as to make a drill jig consisting of various sizes of holes in a block of hardwood, but even then, I had to borrow a friend's press to guarantee accuracy. See Figure 4-15. Of course, there's quite a bit of metalwork in any boat. Here again, a drill press is virtually a must.

In addition to its primary operation, drilling holes, a drill press of adequate capacity can be used for many other woodworking chores: routing, dadoing, planing surfaces, rabbeting, making mortises and tenons, grinding, sanding, cutting plugs, and so on. The garden-variety drill press is capable of speeds up to only 4,200 r.p.m., however, so higher-speed or variable-speed tools must be selected to perform such specialized work. Accessories make the exotic jobs practical and worthwhile.

The standard drill press is designated as, say, 12 inches or 15 inches. This means it will drill at the center of a 12- or 15-inch circle. The throat — the distance from the center of the chuck or spindle to the column — is therefore 6 or 7½ inches. See Figure 4-16. The usual vertical travel of the spindle, and consequently the depth of a drilled hole, is about 3½ to 4 inches. The maximum height from the base to the chuck is about 14 inches. Most drill presses are equipped with a clamp-mounted table on the column, so it is not necessary to raise or lower the head to accommodate work of different thicknesses. The standard chuck capacity is ½-inch drill size. The new high-speed types take up to ⅜- and ½-inch bits.

I regard bench models as portable, for they weigh in the neighborhood of 125 pounds with motor, whereas floor models weigh over 200 pounds. Millions of bench drill presses have been manufactured, so used ones occasionally come on the market. Names to look for are Rockwell, Atlas, Sprunger, Toolcraft, Shopcraft, Delta, Craftsman, and so on.

You should look into the small presses recently introduced that have built-in, variable-speed motors. Ward's and Toolcraft offer machines that feature a rotating head and a solid-state electronic speed control. Thus, one end of the spindle is used for normal drilling and other operations up to 2,500 or 3,000 r.p.m., while

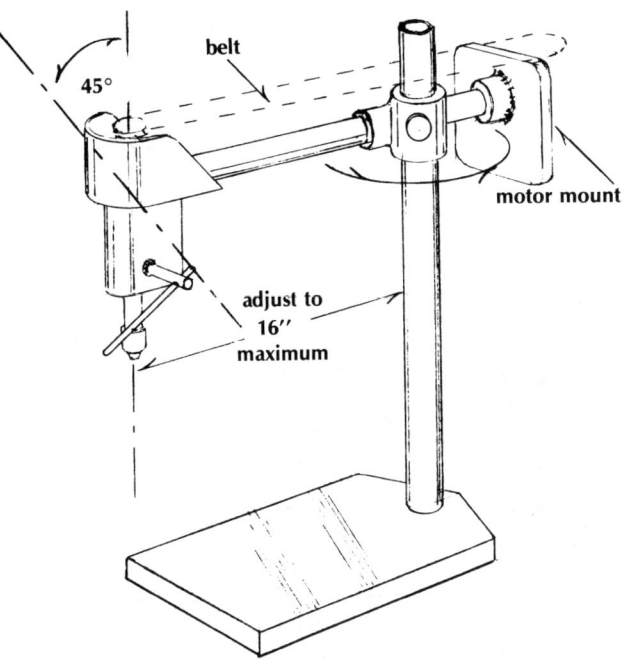

Figure 4-17. 32-INCH RADIAL DRILL PRESS WITH BELT DRIVE

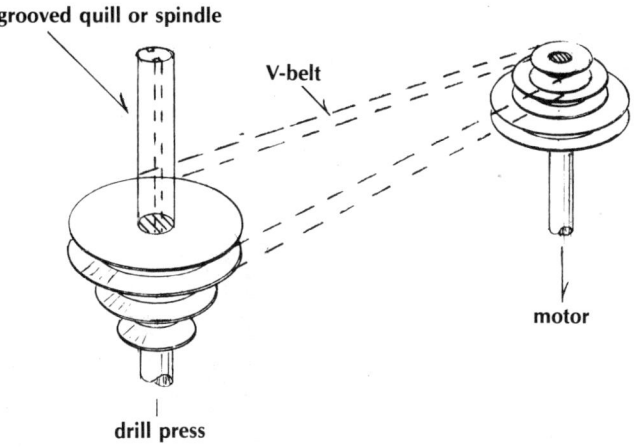

Figure 4-18. THREE-STEP CONE PULLEYS

the other end is available for shaping and routing up to 18,000 or 20,000 r.p.m. With accessories, this tool is definitely a full-fledged shaper as well as a good 17-inch drill press. Price is around $420, including built-in motor. Ward's also has a lightweight model (only 13 pounds). It is about 10 inches with a ⅜-inch keyed chuck. You dial the speed, between 700 and 2,000 r.p.m. The head does not rotate. This tool sells for about $60.

Another development is the light-duty radial drill press shown in Figure 4-17. Radial drills are not new, but these little bench models are. Rockwell has one that drills at the center of a 32-inch circle and the head tilts. This tool takes a ⅓ h.p., 1,725 r.p.m. motor for speeds to 4,700 r.p.m.; the chuck size is ½ inch. The tool's price is about $300. At the lower limit, American Machine and Tool offers a 16-inch model with tilting head and ½-inch keyed chuck. It's under $80. Being able to swing the head of a drill press over the edge of a bench is useful for larger jobs, so plan to locate a radial near an end or edge. In selecting a motor, be sure it has end thrust bearings so it can be operated continuously with the shaft vertical.

The speeds of standard belt-driven drill presses are easily changed. All of this type are equipped with cone pulleys, three or four V-groove pulleys on the spindle (or quill). See Figure 4-18. The motors must be similarly equipped. To change speed, you simply shift the belt from groove to groove. This usually provides a range from about 400 to 5,000 r.p.m. Drilling holes in wood may require the lowest speed. The screw spur on wood auger bits should be filed off so there is no thread; otherwise, the screw will pull the bit into the work faster than it can clear the chips. In addition, the rake angle of the cutting lips of the bit must be filed to a much lower angle to prevent digging in. Of course, the square on the shank also must be cut off.

Another type of bit, the spade (Figure 4-19), works very well. Spade bits cut clean, accurate holes and they are inexpensive — about $6 for a set of six, ranging up to 1 inch. Another fine bit for wood boring is the spur bit. See Figure 4-20. These come with single or double cutting edges and may be operated at 1,800 to 3,000 r.p.m. Those with more than one cutting edge may be used without clamping the stock to the table, but single-lip Forstner or expansion bits over 1 inch require secure clamping of the work. You will find that twist drills (machine bits) have a tendency to wander and to drill oversize or oval holes in wood. Of course, you should always place the work on a block of scrap wood so you don't drill holes into the table.

Accessories for the Drill Press

To use your drill press as a shaper, check to be sure that the top speed is 5,000 r.p.m. or higher. Don't expect a polished finish at under 15,000 r.p.m. Construct a heavy plywood table about 20 by 28 inches with cleats on the underside to fit the drill press base. Sears has a more-than-adequate shaper fence attachment at about $32, or you can make something similar that permits both fences to be adjusted (see Figure 4-21). Remove the Jacobs chuck (it will not hold at high-speed vibrations) and replace with a special collet chuck to take standard two- or three-lip router bits. You can also use ½-inch-bore shaper cutters if there is a tapered socket adapter for your drill press. From this point on, follow the procedures for shaping. Any $50 expenditure for accessories that enable your drill press to do the work of a shaper is money well spent.

One of the handiest accessories for a drill press is a rotary planer. This is a disc-shaped tool about 3½ inches in diameter. See Figure 4-22. Most have a ½-inch shank, but the Sears model has an adapter for replacing the chuck on the spindle. This tool has a single cutter on

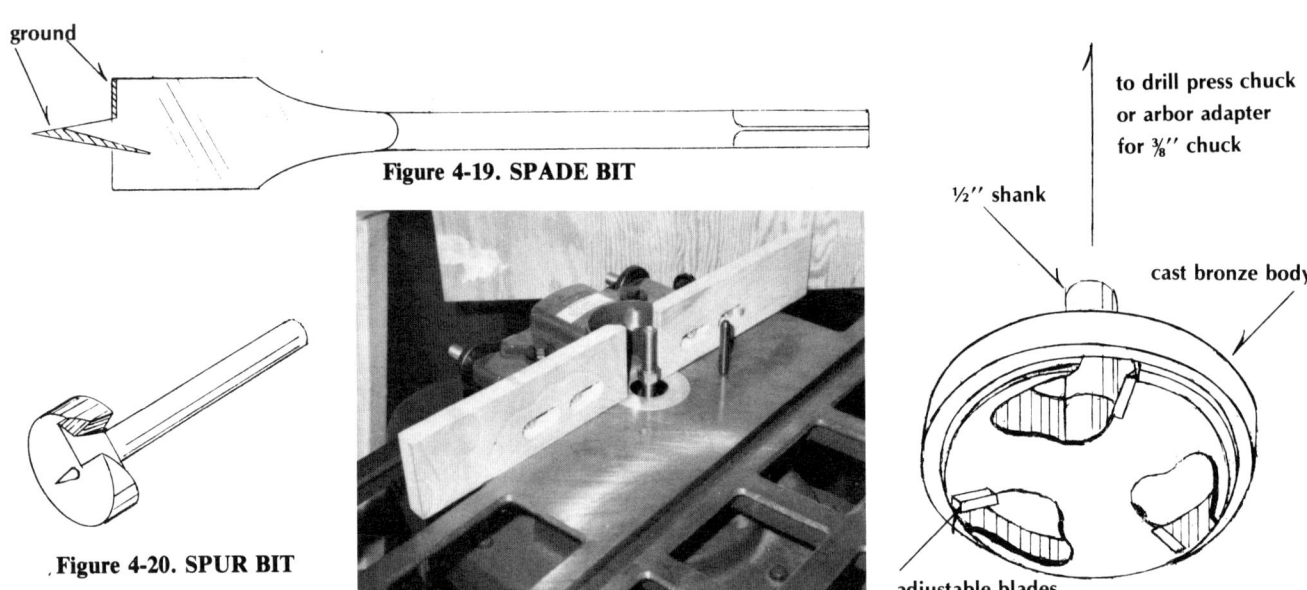

Figure 4-19. SPADE BIT

Figure 4-20. SPUR BIT

Figure 4-21. *Typical shaper fence. Tapped holes in table take guide pins and commercially available spring hold-downs.*

Figure 4-22. ROTARY PLANER FOR DRILL PRESS

the lower surface, but others I have seen (Baron Tool, Detroit) have three carbide cutters. To plane off a surface, feed the work slowly under the rotating disc, holding it down securely. The slightest play up and down will ruin the surface, so it might be a good idea to attach hold-downs to the table. The tool planes a surface 2¾ inches wide, so wider material must be dressed in several passes. A final finish will require a few strokes with a sharp smooth or jack plane, followed by block sanding. The planer may also be used for making handsome raised panels by tilting the table.

Sanding drums, grinding wheels, buffing wheels, hole cutters, and fly cutters are but a few of the drill-press accessories available. Not the least important is a plug cutter. This should be run at moderate speed, and if yours is the open-side, self-ejecting type, you'll need to rig up a carton on the table to avoid ricocheting plugs all over the shop. If you run this type of plug cutter into end grain, you get ⅜-inch by about 1½-inch dowels. Bore a number of these, then saw them loose from the stock in one stroke. Plug cutters and plug counterbore bits are available at marine supply houses or by special order from your local hardware store. The short, nonejecting plug cutters are available everywhere at moderate cost.

Mortising may be done with a spur, dowel, or machine brad point bit if the round end joint is acceptable — and why not? See Figure 4-23. But if not, just square up with a ¼-inch chisel. If you have a lot of joints of one size to make, get a mortising attachment jig, bit, and square chisel (Figure 4-24). The bit turns in a square hollow tool ground sharp on the lower end. This is pressed into the work, cutting the corners square as the mortise is bored out.

We should consider other uses of a drill press for metalworking, even though these are outside the realm of woodwork. When drilling metals, run the press at the proper speed and use a lubricant whenever it is called for. The maximum speed for a small carbon drill bit is about 1,000 r.p.m., except in aluminum, which is drilled at higher speeds. For a ½-inch drill bit, use the lowest speed on the cone pulley, 400 or 500 r.p.m. Brass and cast iron are drilled without lubricant or coolant — not even water. Steel should be kept wet with kerosene or, in a pinch, soapy water can be applied constantly with a brush. For aluminum, believe it or not, except for very shallow holes, soda water is recommended.

If you are using high-speed bits in metal, the speeds can be almost double those for carbon-steel bits. Keep all bits sharp. Look for chipped corners and grind them to the correct angle. If you have a lot of metalwork ahead of you, especially in stainless steel, you'd better pick up a book on the subject. Stainless presents special problems.

To sum up, a drill press is an extremely versatile woodworking and metalworking machine, even if it is only a drill stand that uses a portable drill. Next to your table saw and bandsaws, the drill press might well be your most used machine.

BANDSAWS

The first saw to be discussed in this chapter is small enough and light enough to fit in with the bench tools, but it requires a stand to bring the table to the proper

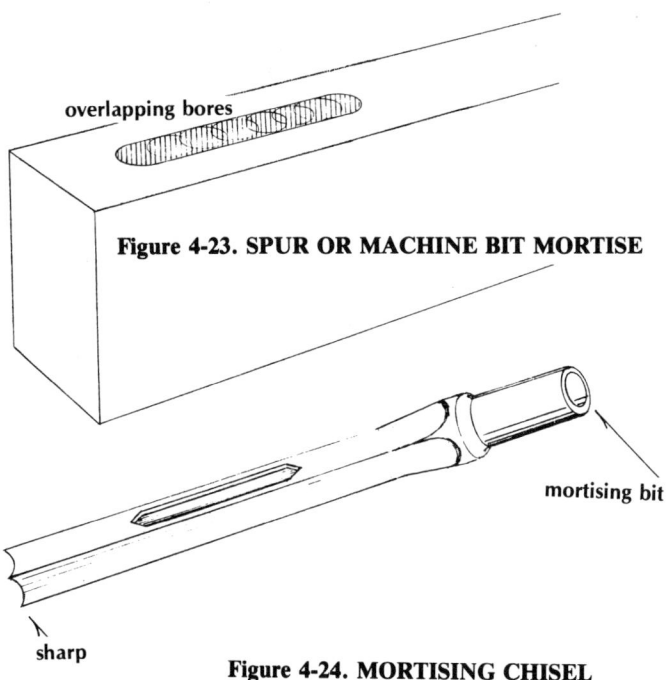

Figure 4-23. SPUR OR MACHINE BIT MORTISE

Figure 4-24. MORTISING CHISEL

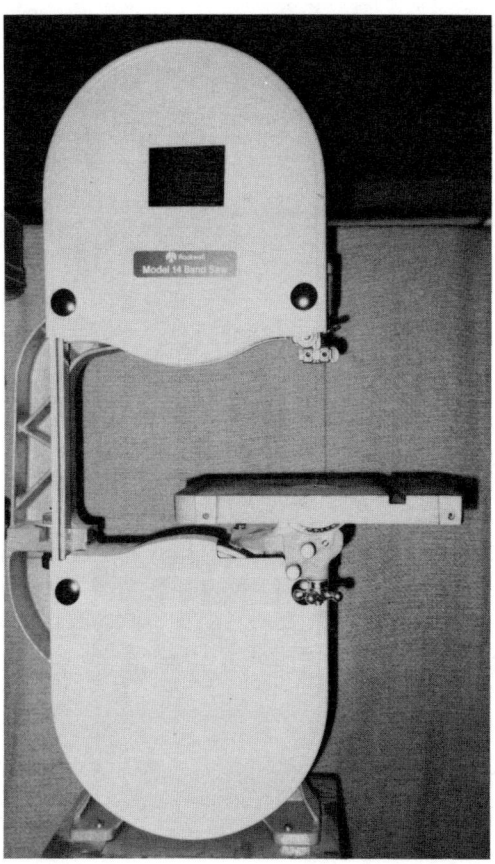

Figure 4-25. *A beautiful 14-inch bandsaw by Rockwell. The difference in utility between 12 and 14 inches is great.*

height. Thus, it becomes a floor machine and a major piece of equipment. The bandsaw is a fascinating tool. It's fun to operate and full of tricks. You'll never regret spending your money on one.

Many bandsaws built in the late 19th century are still around and working. Of course, as they say, they don't make 'em like that any more! In fact, they do, but not for your purposes. In actuality, very little has changed. Fine bearings, accurate wheel balancing, small sizes, ball-bearing blade guides, and other refinements make the modern tool efficient and long lived, but the basic design is the same. Today some of the jobs traditionally assigned to the bandsaw have been taken over by the sabersaw and the portable power saw. Both cut curves. Even a circular saw will cut curves if it has a small blade and a lot of set. But only one tool will cut fine curves, only one tool can duplicate shapes by stacking, only one tool can resaw 6 or 8 inches deep, and only one tool is so much fun to use.

The ideal saw for wooden boatbuilding is probably the 30- or 36-inch capacity bandsaw. (Capacity is the distance from blade to frame.) For heavy work, such as sawing out deadwood and keel oak and other timbers, there is no other realistic answer. But there are exceptions to every rule. I remember sawing 6-inch green oak with a 12-inch Delta bandsaw equipped with a ¾-inch blade. It took forever to make the cut, I broke blades, and I overheated the little half-horse motor, but I got the job done.

If you can find an old bandsaw, 18 to 30 inches, take it. An 18-inch saw, new, may go for $800 to $1,000. Look for slop around the shaft bearings (bronze or babbitt sleeve bearings are all right if relined) and for grooves worn in the rear guide wheel (this is the one the blade presses against). Bearings and guides may be replaceable, but the price should reflect this additional expense. An 18-inch saw should have a minimum of ¾ h.p., and preferably one horse, for resawing takes power. For an old saw, you should pay $150 and up. Used 12-inch saws such as old Deltas, Sears, and the newer Rockwell 14 (Figure 4-25) are extremely popular. Look for at least 6-inch clearance under the guide; more is desirable. Check the saw's balance by running it before you hand over any money. Loose rubber "tires" sometimes cause jumping, making it impossible to follow a line. Replacement, however, is not too much of a task. In Chapter Five, I describe 12- and 18-inch saws I have built from kits. You can do this too.

On a new saw, I would settle for a 12-inch throat, permitting cuts to the center of a 24-inch circle. This is for joinery as well as for general wooden boatbuilding. (I cannot recommend smaller sizes, although some are available.) The Sears tool, for example, is quite typical. It has a built-in work light and a sawdust-ejection system that can be attached to a vacuum cleaner. See Figure 4-26. This tool weighs only 75 pounds and requires a ½ h.p. capacitor-start 1,725 r.p.m. motor.

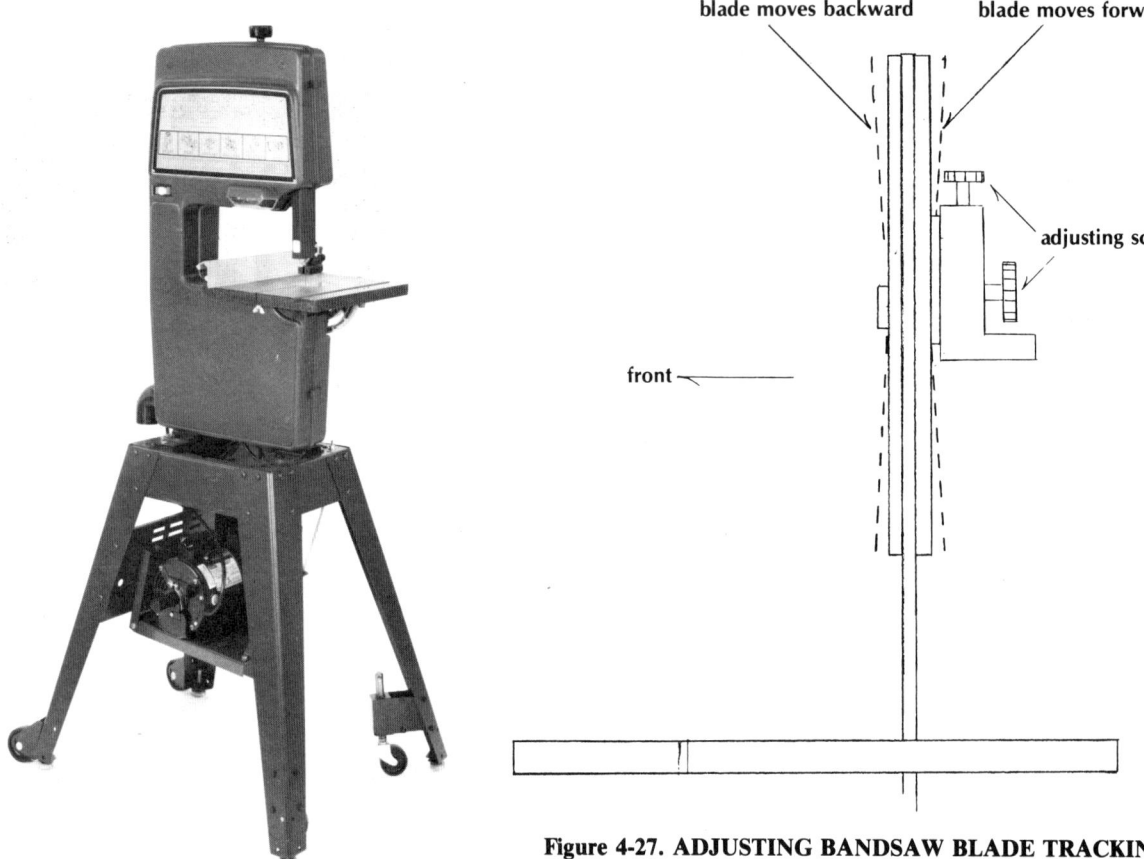

Figure 4-27. ADJUSTING BANDSAW BLADE TRACKING

Figure 4-26. *The popular 12-inch Sears Craftsman bandsaw has a light, dust-ejection vacuum, and other deluxe features. (Courtesy Sears, Roebuck)*

Stands are available. The saw alone goes for about $250. Ward's saw is 14 inches and sells for around $450. Study all the catalogs before you choose.

Bandsaw Pointers

The bandsaw is one of the safest of all power tools. If the upper guide is properly adjusted above the work, it is just about impossible to push your finger into the blade. However, never run or turn on a bandsaw, even momentarily, with the upper or lower guards (doors) open. Adjustments to align the tracking of the blade on the rubber-tired wheels (the mechanism is behind the wheel) should not be made with the saw running until you have some experience.

First, loosen all blade guides so they do not contact the blades. Second, spin the wheel by hand three or four revolutions. (More turns could run the blade off the wheel.) You'll see how a 2-degree movement of the handwheel adjustment changes the position of the blade. If the blade is moving toward the back of the tire, the wheel is tilted back, so screw the handwheel in the direction that moves the blade forward. See Figure 4-27. Make these small adjustments repeatedly until there is no deviation in blade position. At this point, snap the switch on and off quickly for a trial. If the blade wanders again, turn it off and make another small adjustment. The blade does not have to ride at the center of the tire. Frequently it will ride near the forward edge. Its position relative to the side guides and back roller guides is more important.

Tension on the blade is adjusted by a handwheel mounted on a vertical shaft, usually with a strong coiled spring arrangement. Tightening the handwheel (clockwise, face down) forces the wheel upward and increases tension on the blade. Press against the side of the blade on your left, probably in a recess in the frame. About ¼-inch sideways movement for each 6 inches between upper and lower wheel is about right. See Figure 4-28. Spin the wheel by hand again to be sure the blade is still tracking correctly, then turn on the switch. Observe the tracking for a few moments, turn off the saw, and make the next adjustment — the guides.

The guides control the blade so that there is no play from side to side or forward or backward. For accurate work, you want a minimum of movement. In some saws, the guides are small, oil-impregnated bronze blocks or rods held by set-screws (Figure 4-29(A)). In very old saws, these may be blocks of hardwood. In many larger and better saws, the guides are often ball-bearing rollers. Regardless, they should be adjusted in or out, clear of the teeth, so they just *miss* touching the blade, perhaps by the thickness of a piece of paper. The

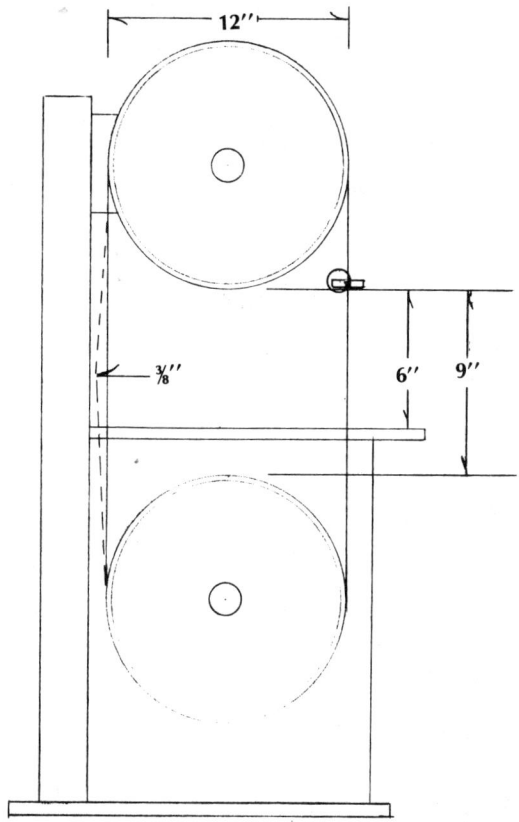

Figure 4-28. BANDSAW TENSION ADJUSTMENT

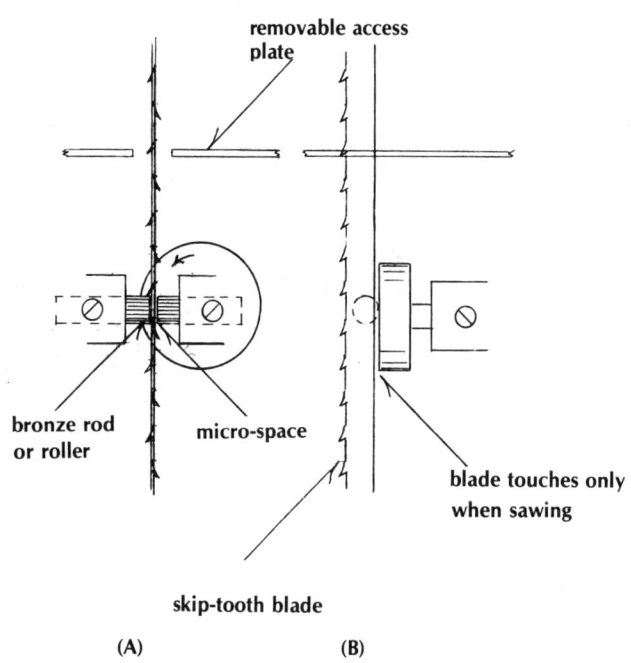

Figure 4-29. TYPICAL BLADE GUIDES

rear thrust wheel or block, upper and lower, should be moved forward or backward so the back of the blade touches only when sawing stock (Figure 4-29(B)). It should not be allowed to spin the thrust wheels at all times, for this could crystallize them and wear them out. Now you have to set the side guides back so they do not touch the teeth, perhaps $1/16$ inch or less from the gullets of the teeth. On some saws, the only way to adjust the side guides forward and back is by moving the entire guide assembly, which is mounted on a horizontal shaft. Other saws have no such adjustment. On these you have to change the tracking of the blade on the wheel so it runs correctly between the side guides, with no contact with the teeth. The thrust block or wheel is always adjustable fore-and-aft in all makes.

After the guides have been set, turn on the switch. If there is a slapping of the blade against the side guides, increase the blade tension slightly until the blade quiets down. It's now ready for work. When your blade becomes dull, open both doors and slack off on the tension handwheel until the blade drops free of the lower wheel. To remove the blade, carefully pull it out from the guides and off the wheels. Take care so that you do not jam or crimp the blade, which can be resharpened. Occasionally a bandsaw blade will break. When this happens, the wheels just continue to spin for a time. Once in a while, however, a broken blade gets jammed into the rubber tires, with sad results.

Coiling the Blades

Bandsaw blades not in use should be coiled and hung up out of the way. Doing this is one of the "mysteries" of the boatbuilder's art — one that you must learn. Hold the blade with your hands about 15 to 18 inches apart, with your thumbs out and the teeth of the blade away from you. Bend enough to rest the bottom of the blade on the floor before you. Place your foot lightly on the blade. Now rotate both hands inward about 180 degrees. This twist will cause the upper portion of the blade to bend down toward the lower section, unless you fight it. Finally, move your hands until they cross and then let go. You will have three loops in the blade, a convenient arrangement for storage. See Figure 4-30.

Most of your joinerwork can be done with $1/4$- or $3/8$-inch blades. I have always preferred a skip-tooth blade, for this tooth is nonclogging. I have a $3/4$-inch blade that I use for occasional resawing, long curves, or straight ripping. Point out to your saw shop that your $3/4$-inch blade is only 78 or 80 inches (for most 12-inch saws), so the gauge of the steel should be somewhat thinner than for a 36-inch wheel. If it is too heavy, the blade will harden and break. Blades are available with fine teeth, 15 per inch, for a lot of very fine work, such as on particle board and plywood. Seven teeth per inch, however, is about right for most work. A skip-tooth blade cuts faster, especially in moist or gummy wood. Because new blades cost about $4, it is not always practical to have old ones sharpened or brazed when they crack.

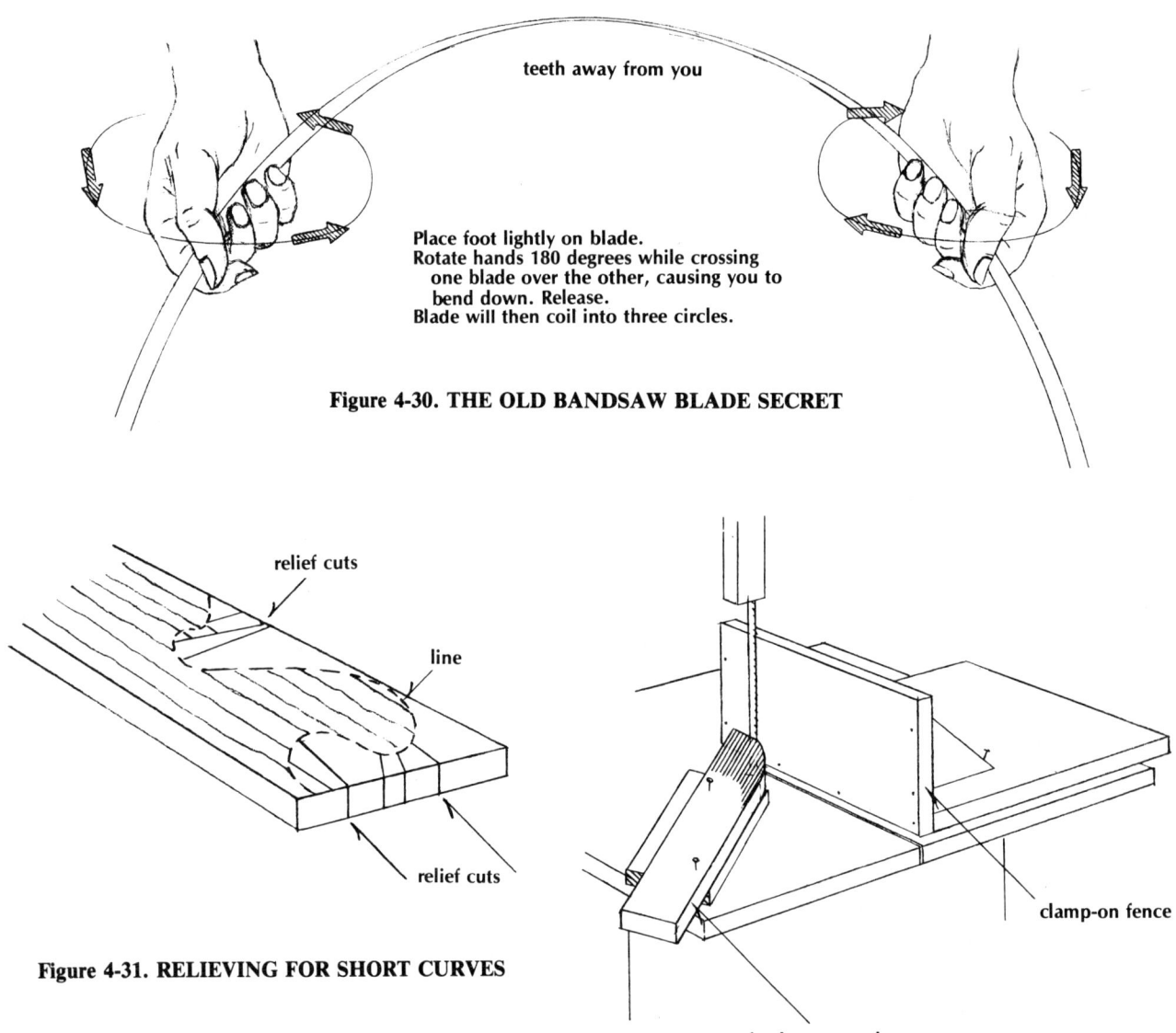

Figure 4-30. THE OLD BANDSAW BLADE SECRET

Figure 4-31. RELIEVING FOR SHORT CURVES

Figure 4-32. RESAW SETUP FOR BANDSAW OR TABLE SAW

Using the Bandsaw

The first rule in using the bandsaw is never to try to force the blade to cut a short radius. It's better to make a number of relief cuts on the scrap side of the line, as shown in Figure 4-31. One way of making two pieces of identical shape — say, berth fronts, hatch beams, or something similar — is to shape the part from stock that is more than double the required thickness and then resaw. The resulting surfaces may be dressed on a jointer or by hand. To resaw accurately on a bandsaw (or any saw), the work must be supported firmly and be exactly perpendicular to the table. Build a fence that can be clamped to the table at the necessary distance from the blade (Figure 4-32). Make a feather or comb to go on the other side of the table. This forces the work against the fence. If the resaw is deeper than 3 inches, raise the feather on a block so the piece cannot wobble. If you prefer, pass the piece between two fences. Try a piece of scrap first. If the pieces have concave and con-

vex surfaces, as shown in Figure 4-33, your blade is not under the required tension, it is dull, it has lost its set, or perhaps all of these problems exist.

The bandsaw table is designed to tilt to angles up to 45 degrees. First check the table at its level position; adjust the screw at the left side so the cut is perfectly square. The pointer on the quadrant under the table at the right should read properly at 45-degree cuts. Check with an adjustable bevel square, then reset the pointer to agree.

To bandsaw parallel (or concentric) to curves, clamp a pointed piece at the required dimension directly opposite the blade. Let the curve follow the guide point. See Figure 4-34. To make exact duplicates, or any

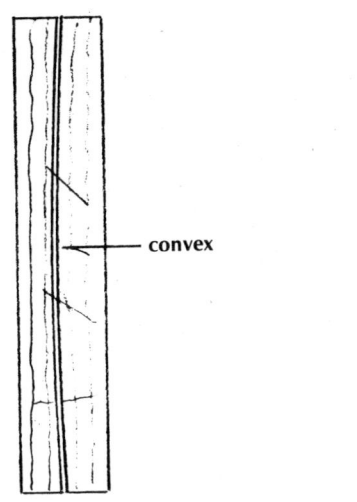

Figure 4-33. FAULTY RESAWING

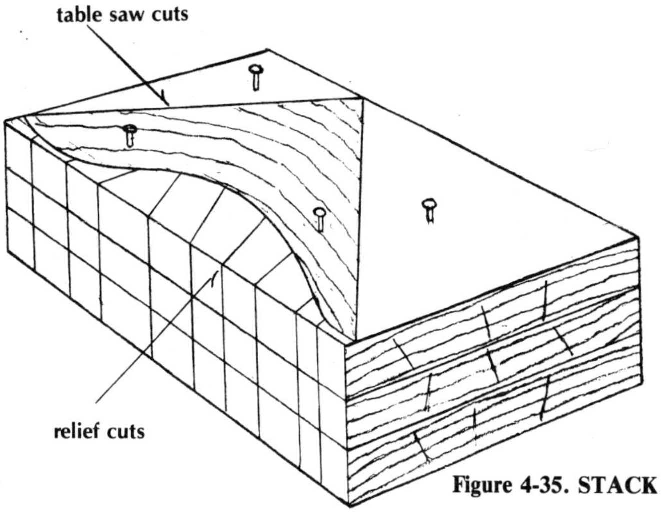

Figure 4-35. STACK SAWING

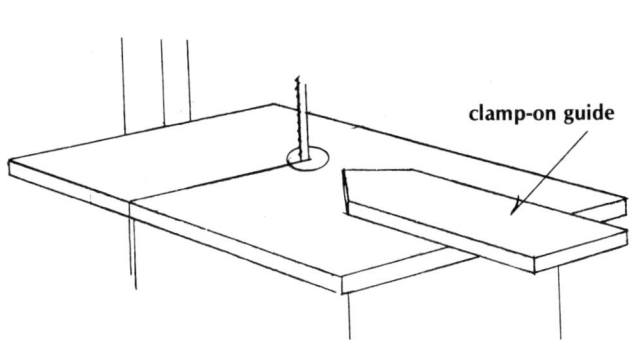

Figure 4-34. GUIDE FOR CONCENTRIC SAWING

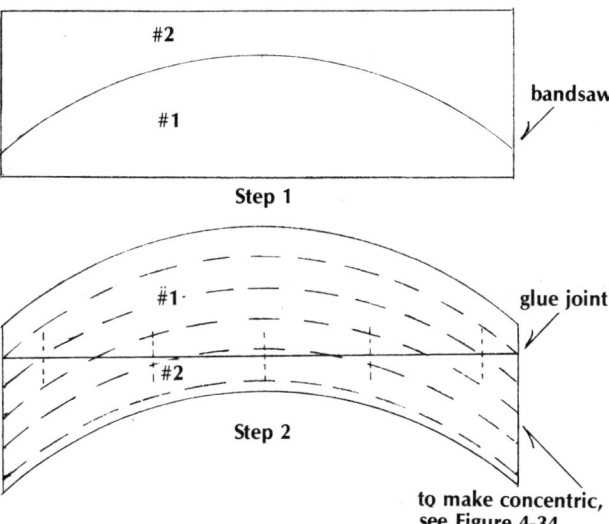

Figure 4-36. SAVING MATERIAL ON WIDE SHAPES

reasonable multiple, nail pieces into a stack up to the capacity of your saw, as shown in Figure 4-35. You can eliminate most of the nails by sticking thin double-faced tape between the layers. The knee shown could well be laminated thicknesses of plywood or ash (oak does not glue well).

You can make wide curved pieces without much waste using a bandsaw. Dress edges square and straight so they can be glued. Plan to use splines or dowels if the assembly is wide. Dowels are mandatory if you want to prevent cupping or warping of the final piece. Mark and saw out the shapes. Epoxy-glue piece number 1 to piece number 2. Dress the edges to the final shape. See Figure 4-36. The dotted lines show the positions of the dowels.

Very old bandsaws may have large oil reservoirs stuffed with waste around each wheel shaft. Keep this sopped with ordinary machine oil. Modern saws are sealed or self-lubricated.

In Chapter Five, you'll learn how to make a simple motor mount for the $2 to $3 ⅓ h.p. used appliance motor. There's also a description of a bandsaw you can build from a kit in less than two days. I can testify to its performance.

Any halfway-decent bandsaw should last your lifetime. Moreover, the beauty of the work one can produce should inspire you to design more attractive joinery for your yacht. When your project is finished, you'll get back almost every dollar you put into the tool. And you will have had fun every inch of the way.

THE TABLE SAW

Sometimes the terms *bench saw, table saw,* and *circular saw* are used to describe the same tool. The bench saw needs a stand to bring it up to a convenient height, thus making it a table saw. The circular saw could be any portable power saw, so let's forget that name. It'll be table saw from here on. See Figure 4-37.

The capacity of a table saw is the thickness of wood it will cut at 90 degrees. An 8-inch saw may have a cutting capacity of 2¼ to 2⅜ inches; most 10-inch saws cut through 2⅞ inches at 90 degrees; a 12-inch saw will

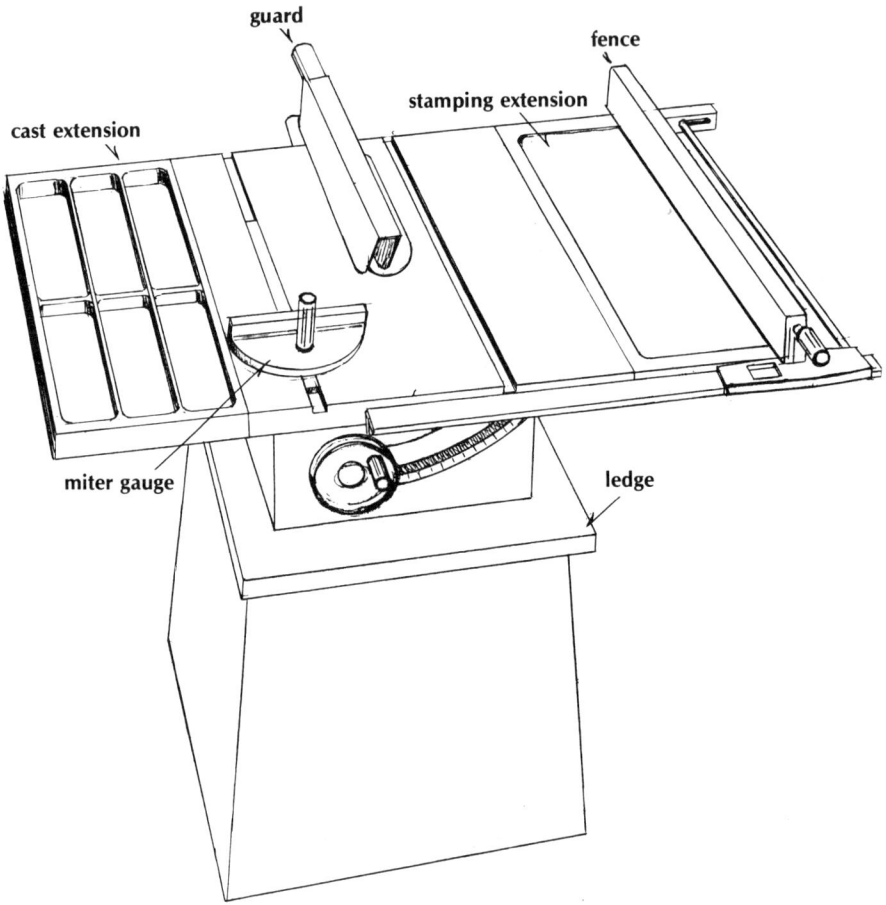

Figure 4-37. TYPICAL TABLE SAW WITH TWO EXTENSIONS

handle up to 3¼ inches. A run-of-the-mill 10-inch table saw should be able to produce all the joinery for your yacht, although I can think of several things it might not handle conveniently.

The original size of the table is less important than the saw's cutting capacity. You just add extensions or wings to both sides. These may be either purchased ones or wooden ones you build (Figure 4-38). The extensions you buy are cast iron or aluminum. They come with various open-grid designs that provide for an extension of the rail for the rip fence. This allows you to rip to the center of a 48-inch plywood panel. Some now have stamped steel extensions.

The area in front of the blade is of considerable importance, especially if you are handling large boards or plywood. This dimension runs from 11 to 15 inches in several 10-inch makes and as much as 16½ inches in 12-inch saws. Table widths are from 17 to 20 inches. Extensions add 10 inches each. You should consider two on the right-hand side and one on the left. Saw tables incorporate two slots for the miter gauge and various devices for locking the fence. Some include micrometer handwheel adjustments for the fence, but the prudent craftsman measures from the point of a tooth to the fence every time he sets it. This is a good habit to get into. You should measure from the back of the blade, too, for fences do not always line up parallel to the blade.

A fairly recent development in table saws is the built-in direct-drive motor. This eliminates the slight nuisance and sound of belt drives. This feature may save you money, for you will not be buying motor, belt, and pulleys. In 1980, the Rockwell motorized 10-inch bench saw with a 17-inch-by-22-inch table, with stand and two extensions, sold for about $400. Rockwell also sells a commercial 10-inch saw with a 27-inch-by-40-inch table. The Sears 10-inch motorized saw with 17-inch-by-20-inch table, two extensions, and stand sold for $420. There are many other good makes to check out, so check all the catalogs or find a good used saw. I have a 10-year-old cast-iron 10-inch Craftsman that does anything I ask of it. I also have a kit-built 10-inch saw that I use for precision cutoffs, dadoing, mitering, and so on. This saw is equipped with a sliding auxiliary table, which I'll discuss later.

Direct drive may appeal to you, but don't overlook an old (or even a new) belt-drive saw. Belt-drive tools for years have been excellent and almost 100 percent foolproof. Belts last indefinitely. Good used motors may be picked up occasionally at far less than new prices. You might start with a "junker" ¾ h.p. motor for your 10-inch saw for a mere $15 to $20, then move up to a better motor later on.

Do not buy an old tilting table saw. I would take a much older tilt-arbor saw first, for this tool is safer and more accurate. Even more important are the bearings in

Figure 4-38. *The author's 10-inch saw built from a kit (see Chapter Five). It is used for precision cut-offs, squaring cabinet doors, cutting moldings, dadoing, and so on. It does anything any ¾ h.p. saw can do.*

Figure 4-40. *Wood that is knotty, gummy, damp, or hard often pinches the saw blade. The splitter, part of the guard, prevents grabbing and kickback.*

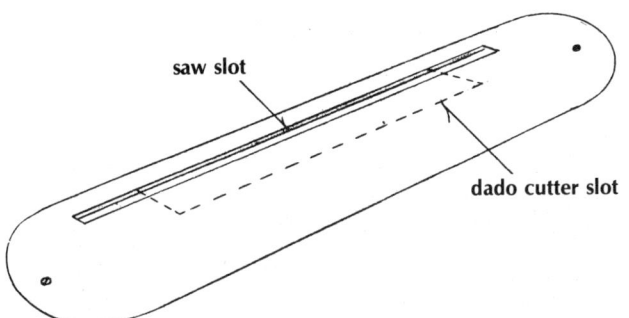

Figure 4-39. INSERTS FOR TABLE SAW

the arbor (they should be ball bearings) and the condition of the table surface. If the surface is badly pitted, think twice. Rust, however, can be removed. Does the arbor-raising mechanism work freely? Is it badly rusted or can it be freed? Does it tilt easily? Can you move the arbor about in its bearings (a sign of wear)? Is the fence-locking device workable and will it slide on its rail? If the saw does not have table extensions, is it a well-known name for which extensions are available? Does the miter gauge fit its slot? Are any blades available, and perhaps a dado set? You must have two inserts for the opening over the arbor, one for the standard blade and another for the dado set. See Figure 4-39.

Most saws are furnished originally with a combination guard and splitter — a vertical affair with a tapered edge that keeps the saw cut open so it does not pinch the blade. See Figure 4-40. This is a common headache when sawing green, damp, gummy, or hard woods. Unfortunately, many craftsmen, especially professionals, remove the guard so they can see the blade, even though the guard can be swung back. Once a cut is started, nothing is gained by not covering the blade with the guard. In addition, it keeps sawdust out of your eyes and hair. The better guards have antikickback fingers or dogs that prevent the blade from hurling the wood like a javelin.

Table Saw Alignments

A new or used table saw should be checked for several alignments. Time and rough handling can cause slight shifting of the arbor in relation to the table. The blade must be precisely parallel to the grooves in the table. Here's a simple way to check the arbor. This test checks for blade flatness as well. Measure from the corner of the miter gauge to a certain marked tooth at both front and rear positions, as shown in Figure 4-41. Use a small block as a feeler. Unfortunately, you have to turn the saw over to loosen the arbor attaching bolts. Perhaps all it needs is a couple of hard hammer taps against a block of wood. Do not touch the shaft; devote your attention to the arbor casting base only. Repeat the test several times.

Alignment of the ripping fence is much easier. You check it by measuring from a specific tooth to the fence, at both front and rear. This is shown in Figure 4-42. Several set screws or bolts are provided for adjustments. The 90-degree position of the miter gauge should be checked regularly by sawing a piece of scrap (the wider the better) and testing the cut angle with a carpenter's square. I have a line scratched into my table against which I can set the miter gauge quite accurately in a few seconds. I rubbed a little white paint into the score for easier sighting. Actually, I never trust a miter gauge; I use a sliding auxiliary table 90 percent of the time. See Chapter Five.

Table Saw Blades

A wide selection of table saw blades is available. For doing strictly joinery (light precision work, with many

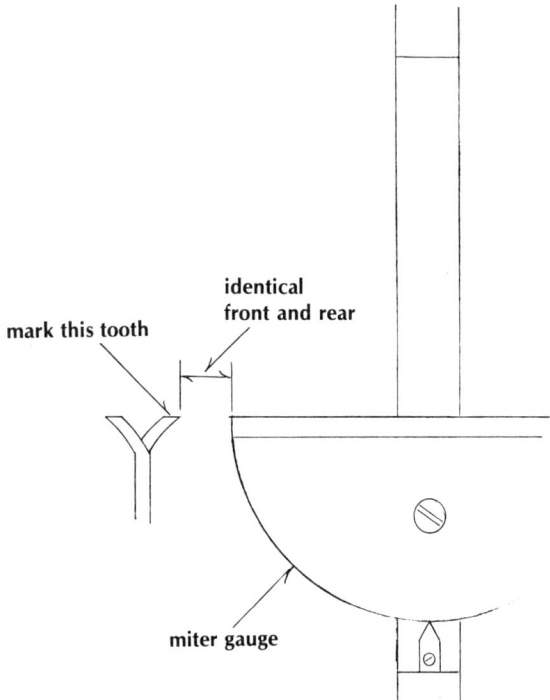

Figure 4-41. ALIGNMENT OF BLADE (ARBOR) WITH GAUGE

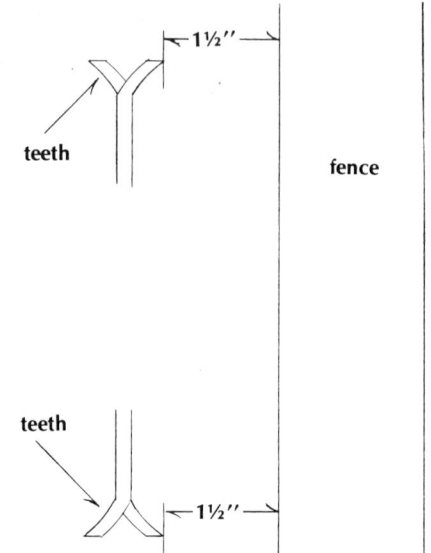

Figure 4-42. ALIGNMENT OF FENCE AND BLADE

Figure 4-43. Left: *Planer or cabinetmaker's combination blade for polished cuts.* **Right:** *Combination rip and crosscut blade performs both tasks adequately but more slowly.*

glued joints), I would recommend a cabinetmaker's combination, also called a planer blade (Figure 4-43: left). This blade is characterized by deep gullets every five teeth. It is either flat ground or hollow ground with no set whatever, and it produces an edge that is almost polished, with or across the grain. It will become dull quite rapidly if used in heavy plywood and very rapidly if used in teak. Having no set, it cannot follow a line freehand and may, in fact, throw the piece at you if you try to force it. The standard combination blade (Figure 4-43: right) has deep teeth that are all uniform. It cuts fast and clean, rip or crosscut. It has a slight set so the surface is not polished. It is, however, far better than the surface produced by a standard crosscut blade. An experienced craftsman can freehand on a table saw once in a while with this blade, but it is not safe to try this often.

For cutting plywood, there are several blade configurations. The first is hollow ground to about 1 inch in from the teeth; it has no set (Figure 4-44: bottom). Do not use this type of blade on ¾-inch plywood, for it will drag, overheat, and warp, ruining the cut. This blade is good for plywood up to about ½ inch in thickness, if you need a fine edge. The other good blade for plywood is a fine tooth, from 6 to 10 teeth per inch. The coarser one (6 teeth) is not made expressly for plywood, but it will produce a nice clean cut, not polished. The finer blade (10 teeth) has to be watched for overheating. A good all-around blade called the cut-off has 5 teeth per inch (Figure 4-44: upper right). This blade is excellent for plywood or any purpose. It is slightly slower than the chisel-tooth combination blade, however. A planer blade is shown in Figure 4-44 for comparison.

Carbide-tipped blades are great time and money savers. They will cut 20 or 30 times as long as an ordinary steel blade without sharpening. My 10-inch, 40-tooth blade cost about $26 at Sears in 1977 and has been running ever since. A carbide-tipped blade costs about $18 to $20 to sharpen, compared with $3 to $4 for the standard blade. But there's no down time, trips to the saw shop, or whatever. And it's just plain beautiful the way a carbide-tipped blade slices through oak! An 80-tooth blade leaves a polished surface, but it may cost $50 or more.

Increasing Table Saw Utility

To increase the versatility of your table saw, several steps must be taken. First, the miter gauge that comes with the saw may be only 5 to 8 inches wide. This, however, is not always adequate for 90-degree or angle cutting. Bolt to the miter gauge a piece of good straight lumber or ¾-inch plywood about 4 inches wide by 24

Figure 4-44. Bottom: *Plywood blade has fine teeth, little set. Friction will cause overheating in plywood thicker than ½ inch. It produces a good surface with little chipping.* **Upper right:** *Cut-off blade will also rip adequately in any wood and produce a fair surface. This is a good all-around utility blade.* **Upper left:** *A hollow-ground planer blade produces a beautiful surface. It will bind in ¾-inch material. All of these blades are available in sizes from 6½ to 12 inches.*

Figure 4-45. *This long miter gauge fence facilitates crosscutting longer pieces. Note adjustable stop rods for producing precise lengths in quantity.*

inches long. Position it so the blade will cut through it (Figure 4-45). Glue and nail a stiffener along the top of the near side. Now you can handle quite long material and prevent creeping by holding the work piece firmly against the fence. Always check the mark on the table to be sure the gauge is still accurate; wrestling long stuff sometimes forces the gauge out of square.

Most miter gauges have holes bored parallel to the fence. This is for a stop rod, an accessory that allows you to cut more than one piece of the same length. You simply turn the hook of the rod so the end of your material butts against it. Set screws provide for adjustment and locking. You can saw exact duplicates up to 6 or 8 feet long by making up wooden stops of about 1 by 3 inches with a wooden block on the left end. C-clamp this piece to the miter gauge, as shown in Figure 4-46. I frequently cut shelves 6 feet or longer, then hang up the stop for the next use. I keep stops in various lengths. They can also be used with the sliding auxiliary table described in Chapter Five.

For resawing, make an auxiliary fence to screw or bolt to the inside of the regular fence. Make the fence from ¾-inch plywood or lumber. It should be 6 inches high and the same length as the regular fence. See Figure 4-47. This will guarantee a square kerf so that cuts in wide material will meet perfectly (Figure 4-48). Always swing the piece end for end; do not simply turn it over. If the stock is too wide for the cuts to meet, rip out the remaining narrow part on your bandsaw. If you have no bandsaw, just use a handsaw.

This auxiliary fence will enable you to cut accurate tenons and halved joints also. Use a cabinetmaker's combination blade for these joints. These fine hollow-ground blades will not work for resawing, however, for there is no set. Resawing, ripping, and all operations calling for continuous steady pressure against the fence require another simple accessory. This is a feather or comb. One is shown in Figure 4-47. The material can be pine, hardwood, or plywood. The "teeth" can be 2 to 4 inches long. Make them by making parallel cuts with the table or bandsaw. To use a comb, clamp it securely to the table so the teeth exert pressure against the stock. Raise the comb up on a block for resawing. This device is especially effective when ripping long, flexible items such as battens. It keeps the piece hard against the fence, and, incidentally, keeps your fingers away from the blade. You can concentrate on shoving the work piece through the saw — by means of a pusher, of course.

A variation of the comb or feather may be used to hold material down against the table. The feather is clamped to the auxiliary fence, as shown in Figure 4-47, at an angle of about 45 degrees. With both feathers in position, neither hand comes anywhere near the blade and there's no chance that the piece will ride up on the blade. Any small stick makes a satisfactory pusher. All of this applies to your jointer as well as to your table saw.

Both of these feathers will be extremely handy if you are using a molding head or dado set on light material, when chatter cannot be tolerated. A better method is to mold or dado the required shape on the edge of a board and then rip off the strip. This way you have the heavy stock backing up the working surface. See Figure 4-49.

Since I have mentioned pushers repeatedly, let me suggest a good shape for one. Make your pusher of ¼-inch plywood or any scrap. See Figure 4-50. Bore a hole in the handle so the pusher is always hanging near your right hand, ready for use. Don't let your fingers come within 4 inches of that blade! Pushers get chewed up pretty fast, so why not gang up four or five thicknesses of plywood scrap and cut out several of them at once on your bandsaw?

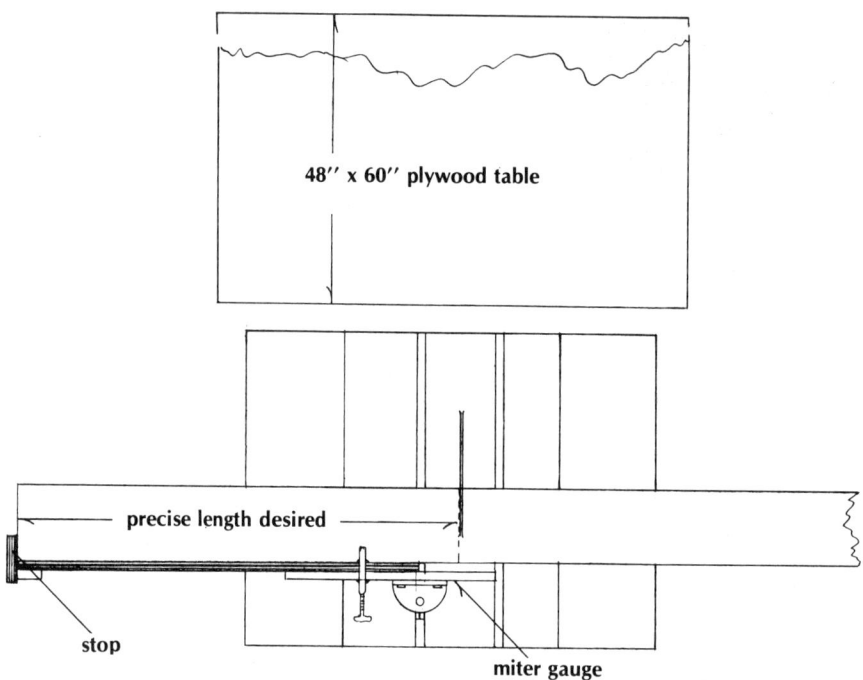

Figure 4-46. TABLE SAW EXTENSION STOP BAR

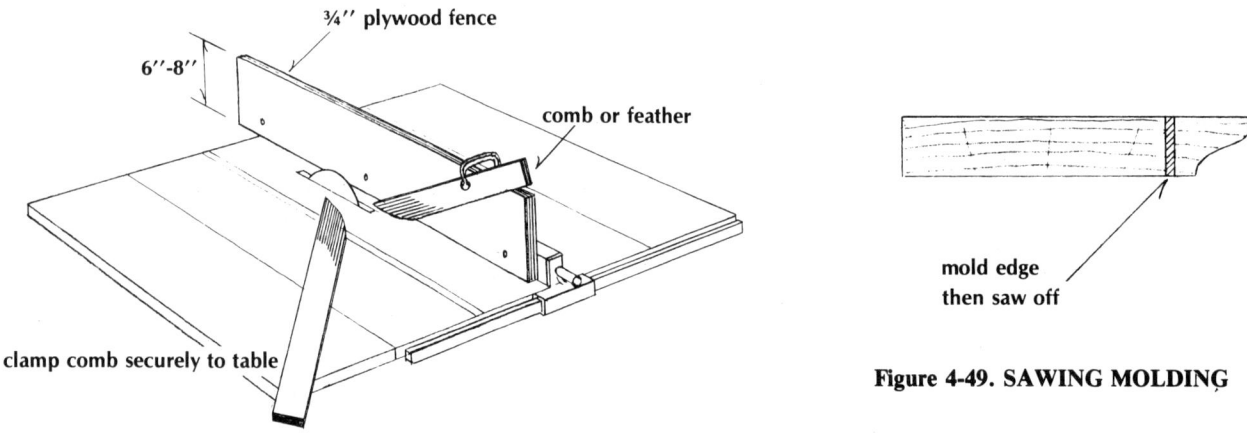

Figure 4-47. TYPICAL HOLD-DOWN FOR SAW OR JOINTER

Figure 4-49. SAWING MOLDING

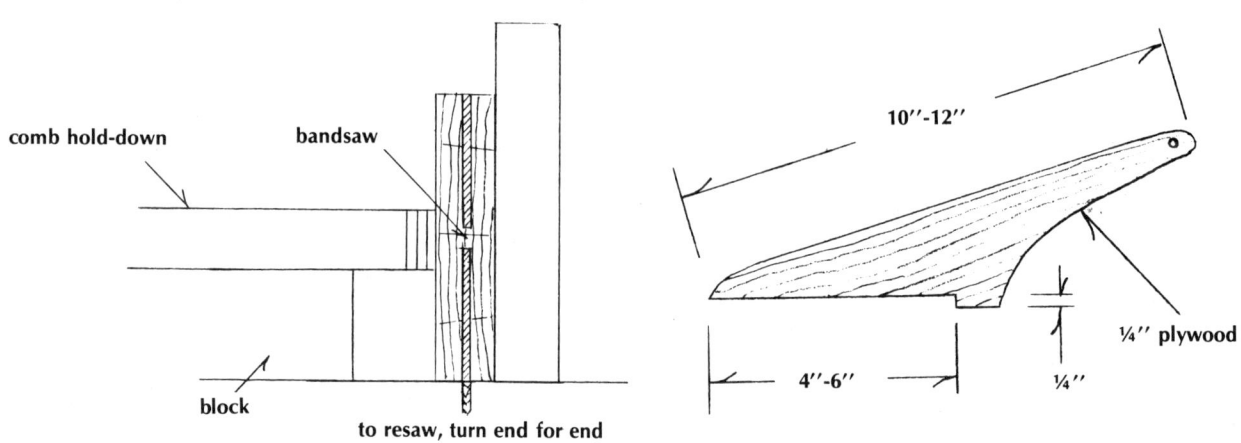

Figure 4-48. RESAWING

Figure 4-50. A SIMPLE PUSHER

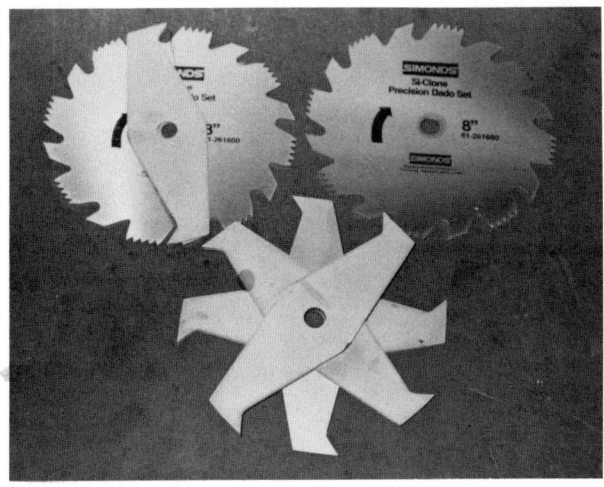

Figure 4-51. *Dado set — two outer cutter blades and as many chippers as required for groove or dado width. An 8-inch set is shown.*

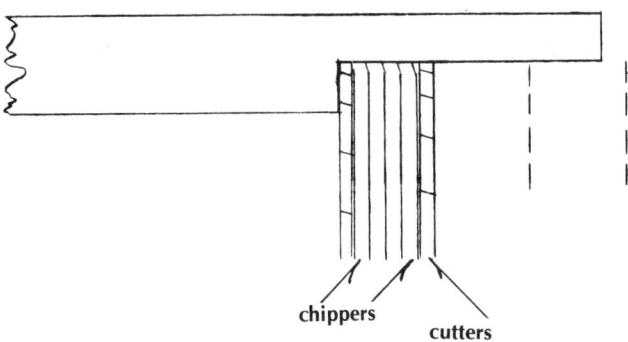

Figure 4-52. DADOING HALF LAP

Stock Supports

Never try to crosscut a long piece without having someone or something supporting the far end. If the piece droops, it will bind suddenly and violently, and possibly split. If you work alone a lot, as I do, you will need some kind of handy support for long stuff, such as plywood sheets. For now, let's say that you will need a simple lightweight table about 4 feet wide and perhaps 6 feet long. Its height should be ½ to ¼ inch lower than the saw table. If you want your support table to do double duty as a workbench, then build it heavier. Place the table about a foot behind your saw when ripping plywood and long lumber. See Figure 4-46. If you have to crosscut long material or plywood sheets, locate the table on your left and toward the rear of the table saw. Be prepared for long boards to drag on the table and cause problems. The answer may be an assistant or a roller supporting stand. Such stands are available from many sources.

Dadoing and Molding

I mentioned a few pages back that your table saw has a large opening in the top. This is to permit replacement of blades and the installation of tools used to fashion grooves, rabbets, dadoes, and decorative edges of all kinds. (Remember: A groove across the grain, as for a shelf support, is called a dado.) Cutting a very narrow groove is called plowing. Any cabinet made with rabbets at top and bottom and snug dadoes for shelves, glued with Aerolite or Plastic Resin, needs no fastenings other than a few hot-dipped galvanized finish nails. Of course, such an assembly must be drawn up tight with pipe or bar clamps while the glue sets.

A dado set consists of two cutting blades on the outside with one to five chippers in between. See Figure 4-51. The ordinary dado set may be from 6 to 8 inches in diameter. Thus, using a 6-inch dado set on a 10-inch saw will limit the depth of cut. Check from the center of your arbor at its highest position to the table top. If this is 2½ inches, your dado can be ½ inch deep. Most dadoes for shelves are ¼ inch deep in ¾-inch sides. Rabbets should be ⅜ to ½ inch to provide the maximum gluing strength. You would be wise to find a 7- or 8-inch dado set, since halved joints and tenons made with a dado probably would require deeper cuts. The maximum width of a dado set is ¹³⁄₁₆ inch, so for a halved joint 2 inches wide, you would make three passes (Figure 4-52). In order to produce precise widths of dadoes and grooves, it is often necessary to use paper shims between the chippers. This process usually takes 10 or 15 minutes of experimentation on scrap wood to make the nice, easy fit required. A press fit forces the glue off the sides of the joint and weakens the structure. A number of press fits in a cabinet or bookcase side causes the side to bend.

When assembling a dado set on the arbor, space the chippers' wide-set teeth so they are opposite the deep gullets in the cutters. This prevents springing and distorting of the chippers when the set is tightened up. It makes for an accurate cutting setup, too. Dado blades and chippers must be kept sharp so that the cuts are invisible. Cutters and chippers usually are ground and jointed together in sets so that their diameters are identical and precisely concentric. Careless grinding results in unsightly and weak joints (Figure 4-53).

The hassle of using traditional dado sets is what forced the invention of the adjustable or wobble dado set. This consists of one heavy blade, 7 inches in diameter, usually having from 8 to 24 carbide-tipped teeth. The rest of the set is various arrangements of large, tapered washers that cause the blade to wobble as it rotates. See Figure 4-54. These washers are calibrated so that the width of the cut, up to ¹³⁄₁₆ inch, can be ad-

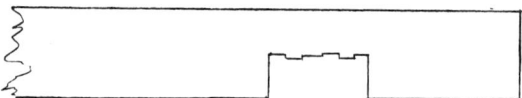

Figure 4-53. RESULT OF IMPROPER JOINTING OF CHIPPERS AND CUTTERS

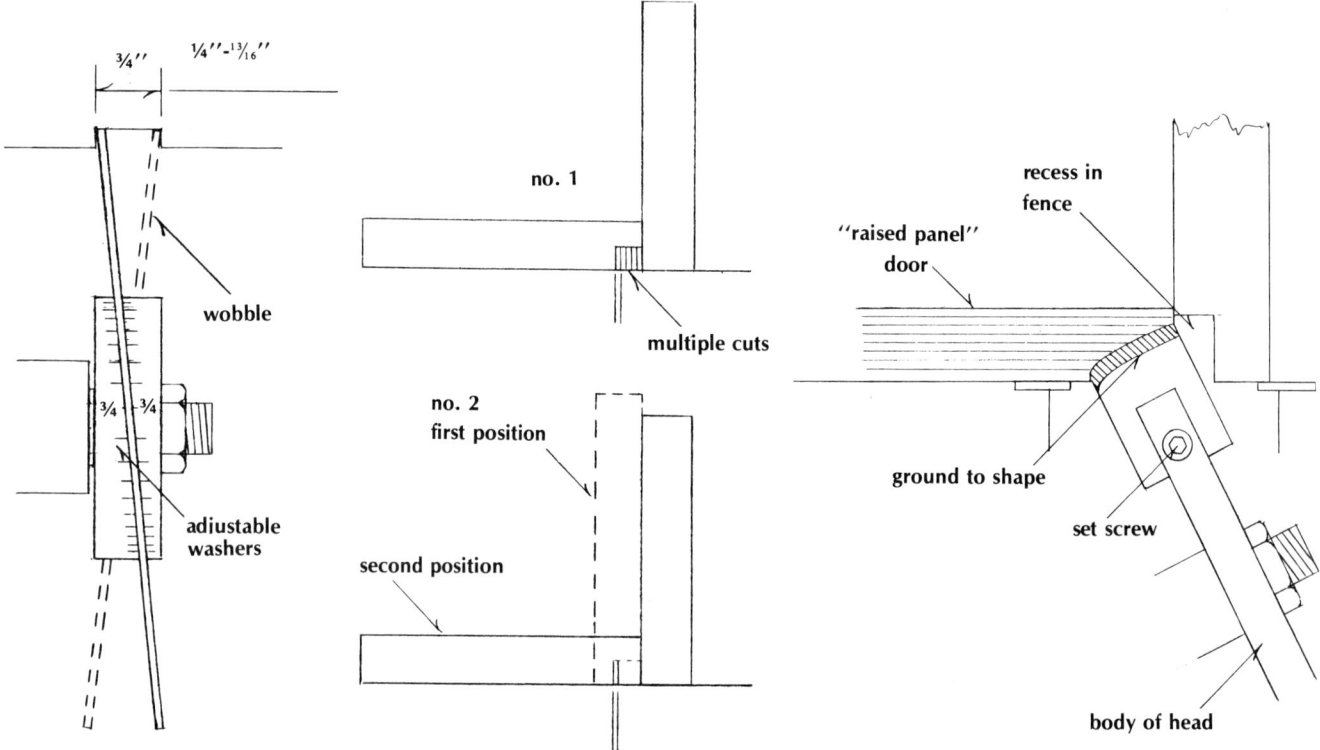

Figure 4-54. DADO, RABBET, OR GROOVE WITH ADJUSTABLE DADO

Figure 4-55. TWO WAYS TO RABBET WITH SAW BLADE ONLY

Figure 4-56. VIEW OF MOLDING HEAD (BLADE SHOWN REVERSED)

justed without removing the set from the arbor. This type of dado set has been around for a good many years; it is quite reliable and saves a lot of time and bother with shims. My adjustable dado set has only eight teeth and does a more-than-adequate job. I see no compelling reason for buying the more costly 16-, 18-, and 32-tooth blades, except for preventing all chipping.

Can you do without this expensive tool? Yes, by making repeated saw cuts. You set the fence for each pass, with the outside cuts to extremely close tolerances the thickness of a piece of paper. This operation takes time and much patience, but it has been done for years and years. Rabbets are easier — one vertical cut with the piece running against a high fence, the second cut with the saw height set to the depth of the rabbet. Figure 4-55 shows this and the multiple-cut method of rabbeting.

There is one more important accessory for the table saw — a molding head. Definition: A head is a device that is slotted to receive one or more blades or knives and is mounted on a shaft or arbor. Thus, the jointer head, shaper head, planer head, and molding head for a table or radial-arm saw. A molding head is a massive steel body with set screws to lock the knives in their sockets (Figure 4-56). The knives are ground to various shapes that produce attractive edges, locking edges for gluing, tongue and groove, cabinet door lips, raised panels, quarter rounds, ogees, beads, V-grooves, coves, and dozens of other useful and decorative effects. The shapes are like those cut with a shaper or router. Infinite varieties may be developed by making more than one pass through different knife contours.

I use a single-cutter molding set from Sears (Figure 4-57). I chose this tool because it has 18 different bits with it for about $35, compared with a three-cutter set making only eight shapes for $37. Of course, you can buy additional three-cutter sets for about $4. The single-cutter set has another advantage, however. Its blades may be ground to different shapes, within reason, and considering the balance of the assembly. I recently ground a straight planer blade to make raised-panel doors; the result is beautiful. The single blade produces a fine surface if the work is passed slowly. The three-cutter set will do as good a job, but a faster one. You would find it very difficult, of course, to grind three blades to identical form and weight.

To use a molding head, you will need a wooden fence

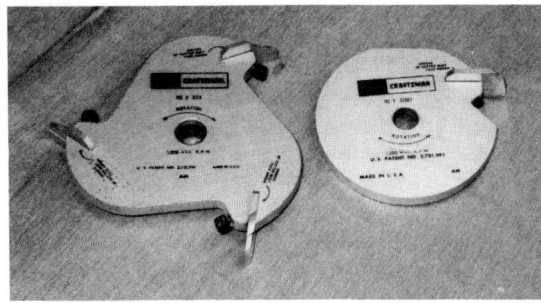

Figure 4-57. *Triple- and single-cutter molding heads. Many forms and combinations are possible.*

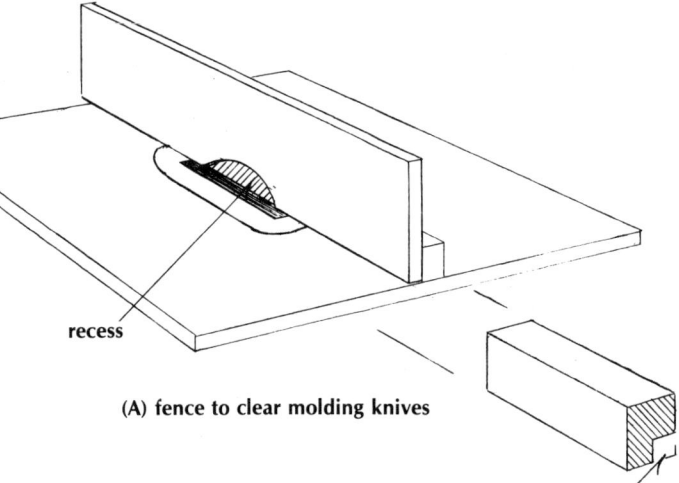

(A) fence to clear molding knives

(B) rabbet to fit molding stock

Figure 4-58. MOLDING TIPS

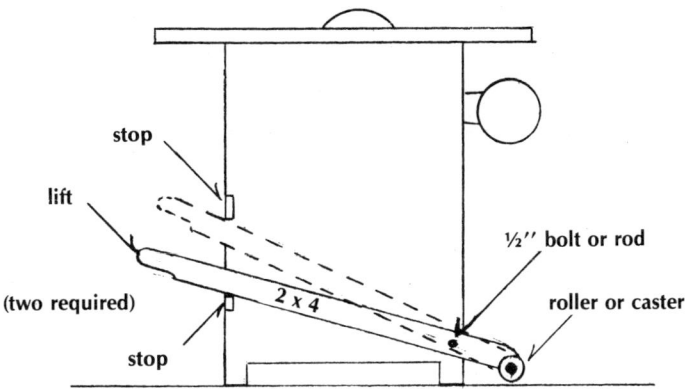

Figure 4-59. MAKING THE TABLE SAW MOVABLE

attached to the regular fence. This should incorporate a recess so the cutters can't touch the standard fence. You make this wooden fence by moving the piece gradually into the cutters until the recess is about ½ inch deep (Figure 4-58). I must warn you that a molding head is very dangerous, perhaps more dangerous than a shaper. A molding head will refuse to take deep bites and may throw the work piece at you if you try to force it. Most cuts must be done in two or three passes; you start with a shallow cut, then raise the head for each subsequent pass. Move the piece slowly; the cutters are taking off far more than a saw blade does, and they can't be rushed. Use the hold-downs described earlier, both horizontal and vertical, to keep your hands away from the head. I usually mold the edge of a board, then saw this off if I need a molding (Figure 4-49). It is not advisable to try to mold a strip of any kind because of chatter. However, you can do this if you build a rabbeted jig to hold the strip. The aperture must fit the rectangular strip quite closely. See Figure 4-58(B).

Fancy molded-edge contours were a mark of quality in fine yachts built in the early part of the century. Then increasing costs of labor, and perhaps changing tastes, gradually phased them out. There is no denying, however, that the judicious use of beautifully molded mahogany and teak woodwork adds much to the beauty and value of a yacht.

Space For Your Table Saw

A table saw requires a lot of space around it for handling material. Ideally, the saw is in the center of a large clear area, perhaps 15 feet on each side and at least 16 feet fore-and-aft. Much lumber turns up in 16-foot lengths.

You can't put a heavy 10-inch table saw down in a hull unless the hull is of impressive dimensions. You might, however, be able to lower a small saw, say, an 8-inch model, into a hull. Just be sure you will be able to get it out through the companionway hatch. For easy wheeling around the shop, you might try the idea shown in Figure 4-59. When you lift the saw like a wheelbarrow, the roller bears on the floor. With this rig, the saw won't creep as it would if it were on casters. The shape of your saw base may present some problems — but that's boat biz! Another kind of solution might be the strictly portable table saw described in Chapter Five.

I know you'll agree that a sweet-running table saw sings a beautiful song and also that it does a whale of a job!

THE RADIAL-ARM SAW

The radial-arm saw is the final major piece of equipment we're going to discuss. See Figure 4-60. To those of you not familiar with this machine, I should point out that its principal feature is that the work remains stationary while the power unit with its blade is moved to make the cut. Unfortunately, there are no radial-arm saws at a price within reason that will crosscut more than about 20 inches. Most will handle only about 15 inches. A radial-arm saw will, however, rip to 24 inches or better at a depth of 2½ to 3 inches, and perform another hundred or so operations with certain ac-

Figure 4-60. *The radial-arm saw is much more than a sawing machine. With attachments, it does almost any job except turning. (Courtesy Sears, Roebuck)*

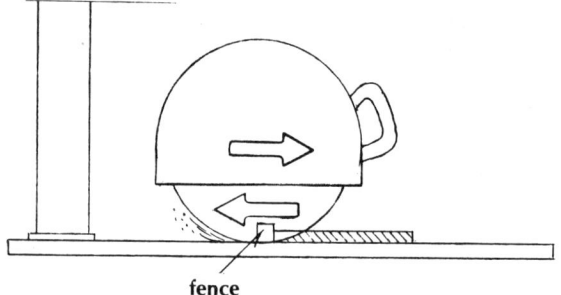

Figure 4-61. SAFE CROSSCUTTING

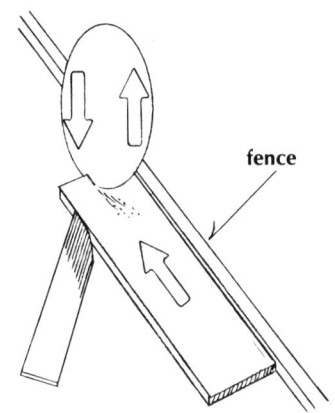

Figure 4-62. SAFE RIPPING

cessories. You can set the machine in the middle of a very large table, if you wish, so there are no stock support problems for either crosscutting or ripping. With regard to safety, the blade's rotation forces the work piece against the back fence, so it won't throw pieces of wood at you (Figures 4-61 and 4-62). Just keep those pinkies away from the saw kerf.

It is true that the radial is a sawing machine (just as the table saw is), but it does so many other things so well that it should have a different name. "Radial-arm woodworker" might be better. There are major and minor accessories available that make this tool extremely efficient for dadoing, grooving and molding, shaping, drum and disc sanding, grinding, planing, drilling, routing, polishing, buffing, and other operations. If you have one of the newer machines with a variable speed control, you can benefit from the high-speed settings desirable for shaping, routing, planing, and other operations. Some of these are available because of the many positions the power unit can be placed in — with the arbor horizontal, tilted at all conceivable angles, or vertical. See Figure 4-63.

A Great Book on Sawing

If you want to risk selling yourself on the radial-arm saw, get a copy of *Fun with a Saw,* by R.J. De Cristoforo, published by McGraw-Hill Book Company, Inc., and first printed in 1961. This book contains more than 200 pages of text, plus line illustrations and excellent photographs. It is written in such a lively manner that you won't be able to put it down. I had no idea of the versatility of the radial-arm saw until I read De Cristoforo's masterful book. I realize now that I used radials in the past as sawing machines, period! I got nothing from them but sawing speed, accuracy, and safety and was unaware of their many other advantages.

Radial-Arm Saw Principles

First, when crosscutting with a radial-arm saw, you hold the work piece securely against the rear fence. The power unit and blade are behind the fence and the piece, so let the blade touch to check its relationship with the mark. Now push the blade back, turn on the motor, and pull the unit across the work. See Figure 4-61. In softwoods this operation takes but a moment. If you want a

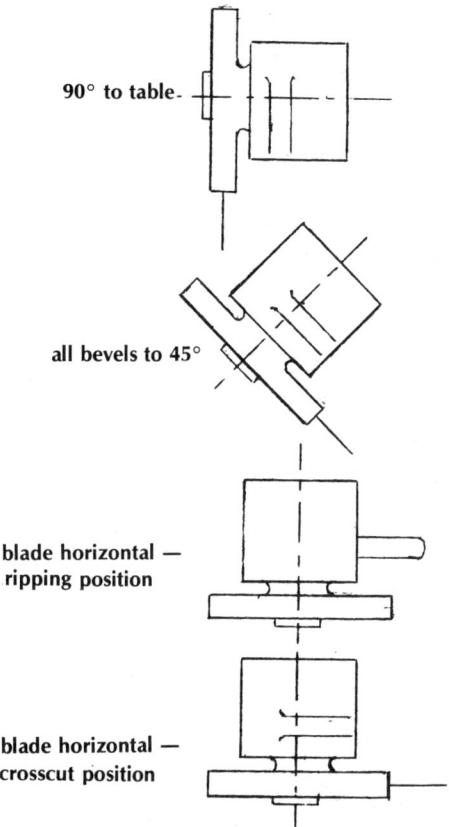

Figure 4-63. POSITIONS UNLIMITED

fine surface, slow the feed down and use a cabinetmaker's combination blade or a carbide-tipped blade. The vertical position should be such that the blade cuts a kerf from about 1/16 to 1/8 inch deep in the table top. Check the two pieces with a square for an accurate 90-degree cut. If they and the kerf in the table are out, check the indexing device for play, the base of the column for loose bolts, and so on. If the blade is aligned properly, you can make 1,000 cuts at one second each and all will be perfect.

To rip, you move the stock against the saw. First, raise the unit, rotate it 90 degrees, and lock it. The blade is now parallel to the fence, as shown in Figure 4-62. Lower the revolving blade until it penetrates the table top 1/16 inch. The piece must be fed against the rotation of the blade, so turn on the motor, press the piece constantly against the fence, and keep it going steadily into the blade, hand over hand for best results. If you can, clamp a comb to the table to keep the work piece against the fence. By this time you know how I feel about using a pusher stick, any old stick.

This is a simple machine, but I like De Cristoforo's advice. "Be alert but relaxed. Be master of the machine, but at the same time don't be so overconfident that you lose sight of the fact that here is a bundle of power that is completely indifferent to who is turning it on. The biggest secret to safe power-tool operation is always to be a little bit afraid of the machine. You'll have this awareness if you are a beginner. The danger lies in losing it as you become more proficient." So remember, your rip or crosscut operation is not complete until the blade has stopped turning and you have removed the work. Never try to remove stock while the blade is still turning, even though the power is shut off. Never feed stock when ripping, molding, grooving, or whatever, in the same direction as the blade's rotation. This could pull your hand into the blade or even wreck the machine.

If angles are to be cut, release the clamp that locks the arm to the column and swing the arm to the correct angle according to the calibration. Try the angle cut on a fairly wide piece of scrap or several pieces so they can be placed in position just as the final parts would be. If the angle is less than perfect, adjust the arm by trial and error and then reset the indicator to read correctly. Swing the blade back to 90 degrees to see if this, too, reads correctly. If it does not, you have an error, the column is loose in the base, or the arm is not locking firmly on the column. This is one of the few faults of radial-arm saws. In some models with automatic or manual stops for 45 and 90 degrees, there is sufficient play in the locking mechanism to require checking after a change of head position.

How do you cut material wider than the capacity of 15 to 20 inches? Pull the blade as far as it will reach, then return the power unit. Turn the piece over end for end, marked side down. Now shift the piece about so the blade can be brought into the fresh saw kerf. Since you are using the blade itself to locate the work piece, your new kerf should match the first one perfectly. You may also locate by tacking a stop block on the table before the first cut is made. Then all you have to do is turn the piece over, but not end for end. Of course, you may mark with a square on both sides of the material if it is over 15 or 20 inches — the capacity of many radial-arm saws.

Material thicker than the saw blade depth capacity (usually about 3 inches) can be cut in two passes. Position the work piece against a stop block, make the first cut, then flop the piece and make the second cut. See Figure 4-64. The second kerf will match the first one perfectly. The stop-block trick (nothing brilliant, really) is used for cutting identical lengths, which you may have to do quite frequently. Another method is to lay several pieces of the stock side by side against the fence and an end stop. Then you cut all in one pass of the blade.

Ripping extra-thick material is simple. Turn the unit to the ripping position, make one pass the full length of the material, then turn it over end for end. The original side must be against the fence. Use a comb to achieve accuracy. The kerfs will meet perfectly.

If the lumber is rough, you may have to joint an edge first. If it is badly bent, tack a straight batten (1 by 3 or

77

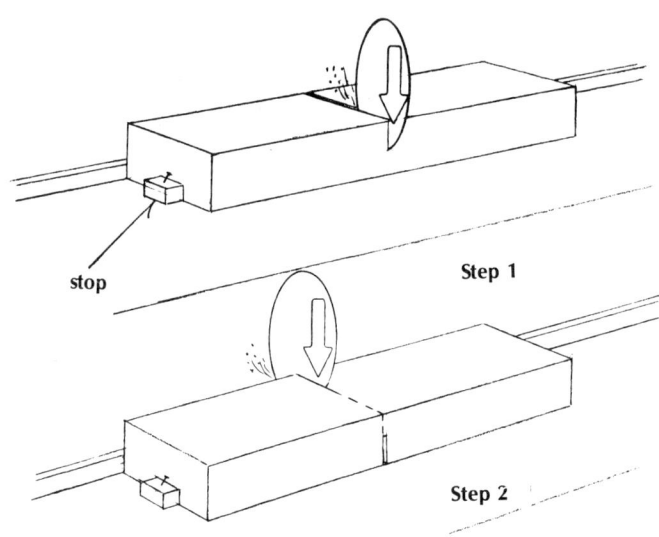

Figure 4-64. SAWING THICK STOCK

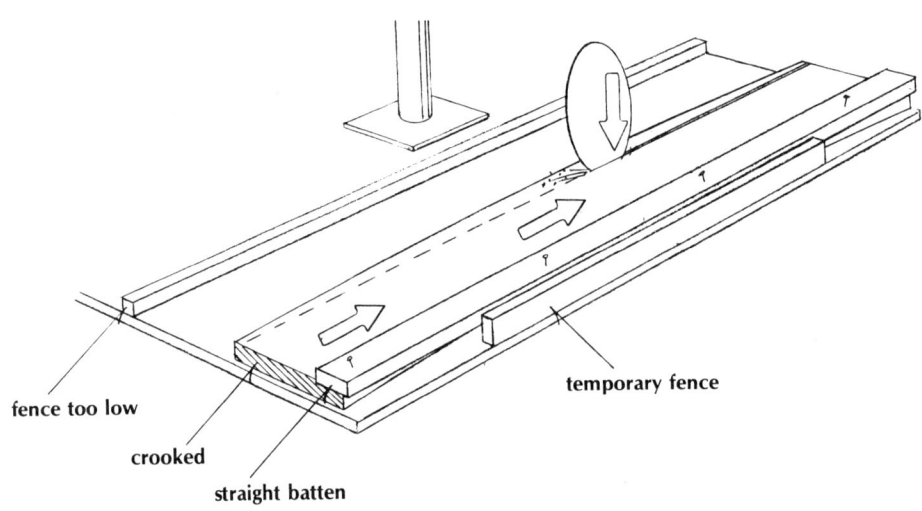

Figure 4-65. RIPPING CROOKED PLANK

1 by 4) to the lumber and run this against the fence. Complications arise if you must turn this piece over, of course.

If the piece is wide, rotate the saw to the out-rip position. If a narrow piece is wanted, turn the unit to the in-rip position so the blade just clears your batten. You now have a straight edge to run against the fence for further ripping. If the fence is so low that the batten will not meet it, you may run the work against a temporary fence clamped to the outer edge of the table, as shown in Figure 4-65. Or you may tack an additional piece to the original fence to give it proper height.

Operating with the blade in its horizontal position, that is, with the power unit on end, offers a number of conveniences. This allows you to make a repeated-pass groove in a plank edge, or a rabbet with the blade vertical for the second cut. This is great for dadoing, rabbeting, or tenoning on a plank end. With the arbor on end, you might find it necessary to raise the stock to avoid interference from the arbor end and nut. Just place it on a piece of lumber or plywood. Use the horizontal position for rabbeting and grooving as well as for dadoing across the plank end. In the latter case, the piece should be raised to prevent the blade from cutting through the fence. A horizontal blade is useful for making many of the joints described in Part Two.

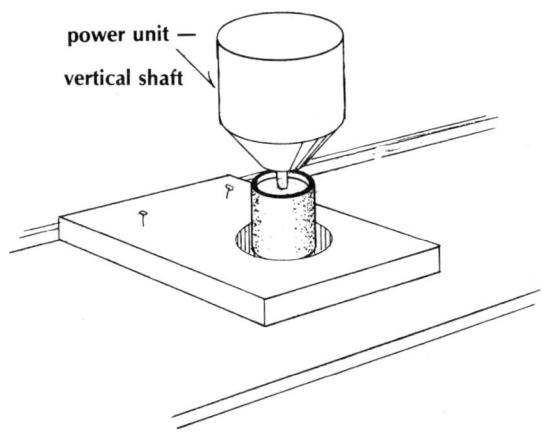

Figure 4-66. DRUM SANDER

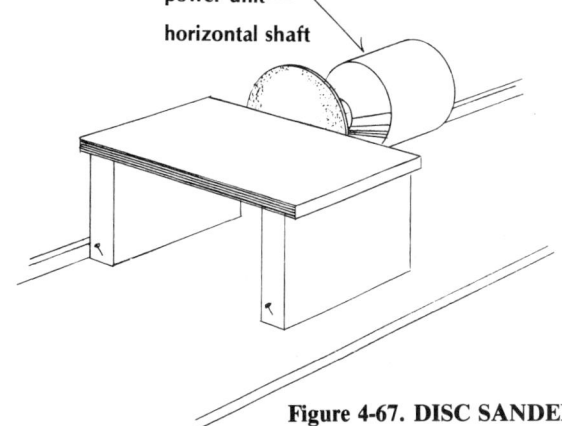

Figure 4-67. DISC SANDER

Accessories

So far I have discussed the radial-arm saw as a sawing machine. All of the accessories used with table saws are used on radials, so I won't go into detail. The horizontal and angled positions possible on the radial make these attachments even more versatile. This applies to molding heads, shaper cutters, router bits, and so on. A planer of the rotary type already described would be very useful. It should be mounted on a collet chuck mounted on the vertical shaft. A sanding drum does a beautiful job on both inside and outside curved pieces. It will work best if it turns inside a cutout in a block, as shown in Figure 4-66. This guarantees that the edges will be square. An 8- to 10-inch sanding disc is set up easily on the arbor in its normal position. Build a little table to clamp up close to the sanding surface, as shown in Figure 4-67.

There are many occasions when holes must be bored edgewise through a wide piece, perhaps a cabin trunk side. Make a horizontal boring machine out of your radial-arm saw by adapting a ½-inch chuck to the arbor. Raise the work piece on a table to approximate the height of the arbor center, clamp the piece to the table (which in turn is clamped to the saw table), and feed the drill into the work just as you feed the blade in a crosscut. I guarantee that a bit, especially a ship's auger, will bore on dead center when set up this way. Don't forget, however, to pull the bit back frequently so chips don't bind it. To do this, simply slide the power unit back and forth on the radial arm.

Need I say more about the radial arm's versatility? The only problem is the cost of the machine and the accessories. Saws for the home shop run in the vicinity of $200 to $375. A DeWalt runs about $400 for a 10-inch industrial model. Rockwell has several in this price range. Of course, you will see them at Sears and Ward's, too. I have seen numerous radial-arm saws on the used-tool market at great prices, but you should take an expert with you to check out a used machine. If you see one with a steel table and two or three accessories — dado sets, molding heads, perhaps a small assortment of blades — you are looking at an additional $75 to $100 in value, new. So anything under $200 that checks out is a buy!

PLANERS

There are many wonderfully productive tools that I cannot include in this book. First, doing so would produce a prohibitively large and costly book. And second, the cost of many of these tools is beyond the reach of the average amateur craftsman. For example, a thickness planer would be a real money saver and a joy to use. The sophisticated types that include setups for moldings would eliminate the need for molding heads on a table or radial-arm saw, but the cost of this accessory is a pittance compared with the cost of such a planer. Sears sells a popular planer-molder with a 2 h.p., 115-230-volt motor, stand, pulleys, belt, and so on. The price in 1980 was $1,200. The planer alone was $700. Figure 4-68 shows such a machine. It will handle anything between 12 inches wide and 6 inches high. Molding cutters come in sets of three for about $6.50.

AN OPEN-SIDE MOLDER-PLANER

I must suggest a possible compromise because yacht joinery often requires thicknesses not available commercially, and the cost of fine millwork in small lots is prohibitive. The open-side planer is not a new idea. The design is probably 50 years old. I used one in 1949 to plane all the oak frames, deck beams, and other parts for my 36-foot *Bay Bird*. The tool was sold by Sears at a very low price. A much finer model is made by Williams & Hussey Machine Corporation. See Figure 4-69.

Figure 4-68. *Every serious boatbuilder performing many joinery operations and sparbuilding should consider a molder-planer. (Courtesy Sears, Roebuck)*

Figure 4-69. *A practical compromise, the Williams & Hussey open-side molder-planer, with a normal capacity to 7⅛ inches wide, planes up to 14 inches wide by reversing the material. The tool handles up to 8¼-inch-thick timbers. (Hamor photo courtesy Williams & Hussey Machine Corporation)*

A short article in *Popular Mechanics* says this tool is "a real workhorse and as versatile as a one-man band. Not only is it a molder and a thickness planer, it's a jointer and edger as well . . . . The 7⅛-inch cutter head can surface a board up to 14 inches wide. Just reverse the board and pass it through a second time. The machine comes in both hand-feed and power-feed models and has an output capacity of 15 feet per minute . . . ." The manufacturer points out that the power-feed model restricts width capacity to 7 inches. Because you will not have any production needs, the hand-feed model probably will be acceptable. The vertical capacity of the tool is 8¼ inches, so it can be used efficiently as a jointer. The hand-feed model requires a ¾ h.p. 3,450 r.p.m. motor. Bare, the price is about $380. The power-feed model is about $500. Many accessories and a wide assortment of knives for moldings are available. The catalog and operator's manual are very thorough.

I hope you will not accuse me of commercialism. I try not to favor any tool over another. If I had the money, however, I would make this molder-planer my next purchase, even though the need in my small cabinet shop does not compare with its many uses in a boatshop. For conventional wooden hull construction, joinery and trim, sparbuilding, and especially when using epoxy laminated systems, this tool should be invaluable. Williams & Hussey Machine Corporation is in Milford, New Hampshire 03055.

Space restrictions do not permit more detailed information on all of these wonderful power tools. But believe me, there is much more to be learned. It will be up to you to pick the brains of any experts you know or to spend some time at the library. Elsewhere in this book, you will find a list of books that I think will be useful. These books are not just on tools, but on the many ways to make them work for you as well.

FIVE

Tools, Jigs, and Accessories You Can Build

Most woodworkers derive immense satisfaction from owning and using top-quality tools and equipment. I have a few such items, and I prize them highly. You do not, however, have to use only the best of everything to turn out quality workmanship.

For those of you who must stay within a budget, I have a suggestion. Get acquainted with the kits manufactured and sold direct by Gilliom Manufacturing, Inc. Gilliom provides complete sets of the metal parts for a number of power tools. You supply the plywood, hardwood, and labor needed to complete the tool.

A GREAT 10-INCH TABLE SAW

Let me describe my Gilliom 10-inch table saw. (See Figure 5-1.) It includes a ball-bearing $\frac{5}{8}$-inch arbor and an arbor tilting system that enables one to tilt the arbor up to 45 degrees by hand. The arbor raising and lowering device is based on the teeter-totter principle. The motor and arbor are mounted on opposite ends of a husky oak platform that is moved easily by a handwheel. The motor is lowered as the arbor is raised. Two aluminum channel extrusions mount on the front and back of the table; the oak rip fence slides on these.

There is no micrometer gearing, just a simple clamp on both ends of the fence. Alignment is adjustable; once set, it is reliable. Spacing of the fence may be set accurately by a light tap or two. (Always measure from a tooth to the fence, of course.)

I mounted the fence rails to permit ripping 24 inches wide, or better. Thus, I can cut to the center of a 48-inch-wide sheet of plywood. In addition, I covered the table top with plastic laminate. This wears well and minimizes friction. Be sure to do this before drilling for fastenings and installing. Otherwise, it will be impossible to remove the top for servicing.

Gilliom provides paper patterns, a great time-saver, to trace the rather intricate plywood and oak parts. The design shows construction of a regular floor-model stand. It is totally enclosed and holds several bushels of sawdust. A door in the right side permits easy emptying. I added 14-inch extensions made from scraps of kitchen countertops, in addition to increasing the dimensions of the table top three or four inches each way. The result is a large saw. I found a used ¾ h.p., 3,450 r.p.m. motor based on the necessary long low-profile frame at a cost of about $20. For heavier work (1½-inch oak, for example), you would need a 1 h.p. motor.

I have used this saw every day for eight years for custom cabinetwork of furniture quality, including

Above: Figure 5-1. *Built from a Gilliom kit, this 10-inch saw has produced precision results in the author's cabinet shop for years. He considers it the bargain of a lifetime.* **Right: Figure 5-2.** *An 18-inch homebuilt bandsaw that performs like $700 saws. Assembly time was about 10 hours.*

dadoing and molding. I frequently turn out large parts within 1/64 inch and absolutely precise miters. The cost of the Gilliom kit in 1980 was about $60. Completing the saw requires a sheet of ¾-inch plywood and a bit of 2-inch oak and glue. All hardware and fastenings are in the package. Later in this chapter I'll show you how to make a sliding auxiliary table for this or any table saw, and also how to cut out the miter gauge grooves.

BUY-N-BUILD 18- AND 12-INCH BANDSAWS

When I bought the Gilliom table saw kit, the company whose production I managed ordered Gilliom's 18-inch bandsaw kit. The business then took a nose dive and I was able to acquire the unopened package. All metal parts and fastenings were there — from wheels, rubber tires, and guides with ball-bearing wheels to alignment mechanism, tilting table quadrant, and all the bolts, screws, and wing nuts needed. I bought one sheet of ¾-inch plywood and about six board feet of oak. Assembling the saw took two days of patient effort. I found that shortcuts got me into trouble because the beautifully illustrated sequence of operations is quite rigid. This machine does everything that any 18-inch moderate-duty saw can be expected to do with ease, precision, and freedom from vibration. See Figure 5-2. The 18- and 12-inch bandsaws account for 60 percent of Gilliom's sales. Ease of assembly, people say, is one reason why.

I have used a Gilliom 12-inch bandsaw also. This tool has been used without any problem to build hull mold sections of ¾-inch pine and many other items. I use it almost every day and it has always done everything demanded of it, smoothly and quietly. It will admit 6 inches under the guide. So far I have not had occasion to run anything over 4 inches through it, but it did a fine job of resawing 4-inch mahogany without so much as slowing down the 1/3 h.p. appliance motor. The kit calls for a sheet of ¾-inch plywood, a little bit of 2-inch oak, and a $3 motor. The workmanship required on the oak parts may be a bit closer than anything on the 10-inch table saw, but if your tracing is done carefully, it's all very easy. I made no changes or additions other than the application of plastic laminate to the table.

To build these machines you need a sabersaw and a power handsaw or access to a table saw. You may find it safer and more accurate to mount the sabersaw upside down so that small parts can be manipulated with two hands. Try clamping the sabersaw firmly in a vise, but do not crush it.

BUILDING A SHAPER

Gilliom's ½-inch shaper is even simpler to build than the table saw and bandsaws. I put together the one shown in Figure 5-3 in about five hours. In a few weeks I have shaped nearly 1,000 feet of moldings and molded edges and a dozen sets of hull mold templates. I found that a ½ h.p., 3,450 r.p.m. motor permits feeding ash as fast as it can be pushed. This machine has a split fence and guide pins for shaping curved or irregular

Figure 5-3. *This shaper, from a Gilliom kit, was built in less than a day. It turns out a precision mold frame in under two minutes. The same part takes two hours to make by hand.*

pieces against a collar. The raising and lowering system is simple, accurate, and fast. The table is a generous 18½ by 28 inches, with a durable surface of ¼-inch hardboard glued and screwed on. The groove for the miter gauge is easily constructed without tricky routing or sawing. The large instruction sheets are clear and well illustrated and include templates for precise location of mandrel, fences, pin anchor nuts, screws, and so on.

The materials needed are simple: about two-thirds of a sheet of ¾-inch plywood, a scrap of Tempered Presdwood, and about 6 feet of 1 by 3 hardwood or plywood. All fastenings and hardware are in the kit.

Gilliom manufactures other tools in kit form that I have not used. I'll wager that they are just as ingenious and efficient as the two bandsaws, the table saw, and the shaper described above. Contact Gilliom Manufacturing, Inc., at 1109 North Second Street, St. Charles, MO 63301.

SLIDING AUXILIARY TABLE — SLAT

Whatever the size of your table saw, you must provide extensions on each side, or even two of them on the right side. And then you must have a sliding table that works on top of the original table. This is essentially a much larger piece of ¼-inch plywood with a hardwood batten glued to its underside and fitted accurately into one of the miter gauge grooves. See Figure 5-4. A sturdy fence on the side toward you locates everything right up to the stationary blade before the cut is begun. If the fence is square to the groove and blade, everything you cut will be right on the money!

Here's an example. Let's say you are about to fit a counter or dresser top between two partial bulkheads. This piece of ¾-inch mahogany plywood can be sawed quite square by using your 90-degree saw guide or by ripping on your table saw. The miter gauge, on the other hand, is unreliable for squareness. Unfortunately, if the piece comes out $\frac{1}{32}$ or $\frac{1}{16}$ inch under the fore-and-aft dimension required, you can't stretch it to achieve the gentle press fit it needs. And if it comes out $\frac{1}{32}$ inch over, it will take precious time to plane off, try, and fit. If you have a sliding auxiliary table (let's call it SLAT from here on), however, you can line the piece up to the tooth of the saw blade while it is stationary and actually split the pencil or knife line. You can even make a tentative saw cut; $\frac{1}{16}$ inch deep is enough to show where the final kerf will be.

Here's another example. You want a number of 45-degree miters. Brad two pieces of 1 by 2 about 12 inches long to the table, but don't allow the points to come through. See Figure 5-3. Experiment with two pieces of scrap until you get a perfect 90-degree joint by shifting the little fences, then add another couple of brads. Save these pieces so the brads can be pressed into their respective holes for future use; mark around the fences so they can be located rapidly. Another way is to use a 90-degree corner off a plywood sheet for the fences. If you use a cabinetmaker's combination or a multitooth carbide blade, you will get beautiful miters.

A third important example is the technique for making repeated cuts to length. Tack a stop block to the fence or surface of the SLAT. Now all cut pieces will be identical. For producing pieces longer than the width of the SLAT, use a 1 by 3 or 1 by 4 with a block glued to one end as a stop rod. Clamp this bar securely to the front fence. Now it takes just seconds to make precise duplicates of any number. Here's a tip: Mark with a knife for accuracy and the cleanest possible cut when sawing across the grain.

How to Build a SLAT

The drawing in Figure 5-4 shows the general dimensions taken from my own sliding auxiliary table. The SLAT extends slightly beyond the table extensions. As a result, it must be reinforced adequately on the underside. Make it not less than 48 inches wide. The depth should be 33 inches or more. This enables you to saw material as wide as 24 inches (remember the blade width). The fences should be about 4 inches high, and of hardwood, fir, or ¾-inch plywood. The drawing shows additional pieces against each fence for stiffening and to absorb the saw

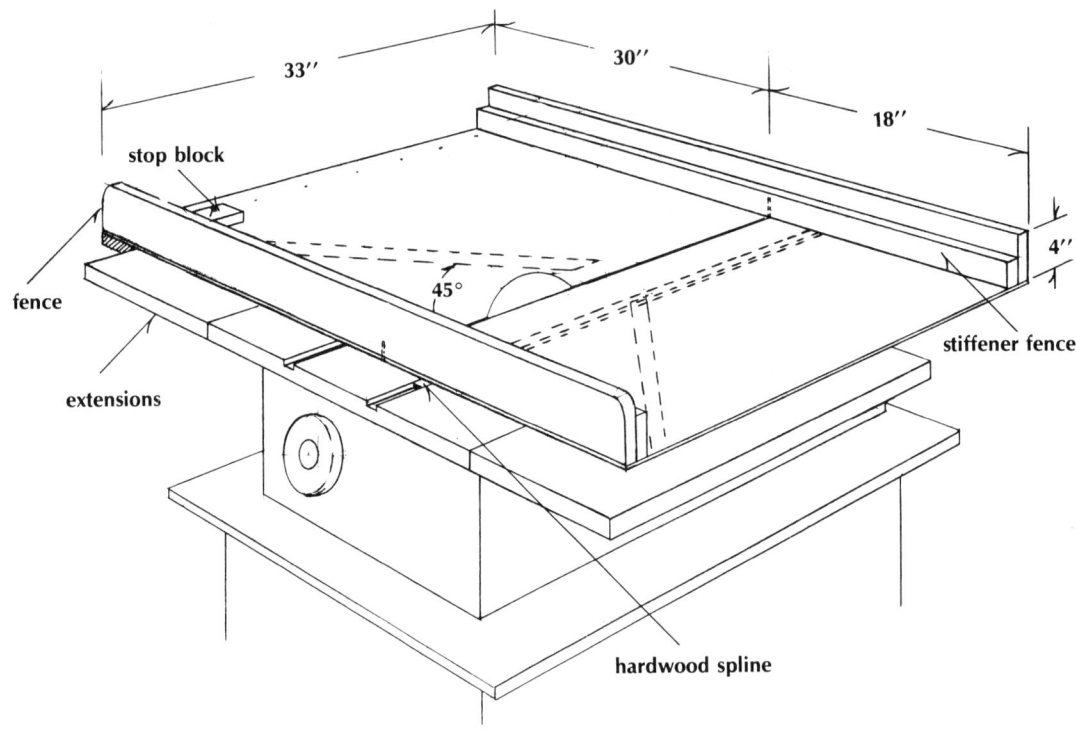

Figure 5-4. SLIDING AUXILIARY TABLE (SLAT)

cuts. These may be anything, even particle board. Because they are expendable, don't use glue.

Here's the assembly procedure. Make a straight hardwood spline or batten that will fit snugly but slide easily in one of the grooves in the saw table. The sliding panel itself may be ¼- or ⅜-inch plywood. A greater thickness will do also, but this reduces the cutting depth of the blade. Now lower the blade below the table top. C-clamp the 33-inch-by-48-inch panel to the saw table so it is flush with the front edge. This assumes that the front edge is square to the blade (check it, to be sure). Tack five or six brads through the panel into the spline in the groove. The assembly should now slide back and forth easily with no measurable side movement. If there is side movement, make a new spline. Otherwise, your workmanship will be inaccurate. Now pull the batten off, spread white glue on its top surface, find the same holes for the brads, and drive them through and clench over. Check the sliding action. If the batten binds in the groove, check it with a plywood straightedge and correct with a gentle tap here or there until the action is perfect. Add three or four additional brads and allow the glue to set.

The rear fence can be glued and nailed permanently in place and the stiffener fence screwed to it. Don't glue the stiffener, for it is to be expendable. Fasten the front fence temporarily with brads, aligning it with the table front edge and the plywood panel. Place the panel on the table, with the batten in its groove, located so the blade will penetrate fairly near the rear fence. Now turn on the saw and slowly raise the blade until it penetrates the plywood. Push the panel back so you have a kerf or slot about a foot long. Shut the saw down. Check the slot with a carpenter's square against the front fence. If the fence does not line the square precisely along the slot, tap the fence until it does. Be sure the fence in its final position is absolutely straight. You may now cut the kerf from the front fence to near the back fence.

Test with a piece of plywood scrap about 12 inches wide. Hold it securely against the front fence, positioned so you are about to slice off a narrow piece. Turn on the saw, and slide the SLAT back until the blade barely cuts into the front fence. Then pull it toward you again and turn off the machine. If this test does not produce a perfectly square cut, your fence is bent or out of line. Give it a few taps and try again.

Here's another test. Saw another wide piece of scrap in two, then flop one part over and move the freshly sawed ends together. If they do not meet, your fence is out of line or it is slightly curved. Check with a good straightedge. When you are satisfied, hold the fence in place against the panel securely with clamps, then remove it from the saw table. Drive five or six screws temporarily, then remove the screws. Coat the surfaces with white glue and replace the screws. Test once more before the glue sets. Any corrections done at this point should be minute and can be made easily with a couple of taps.

Figure 5-5. *The sliding auxiliary table (SLAT) set up especially for mitering.*

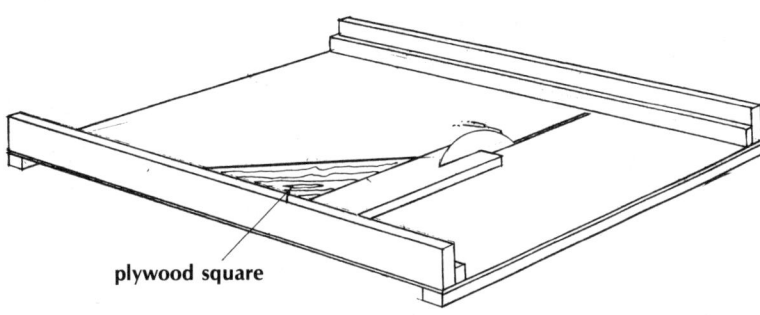

Figure 5-6. SMALL RIPPING JOB ON SLAT

If you have overhangs that are wide enough, add a stiff batten under each end to provide additional rigidity. Now let the whole thing set up.

When using the SLAT, be wary of the blade cutting through the front fence. It will do this if the work piece is thick. Just replace the expendable stiffener from time to time.

A dado set will cut a wide slot in the panel. This is not serious, but you can make a separate SLAT for dadoing. I have an additional small SLAT for mitering moldings. I use this rather than set up two tack-on fences (Figure 5-5).

To shave an edge, say, by $1/64$ or $1/32$ inch, place the edge firmly against the saw teeth, hold it down, and tap it slightly against the blade. This will cause a very small deflection, just about the amount you want to shave off. Back up and start the saw. You'll see it take off a mere sliver. For a polished edge, use a cabinetmaker's combination or a carbide-tipped blade. Short lengths may be ripped if one end is square, but you can achieve precision by using a square to line the piece up against. See Figure 5-6.

The SLAT described here is a simple device. I have seen sliding tables made by cabinetmakers that look like furniture, with brass corner reinforcements, handles, and so on. These are passed down through the generations. When you discover how valuable this accessory is, you may decide to use mahogany or teak in your next one.

A ROUTER-SHAPER

In Chapter Three I described a router as a shaper turned upside down. Let's build a table with a cutout to receive the base plate of your router with the collet pointed up. See Figure 5-7. Make the outside dimensions of the table approximately 16 by 30 inches, and use ¾-inch plywood. The legs should be 10 to 12 inches long, that is, high enough to be comfortable when in use on a bench. The rails to stiffen the top can be pine 1 by 3s. It may all be nailed together if well glued. The cutout in the center should be a nice fit for the plastic base of the router.

You will probably find it convenient to remove the handles of the router before mounting it. Otherwise, it will have to be passed up through the hole from beneath. The removable turnbuttons (A) may be 1 by 2 or smaller, and held by a ¼-inch flathead stove bolt and

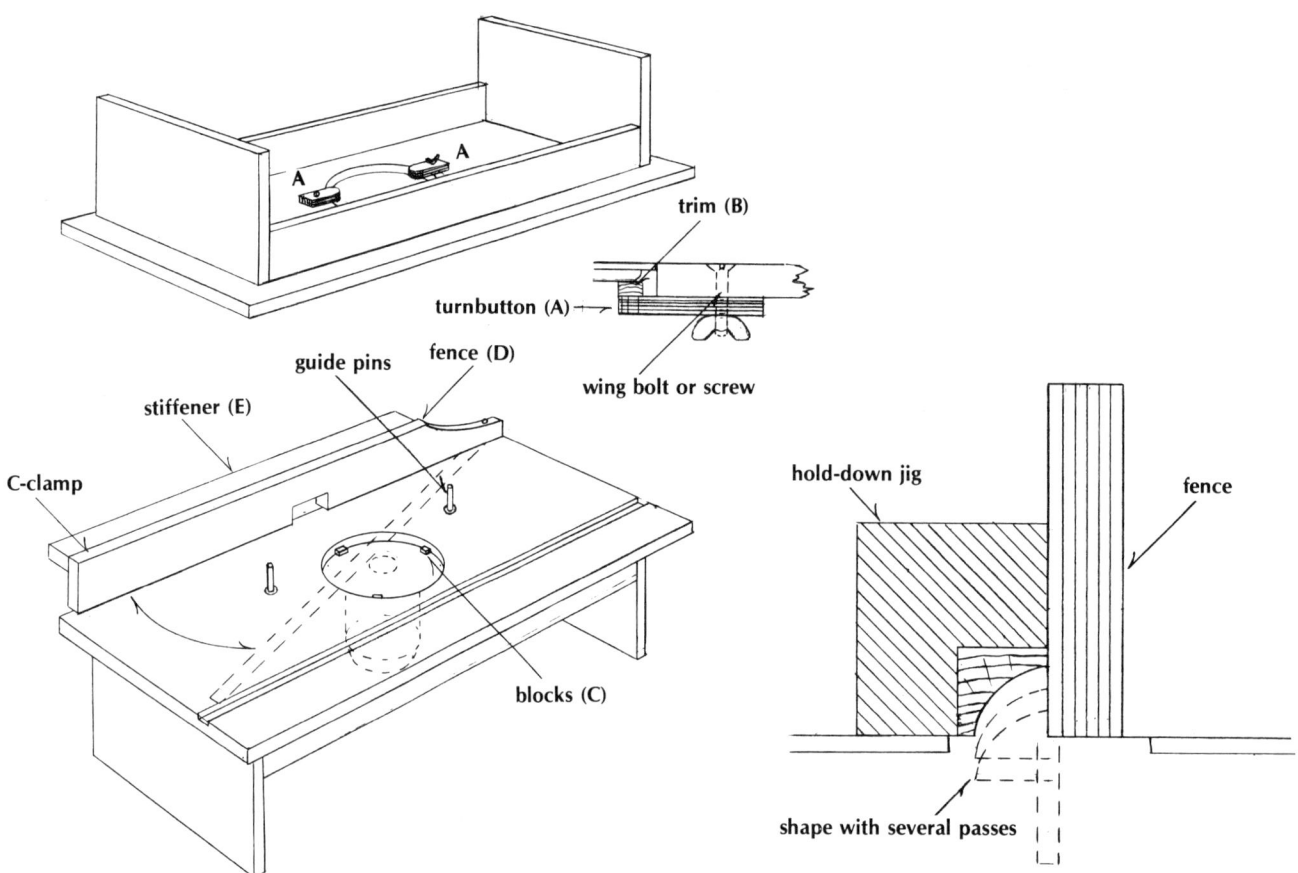

Figure 5-7. CONVERTING ROUTER TO SHAPER

Figure 5-8. HOLDING JIG

wing nut or screw. Insert the router in the hole. It may not want to lie flush with the surface of the table, but it must. If it is too low, glue a tiny shim (B) on the tip of each turnbutton. Trim this with a chisel or coarse sandpaper until the router lies flush with the table top. Position the router with the chip ejector aimed toward the back of the table.

Another way to install the router requires some careful work with a chisel. Mark around the base plate, but saw 1/8 inch to 1/4 inch inside the line. Then chisel a rabbet to the depth of the base plate. Or you can run the router around the opening using a collar and rabbeting bit. Finally, you can saw out to the line and glue and brad three small blocks (C) inside the cutout to support the router at the proper height. Routers differ, so the choice is up to you.

Most shaper operations require a fence or other stop to guide the work piece. Figure 5-7 shows a simple one-piece fence (D) that can be adjusted by pivoting at one end. This is shown by the dotted line in the drawing. Clamped to the table, the 1 by 2 stiffener (E) keeps the fence straight. Note the cutout to clear the router bits. The fence is adjusted by trial and error on a straight piece of scrap. The single fence shown is good only for forming radii, rabbets, and other shapes or straight edges where the piece is not reduced by the shaper (in contrast to jointing).

It is dangerous to run light stock in this or any shaper without good hold-downs. Moreover, you would get chatter and a poor cut surface. I prefer to rout the edge of a larger piece and then rip off the molding, but you may want to saw out a holding jig (Figure 5-8). Don't try to shape a molding in one pass. Raise the bit in two or three stages as shown in Figure 5-8. You can use a feather or comb hold-down, but neither of these will support the molding at the bitter end. On the first pass, always try to run through as much molding as you can foresee a need for. Then run all of it through on the second pass, and so on.

Solid router bits for radii (rounding) have pilots (extensions) that are designed to ride against the edge of the piece. See Figure 5-9. A pilot eliminates the need for a fence, but there is a chance you will burn the edge of the work piece. Two-piece bits mounted on a shaft, spindle, or arbor may be set up with a ball-bearing collar, thus ending the burning problem. The collar may be used with rabbet bits and other shapes also, so try to acquire this type (Figure 5-10). Get carbide bits if you can. They

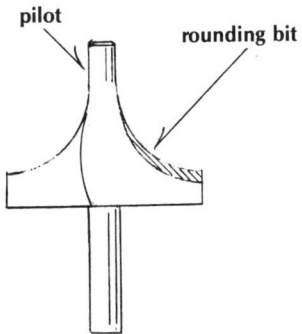

Figure 5-9. PILOT FOLLOWS STRAIGHT OR CURVED EDGE

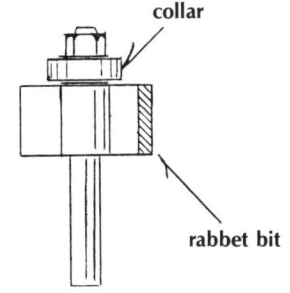

Figure 5-10. COLLAR PREVENTS BURNING

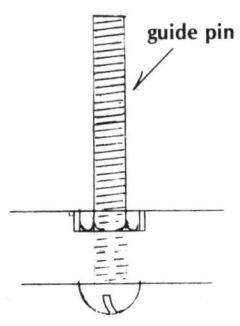

Figure 5-11. SHAPER GUIDE PIN

Figure 5-12. *Constructed in hours, this inexpensive (about $10) disc sander does the work of machines costing hundreds of dollars.*

cut faster and more smoothly and do not need sharpening.

Sears offers light-duty split fences. And Gilliom sells the castings for a good split fence. Such a fence permits using the shaper for edging, like a jointer.

To get the most out of your shaper, there must be provision for guide pins. See Figure 5-11. Let's say you want to shape a molded edge on a round or curved piece. A collar on the spindle is needed to carry the squared edge of the piece, but it is dangerous to simply push a work piece into the rotating bit without some means of control. Otherwise, the bit can chew into the wood and throw the piece across the shop. To prevent this, pins are inserted into the table 4 inches from the center of the spindle (Figure 5-7). The work is placed against the pin and slowly fed into the bit until it rides against the collar. Then you start moving the piece against the counterclockwise rotation and keep it going so it doesn't burn. You keep a firm grip on the work piece and move it as steadily as possible. Any imperfections in the original edge of the work piece will be reproduced in the molded edge.

One disadvantage of this router-shaper arrangement is that the router's built-in switch may be awkward to reach. For safety, you might have to lock it "on" and use a cord with a line switch.

You may wish to add a groove for a miter gauge, a real necessity for molding the ends of narrow pieces such as drawer fronts. You can dado the groove or saw it out by making repeated cuts with your power saw, being very careful with the positioning of the guide piece so there is no slop. You can also use a router and a ¾-inch straight bit, but be sure the miter gauge fits the trial groove you cut in a piece of scrap. A third way is to cover the top of the table with two pieces of ⅜-inch tempered hardboard or plywood spaced correctly by using the miter gauge itself as a spacer. If you choose this method, brad and glue the cover on before any bolt holes are drilled.

AN INEXPENSIVE BENCH DISC SANDER

I designed and built the inexpensive and totally efficient disc sander shown in Figure 5-12. Anyone with basic woodworking skills can do it. The sander's cost without motor should be under $15. You can pick up a junked appliance motor for $2 or $3.

For my sander, I found a rusty swimming pool pump motor whose base was completely eroded. It was rated at ½ h.p. and turned 3,450 r.p.m., far more than enough for an 8-inch Sears sanding disc. The disc was fitted to the shaft by means of an arbor extension. The only disadvantage to this machine is that 3,450 r.p.m. can eat up any piece you touch to it unless you are extremely cautious. An old appliance motor of ⅓ h.p. and 1,725 r.p.m. would be more than adequate for light duty.

The obvious uses for a disc sander are rounding corners and convex edges accurately, sanding and squaring sawed ends, fitting miters, and so on. Every plywood cabinet door, bulkhead edge, and shelf in a vessel must be covered with a neat strip of pine, mahogany, or other

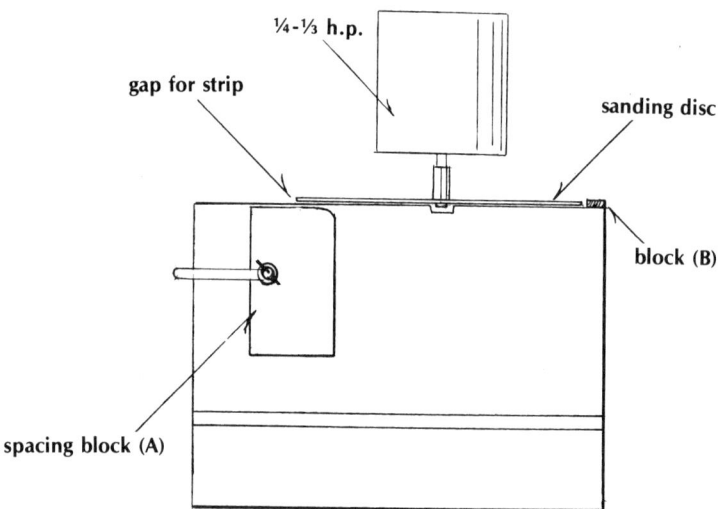

Figure 5-13. SETUP FOR "PLANING" STRIPS

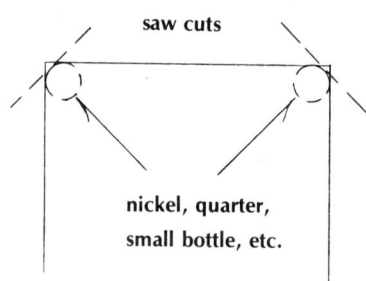

Figure 5-14. ROUNDING A CORNER

hardwood. A disc sander does a fine job of sanding out the rough surfaces left by your saw on such strips. In addition, it reduces the strips to a uniform thickness, much as a thickness planer does. Yes, the strips must still be sanded later with the grain to erase the fine diagonal scratches left by the disc. Even so, it beats trying to plane hardwoods or curly or unruly grains such as those of birch, mahogany ribbon grain, ash, and especially flat-grained fir.

There are two ways to make these strips. One is simply to rip them out one after another until you have the number required. If you like to use a jack plane or jointer, however, you dress the edge *before* you rip out the next strip. This way, one surface is good for gluing, even if it's imperfect. It's much easier to dress the edge of a board by hand in a vise, or on the jointer, than to try to plane a thin strip. So now you have a supply of strips about 3/16 inch or 1/4 inch by 3/4 inch rough on both sides, or rough on one side and planed one side, depending on which way you decide to go.

Round a corner of a block (A) about as shown in Figure 5-13 and clamp it to the table. Leave a gap of about 3/16 inch between it and the sanding disc, according to the dimensions of the strips. If the strips are 1/4 inch, this gap will remove all saw marks from one side. Practice on scrap. If both sides are rough, allow for passing the strips through in two passes by adjusting the gap closer for the second pass. Note the block (B) near the up side of the disc. This prevents the strips from touching the disc as they are passing through. Pull the strips through the gap in a steady, quite rapid motion without slowing or stopping. If you stop, the strip will simply disappear or at least show undesirable low spots. Surface one side of all the strips with one setting of the block. If you planed one side previously, the strips are ready to use. The sanded side is the glue side — a slight tooth is wanted.

To sand both sides, give the block a tap to close up the gap about 1/16 inch. Try a piece of scrap again. When the gap is right, pull the strips through as above. Disc sanding this way will not leave a perfect surface for finishing. I usually finish-sand after the strips are glued to the shelf, door, or whatever, using a block. Another way is to tack or staple a couple of sheets of 80- to 100-grit aluminum oxide or garnet sandpaper to a board. Tack the board to a bench, then slide the strips back and forth rapidly over this long sanding surface. Press down with your fingers so the entire strip contacts the paper. This will take out disc marks in a hurry. A portable or bench belt sander will work even faster.

To dress ends square, place any work piece firmly against a miter gauge with the end just kissing the moving disc. Then slide the piece rapidly across the disc. If your saw cut was square, this will give the end grain a final finish. If it was out of square, a couple of strokes should do the job. Don't let the work piece shift on the miter gauge.

To round corners, mark the desired radius with a dime, penny, or whatever. If a larger radius is desired, it would be best first to hack off most of the material with a bandsaw, table saw, or chisel (Figure 5-14). The disc will do the job, but you would be heating it up and filling the sanding surface unduly. Practice with this tool will enable you to take off just a smidgen and leave a beautiful surface. For example, you can fit miters perfectly by tacking a stop at exactly 45 degrees to the face of the disc. Get the exact angle with a piece of scrap. Then slide your work piece along the stop until it just touches the moving disc.

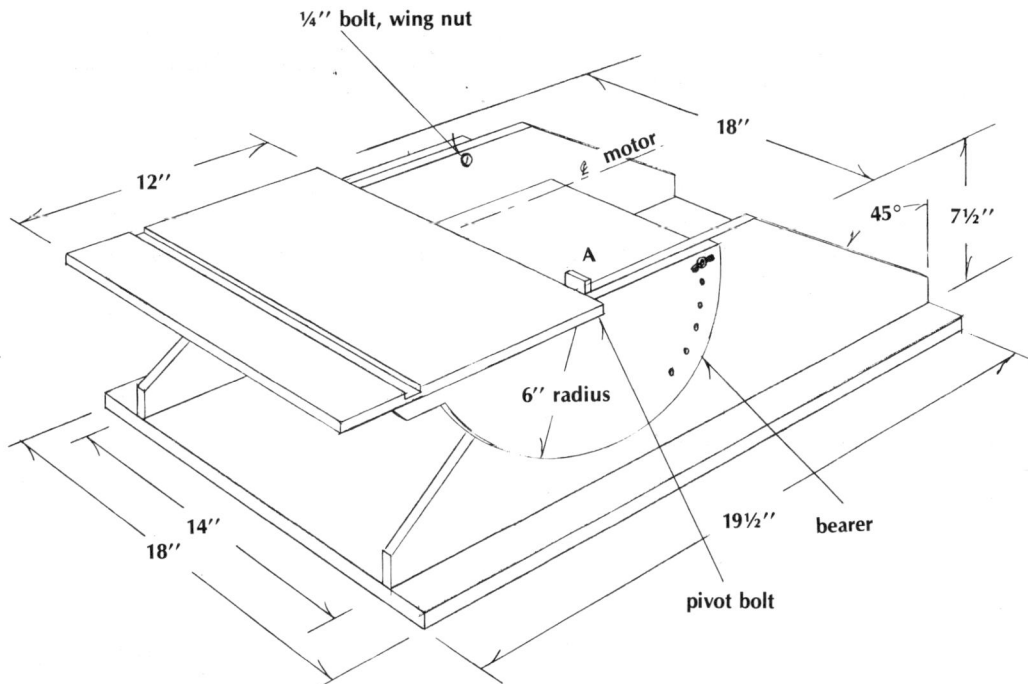

Figure 5-15. BUILD A DISC SANDER FOR PEANUTS

How to Build a Disc Sander

Now you can construct your bench sander, which is simply a firm support for a motor with a metal disc on its shaft against which a worktable is mounted. That's all there is to it. See Figure 5-15. The tilting table is a refinement you may add if you like.

The base can be ½- to ¾-inch fir plywood. On this the side pieces are fastened with glue and nails. Leave 14 inches between the sides to receive the motor mounting shelf. Locate this shelf at a height that places the motor shaft just below the top of the side pieces. Glue blocks under the shelf to support the weight of a motor.

If you choose to eliminate the tilt table, ignore what follows and just make your side pieces as the drawing shows. The tilt arrangement, however, can be very handy for yacht joinery, so let's do it. Saw out the two tilt-table bearers with your sabersaw or bandsaw to the 6-inch radius. Also make the 5½-inch radius for the pinholes. When the two bearers are cut out, tack or clamp them together and plane off the top edges straight and square. Lay out the location of the holes every five degrees with a protractor and mark each location with a punch or sharp nail. Drill ¼-inch holes along the radius and another at the radius center for a pivot. Separate the two pieces and put them aside.

Next, make the table of ¾-inch plywood. If you want a size that will handle quite long stuff, make it 12 inches deep and not less than 18 inches wide. If you want the convenience of an occasional use of a miter gauge, you can cut the groove with a dado set or with a router. Try it on scrap wood until you get a perfect sliding action. If the groove is wide enough to admit the gauge but too tight to allow easy movement, wrap a piece of sandpaper around a piece of ½-inch plywood and sand the sides of the groove until it's right.

Clamp the table bearers or supports on the outside of the side pieces flush with the top surfaces. Drill a ¼-inch hole for the pivot pin or bolt on each side. Lay the table on the bearers and square it up, then clamp it securely so it can be nailed and glued while everything is in the proper position. You'll need another ¼-inch hole at the top end of each quadrant. Put bolts with wing nuts in these and in the pivot bolt holes. Let the rig stand while the glue sets.

A SIMPLE MOTOR MOUNT

Does your motor have a base? If it is an appliance motor or a cruddy old junker like mine, you'll probably have to make a base to keep the motor from crawling around each time you turn it on. Refer to Figure 5-16. Cut two pieces of 1 by 3 about 5 inches longer than the diameter of the motor case. On one of these, scribe the outline of the case, centered on the piece. Bandsaw or sabersaw this out, then smooth it with a rasp to fit the motor. Mark the other piece from the first one, and repeat the fitting. Now fasten both pieces to a base of ¾-inch plywood with glue and screws or nails. Cut two pieces of perforated strapping long enough to reach over the motor to the ends of the base pieces. Screw

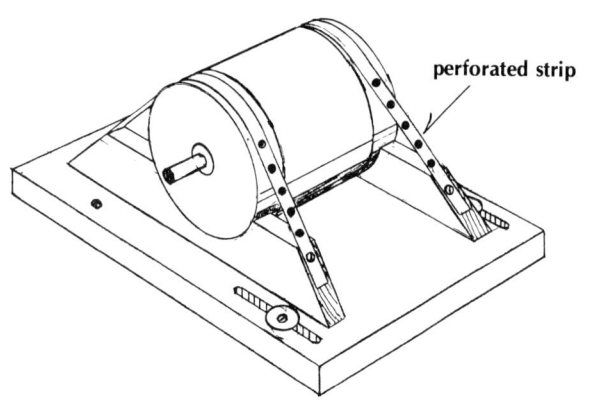

Figure 5-16. A 50-CENT MOTOR MOUNT

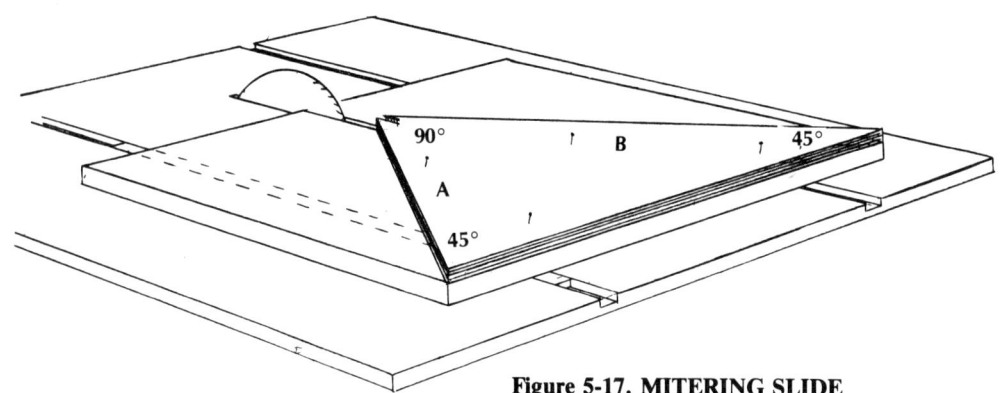

Figure 5-18. MITERING MOLDINGS

Figure 5-17. MITERING SLIDE

these strips down securely at one end, bend the other ends over the motor, and then fasten the loose ends with 1½-inch roundhead screws and washers at an angle that will tighten the strips as the screws are driven. This motor base will last indefinitely.

Place this assembly on the motor support shelf with the disc mounted on the motor shaft. Bring it right up to the table. You may find it necessary to cut a notch in the table to clear the nut holding the disc. The disc should clear the table by about $\frac{1}{16}$ inch. Check the distance from each end of the disc to the groove in the table. The disc and groove must be parallel. Drill four ¼-inch holes for hold-down bolts through the motor bed and the shelf. Fasten with wing nuts or ordinary hex nuts. The alignment of motor, disc, and table can be adjusted at any time by giving the base a light tap. Finally, put a line switch in the motor cord. That's all there is to this inexpensive sander.

A MITERING SLIDE

Moldings for doors, drawers, and other trim require clean, accurate miters. It would be well worth your time to construct a mitering slide, a smaller variation of the sliding auxiliary table (SLAT). See Figure 5-17. Because your slide will not be supporting panels or boards of any size, 20 inches wide by 16 inches deep on ⅜- or ¾-inch plywood should be adequate. Saw a 90-degree corner off a plywood panel. Precise measurements on each leg make a perfect 45 degrees. This must be planed off carefully on the sawed sides so that when it is bradded to the slider, sides A and B make a perfect 45-degree angle to the slot. To test this, cut two 10- to 12-inch pieces of 1 by 2 scrap on the right side. Try not to let the blade cut into the triangle any more than is necessary, because it must be kept intact for future use. These two pieces should make a perfect 90 degrees when held together inside a carpenter's square. Now cut a piece on each side of the triangle and try these in a square. If these tests do not check out, take a shaving off the base of the triangle and check again. Keep trying until you achieve a perfect joint. Then set the brads in, but don't let them touch the table top.

Of course, to get quality mitered joints, you must use a cabinetmaker's combination or a carbide-tipped blade. The great advantage of the mitering slide is that with the blade stopped, you can position the mark right up to the tooth, leaving perhaps $\frac{1}{32}$ inch over until you get all parts together, then come back and shave off that $\frac{1}{32}$ inch, if needed. If you are working with odd-shaped molding like the piece shown in Figure 5-18, don't miter

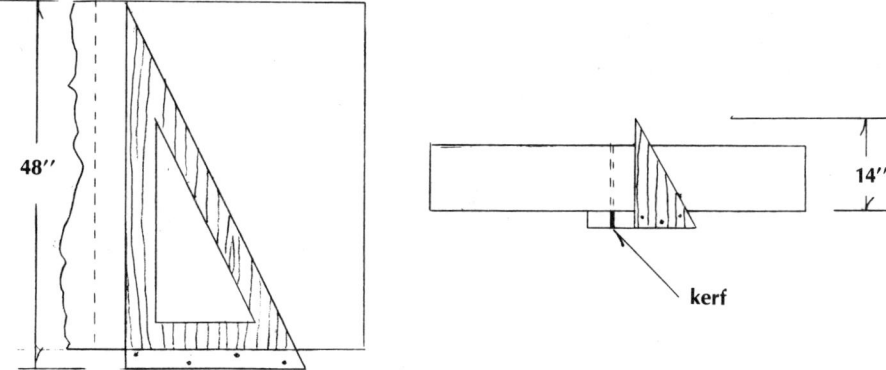

Figure 5-19. CUT-OFF SQUARES

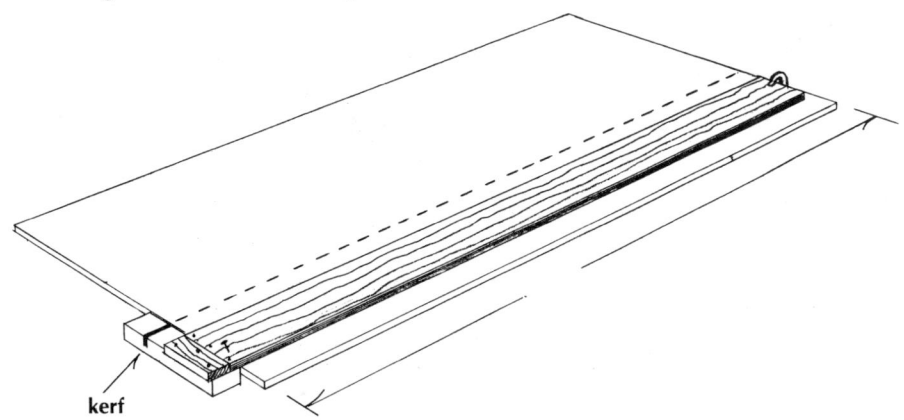

Figure 5-20. PANEL RIPPING GUIDE

with the molded side down; this throws off the angle. If you are mitering moldings on edge, add enough height to the triangle sides so that the pieces cannot slant or wobble. If the moldings run wider than 2 inches, you may have to use a miter box and backsaw. Or you can set the table saw blade to 45 degrees and use the miter gauge. There are always three or four ways to cut for mitered joints.

SQUARE AND RIPPING GUIDES

From the complexity of the SLAT and mitering slides, we turn now to the basic square and ripping guides. The square guide is simply a triangle cut off the corner of a sheet of ¼-inch plywood with a batten glued across the base on both sides (Figure 5-19). You press this against the sheet of plywood or other material to be cut, and clamp or brad it in position. The power saw is then run along the edge of the square. I have a large one measuring 48 by 24 inches, and a small one about 14 by 10 inches for smaller stuff when I am away from my table saw. Let the end of the 2 by 2 cleat on the base be cut by the power saw. This provides a fast way to line up to the mark.

The ripping guide is simply a piece of ¾-inch plywood 5 to 7 inches wide and 8 feet long. If you nail a piece of 2 by 4 on the underside of the near end, it will show you where the kerf will be. See Figure 5-20. To line up, measure from the saw tooth to the right-hand edge of the saw's sole plate, add that to the dimension you need, and clamp your guide in place. Repeat on the other end, using the measurement from the guide to the edge of the sheet. Double-check and adjust by light taps. A ripping guide is a great help for cutting large sheets of plywood to sizes more convenient to handle on a table saw. Sometimes I rip slightly oversize, and then rip on the table saw with a fine carbide blade. A cutoff blade will rip or crosscut ¾-inch plywood and give you a surface requiring very little dressing with a plane. A fine-toothed plywood blade will overheat and warp on anything over ½ inch, but it will produce a slightly better surface. The cabinetmaker's hollow-ground blade cannot be used on ¾-inch plywood, and only with caution on anything over ⅜ inch, but the edge is beautiful.

My apologies to those of you who find these guides elementary. They are time savers. I have seen workmen follow a line on plywood freehand, then saw the piece more accurately on a table saw. With few exceptions, this approach is a complete waste of time if the cut can be done right the first time.

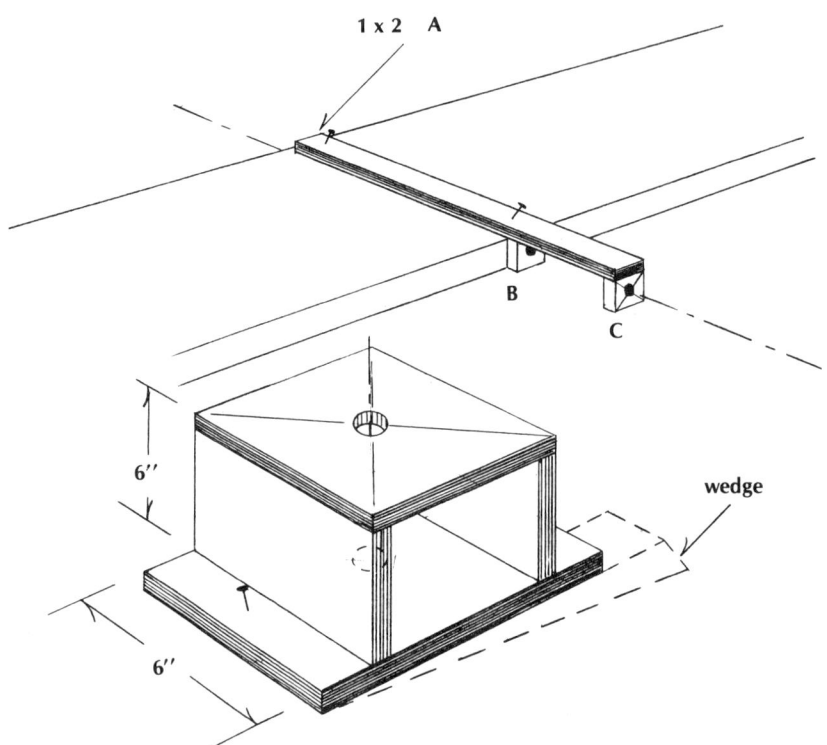

Figure 5-21. BORING JIGS

BORING JIGS

Not long ago I read an article describing a method of deep hole boring. I believe the hole was through a trunk cabin side. The writer recommended clamping a batten across the work piece and having a second person visually line up the long bit with the batten, while the borer tried to keep the bit parallel in the other plane. Now, this might work — or it might not. Trying to hold a drill motor firmly, or, worse yet, a brace while sighting down the bit, is asking for trouble, as well as taking up another man's time. The jig shown in Figure 5-21 works, it takes minutes to construct, and it can be used repeatedly.

If the material to be bored is 1¼ inches thick, blocks B and C should be twice that, or 2½ inches thick. Find the center on one by crossing diagonals, and then punch the center. Stack the blocks and brad them together so you can drill the hole on your drill press. The blocks will then be identical. You can use a ship's auger in the jig either with a brace or an electric drill. Be sure this bit is backed out frequently to free it of chips. It could twist off if it jams. If your bit has a screw on it, grind this off. These screws sometimes hit hard grain or a knot and are deflected.

The lower jig in Figure 5-21 is for boring at right angles to a surface. There is a good base for clamping to the surface. This jig could also be used for boring at a specific angle by making two wedges to fit under it.

A JIG FOR ADJUSTABLE SHELVES

Small cabinets often contain adjustable shelves. In order to make such shelves seat precisely, the holes must be spaced with care. Make the jig shown in Figure 5-22 of ¾-inch 1 by 2 oak or other hardwood. Use a scriber or knife to lay out the pattern of holes on 1-inch or 1½-inch centers, 1 to 1½ inches from the edge. Drill on a press so the holes are perpendicular. Attach the spacing leg B so the series of holes starts a uniform distance above the bottom of the cabinet. Clamp the jig in position, drill a hole at each end, and insert a dowel in each hole. This prevents any movement while the rest of the holes are being drilled. If the row of holes is to continue, again locate the jig with a dowel so accuracy is maintained. Once you have this jig, the entire layout of holes for a good-sized cabinet can be bored in 15 or 20 minutes. Cabinet hardware supply houses have molded plastic brackets to fit. They are noncorrosive, of course, but not as romantic as birch dowels with chamfered ends.

Watch out for the possibility that your bit will go all the way through the cabinet side. A quick remedy is a piece of masking tape wrapped around the bit to show when you are approaching the correct depth. See Figure 5-23(A). A better stop is shown in Figure 5-23(B). Bore the ¼-inch hole in a piece of ¾-inch oak or plywood, then bandsaw the piece to about 1 inch in diameter. Chamfer and smooth it up on your disc sander. In use, it may creep up on the bit, so watch it! Glue helps.

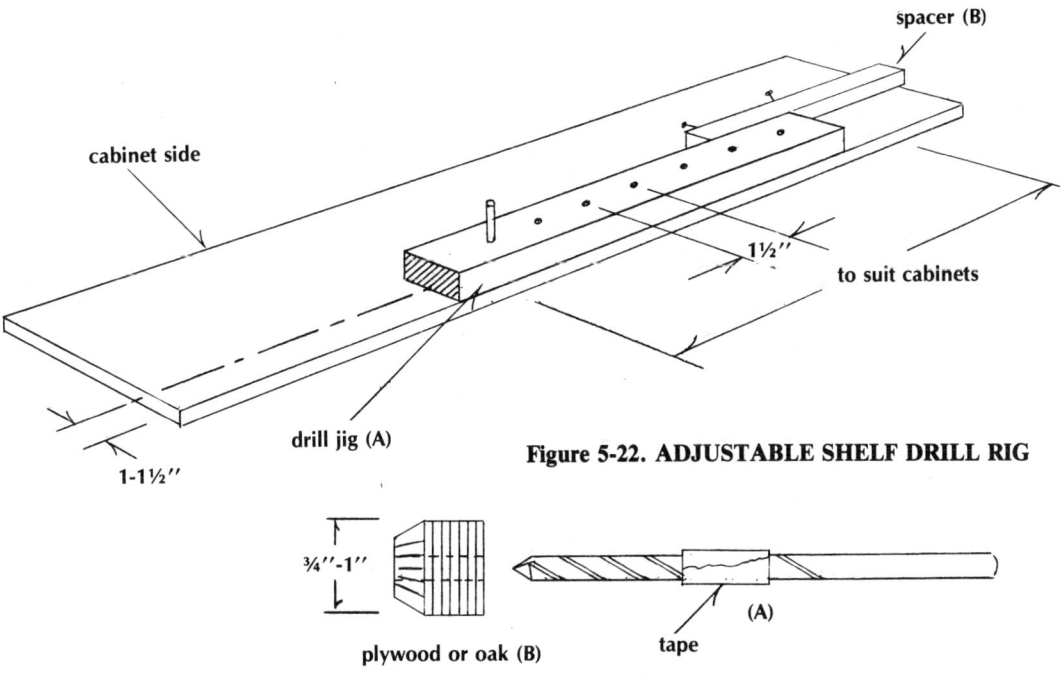

Figure 5-22. ADJUSTABLE SHELF DRILL RIG

Figure 5-23. SIMPLE DRILL DEPTH STOPS

HAPPINESS IS A $5 TABLE SAW

Some years ago I needed a table saw that I could hoist up and down ladders, lift in and out of a companionway hatch, and stow in the trunk of my car. Also, I wanted to get it for nothing — or less. Perhaps I reinvented the wheel, as they say, but I had not heard of or seen the contrivance I invented (Figure 5-24). Since that time, I have built several of these tools, with improvements. If you need portability, this saw could solve a lot of your problems. You can use surplus materials that cost very little (about $5 in 1980) and you'll find that the saw does about 90 percent of the jobs of those costing $200 and up. (Cutting dadoes is the main exception.)

First, determine the size of the table. There's no law on this, but you will find that the area between you and the blade is important. See Figure 5-24. This span provides support for your work piece and also allows a sliding gauge for cutoffs. Width, too, is important. Because you will be handling fairly long pieces, I suggest a minimum of 30 by 30 inches. If you have a larger piece of ¾-inch plywood lying around, just dress it to accurate squareness instead of reducing it in size.

Power saws of different makes have soles of different sizes. It makes no difference what make of saw you use, but I do not recommend a blade size smaller than 7 inches. The cutout that will receive the saw must be quite accurate in width. It should be located approximately as shown in Figure 5-24, and its sides must closely parallel the sides of the table. If you can borrow a friend's table saw, the cutout will be a cinch. Try this procedure on a piece of scrap first. Place the piece against the fence, spaced correctly, then crank up the running blade slowly until you see it emerge to about ¾ inch above the work. Do not remove the piece until the blade stops turning. Now do the same with your actual table top, being sure to hold the piece down firmly. Next, move the fence to saw the opposite side of the opening and repeat the procedure above with no sloppiness. The cuts will be precisely parallel. You can connect the cuts at the ends of the opening with a sabersaw. The sole of the saw should fit snugly, and the blade should come out parallel to the left side of the table. If you somehow missed, you can use a rasp or glue a thin shim here or there. It's up to you.

If you are unable to borrow a table saw, you can make these cuts by clamping a straightedge to the table and lowering your power-saw blade with care just within the lines. This, you will recall, is a plunge cut. You'll get the best results if your guide piece is quite thick, perhaps a length of 2 by 4.

When your saw fits the opening, you'll need a support to hold the surface of the sole flush with the table top. If the saw has projections, such as a wing nut for the rip gauge, for example, notch the opening as needed. See Figure 5-25. Rip out a little piece of pine to about ¼ inch by ½ inch; you'll only need 6 or 7 inches. Glue and brad this in the back end of the opening so that it holds the saw sole flush. The forward end also needs support, but it may be best to brad and glue bits of batten about ¾ inch long into the corners instead of full length. This facilitates juggling the saw into the opening. You may have to experiment.

This is the time to admit that the portable table saw has one disadvantage. You can't operate the built-in switch while you saw. Thus, each time you set it up, you

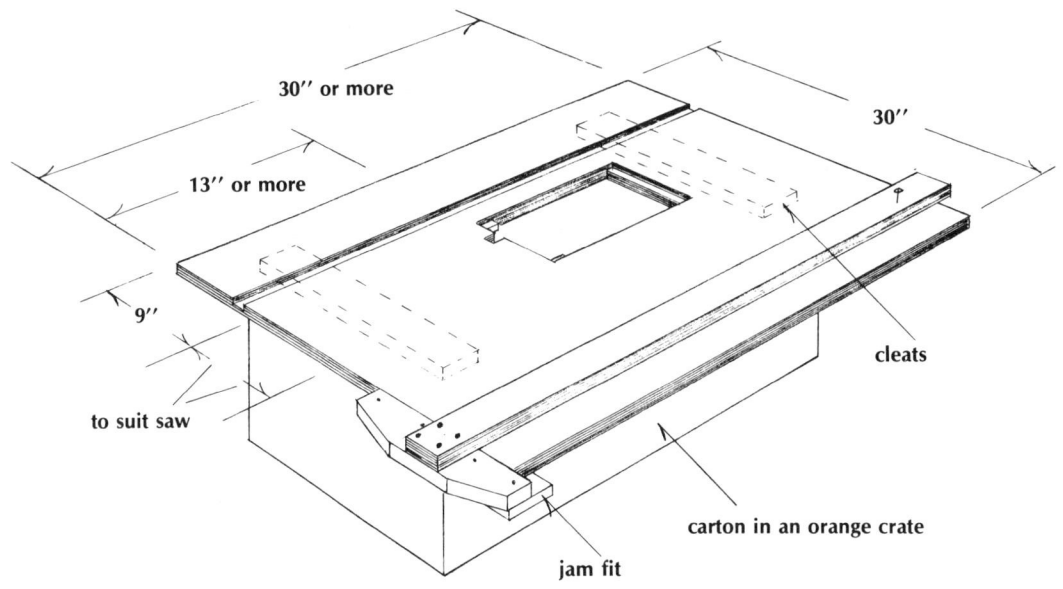

Figure 5-24. A $5 PORTABLE TABLE SAW

Figure 5-25. *Portable table saw top. Note notches and supporting blocks glued and bradded in.*

must tape, wire, or tie the switch to "on." It's disconcerting to have the saw start howling as soon as you plug it in, and it's dangerous! For safety's sake, install a line switch in an extension cord where it can be reached quickly, or build in a proper switch.

You'll find that the saw's movable guard is a nuisance, especially if you are ripping strips narrow enough to catch inside it. An uncovered blade is dangerous, however, so you must learn to respect — even fear — this machine just as you respect your jointer, bandsaw, or sharp chisel. Fear generates caution. To hold the guard down and keep little cutoff pieces from falling into it and jamming the blade, tack a piece of ¼-inch plywood to the underside of the table so there's just clearance between this piece of scrap and the blade. This holds the guard down and catches any cutoff pieces so they can be removed after the saw is shut off.

Now that your saw is working, how about a stand? A carton inside an orange crate worked well for me. The carton catches the sawdust. Place the crate on a couple of sawhorses to support it at the right height. Cut an aperture for the projecting motor housing. Nail two cleats on the underside of the table to fit inside the crate and keep the thing from creeping around, and lightly nail the top to the crate to prevent tipping.

Figure 5-24 shows a simple rip fence. Fasten the T crosspiece with finish nails until you get it truly in line with the blade and have tried it a few times. Then glue and nail it with four 1½- or 2-inch galvanized finish nails, or use screws. Don't overlook the piece glued on the underside of the T. This can be ½-inch plywood. This piece gives you a jam fit that can be augmented with a C-clamp. A clamp at the far end is good insurance, but if you made the fence out of ¾-inch plywood and 3 inches wide, I don't think there will be any visible deflection. You can use a manufactured miter gauge if you want to tackle the job of cutting out the groove. This procedure was explained earlier in this chapter for a router-shaper.

This little saw's usefulness is greatly expanded if you equip it with a SLAT. See Figure 5-26. However, you don't need a groove in the table if the sides are exactly parallel. Just glue battens to the underside of the SLAT

Figure 5-26. *An inexpensive portable table saw based on a hand power saw. The sliding auxiliary table (SLAT) has an additional mitering jig in place.*

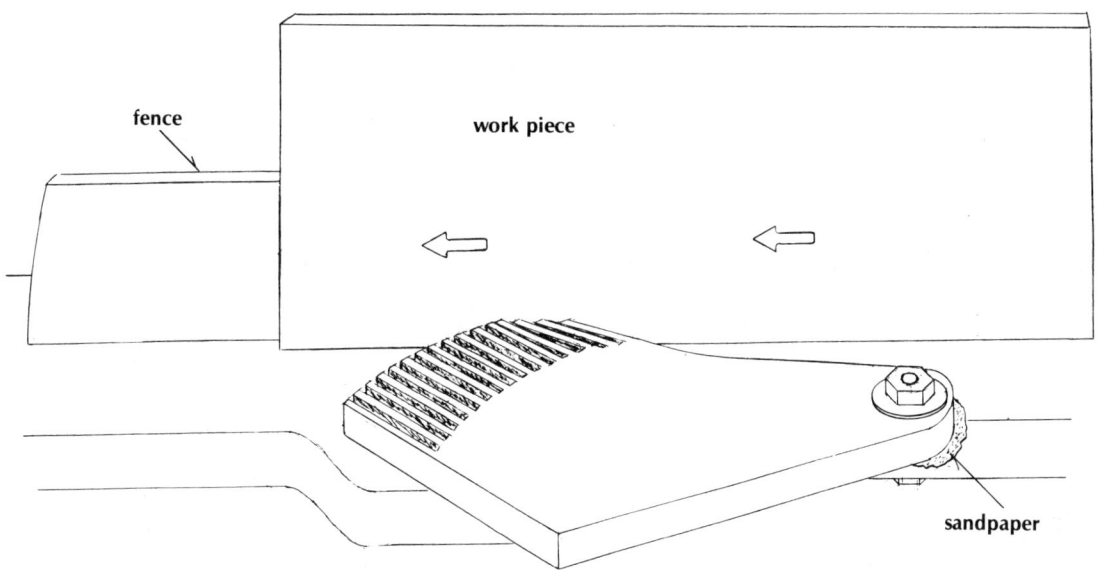

Figure 5-27. JOINTER HOLD-DOWN REPLACING GUARD

so they slide nicely along both outer edges of the table. There should be no binding, no slop. Glue the fence on after the action is perfected. With regard to ripping, the more powerful the saw, the better. My old 7¼-inch Skilsaw handles 1½-inch fir without any problem, but I don't do this all day, of course.

A JOINTER HOLD-DOWN

In order to joint edges truly square, the entire length of the work piece must be held securely against the fence. A feather or comb does this job very well and has the advantage of freeing the hands to feed the work. See Figure 5-27. The guard must be removed. In most jointers it is impossible to bolt through the hole for the guard pivot pin. Bore a 5/16- or 3/8-inch hole through the table at a point where a wing nut can be set up on either end of a hex bolt and as near the edge as feasible. You may have to tap a threaded hole. The feather may be done on the bandsaw or table saw. The splines should be about ⅛ inch wide. Place a couple of large steel washers and several cuts from coarse sandpaper between the piece and the table (this helps prevent movement). You will be surprised at how little pressure is needed to hold the work piece properly against the fence and how easy it is to feed the work through.

When jointing the edges of wide boards, avoid wobbling. Most jointer fences are not high enough to prevent movement, so bolt on a ¾-inch plywood extension to increase the height of the fence to 10 or 12 inches. (This was shown in Figure 4-9.) The combined pressures of the feather and your hand, holding the work piece against the upper part of the fence extension, will

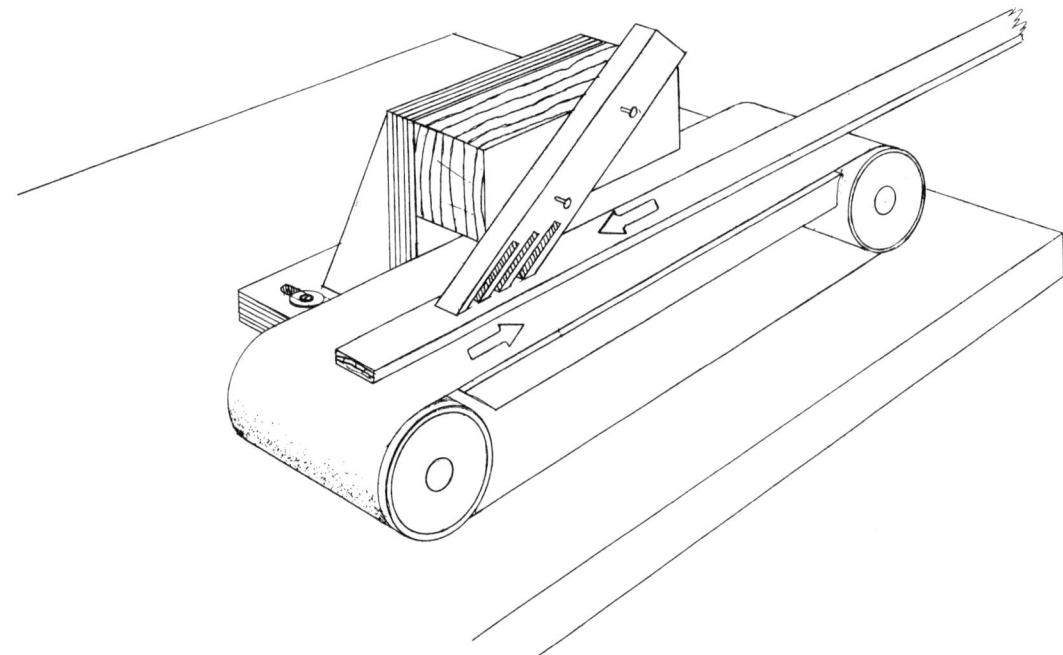

Figure 5-28. BELT SANDER HOLD-DOWN

guarantee accuracy. To joint smaller stuff, bolt an additional hold-down to the tall fence. Now the job is simply to feed the piece through. This idea is adaptable to your table saw as well.

To joint small rectangular pieces with safety, make a jig similar to the one shown in Figure 5-8. Use the same jig if the dimensions are correct, or add a shim to the top and/or side of the rabbet if that's faster than making a new jig. There is almost no limit to the small sizes that can be jointed, routed, or sawed by this method, except that the tools can tear the pieces apart if you try to cut too fine.

A BELT SANDER HOLD-DOWN

Surfacing on a bench sander, even a light 4-inch type, can produce very satisfying results if uniform pressure is maintained for the entire length of the work piece. This is not always easy, for one hand pulls and the other holds the piece down on the belt. It takes a lot of practice to avoid a fits-and-starts pass, especially if the pieces are more than 2½ to 3 feet in length. To solve this problem, make the device shown in Figure 5-28. The 2-inch block places the feather near the center of the belt and over the center of the work piece. The whole affair is screwed to the bench. Leave enough clearance under the block so the jig can be left in place when sanding other work. Of course, the feather may be C-clamped to get the right pressure.

A BOX JOINT JIG

Some people refer to a box joint as a finger joint. See Figure 5-29. Strong and easily made, it has many uses in yacht joinery. Next to a dovetail, it is the strongest for drawer construction if glued with Aerolite, epoxy, or Plastic Resin glue. I feel it would be superior to the half lap for hatch coamings and frames. If you were to run a dowel through a finger joint, it would be second to none.

To cut a finger joint, it is almost mandatory that you use a dado set adjusted to the desired slot width and depth. You could, however, set up two or three identical saw blades with plywood or doorskin shims in between like big washers. On the other hand, I have seen box joints cut with spacing made to match a wide saw kerf, perhaps ³⁄₁₆ or ¼ inch for small boxes. You might try to have extra set put in an old blade if you have many such joints to run.

Refer now to Figure 5-29. Pick a piece of scrap (A) to screw or clamp to the wooden face of your miter gauge. Let's try a dado set adjusted to the material thickness of ¾ inch, and ¾ inch high. Cut the notch (C) in the backing (A). Glue into this notch a block (B) ¾ by ¾ by 3 inches, letting it project 2¼ inches. This is to space repeated cuts and duplicate pieces for an accurate fit. Now shift the backing piece to your right, as you face the saw table, twice the width of the cut. Use two thicknesses of the material as a gauge. Screw or clamp to the gauge face and make the trial cut (G). Try this measurement with two nice pieces of scrap (D and E). Hold D over the slot (G) and take out corner F. Now

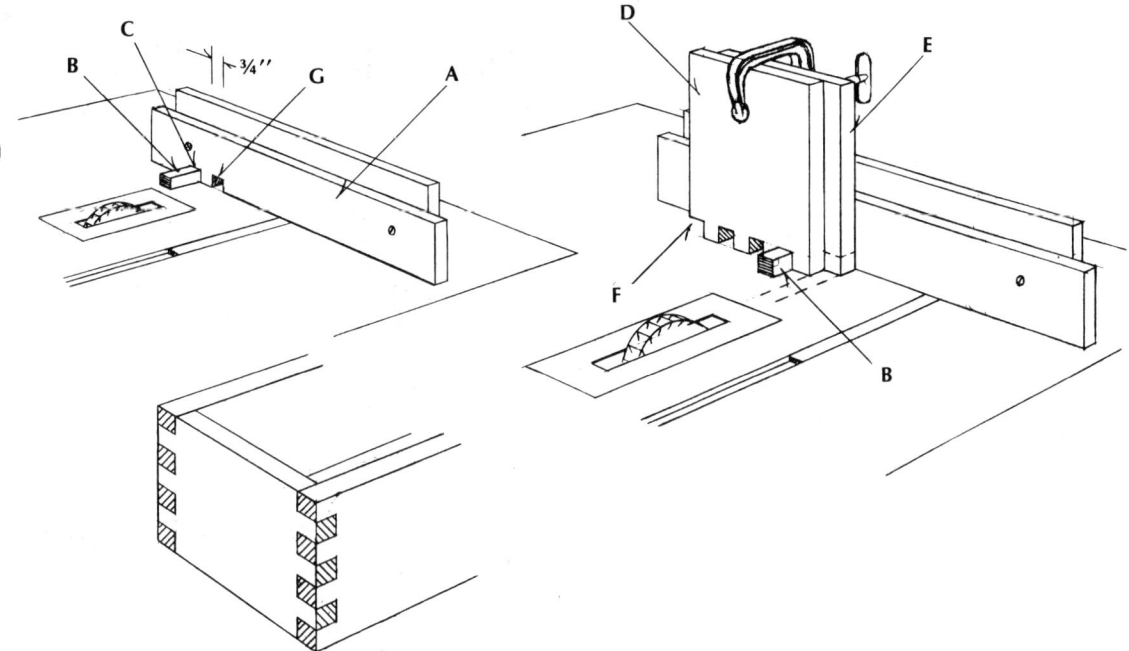

Figure 5-29. BOX OR FINGER JOINT JIG

place piece E against the block and corner F over the block so the two pieces are in staggered arrangement. Clamp them together. Now this pair can be notched simultaneously by making a pass over the dado cutter, shifting that notch over the block, cutting another notch, and so on, for the width of the piece. The drawing shows the final notch about to be cut (dotted lines). Try these pieces for fit. The widths of the notches can be increased or decreased by adjusting the dado set. Drive three or four screws through A to ensure precise replacement next time. The height of the notch is the height of the dado set, of course. When you are satisfied with the fit, cut four scraps to identical lengths, number them to avoid error, notch them out, spread glue between the fingers, tap all four together, check with a square, then tack a diagonal across from corner to corner. In a few hours this should prove to be tremendously strong and, after sanding, very handsome.

Making this box or finger joint jig may sound like a very complicated process, but it is not. It does require accuracy to create something you'll be proud to display. If you don't have the patience, take heart, because a glue such as Aerolite will fill cracks without losing strength. The right way, however, is one of the little differences between a boat and a yacht.

BENCH HOOKS AND STOPS

The bench hook is a simple device for holding small work pieces being planed. A 3-foot length is handy. So is a short one for using across your bench. See Figure 5-30. The stop (A) need not be more than ¼ inch thick, and any width will do. Piece B, however, should be a 1 by 2. Bench hooks can be clamped or bradded to the table to prevent creeping on the back stroke.

Figure 5-31 shows two variations, the taper stop and the wedge stop. These are used for planing pieces on edge. They should be made substantially of ¾-inch plywood or hardwood and be nailed and glued to a rather longish bench hook or screwed down to a bench.

SHOOTING BOARDS

I wish I knew the origin of the name of shooting boards. It's a simple little bench jig that enables you to plane the edges of a piece square with almost no thought. A shooting board can be tacked to a bench or clamped against a stop to prevent creeping. The work, as shown in Figure 5-32, is held flat on the shelf (A) and the plane is stroked back and forth on its side on the board (B). Make A of ¾-inch material. It is sufficiently above B so that it will work well with a smooth, block, or jack plane. The surface of B should be waxed. The stop (C) should be removable so long stuff can be handled. I keep a 40-inch-long shooting board handy so it can be used across a couple of sawhorses.

CUTTER GRINDING JIGS

Earlier in the book I promised to describe several ways to hold power plane and jointer blades or knives for grinding. Most grinders have adjustable tool rests that

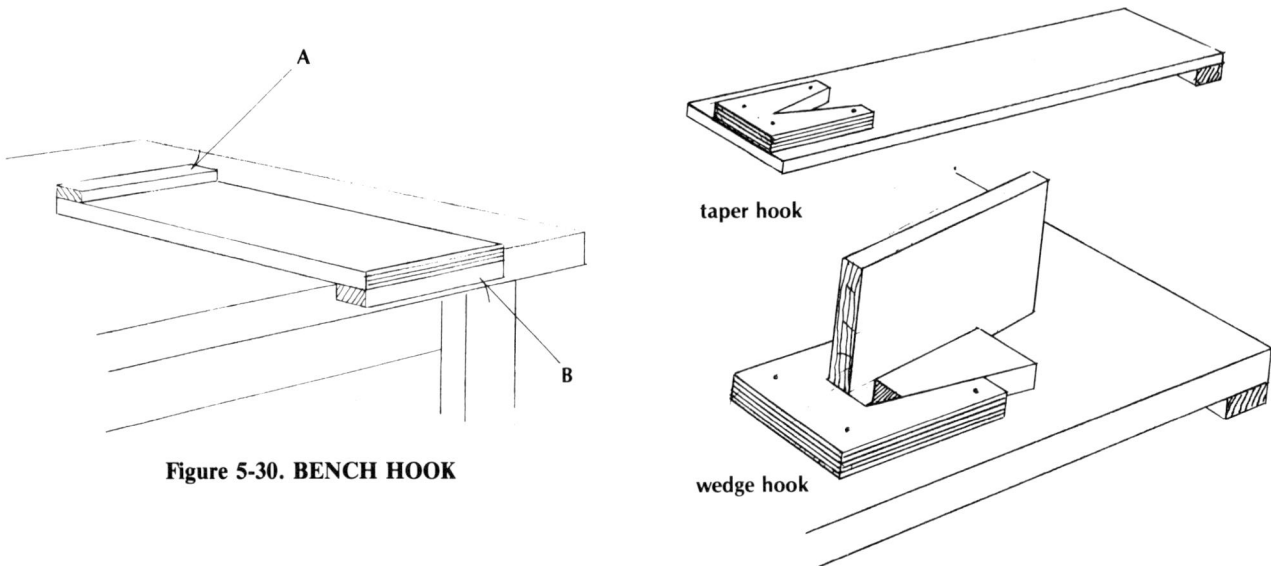

Figure 5-30. BENCH HOOK

Figure 5-31. WEDGE AND TAPER HOOKS

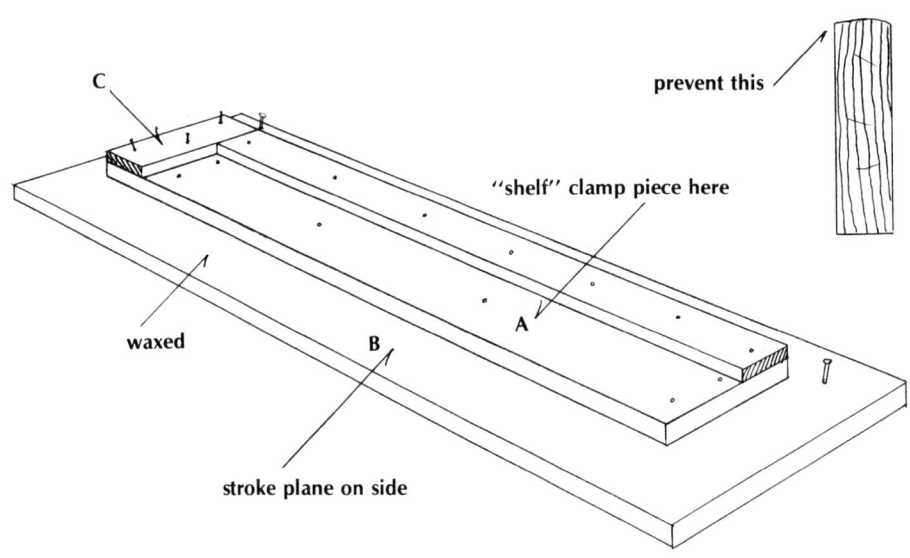

Figure 5-32. SHOOTING BOARD

allow you to bring the tool bevel to the grinding wheel at the proper angle. But this works only with tools long enough to be grasped. The tool holder shown in Figure 5-33 (top) is like an extension to the narrow jointer blade. It can be moved up to the wheel properly and slid back and forth across the face, guided by a stop. Pick out a block of oak (A) about 1 inch thick and perhaps 4 inches wide. Saw out a slot (B) about one-half the depth of your blade so the blade has a depth stop. Then cut a finer kerf (C) 2½ inches deep with a bandsaw or backsaw. Bevel under the blade holder to clear the wheel. Drill for a ¼-inch flathead stove bolt, with washer and wing nut. The hardwood stop (D) is bradded square to A so that the blade touches the wheel at the approximate original angle. Fine adjustments can be made with the original adjustable tool rest. Start the wheel and run the blade about four strokes end to end. If the original bevel was flat ground, it may take a few more strokes for the hollow grind to reach the cutting edge. Take off no more than absolutely necessary. Whet this new edge on the oilstone as described in Chapter One.

The tool grinding stand shown in Figure 5-33 (bottom) is quite simple to make, but some of the angles must be worked out by trial and error. The vertical block (A) is loose and free to slide against the batten (B). Its height is determined by the height of your grinder above the bench. Saw a slot to receive the jointer knife (C). Drill down into the end grain for a no. 10

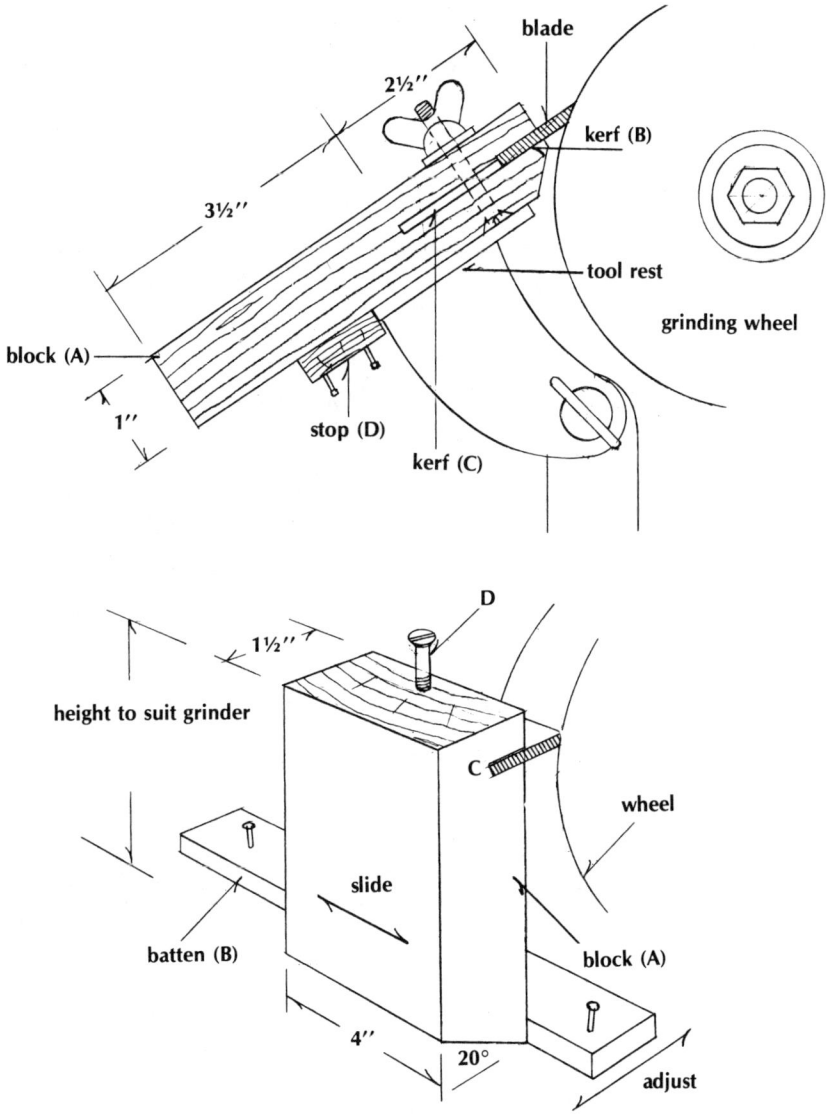

Figure 5-33. JOINTER BLADE GRINDING FIXTURES

wood screw or stove bolt (D), located so its point bears against the blade, locking it in the slot. The lower end of the block should be cut off at a slight angle so it can be rocked against the wheel and away. To make the knife contact the wheel at the proper bevel, move the batten (B) until you are satisfied. The tool bevel is run across the wheel lightly by sliding block A back and forth. A little soap or wax rubbed on the block and the batten helps.

A SCARFING JIG

When you get into constructing hollow box spars, you'll have to become an expert at making long, thin scarfs. A properly made scarf on a ratio of 12 to 1 is stronger than the original material, so it is practical to join shorter lengths of costly material. This applies not only to spruce or fir spar stock, but to mahogany as well. It does not apply to oak. Glues like Aerolite set up clear, so discoloration should be minimal. However, I would not advise scarfing a piece where the joint will jump out at you.

Sawing and planing to a paper-thin feather edge is a job no man in his right mind wants. This makes a scarfing jig (Figures 5-34 and 5-35) a necessity. The one shown is dimensioned for a router mounted on a plywood base with a length about three times the width of the jig. On the underside are stops to keep the router bit from running into the sides. This job can be done with a jack or longer plane also, but the jig would have to be much wider. Otherwise, you would simply plane it away inadvertently. Rent a router and a straight bit up to ¾ inch and avoid a headache.

Make the jig of hardwood or good plywood, screwed and glued to last. See that the inclined faces are dead straight. The chip ejection chute is advisable. Remove the plastic base of the router and mount the plywood

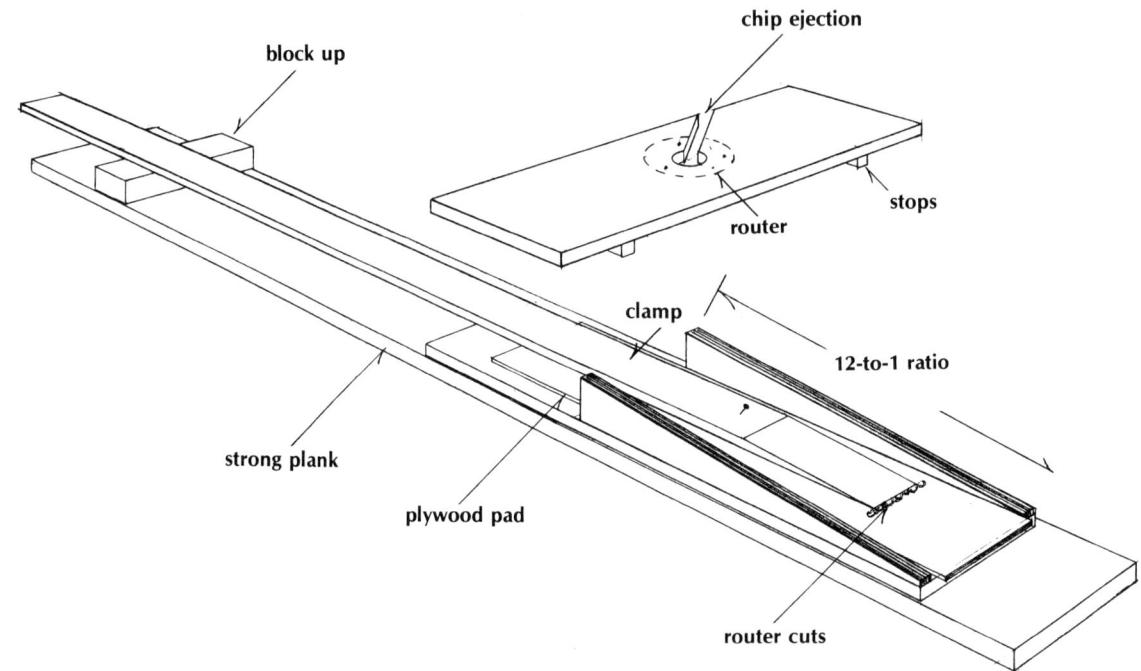

Figure 5-34. SCARFING JIG

Figure 5-35. *This 12-to-1 scarfing jig is made of three pieces of ¾-inch plywood glued up.*

base with three screws centered over the hole. Clamp the jig to a strong plank or bench. Place several blocks to raise the stock to the level of the jig and its pad. Note an expendable piece of plywood added to absorb the router cuts as you form the feather edge. Place the work piece so the router will take off a good ¼-inch bite in the first pass. C-clamp it securely equidistant from the sides, with no vertical spring. Now just run the router back and forth or with the grain, no matter. Lower the bit until you get close to the feather edge. Run a cut along each edge to eliminate splitting at the corners, and then run a fine and final cut. Rout off the rest to a nice flat surface, with no grooves or ridges. Do not plane or sand this surface, as the "tooth" produces the best glue joint.

AN "INSTANT" VISE

This vise, usually called a planking vise, is an old-timer. It is great for dressing the edges of anything. I ran a boatshop once that had no other vise, and we got along just fine. Your bench is probably constructed of 1½-inch material. To the underside of the top, bolt and glue a piece of 2 by 6 fir (A) about 14 inches long, as shown in Figure 5-36. Let this project from the edge about 5 inches, square to the bench. Now make a wedge or tapered piece of fir or oak (B) 14 inches long, 2¼ inches at its greatest width, and 1 inch wide at the small end. Smooth this up. Then a piece of 2 by 6 (C) must be bolted and glued to piece A projecting from the bench. The taper of C must match the taper of the wedge (B). So clamp the wedge plus a ¾-inch piece of scrap to the projection, then clamp the 2 by 6 block while you bore holes for three ⅜-inch carriage bolts. Glue and bolt piece A to stay. Much of your work material will be ¾ inch or less, so the angle of the block now matches the wedge. To use, place your work piece on the projection and against the bench edge, slip the wedge in the gap, and give it a light tap with a hammer or block. The work piece will be held absolutely rigid. For stock much lighter than ¾ inch, insert a piece of scrap to make up the difference. To handle long work pieces, provide one or more supports (D), 4 to 8 feet from the vise. To

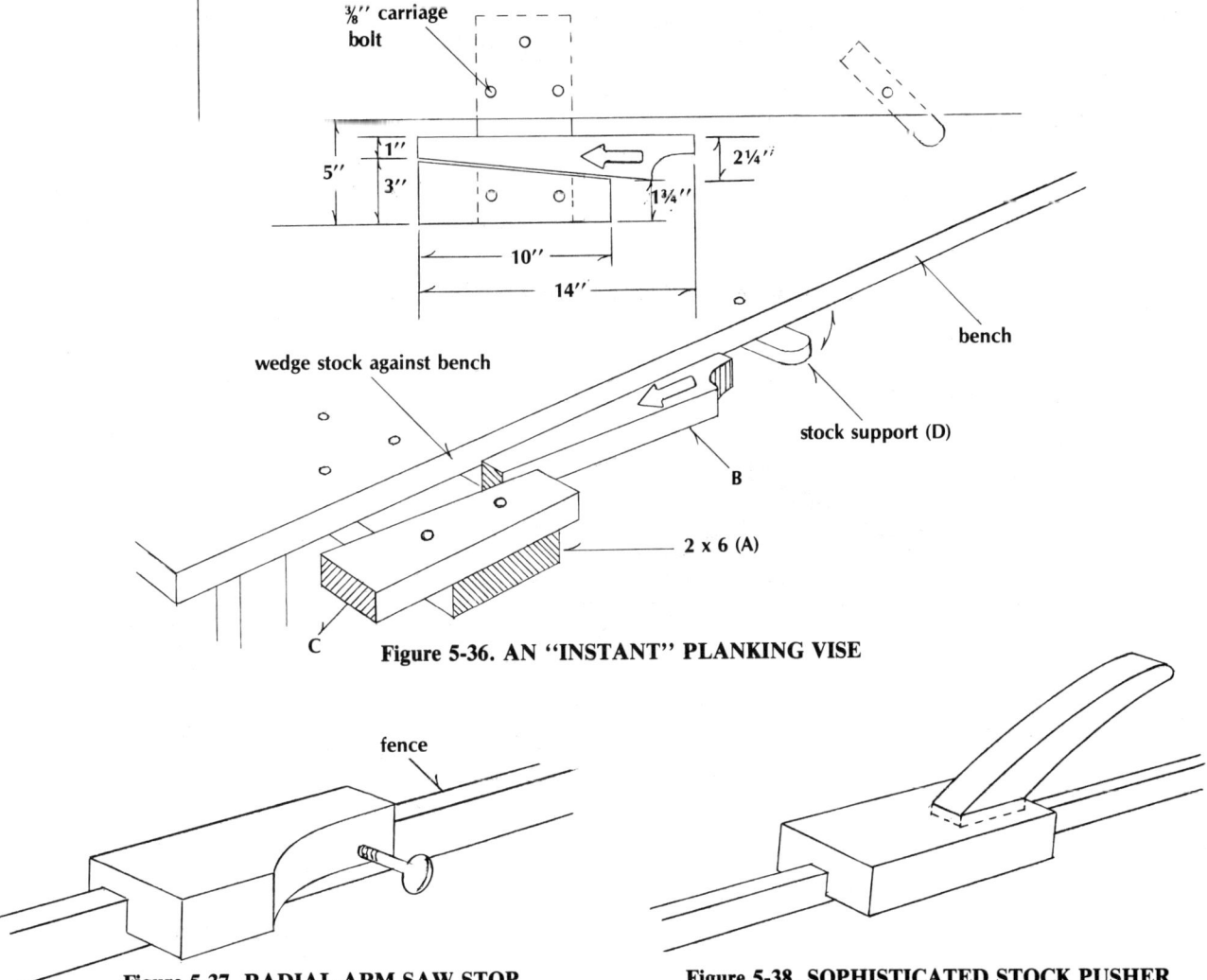

Figure 5-36. AN "INSTANT" PLANKING VISE

Figure 5-37. RADIAL-ARM SAW STOP

Figure 5-38. SOPHISTICATED STOCK PUSHER FOR RADIAL-ARM SAW RIPPING

remove work from the vise, just wiggle the wedge or give it a light tap.

RADIAL-ARM SAW STOPS

For crosscutting multiples to exact length, you can just tack a bit of scrap to the table or fence. But here's an idea from De Cristoforo's book *Fun with a Saw* that looks neat and efficient (Figure 5-37). This is a grooved block that straddles the fence. The wing bolt or set screw is threaded through the wood so it hits the fence. De Cristoforo also shows a refined pusher stick for ripping. See Figure 5-38.

HINGE JIG

There will probably be a dozen or more cabinet and passage doors in a 35-foot yacht. This makes the installation of hinges a major task, and a real problem unless you have skill and patience. Plywood doors in particular are a nuisance because it is more difficult to chisel out the gain (the recess into which a butt fits) and achieve the exact depth (Figure 5-39). If the gains are too deep, the doors will refuse to close. If they are too shallow, there will be an ugly gap. Gains routed in a jig, on the other hand, are uniform in size and done quickly and easily. Some hinges have rounded corners that fit a routed gain. If your hinges are square-cornered, you'll have to chisel out the corners of the gains.

The jig shown in Figure 5-40, made of scrap plywood and a piece of 1 by 2, is easy to put together, but watch the arithmetic. The guide piece (A) can be ½ inch by 8 inches by 14 inches or more, cut carefully with a sabersaw or bandsaw. The router is supported on B, which is bradded and glued to A. Piece C, cut from 1 by 2 stock, enables you to clamp the jig securely to the door. Now pay close attention, for the arithmetic that follows can be confusing.

101

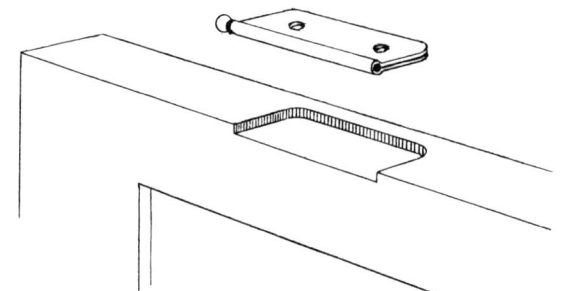

Figure 5-39. TYPICAL HINGE GAIN

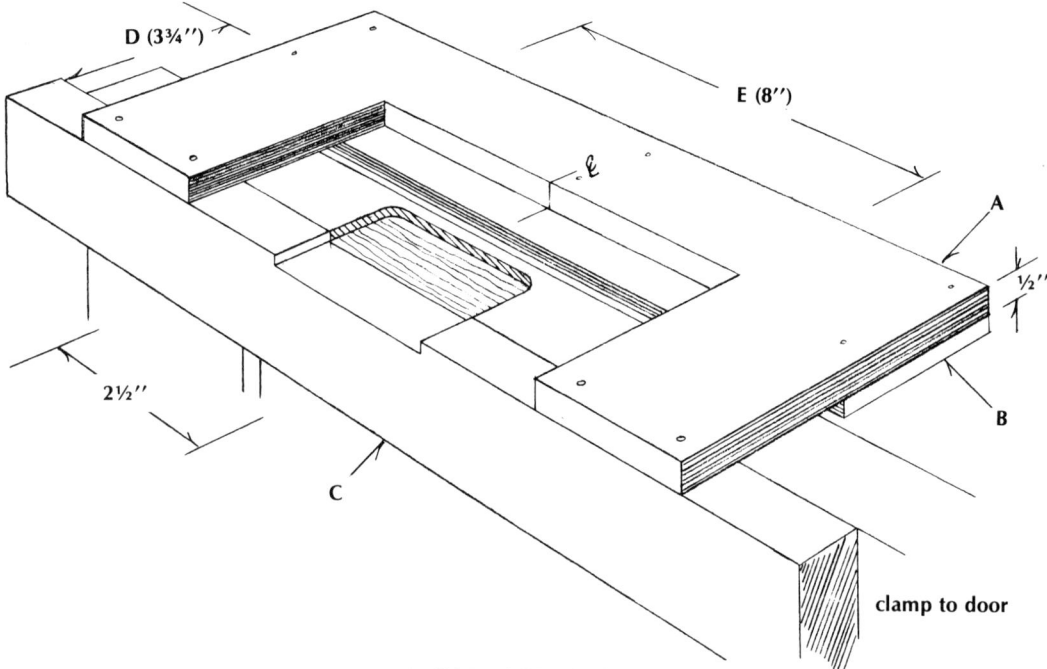

Figure 5-40. GAIN ROUTING FIXTURE

Dimension D is the sum of the width of the hinge leaf (1 inch) plus the measurement from the cutting edge of the router bit to the outside of the router base plate (2¾ inches), a total of 3¾ inches. Dimension E is the length of the hinge (2½ inches) plus 2¾ inches twice, a total of 8 inches. Warning: If you use a larger or smaller bit, the gain will be changed accordingly.

The same jig can be used for several sizes by making the cutout suitable for the largest hinge, perhaps 3 inches. For smaller hinges, just tack in filler pieces or shims to reduce the sides and back. Save the shims, marked for size, for future use. Of course, you can buy butt guides that require manufactured guide bushings. These are quite reasonable, but they are not adaptable to various hinge dimensions, and they won't do work any better than this gadget that you can make in just a few minutes.

Incidentally, if you are going first class, you'll rout gains in the jambs as well as in the doors. Set the router bit only as deep as the thickness of the metal. (Always use brass hinges, not plated steel. Check with a magnet, to be sure.) If all the gain is to be in the door, set the bit to slightly less than the thickness of both leaves of the hinge when they are in the closed position. Refer to Figure 5-39. Once your jig is clamped to the door, the job takes about 10 seconds, running the bit back and forth or lengthwise.

HALF-LAP JOINT JIG

There are many uses for the strong and versatile half-lap joint. Half laps are easy to make, but they must be uniform, which means fairly precise. All you need is a way to hold the parts firmly and parallel to the table saw blade. Double-check the blade setting to be sure it is ex-

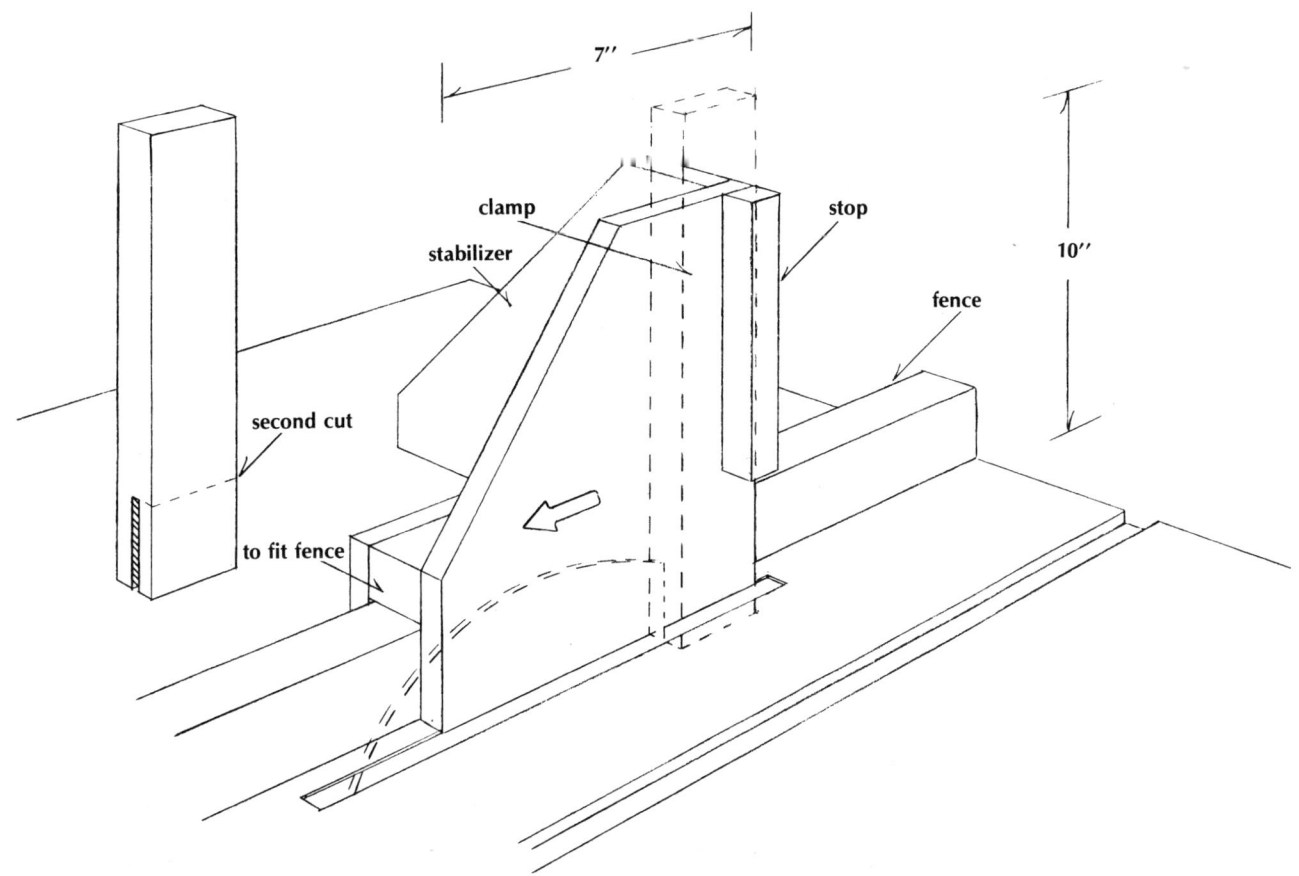

Figure 5-41. HALF-LAP JOINT JIG

actly 90 degrees to the table. The jig (Figure 5-41) works very well. You should be able to put one together in about an hour. It's designed to slide along the rip fence without visible play; the stabilizer maintains squareness to the table while it moves. The parts to be cut could be C-clamped against the stop. With a little practice, however, you should be able to hold them in position while sawing.

The second cut too must be accurate. This is simple if you have a sliding auxiliary table with a stop tacked to its fence to ensure precision. The second cut may also be done by tacking a stop block to the face of your miter gauge. You'll get good, clean cuts if you mark these shoulder cuts with a deep knife mark.

BEAM MOLDS AND PATTERNS

The beam pattern for decks and cabin trunks is called a beam mold. It is used to lay out the crown or camber on the lumber for sawing beams to shape. It is used also for holding carlings in the deck framing so these members match the designed camber in the deck. Thus, the beam mold must have considerable strength. You may find two or three handy so that the full-length carling can be forced into the sweep caused by the sheer of the vessel while the short deck beams are being fitted. First, however, the proper camber or crown must be laid out on the pattern material. This can be done either mechanically or geometrically.

The first system is quite simple. See Figure 5-42. Use seasoned pine or fir of double thickness so the possibility of distortion is eliminated. Select two straight pieces of material ripped to about 1 by 6; plywood would be fine. Drive nails near the ends of the pattern material and another at the midpoint, this one being the height of the crown specified by the designer (so many inches per foot of beam). Lay the two straight lengths so they cross at the centerline and bear against the three nails. Nail securely. Remove the center nail. Hold a pencil at the intersection and swing the two battens from one side to the other, keeping them tight against the nails. It may help to backsaw a tiny nick at the intersection so the pencil can't creep. This produces a perfect arc.

The pattern can be bandsawed out, or a small power handsaw might handle this easy curve. Dress very carefully to the line so the beams will be precise. Make several duplicates from the first one cut.

The second layout method, shown in Figure 5-43, is a bit tricky; your lofting, that is, drafting, must be ac-

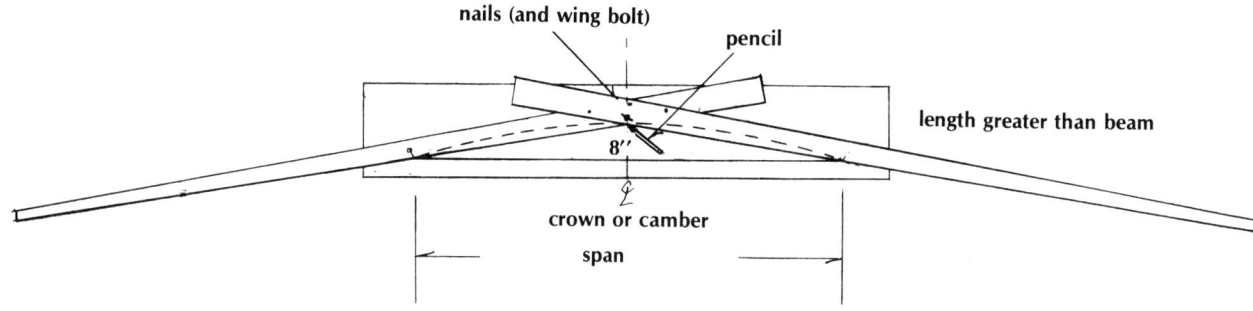

Figure 5-42. JIG TO SCRIBE ANY CAMBER

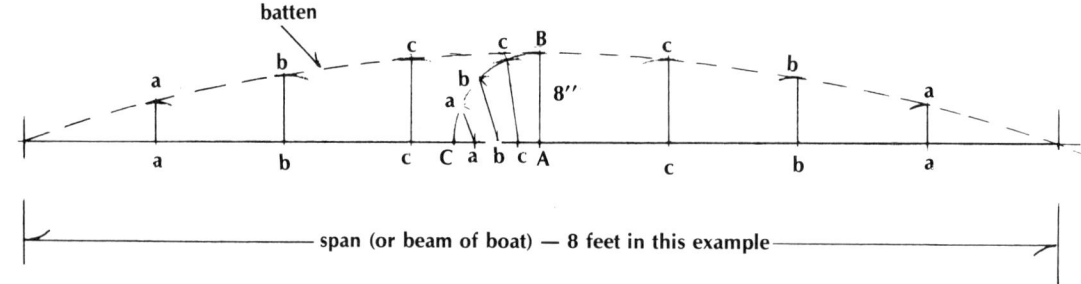

Figure 5-43. GEOMETRIC LAYOUT OF ANY CAMBER

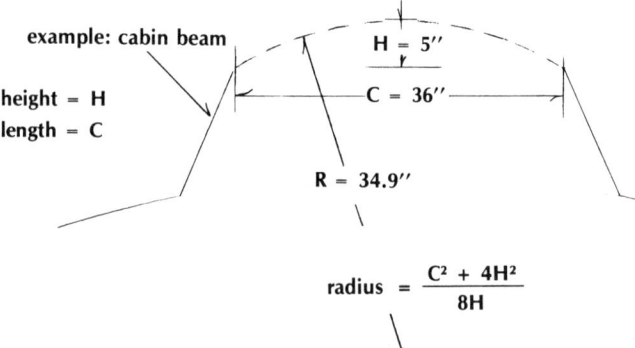

$$\text{radius} = \frac{C^2 + 4H^2}{8H}$$

Figure 5-44. CAMBER BY SIMPLE ARITHMETIC

beam. This must be rigid, so double it. A 2½-inch-wide pattern is quite flexible otherwise.

The arithmetic method of finding the radius to produce a certain camber between two known points must have been worked out by Archimedes (or was it Noah?). See Figure 5-44. Square the span, add to this the height squared multiplied by four. Divide this total by eight times the height. The result is the required radius. If you had to build a set of forms for a cabin trunk top, no two alike, you could use this method or the straightedges in Figure 5-42. But sometimes the dimensions of the shop interfere or they are just plain awkward. In this case, use the arithmetic method.

curate. On the centerline swing an arc equal to the height of the camber A – B to point C; divide this by four. Divide the arc (B – C) into four. Connect the points (a – a, b – b, and c – c). Now divide the baseline into eight, and at each point erect the heights of a – a, b– b, and c – c. Drive small brads in at these points, and bend a good batten around the nails, using weights to hold it. (Never drive nails through a batten.) Mark inside the batten and you have it.

Because many deck beams could be laminated, the beam mold would be used for locating the blocks or forming the mold to which the laminations are to be clamped. Remember that this is the pattern for the upper surface of the beam. Make another pattern for marking lower and upper surfaces, the total depth of the

WOODEN PLANES

There are just a few uses for wooden planes in yacht joinery. Spar work and backing out of hatch rails are examples. John Gardner, technical editor of *National Fisherman,* wrote a series of articles on the origins, uses, and construction of wooden planes (November and December 1972, and January 1973). Reprints may still be obtained from the magazine.

Gardner describes one secret of old boatbuilders that I feel bound to pass on to you. Working woods with cross grains is extremely difficult, for even the sharpest blade may tear the surface. In Gardner's first article, he says, "He honed the cap on the oilstone until it was sharp and fitted the surface of the plane iron perfectly. Then the edge was turned down with a burnisher as if it

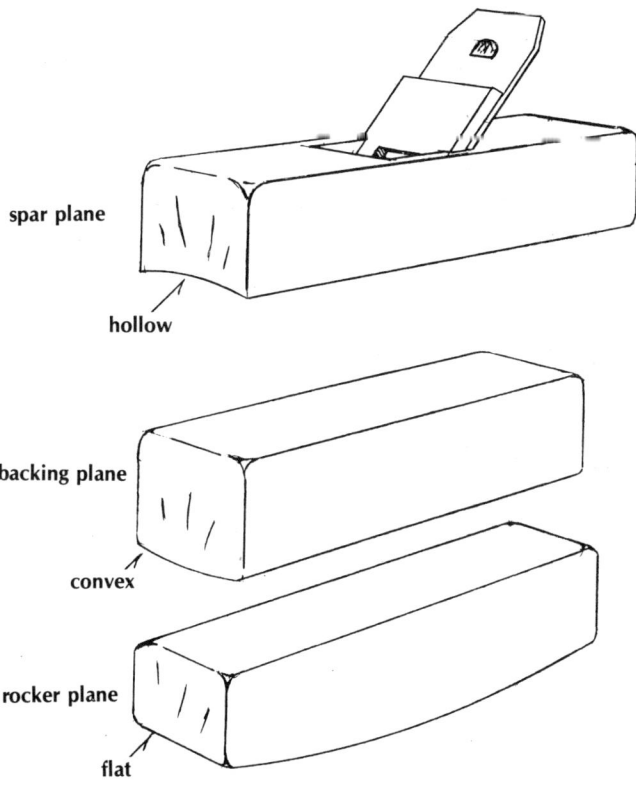

Figure 5-45. PLANES

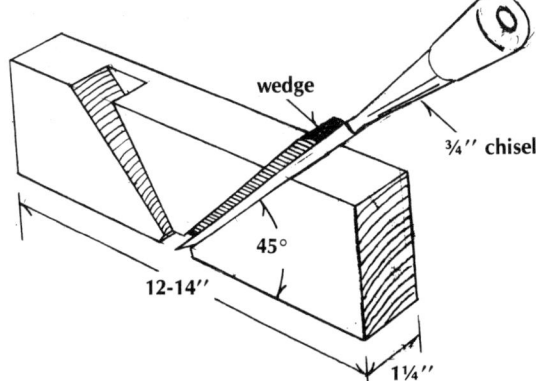

Figure 5-46. RABBET PLANE

were a scraper. The cap was then fastened to the iron with its burnished edge set very close to the sharpened edge of the iron, within $\frac{1}{32}$ inch or thereabouts. A plane set in this manner is harder to push, but it will smooth the most difficult and treacherous cross-grain wood without catching, digging in, or tearing." I can report to you that this is almost as effective with a smooth plane blade ground almost perfectly square, but with an arc of less than $\frac{1}{32}$ inch. It's great for smoothing joints such as the meeting of stiles and rails, for even planing across the grain takes off a shaving you can read newsprint through. I have used this technique on flat-grained fir to remove planer corrugations.

Figure 5-45 shows just three of the many configurations of wooden planes. One of my old craftsmen had a trunkful of planes he had made or otherwise acquired in his 40 years. And he performed wondrous magic with them. But perhaps we should be content with a little less than magic.

How about cleaning up a rabbet after you have dadoed or sawed it out? The tool in Figure 5-46 is based on an article by Jim Emmett in the November 1962 issue of *Rudder*. You can make this rabbet plane if you have just a little skill and a lot of patience. Lay out the angles of the two sockets with a sharp knife. Saw with a backsaw to a depth slightly less than the width of the chisel. Clean out the side of the socket with a ¼-inch chisel. The hardwood wedge must be a perfect fit for tapping in to hold the chisel. Minute depth adjustments are made by tapping on the appropriate end with a mallet or hammer. Live oak would be the ideal wood, but you may have to settle for beech, birch, maple, or ash.

I could go on for a few pages more about accessories, jigs, gadgets, and gimmicks. Similar information, however, will emerge in Part Two as we go through the actual construction of doors, drawers, tables, hatches, rails, spars, and all the rest. So let's drop anchor here for now.

SIX

Tips, Techniques, Facts, Opinions

This chapter is a slop chest of tricks, standards, common practices, and advice on several subjects important to the builder of wooden boats. To some of you, what follows may seem elementary. I must assume, however, that other readers are less familiar with the subject. A good part of the chapter consists of facts and opinions from experts far better qualified than I to instruct less-knowledgeable yachtbuilders. So please bear with me.

POWER TOOL SPEEDS

To achieve maximum efficiency, every shop power machine must make the correct number of revolutions per minute. Adapting used motors (as is often suggested) is easy if you know the r.p.m required, and the pulley sizes needed to achieve the desired r.p.m. Here are recommended speeds:

Machine	Size (inches)	Motor Speed	R.P.M.
Table saw	10	3,450	3,100
Table saw	8	3,450	3,400
Bandsaw	12	1,725	700
Bandsaw	14	1,725	600
Jointer	4-6	3,450	7,000
Jointer		1,725 (less efficient)	5,000
Drill press	all	1,725 (with 2-, 3-, 4-, 5-inch cone)	600-5,000
Bench disc sander	8	3,450 (direct)	3,450
Bench disc sander	10-12	1,725 (direct)	1,725
Shaper	½	3,450	8,000-10,000

SPEEDS AND PULLEY SIZES

It is simple arithmetic to work out the pulley sizes required to give reasonably accurate tool speeds. Just apply these formulas.

$$\frac{\text{tool r.p.m.} \times \text{tool pulley dia.}}{\text{motor r.p.m.}} = \text{motor pulley dia.}$$

$$\frac{\text{motor r.p.m.} \times \text{motor pulley dia.}}{\text{tool pulley dia.}} = \text{tool r.p.m.}$$

$$\frac{\text{motor r.p.m.} \times \text{motor pulley dia.}}{\text{tool r.p.m. wanted}} = \text{tool pulley dia.}$$

Figure 6-1. *The twisted belt reverses the arbor direction on the jointer.*

THE TWISTED BELT REVERSE

Frequently you will find that a motor turns opposite to the direction needed. On a 4-inch jointer I use a ⅓ h.p., 1,725 r.p.m. washing-machine motor mounted on a shelf directly under the tool pulley. The motor is set at an angle of about 30 to 40 degrees so the belt can be twisted. This reverses the direction of the jointer. Friction is minimal; the jointer has been running for four years with no sign of wear. See Figure 6-1. Some motors can be reversed by changing the wiring, but cheap motors are not worth working on. Besides, you still have the original direction if you want it for another kind of tool.

SANDING TRICKS

You may find a long sanding board preferable to a belt sander wherever a fair surface is required. Try a flexible board, as shown in Figure 6-2. The board should be of ⅜- or ¼-inch fir plywood just long enough to take two halves of a sheet of sandpaper. Make a number of shallow saw cuts about one-half the thickness of the board if flexibility for quick bends is necessary. Secure the two halves of the sandpaper sheet with staples into the end blocks. Then fold the paper over the back and staple. Or use Glop, the aptly named cement used for sanding discs. It permits immediate use and rapid replacement of sheets.

If you can pick up a remnant of a sandpaper belt, say, 80- or 100-grit open coat garnet or aluminum oxide production paper, you'll need staples only at the ends. This paper lasts longer, too. I use about 36 inches of such a sanding belt stapled to a board clamped on a nearby bench. It's great for instant sanding of small pieces such as cabinet stiles and rails without taking them to the bench belt sander.

Sanding concave curved edges using a drum mounted on your grinder shaft is all right, but a drum in the chuck of a drill press is better. Place the work piece on a block fitted to the drum so you can control the cutting action and always maintain a square edge — not easy on a shaft-mounted drum. To get into concave spots when the piece is too large to handle, make a cylindrical block out of a length of carpet-roll tubing. Such tubing is about ¼ inch thick and holds staples quite well. (Figure 6-3). This, too, is a good place to try Glop. The tubing idea works well for sanding small spars also. Simply shape the sandpaper to the inside of a split tube.

Tooling foam makes great sanding blocks and shapes. Ask fiberglass buffs where to buy it. You can plane, rasp, saw, or sand this foam to almost any shape. Use it to sand round or rectangular spars, moldings such as ogees and coves, and so on. See Figure 6-4. Do not sand a flat surface without a block of some kind. When you get into fine sanding (220- to 400-grit), use a rubber block whenever possible. Never sand plywood until it has had several coats of primer, sealer, or thinned-out varnish.

SAW KERF BENDING

There are occasions when it is necessary to make a sharp bend in thick material. If great strength is not required, the piece may be slashed with saw kerfs across the inside of the area to be bent. See Figure 6-5. The idea is to space these cuts so they close up completely when the bend is made. A thickened glue fills up the wedge-

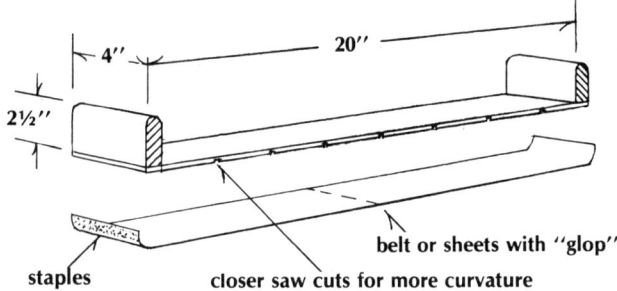

Figure 6-2. FLEXIBLE BOARD FOR SANDING

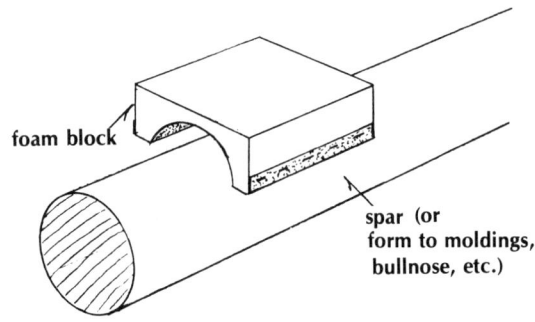

Figure 6-4. A SANDING DEVICE

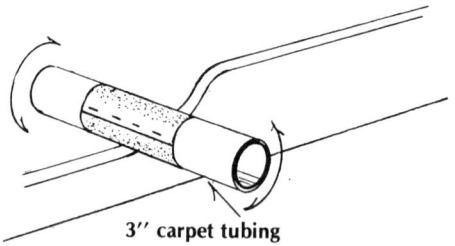

Figure 6-3. TUBING FOR SANDING

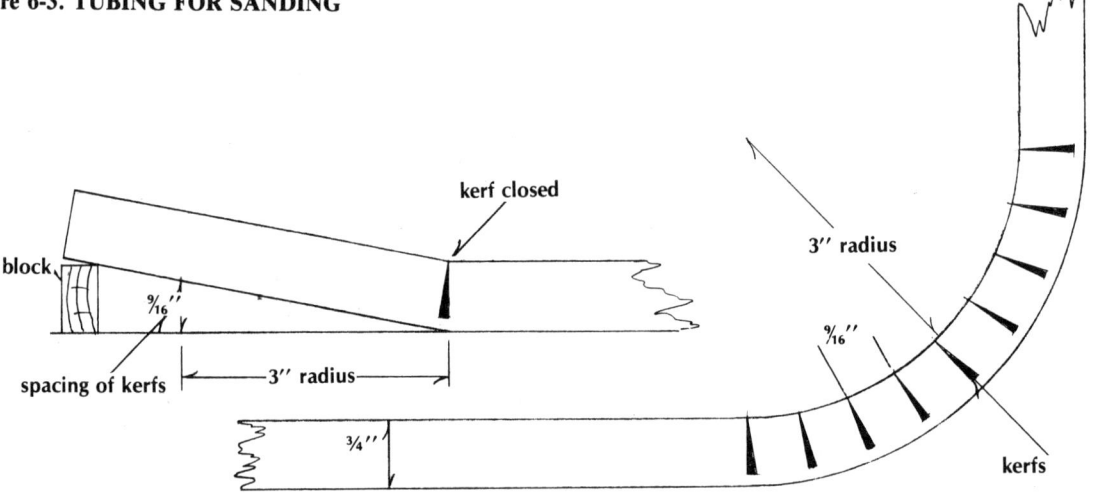

Figure 6-5. BENDING TO GIVEN RADIUS BY KERFING

shaped spaces. Here's a formula used for centuries in furniture building.

First determine the approximate radius of the inside of the finished piece. Let's say 3 inches in ¾-inch material. Find a piece of scrap 1 inch thick. Set your table saw to about a ⅛-inch depth of kerf. Make a cut in the piece of scrap, then clamp it to a bench with the open kerf up. Raise the free end until the kerf closes fully, and block the piece in this position. Now place a mark 3 inches from the kerf on the raised portion. The distance between the bench and the raised piece at that point is the exact spacing required for a 3-inch radius. Experiment with scrap to determine how many cuts will be needed. For looks and strength, fill the kerfs before bending with glue and sawdust mixed to a heavy paste. Plastic Resin or a two-part epoxy would be satisfactory.

If your piece is hardwood and visible, sanding with a hard block will fair out any irregularities on the outside surface. This method can be used for forming lightweight blocking for laminated cockpit coaming corners, for table framing, and for bending dummy frames to take ceilings in fiberglass hulls, among other uses.

FASTENINGS

This will not be an exhaustive discussion of the many types of fastenings used in a wooden vessel. Your best

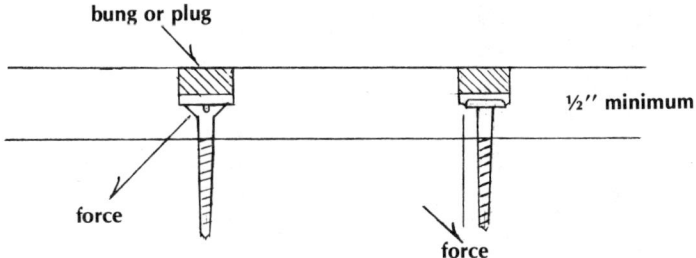

Figure 6-6. FLATHEAD SCREW VERSUS PANHEAD SCREW

Figure 6-7. SIZES FOR SCREWS IN PLANKING AND JOINERY

Material Thickness	Screw Size[1]		Screw Dia.	Shank Drill	Lead Drill[2]	Plug Dia.
3/8"	3/4"	#7	.150"	9/64"	#44	none
1/2"	1"	#8	.163"	5/32"	#40	none
5/8"	1 1/4"	#9	.176"	11/64"	#37	3/8"
3/4"	1 1/2"	#10	.189"	3/16"	#33	1/2"
7/8"	1 3/4"	#12	.216"	13/64"	#30	1/2"
1"	2"	#14	.242"	15/64"	#25	1/2"
1 1/8"	2 1/4"	#16	.268"	17/64"	#18	5/8"
1 1/4"	2 1/2"	#18	.294"	9/32"	#13	5/8"
1 1/2"	3"	#20	.320"	5/16"	#4	3/4"

[1]*May be reduced one gauge for decking*
[2]*For hardwood*

sources are the excellent books mentioned earlier. Reliable guidance is available in Howard Chapelle's *Boatbuilding,* Robert Steward's *Boatbuilding Manual,* L. Francis Herreshoff's *Common Sense of Yacht Design,* and others.

For exposed work that is to be finished bright, it is best to use bungs (plugs) over screws. Galvanized hot-dipped flathead screws are more than adequate, for their life and holding power are excellent. They drive harder, however, because of the rough zinc surface. Also, the slots are not always clean. Stainless steel screws are used in large numbers by production shops because they drive easily, the slots or Phillips sockets are clean, and they are available with pan-type heads. As shown in Figure 6-6, these have less tendency to split the wood than cone-shaped flathead screws. Many situations require glue even with screws. This is true for the cleats supporting berths and settees, for example, and when the fastening is in shear, it should always be glued.

Some cleats can be glued and nail-fastened. The glue does the actual work; the nails may be hot-dipped finish, Anchorfast, or headed nails if the spot is not seen. (If the bulkhead is thin, fasten from it into the cleat.) Serrated nails of bronze or Monel are great almost anywhere, but their cost is high. They drive fast in softwoods and hold forever! These nails require drilled lead holes in hardwoods and sometimes in softwoods. Where the joint is visible, serrated nails must be bunged just as screws are. It's best to set them with a large nail-set into the same 3/8-inch counterbore you use for screws.

The table in Figure 6-7 shows the screw sizes to be used when bunging is required. Robert Steward recommends using white laundry soap on screw threads; this certainly makes large screws drive more easily. However, paraffin and tallow have none of the chemicals found in soap. They, too, make excellent lubricants.

Light trim and moldings of mahogany and teak should be fastened with hot-dipped galvanized finish nails set in and filled after staining and one or two coats of varnish. The thinnest material you can bung is generally about 1/2 inch. Even this leaves very little to secure the bungs. You might have better luck with pan-head stainless steel screws, for this head does not have the conical shape of the flathead screw and thus has less tendency to split the trim when driven in hard. If you are careful, you might successfully bung pan-head screws in 3/8-inch material. Where the trim or molding is being applied to a glass liner or other part, your only choice, in my opinion, is the pan-head sheet metal screw, which cuts a pretty fair thread.

Figure 6-8. *Deck seams caulked and filled with compound. Note handmade locust or ash halyard cleats. (Bruce Bingham photo)*

BUNGING

Remember that bungs must be set in with grains matching. Tap bungs in lightly, but not hard against the screw head. If a bung swells, it has nowhere to go but out. Slice off bungs with a sharp chisel above the finish surface so you can see whether the grain is running up or down, then pare them off flush with the surface. Any bung that cracks off below the surface must be replaced. Remove a defective bung by splitting it with a screwdriver. The pieces are then removed easily without damaging the counterbores. This is important.

DECK FASTENINGS

The most common deck built today is fiberglass over double plywood. This can be fastened with galvanized or bronze screws sunk just below flush. I would use serrated bronze nails, set in slightly. Hot-dipped headed nails are less desirable for this purpose, but they will hold if toenailed. Galvanized finish nails can be used only if the plywood is glued to the beams. In fact, it is preferable to glue all plywood decking to fir or spruce framing, regardless of the kind of fastening used. The sunken heads of the screws or nails should be glazed with a filling compound compatible with polyester and/or epoxy resins. If you canvas your decks, the popular glazing compounds are satisfactory. It's too bad more owners can't see the ease of application and the other advantages of canvased decks. But that's another topic.

The best-looking deck is probably white pine, fir, or teak sprung to the curvature of the deck edge or covering board. Traditionally, this type of decking would have to be 2-inch strips a minimum of 1½ inches thick, each fastened with two bronze screws into the beams, with one or two hot-dipped nails holding each pair of strips. The seams would be caulked and filled with a black compound, as shown in Figure 6-8. I believe the most common practice today, however, is to lay a plywood deck, spring the decking strips over it, bed in Thiokol or epoxy, then drive screws from the underside between deck beams into the decking to pull it all together. Use roundhead bronze or galvanized screws up through the plywood. If thin, the decking can be fastened to the beams with galvanized finish nails and toenailed to draw the strip against its neighbor. The decking can be screw-fastened and bunged if it is heavy enough. Use weights to hold the decking firmly against the plywood until the screws are set and the glue has cured. Four or five strips can be bonded at once if you place boards and concrete blocks on top. There is more on decks in Part Two.

GLUES

John Gardner wrote about glues in a 1976 *National Fisherman* article called "Excellent Foreign Glue Liked by U.S. Builders." The comments about Aerolite 306 from several authorities who tested it were overwhelmingly favorable, even enthusiastic. This glue has been used for over 30 years in England and Canada in both aircraft and marine applications. It has been distributed in the United States only since 1974. Classified as a urea-formaldehyde resin adhesive, it is a product of Ciba Co., Ltd.

Aerolite 306 differs from all other formaldehyde systems. The Aerolite liquefied resin (one part dry powder to four parts water) is applied to one side of the joint, and the activator liquid is applied to the other side. Curing does not occur until the two are brought together. No heat or pressure is required, just firm contact. Glue line failures that occur with other urea-formaldehyde glues are prevented.

In an article called "Gluing Can Be Easy," published in *Sport Aviation* in 1965, Clint Lillibridge said that the advantages of Aerolite are:

1. It fills gaps up to 1/16 inch wide and still produces a strong bond.
2. Firm contact of joint faces and pressure of a pound or two are all that are required.
3. Assembly time may be extended as long as coated surfaces remain moist, and they may be remoistened. Curing time is uniform.
4. Excessive moisture in the wood slows curing but does not weaken strength.
5. Aerolite will cure at temperatures as low as 50 degrees F.
6. Joints are entirely waterproof and will withstand exposure for many years.

A couple of advantages Lillibridge did not include are: (1) The glue is crystal clear when cured, and (2) there is very little waste, as pot life of the resin mix is several days.

Comparisons of Aerolite with other glues showed it to be superior to all. Plastic Resin was a close second. The cost is considerably lower than epoxies. Distributors are Aircraft Spruce and Specialty Co., 210 W. Truslow Ave., Fullerton, CA 92632, and Woodcraft Supply Corp., 313 Montvale Ave., Woburn, MA 01801.

I used Aerolite 306 to glue the laminated stems to the keel batten on a very lightweight duckboat, intending to add bolts later. Completion has been postponed. This assembly has been kicked around my shop for several years, really mishandled, and it appears that no bolts are necessary. One day, however, I shall add fastenings to calm the doubters. I have used Aerolite in a dozen critical spots with complete satisfaction.

I have been using Weldwood Plastic Resin (also a urea-formaldehyde) for many years. Before that I used its predecessor, Borden's Casein, mainly for spars. All my plywood boats were glued everywhere, including plywood planking butts, which were also bolted. Charles G. MacGregor, the designer and pioneer in plywood construction, said one could remove the fastenings in such a boat and it would stay together. I never had the guts to try it. A number of sailboats up to 27 feet long built by me in the late 1930s and early 1940s, however, were still sailing in the mid-1970s. If Casein will do this, why worry about Aerolite and Plastic Resin? Of course, Plastic Resin requires a lot of pressure, lots of clamps, and fast action. The great advantage of Aerolite is that nothing happens for quite a while after the parts contact.

A word or two about Resorcinol seems in order. Many builders use it. This means their shops must be at least 70 degrees F. The moisture content of the wood must be below 15 percent. The glue line with Resorcinol is black and unsightly. The glue's most critical characteristics are its dependence on glue line thickness and clamping pressure. U.S. Plywood Bulletin 400 states: "In general, for best results, sufficient pressure to reduce the glue line to a thickness of 0.005 inch is required. Thicker glue lines will result in an inferior bond . . . . But high pressure should not be substituted for poor-fitting joints." Smears and runs make unsightly stains that are difficult to remove. Moreover, relatively thin parts fastened with screws and Resorcinol may fail because sufficient pressure is generated only in the area of the screws. This effect is more pronounced with serrated nail fastening. Amateurs can build sound boats with Resorcinol adhesives, as hundreds of professionals have, but care and skill are needed to achieve the strength the glue is capable of.

A fine article, "Adhesives and the Boatbuilder," by Gerald Schindler, published in *WoodenBoat* in 1975, says " . . . all joints are variations of four basic types, as defined by the manner in which they are stressed. These are shear, tensile, cleavage, and peel. Since the nature of the stress in a joint has a great influence on the characteristics of the adhesive required to function most effectively in that configuration, before we talk much about adhesives we ought to consider the stresses that must be withstood." The four stresses are shown in Figure 6-9.

Schindler continues: "1. SHEAR. Force is exerted across the adhesive bond. The bonded surfaces are being forced to slide over each other. All of the adhesive contributes to bond strength.

"2. TENSILE. Force is exerted at right angles to the adhesive equally over the entire joint. All of the adhesive contributes to bond strength.

"3. CLEAVAGE. Force is concentrated at one edge of the joint and exerts a prying force on the bond. The other edge of the joint is theoretically under zero stress. Only a portion of the adhesive resists load.

"4. PEEL. One surface must be flexible. Stress is concentrated along a thin line at the end of the bond where separation occurs. A very small portion of the adhesive carries all of the peeling force.

"Most adhesives perform better when the primary stress is shear or tensile. However, in most applications a combination of stresses is involved . . . other factors influence the selection of an adhesive. Environmental exposure is an important consideration — moisture, temperature extremes, impact, vibration, chemical contact, dimensional changes, and biological attack all impose added requirements on the adhesive.

"Next, application requirements or process limitations must be examined. Is the adhesive easy to use? Are special tools required? A weight scale? How much working life is needed? What is the range of application and curing temperatures? How critical is the condition and fitting of the surfaces? Is clamping pressure important to the ultimate strength? Can dissimilar materials be bonded?

"Finally, the nature of the cured product is of concern. Is color important or will staining detract from the finished product? Will the adhesive be compatible with materials applied later? What is the anticipated life under the expected service conditions?"

Schindler's article reiterates most of what has been stated above about urea-formaldehyde and Resorcinol

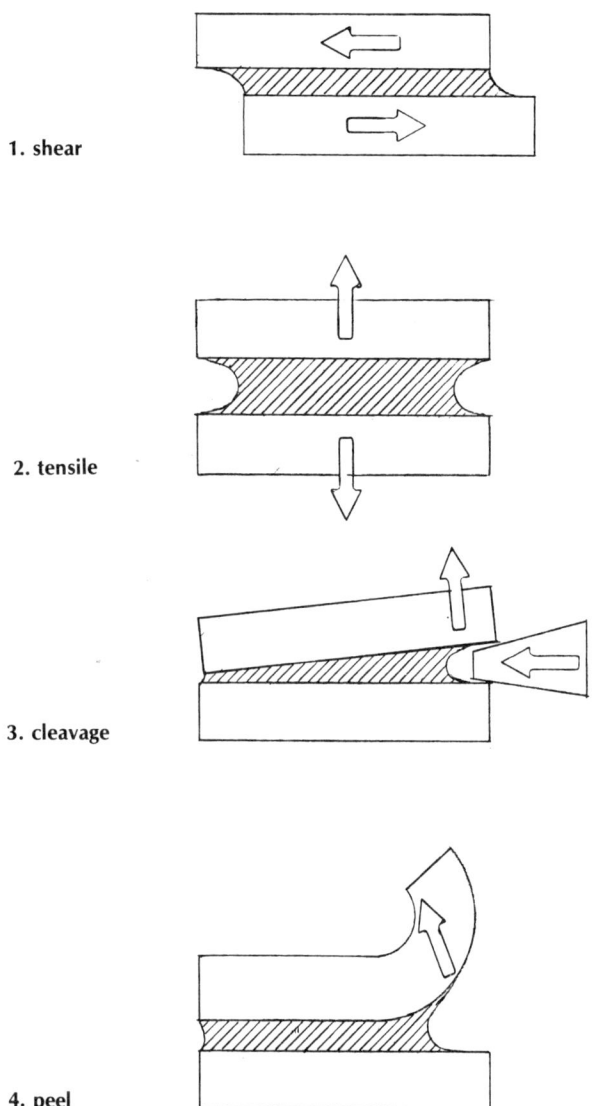

Figure 6-9. STRESSES ON ADHESIVES

adhesives, but he includes information about an interesting epoxy, Chem-Tech T-88. "Although T-88 is tailored to the needs of boatbuilders, and particularly amateur boatbuilders, many of its properties are shared by other epoxy adhesives, although no other epoxy duplicates all of its characteristics.

"T-88 is supplied in kits consisting of two bottles of rather viscous liquids designated A (resin) and B (hardener). These are mixed in equal amounts by volume . . . . At 70 degrees F, the user has about 45 minutes to apply the adhesive if he has mixed a total of 8 ounces or less . . . .

"The epoxy is easily applied with a flat stick, and because resin and hardener are mixed in the same cup, it need only be applied to one of the mating surfaces . . . . T-88 differs from most adhesives in that it may be applied to damp surfaces, which is helpful in making laminated curved structures where soaking or steaming is required.

"Fit and clamping pressure do not present any problems either, since epoxies are truly gap-filling and require only sufficient pressure to hold the surfaces together . . . . Where gaps are really bad, a thickening powder furnished with the adhesive can be used to keep it from running out of the joint . . . .

"T-88 will remain workable in a joint for two hours or more, allowing for more leisurely clamping and fastening of large panels without concern that the joints may not fully close . . . . T-88 is light amber in color, won't discolor wood, and becomes invisible when varnished."

T-88 can be applied in temperatures below 70 degrees F, down to 50 degrees F, but the curing time is extended from six to eight hours to as much as a full day. This temperature range, however, adds many working days during the winter, an important consideration.

WOODS

The following comments may be a bit late if you have already built your wooden hull. On the other hand, if you bought it, or you are rebuilding an older vessel, or you are about to finish a fiberglass yacht with decks and structures of wood, then what follows might be useful at this point.

All yacht joinery woods should be air dried, not kiln dried. Lumber right out of the local yard (Oregon fir, Douglas fir, pine, white or red oak) is apt to be high in sap and oils. Such wood is bound to shrink, warp, and check as it dries. Warping and shrinking place great stresses on fastenings, including glue; serious splits may occur. Moreover, wide-open joints are next to useless. Of course, appearance suffers. If your lumberman knows anything about boat construction, he should be willing to find the quality of air-dried material you need. If not, settle for green lumber and stack it yourself for proper air drying. Even the kiln-dried stuff can be made reasonably serviceable by stacking, so purchase everything you can far in advance of your needs. Paint the ends of boards with any old paint to prevent drying and checking of the end grain.

Here's how to stack lumber. Find a flat spot where you can cover the material with a plastic cover, sheets of plywood, or a simple framed-up shed roof covered with plastic, roll roofing, or whatever. Space out four or five strong timbers. These should be 4 by 4, 2 by 6 on edge, or heavier. Level these timbers with blocks. See Figure 6-10. Now put down a layer of lumber with 1-inch spaces between the planks. Next, lay down four or five sticks ½ to ¾ inch thick (laths, tomato stakes, or scrap) across the lumber at right angles to it. Repeat this layering for your entire stock. Finally, arrange the cover

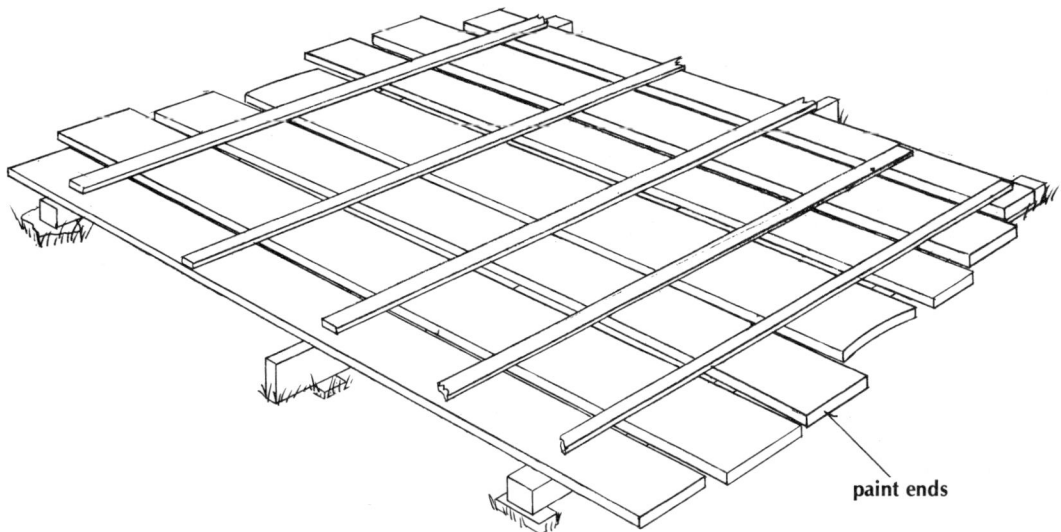

Figure 6-10. TO DRY LUMBER, BEGIN BY "STICKING"

loosely so it sheds rain, but leave the ends and sides open. The lumber should be shielded from direct hot sunlight, too.

Drying must be slow and uniform, so every two or three weeks unstack the pile and turn each piece over. Watch for crooks. Wedge badly bowed boards between straight ones or stand them on edge so the weight of the pile forces them straight. Don't be too concerned about the graying, especially if the lumber is still in the rough.

Avoid lumber called *construction grade*. This is used to frame houses and buildings and has no place in a vessel. It will rot in several years in a moist atmosphere. Clear vertical-grain Oregon fir is excellent lumber. It is heavier than spruce, but very strong. Thus, lighter sections may be used. Clear Douglas fir is good spar lumber. Fir is excellent for framing, and it is used for keels and deadwood also. Fir should be treated for rot resistance, particularly if the vessel is going into warmer climes.

I assume that all modern wood boatbuilders will treat all materials against fungus, perhaps by epoxy saturation techniques, or by direct application of Cuprinol, or by other preventive measures (more on this later). However, the wood should be quarter-sawn. This is called *vertical grain* or *edge grain* also. Look at the ends of quarter-sawn boards. The grain runs more or less vertical to the wide surface. The boards were sawed from the log in quarters, as shown in Figure 6-11. This grain pattern increases a board's stiffness, compared with a flat grain. It shrinks and warps less and is also easier to plane.

Oak or fir may be used for structures below the waterline, such as sole beams and supports, but these woods are too heavy for deck beams and framing. Spruce is best here. Laminated beams are excellent and conserve lumber. Moreover, they look rich with the entire beam finished bright. A lower grade of spruce other than Sitka or aircraft would be perfectly satisfactory. Long lengths of any grade are now rare. That's why you have to learn how to make strong scarfs.

Western red cedar is sometimes used for relatively light planking. It is more than adequate for laminated or cold-molded planking saturated with epoxy. Philippine mahogany is almost perfect for any use, but it is much heavier than any cedar. While planking is not the concern of this book, you should remember that laminated systems can be used for streamlined deck structures, bent coamings, and so on. For such purposes, if economy is vital, you can use cheaper grades of wood such as the so-called knotty pine and even construction-grade fir. Just cut out the knotty areas, and rip the wood in between into strips and/or resaw for laminating.

Some of the so-called hardwoods may actually be soft. Philippine mahogany, teak, and Honduras and African mahoganies are all softwoods. They are delightful to work, although the last two are rare indeed, and teak is deadly to cutting tools. The most desirable Philippine is Lauan, which should be selected for color (a deep red), straight grain, and perhaps some ribbon grain for beauty. This grade is called first, meaning "clear of knots on one side and free of rot, shakes, and checks and other faults on the other side," according to Howard Chapelle. For steam bending, use oak firsts only. This will have to come from young green trees, with no drying at all. Ask your lumberman for bending stock. Or try to find a country mill that is cutting oak.

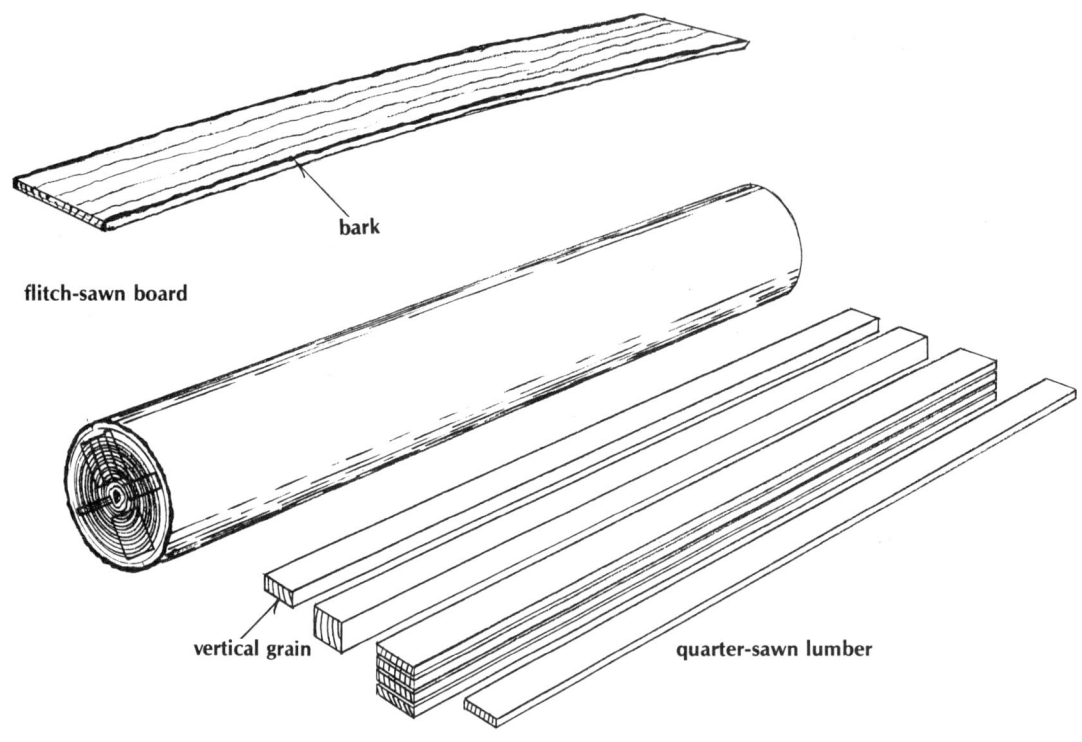

Figure 6-11. LUMBER CUTS

DECKING

The best deck for footing, wear, and appearance is teak left bare. See Figure 6-12. Teak weathers to a beautiful silver gray color, or it can be oiled. It is costly, but because it requires no finish, even on interior trim, the final cost is moderate. Sometimes exterior trim, grabrails, hatches, moldings, and even cabin trunks of teak are varnished. Many swear there is nothing handsomer. You'll see varnished teak on some of the world's finest yachts — especially those with crews. For decks, however, bare teak is superb. You can't varnish any deck, for it would be too slippery. This means Philippine mahogany is out for decking; it can't be left bare.

Clear white pine also is a beautiful decking wood, especially with its seams filled with a black compound (Figure 6-13). White pine must be sanded to keep it clean, and it does absorb suntan oil and grease. Vertical-grain Oregon fir makes a great deck, and it may be treated with sealers such as Rez, Firzite, or special oils made for this purpose. You can buy kiln-dried Oregon fir at most yards as stair tread, dressed from 1 inch to $1\frac{1}{8}$ inches. All decks are assumed to be laid over plywood, so $1\frac{1}{2}$- to 2-inch pine is not necessary. All in all, this reduces total weight, saves precious lumber, and makes a watertight deck — something most traditionally laid decks cannot claim. Details on decking follow in Part Two.

Figure 6-12. *A bare teak deck. Note beautiful Dorade vent. (Bruce Bingham photo)*

Figure 6-13. *A white pine deck with contrasting compound. Note traditional pinrail. (Bruce Bingham photo)*

DECK OIL

I must mention a well-advertised product for finishing decks as well as other exposed areas such as hulls, cabin trunks, and so on. The name is Deks Olje, which translates freely as deck oil. This product is distributed by The Flood Company, 377 Barlow Road, Hudson, OH 44236. You put one coat of No. 1 right on top of another without drying until the wood is filled. Then you apply multiple coats of No. 2 with 24 hours' drying time between coats. The 1978 advertising quotes a highly respected yacht designer, " . . . the cost is low compared to varnish and paint, it is beautiful, easy to apply, lasts longer, does not soak up dirt and turn dark, and it is easily maintained with soap and water wash and an additional coat or two each year." The footing provided by this deck oil was not mentioned, but I assume that it is more than adequate, for this designer had used it for several years.

LET'S HEAR IT FOR "AIRBALL"

Now let's go to the other extreme and mention a product that to my knowledge has never been advertised, yet it has a navy of rabid fans up and down the West Coast. This product is Arabol, called "Airball" by those familiar with it. Arabol is classified as a lagging adhesive. It's not for the decks of spit-and-polish yachts, but I suspect that some owners who would be satisfied with fiberglass over plywood or old wood might find it very acceptable. It should be considered for rugged deep-water cruising yachts. You might class Arabol as a substitute for resin on glass or paint on canvas. It dries to a hard rubbery consistency and works best on a loose-weave fabric such as burlap. A loose weave allows more complete penetration than in canvas and provides a nonskid surface. If you use canvas, both sides must be coated. Arabol has been used successfully on fiberglass door screening.

Arabol applications require a plywood base, for it may crack over seams in decks or cabintops. Thus, an old wood deck would have to be covered with plywood first. I haven't given you all the information you need to judge Arabol, but at about $2 per gallon, it would pay you to look into it thoroughly. Contact Borden Inc. Chemical Division, 41100 Boyce Road, Fremont, CA 94538, or 56 Nostrand Avenue, Brooklyn, NY 11205.

YOU CAN AVOID DRY ROT

In the July and August 1978 issues of *National Fisherman,* there were two articles on dry rot, its causes and cures. The author stated that inquiries would be welcome, so I am going to summarize the information in the two articles. For more information, contact the expert, Robert L. Kocher, Electrical Engineering Department, College of Engineering, University of Maryland, College Park, MD 20742.

First of all, Kocher says that the term *dry rot* is a nickname. We see deterioration when the wood is dry, but the dry rot fungi require damp wood. Most of these fungi simply go dormant when wood dries, then reactivate when it becomes damp again. Alternating damp and dry conditions promote rot, as in occasional rain or salt spray on a hull or deck. Salt water does not prevent rot. There is, however, less oxygen available in the soaked wood below the waterline or in a wet bilge, and it is harder for the fungi to grow. When a boat is put into dry storage, on the other hand, more oxygen becomes available, and the reserve of moisture slowly moving out of the interior of soaked wood promotes fungus growth. Because drying out takes weeks or months, there is ample opportunity for the spores to reduce wood to "the texture and strength of a semi-dried cow-pie," to quote Kocher.

Dry rot fungi become dormant in temperatures below about 35 degrees F. They are most active between 65 and 80 degrees F. Ordinary high temperatures do not bother them at all. Heating a boat means nothing. Kocher also points out that dry rot spores can survive for years, just waiting to come into contact with damp wood.

Fiberglass can be the most destructive thing that can happen to a boat, Kocher claims. Wood is porous to oxygen and water, but fiberglass is not. " . . . residual dampness remains longer in the part of the wood farthest from the unglassed surface, which is the surface where the water has to leave if any drying occurs," according to the author. "Hence, the area where the fiberglass bonds to the wood develops a type of continual dampness which makes a good growing place for rot fungus." The result is the appearance of good wood on the unglassed surface, but under the glassed area the wood is soft, spongy, and infested. Of course, the glass eventually will separate. This will happen with many paints also. A slight bulge or deformation of the paint surface, or flaking, is the first sign.

So-called unexplainable conditions contribute to the confusion, myths, and superstitions surrounding dry rot. One owner paints his deck dark to absorb the sun's heat and his dry rot problems are over. Another paints his decks dark and his boat caves in two years later, completely rotted out. The sun's heat probably caused the first boat's decks to dry out more quickly, but the sun heating the second boat's decks no doubt raised the temperature to the point where the fungus thrived. The moisture content of the second boat was higher. Why?

According to Kocher, perhaps the first boat's bilges were pumped drier, leaving less water to condense on the underside of decks at night. Or perhaps it's the way vents were arranged, or whether the boat faced into the wind in its berth. A difference in engine heat, too, could account for the difference in dryness. Or the second boat could have been using some kind of a heater, leading to condensation on the decks and hull. On the other hand, what if the lowered bilge water in the first boat suddenly produced moisture levels in exposed timbers that feed the dry rot spores? Positive answers can't be found for each problem situation, so we must find ways to kill dry rot fungi in their tracks.

TWO WOOD PRESERVATION SYSTEMS

We can't prevent dampness in a marine environment. Instead, we resort to chemical treatments that attempt to make wood resistant to attack. One of the treatments to be discussed here is petroleum-based, the other is water-soluble-salt-based. Kocher points out that the two systems are completely incompatible. Oil and water do not mix, as you well know.

Pentachlorophenol, or penta, is dissolved in petroleum-based solvents. An 18-hour soaking in penta will raise the lifetime of test wood to about 10 years. Even a one-minute dip adds a couple of years of life to wood under tropical test conditions, according to Kocher. Thus, yearly brushed-on applications are bound to be effective. Kocher points out that when penta is used with heavy oils, painting becomes difficult; light mineral spirits leave less residue. Be sure to create forced ventilation when you work with these substances.

Copper naphthanate is a powerful preservative when it is forced into wood under pressure. Test samples put out in various climates in 1941, while not in good condition, were in serviceable condition in 1977. A simple three-minute dip raised test-wood lifetimes to 5.2 years in the tropics and 9.8 years in northern climes. This indicates that yearly brushed-on applications on dry wood can definitely be effective as a preservative, according to Kocher. I agree, for I have made this my practice since 1936. I never paint the inside of a hull unless the owner forces me to do it.

I must emphasize also that during construction or repair, all hull parts should be treated by dipping or repeated brushings after final fitting and before installation. Bolt holes should be plugged lightly and filled with the preservative, which will allow it to penetrate to the center. Unfortunately, copper naphthanate has a green color that sometimes bleeds into paints. The color, however, is included to show areas treated. You can get the clear type, if you prefer. In addition, the green will discolor polyester resins, but it does not seem to affect epoxy. Both resins adhere satisfactorily after a week's drying period. Zinc naphthanate is colorless but less effective in decay prevention. A trick that Kocher describes is to cover temporarily multiple brushed applications with a thin polyethylene sheet. This helps to soak the wood fully. Remember, none of the above preservatives will work when applied to damp wood.

WATER-SOLUBLE PRESERVATIVES

You will recall that many antifouling bottom paints contain copper. You may remember also that aquarium instruction books warn against putting copper into the aquarium because, in Kocher's words, "... three coins in the fountain will wipe out your prize guppy collection ...." The most effective water-soluble preservatives contain copper. The most-used one is chromated copper arsenate, which is sometimes called copper chrome arsenate, or CCA. Quoting Kocher: "Most of the experimental wood appropriately pressure-treated with CCA is still in good condition after 27 years of testing. Similarly, wood pressure-treated with ammoniacal copper arsenate 32 years ago is still in good condition .... The untreated wood used as a comparison lasted only 1.9 years. What more can be said?"

Kocher continues: "... the copper reacts with the arsenic and/or chromate to form an insoluble copper arsenate of copper chromate which then cannot leave the wood. Thus, the preservative becomes locked in permanently even though the wood subsequently may be subjected to moisture." He goes on, "The soaking in copper sulfate solution followed by sodium chromate or arsenate is called a double-diffusion process and works fastest on green or wet wood."

It's possible to paint over water-soluble copper salts as well as covering with polyester or epoxy resins.

Can you pressurize wood preservatives into a completed boat? No, but remember the trick of covering treated areas with polyethylene sheets to retard evaporation. Remember too that cold weather retards evaporation of petroleum solvents. You can use these tricks to greatly increase the effectiveness of preservatives, even for hulls no longer young. Another point: copper salts barely penetrate dry oak by brushing on. "However," Kocher says, "copper salts will penetrate water-soaked oak about ten times as fast. This is why the double-diffusion process works even better with green or wet wood . . . . Copper chloride follows water, even when that water is in wood. In other words, while dampness is ordinarily a prohibitive factor in applying paint or preservatives, it *aids* in the application of waterborne salts."

So bare the wood of your vessel immediately after the fall haulout and wet it well, even going so far as to use a lawn sprinkler on decks. Apply copper solutions, and then cover with polyethylene sheets. Hold the polyethylene sheets with weights, not staples. Kocher says: "The chemicals can sit under there for days or weeks, and new water or solution added periodically. If dryness occurs under the polyethylene and crystals can be seen, addition of more water will redissolve the crystals for further absorption into the wood. The longer the application, the deeper the penetration and the more dry rot resistance. After a deck has absorbed copper sulfate or chloride, it should be flushed off briefly, dried, then the process repeated with sodium chromate."

You can use water in the bilge for rot treatment. If the hull has been leak-proofed with glass or epoxy, dump some copper sulfate or chloride solution into the bottom and let it soak in. Plug the limber holes so you can soak one section at a time, then use a plastic bilge pump to soak timbers and other areas and to transfer the solution from one section to another. This is great for all those nooks and crannies the fungus loves.

The chemicals come in crystal form. They are applied by brushing the dry crystals onto wood that has been soaked thoroughly so the crystals stick to the wet surface. A very fine spray is then used to barely wet the crystals without washing them away. In about 25 minutes, the copper chloride crystals will dissolve completely in the water in the wood. The copper chloride will then continue to spread throughout the structure. After the copper application, the process is repeated with sodium chromate or sodium arsenate both to complete the preservative action and to lock it into the wood permanently.

The goal is to get about a pound each of copper and chromate salts into a cubic foot of wood. This is a lot, but it's worth it. For example, if you have planking 1 inch thick, 2 ounces of each type of crystal by weight will be enough to treat each square foot of surface. This means that a pound of each will treat about 8 square feet. When treatment is finished, keep the wood moist for four days to a week, as described above. Note that the wood surface will have a terribly milky appearance following treatment. The residue can be sanded off. Some can be squirted off with a hose first.

PART TWO

SEVEN

Nineteen Useful Joints and How to Make Them

Portions of Part Two may not be new to those of you with extensive woodworking and yacht joinery experience. On the other hand, the information presented should be useful to readers with less skill and limited tool inventories. Included are descriptions of the construction of scores of components from sole beams to spars. I'll show you several ways to make parts, taking into account tool availability and differing degrees of skill. In general, I prefer a simple method if it produces a strong part, even though appearance may suffer a bit in rare instances. In other cases, a complicated procedure is more likely to create the better result. I'll attempt to show why these steps are preferable, if not mandatory.

In my opinion, a simple, low-cost approach often can create an equally functional and eye-pleasing effect. Thus, I hope to help those who want to save time and dollars and still turn out a respectable yacht.

A THOUSAND WOODEN JOINTS

If you have never spent some time in a hard-working wooden vessel, your life is incomplete. The sound of a ship as her hull drives to windward against a sea is music. You hear the soft sighing and bubbling of foam caressing her planking, a muffled thud far up in her bows, and the whoosh of spray and green water shooting over her bulwarks. Then there's the hurried gurgling of water cascading across her decks and pouring from her scuppers. In addition, there are the voices of the ship as she butts her path through the seas. You hear the creaking, cracking, and groaning of thousands of joints protesting the forces battering the hull. No orchestra can match this music. Moreover, the tighter the ship's joints, the sweeter the symphony.

It is sometimes said that it isn't the fastenings that hold a ship together, it is the joints. If this is true, then each joint must be appropriate to its function, and it must be fitted with care. Of course, these comments pertain primarily to traditional wooden vessels. There is, however, much joining of wood in modern laminated, fiberglass, metal, or ferrocement vessels. The sounds of such a vessel when underway may not be the same, but the satisfaction to be found in quality workmanship surely is.

The fitting of a bulkhead into a hull is a joint. A drawer contains many joints, and a deck consists of hundreds of joints. This chapter will tell you how to fit many common joints with a variety of tools and techniques. Three or four ways are often described. Method A may take five times longer and be painfully difficult because it uses only hand tools. Method B may show how the use of hand power tools improves matters. Method C will show how speed and accuracy are attained with sophisticated tools and accessories.

Do give this chapter some attention. Later, when I describe yacht joinery problems, I shall not repeat recommendations given here. It would help, too, to review the suggestions given in Part One. Not all of these will be repeated.

Because naval architects and designers do not always spell out the details of joints, you may have to decide which joint to use. Often there are several choices. The joints shown in this chapter are basic. Many variations are commonly used. To supplement what follows, I recommend *Woodwork Joints,* by Charles H. Hayward (published by Drake), and *How to Work with Tools and Wood,* by Robert Campbell and N.H. Mager (published by Pocket Books).

Keep in mind that you must use tools that are sharp. Your backsaw must be fine-toothed and properly sharpened and set. Your table saw must be equipped with a cabinetmaker's combination or a fine carbide-tipped blade. Your jointer knives should be honed just before you tackle wild grain hardwoods. Your plane blade or chisel should be razor sharp. Sharp tools save hours and produce fine workmanship with less effort.

Now let's fit those basic joints.

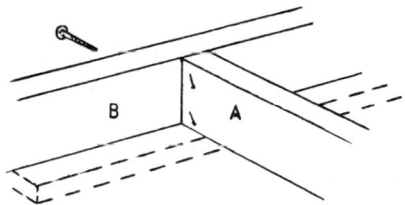

Figure 7-1. T BUTT

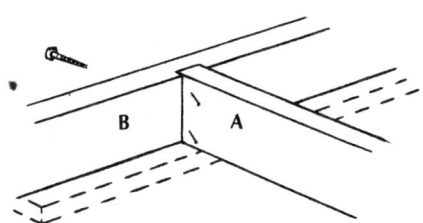

Figure 7-2. DADOED BUTT

BUTT JOINTS

Butt means to join end to end. It means end to side, also. End-to-end butt joints are used in yacht construction only when backed by a long block of similar thickness, as in a planking butt joint. Should you elect to butt-block a sheer clamp or bilge stringer (they really should be scarfed), you can achieve a perfect fit of the ends. Clamp up and then run a handsaw between the ends two or three times, closing up with a crack of a hammer on the outer ends after each try.

The 90-degree side or T butt shown in Figure 7-1 has some uses. This joint is extremely weak, however, for it is entirely dependent on fastenings. Glue is of little value on end grain. Toenailing, in addition to nail or screw fastenings from the back side, adds some strength. If this joint were supported by a shelf or riser, as indicated by the dotted lines, it might serve.

Method A uses a backsaw in a miter box. The members of this joint must be square to each other to have any strength. Method B uses a hand power saw, using a carpenter's square or a plywood square guide. Method C is done on a table saw, using the miter gauge or a sliding auxiliary table (SLAT) as described in Chapter Five.

DADOED BUTT

The dadoed butt is a joint that provides greatly increased gluing area and quite rigid construction if carefully made. See Figure 7-2. Fasten the same as the T butt joint. Excessive tension and/or working can make this joint fail, for it is greatly dependent on glue.

If you are using method A, mark the dado with a knife and make several cuts with a backsaw to a depth equal to a third of the thickness of the material. The material between the cuts is then removed with a sharp chisel narrower than the dado groove. Swing the chisel from side to side in a paring motion, coming in from both ends of the dado. If the dado is more than ¾ inch wide, make three or more cuts so the chips are small and you have control. Cut off the end of A in a miter box. Method B is identical except that the cuts are made with a hand power saw set just less than the wanted depth. Use a guide clamped to the piece to control the cut. Or use a router. Clean up the dado surface with a chisel.

Method C is done on your table saw with the blade set to the depth of the dado. The knife marks should be on the edge of the piece so the line can be sighted along the blade while it is stationary. If you trust your miter gauge, make repeated cuts to clean out the dado groove. A SLAT would be more accurate, for when one is used, there is less tendency for the piece to creep. Even better is a dado set or adjustable dado cutter used with either a miter gauge or a SLAT.

Glue the dadoed butt joint by coating the sides and bottom of the groove with Aerolite. Paint the catalyst on the entering piece. Do not make a squeaky fit, and clamp only enough to hold the pieces in position while the glue is curing. It's OK to rely on the fastening through the back. Do not squeeze the glue entirely out of the joint. Any epoxy glue would be adequate. If Plastic Resin is preferred, coat both surfaces, clamp, and screw fasten. Glue and C-clamp to the underlying shelf, if one is to be used.

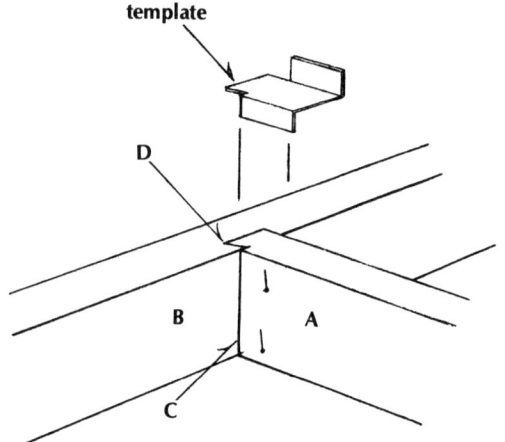

Figure 7-3. DOVETAILED DADO

DOVETAILED DADO

The dovetailed dado is an extremely strong joint that has many uses — for example, joining the short side deck beams to the carlings — but it is one of the more difficult to construct with accuracy. See Figure 7-3. If you plan a number of these joints, I recommend that you first make a sheet metal pattern of aluminum. Use this template to mark off the angle and other dimensions of pin A, the part fitting into the recess — the dovetail. Save the template. The depth of the socket should be one-third the thickness of the piece and the depth of the shoulder (C) in A should be one-third or less. Fashion pin A first.

Method A squares the end of part A, then clamps the template to it so you can mark it accurately, top and bottom, with a knife. Use a miter box to backsaw the shoulder (C) just shy of the line. Secure A in a vise vertically so you can saw the angle that locks to D. A dovetail saw (a small, fine backsaw) is almost a must. Try to leave a little stock for trimming back to the line carefully. The best way is to clamp the beam flat on a bench and chisel back. Check repeatedly with the pattern and a try square until you shave down to the knife marks. Now for part B. C-clamp the template over the desired location and mark. Square across B and mark on the bottom from the template. Backsaw just inside the marks with repeated cuts to ease removal of the material. Your chisel should be a socket firmer (with beveled edges), for this shape enables you to get into the corner (D).

Try dropping part A into the dovetail, marking with a pencil where more wood has to be removed. Pare in carefully, cutting from both ends of the dovetail at both top and bottom. In theory, you come right down to the knife marks, but life is not like that. It will take a great deal of fit and try to attain a snug fit. A squeaky fit here would be best to resist tension. If you see some daylight, however, don't despair. Aerolite glue is coming to the rescue. It fills cracks wider than 1/32 inch with full strength (but don't let your workmanship slide). Coat the dovetail sides, back, and shoulder with the resin, and wet the pin with the catalyst. Press the pin in and fasten with a couple of galvanized toenails.

If you are fitting from sheer clamp to carling, don't glue any joints until all are completed. You may have to disassemble the whole thing a dozen times as you fit one after another. It's far better to fit all into the clamp, then clamp the carling to a couple of strong beam molds while you mark the locations and lengths. Then you can do the actual cutting of dovetails on a bench. By the time you finish four or five, you'll be a pro.

Method B is a bit different. Use a square guide on part B and a fine-toothed blade in your power handsaw. Most of the material can be removed with repeated passes, but not much faster than with a backsaw. The last cut is the shoulder angle (D). Once you get the angle right, saw all of it. Then it's back to the chisel for cleaning up. I would not try to use a power saw for shaping the pin on part A.

Method C uses your table saw to cut the rough socket, but of course, only if it is not installed. Thus, this lets out the sheer clamp. It's all right for the carling, though, and also for the pins. I would much prefer to use a SLAT for this job, but this is a handmade joint. The rough cut could be made with a dado set, but the setting-up time is not justified unless you have a number of cuts ready to go.

There is a method B, however, that uses a router with a dovetail bit. In this method, you follow a square guide clamped to part B. Be sure that the bit angle and the cut angle of the pin coincide. Make the dovetail pass, then dado out the remaining material to the mark. This can be done precisely on a SLAT. None of this, however, is practical unless you have a sufficient number of joints to fashion in one setup.

In Chapter Five, I described a lap joint fixture for your table saw. This would be great for cutting the dovetail angles on the pins. Just set the saw blade or dado cutter to the proper angle, then stand the beam on end in the fixture. This should produce a high level of precision.

MORTISE AND TENON

A mortise and tenon is one of the strongest joints available. It is used more often in furniture than in yacht joinery, but you may find applications. This joint is a real test of your skills. There are many variations. See Figure 7-4. Parts A and B, for example, constitute a plain mortise and tenon. Some of these joints include wedges inserted into saw kerfs in the tenon. Some are pinned by a dowel. Others have an extended tenon through which a wedge is fitted. This is sometimes seen in yacht table construction.

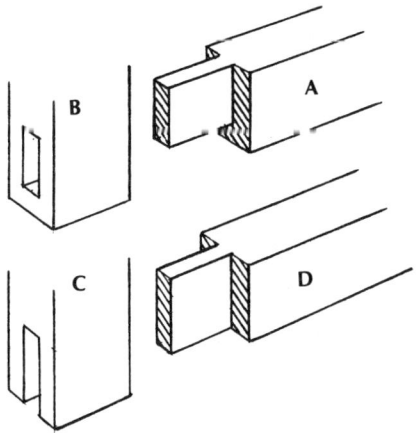

Figure 7-4. MORTISE AND TENON

An easier joint is the open mortise and tenon, parts C and D in Figure 7-4. Not being totally enclosed, this joint lacks some of the strength of the plain mortise and tenon, but it can be made on a table saw. The open mortise and tenon is excellent for supports for cabin soles, for transom berths, for hatch screens, and so on.

The plain mortise and tenon can be made by method A. First, you backsaw the tenon to knife marks. The mortise may then be cut out roughly by boring four or five holes with an auger or spur bit smaller than the width. The rectangular socket is then opened up with a thin, narrow chisel, working in from opposite sides of the opening. A wider chisel is best for cleaning up to the marks. Again, this is try and fit. When a fit is satisfactory, insert the tenon and mark and trim the shoulders to a square fit. Then finish off the exposed end of the tenon.

Routing, a method B, is commonly used to cut mortises, provided the machine's depth adjustment is sufficient for the bit to reach the bottom of the mortise. Extra depth can be gained by moving the bit out of the collet somewhat, but be sure it is locked securely. Clamp a piece on the side so the router has a wider base to ride on. Rocking will ruin the work. A rather deep guide must be attached accurately so the bit starts right on the line. It takes practice and skill to start and stop the slot within the end marks. A fast-turning drill press with a router bit simplifies this job, if you can keep the bit secure in the chuck. Vibration and high speed have a way of loosening bits. Clamp a fence to the drill press table and slide the work piece slowly the length required. Now that you have rounded ends in the mortise, round the tenon to fit.

The open mortise and tenon also may be made with a backsaw and chisel, but its design cries for a method C approach using a table saw. Start by adding an extension to your fence, a piece 6 to 8 inches high. Check the extension for squareness to the table. The work piece (D) for the tenon must be truly vertical when the cuts are made. Make both cuts in all your pieces right up to the line, then set the fence back that dimension and lower the blade so it just cuts out the piece to form a nice shoulder. The thicknesses of all tenons will be identical because they were made by rotating the work piece.

Now make the open-end mortise the same way. Practice on scrap, adjusting the fence as needed, until you get a snug fit on the tenon. Make all these cuts in sequence, resetting the fence once or twice so the multiple cuts remove all the material.

This entire joint can be made on a bandsaw using a temporary fence, but it is less likely to be accurate with smooth surfaces. Whether you use a table saw or a bandsaw, push the work through with a square block sliding along the fence to hold the piece vertical. And set up a feather or comb to hold it against the fence so it is vertical in both planes.

Both of the mortise-and-tenon joints should be glued, especially if screws would be visible. Coat the mortise with Aerolite and the tenon with catalyst. Clamp lightly.

DOWELED BUTT

A doweled butt is a form of mortise and tenon that eliminates the difficult hand work at a sacrifice of some strength. See Figure 7-5. It is a good joint for hatch screens, paneled doors, and so on. You'll need a drill press (for method C), because the holes must be precisely parallel and on center. The layout of the centers must be done with a knife, not a pencil. It is essential that the dowel holes in part B be drilled first, for drilling in end grain frequently causes wandering, unless you use a Forstner or machine spur bit. Never use a twist drill.

There are several ways in addition to a scribed layout to transfer center locations from B to A. The best is the use of dowel centers. These are button-like devices available in sets to fit several sizes of dowel holes. The dowel centers are inserted in one set of holes, then the parts are pressed together so the points make an impression in the opposite part. Try clamping both pieces flat and square on the saw table or a bench, then tap sharply with a mallet. Drill the holes about ¼ inch deeper than the length of the dowels so glue and air have somewhere to go.

There's another method for marking dowel centers. Grind the heads off brads, and then grind the ends to a sharp point. Next, drive another pair of brads or small nails into the dowel locations, leaving the heads out for easy removal. Remove these brads. Now insert the sharpened brads in these holes, leaving enough protruding to be grasped with pliers. Press the two parts into careful alignment so the sharpened brad tips press in just enough to make a center mark for your bit. (Don't press the pins below the surface of the wood. You'll never get them out.)

If you don't have a drill press, you can make a boring guide on the order of the one in Chapter Five. Or use a metal dowel jig, which is available wherever tools are sold at a cost of $15 and up.

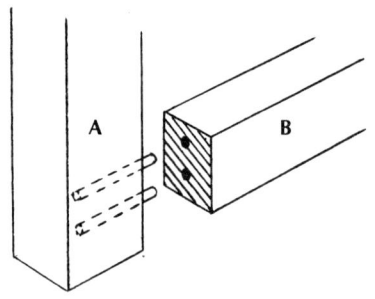

Figure 7-5. DOWELED BUTT

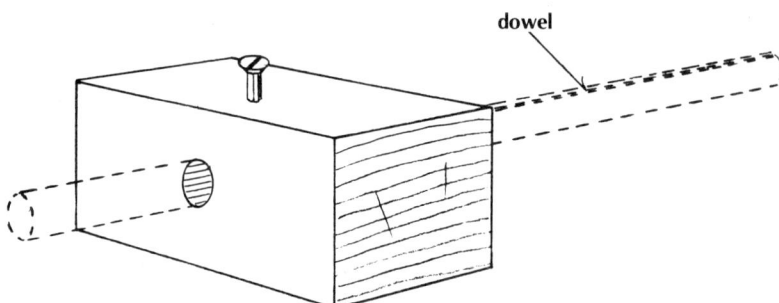

Figure 7-6. DOWEL GROOVE JIG

A third way is strictly method A. I have used it many times because it is fast and simple. Clamp the parts together exactly in position on a flat surface, then bore through part A into part B. This eliminates all the problems of surface matching, hole centering, boring alignment, and so on. In my opinion, the exposed ends of the dowels contrast nicely with mahogany, teak, or walnut, creating a pleasing effect.

You can make your own dowels, if you don't mind the effort required. Dowels must have a couple of grooves running full length so air and excess glue can escape. Otherwise, part B of the joint might split. You can build the simple grooving jig shown in Figure 7-6. Make the hole an easy fit for the dowel. Turn the screw until its point enters the bore in the block $1/16$ inch or better. Now just drive the dowel through two or three times so the screw scores grooves along its full length. Cut the dowel to length and chamfer one end on your belt sander or even a sheet of sandpaper on a bench.

But let's face it — ready-made dowels are perfect with their spiral grooves. You won't be using them by the hundreds, so save time and invest in what you need.

MITER JOINTS

Miter joints (Figure 7-7) are extremely weak in themselves. However, there are dozens of uses for them in yacht joinery where their neat appearance is desirable. Door frames, trim, and drawer fronts are examples. Miter joints are quite easy to make with a miter box and saw, preferably a miter or dovetail saw. This is method A. If trim goes around four sides of a door or its opening, the fits cannot be too long or too short. Miters must be clean and sharp, with no visible opening.

I cut the first piece about $1/32$ inch long; tape, tack, or clamp it in position; then try the corner with a short piece I call a fitting piece (Figure 7-8). Your first length can be reduced with a sharp block plane until the fitting piece meets the corner perfectly on both ends. You may need a right and a left fitting piece. Tape, brad, or clamp the first length in position. Start your second piece by placing the corner miters as they belong while you mark with a knife where the next miter is to be cut. Again cut slightly long in the miter box, unless you have a lot of confidence. Tape the second piece against the first at several points along its length, if needed, and again try the fitting piece. Trim off if needed. Once more, tape, brad, or clamp this piece to the door or drawer, or whatever.

Fit the third and fourth pieces in the same manner. When all the miters look perfect, glue and fasten everything in place permanently. I use pipe clamps if I can't use brads or finish nails, sometimes three or four across one face of the door, and as many across the other. It's possible to use nothing but tape, but be sure the joints are fully closed if you go this route. Tape and clamps work well together, and so do brads set in. The miter joint is a good place for Aerolite glue.

Method C uses your table saw miter gauge set at 45 degrees, or the miter gauge at 90 degrees and the blade set to 45 degrees. Using a SLAT on the table saw, however, is so superior in speed and accuracy, and also in its ability to take off $1/64$ inch, that it is the only way to go. See Chapter Five. You can tack 45-degree guides right on the sliding panel itself and get perfect joints.

There is a fine method B that uses your power handsaw. Remember the little portable table saw described in Chapter Five? For this mitering job, that saw will produce the same accuracy as a table saw, at the same speed. But with a simple SLAT, of course. So build one now.

Let me interject a couple of hints. Always use a cabinetmaker's combination blade to get a polished miter surface. Otherwise, the miter will absorb a lot of filler and stain that will show. Second, position the piece about to be sawed on the right- or left-hand guide so the edge you want to keep does not splinter. The blade must not go against the grain in the piece you keep. See Chapter Six on sabersawing a panel. The same rule applies.

SPLINED MITER

A splined miter is made and fitted in the same way as the plain miter, but the spline (Figure 7-9) adds greatly to

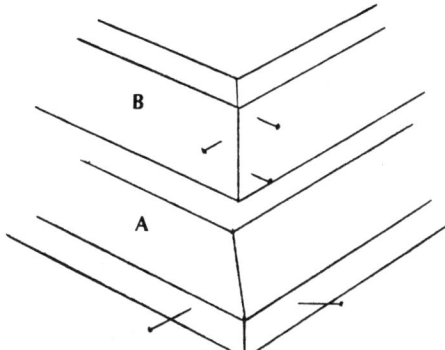

Figure 7-7. MITERED JOINT

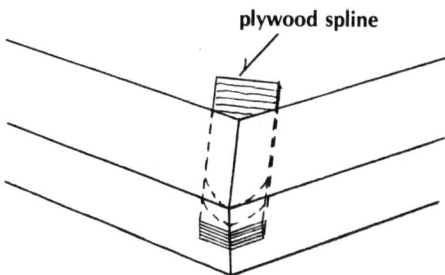

Figure 7-9. SPLINED MITER

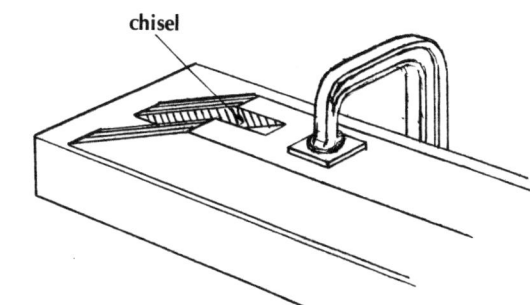

Figure 7-10. MITER SPLINE GROOVE

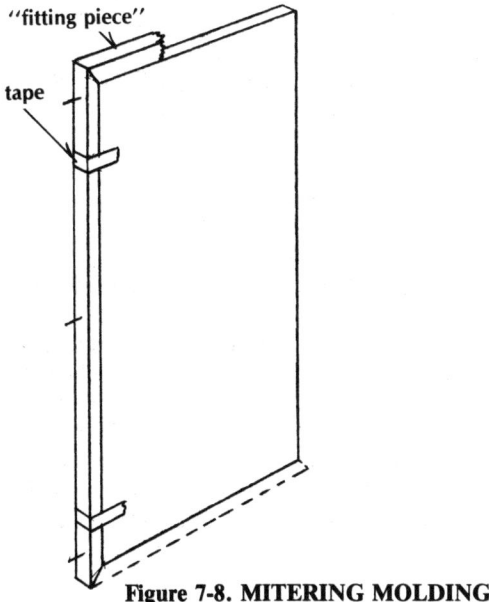

Figure 7-8. MITERING MOLDINGS

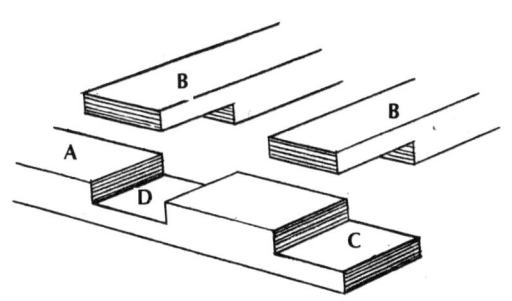

Figure 7-11. MIDDLE AND END HALF LAP

the joint's strength. While this is a time-consuming task, it should be done where there is a possibility of stress. For example, hatch screens might be wracked by careless stowing. The splined miter is one way to reinforce such structures. Also see the splined joint, which is described later in this chapter.

Method A is the same as for the plain miter. Then, after the miters are done, lay out a groove on the joint surfaces (¼ inch wide by ⅜ inch deep in ¾-inch stock). Use a dovetail or fine backsaw to saw to the full depth, then chisel out the material between the kerfs, as shown in Figure 7-10. There is a danger of splitting off a chip as the chisel approaches the thin end, so back up this edge by clamping it to a piece of scrap. Make the splines by sawing a ¾-inch strip off the end of a sheet of ¼-inch plywood. A plywood spline is less likely to split than a strip of wood. Fit the splines, cut the V on the inner ends, and let the outer ends protrude. Now assemble the entire rig with glue and pipe clamps. Check with a square as you go, and secure by tacking on a light diagonal. Weight the assembly on a flat bench or the floor to hold it flat.

The only method B I can suggest is to mold the grooves with a ¼-inch router bit. In method C the grooves are sawed or dadoed on a table saw.

LAP JOINTS OR HALF LAPS

End and middle laps are used frequently in yacht joinery. See Figure 7-11. The end lap is adequate as a substitute for the mortise and tenon, doweled butt, and mitered joints. The end lap is not as strong as the first two, and perhaps not as attractive as the miter. End and mid-lap joints would be excellent for supports for sole beams, settees, berths, and so on. The end lap will support a weight. If used in a frame, however, such as in hatch screens or in a paneled door, it would be entirely dependent on the glue for strength. The material thickness usually won't take mechanical fasteners.

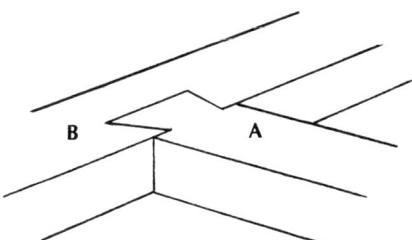

Figure 7-12. SINGLE DOVETAIL

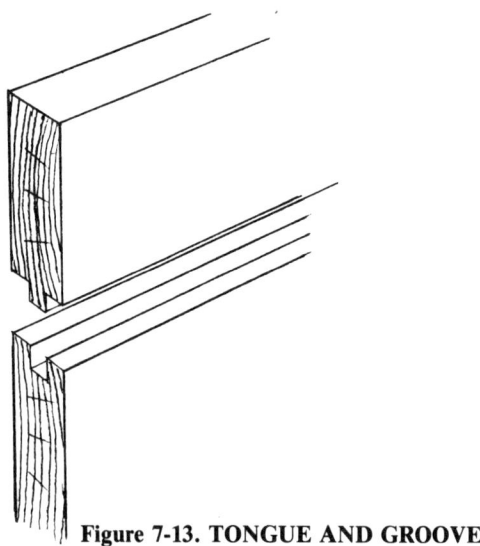

Figure 7-13. TONGUE AND GROOVE

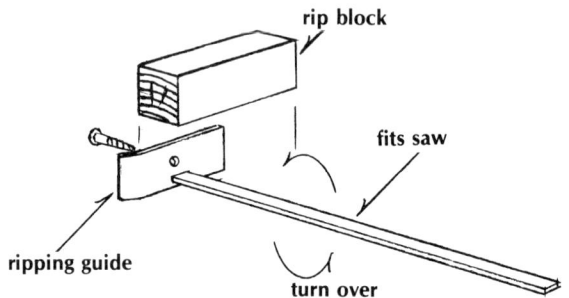

Figure 7-14. JIG FOR TONGUE AND GROOVE

there are two shoulders. See Figure 7-12. The joint is easy to make. In method A, the pin can be cut with a backsaw or dovetail saw; in method B, with a sabersaw; in method C, with a bandsaw. Pare the edges with a sharp chisel. Clamp the pin square on the part (B) to be dovetailed, and mark with a knife. Cut out and trim to fit part A. Secure with epoxy, Aerolite, or Plastic Resin glue. This joint is good under tensile stress.

TONGUE AND GROOVE

The tongue-and-groove joint (Figure 7-13) is used more and more these days because of the scarcity of wide lumber. It is used also to join pieces with alternating grain. This helps prevent warping. A wide structure such as a cabin side, if built of one width, would be subject to a lot of shrinkage and possibly even splitting. A tongue-and-groove joint here, however, would remain watertight even though the joint separated. Of course, this applies also to the splined joint (Figure 7-18). Tongue and groove is standard procedure for table-top construction if solid hardwood lumber is used. Such long joints can be doweled, as discussed earlier.

Any method A for building a tongue-and-groove joint is likely to be reminiscent of the 17th century. Even with a special combination rabbet plane, it would be an extremely laborious task. Modern rabbet (or filister) planes have matched tongue-and-groove sets, including blades and fences that adjust for the material thickness. You should have plenty of such work ahead of you to justify the purchase of such tools, for they are costly. Old-style wooden rabbet planes provide blades for tongue and groove. These must follow a guide such as a clamped-on straightedge. If the cost of such specialized tools does not suit you, try to make do with doweled joints.

Method B is less laborious but still primitive. First, you must pad the ripping guide of the power handsaw if it can't be adjusted close to the blade. This is done by screwing a small block 1 inch thick by about 2½ to 3 inches long to the T on the guide. (See Figure 7-14.)

Try the tongue cuts on scrap. Cut the side of the tongue first. Your saw will need a broad base to ride on, so clamp a 2 by 4 on one side, as shown in Figure 7-15. Use two if you don't feel confident. Make the second

Method A for these joints is a backsaw job. Mark with a knife and make repeated kerfs in the portion to be removed. Use paring strokes of the chisel, working in from both sides. Use care so that the mating pieces match up to make a smooth surface. Use Aerolite glue or Weldwood Plastic Resin. You can use five ¾-inch brads in a pattern if the stock is ¾ inch or more in thickness, or you can set the brads at an angle. Plugging over screws in a ⅜-inch thickness is too close for most craftsmen.

Method B is to cut repeated kerfs with your power handsaw after the square cuts, followed by cleanup with a chisel.

Method C is to cut the B parts and cutout C using the lap joint jig described in Chapter Five. Cutout D can be done on your table saw, using a SLAT, or with a miter gauge and repeated cuts, or with a dado set. Allow for fitting with a chisel if appearance is vital. Much of the cutting for this type of joint can be done on a bandsaw, with practice.

SINGLE DOVETAIL

A single dovetail is essentially the same as the dovetail butt joint, but the long dimensions are horizontal and

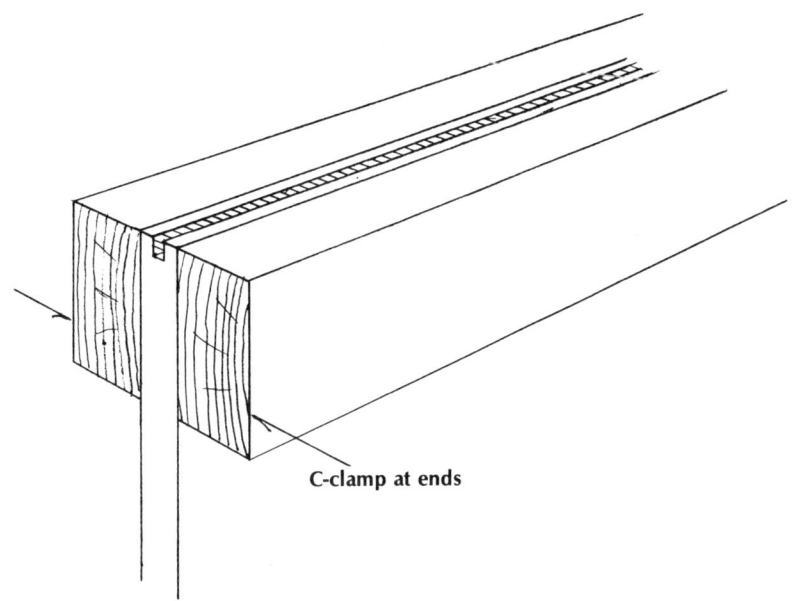

Figure 7-15. ONE OR TWO 2 x 4's MAKE BASE FOR SAW

cut to leave a tongue ¼ inch thick by about ⁷⁄₁₆ inch high. Cut steadily, for parallel sides are needed. Now lay the piece on its side and rip out the second dimension to form a ¼-inch by ⁷⁄₁₆-inch rabbet. Repeat on the opposite side.

To saw out the groove, repeat the 2 by 4 step, but make the depth a bit more than that of the tongue to allow space for glue and air. Experiment on scrap. The tongue should slip without pressure.

Another method B uses a ¼-inch router bit and a guide attached to the sole plate. You can make both the tongue and the groove this way. In addition, you may use router tongue-and-groove bits or glue joint bits, if desired. To do this, you will need a router-shaper table, as described in Chapter Five.

Method C, the table-saw approach, offers several ways to go. First, you can get by with any reasonably fine-toothed blade and a tall fence attachment. Flip the piece end for end so the tongue will be centered. Do the groove the same way. Be sure to make these cuts on scrap first, so they fit. Second, you can set up a dado cutter for a ¼-inch groove, and take out both the shoulders of the tongue and the groove itself. The third way is the best. It uses a molding head with matching tongue-and-groove or glue joint blade. In all of these methods, be sure to use a comb hold-down to keep the piece against the fence.

The ultimate method C is to form with a shaper, using matched cutters. These can be found at most tool shops. These cutters are not cheap, so be sure you have plenty of work ahead of you before buying. If you build a shaper table for your router, you'll get the same results. This kind of molding requires only a straight fence, or you can shape against a collar. If your tool inventory includes a head and set of molding cutters for your table saw, a third good method is available to you. With these tools too, be sure to use adequate hold-downs so the grooves don't wander.

Long pieces joined lengthwise have two characteristics you should be aware of. They warp and tend to open up at the end of the joint as the pieces shrink. The answer to the first problem is alternating the grain, as shown in Figure 7-16. This is mandatory if the pieces already show warping. The second problem is solved by planing the edges so they meet evenly full length, as shown in Figure 7-17. You then take off a couple of shavings so the ends close up first. Thus, the pieces are able to shrink slightly without showing an open joint. The drawing shows an example of clamping. In practice, you would need three or four clamps, rather than just one. The clamps should be alternated. The crosswise pieces shown keep the assembly from buckling. Thus, there should be one on each side, like the bread of a sandwich.

If you are using plywood, all of this is unnecessary. Two good plywood remnants, however, can be joined by tongue and groove or splines. The gap procedure described above can be skipped, for plywood is dimensionally stable.

SPLINED JOINT

There are other methods for forming good tongue-and-groove joints, but the complexity and cost of tools lead one to a simpler joint. The splined joint (Figure 7-18) has all the strength of a true tongue and groove, yet it can be made in a few minutes with a rabbet plane, a

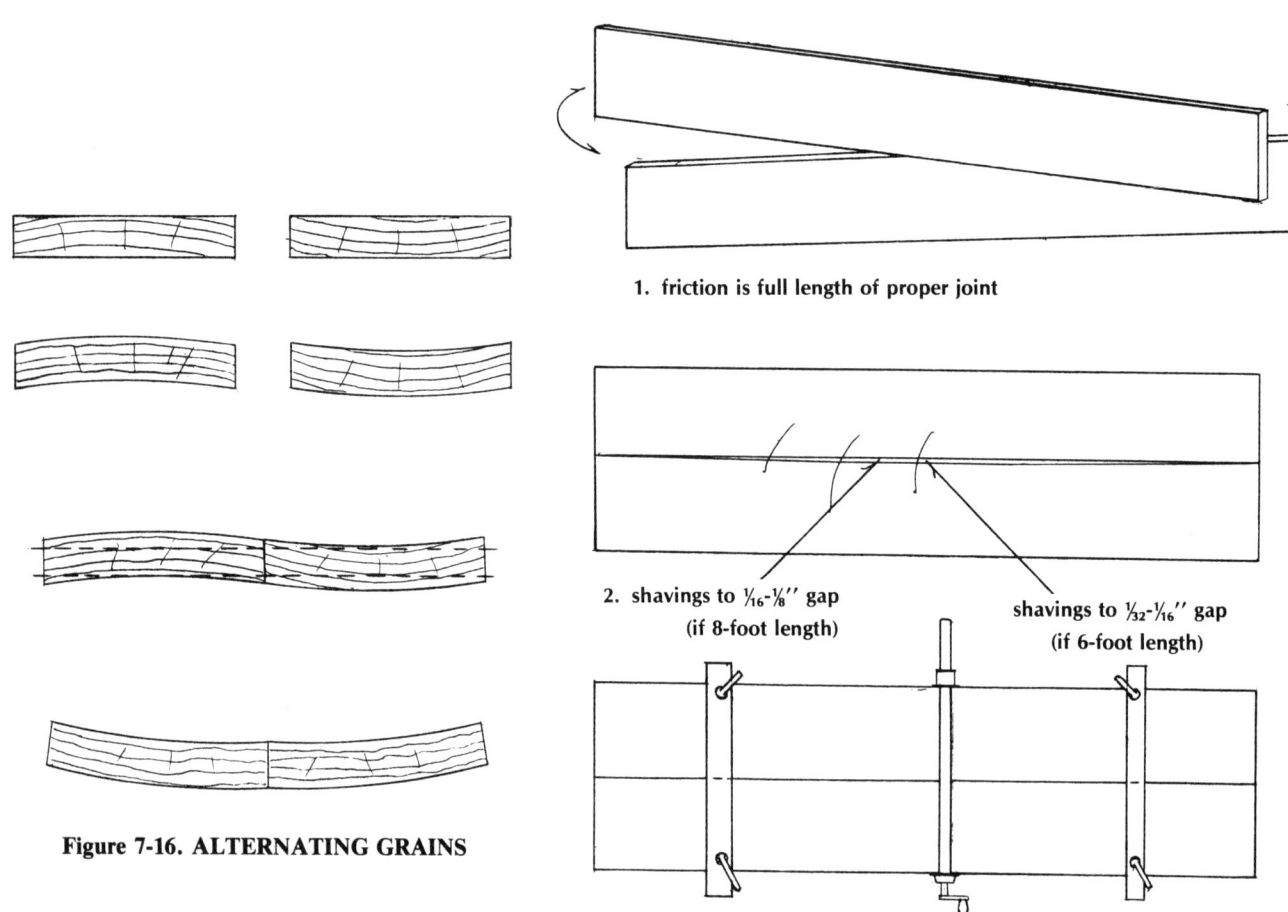

Figure 7-16. ALTERNATING GRAINS

Figure 7-17. LONG PIECES JOINED LENGTHWISE

power saw, a table saw with a regular blade, or a dado set. You don't need a router or a shaper. Another advantage of the spline is that the groove and spline need not be visible at the finished ends of the joints. You simply stop the planing, sawing, or dadoing before the tool reaches the end of the work piece. This produces a blind groove, as shown in Figure 7-19. A ¼-inch spline is fitted in and glued with Plastic Resin or Aerolite glue, then the opposite groove and surfaces are coated in the same way. Pull the assembly together with bar or pipe clamps.

Similarly, the use of a spline can make a miter joint quite strong. In a wide joint — say, for a panel door — the groove can be blind.

RABBETED CORNER

Bulkhead corners and others, such as on dressers, lockers, and so on, in a yacht must have strength. A body can be thrown about a bit on occasion in a vessel. If this projectile meets a stationary object, both might be wrecked. The basic corner (Figure 7-20) is rabbeted and glued and screwed or nailed. (Later I will describe a more involved type of construction in corner posts.) The procedures for rabbeting are similar to those for tongue-and-groove joints, but because of the large sizes you might have to handle, working on a table saw is just about out of the question.

The rabbet can be made by a method B using a power handsaw with a rip guide. To cut surface A parallel to the sides of the plywood, clamp on a straight 2 by 4 so the saw has a reasonable platform to run on without wobbling. Surface B is no problem, but accurate setting counts. Another method B is making a couple of passes with your router rabbet bit. To ensure a nice clean edge on B, score a knife cut to eliminate splintering. Fasten the joint with Aerolite and galvanized finish nails. If the corner is not covered by a hardwood molding, round it with a router after installation, but be sure the nails are set in sufficiently. Alternatively, you can hand plane the radius before installation.

GLUE BLOCK CORNER

This joint (Figure 7-21) does about the same job and forms a structure equally as strong as the rabbeted cor-

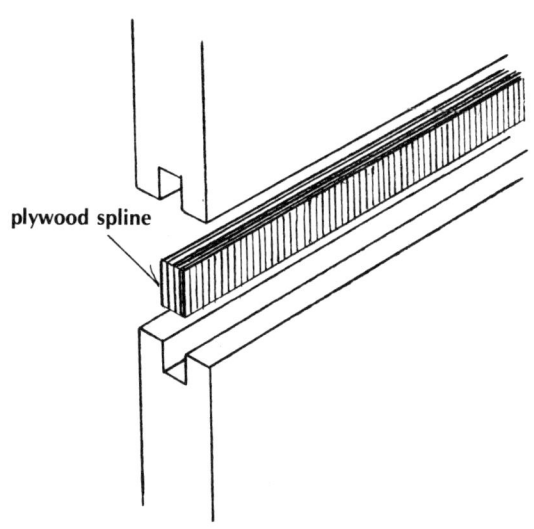

Figure 7-18. SPLINED JOINT

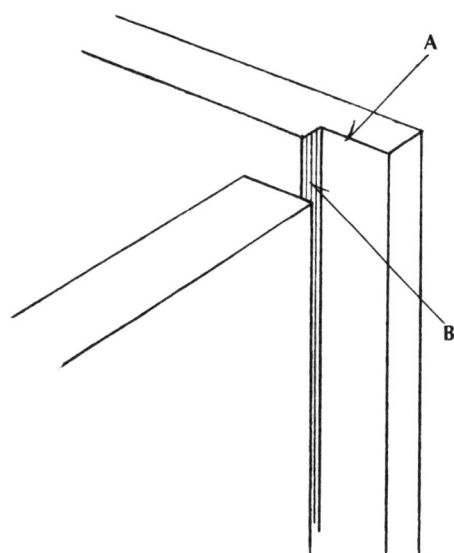

Figure 7-20. RABBETED CORNER

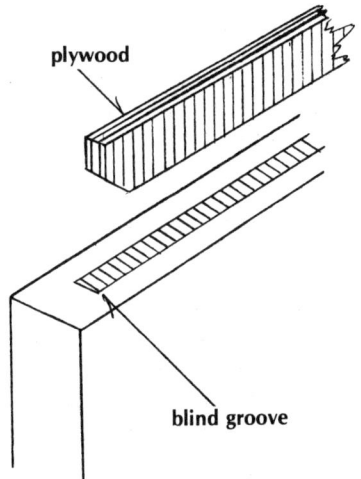

Figure 7-19. BLIND GROOVE

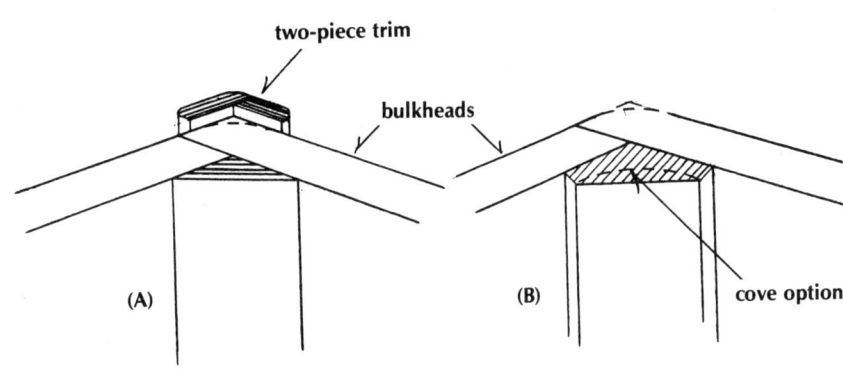

Figure 7-21. GLUE BLOCK CORNERS

ner. The block may be of mahogany or teak. It increases the effective gluing surface 100 percent or more, depending on the size of the piece. There is no method A, unless you are masochistic enough to want to rip out the block with a handsaw. With your table saw set to 45 degrees, it's a cinch. The appearance and strength of the glue block can be improved by cutting off the corners of a rectangular piece, as in Figure 7-21(B). Use Aerolite or Plastic Resin glue, and finish nails or screws driven from the outside of the bulkhead. Or fasten from the inside with bunged-over screws.

The outer corner looks best if covered with a corner molding of mahogany or teak. A spartan yacht, however, can have the sharp corner routed to about ½-inch radius. A rabbeted joint backed up by a glue block is considerably stronger. A third option is to miter the plywood panels, but this is not an easy task in lengths greater than six feet. Such a miter can be done successfully with a power handsaw and a clamp-on guide, or on the table saw or radial-arm saw if the panels are held down flat while cutting the miter. Any slight upward flexing will cause the mitered edge to wander. I have used weights and an assistant with satisfactory results.

RABBET BLOCK CORNER

This joint is deluxe construction, and very strong. Figure 7-22 shows a two-piece option with the rounded outer corner fitted after the inner piece is glued and screwed. Actually, while this saves a bit of material, the one-piece block is easy because the two rabbets can be sawed or dadoed out in minutes on a table saw. These could be fashioned with a power handsaw, a method B, and, of course, laboriously with a rabbet plane in a method A. Be sure to allow ample room for the bulkheads and plenty of stock for screws into the rabbets, or

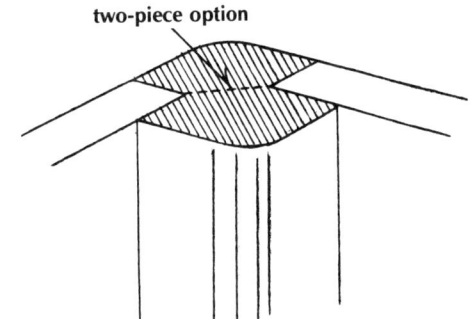

Figure 7-22. RABBET BLOCK CORNER

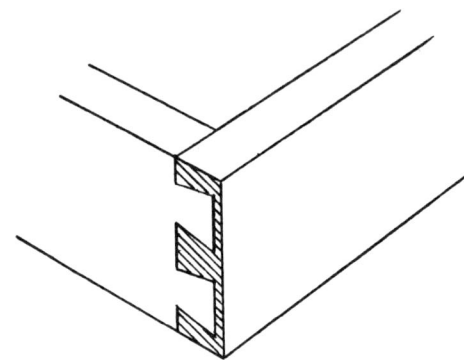

Figure 7-24. "SECRET" OR "BLIND" DOVETAIL JOINT

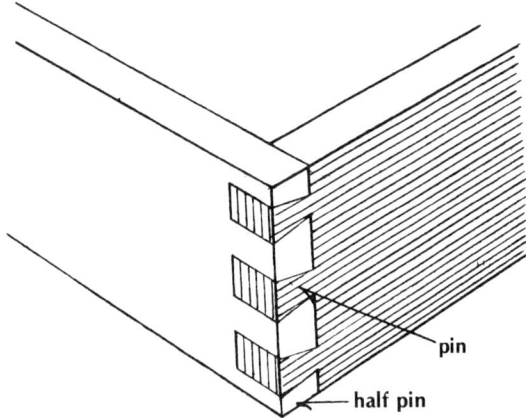

Figure 7-23. DOVETAILED CORNER

a split could result. A nice touch is to make the rabbet ⅛ inch deeper than the material thickness, so the corner block stands out from the bulkhead. Finished bright, this makes a very handsome corner.

DOVETAILED CORNER

This joint (Figure 7-23) is extremely strong because of the wedge effect of the pins locked into sockets (the dovetails or mortises). Slamming drawers full of heavy stuff quickly destroys most other joints, but not the dovetailed corner. This is a very difficult joint to make, however.

The first step is to divide off the height of the drawer (or box) into a number of dovetails. Let's assume this front will be covered by an attractive overlay. If the front and sides are ½-inch material, mark the dovetails with a knife, ¼ inch wide at the thin end and ⁷⁄₁₆ inch wide at the outer end on the side pieces. The material left over at the top and bottom is called a half pin. In fine furniture, the pins are sometimes very narrow. For our purposes, however, the base of the pins should not be less than ¼ inch wide.

For method A, you'll need a fine backsaw or dovetail saw, ¼- and ½-inch chisels, a light mallet, and, of course, a bevel square. Saw the angled sides in the dovetails and random kerfs in between, but stay within the knife cut! Chisel out to the lines, paring off the sides until you "split the line." Be sure the socket ends are square and clean. Now clamp the side against the front and mark around all the pins. Put an X in each. Repeat the sawing and chiseling as above. Try for fit and pare off any small corrections. Use Aerolite or any epoxy or Plastic Resin glue. If you choose to make many dovetails by hand, I suggest that you make an aluminum sheet-metal template.

Method C, using a bandsaw for the picky sawing, would save much time. Tilt the table to cut the pins. Method B, using a dovetail fixture and router, might be satisfactory, but I can't recommend it fully. Several companies manufacture jigs and templates for a special router dovetail bit and guide bushing that follow the form with both pieces clamped together in the device. It takes about 20 seconds to dovetail both. See Figure 3-19.

Dovetail fixtures are available to accommodate various thicknesses of material. One at about $40 to $60 handles stock from ⁷⁄₁₆ inch to over 1 inch thick and up to 12 inches wide. A lower-cost model sells for about $30 and dovetails stock from ¼ to ½ inch thick, and up to 8 inches wide. The necessary bushings for the router are included, but the special dovetail bit is extra. I have used one of the smaller fixtures with success, but I have also ruined some work because the instructions were confusing. Practice for a few hours on cheap scrap. Once you have it down pat, you can dovetail both parts literally in seconds.

An interesting feature is that the dovetail fixture allows you to fashion secret or blind dovetails (Figure 7-24). Such a dovetailed drawer front does not have to be covered by a false front. Thus, it can be fitted flush with the cabinet face. In Chapter Twelve I describe several other ways to build drawers. You don't really have to learn to dovetail with your eyes closed.

To learn more about the different types of dovetails, read *How to Work with Tools and Wood,* mentioned at the beginning of this chapter.

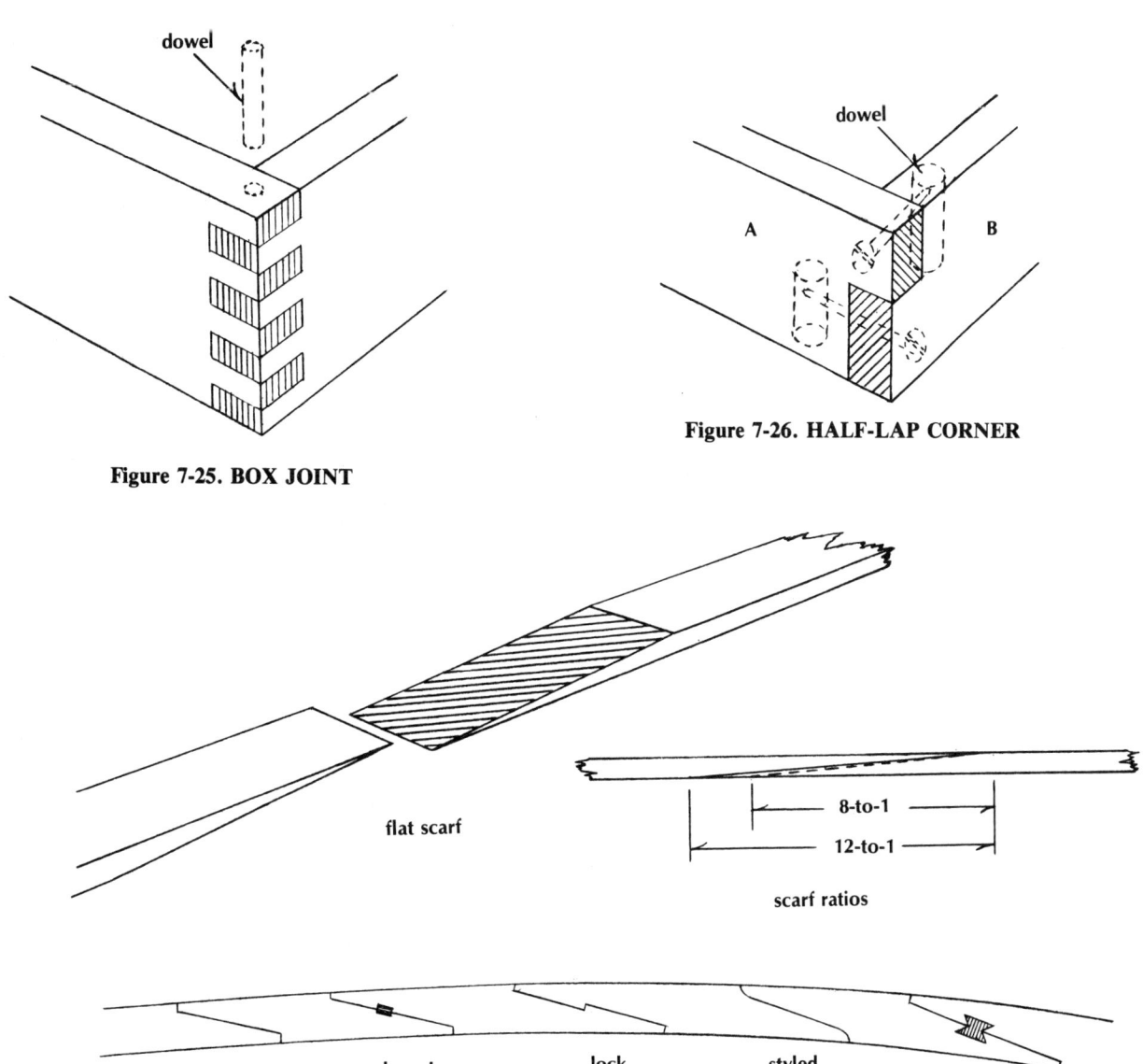

Figure 7-25. BOX JOINT

Figure 7-26. HALF-LAP CORNER

Figure 7-27. RAIL, COVERING BOARD, AND FLAT SCARFS

BOX JOINT

This strong, simple joint (Figure 7-25) was described in Chapter Five, together with detailed instructions for building a jig to produce it. In Chapter Thirteen you'll find a photograph of a beautiful example of box joints in a deck storage box.

I can't understand why anyone would try to make this joint with hand tools. Dovetails are only slightly more difficult. So there is no method A or B. The section in Chapter Five mentioned above covers very thoroughly method C, using a table saw and dado set, so there's no point in repeating it.

HALF-LAP CORNER

The corners of hatch coamings and hatch frames quite frequently are made with half-lap joints. See Figure 7-26. Keeping such joints from working as a result of expansion and contraction of the parts is difficult. A screw into end grain does not hold well, and a single screw down into good grain is inadequate.

The half-lap joint is used by furniture and cabinet builders. I see no reason why it should not be used in yacht joinery. Moreover, it is not as difficult to make as the sketch makes it appear. As shown, the whole frame or coaming would be assembled, completely fastened, and then installed. The dowel in part A, however, could be bored for and inserted from the top so the coaming could be assembled right on the deck. (I have not shown an additional screw that is driven from the top of A into the lower lap of B.) Screws passing into or through the hardwood dowels will draw up tight and stay that way. Use epoxy, Plastic Resin, or Aerolite glue.

SCARFS

This section will be brief, for a router scarfing jig is described in Chapter Five. See Figures 5-34, 5-35. The principal purpose of this type of scarf is to join short lengths of good material to make a longer piece, such as a stave for a hollow box spar. The shortage of Sitka spruce for spars makes a knowledge of this process mandatory. There is no method A, for no man in his right mind would saw out a 10-to-1 or 12-to-1 scarf and plane it to the paper-thin feather edge needed. There is a fine method B, so why ask for more?

A method B using a router allows the construction of scarfs that join short lengths around a curve. Two examples are covering boards and rail caps (Figure 7-27). These joints must be very strong, for the topsides of a vessel sometimes receive stresses, even blows, that strain the frames and clamps inside the hull. A covering board must be strong enough to absorb such stresses, yet flexible enough to yield without splitting and still return to its original close fit. Many such scarfs are hooked or locked together. See Chapter Fourteen.

EIGHT

Tying It All Together

Unless they are somehow held to their designed shapes beforehand, all fiberglass hulls and many plank-on-frame ones go as limp as a handful of spaghetti when their mold sections are removed. Glass hulls from a female mold have several bulkheads glassed in to hold the hull's lines. Both conventional and laminated wooden hulls present no problem. In the former, cross spalls and diagonals can be fastened athwartships from frame to frame and bulkheads built right in as the mold sections are removed. Laminated hulls often have bulkheads as part of the mold.

RECEIVING CRADLES

One-off glass and foam-sandwich hulls require special treatment. In both types, if you wish to preserve the major part of the mold and will not be installing bulkheads, you have to provide a receiving cradle. See Figure 8-1. There are two ways to go. Tear out some of the mold ribbands and glass in diagonals or cross spalls at two or three favorable locations. Then turn the hull and place it in a receiving cradle fitted and padded to the hull. Or fit the cradle, as shown in Figure 8-1, and turn. Another way is to build a receiving cradle on the inverted hull, including the carpet padding, and then drive screws from the inside into the plywood or lumber of the cradle. Use large washers. Actually, there isn't much stress, because the hull is held to its shape by the mold while being turned over.

If you plan to save the mold, lift it out with a crane or chain falls. If you insist on pulling the inverted hull off the mold without cross spalls and diagonals, don't depend on the screws to lift it. Use at least four hydraulic jacks to break it loose, and don't let one jack get ahead of the others. Once loose, the hull may be lifted by glassed-in iron rings or chain on the keel. It's not good practice to lift the hull or break it loose by tugging on the receiving cradle. That puts a lot of stress on the screws. If you decide against a crane and your beams won't support a chain fall, you can roll the hull and cradle on a couple of rows of tires for padding.

What you've just read is far beyond the scope of a joinery book. There is, however, a fine section on turning hulls in Bruce Bingham's book *Ferro-Cement Design, Techniques and Application*. About 98 percent applies to any kind of hull. Bingham describes in detail the rolling sling and rolling wheel methods.

AN IN-HULL SCAFFOLD

I've tried laying loose timbers, planks, and plywood in deep wineglass hulls, but it's not worth the time. In-

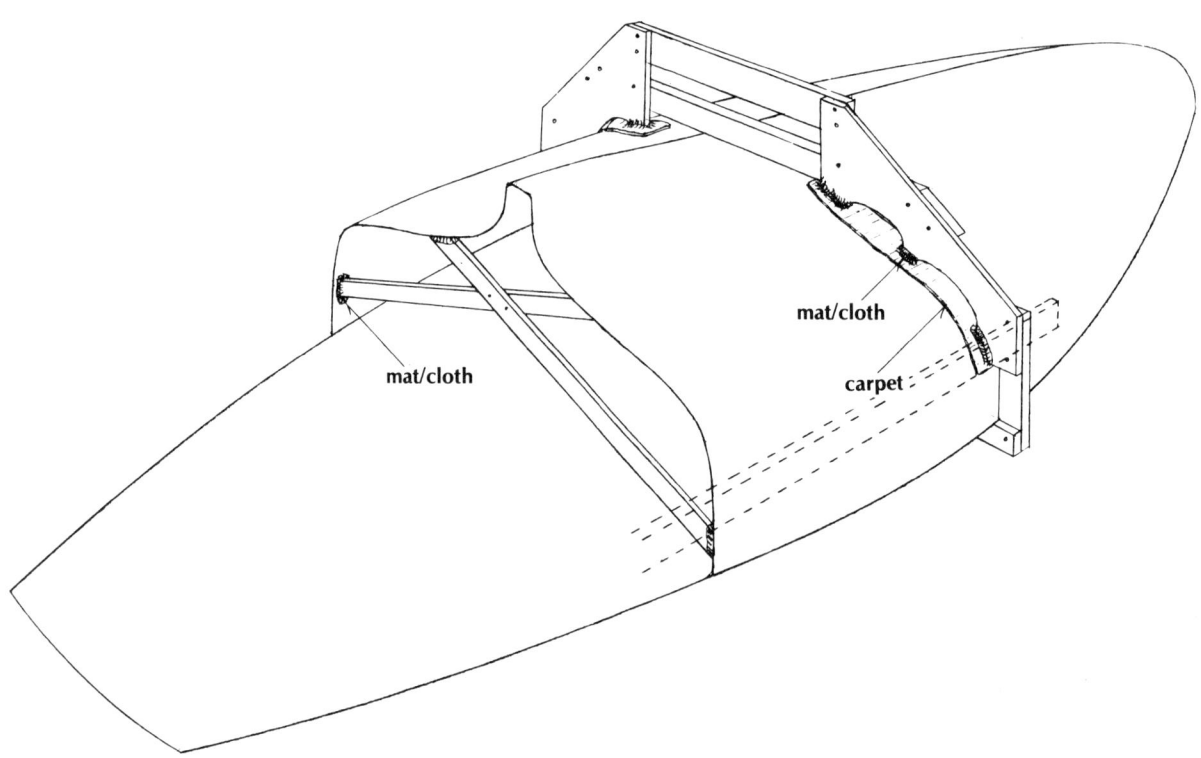

Figure 8-1. RECEIVING CRADLE FOR FIBERGLASS OR AIREX HULL

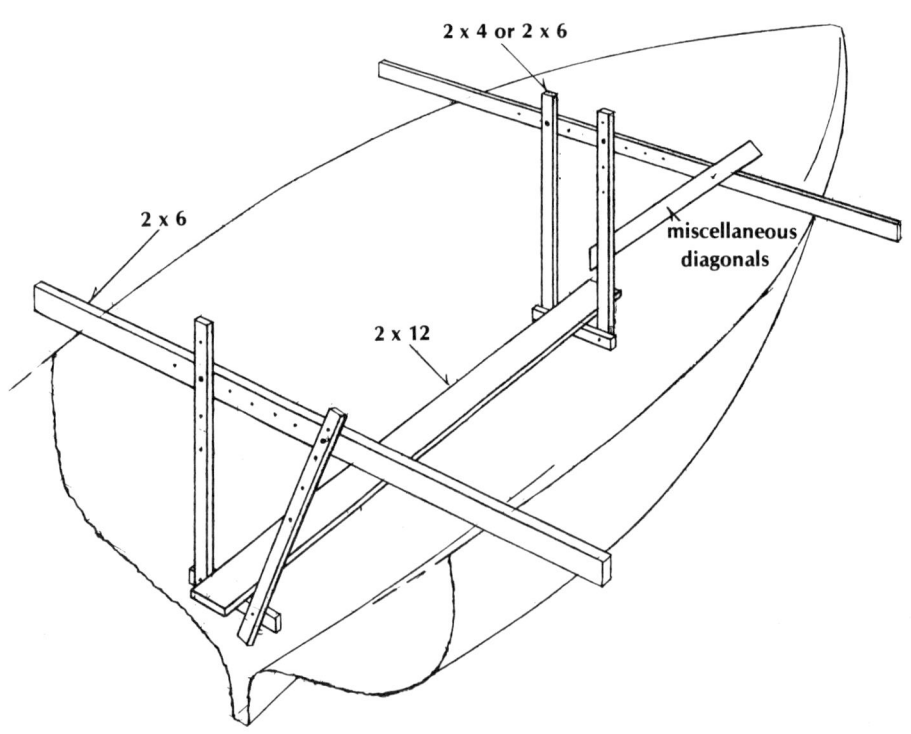

Figure 8-2. ADJUSTABLE IN-HULL SCAFFOLD

stead, hang a scaffold from the sheer as shown in Figure 8-2. Make the vertical 2 by 4's long enough to reach into the keel cavity, and bore plenty of bolt holes for vertical adjustments. The 2 by 4's or 2 by 6's on which your planks rest should be short so they can be placed low in the hull. Nail longer pieces on top of these when you have to reach out to the greater width of the hull. When installing a bulkhead, place this rig a foot or so away. This will let you sit on the plank end and/or work down in the bilge without hanging by your tail.

WHICH COMES FIRST, SOLE OR BULKHEAD?

Some designers prefer to erect bulkheads on top of a continuous cabin sole. This makes everything easier and faster, and permits alterations in the future. Other designers, however, value the strength of bulkheads extending right down to the keel timber or bonded into the fiberglass or ferrocement hull all the way to the covering over the ballast. If your hull is built on the cold-molded or laminated system, the bulkheads may be part of the mold, with the laminated planking built up on top. Even in this system, however, partial bulkheads may be installed later.

Your first step is to provide a positive location at the sheer batten or clamp. Nail together a straight 2 by 4 and a 1 by 6 to form an L-shaped beam. Nail or clamp this across the hull on the bulkhead marks as lifted from your lofting. Or, so many inches from station such-and-such. Use a plumb bob or a level and straightedge to find the position of the bulkhead at the turn of the bilge and on the keel timber. Make four or five marks. If your hull is wood, tack three or four blocks against these marks on each side of the hull. See Figure 8-3. If the hull is glass or cement, bond these blocks lightly. They'll be chopped off later.

The Tick Stick Method

Don't fool around with dividers or scribers to shape the bulkheads. Find a straight piece of plywood that reaches from the keel to the top of the cabin trunk. The width of this piece should be sufficient to come within 12 to 18 inches of the hull when the inboard edge is placed vertically on the bulkhead location. If necessary, hack off a corner or two so it will enter the bilge area, as shown in Figure 8-3. Tack or clamp this tick board to the locating girder and to a block low in the hull or on the keel.

Now for the tick stick. This can be a straight 1 by 1 long enough to reach from about the center of the tick board to the hull. Cut one end to a sharp angle. Hacksaw two nicks to hold a pencil point. You make the ticks by holding the stick firmly against the board with the sharp tip touching the hull, shelf, clamp, bilge stringer, and so on, down the surface to the keel. Mark along the side of the stick and tick your pencil point in the nick and at the inner end of the stick. The more tick marks the better. If your stick is too long for some areas, just use the second nick. Mark on the board its position relative to the centerline of the hull. Now it is a simple job to transfer these ticks to your plywood bulkhead material or pattern. Be sure to leave ample room above the sheer for later shaping of the cabin trunk.

Full-Width Bulkhead

Most of the preceding instructions apply to partial bulkheads. For a full-width bulkhead, set up a tick board to port first, then to starboard, positioning it relative to the centerline. Or you can use a wide board or two cleated together to pick up all the ticks simultaneously. Before ruining good material, make a pattern of cheap plywood, transfer the marks, connect them with a flexible batten, and cut out with a sabersaw. If your hull is accurate, there will be small differences only. If the differences are greater than 1 inch from the lofted shape, you no longer have the lines designed for the hull.

The bulkhead can be built of two thicknesses, perhaps fir plywood on one side and teak plywood on the other. To save this precious material, be very careful when fitting the template or pattern around the intricate clamp and bilge stringer areas. Drop or swing it into place against the locating blocks. You'll see immediately where it is too fat or too thin. Saw, plane, or grind away until the template fits accurately. If this is one-half of a full bulkhead, leave the template in place and fit another to it and to the other side of the hull. Nail substantial 1 by 4 or 1 by 6 cleats across the two sides. If necessary, pull nails to remove the template from the hull, then replace the nails, lay the template on the bulkhead material, mark, and saw out.

It may be necessary once again to insert the bulkhead against the blocks in two pieces, joining them after positioning. There's always a smarty who suggests that we could have just made the starboard template and flopped it over to make the port side, thus saving a lot of work. The two sides of a hull, however, are never truly identical. If you want to sleep soundly, don't even think about this, because the differences will probably shock you. The point is that while the sides vary slightly, each one is fair and the "slow" side always seems to keep up with the "fast" side.

These large pieces of template material, of course, can be used for fitting the smaller bulkheads. This applies to the tick boards, too, so there is little waste.

Laminated Bulkheads

Many designers prefer to use a double thickness of plywood for bulkheads. Obviously, it takes no time to

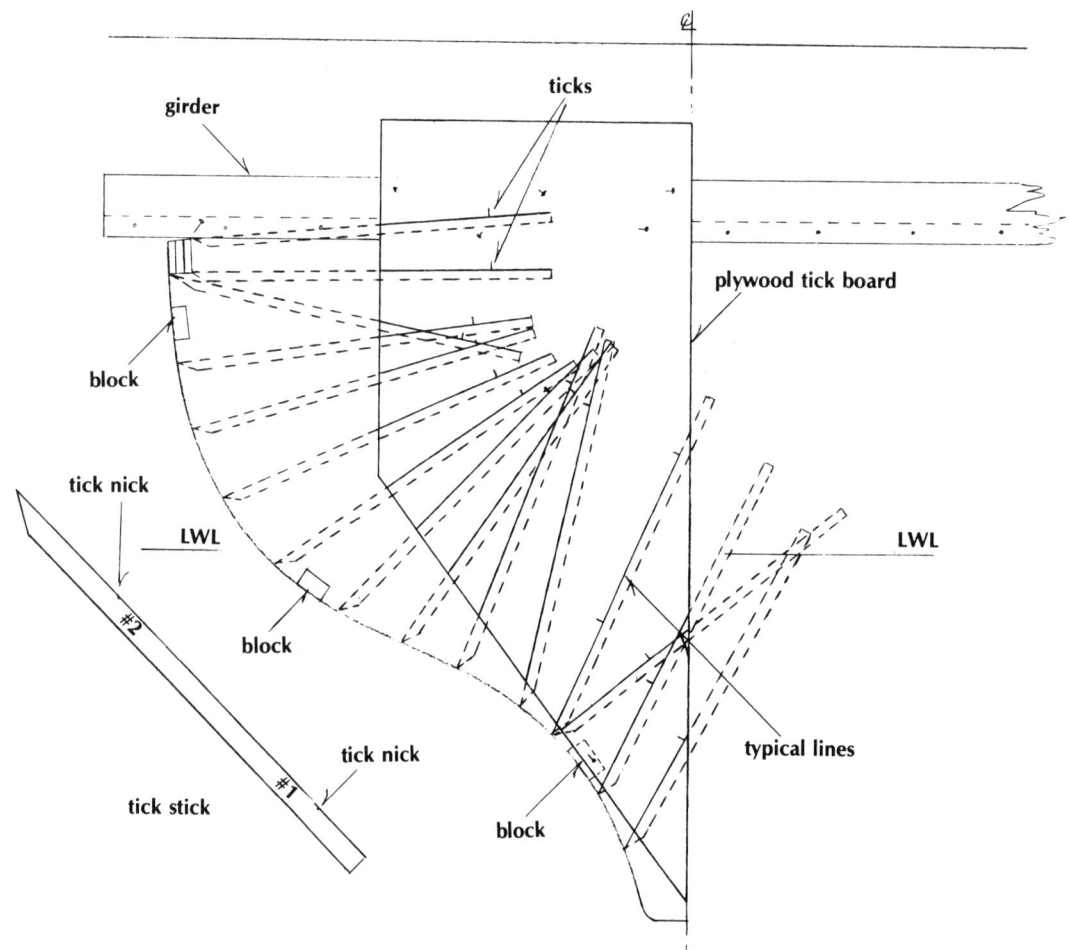

Figure 8-3. BULKHEAD FITTING WITH TICK STICK

make a second thickness from the first, allowing for the tapering of the hull. However, lay out the second lamination so the joints overlap the joints in the first thickness by about 4 inches. Shift the pieces around so you don't have to saw out large door openings (Figure 8-4). Do not permit joints to form a cross. Brad the two laminations together, making sure that all joints are snug. When you are satisfied with the fits, lay down a sheet of polyethylene plastic so your glue won't bond the whole thing to the floor.

At this point, you have a decision to make. Can the entire bulkhead be located in the hull in one piece, or must it be joined after it is in position? The assembly may be very heavy, and there will be interference from the clamp and bilge stringer in your wooden hull. If the two templates cleated together can be horsed into position, you can assume that the lamination will go in. If some of the locating blocks are in the way, knock them out. If there's no way to fit the entire bulkhead in, just plan to join the pieces at a convenient spot. We'll discuss fastening the pieces later on. Let's make it in two parts.

Coat the joining edges with Plastic Resin or epoxy adhesive. Hold the parts together by nailing blocks around the perimeter of the bulkhead. Since this is a two-piece bulkhead, do *not* coat those edges and overlaps that make the final assembly joint after the parts are in the hull. You can tape plastic strips to those spots to be safe. Now pour cups of the adhesive here and there and spread it evenly, preferably with the type of serrated tool used to glue down floor coverings. Work fast, especially in sunlight. Presaturate the panel with penetrating-type resin if using epoxy.

Next, coat the edges of the second lamination piece (also presaturated) and lay these on the first panels. Fasten with a dozen brads so nothing can shift, and wipe away all excess glue. The entire assembly must now be weighted down with as many concrete blocks as you can crowd on top. The weight will force the glue out through the joints, so stand by to wipe it up. It may be necessary to fasten the piece with four-penny nails and blocks here and there. Be sure to put bits of plastic under the blocks. The two halves of the bulkhead should lift up easily in about 24 hours.

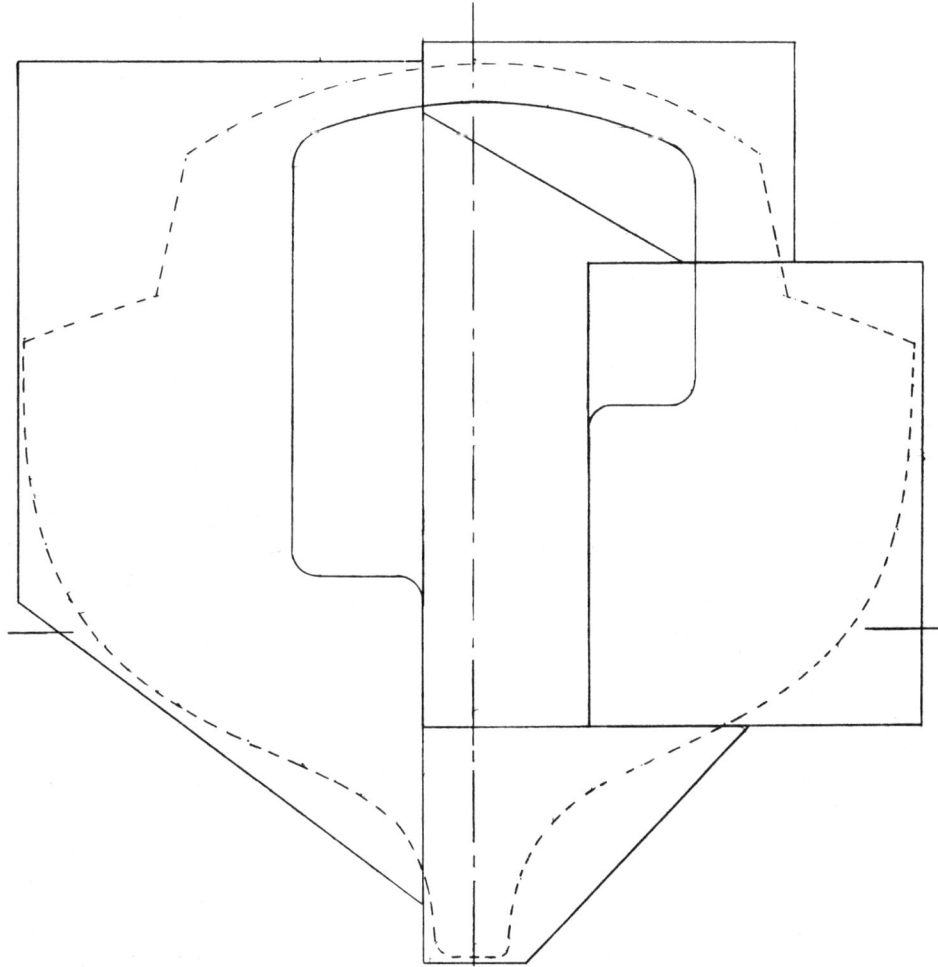

Figure 8-4. TYPICAL LAMINATED BULKHEAD PANEL LAYOUT

The matter of excess glue is extremely important. If you are laminating costly material such as marine teak or mahogany plywood, you'll have to be careful. The glue must be spread carefully, with no excess. Do not glue the joining edges, unless you are prepared to clean up small dabs immediately with a damp sponge or rag. Glue in the grain can cause permanent disfigurement — a spot that will not take stain. If in doubt, try applying masking tape along the surfaces next to joining edges. Aerolite glue cleans up with water before it cures and it can be removed completely if thoroughly wet. This is costly for large areas, however. Experiment with scraps, if you can, and glue up one or two of the small bulkheads first, just for practice.

Joining Bulkheads

You have tried the two parts for successful fit at the hull and at the inner joint. This may or may not be on the centerline. Have on hand a long pipe clamp, about six C-clamps, two 2 by 4's, and the necessary glue (Plastic Resin or Aerolite). Apply the glue to the part clamped in position to the girder. Place the second part in position and quickly and lightly C-clamp the joint, using long blocks over pieces of plastic to flatten and protect the plywood. Now place the 2 by 4's across from side to side, and C-clamp at the opening so the assembly is rigid. Position the pipe clamp athwartships so it pulls the joint closed. Move the C-clamps and blocks so you can see that the joint is flush and smooth on both sides. This is where a careful laminating job shows up.

If you want to play safe, you can drive flathead screws from the side you don't care too much about. Space the screws vertically about 4 inches apart in two rows. The points must not come through on the good side. Actually, these short screws may help to pull the laminations together and hold the parts securely until the glue is cured. In themselves, however, they do not add much strength because the threads have little to hold to. Years ago, when building plywood boats, I placed many small bolts through plywood butt blocks and planking. These were removed in some cases after the glue cured. Often we used brass or bronze stove bolts or flathead machine screws that stayed in the hull. I never had such a butt fail or be detectable from the exterior after finishing. Your joint, too, should remain invisible from one side.

BULKHEAD-TO-HULL FASTENING

If the designer of your wooden hull specified fastening the bulkhead to the side of a frame, you can do it by simply driving screws. I assume the frame is straight, so this will place no strain on planking fastenings. If the frame isn't straight, shim under the screw area. The next stronger method is the addition of a layer of mat and cloth and polyester resin in between. Figures 8-5 and 8-6 show several variations for most hull types, including a situation in which the bulkhead lands on a frame. These bonding systems all call for large fillets (formed with a bottle, glass, or large spoon) composed of a mush of chopped mat, or microballoons, or Cab-O-Sil covered by neat strips of mat, with cloth tape over that.

The beveled edge is generally quite strong, but the routed rabbeted corner permits a flush finish and better appearance. To make these bevels in a hurry, rent a high-speed disc sander, put on one of those extra-coarse discs that look like gravel and just eat away the plywood. This leaves a rough surface that is best for bonding.

You can combine any of these ideas, of course. Don't overlook the Airex foam pad shown against a fiberglass hull. This, however, can be shaped from ¾-inch plywood and kerfed. It forms a more positive anchor than the foam sandwich. I strongly advise that you use only epoxy glue and/or mat between the pad and the hull. There should be a strip of mat between the bulkhead and the pad also. A rabbet is an unnecessary refinement here, if you don't mind the look of glass tape all around the bulkhead.

Anyway, all this mess should be covered by a nice mahogany or teak frame that follows the contour of the hull. Need I suggest that you study one of the excellent references on fiberglassing procedures? Note also that epoxy is always preferable to Plastic Resin for bonding anything to wood.

Don't forget that such methods, or even simpler modifications, should be used to bond smaller partial bulkheads, and also such horizontal members as berth and counter tops, long bookshelves, and so on. These become structural and contribute substantially to the strength of a hull, especially hulls of light fiberglass, wood laminations, or foam-sandwich designs. Horizontal bonding is difficult and messy in a plank-on-frame hull. Nor is it as essential, for the inherent strength of planking generally is adequate. Always build up a broad base along the juncture of any part bonded against a glass or foam-sandwich hull. If you don't, a disastrous "print through" will show up on the hull exterior.

BULKHEADS ON THE CABIN SOLE

Clearly, there are fewer problems when bulkheads are simply mounted on the cabin sole. Fitting is identical, using the tick stick and the tick board. The bulkhead can be fastened to a substantial cleat or into a rabbeted sill. The latter method is good practice, and the sill is made easily with a table saw. Be sure the rabbet is deep enough for adequate fastening with screws and glue. See Figure 8-7. If the sill is finished bright, like a baseboard, the bulkhead can be fastened from the exposed side and bunged over.

Much might be written on bulkhead options, especially if we discussed the nostalgic paneled bulkheads of an earlier era. Do look into plywood faced with hard surface material. Think about panel effects made with delicate moldings. Don't forget that mirrors can be mounted on bulkheads to brighten an interior. They don't have to be large, either. I had one about a foot wide on a forward bulkhead that just happened to be located so that I could admire myself as I lounged at the tiller. Uplifting and useful, that mirror.

CABIN SOLE BEAMS

Let's go back a bit to where we talked about deep bulkheads reaching down into the bilge. Here's an easy way to line up your cabin sole. Having found the height on the bulkheads, glue and screw a strong cleat at this level clear across the hull.

Incidentally, have you learned the trick of leveling with a transparent tube and water? Find a tube quite a bit longer than the space. Have a pal hold the tube against the cleat while you fill the tube with water until it reaches the height of the cleat. Now move this over to the next bulkhead and mark at the water level. That's the location of your next cleat. This trick works anywhere in the boat — on opposite sides of bulkheads, way up forward, it's all the same. I'm assuming, of course, that your vessel is dead level.

With the cleats securely in place, you'll next need three good lumber straightedges reaching fore and aft from bulkhead to bulkhead, with one on the approximate centerline. Clamp these or nail blocks to keep them vertical and secure (Figure 8-8). To find the locations of the beams at the hull, you use a smaller pointed straightedge along the underside of the first three. Mark all along the hull where the straightedge touches. Try a sharpened piece of chalk, a crayon, a grease pencil, or a fine felt pen — except on wood, of course. As an alternative, use the same transparent hose all around the perimeter of the sole.

Much of the following applies to yachts with beams of 9 or 10 feet or more, so use your judgment on the details that fit your circumstances. For example, Allegra has a sole less than 24 inches wide; only a couple of bilge access openings are needed. *Idler,* designed by the late

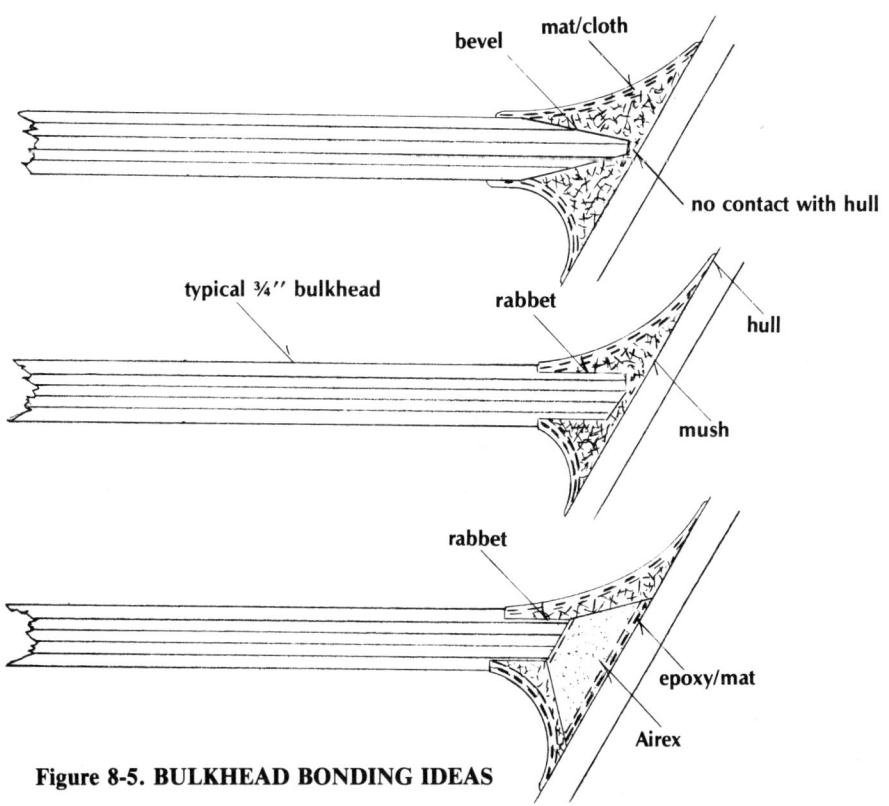

Figure 8-5. BULKHEAD BONDING IDEAS

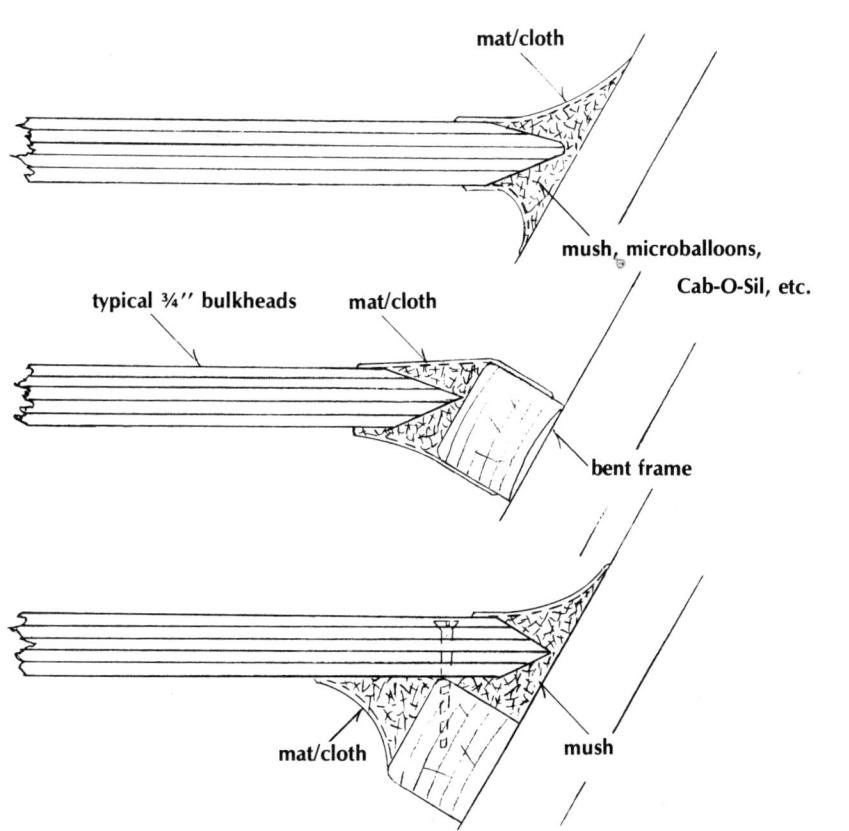

Figure 8-6. BULKHEAD BONDING IN WOODEN HULLS

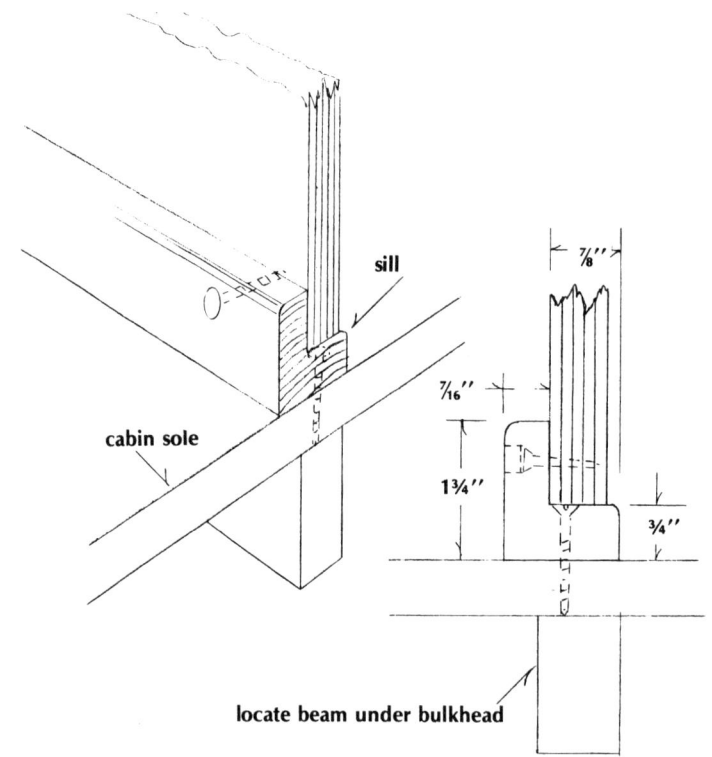

Figure 8-7. BULKHEAD IN RABBETED SILL

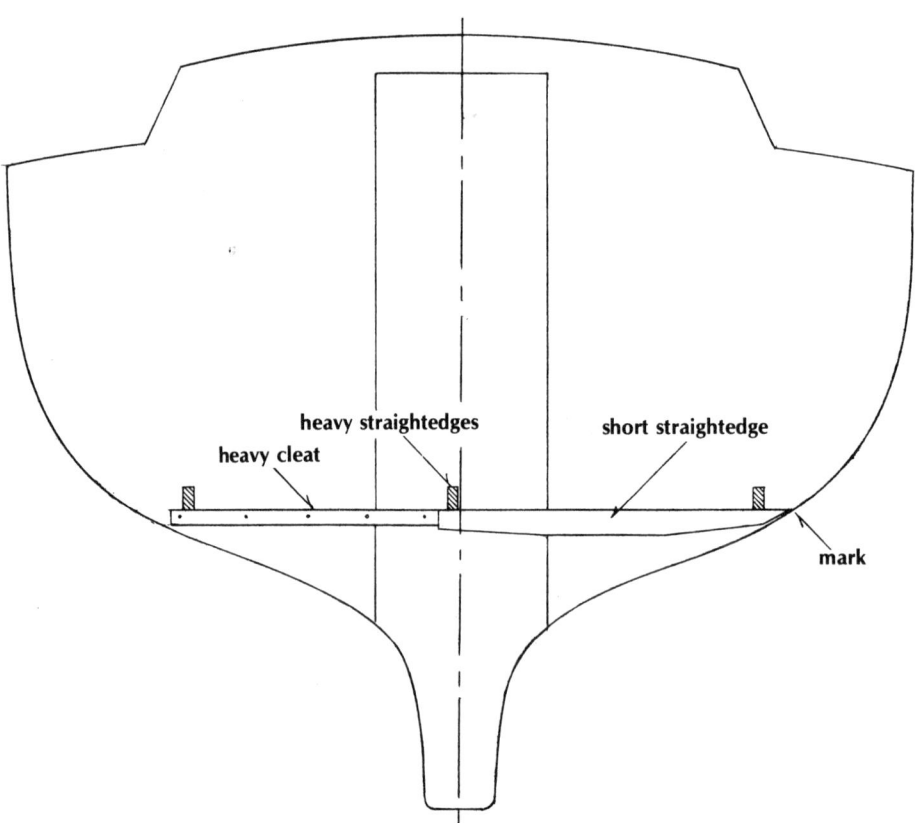

Figure 8-8. FINDING PERIMETER OF CABIN SOLE

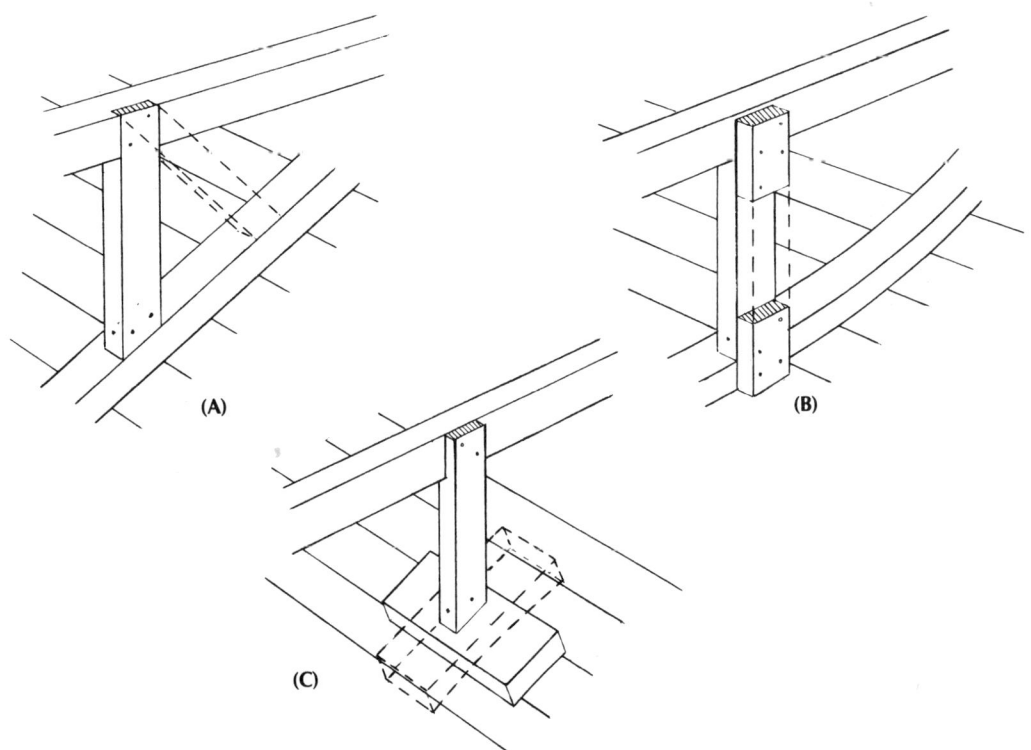

Figure 8-9. SOLE BEAM SUPPORTS

Philip L. Rhodes, has a wider sole, but the ½-inch plywood rests directly on the floor timbers, with no beams (risers) needed. Rhodes's 31-foot *Dog Star* is a beamy craft, but with a simple knuckle garboard and a shallow bilge, so her sole beam structure is almost as plain. Rhodes's 41-foot *Reliant* has a deep wineglass section. It needs a solid structure in both the wood and fiberglass versions. This is what I want to discuss, because the solutions may be helpful.

SOLE BEAM SUPPORTS

Openings in a deck or sole are framed at the fore-and-aft ends by heavy beams that span the hull. These heavy beams receive and support the timbers running fore and aft along the openings. They are called carlings, headers, and other names. Some builders use simple half-lap joints. Because it is best to have the supporting leg rest on a frame or floor timber, the beam itself may be shifted according to the way it is joined to the hull. Thus, the leg may be let into the beam or not, as shown in Figure 8-9, (A) and (B). The joint in Figure 8-9(A) weakens the beam somewhat, and its lower end would tend to creep down the frame if the angle were acute. An alternative, then, would be to cant the leg as shown in the dotted lines. The leg in Figure 8-9(B) serves the same function but is not lapped. This leg is secured by nailed and glued cleats or even doubled full length. The lap could be in the leg only, as in Figure 8-9(C). All of these joints can be made with a backsaw, power saw, or table saw, as previously described.

If the heavy beam is located where it cannot land on a frame or floor timber, do not place the leg directly on the planking or the glass of the hull. Bond down a large pad shaped to the hull, and toenail the leg to it or to a block on the pad, as shown in Figure 8-9(C). Or span the block across two frames. This is done because weights or heavy stresses on the sole could be transmitted and concentrated in a small area of the hull. Whenever possible, stand a leg on the keel. It's all right to shift the location of a tank slightly to permit this. You never know when a 200-pounder is going to jump off the companionway ladder. Solid support for the sole could avoid a lot of destruction. Glue every joint, preferably with epoxy. Make them strong, and these structures will even help to stiffen the hull.

It's assumed that you have installed all plumbing, tanks, batteries, and so on, before the framing goes in. Keep in mind that openings must be ample to service these areas and also to maintain the hull.

BEAM-TO-HULL ATTACHMENT

The heavy beams must be tied to the hull. In a fiberglass hull, this problem is quite easily solved by bedding the beam in a mush of chopped asbestos or mat and then

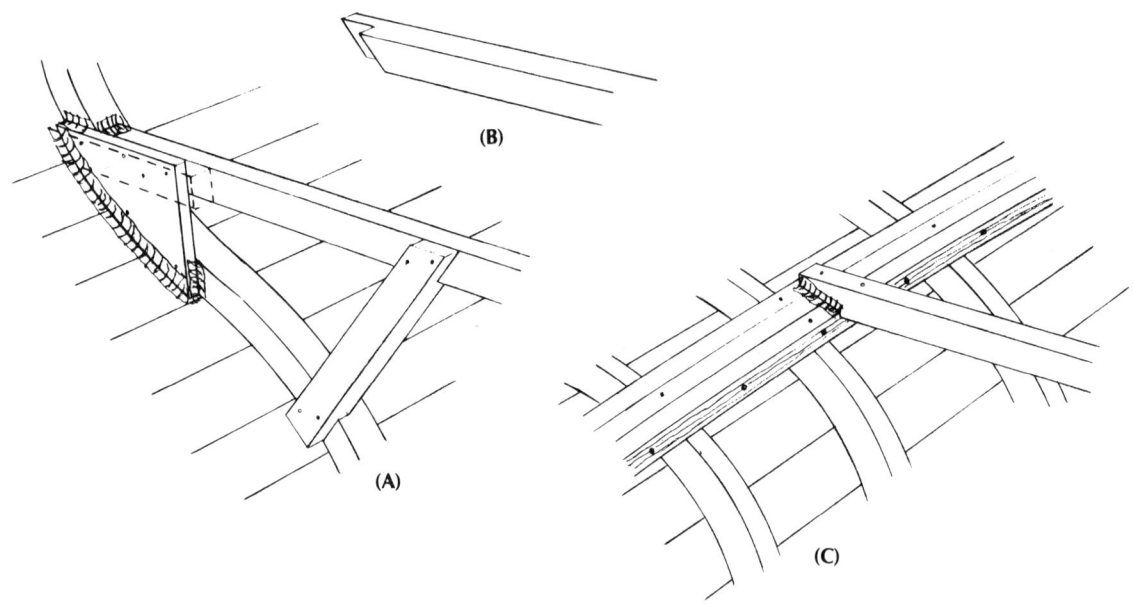

Figure 8-10. BEAM-TO-HULL ATTACHMENTS

covering it with a nice fillet of mat and cloth. It would be good practice to lay the beam end on a ¾-inch plywood pad bonded to the hull. This will prevent print-through from the beam.

If your ferrocement hull was properly designed, brackets were constructed for bolting the beam ends. If these are not provided, attach the beams as described for fiberglass, but use epoxy.

You have several choices for installing sole beams in your wooden hull. Ignore my suggestions, however, if your designer has provided specifications. My subject is not design, even though there are many options in actual construction. Many designers leave much to the discretion of the more experienced professional builder. And that's the way it should be. Otherwise, the fees for yacht designs would be beyond reach for most of us. Detail is costly!

If you are free to choose, fit the beam right on the frame, as shown in Figure 8-10. This is fine if it locates the heavy beam where the opening is desired (Figure 8-10(A)). You can attach a cleat to the side of the beam (*dotted lines*) with screws and glue. I would bond all this to the frame with mat and cloth and no more than one or two small nails. Make this a form of gusset if you want greater strength. Believe me, a series of beams all tied in this way can give you a nice, warm feeling in a really severe grounding. Half-lapping the beam over the frame would be a refinement of some small value, but do not drive fastenings into bent frames unless they are at least 1½ inches in depth, as in Figure 8-10(B). Any beam end termination becomes immensely strong if there is a substantial triangulated leg under the beam.

Another way to land beams on a wooden hull is to build in a pad spanning two or more frames — or, better yet, a continuous stringer, as shown in Figure 8-10(C). This has nothing to do with the bilge stringer in a wooden hull. It's actually a shelf to lay the beams on, but there is no denying that it adds strength. Because of the great curvature of this shelf, it may be advisable to build it up strip-fashion, edge-nailing and gluing each strip to its neighbor. Bonding all the short beams as well as the heavy beams to the hull in this manner would make your cabin sole a major structural unit. This permits locating the beams anywhere — a definite plus.

You have noticed, I'm sure, that I like to reinforce many joints with fiberglass fillets of chopped mat covered with mat and cloth (or roving). I haven't shown this in detail in my sketches, but where I indicate it, I mean that the mush is between the parts as well as in a fillet around the exterior. Repeated wetting and drying is one of the promoters of dry rot. I try to avoid if not prevent this by making it difficult for water to find a place to collect. I don't want it, for example, in a pocket between the gusset and the frame in Figure 8-10(A). Polyester is not impermeable to water, but it is nearly so in such a situation. Years ago we had nothing like this to strengthen and protect a joint. Let's take full advantage of the good characteristics of polyester and epoxy resins wherever we can.

CARLINGS

The beams running fore and aft, called carlings, must be attached securely to the main or heavy beams. These

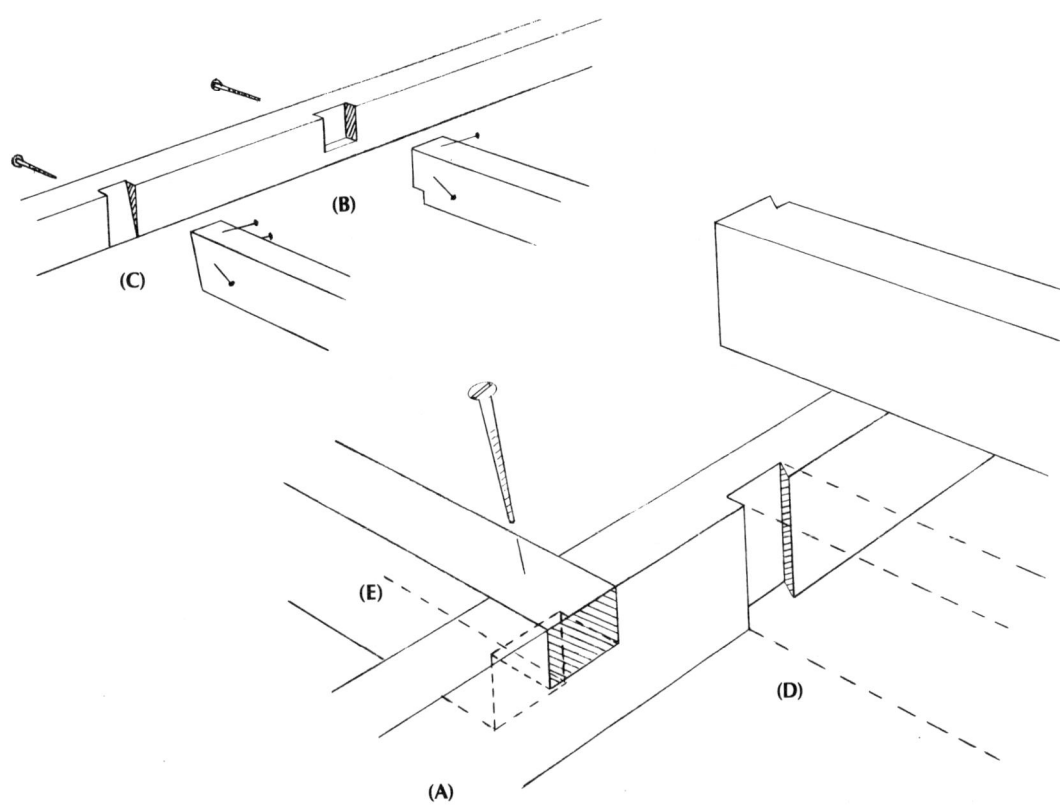

Figure 8-11. JOINTS: CARLING TO HEAVY BEAM, SIDE BEAM TO CARLING

carlings then receive the short side beams extending out to the hull, as just described. Most builders and designers specify an ordinary half lap (Figure 8-11(A)). This is sometimes used in the main deck from clamp or sheer batten to the cabin trunk carlings. This joint has several obvious weaknesses. First, the side beam has a tendency to split from the corner where it rests in the carling notch. Second, one-half of the carling has been removed, creating a weak spot, unless the area is supported by a leg. However, this is not 100 percent true if the side beam (E) is a snug fit into the half-lap socket, for the socket would not be able to close up under stress if filled completely. I prefer Figure 8-11(B), a haunched dado. This is a much more difficult joint to make, but it retains three-quarters of the original strength of the short beam and weakens the carling very little. It would not resist tensile stress as well as the joint in Figure 8-11(A), but these situations rarely experience that kind of force. All of these joints are highly resistant to compression.

The joint in Figure 8-11(C) weakens the carling very little and the short beam not at all. It must rely on the friction of the wedge form, and the fastenings and glue to resist excessive downward stresses. Note, however, that a glued decking over the joint would eliminate that weakness almost entirely. This is much easier to construct than the joint in Figure 8-11(B). I think it would be very adequate. The joint in Figure 8-11(D), a single dovetailed dado, resists tension well. It is a bit more difficult to fit closely and it also has little resistance to downward force. Like the joint in Figure 8-11(C), however, it would be amply reinforced by a glued deck on top. This was described in Chapter Seven. Be sure to use Aerolite or Plastic Resin glue.

CABIN SOLES

One owner I know built his sole of beautiful vertical-grain fir with strips of dark mahogany glued in between, and then varnished with about six coats. This is great to look at, but that skipper will need three hands and a tail when the boat is heeling and pitching and a few drops have come aboard. Bare wood would be good, but that's difficult to keep clean unless it's teak. There is a teak plywood with holly strips that make it look like the costliest sole available. Some production yachtbuilders use it. You might be able to pick up the few pieces you'll need at a reasonable price.

To go this route, first fit your underlay of ½- or ¾-inch plywood all the way out to the hull, using the tick stick. Bevel the top corner back about 1 inch as you did with the bulkheads so it can be glassed to the hull (see Figure 8-5). This means the underlay must be notched around frames in your wooden hull, but do it rather casually to allow for filling the gaps with chopped

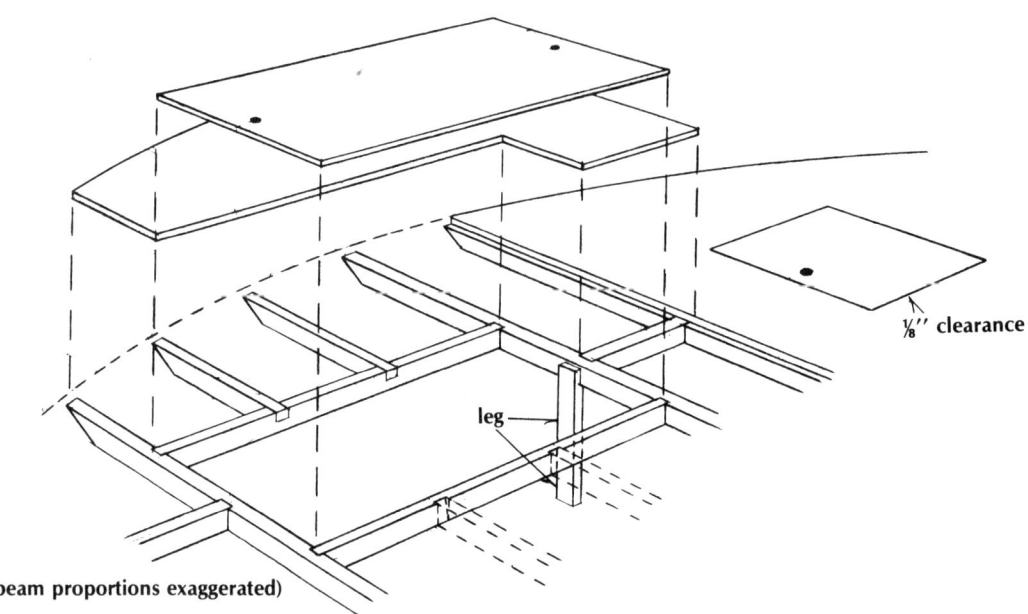

Figure 8-12. TYPICAL SOLE APERTURE FRAMING

mat later. Be sure to provide about ¾ inch around the access openings so the hatches rest securely on the frame. See Figure 8-12. Make the hatches with ⅛-inch clearance to avoid swelling and jamming. Juggle the plywood so all second-layer joints fall on beams, and do not allow joints to meet to form a cross. There should be T's only, as in Figure 8-4. Keep in mind also that the teak overlay joints should form pleasing patterns equidistant from the centerline, and so on, so underlay joints must be staggered accordingly.

You can nail and glue these sections to the beams and frames with bronze, galvanized finish nails, or box nails. Pack the chopped mat or asbestos all around the perimeter of the sole, forming a nice fillet with a spoon or bottle. Cover this with mat and cloth tape. You have just added tremendous strength to your hull if you used epoxy resin, less if you used polyester.

When this has cured, sand off high spots and clean up with a vacuum cleaner, if possible. Be sure the surface is fair and smooth. Assemble the teak overlay. It is not necessary that these pieces be fitted close to the hull. Brad each piece so it cannot shift. Lift one piece at a time and spread Plastic Resin evenly over the area (but rather thinly near the edges) with a brush, block, or squeegee. Replace the brads. When two pieces have been laid in the glue, cover the area with plastic, walk all over it, and then lay concrete blocks on the plastic. Be sure all joint edges meet flush, and immediately sponge off any glue that oozes out. No other fastenings are needed, but you can use more brads if you wish. Repeat this process with the remaining sections. Give the sole about a day to cure.

If you are willing to settle for a plain, painted, plywood sole, use ¾-inch marine-grade plywood. The exterior grade has many voids in its core that will pick up moisture in time and thus start to decay. In addition, such voids create weak spots. Do not for a minute consider covering with linoleum, carpeting, or so-called indoor-outdoor stuff. Linoleum is exceedingly treacherous when damp, and moisture always creeps under it. This also applies to any kind of carpeting. All coverings prevent evaporation and drying for weeks at a time. Nylon carpeting may be laid for use in port only.

Cabin soles vary with the type of vessel. On one of our old boats, we had ½-inch plywood pieces laid loose on top of the floor timbers. We liked this because we were able to clean the bilges occasionally with ease. Smaller areas in your boat should be planned this way — that is, simple, inexpensive, and handy. Regardless of the type of sole, miter a small decorative molding to cover the deck corner joints at bulkheads and berth fronts. Finish it bright for a nice touch.

Strip Cabin Soles

While teak plywood with artificial holly strips may satisfy some people, there are those who favor a genuine teak sole with raised holly strips. See Figure 8-13. First of all, the narrow decking generally specified needs sup-

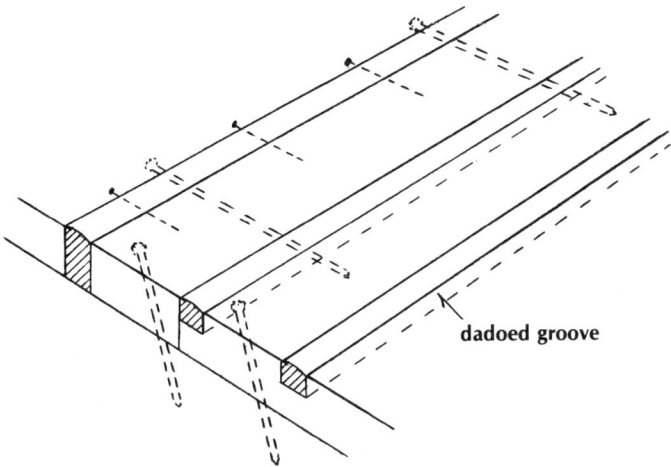

Figure 8-13. THREE WAYS TO DECK WITH HOLLY STRIPS

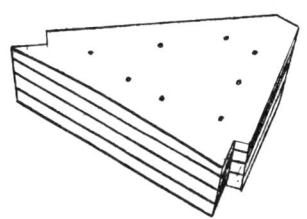

Figure 8-14. BUILT-UP BREASTHOOK

port from an underlay as described. Even with that, I would not try to deck with less than ⅝-inch teak because of fastening problems.

Figure 8-13 shows three systems. The first, on the left, uses strips about 1¼ to 1½ inches wide. These are toenailed into the beams through the edge (drill pilot holes first) while clamped or weighted to the beam. Then 2-inch or 2½-inch finish nails are placed horizontally, two or three between beams, from each strip into its neighbor. The ½-inch holly strip with its upper surface slightly rounded and raised goes in between. Epoxy glue is required, along with 1- to 1¼-inch finish nails through the holly. Both the teak and the holly must be bedded in viscous epoxy glue painted on the underlay. The second system, at the center, shows the teak rabbeted to take a smaller holly strip about ⅜ by ½ inch wide. Pilot holes are drilled for nailing the teak to the underlay and to its neighbor. It is necessary to drill completely through both pieces of the holly because the nail locates right on a joint. Use the type of long, flexible drill bit common in aircraft assembly. As an alternative, you can lay all the rabbeted teak strips, clean out the resulting grooves with care, then press in the holly strips. If you omit glue under the holly strips, they can be replaced much later when they wear. The third approach is the easiest. Using a dado set, groove out ½-inch slots into which the holly strips are then pressed. You can use pieces of teak from 6 to 8 inches wide.

This laid sole will not need finishing, but if it is left bare, it will show grease spots. Perhaps a teak cleaner will take care of that. If the teak, or even mahogany, were varnished, the holly would provide good footing and reduce wear on the base surface. All of this looks like a lot of work, but isn't it worth it to make your boat a yacht?

THE BREASTHOOK

It is assumed that your design gives the breasthook details. If it does not, study the fine boatbuilding references mentioned earlier in this book. Traditionally, the breasthook is oak, but you can build up a perfectly satisfactory one using three or four thicknesses of ¾-inch fir or mahogany marine plywood — glued with epoxy and Anchorfast nailed (Figure 8-14). The angle of the topside flare can be bandsawed if there is a slight curvature. Most of the slight camber should be dressed before it is installed. This applies, too, to the notches to receive a sheer batten, if any. If there is a clamp over bent frames, spring it up slightly and notch it snug to the aft edge of the breasthook, then bolt through. In a fiberglass or ferrocement hull, bed the breasthook with epoxy adhesive and drive heavy screws through the hull. Wooden planking also must be screwed and glued. Fill all open joints with epoxy, then grind off the top surface smoothly to receive decking or the king plank.

SHEER BATTENS

Perhaps I should not have assumed that sheer battens were installed previously in your fiberglass hull. Of course, no builder would allow a hull to leave his shop without sheer battens and several bulkheads or numerous cross spalls in place. Nevertheless, here's one way to install a sheer batten. First saw out the bulkhead apertures to size. The sizes of the sheer batten members will vary, of course, with the size of the hull. There must be ample height — about twice the molding of the deck beams would be safe — but follow the designer's scantlings if they are in the plans. The siding (thickness) should be enough for the canted half-lap joint and a bolt or heavy screw.

The batten can be built up of two or three thicknesses of clear fir in long lengths. This timber could be replaced by three or four thicknesses of ½-inch plywood for comparable strength, but more work. See Figure 8-15. Both would be scarfed to a 1-to-8 ratio. The fir can be scarfed full length on the floor, then sprung to the sheer the hard way, one at a time. Try a shorter

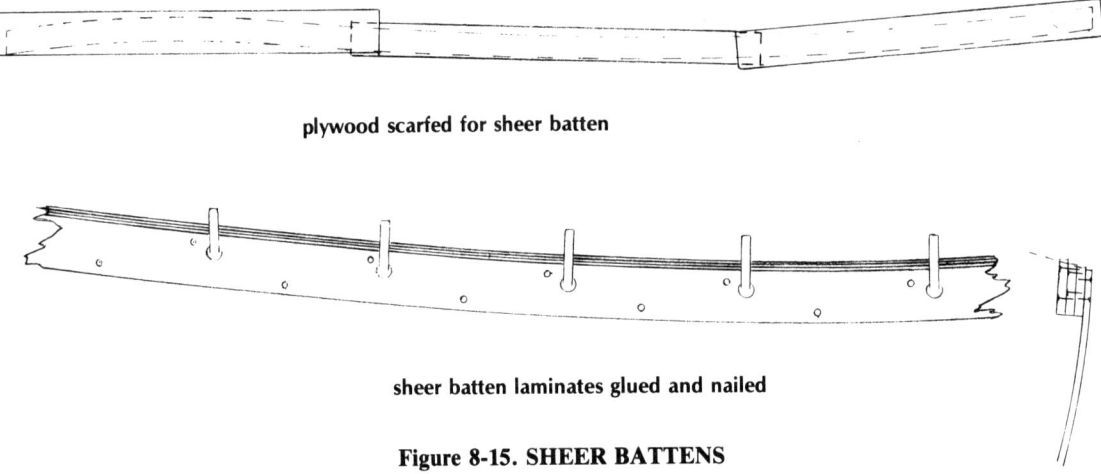

plywood scarfed for sheer batten

sheer batten laminates glued and nailed

Figure 8-15. SHEER BATTENS

length first to be sure it can be urged into this curve. If not, you'll have to use wider material and cant the scarfs as shown to save material. Each component may have to be sawed to the sweep of the sheer before joining. In this case, it would be easier to glue the scarfs with the batten parts clamped temporarily to the hull. Fit to notches in the breasthook and to the transom frame quarter knee. When scarfed from bow to stern, lift it up, and apply epoxy glue to the surfaces of hull and batten and to the scarf areas. If you are short of clamps, install one piece at a time. Bore for flathead through-bolts with a counterbore for the nuts, or use temporary short screws. This is insurance — you can rely on the epoxy to hold. The second and third laminations should be fitted the same way but fastened with ringed nails and epoxy glue (or through-bolted after pulling the temporary screws).

For plywood battens, the procedure is much the same, except that you cannot count on springing the material the hard way. And you cannot counterbore deep enough for recessed nuts in ½-inch plywood. The best way is to clamp easily handled widths of the material to the hull, saw to shape, fit to breasthook, and so on. Then fashion the scarfs. A small amount of edgewise springing will be possible in the final installation. Fairness is required, but not hair-splitting precision. A power saw should be able to make any of these easy curves, especially with a small-diameter blade. The finished shapes may be more exotic than I have sketched, depending on the flare of the hull. Incidentally, there is a saw attachment called a Scarffer that enables one to scarf the full width of plywood panels up to ½ inch thick. This could be easier than several dozen separate scarfs. It will save a bit of material, too. The Scarffer is sold by Gougeon Brothers, Bay City, Michigan 48706.

I have shown the upper edges in a sort of step arrangement so the rise for the deck camber can be accommodated. This can be planed down or ground off with a high-speed disc sander using 20-grit paper. Be careful not to cut below the line of the sheer.

You may elect to fasten the guard or fender at the same time as the batten, so the through-bolts will be the only fastenings. This takes some large clamps and a lot of planning, because all the bolt holes must be bored through, then the whole assembly taken apart for gluing. The safe way would be simply to glue the first lamination, the second, the third, and so on, fair off the camber, then bore through the guard (fender or rubstrake) after the glue is set. Be sure you space bolts, nails, and screws where they will not interfere with notches for the deck beams — about 8 inches center to center.

Some builders swear by the use of mat and polyester resin as an adhesive in situations like this. I think this would be very strong if there were mechanical fastenings too. Holes would have to be predrilled without the mat in place, for wet mat will ball up on the drill bit. It may cause some of the same difficulty with screws, but you may be able to tap them through the wet mat, then drive them.

DECK BEAMS

Framing the deck is a large subject that is covered extremely well by the fine books by Chapelle, Steward, Herreshoff, Verney, and others. However, it is a joinery subject and for that reason should be included here. I have several ideas on simplification and the use of glues to save materials.

First of all, avoid beams sawed out of a wide plank. Cutting this kind of beam consumes horrendous quantities of costly wood. If there is considerable camber, the beam is very weak because of the run-out of the grain. There are two ways to go. If the beams are normal camber, that is, ½ inch per foot of beam, or somewhat more, they may be sawed from a broad glued-up plank as shown in Figure 8-16. Second, for all purposes a laminated beam is far better and can be extremely handsome. Laminated beams can even be

146

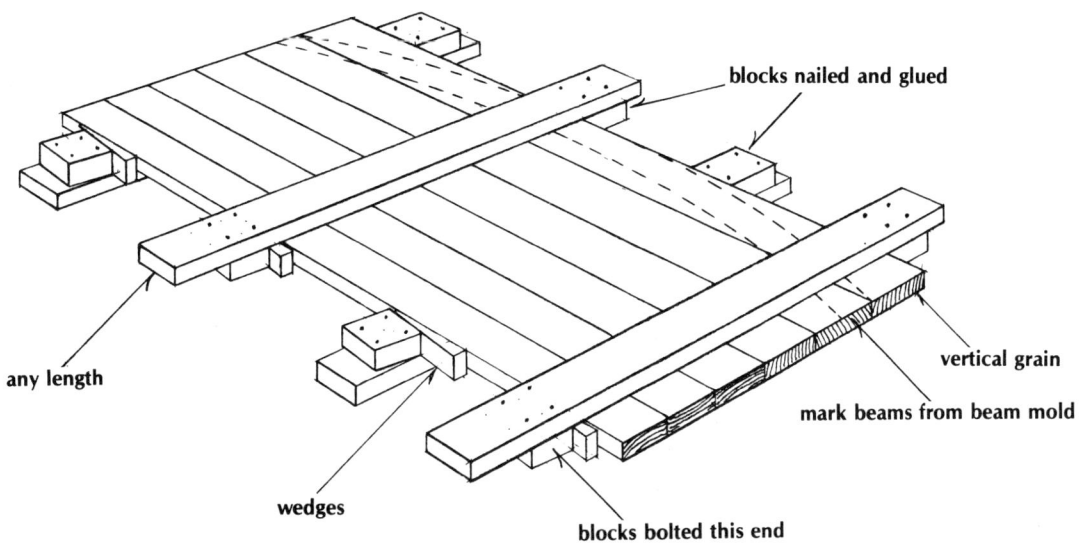

Figure 8-16. MAKE-DO CLAMPS FOR SAWED BEAMS

finished bright. See Figure 8-17. Don't use oak. Oak is far too heavy for this location so far above the waterline. This tenderizing effect is multiplied if oak is used in the cabin trunk beams. In addition, oak does not take glues well.

Spruce is by far the ideal beam material, but it is costly. Ash is a good substitute for oak. It is strong, lighter than oak, takes glues, and finishes beautifully. It is not known for its resistance to rot, but today it can be sealed with a penetrating epoxy. Oregon or Douglas fir makes a very good beam. It is midway along the weight range, very strong, glues well, and finishes nicely to a deep golden yellow. It does split, however, if not properly bored for fastenings. All in all, next to spruce, Oregon or Douglas fir would be my choice. Spruce or fir with alternating laminations of mahogany or ash makes a beautiful beam. The traditional beam has a mahogany or teak cap along its lower edge.

Sawed Beams

Let's assume you have some good clear fir on hand with vertical grain. If in the form of 2 by 4's or 2 by 6's and your beams are to finish to 1 by 2½ (a good ratio), the boards may have to be run through a planer to bring them down to about ⅛ inch over the final size. Or you can reduce them after sawing, but this is a lot of work with a plane or jointer. The job is to edge-glue these boards.

Figure 8-16 shows an easy and inexpensive way to clamp up a very wide structure, using wedges. The crosspieces may be of any convenient length. The blocks on the wedge end should be bolted for adjusting to another use. The fixed blocks should be nailed and glued. I think 2 by 4 material would be adequate, but use 2 by 6 for a very heavy beam, and 1 by 6 for light beams. You may need more clamps than I have shown to spread the pressure equally. I prefer epoxy glue here, but Plastic Resin would be acceptable. Place plastic sheets between the fir and the clamps. Try to line up the edges as you wedge up so you won't have too much to plane off later. If the pieces are edge or vertical grain, but show some cupping (warping), alternate them as explained in Chapter Seven. If they are flat grain, they must be alternated. Let the glue ooze out for a few minutes, then scrape and wash off the excess. Let the assembly cure for about 24 hours. Chisel or plane off the hardened glue.

When the surfaces are clean, lay out the beam with a beam mold (see Chapter Five). If you have a template or pattern of the upper camber only, don't forget that the bottom curve is different because it has a shorter radius. You either make a beam mold or you set up your bandsaw for sawing concentric to the upper curve. Again, see Chapter Five. This requires considerable care. To plane the concave surface, stroke your plane at an angle of about 45 degrees, then finish with a belt sander or coarse (60- to 80-grit) sandpaper on a block.

The production method uses a shaper. Run your beam mold against collars with a straight cutter on the spindle. If the beam is sided too thick for your cutter, make it in two passes by raising the spindle. Take care when the cutter begins to shape against the grain. You may have to slow the feed to avoid chipping the surface. It's best to bring the beams down to their specified siding on a small jointer or let a mill put them through its planer. Of course, you can use a roughing plane, a jack, and a 24-inch jointer plane, with a final run over a bench belt sander. The appearance of any beam is

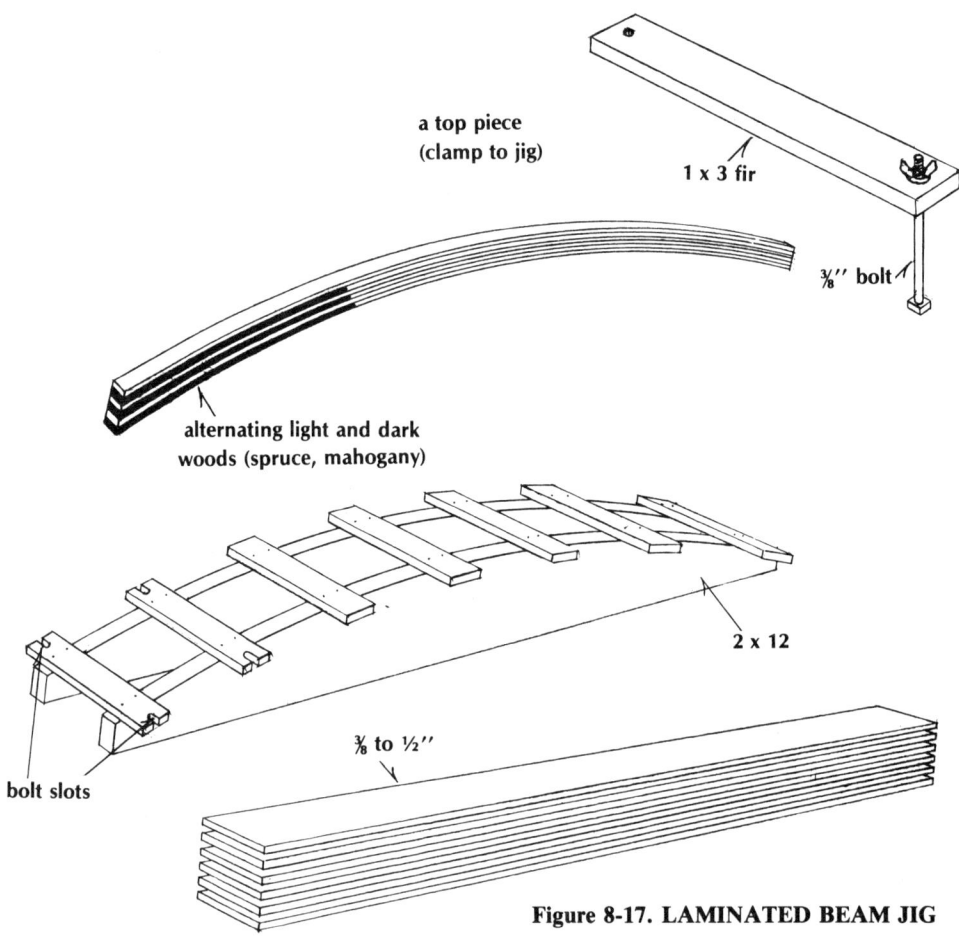

Figure 8-17. LAMINATED BEAM JIG

enhanced by routing a small radius, ogee, or chamfer on the lower corners. Or you can cap with hardwood in traditional yacht style.

Laminated Beams

I recommend strongly that all beams be laminated, so let's build the form now. See Figure 8-17. Start with a couple of 2 by 12's cut to the necessary crown. This means the camber of the beam mold, less the molded depth of the beam, less ¾ inch — the thickness of the crosspieces or staves. By laminating wide pieces together, we wind up with a bent plank that we then rip into three or four beams. The more laminations, the stronger the beam. For a small beam, the laminations should be ¼ or $\frac{5}{16}$ inch thick; for a large beam, ⅜ to ½ inch thick. This means that your spruce, fir, mahogany, or whatever may have to be run through a planer.

If you want four beams 1 inch wide (sided), use laminations 5 inches or more wide. This should rip out to at least 1⅛ inches. If you need four 1½-inch beams, use 7-inch material. The wider the laminations the better, for the staves tend to bend considerably over narrow stock. You may have to place C-clamps so there are no air pockets in the lamination. The staves should be about 8 inches longer than the material, leaving the ends for clamps or bolts. Glue the staves to the 2 by 12 so they overhang 2 inches. The slots permit rapid setting up with bolts and wing nuts, but you'll need a wrench, too, for power.

Try a dry run. Stack your material over a center mark. Clamp the staves down one by one, working from the center. Light laminations can be sprung down easily by hand. Remove them and get the glue ready. I prefer Aerolite here because the glue line is crystal clear and nothing happens until the two parts come together — and then it happens slowly. Epoxy adhesive is the most powerful, especially if you presaturate. Working time with either is ample. As you tighten the clamps, be sure to align the sides of the stack of laminations and finish nail the bottom one to the form to keep the pieces centered.

Bolt up the center stave first, then work toward the ends, clamping loosely. Watch the side alignment closely. The laminations will want to creep about. Place C-clamps near the center of each stave and pull down all the bolts and clamps. Wipe and wash off all the glue for

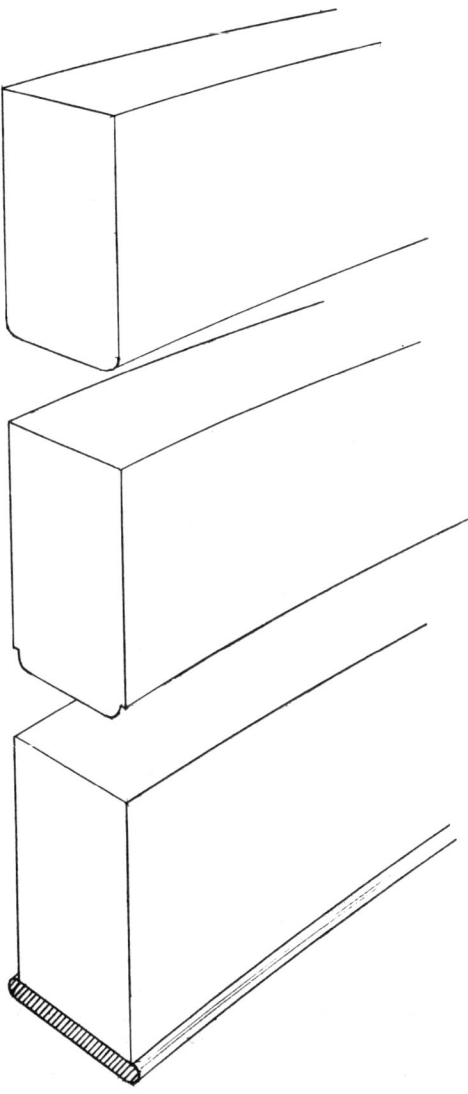

Figure 8-18. BEAM TREATMENTS, YACHT STYLE

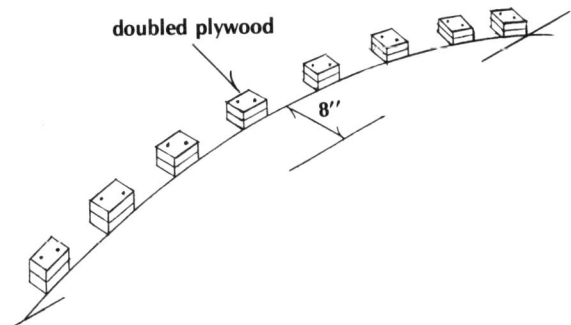

Figure 8-19. FORM FOR LAMINATING SPECIAL BEAMS

an hour or so, and then cure for about 24 hours before releasing the beam from the form. If you remembered to cover the staves with plastic, the lower side of the bent plank should be fairly clean. Plane one side so it is fair and rip slightly oversize on your table saw or bandsaw. The final dressing to the required dimension is best done on a jointer, with a finish sanding. Once again, a nice touch is a routed radius or ogee or a hardwood cap installed after the beams are set. See Figure 8-18.

Special Laminated Beams

Sometimes a special beam is needed in the deck just abaft the breasthook, or the cabin trunk may require all beams to be crowned to a special radius. To make a series of special beams, first cover an old bench, plank, or heavy plywood panel with plastic sheet. Nail blocks along the beam pattern (or a pencil line under the plastic) about 6 to 8 inches apart. Make them of ¾-inch plywood or 2-inch lumber and high enough so you can turn the clamp screws (Figure 8-19). Go through a dry run. After the glue has cured, save the blocks for the next special beam, and then the next, and so on. Of course, there's the tiller and very light beams in hatches, too. Nothing equals laminating for strength. Alternating laminations of light and dark wood are very attractive. You'll never regret taking the time to do a proper job of laminating.

Short Beams

You'll need beams extending from the carlings — to which the cabin trunk is eventually fastened — out to the sheer plank. These will be mortised into the sheer batten if there is one, and bolted to the clamp or shelf. The easiest practical way is to saw these out of short pieces left over from other work. You can also laminate a couple of long beams and saw them up into the lengths required. If you do this, there is less chance of the laminated beams being split by bolts near their ends.

CARLING AND BEAM ALIGNMENT

I have already discussed the sweep of the beams in the foredeck. If there were no opening for the trunk cabin, all beams would have to line up similarly, forming a very fair line down the center. This would be much flatter than the sheer, depending on the amount of camber. The short side beams and all other beams must be cambered to meet the invisible centerline. Likewise, the carlings must be sprung down to match the cambers.

To start with, the main beams at each end of the opening in the deck have been installed. Let's say they are 2½ inches molded (depth). The beams in the foredeck have been lined up and installed as above. I would now stretch a 2 by 4 or 2 by 6 strongback from bow to stern under the main beams, either doubled or with long butt blocks to keep it fair at the joints (Figure 8-20). The forward end must be clamped under the

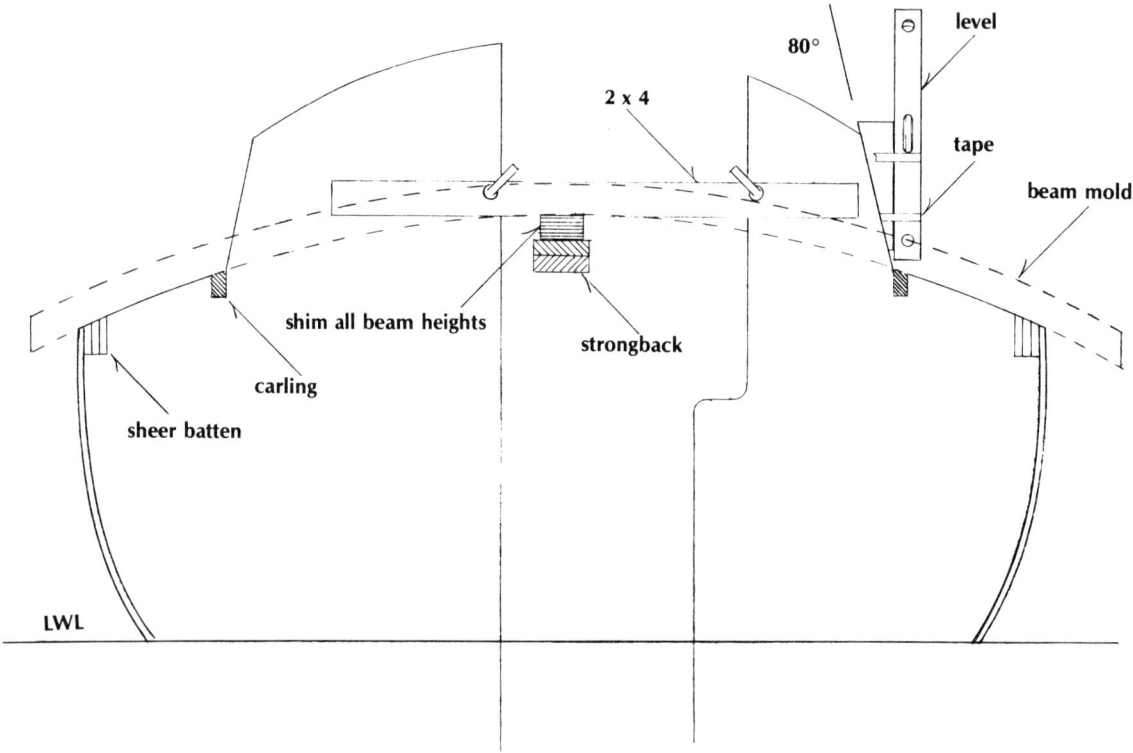

Figure 8-20. SPRINGING THE CARLINGS

breasthook with shims to position it 2½ inches under the decking. The aft end must be clamped under the transom frame, cleat, or beam the same 2½ inches under the deck level. Clamp the strongback to the main beams of the trunk opening also. If the strongback does not form a fair sweep, prop it up or pull it down until it does.

I know that some boatbuilders lay this strongback over the beams, but now you have a useful shelf to support other beams while they are being fitted. You also have a sure way of measuring the required cambers anywhere by stretching a taut chalkline across the hull and measuring up to the strongback and shim. All you have to remember is that some beams are molded to different depths so shims will be necessary. Just tack them to the 2 by 6.

Where bulkheads are in, but not the main beams, clamp 2 by 4's across at the designed height for each beam (beneath the beam mold). Place a removable shim between the strongback and the 2 by 4. Remove this when fitting a main beam into the sheer batten, or on the clamp or shelf.

I mentioned earlier that you will need several beam molds. The height of the carlings is fixed where they pass through bulkheads, but elsewhere they must be forced down into a fair curve. This is where you'll need the beam molds. See Figure 8-20. Clamp these to the sheer battens or clamps and to the strongback. Now you have something solid with which to pull the carlings down to their proper sweep. The carling notches through the bulkheads should have been cut out from the lofting before installation. If not, mark the locations from the beam mold and saw out with a keyhole saw or sabersaw. Remember that the face of the carling generally is vertical, while the upper surface has to be sawed off to match the camber of the beam mold.

The carlings must be jointed into the main beams fore and aft and carefully fitted, allowing for the sweep. Once they are installed, tie them down to the hull and to any partial bulkheads with a couple of 1 by 3's. The tie-downs may be glassed in temporarily and chopped off later, if your hull is glass. The beam molds may be removed, if you wish, but they help to stiffen the carlings while they are being notched, as shown in Figure 8-21. Some designers prefer half laps, others dadoes and dovetailed dadoes. If the canted half-dado is strong enough for one end of a beam, however, it's strong enough for the other. Note the simple notching of the beam into the sheer batten.

SETTING THE BEAMS

I assume you know that beams must fit nicely to the inside of your hull, whether it's wood, glass, or ferro-

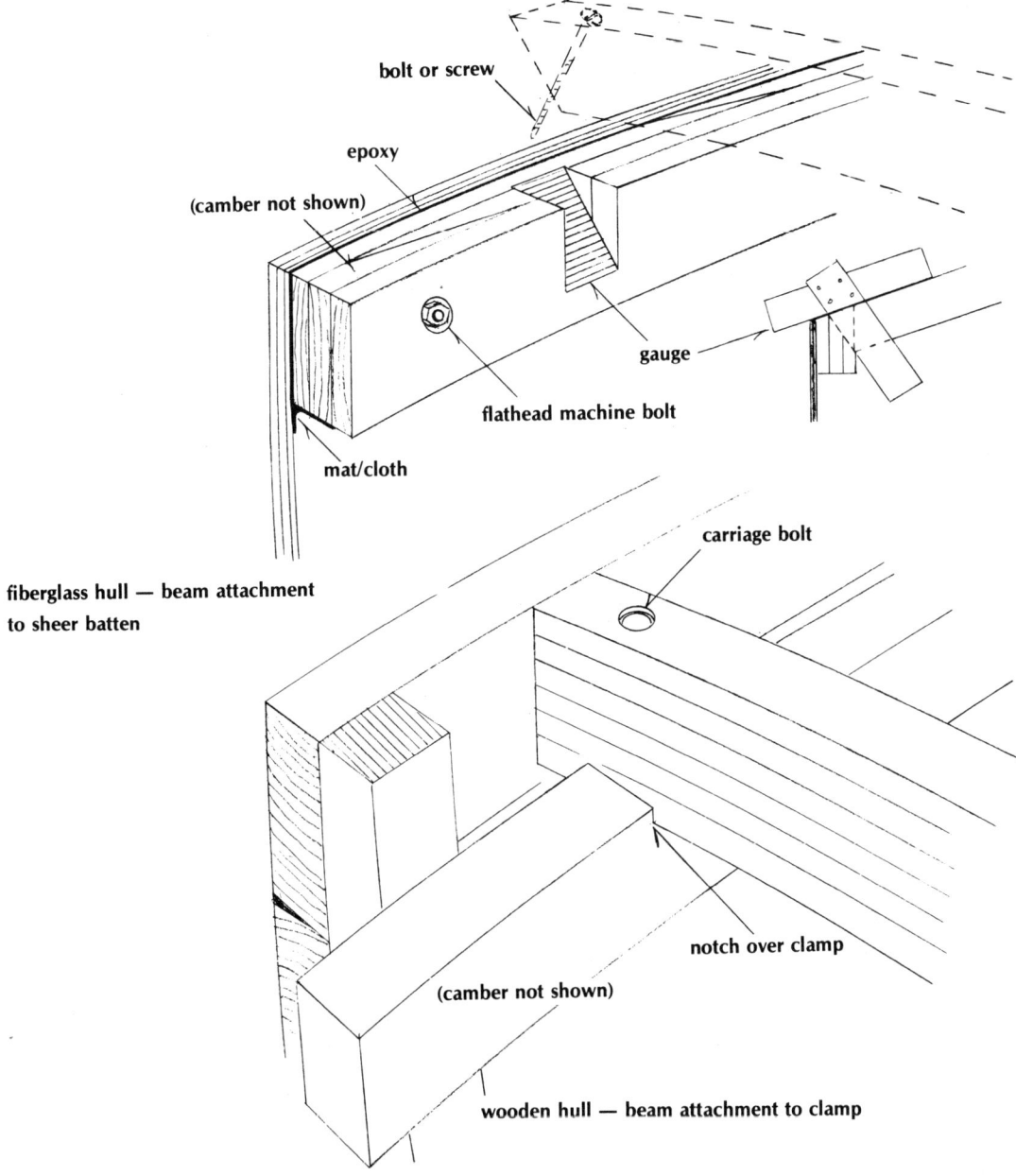

Figure 8-21. BEAM ATTACHMENTS

cement. This prevents the hull from springing in (when rolling against a dock?) and splitting near the beam end around the fastenings. In addition, if there is a sheer batten, it must be cambered like the beam mold and fair into the true sheerline (see Figure 8-21). Again, the clamp in your wooden hull must be bolted through the frames and planking. It is essential that beams be notched over the clamp, the sure way to prevent panting — athwartships in-and-out movement. So locate the clamp below the sheer the molded dimension of the beams less the depth of the notches. This construction reduces strain on the hold-down bolts running through the clamp. If the plan calls for a few lighter beams of less molded depth, shim sufficiently to raise the beams flush with the camber of the sheer plank. Be sure all beams fit neatly against the inside of the hull. I do not advise screwing or bolting deck beams to bent frames, since any movement could split one or the other member.

You can get the exact length of a beam between notches or sockets from batten to batten or batten to carling, let's say, by laying the beam upside down over the sockets. Mark at the outboard corner of both sockets. Use your bevel gauge or square to get the taper of the hull. If you make a gauge as shown in Figure 8-21, you can transfer this cant of the socket to the

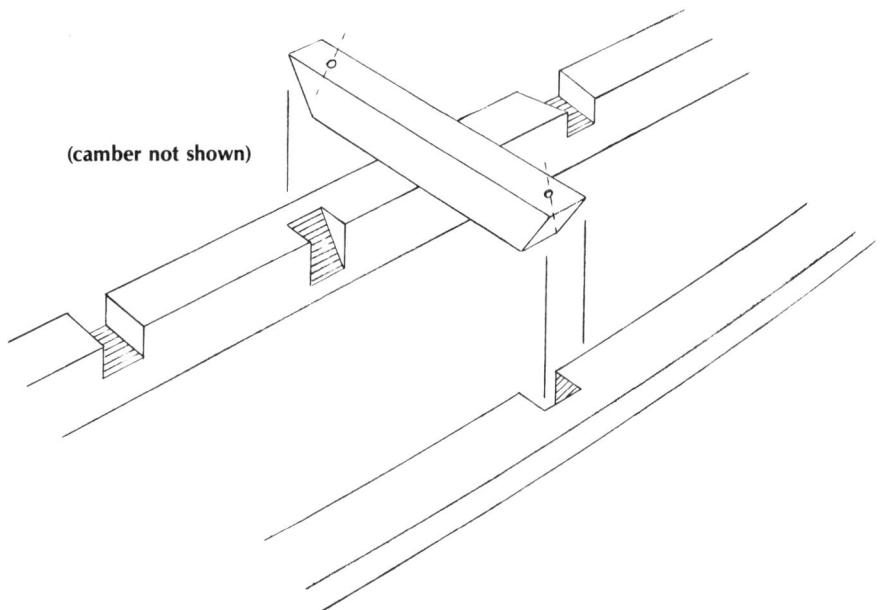

Figure 8-22. SIDE DECK BEAM JOINTS — SHEER BATTEN TO CARLING

beam (or to the socket, whichever way you prefer to fit). A little blue chalk on the end of the beam will show you where to shave off a little in the notch. The gauge works well in areas of greater beam but does not make allowance for the flattening of the beam as the hull narrows. Here I would construct the socket, then take off the angle with my bevel gauge.

This kind of construction of side deck framing is satisfactory with glued plywood and plywood underlay decks. It used to be standard practice to place tie rods between the carlings and the clamps, because laid decks would not prevent opening of the joints. All dovetailed half laps would provide a similar tie-in. This, however, would be a waste of time with a canted half lap. Figure 8-22 shows the weakening effect of the half lap, then the canted half lap, and then the dovetailed half lap in the carling. It is difficult for me to remember that epoxy glue eliminates almost all of the weakness of these joints. It does, after all, fill cracks without loss of strength. It can, however, be a bit disconcerting to lie awake in your berth counting the sloppy joints overhead. And if the joints you can see are bad, how about the hidden ones?

It is interesting at this point to note that L. Francis Herreshoff says to prevent a hull from panting, "Lloyd's Rule . . . calls for the deck beams to be different spacing from the frames so the head of the frames cannot be bolted to the deck beams, which is a very poor arrangement indeed, for the usual single fastening through the clamp does not support the frames or deck beams rigidly." Now, I hesitate to dispute Herreshoff, and believe me, I still hang on his written or spoken words. If I really wanted to split a frame head or a beam end, however, I would stick a bolt or rivet right close to its end and then bounce a heavy load on the deck. The beam loses a bit of its camber for a second, then it stretches, and you have a split in one or both parts. Or possibly a started plank. Notch the beams over the clamp, friends. This resists tension and compression, which occur daily. Herreshoff mentions other things to reduce panting or a change in shape of a section — bulkheads and partitions strongly attached to deck beams and frame, and cabin sole beams. These have been covered.

A strengthening system down the center of the deck usually is required. It is not uncommon to see a strongback let into the beams of the foredeck. This is not too bad if it is a light piece, say, ½- or ¾-inch plywood let into a 2½-inch beam. It is a crime, however, to cut out one-third or one-half of the strength of five or six beams where it is needed most. It is far preferable to fit blocks (say, 1½ inches thick) between beams, toenailing into one beam and nailing from the other. The tops must be planed off flush with the beams, of course, for there should be no air space between the blocks and the deck. See Figure 8-23. In addition, blocking should be installed all along the deck edge between beams where the covering board joint falls. Even a plywood deck must have blocking for deck hardware so that cleats, padeyes, fairleads, travelers, jib tracks, winches, and so on, can be bolted down securely.

All members that penetrate the deck must be blocked — for example, the rudderport and cockpit scuppers. Winches, especially those on the cabin trunk, should be blocked to the second beam forward. The blocks should

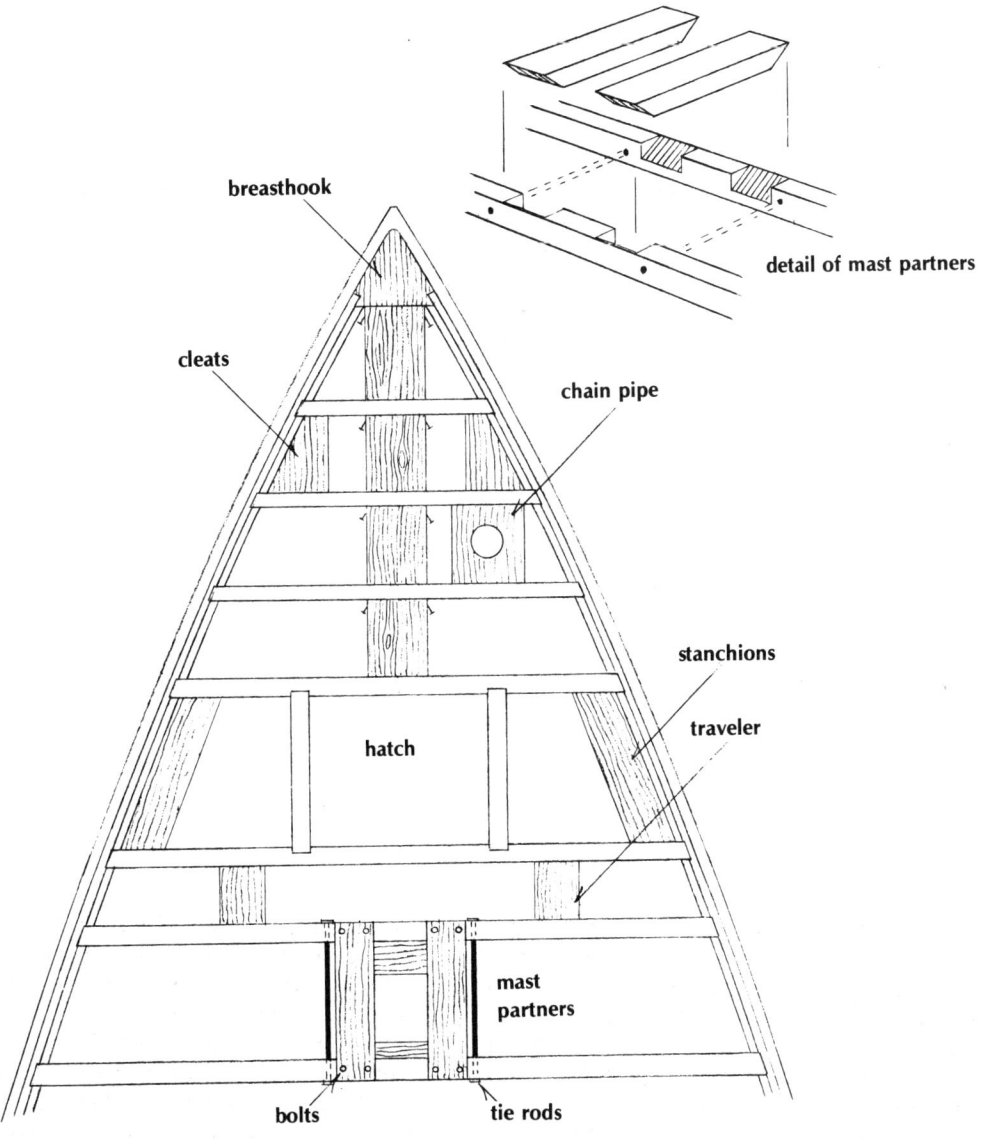

Figure 8-23. TYPICAL DECK BLOCKING

be of attractive hardwood with decorative edges if they will be visible from below. With regard to foam-sandwich decks, I need only remind you that foam cannot take compression or permit shear on the bolts. The answer is blocking in place of the foam in such areas, either by scraping it away before the upper surface is bonded on or by inserting the blocking during lamination. Compression tubes around the bolts instead of blocking would not provide complete resistance to shear, such as from a winch.

The placement of hardware often requires shifting from one location to another. Always install new blocking. This is one of the disadvantages of foam-sandwich decks. The block area has to be routed out; an ugly repair job may result. If your construction plans do not detail blocking for everything, ask your designer's advice.

This concludes my suggestions on basic framing for your vessel. Now you can cover the deck area with plywood, tarps, or plastic for a temporary cover to permit you to work on the interior when it's freezing out and on deck when the sun shines. You might review the construction of some of the joints described in Chapter Seven before starting anything to make sure you have all the necessary tools and materials.

NINE

Decks

The decision on the type of deck most appropriate for your vessel, your tools, and your skills must be made months ahead. Many factors influence deck construction. For example, plywood decks eliminate the need for lodging knees — reinforcements between beams and around openings in the deck. See Figure 9-1. If you choose a laid deck, however, many lodging knees must be fabricated and installed meticulously. Also, if there are few plywood structural bulkheads, many hanging knees must be built.

This chapter is devoted primarily to the lower-cost, practical types of deck that many nonprofessional builders seem to prefer. Traditional laid or bright decks are discussed only briefly in the last few pages of the chapter. If you are highly skilled and have a hefty bank account, skip right along now to those pages without hesitation. Just be sure you know exactly what you're getting into. If, on the other hand, you want to learn a little about some of the compromises available in deck construction, read on.

PLYWOOD DECKS

Plywood decks must be built with genuine marine-grade plywood, not exterior grade. Such decks should be laminated of two thicknesses, except on small half-decked craft. It is difficult to lay a deck in a single thickness of ½- or ¾-inch plywood and not have the joints show if the camber is more than ½ inch per foot of beam. This occurs because of the stiffness of plywood. Even butt blocks between beams may fail to fair out such joints because of the curvature required by the deck. Laminated decks prevent this problem by staggering or scattering the joints (Figure 9-2). Moreover, lighter plywood does not resist a slight compound curvature.

Thus, the joints in the top lamination are always backed up by the bottom layer, with both on beams. These joints cannot leak and the flexible sheets form a fair surface and a rigid structure. Two layers of ½-inch fir marine plywood — or mahogany, in combinations — would make a strong deck for about a 40-foot-overall sailing yacht. Combinations of thicknesses can be used to get the total required. Even a light deck of ½-inch plywood with ⅛- to ³⁄₁₆-inch teak strips on top will work.

Shift the arrangement of the panels so that no joint falls on a corner of a deck opening. There are no lodging knees under a plywood deck because working is eliminated by the nature of the laminated material. If a plywood joint is in a corner of an opening, a stress point is created and working may result.

Do try to keep the weight of your deck down to avoid the unhealthy effect of excessive weight above the

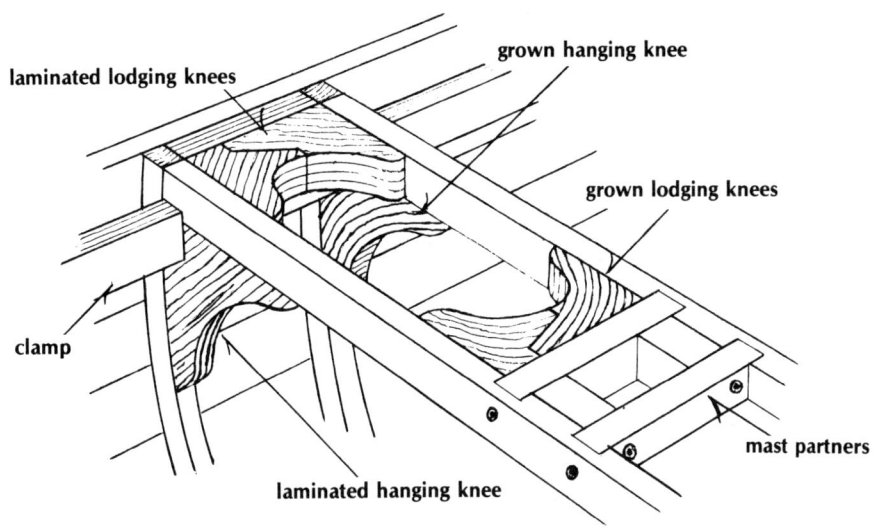

Figure 9-1. LODGING AND HANGING KNEES

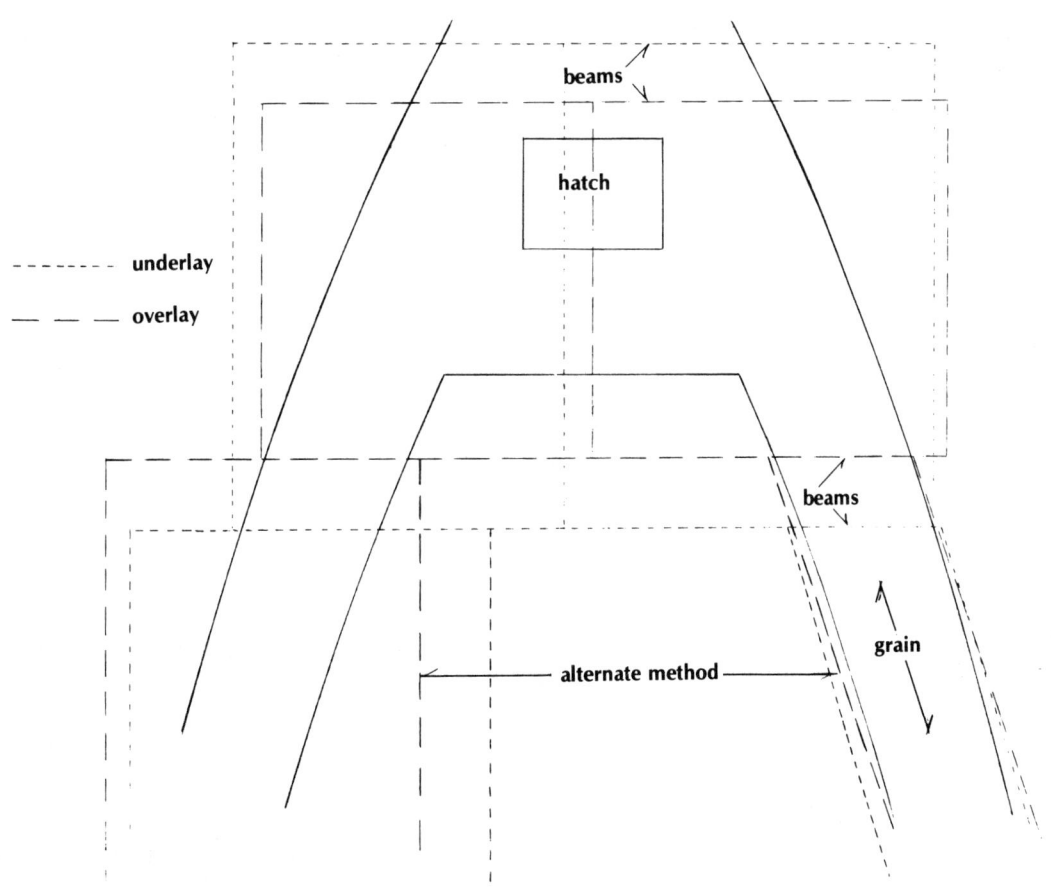

Figure 9-2. SCATTERING JOINTS IN PLYWOOD DECKING

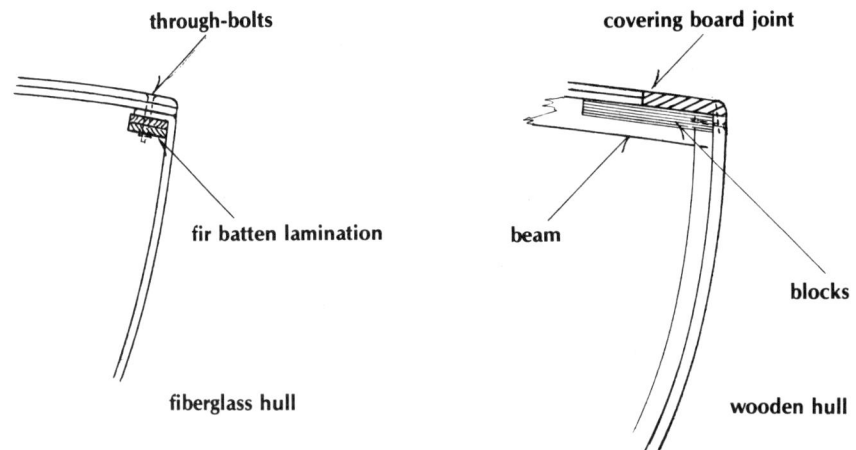

Figure 9-3. DECK-EDGE CONSTRUCTION

waterline. Massive strength here does not make a superior vessel. Get your designer's advice if this is a potential problem.

A simple plywood deck must be fastened directly into the sheerstrake properly beveled to conform to the crown of the beams. Use galvanized or bronze wood screws or Anchorfast nails. Glue this joint and/or lay a tape of fiberglass mat on it. Glass or ferrocement hulls should have a full-length husky sheer batten as described above. If the glass hull has a flange turned in, I suggest you back this up with a laminated fir batten so the pressure of the through-bolts is spread out. Quite large wooden vessels have blocks between the beams and tight against the planking, fastened with screws from outside and nails through the beams. See Figure 9-3. The top surfaces must be planed off fair with the beams so there are no openings where moisture can enter.

Plan to glue plywood to beams and carlings with epoxy or Plastic Resin. Lay down the first layer, fasten temporarily so you can see that all joints match up, mark on the underside where glue must be applied (for Aerolite or other two-surface applications), remove, and trim close to size. Glue and fasten the first panel, then the second, and so on, being sure all butting edges are adequately coated with glue. Wipe off all excess glue at once, before it sets up.

LAMINATING THE DECK PANELS

There must be no possibility of voids between panels. The adhesive must be watertight or water-repellent and it should be crack filling, that is to say, void filling. Some cracks can be eliminated by using the right adhesive. Aerolite is crack filling, waterproof, has several days' pot life, and can be used at fairly low temperatures. It has the disadvantage of requiring application of the activator to all of one side while the adhesive goes on the other. Chem-Tech T-88 may be applied to only one panel. It works at temperatures in the low 50s and loses no strength in gaps up to $\frac{1}{16}$ inch wide. High clamping pressure is not required with either of these adhesives (see Chapter Six). Plastic Resin is not crack filling, but it costs less.

When you are ready for the second thickness, spread the adhesive with a laminator's squeegee or a tile-layer's toothed tool. Fasten first near the panel center so the air is squeezed out. Galvanized finish nails into the beams are acceptable, but use Anchorfast nails or screws around the perimeter. Fore-and-aft joints may require a series of blocks if the panels are too thin to hold screws. Fastened from the underside, they are not offensive. A line of roundhead screws between beams would be good insurance if the top layer is heavy enough. You will definitely need weights on the deck here and there. Put concrete blocks on 1 by 4's laid fore and aft. Or try the type of plastic sandbag used on pool covers. If you still feel a springy place, drill a couple of $\frac{1}{16}$-inch holes through the outer layer, then tread around the spot. This should force out any trapped air. Give the deck a day to cure.

COVERING THE DECKS

You have just laid the simplest possible deck. It is not complete, however, until it has been protected from weather and wear and tear. The mania for glassing everything has generated many books and articles describing how to use polyester resin. Unfortunately, even when painted up to make it more attractive, such a deck is inadequate. After just a few years of use, water enters any bruises. Delamination then begins, and dry rot follows. Remember, too, that polyester is moisture-permeable and that the plywood expands and contracts. Thus, moisture is bound to pass through it in time, bruises or not. The only answer for glassing over is epoxy, because it will not let go and it is nonpermeable.

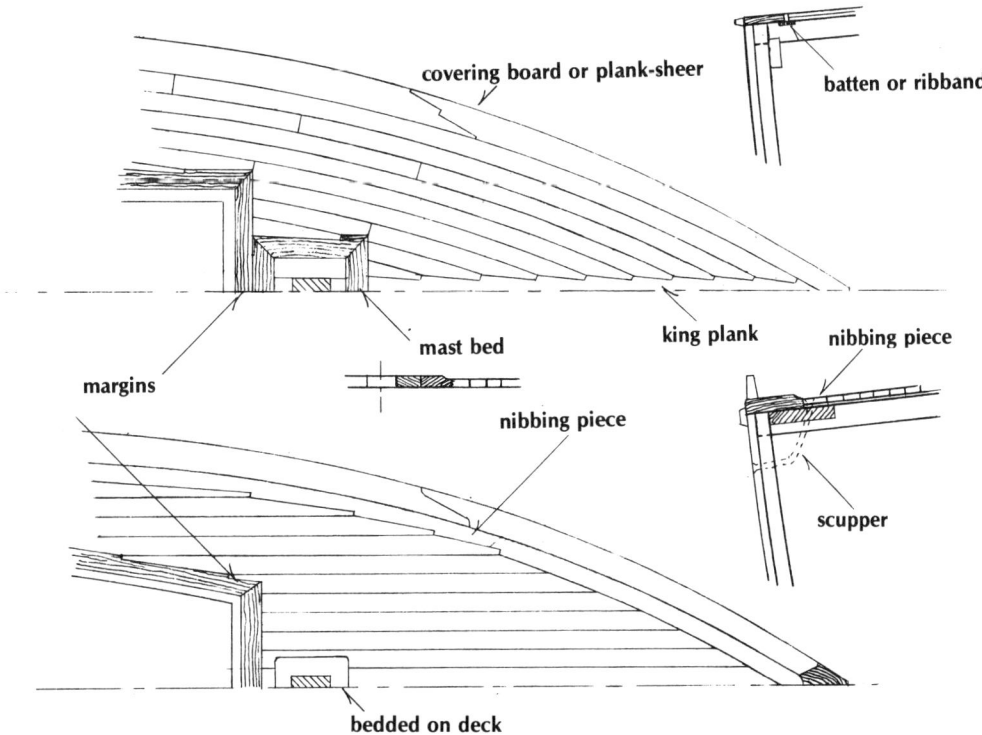

Figure 9-4. SPRUNG AND STRAIGHT DECKING, DECK MARGINS

The best reinforced plastic deck coverings are Dynel, Versatex/L-26, and Vectra, and epoxy resin. It is recommended that a thinned coat of resin be applied to the bare panel to increase impact resistance, and that this be allowed to cure. Dynel stretches, so it's best to lay this on a wet coat of resin, pull it out, and then staple or tack all around the perimeter. Vectra, or Versatex (polypropylene), stretches slightly and is lighter. It absorbs less resin and is extremely resistant to wear and impact. Get full information on the Versatex/L-26 system from Chem-Tech, 4481 Greenwold Road, Cleveland, Ohio 44121.

Be sure the deck has been vacuum cleaned or well swept before you lay out any cloth. Smooth out the wrinkles, stretch taut, and staple around the perimeter, covering the deck-planking joint. Resin may be applied with a large, cheap brush or a paint roller, or poured on and squeegeed all over. Experts swear by the rollers, for they avoid a buildup of excessive resin. The cloth will be transparent when it has fully absorbed the resin. Don't try to fill the fabric surface to a glaze, for this destroys its excellent footing. As soon as you see the grain of the plywood, stop. This means that the surface is well wetted. Watch for the resin to kick off, then trim immediately with razor blades or a sharp knife while the cloth is flexible.

Where it is necessary to join panels, allow for a lap of about two inches. Sand the under panel to a feather edge to minimize the hump. After the second panel has set up well, sand the joints with 80-grit paper and go over the entire surface lightly to remove the hard fuzz. If you insist on a really smooth surface, fill the fabric with a surfacing compound using a hard squeegee or spreader. Chem-Tech has a filler called F-9. It would be satisfactory, however, to give the cloth a coat or two of thinned paint. The barren tennis-court look of your deck will be relieved when you add toerails or bulwarks.

COVERING BOARDS

While covering boards or plank-sheers are essential with any laid deck, they may be used to frame fabric-covered decks, too. Covering boards add to your work, but also to the yachtlike appearance and repairability of your vessel. See Figure 9-4. I'll show you later how this was accomplished on our old R-class sloop, *Mouette,* with a toerail over the inboard edge of the covering board to cover the canvas edge. Of course, what follows has to be done before any actual deck work is begun.

Your first task is to line off the sweep of the covering boards on the deck plan, tapering toward the ends gracefully to about two-thirds the greatest width. Transfer these rough dimensions to the deck beams. Next, spring a ¾- by 1-inch fairing batten by tacking small nails in the marks. Never nail through a batten. Keep shifting the nails slightly until the batten springs fair, then mark on both sides. Don't move the batten.

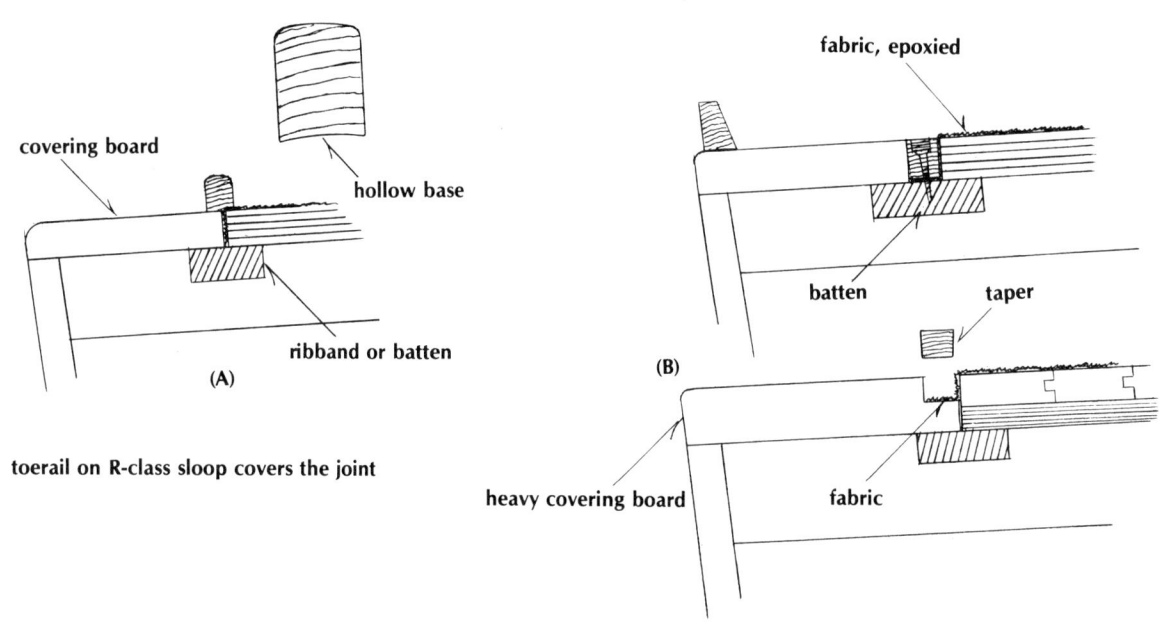

Figure 9-5. COVERING BOARD JOINT VARIATIONS

Here's how to transfer that curve to the deck panels. Screw the panels temporarily but accurately in place — at the outer edge, of course, resting on the batten. Go below and mark along its inner edge. If there will be no king plank, the deck panels can be dressed to the marks, including first and second layers, but do not fasten. If there is to be a king plank, complications arise that I'll try to dispose of a few pages farther on.

Remember that the deck and covering board edges must be supported. This is usually done by a batten or ribband let into the beams, and sometimes by blocking, as in Figure 9-4. Locate the ribband notches about 1 inch to 1¼ inches inboard from the marks and saw them about 2½ inches wide, ¾ inch deep. Screw and glue the ribband securely, using butt blocks at end joints. Now, if you never expect to replace the deck covering, you can go right ahead and lay it, stapling or tacking into the decking edge (this is preferred to fastening into the ribband).

You should provide for eventual replacement. In general, canvas decks are good for 12 to 15 years, fiberglass for who knows how long? If you go the *Mouette* route, you fit the covering boards right up against the deck edge; a toerail, its mounting edge well hollowed out, is fastened over the joint and the fabric. The toerail can be removed by digging out the bungs and refinishing the whole thing. See Figure 9-5(A).

Another yachty style is to insert a ¾-inch sided mahogany spline against the fabric-covered deck edge, with the covering boards fitted against the spline. Well seated in sealant, this spline can be removed easily when necessary. If the covering boards and deck are very heavy — say, 1¼ inches — the spline may be fitted into a rabbet in the covering board. See Figure 9-5(B). Carefully plane down to a hairbreadth of the deck, bung over the screws, sand, stain, and fill, and you have a fine joint. But what about covering boards?

Construction of a covering board or plank-sheer is another task requiring skill and patience. Because of the curvature of the hull and deck, these pieces must be made up of short lengths, unless you have on hand a lot of long and wide teak or mahogany. Remember, the procedure above is for a plywood deck. If you go for a laid deck, everything is reversed. The covering board is made up first, with the decking being sprung against it, as I shall describe later. All covering boards are joined by meticulously fitted scarfs in a half-dozen configurations. The box scarf shown in Figure 9-6 is more than adequate if well done. Make ¼-inch plywood patterns of both sides, A and B, fitted so you can't see daylight. This way all scarfs will be identical, and you won't be heaving large boards all over the vessel. You could do this by a method A, using the patterns only for marking. You should, however, rent a router and save many hours as well as get accurate joints. Use a ⅜-inch combination panel bit. This tool has a shank designed to follow a pattern with precision and dispatch. It is carbide tipped for sharpness and long life.

Always leave the outer edges of the covering boards to the very last, after all scarfs are fitted, so small adjustments can be made. Position piece no. 1 against the stem or the king plank, or to the centerline. Tack pat-

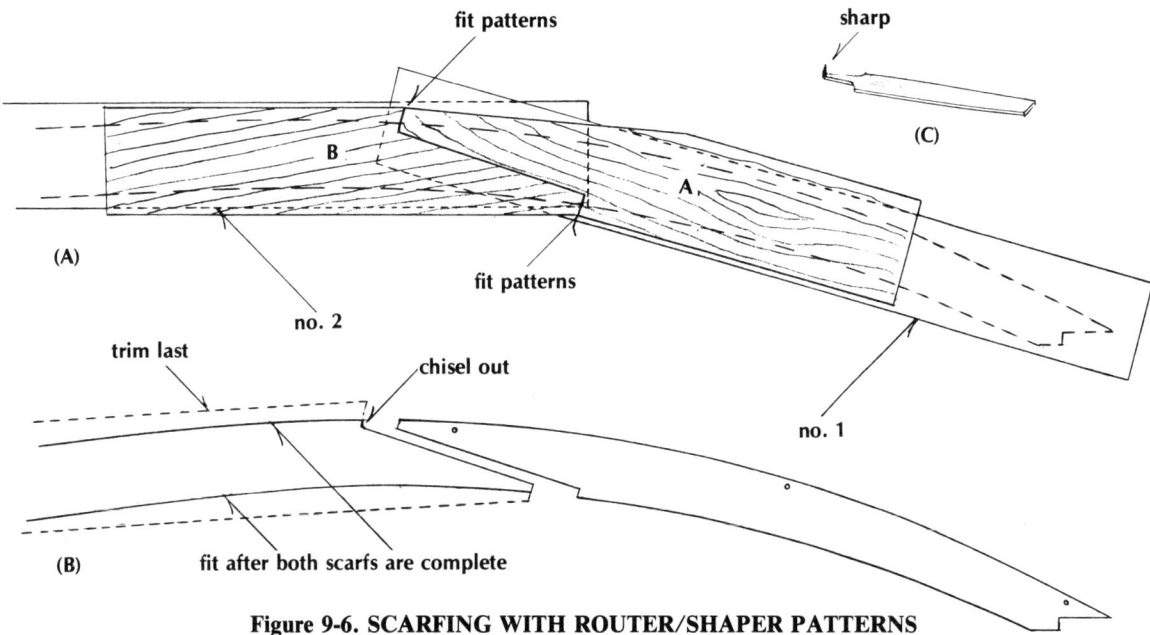

Figure 9-6. SCARFING WITH ROUTER/SHAPER PATTERNS

tern A to it so the nib lines up ¾ inch inside the plank-sheer and the center of the joint ribband (Figure 9-6(A)). Mark the scarf, saw out roughly, tack the pattern to the underside, and rout out. Clean up the corner radius in the nib with a sharp chisel. Bore and fasten no. 1 temporarily in place.

Now lay no. 2 on no. 1. Slip blocks under it to bring it up to the same plane. Use a bent and sharpened pick or small file (Figure 9-6(C)) to mark the joint underneath. Saw out roughly, tack pattern B in place (on the underside again), and rout to size. Chisel out the nib and try the fit. If the far end of piece no. 2 does not lie over the plank-sheer with ample room for trimming, adjust the position of your pattern, leaving a bit to trim off, and try again (Figure 9-6(B)). You really should not need this second try, but if you are careless, you might. Precise fitting of the length of the scarf may also be completed by trimming a bit off the male end of the nib. Make the far end scarf and bore and fasten down temporarily. Fit the inner and outer edges only after all scarfs are made up for the full length of the vessel.

As you can see, some of this joinery has to be done with a chisel into and across the grain. This takes much control and patience, and very, very sharp chisels. You should have joints that you can't see daylight through. When all the covering boards are fitted, bored for fastening down, and bedded in Thiokol, bore for additional screws, these running edgewise. Some designs call for through-bolts, a possibility if there is no decking in way of the inboard edge. The last touch is to bore parallel to the nibs and tap in a pine dowel called a stop-water. The covering boards will not swell lengthwise at the nibs, so leakage could occur, followed by discoloration of the fine finish, and possibly dry rot. Of course, blocking is to be used under all scarfs.

It is superior yacht practice to run a covering board over the transom, a fashion piece similar to your rail caps. Support blocking must be constructed to keep the decking and covering board from working (Figure 9-7). The sketch does not show decking running straight out over the transom, but it's not uncommon. This should at least be covered by a continuation of the rail or bulwark cap called the taffrail. (This is shown in Chapter 14, in Figure 14-3.) The transom covering board may join the side board in a simple miter, but do not allow the sharp ends to extend to the extreme outer edge. A careless helmsman might tear off a lot of nice hardwood as he swings away from a pier.

Figure 9-7 shows another style of deck — the herringbone. If any sprung decking meets the fashion piece at a more acute angle than indicated, it could be nibbed in as shown by the dotted lines. Blocking under the deck and fashion piece is also indicated by dotted lines. A great many variations in the quarter knees here are possible, both straight and crooks. All of this joinery must be first class, and all precautions must be taken against leakage. Counter sterns are highly susceptible to rot resulting from frequent doses of rainwater and little fresh-air circulation under the deck.

It is good form and sound construction to build frames or margins of teak or mahogany forward and aft of hatch openings and mast partners, even all around the cabin trunk and cockpit well. (See Figure 9-4.) This type of framing and king plank is often quite a bit heavier than the decks, with the step-down usually in the form of a routed cove. Again, such deluxe construction is more often used in conjunction with laid decking, but it can produce an impressive effect with fabric-covered plywood decks, too. Note the optional nibbing piece, to avoid nibbing the covering board. In the description of

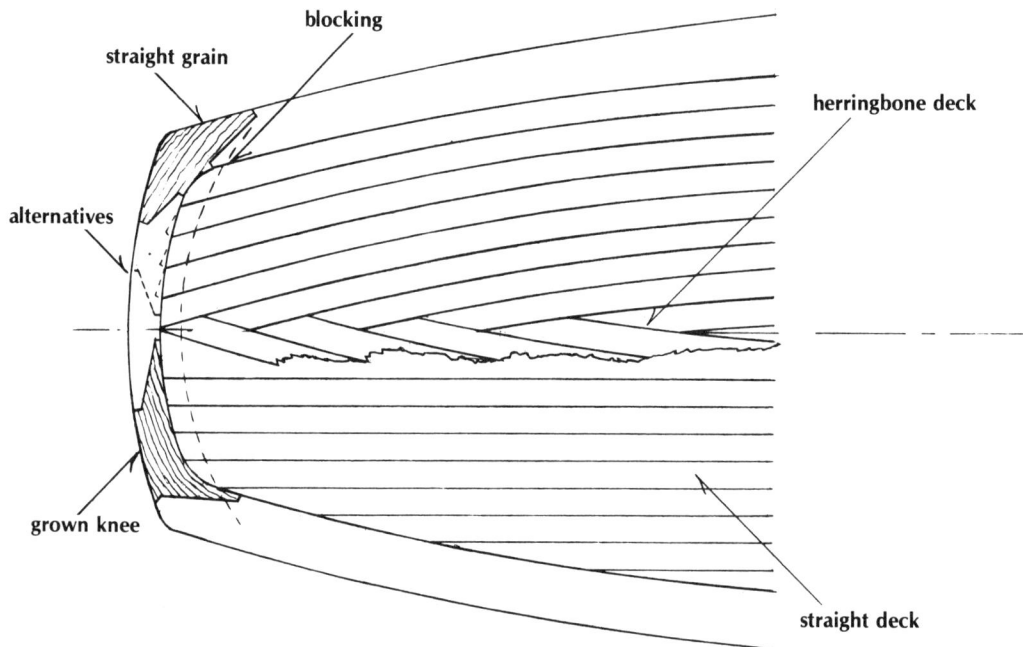

Figure 9-7. TAFFRAIL OR FASHION PIECE AND QUARTER KNEES IN TRANSOM COVERING BOARD

canvas-covered decks, I will cover some difficulties and possible solutions.

CANVASED DECKS

Along with the resurgence of interest in wooden yacht construction, canvasing of decks has, to a lesser degree, regained some recognition. Canvasing has advantages important to the nonprofessional builder. These include lower cost of materials, excellent footing, simplicity of application, long life, and easy maintenance and replaceability. In my opinion, canvasing does not promote rot as polyester resin fiberglassing does.

Cosmetically, it is preferable to use canvas wide enough to eliminate the joint fore and aft (Figure 9-8). Material 96 inches wide is readily available. Check your local awning or sailmaker for sources of canvas up to 12 feet wide. Decking weights would run from 8-ounce to 12-ounce; do not confuse these terms with #8 or #12. Use 12-ounce for really hard service. For small half-decked boats I have used heavy cotton sheeting, but of course this fabric is likely to fill with paint in a few years. I made it a practice to brighten the color each spring with one coat of paint well thinned with turpentine to preserve the fine nonskid surface. Joints athwartships are less objectionable if they occur on the side decks only. Such joints may be double-stitched by your sailmaker, or they can be folded and double-tacked. They'll be highly visible even if you try to butt them, so why take a chance on a nasty leak? A certain amount of feathering can be done to produce a lapped joint, but this is not as effective as with fiberglass.

Let's assume you are doing the simplest canvasing job. The canvas is to be pulled over the deck edge and covered by the usual rubstrake. This can't be done by one person. I suggest that you pick up a couple of pairs of clamp pliers with jaws about 2½ to 3 inches wide. This is the type used by welders. With these pliers (Figure 9-9) you can pull the canvas tight without poking holes through it. You might be able to roll the canvas around a stick, but this is tough on the fingernails. In addition, it's difficult to get enough local tension. Fasten with copper tacks with large heads or bronze staples. (Anything made of steel will promote rot.)

Do not lay the canvas in wet paint, as some advise. There will be minute working of the deck panels as a result of infinitesimal expansion and contraction of the joints. Cementing to the plywood with paint will eventually cause cracks. Do seal the plywood or tongue-and-groove lumber with thinned epoxy resin or at least the commercially available Firzite, or Rez, or something similar. Keep brushing or rolling it on until the surface refuses to soak up any more. This hardens the surface, giving it a resistance to dents, and prevents moisture from entering. Vacuum clean or sweep the deck. A particle the size of a pinhead will create a bump you'll hate for a lifetime.

Have a gallon or two of ordinary house paint ready to use later. Lay the canvas in position, tack or staple it to the deck at the forward end of the main opening, then

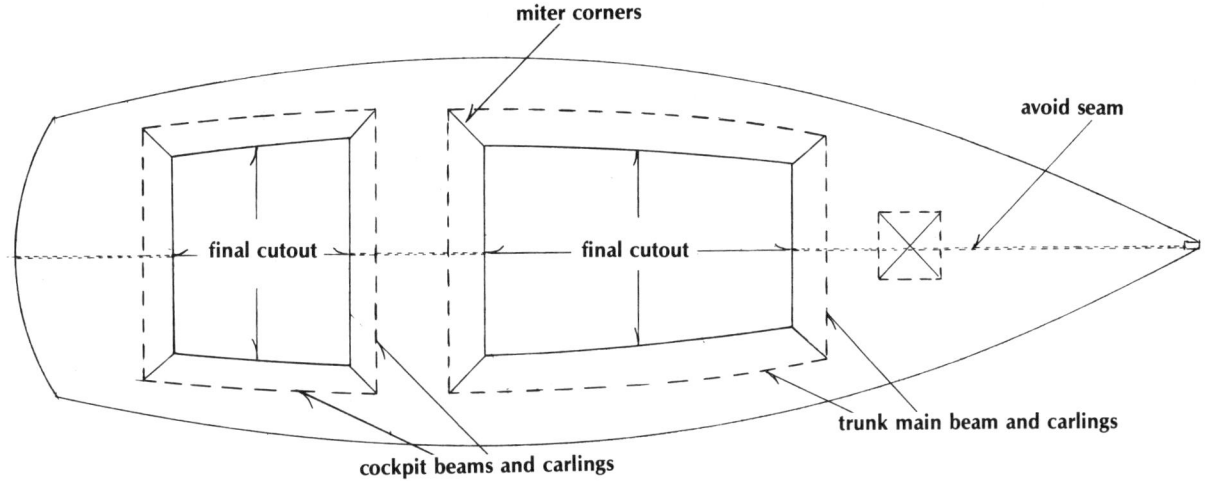

Figure 9-8. DECK CANVAS LAYOUT

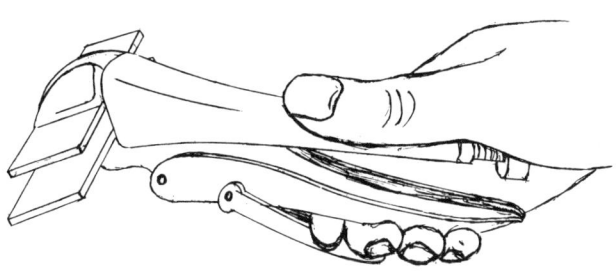

Figure 9-9. HAND CLAMP FOR PULLING CANVAS

stretch it taut along the centerline and fasten it to the planking on both sides of the stem. Do not trim yet. At this point, a man on each side starts pulling. These two work from the big opening forward, fastening to the plank-sheer just under the deck joint as they go. The canvas must be bent down and stretched over the deck edge while a helper shoots in a couple of tacks or staples.

Continue hauling the canvas out as you move forward. By the time you approach the stem, you'll see that the material has stretched and is causing large wrinkles at the stem. Pull out the original temporary fastenings and replace them. If yours is a projecting stem, trim carefully there but let the surplus canvas hang down over the planking until the rubstrake or fender is installed.

This leaves the canvas drum-tight across the cabin opening, unless you have already split the material. Do not cut unless you are positive about how you're going to handle it where it joins the trunk. As usual, there are several options, as shown in Figure 9-10: (A) bend up inside the trunk; (B) bend up outside against the trunk and cover with moldings; and (C) hide in a rabbet in the trunk side at the deck. The first is the easiest. It is almost 100 percent leakproof, but you would have to remove the trunk to replace canvas. Also, you might create a pocket where moisture from sweating and leakage could collect. It is standard practice to cover with a mahogany or teak facing piece. I have shown the carlings in both vertical and canted positions — take your choice. The second approach is neat and easy to make, although it is a nuisance to deal with the changing angles of the molding. The possibility of water lodging under the molding and soaking the fabric must be considered. Here, too, the fabric should be soaked with paint, resin, or glue, and the molding bedded in Thiokol. Set the molding with screws so replacement of the fabric will be simpler. The third design is the best if the weaknesses discussed above are taken care of, but it does require a heavy trunk side. Of course, the rabbet must be cut in after the trunk sides are fitted but not finally installed. The recessed spline or molding should not be trod on. The molding in Figure 9-10(B), however, may be walked on freely.

The fourth approach is a compromise. I have never done it. The rabbet should be quite shallow compared with the one used in the third approach, and the screws or finish nails should go into the deck instead of into the trunk side. Bedding and the other precautions are just as necessary here as in the first three approaches. I think the finished appearance would be rather good. Bringing this or any molding around a forward corner post is a job that will test the skill of any craftsman. I suggest that you get a consultation locally.

These approaches apply in general to fiberglass, Vectra, Versatex, Dynel, and any other fabrics, in addition to canvas. Note too that the decision as to which approach you will use must be made long before you build the deck or the trunk cabin. For example, the rabbet just described must be routed out before the sides are assembled and bolted down.

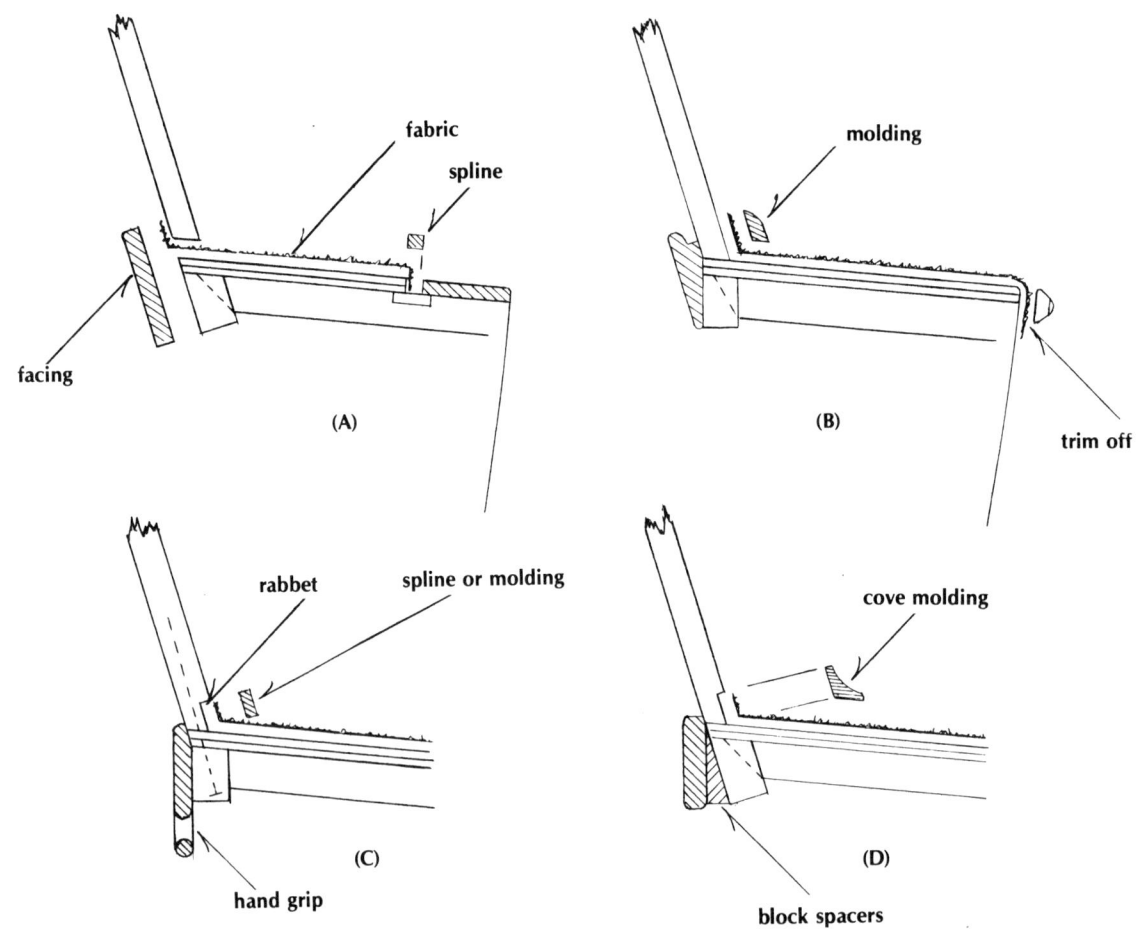

Figure 9-10. FABRIC INBOARD EDGES — AND IDEAS

If the beam of your yacht is somewhat greater than the width of the material, take advantage of the cutout for the cabin and cockpit to spread the canvas perhaps as much as a foot or more (Figure 9-8). Bending it too far, however, will create wrinkles. If the design includes a bridge deck, you may be able to hide joints under the coaming to port and starboard. Just a small piece of surplus would cover the bridge. If you can reach all the way to the transom with one piece of fabric, you may increase the resale value of the vessel by $1,000 for just the price of a couple of square yards of canvas.

INSTALLING KING PLANK AND CANVASING

In Chapter Eight I described blocking that runs the length of the deck between beams or a strongback let into the beams. This is similar in function to the ribband to which the outboard deck edge and covering board are fastened. Such construction is necessary for any deck that includes a king plank. Also, any margin or framing of trunk, hatches, or other openings must be supported in the same manner, whether the deck is fabric-covered plywood or laid strakes. Nibbing, especially, must be backed up. Another method, one lacking the strength of the above, is to let in two ribbands to which the king plank and decking are fastened (Figure 9-11(A)). This saves some weight, increases labor, and decreases strength. I would hesitate to place cleats on this. It might be accepted in a light-displacement sailboat, in which case I would make the ribbands of plywood to prevent splitting.

Here, as at the covering board, the fabric may be made replaceable by covering its edge with a spline pressed into a groove. The splines should be made with a slight taper, as shown in Figure 9-11. Fasten the panels down as described previously, making sure the groove is of precise width to take not only the spline but also the thickness of the fabric. Now it's a simple matter to stretch the fabric hard fore and aft, trim to cover the groove, soak with paint or glue, and press or tap in the spline. This should pull the fabric into the groove, but don't permit the fabric to bunch up under the spline. Bore the spline for screws and plugs and screw down. Now stretch the fabric across the deck to go under a similar spline next to the covering board described above.

I suggest that covering boards, king plank, splines, and so on, be filled, stained, and varnished before the deck fabric is started. This keeps paint and glue from getting in the pores of the wood. Taping is still ad-

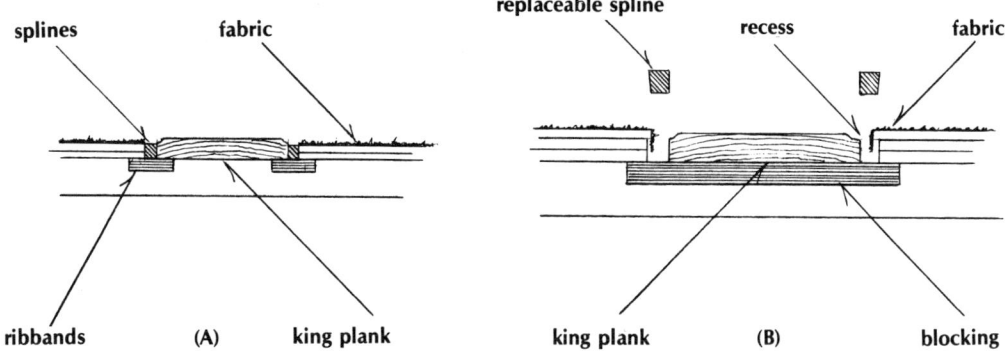

Figure 9-11. KING PLANK AND CANVASING SYSTEM

visable. It is mandatory if these parts are teak. This applies whether the deck is to be painted or filled with resin.

PAINTING THE DECK

After the canvas has been fastened properly, it's finally time to paint. The first thing you do is wet the canvas thoroughly with — of all things — water. Yes, the paint goes right on the wet cloth. If you tried to paint on dry canvas, your entire brushful would soak instantly into the cloth. The job would require perhaps five times as much paint, and it would appear blotchy. In addition, some of the paint might soak through and cement the canvas to the plywood, an effect you do not want. After two coats have dried for a day or two, go over the deck with a sanding block to remove the fuzz, if any. To brighten up the color once or twice a year, use paint thinned down about 30 percent with turpentine. This dilution acts more like a stain. Heavy coats cause buildup, checking, and cracking, all of which destroy the excellent nonskid surface.

LAID DECKS

The process of installing decks of pine, fir, cedar, or teak is covered fully in the boatbuilding books recommended earlier. I included a few words on fastening decks in Chapter Six. Now I'll add some material on the drawings in Figures 9-4 and 9-7. These show the two main classes of decks — sprung and straight laid. The sprung deck, in my opinion, is the most beautiful of all, but a straight-laid deck is also worthwhile. The sprung deck was originally a means of simplifying construction when the deckhouse curvature followed the plank-sheer closely. Today this is rarely found. The straight-laid deck matched trunk construction parallel to the centerline, a feature found in many older designs, especially workboats and the yachts of designer Billy Atkin. Both styles are considered obsolete now.

Either system requires nibbing of the deck strakes where they run out to a fine end. The sprung deck may be nibbed into the king plank (Figure 9-4) or laid herringbone-fashion (Figure 9-7). The latter is much easier to build and very handsome. Nibbing is time-consuming because each strake end is squared off, then tapered to its intersection with the covering board or king plank (or to a nibbing piece). It is good practice to outline a margin around all deck openings and the deckhouses (Figure 9-4). This means more nibbing, of course. It is customary to build these margins and king planks of mahogany or teak, perhaps ¼ to ⅜ inch thicker than the deck strakes. All nibs should be of the same depth everywhere, and should match port and starboard. Decking is sometimes nibbed into the transom covering board or fashion piece. It must be if the piece is very rounded and the strakes come in at an acute angle.

Very narrow teak deck strakes might not be nibbed. Also, such narrow decking, if laid herringbone, may be doubled in these staggered joints. This deck may be laid up without a caulking seam. Of course, all joints and butts must be properly sealed with Thiokol, or epoxy, or their equivalent. The bevel required on all caulked seams was described earlier.

One more point. The traditional laid deck is nearly square in section so the sprung deck can be clamped or wedged to the covering board without more than the usual sweat. Moreover, most of the remarks above apply to a deck laid over a plywood underlay (the *only* way to go!), except as follows. The thinner deck material (say, ½ to ¾ inch by 2 inches) will try to pop up into your face when you spring it the hard way. This is very dangerous. One solution is to have assistants stand on

Figure 9-12. *A WEST System teak deck laid over plywood. This handsome deck provides excellent footing and is easily maintained. (Gougeon Brothers photo)*

the strake while you draw up the bar clamps and get a few fastenings into the beams. I have seen a half-dozen body-builder's 20-pound weights perform this duty. The ones I saw in use were covered with plastic. This eliminates bruises.

After the seams have been payed, scrape off as much as you can of the messy compound before it sets up hard. You can sand with a regular belt floor-sanding machine, then finish the job with a portable belt sander and a sanding block. Use 80-grit open-coat aluminum oxide or garnet paper.

A TEAK STRIP DECK

The Gougeon Brothers on Boat Construction is a book about laminating systems. It is a true gold mine of information on modern methods. Much of it would be of benefit to you. I was particularly impressed by the section called "Teak Veneer Deck System." This describes the laying of teak only $\frac{1}{8}$ to $\frac{3}{16}$ inch thick over an underlay of $\frac{3}{8}$- or $\frac{1}{2}$-inch plywood (or heavier, depending on the size of the vessel). Teak no thicker than $\frac{3}{16}$ inch, however, is required. You must resign yourself to a copious use of epoxy resin adhesive (the Gougeons' No. 403 and No. 423 graphite powder), and you will need a double coating of WEST System epoxy resin on the bare plywood before starting the teak lamination.

Here's a brief rundown of the Gougeon system. The teak is rough sawed from full 2-inch flat grain or 2 by 2 stock. Saw out edge-grain strips to $\frac{1}{8}$- or $\frac{3}{16}$- inch strips. Do not plane to thickness. The "tooth" improves the bond. Square the ends precisely on lengths ranging from 6 to 12 feet. Mix up an adhesive mixture of No. 403 fiber and No. 423 graphite powder to a thick, syrupy consistency. Add 10 percent (by volume) graphite. Try some sample bonds. Apply the mixture liberally to both the underlay and the strips. Staple with $\frac{1}{2}$-inch-long bronze staples of the wide crown type, set so the staples are slightly above the teak surface. Use only enough to hold the strips in position until the adhesive cures, about one staple every 9 inches along the center of the strip. Use more staples if the strip curves severely.

Gauge a gap of about $\frac{3}{32}$ inch between strips. Resin must be seen oozing up in the gap. The deck is now a mess. Start to clean up by nipping off the staples with a sharp wire cutter. Sand with 50-grit on a portable belt sander or a disc with a foam pad. On a large deck you may use a belt floor sander. This is the rough sanding stage. Now fill all gaps with a WEST System resin putty mixture of 406 Colloidal Silica with WEST System resin. Add 10 percent graphite powder. This protects the resin from ultraviolet attack.

Final sanding is with 80-grit on a soft foam disc pad. I see no reason why a portable belt sander would not work as well. There will have to be some final sanding with a block around tight areas, of course. The bronze staples are almost invisible. The Gougeons say this deck should stand heavy foot traffic for "at least 20 years." See Figure 9-12. I think it is a system the amateur builder should use if he wants his boat to become a yacht. The extensive work involved in laying any of the decks I have described will pay off in pride when you hear someone say, "Now *that's* what I call a yacht!"

TEN

Cabin Trunk Construction

The design of your cabin trunk or house is subject to many variations. It may be of the old style, with sides inclining inward from ½ to ¾ inch per foot of height. Look at the superb creations of such designers as Philip L. Rhodes, S.S. Crocker, Charles D. Mower, Charles G. MacGregor, Murray Peterson, and others. Their deckhouses usually show a moderate camber. The beams are more often sawed than laminated. Forward corners are slightly rounded, unless cost was no problem. In other words, their cabin trunks are simply constructed, straightforward, conservatively proportioned, and always handsome. In many other ways, too, the older designs are totally satisfactory, and they should be considered by any of you making design decisions.

In contrast, the deckhouses of moderate yachts always tumble home greatly (three inches per foot of height is considered moderate). Many have cambers of more than 1 inch per foot of breadth, and they have not only extremely rounded forward corners, but also raking forward ends. Combined with a high cambered deck, these features mean increased material and labor costs, shaped carlings, very wide cabin sides, laminated beams, intricate corner posts, laminated or steam-bent forward ends, and so on. No wonder the modern wooden yacht is costly. Because of the complexity of the deck plug and mold, plus the quantities of resin and glass required, the production fiberglass vessel is also costly.

In deference to those who are convinced they must be "modern," I will discuss a few procedures that apply to contemporary designs. Fortunately, these procedures can be used on older vessels as well. Either way, tumblehome and smoothly rounded forms, especially the blister-shaped structure, tend to reduce windage created by height. High cambers pay off in increased headroom in small boats, so it's not all bad.

TUMBLEHOME

Your first job after completing the deck is to set up a structure around which the cabin trunk sides can be bent, thus securing them at the designed tumblehome. I'll refer to this as a form and the separate cross sections as strongbacks (Figure 10-1). Strongbacks can also be used to provide a rigid support for laminating a beamless cabintop, if you choose to go that way. This form is mainly 1 by 4 or 1 by 6 construction, with the curved top piece of ¾-inch plywood or lumber. The several radii of the strongbacks may be swung with a wire or with a camber scriber. I said "several" because there is a slight sheer to the cabin side when it is viewed

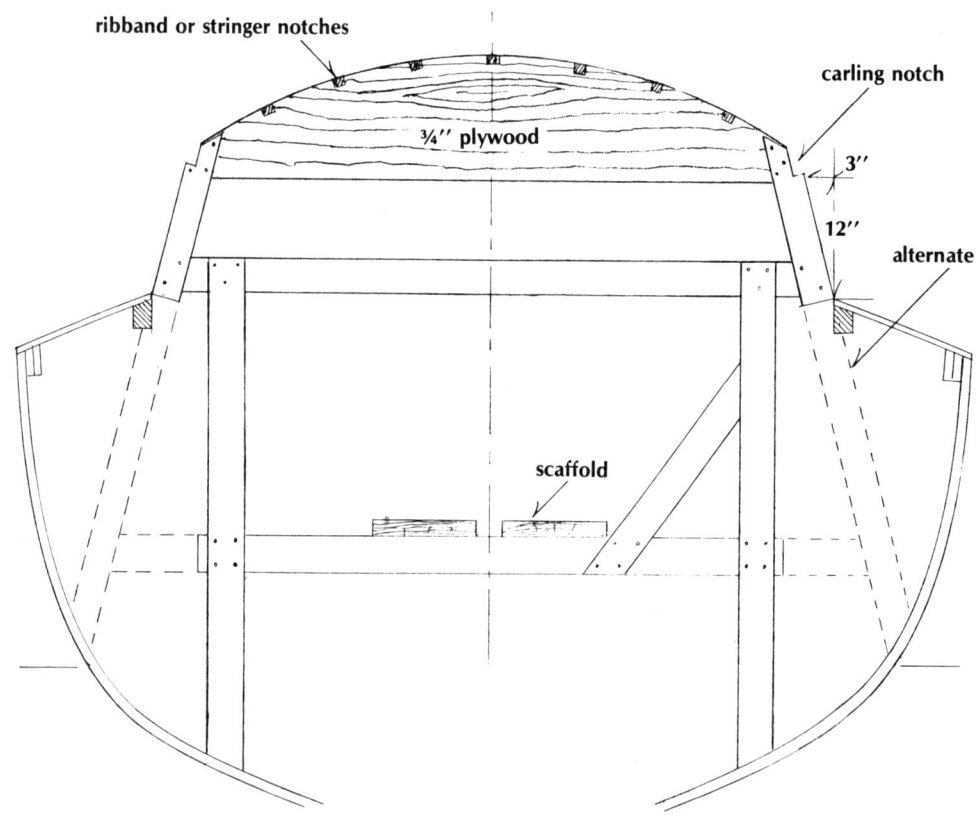

Figure 10-1. STRONGBACK FOR TRUNK SIDES AND TOP

after bending (this must be spelled out in detail by your designer). Thus, if you desire a straight centerline profile (and most people do), each strongback must be laid out and supported so as to reach a strong, straight board clamped on the centerline.

It is assumed that your main bulkhead aft and another one forward have been proportioned correctly so you can run strong battens from these over the two or three (or more) strongbacks and along the sides so the trunk sides and cabintop will be fair. A level with a wedge taped to it would be handy to make the sides fall to the same tumblehome. See Figure 8-20. You can simplify this by making the strongback all one piece. Then you can screw legs to it, eliminating the 1 by 4 cross frame. Don't forget notches for the cabintop carlings, and the many notches for stringers for forming a beamless top. (If there are to be beams, ignore the cambered strongback and laminate the beams, as described in Chapter Nine.)

A simplified trunk tumblehome form is shown in Figure 10-2. This construction is not strong enough to support the weight of a couple of men laying a laminated top. It should be adequate for a beamed top, however. You can use scrap plywood instead of the open framework. The strongbacks must be tied together temporarily with battens to maintain their vertical alignment as the sides are being bent and fitted.

A TRUNK SIDE PATTERN

You will need a pattern of the cabin side to make sure both sides are identical and to show up differences in the sweep of the carlings, and so on. This can be pieces of ¼-inch plywood nailed together with butts between the strongbacks (so they don't interfere on the opposite side). Heights to the sheer of the side can be taken from the lofting or from a reference line in the design. This sheer, when finished, is almost invisible, unless it is wrong. In that case, it stands out like a three-legged man at a dance. Give this your careful attention, for insufficient sheer could make the side appear to be hogged because of the tumblehome. If the side is to be laminated of two thicknesses of plywood, make allowances for the bevels at the deck and at the juncture of side and top. Lay out the ports and window shapes, and the locations and incline of forward corner posts. Do the same if the main aft bulkhead rakes forward (a nice backrest, but a more difficult piece of construction, of course). With the pattern tacked around the strong-

166

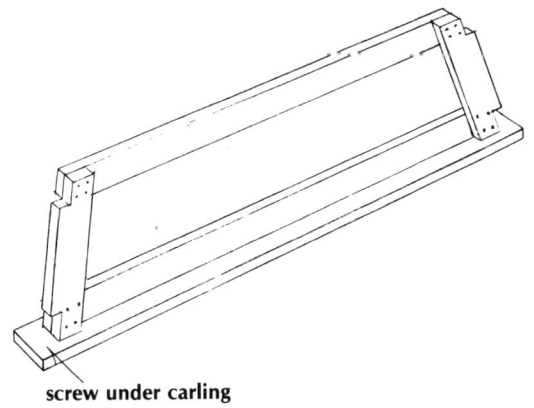

Figure 10-2. SIMPLE TRUNK TUMBLEHOME FORM

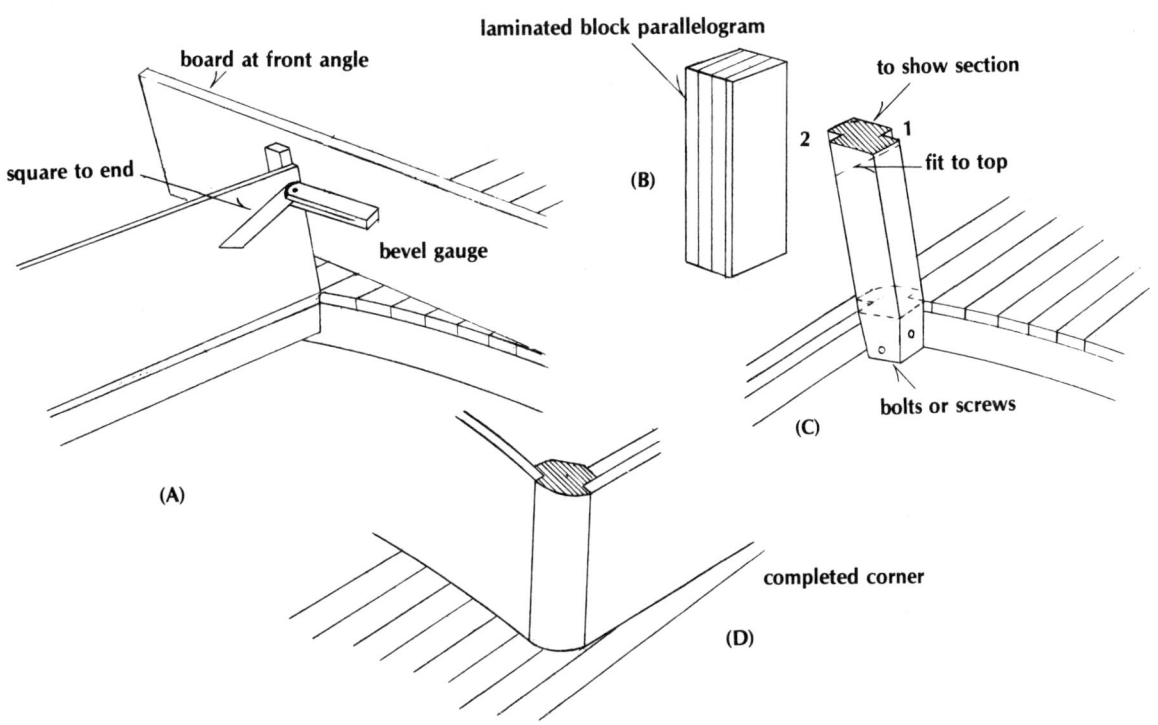

Figure 10-3. CABIN TRUNK CORNER POST LAYOUT

backs and a couple of light battens laid fore and aft, you should now be able to get a pretty fair picture of what your cabin trunk is going to look like.

CORNER POSTS

Now we come to a hazardous and frustrating problem — the forward corners. A simple solution would be to butt the sides against the end with a cleat in the corner. This is lubberly construction. It is unsightly, prone to rot, and seen on cheap boats. The proper method is to construct a pair of rabbeted corner posts to receive the cabin sides and the front piece. See Figure 10-3. The main problem is the tumblehome of sides meeting the rake at the forward end. This is compounded by the need to fasten the post to the beam and/or deck. This task calls for the finest joinerwork. I hope your designer has detailed it well. Herreshoff, Chapelle, Steward, and other authorities have not paid attention to this problem. I have not found a source to which to refer you, so here goes!

To start, build up a laminated timber of mahogany or

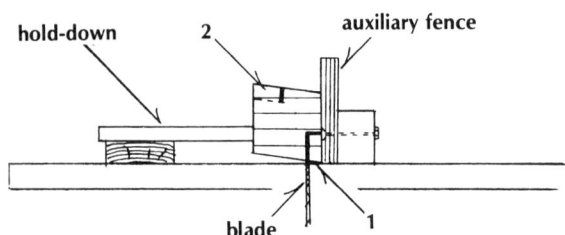

Figure 10-4. RABBETING THE CORNER BLOCK

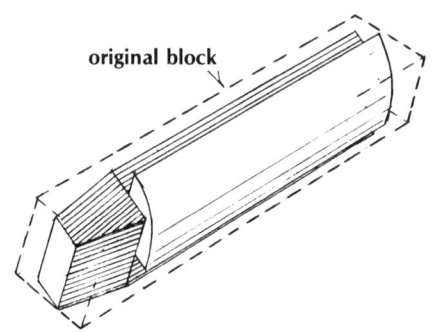

Figure 10-6. CORNER POST COMPLETED

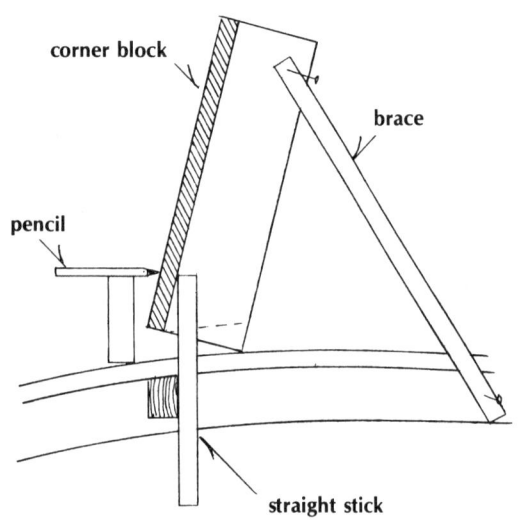

Figure 10-5. SCRIBING TO DECK AND BEAMS

teak at least 4 inches wide and 4 inches deep, and long enough to make considerably more than two corner posts or blocks. This will be worked into a parallelogram (Figure 10-3(B)) when fitted, so allow plenty of stock. The final section will look like the sketch because of the sloping side and front. To get this peculiar shape, clamp the plywood pattern or lumber to a couple of the cabin strongbacks. Erect another one athwartships temporarily supported at the angle of the forward end. The side pattern, while in position, should be marked to the desired angle of the front and sawed off. See Figure 10-3(A). Tack them together to produce a mock-up of the corner. Check the tumblehome and rake with your level. Make a mark on the side pattern square to the forward end and place a bevel gauge flat against this mark, the blade against the front piece. This gives you the true angle of the vital corner of the parallelogram. Now you can saw out that angle on your table saw and plane it carefully to fit inside the temporary corner. Dress the two inner sides so they are parallel.

Assuming your cabin side and end pieces require rabbets 1 inch by 1½ inches wide, use the same saw setting to make all the deeper cuts. Then reset to 90 degrees for the 1-inch cut. Figure 10-4 shows another method. The block is held securely against an auxiliary fence by a hold-down (comb or feather) raised on a block. This is faster than changing saw angles back and forth several times.

Fitting the lower end against the carling and beam is a fussy job. Set up the cabin side pattern so the corner block fits, with its end standing on the deck above the beam (Figure 10-5). Use a block a bit higher than the total thickness of deck and beam as a gauge (or a compass) to mark both the front and the side above the deck. This indicates where the horizontal or deck rabbet will come. This is pretty close to the final shape required, but you still have to get the faces that meet the carling and beam. Just place a little stick against these and mark so they intersect parallel to the deck. Backsaw or bandsaw on the safe side of all lines and chisel to a snug fit so all angles check out.

It might be easier to fit the side of the block against the carling, then the front against the beam. A carling canted to parallel the trunk side (see Figures 10-9 and 10-10) might simplify this operation, but that, too, is a trade-off. Trim off the lower end to conform to the facing piece to come. Bevel the inside corner or round it off as you please. Finally, the outside corner must be rounded to blend into side and front, as shown in Figure 10-6. The upper end must be trimmed to meet the camber of the cabintop after the final assembly — or bandsaw approximately, then plane off. When all is perfect, counterbore for bungs over bolts through beam and carling. Leave this for now, but plan to use epoxy or Aerolite in the final assembly.

SIMPLE CORNERS

There are several easier ways to construct cabin trunk corners. This same one-piece rabbeted post can just sit comfortably on the deck 6 or 8 inches forward of the heavy beam, forming a convenient shelf. See Figure

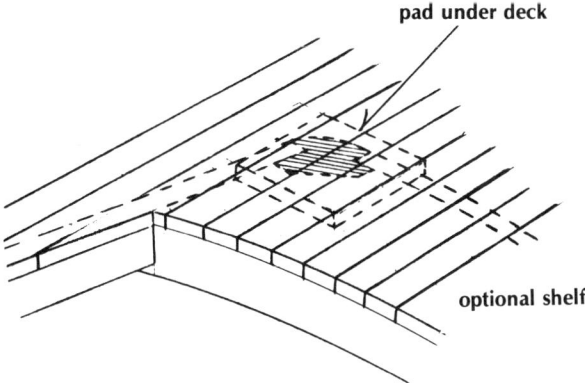

Figure 10-7. POSITION OF CORNER POST

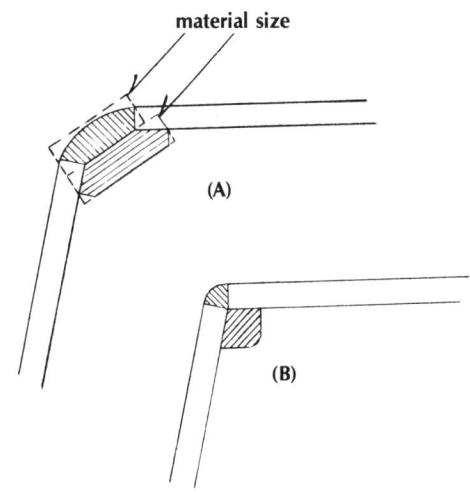

Figure 10-8. TWO-PIECE CORNER POSTS

10-7. Nice cabinets on each side of an opening port make a fine yachty touch, but first the post has to be set up rigidly so that both angles are correct. Then you scribe with a block or compass around all four sides, as in Figure 10-5. One or two lags driven from the underside is the usual way this is fastened. Blocking under the deck is required. Bed the post in Thiokol or other luting. Once the sides and end are glued and screwed into the rabbets, this will be a strong structure. The forward end must be epoxy glued and fastened from under the deck with long lags, screws, or through-bolts.

Another system used frequently is the two-piece post. This requires taking angles from sides and end as above. The style shown in Figure 10-8(A) is only a bit more difficult than the one shown in Figure 10-8(B), and the larger radius is handsome. I would not try to bolt this inside the carling and beam, however, without a filler piece in the corner. The rounded outer corner is fitted after everything is set up, and fastened from the inside. The post in Figure 10-8(B) could be screwed into the corner if the tumblehome and rake are slight and if you make the post ample, not less than 2 inches on a side. Somehow I find the appearance of this just a little less than first class, but who am I to complain?

The trunk aft end has corners that may rake forward (this makes a good backrest for a bridge deck). The answers are the same — tough! More frequently, however, the end is vertical, so construction is easy. Some small sailboats with low trunks continue the side into the cockpit coaming. If the coaming is lower, some of the cabin-side end grain above may be exposed. I can't say this is bad, but I would prefer to see a corner something like the one shown in Figure 10-8(B). Don't forget to plan for a coaming fairing block to mate with the sloping coamings (this will be detailed in Chapter Thirteen).

Bulkheads meeting the cabin sides must be cleated attractively to provide an ample surface to which to fasten the trunk sides. The side cleat should be mitered to the overhead cleat, which is really a short beam. Run your router around the corners to form a radius, chamfer, ogee, or whatever pleases you.

TRUNK-SIDE CONSTRUCTION SYSTEMS

Sometime prior to this point, you must determine the kind of trunk side that is best for your boat. Your choice is quite broad. Each type has its good and bad points:
A. For a painted trunk, single-thickness plywood, scarfed or butted;
B. The same, but laminated of plywood, two or more thicknesses glued;
C. Solid mahogany or teak for a bright finish, probably jointed, splined, tongue and grooved, or rabbeted;
D. Also for a bright finish, strip-built, small sections sprung around the strongbacks nailed and glued to each other.

PLYWOOD TRUNK CABINS

A single thickness of ¾-inch plywood 15 inches or more in width is not easy to bend, especially in short lengths. If scarfed on a 10-to-1 ratio for a total length of 10 to 12 feet, this might be possible. The other difficulty is the fastening from beneath into the plywood edge, passing long lags, or whatever, through the carling and deck with accuracy. Years ago I built a number of small plywood yachts designed by Charles G. MacGregor. He was a genius at simplification combined with excellent engineering. His 27-foot *Threesome* (my name for her) specified a trunk with ½-inch plywood sides. His design is similar to the sketch in Figure 10-9(A), except that there is no carling in the accepted sense. Instead, what I label a cleat or sill is sprung down to the necessary sweep of the deck and closely screwed and glued from beneath, with no carling. Long screws go through the beams into

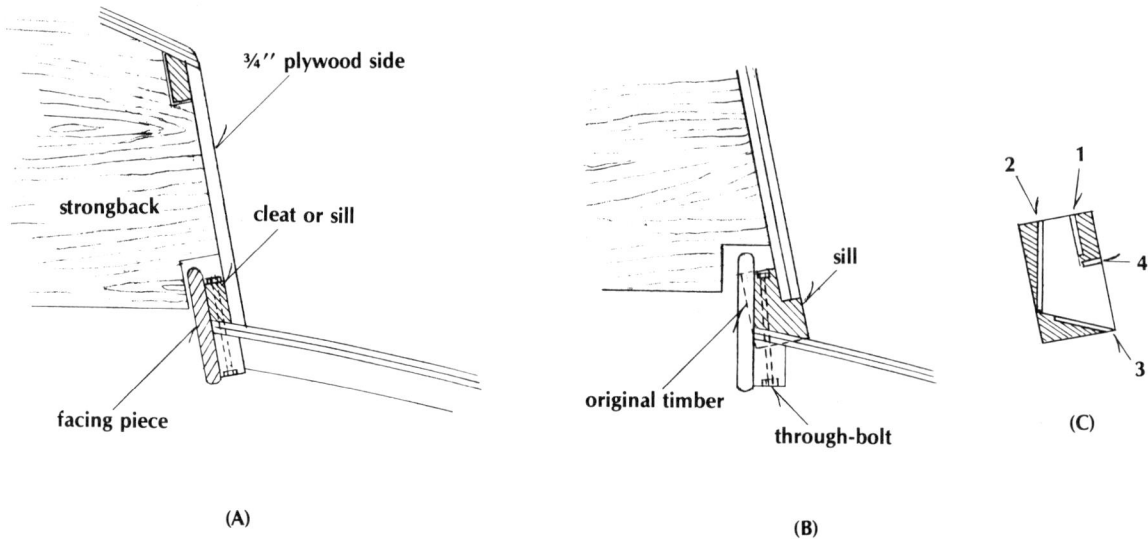

Figure 10-9. CABIN TRUNK SIDE CLEAT OR SILL CONSTRUCTION

the sill. We bent the ½-inch sides around a couple of strongbacks, spiled them to the deck sweep, and screwed and glued them to the sills. Years later, this proved to be very strong construction in spite of its oversimplification. There were no signs of opening or movement along the long joint. My construction is massive by comparison. It is further strengthened by the facing piece fastened to both the carling and the sill. Of course, the upper edge had its conventional batten or clamp to take the cabintop beams. This clamp was sprung in, glued, and screwed from the outside. The point of my drawing is to show that the sill (when 1 inch or more) is strong enough to withstand the stresses of bending ¾-inch plywood.

CANTED CARLINGS

Note that Figure 10-9(A) shows a carling inclined to match the tumblehome. A variation for plywood sides is the strong rabbeted sill shown in Figures 10-9(B) and 10-9(C). This shows the inboard surfaces of the carling and sill vertical, but the outboard surface of the sill tumbles home and is rabbeted for the side. This sill is not as hard to make as it appears. I show the sequence of saw cuts you need to shape this piece.

There are several systems you should consider, even though I do not approve. See Figure 10-10. The first is the cabin side fastened inside the carling and deck. The second is the cabin side screwed directly to the facing piece (or vice versa). This is seen in some extreme racing machines. If the facing piece is very heavy, say, 1¼ to 1½ inches, with a shaped hand grip formed in it, it should be substantial enough. Bolts, screws, and glue are advisable. The last, with a wedge-shaped filler full length, beefs up the construction even more. This could be one piece, of course.

LAMINATED TRUNK SIDES

Plywood in two thicknesses is easy to bend. The two sheets may be a combination of ⅜ inch with ½ inch, both ½ inch, or whatever. The first lamination had better be stiffened and faired along its upper edge before the second is glued to it, especially if you see any hard spots over the strongbacks. Do not cut out any openings at this time. Your pattern should be useful in fitting this piece into rabbets fore and aft and to the deck or sill. Fasten here with glue and screws.

The installation of shelf, clamp, or batten should fair the side. See Figure 10-11. If you are using laminated beam construction, your choices are a shelf (Figure 10-11(A)) or a notched batten (Figure 10-11(B)). The former is strong and quite simple. Constructing it is just a matter of sawing the correct bevel so the shelf sits level. You can fasten the beams with screws and glue from above or below. If A were turned flat, it would be called a clamp, and it would need to be somewhat heavier so fastenings would be more effective. In B there is no mechanical fastening of any real effectiveness. The joint is fully dependent on epoxy glue. The batten (Figure 10-11(C)) provides a nailing and gluing area for a laminated beamless top. Because of the great camber, the tops in A and B would have to be two thicknesses of 3/16- or ¼-inch plywood (not shown). Be sure the angle of the upper surface of these battens is sawed accurately for close fitting of the top material.

Fit the second lamination carefully all around, then coat both surfaces with epoxy or Plastic Resin glue.

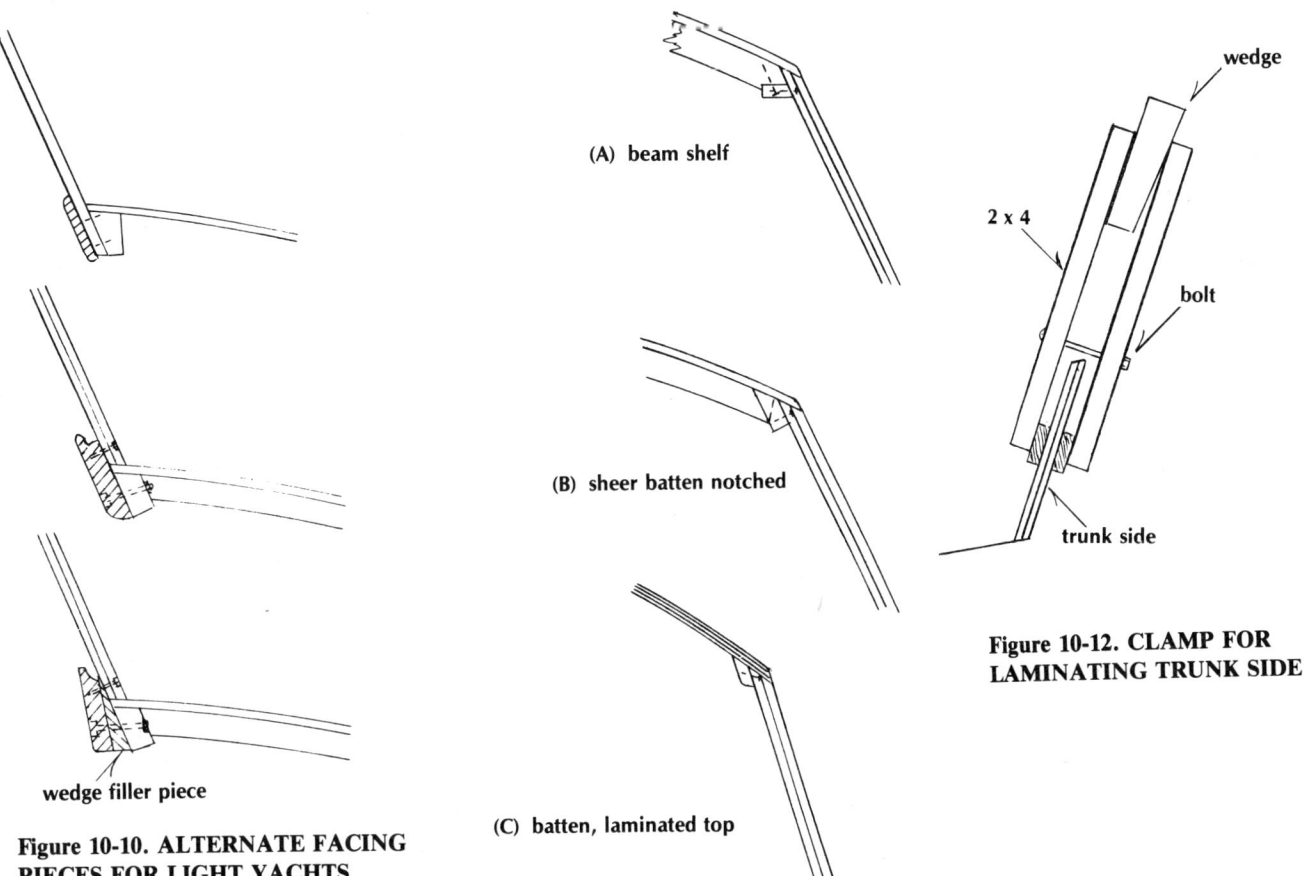

Figure 10-10. ALTERNATE FACING PIECES FOR LIGHT YACHTS

Figure 10-11. UPPER REINFORCEMENTS

Figure 10-12. CLAMP FOR LAMINATING TRUNK SIDE

Four or five large cabinetmaker's screw clamps (the wooden kind) would help prevent air pockets. It's best to place 1 by 4's inside and out, under the clamps. Even with these, however, additional temporary clamping might be required. Try a dozen nails through small plywood blocks inside and out to draw the plies together. Screws or serrated nails and glue in the end rabbets fore and aft should hold well. It should not be necessary to use screws along the top edge. Here's a tip. If you run into heads of screws in the inner ply when fitting this bevel, use a disc sander very carefully.

Figure 10-12 shows a very useful clamp for gluing up trunk sides or other wide assemblies. You might need four of these at a time. Place the 1 by 4's mentioned above under the clamps to distribute the force. A length of 30 to 36 inches should be ample. Tap the wedge in gently. Before the glue sets up, go all over the side with a hammer and a block. If you find any hollow spots, drill a $1/16$-inch hole to allow the trapped air to escape, then place a clamp over the area or run small-diameter screws through blocks. Lay scraps of plastic between the blocks and the plywood, for glue might ooze out of the hole. The hole can be patched up later.

Perhaps you have already thought of applying an attractive overlay of mahogany or birch doorskin to the inner surfaces. This can be bonded without mechanical fastenings using lots of clamps and blocks. You can use contact cement if you are experienced with the stuff. Follow instructions carefully. Once the parts touch, they can't be moved. This extra lamination adds enormously to the strength of the side. This permits you to reduce the thicknesses of the first two sheets accordingly. As you know, weight reduction is vital, especially high above the waterline. Do not overbuild.

Here's another idea. One of the side laminations could be a finer plywood, say, mahogany or teak. This would give you a more attractive trunk, either inside or out. Teak plywood is costly, but it is much less so than solid timber. The corner posts, of course, should match whatever you use, so this is something to be planned well in advance.

TRUNK SIDES OF SOLID TIMBER

Solid timber is the traditional approach for trunk sides. It is an excellent method. For one-piece construction,

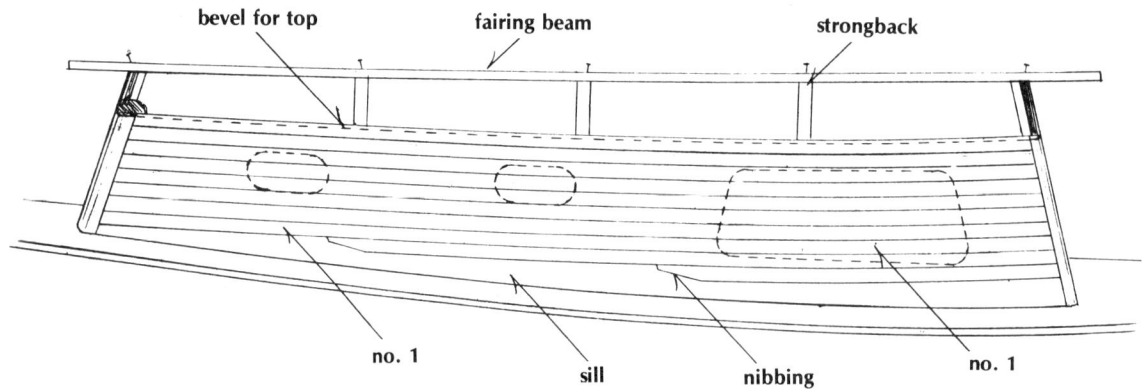

Figure 10-13. STRIP-PLANKED CABIN TRUNK WITH OPENING LAYOUT

however, it requires widths not easily found. You will have to run drifts or through-bolts all the way through the carlings to prevent warping of the wide plank. (More on this below.) The sides can be set into rabbeted sills, but you still need the rods for stiffening. I would consider 1⅛ inches as the minimum thickness unless you have the skill to bore edgewise through 1-inch stock. A boring guide for this task is described in Chapter Five. I think the best way is to clamp the side to sawhorses, bore from the top edge all the way, then clamp the side in position and run your bit down through deck and carling. This is for through-bolts. Bore slightly undersize (1/32 inch should do) for galvanized drifts. Have someone on top of the timber with a heavy weight while you are driving the drifts from below. Otherwise, you might knock everything loose. Slip a washer on the rod first, for the end will upset as you drive. There should be a counterbore for the washer, for looks. Place a drift every 20 to 24 inches, but watch out for openings. You can use rods purely as stiffeners, the actual holding being done with lags screwed up through the carling. This is not, however, the first-class way to go in a vessel greater than 35 feet on deck.

An alternate method is to thread the lower end of the drift so it can be pulled up in a counterbore in the carling. The bore in the side should be just undersize (say, 1/64 to 1/32 inch) and the drift driven from above with your partner supporting the carling. Let the thread appear about 1 inch, place the washer and nut, and pull it up. The chances are good that you will not need a washer and nut on the upper end of a properly fitting drift. If, however, your cabin side timbers are well over 1 inch thick, you can add this insurance and ease the drive fit, too. Fill the open counterbores above with thickened epoxy.

If full-width material is unobtainable, use the splined joint described earlier. The lower piece is fitted, then the upper piece to it. This long joint must be daylight-proof. The grooves can be cut using methods given in Chapter Seven. Be sure the spline is about ⅛ inch narrower than the total depth of the two grooves so there's space for air and glue. Replace the lower piece on the form and glue and fasten all around, or drift or lag as described above. Brush Aerolite glue in the groove and tap the spline in after wetting it with Aerolite catalyst. Brush glue in the mating groove and joint. Clamp the upper half loosely on the forms and start tapping it down so the spline enters the groove. Check the alignment at the end before you go too far. When satisfied, drive the piece down and pull together with pipe clamps. Glue and fasten all around. Although this side is less likely to warp and shrink because it's in two parts, I believe you should bore for through-bolts or drifts for a positive and super-strong hold-down.

STRIP-PLANKED TRUNK SIDES

Strip planking is a kind of construction sometimes used on hulls. Strip planking, in general, is easy, monotonous to apply, very strong, and beautiful if done right. See Figure 10-13. If built from ribbon-grain mahogany or teak sawed into strips about 1¼ inches wide, glued with epoxy, and sanded thoroughly to remove slight irregularities, strip planking would be impossible to beat. You can't use metal fastenings in the cut-out areas, but ⅛- to ¼-inch dowels work fine. Alignment of each strip with its mate is fussy work.

The first step is to lay off with a batten the sweep of the upper edge of the side. Or you can use your pattern, if it is perfect. Mark each strongback. This is the location of the last strip to go on, making allowance for the upper bevel, and so on. Multiply the width of the strips (I suggest not over 1¼ inches per strip) by the number

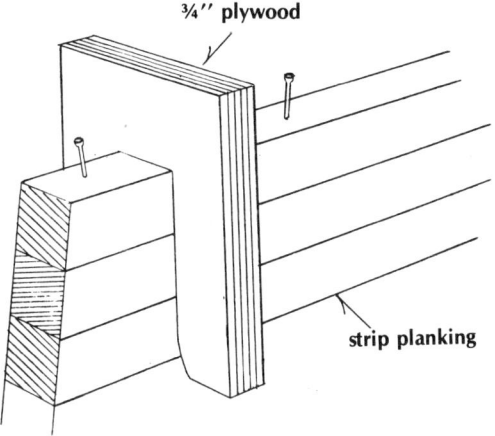

Figure 10-14. STRIP ALIGNMENT TOOL

the exterior with a very sharp plane set fine. The concave inner surface, however, is another matter. Plane diagonally across the grain, if necessary, then go over the surface with a belt sander, a cabinet scraper, and finally a block sander by hand. It pays to watch the alignment of the strips while nailing.

No doubt there are other ways to build a trunk cabin side. Regardless of how it's built, however, it is customary to cover the carling and deck edge with a nice facing of mahogany or teak. On small sailboats the facing piece can be put in first with a bevel to match the tumblehome of the sides. These are glued and screwed right to the facing and from beneath with long screws or lags. All deck structures — trunks, coamings, hatch runners, and so on — must be bedded in an elastic compound such as Thiokol or in a glue that is crack-filling. The traditional way is to lay a string of cotton caulking well soaked with white lead under the structure before fastening. Never caulk such a joint after it is done.

CABINTOPS

Let's start with the accepted type of cabin deck — laminated beams with plywood over. The camber here is much greater than on the main deck. Sawed beams are out. You might be able to use a laminating form for three or four beams, but be prepared to form most beams individually on the floor or bench. (See Figures 8-15 and 8-17.) Spruce is ideal, or a combination of spruce or ash with mahogany will do nicely. Traditionally, such beams are capped with a piece of mahogany about ¼ inch wider than the beam siding. Laminations should be ⅛ to ¼ inch thick. Because of the rapid change in the cabin width, you'll find variation in the beam cambers necessary to keep the centerline straight, as in the design. Clamp a strong batten on the centerline and get your cambers from it. A slight difference, say, ⅛ inch in height, can often be adjusted by cutting the beam a bit long to squeeze it in and raise it. Or shorten it and let the strongback press it down. As soon as the decking is installed, these beams will stay put. You can fasten with long screws going into the shelf, or fit fillers between beams so there is ample wood to fasten to when the deck is laid.

Construction of hatches, skylights, and so on, is handled the same as in the main deck. Beams should be half-dovetailed into the hatch carlings, for these beams are much smaller and it is essential to build in all the strength you can without a lot of weight. The excellent crack-filling glues Aerolite and T-88 save the day. Check for high spots with a batten, being sure that the corner posts are trimmed off so they meet the cabintop or decking neatly.

The decking is usually two thicknesses of ¼-inch plywood glued to the beams and between the laminations. If your trunk is more than 4 feet wide, you can avoid the appearance of a joint by placing the panels

required to come within about 1½ inches of the deck forward. Mark this dimension on all the strongbacks and the corner posts at both ends. This is where your first full-length strip goes on. (It is No. 1 in Figure 10-13.) Because all additional strips sweep the same as No. 1, you wind up with the beveled edge exactly as designed. But there has to be something on which to nail No. 1. I show a fairly intricate piece that I call a sill (for want of a better name) into which two short strips or stealers are nibbed. If you insist on avoiding this work, the sill can be made full width to the marks for strip No. 1. This, however, will not look as good. Do not make the sill with its upper surface following the sweep of the deck, for your strips will run out to feather edges, a bad practice. Whatever the width of the sill, it must be through-bolted to the carling and deck.

The strips should be nailed with galvanized finish nails or bronze serrated nails 2 to 2½ inches long, on about 6-inch centers. Clamp a piece of scrap on the side to guide your drill so there is no chance that a lead hole or a nail will run out, a real tragedy. In the areas of the openings, however, fasten with ⅛-inch dowels. Coat the dowels with epoxy glue and work a little into the holes with a pipe cleaner. This will produce very strong construction. The joints must be painted liberally with epoxy or Aerolite glue. Clamp the strips to the forms and line them up, one on top of the other, with a little clamp, as shown in Figure 10-14. This alignment is vital, for otherwise you will have to dress down both surfaces. Do not permit this clamp to smear glue over the sides of the strips. For this reason, you should consider using Aerolite glue; it can be washed out with a wet rag for a few hours after application. It is crystal clear, too. Fasten your top strip with small dowels so the bevel can be planed.

Jointed trunk sides might show slight misalignment and unsightly seams. These can be planed out easily on

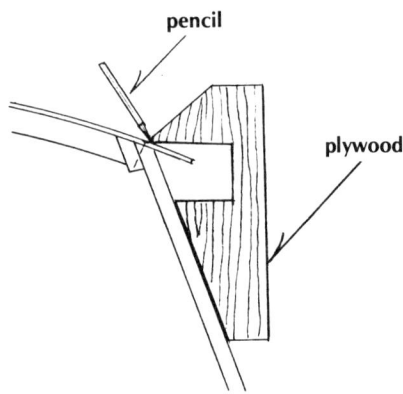

Figure 10-15. HIDDEN EDGE GAUGE

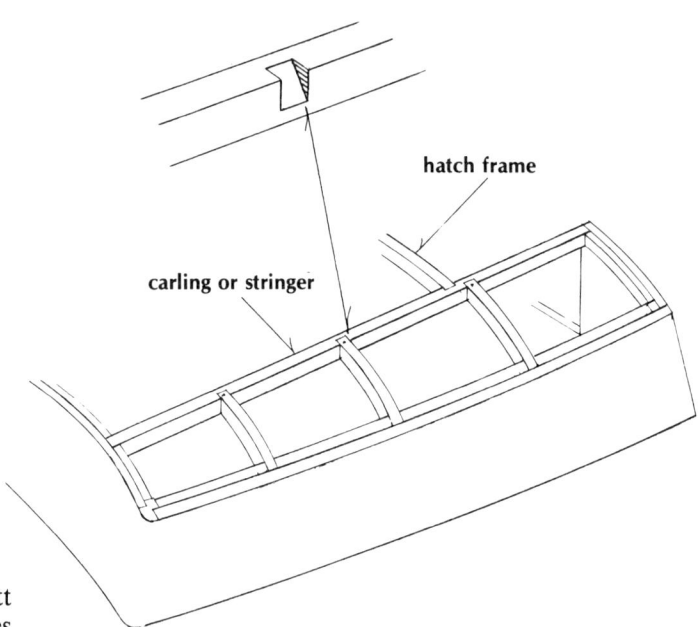

Figure 10-16. CABIN BEAMS IN A SHARPIE

with the grain running athwartships. They must butt over a beam. Do not, however, join both thicknesses over the same beam. If you must have the grain running fore and aft, the job is a bit more complicated. Lay the side panel so it is dead on the centerline and roughly cut to overhang the cabin side ½ inch or less. Epoxy glue and nail to the beams, using ¾- to 1-inch bronze Anchorfast nails 3 inches apart around the perimeter. Make yourself a hidden edge gauge (Figure 10-15) so you will know just where the outside trim will come. Place the fastenings well inside, allowing for a generous radius.

Repeat with the other panel. As soon as possible, start the second lamination so the new fastenings will take hold before the original glue application kicks off. Mark the joint about 4 inches from the first. Roll on a good wet coat of Plastic Resin or epoxy and nail the second panel into the beams, sides, and ends with 1¼-inch bronze nails. If there is no king plank or blocking between beams on the centerline, fasten along the joint with closely spaced screws (⅝-inch no. 4 flathead brass) about ¾ inch from the joint edge. It's best in general always to start nailing near the center of the panels and work outward to avoid trapping air.

Soft spots can be cured by laying weights on them quickly or by weighting down a 2 by 4. Saw around the perimeter but stay away from the sides at least ⅛ inch so you don't damage the surface. Trim closely to the hatch framing, and so on, and plane a nice radius all around outside. After sanding off high spots, cover with Vectra or Versatex (polypropylene), because it is very resistant to wear and abrasion. Read up on it. Help is needed for this entire job.

A STRINGER/BEAM SYSTEM

Here's an easier system that provides that extra 2 inches or so of headroom. We used it successfully on an old modified sharpie. See Figure 10-16. You install two stringers or carlings spaced out for the width of the main hatch extending the full length of the trunk. Clamp on a couple of supports so there is no sign of sag. Now let short sawed beams into the carlings, as shown in Figure 10-16. Do not half-lap these, for this would weaken the stringers (unless, of course, they are supported by bulkheads).

Shore up a lengthwise 2 by 4 for additional temporary support along the centerline. At this point you have two choices. The easy way is to lay plywood panels with the grain athwartships (if the trunk is over 7 feet wide). The other method calls for the panels lengthwise, with the fore-and-aft joints centered on the stringers, so there is a limit. It would be possible to butt these on the centerline, but there is less chance of making the joint invisible outside. The inside could be trimmed with a small, flat molding. This method looks very neat, and there are no beams to bump your head against.

A BEAMLESS CABINTOP

There's still another way to construct a trunk top. Eliminate the beams entirely. Call it cold-molded. The first step is to set up strongbacks as described, but in this case they must be spaced more closely. Then they are to be notched to receive stringers fore and aft, as shown in Figure 10-1. Because the camber of each strongback will vary as the trunk narrows, you must swing each one, using the camber scribers detailed in Chapter Five. Or you can lay them out geometrically. If the resulting form is a section of a cylinder or a cone, you will have no problems. If a compound results, another system will be necessary. This is laminating in diagonal strips, a method I cannot cover here.

With each individual strongback clamped but removable, swing the scribers across the sides of the trunk, marking with a pencil as you go. Then bandsaw close to the lines, set them back in position, and fair them with stiff battens. They must be perfect. Next tack the ribbands spaced nicely across the strongbacks and mark for notching. Set them all down in the notches so the surfaces are flush. Cover this form or mold with plastic sheet, except around the perimeter, where it will be glued.

Now for the top. We built a new cabin trunk and low doghouse on the sharpie using ¼-inch fir plywood in three laminations. This was unbelievably strong, but heavier than I now would recommend. I believe $3/16$ inch would be more than ample, and four thicknesses of $3/32$-inch doorskin might work well. Join the first thickness straight down the centerline, nailing ¾-inch brads into every second strongback. Joints athwartships must fall on strongbacks also. Glue and fasten around the perimeter with epoxy and bronze Anchorfast nails. Trim off the excess overhanging plywood.

The next step is to tack the second laminations in position for trimming. Allow the joints to overlap the first about 2 inches. Drive a few temporary ¾-inch brads in the same strongbacks as in the first step. Get your glue ready. We used Plastic Resin because it was the best available. Today you should use epoxy glue (or Aerolite). Read up on these. Brush on the glue as required, place in position so brads enter the same holes, and again nail to the same strongbacks on about 4-inch centers. Use Anchorfast nails around the perimeter. The third lamination goes on the same way — quickly! If there is any sign that the brads are not pulling the plywood down flush, place weights all over it — fast! Lay these on 1 by 3's running fore and aft to distribute the load. Don't do any trimming until the epoxy has had 24 hours to cure.

Now you can crawl below and start dismantling the forms. You will see lines of brads where the strongbacks were. It's better that these be pulled through rather than nipped off, for they will rust. Finally, cover this line of tiny holes with nice, small battens of mahogany or teak. The center joint will probably need the same treatment in short lengths. If you use a light-toned plywood such as waterproof ash or birch, the contrast will be very pleasing. Doorskins (⅛ inch) make a fine appearance overhead.

The exterior, of course, must be trimmed flush and nicely rounded. The bronze Anchorfast nail heads that interfere can be ground off with a sander, either belt or disc. Saturate the entire deck with epoxy. Place a modest half round or other molding well below the radius. Bullnose the ends of the trim moldings where they meet the corner posts unless you choose to fashion molding bends laboriously around the corners. This is very difficult — I doubt whether I could describe it to you. Years ago you could buy lead molding to form around these corners — to be painted later, of course. Oh, well, that's progress.

PORTLIGHTS, DEADLIGHTS, AND WINDOWS

There are many types of hardware designed to enclose cabin trunk apertures. In addition, installation is complicated by the different types of trunk construction. It would take many pages to cover all possibilities. I will cover three situations only:
  A. Traditional opening ports of cast metal and molded plastic;
  B. Fixed (nonopening) deadlights, framed and frameless;
  C. Opening windows and shaped deadlights.

First, a few definitions. A portlight swings open. A deadlight may be of similar round, rectangular, or oval shape, but it does not open. I hate to use the word *window* on a vessel, but what else can one call the large areas of plastic or glass so common today? If it opens, I'd call it a window. If it is fixed, I would call it a deadlight, no matter what its size and shape.

Whether of cast bronze, stainless steel, nylon, or molded plastic, most portlights are designed with a collar or spigot that fits into the opening. See Figure 10-17. A frame or bezel can be bedded and screwed to the trunk side to cover the joint and bolt heads, if any. Many prefer to omit the bezel, for it emphasizes the size of the light. Some portlight bezels are designed to be through-bolted. Bolted or heavily screwed, this type is probably best able to withstand the force of solid water. The "glass" may be Plexiglas, Lexan, or plate or shatterproof glass. I suggest Lexan because it resists scratching and is very strong yet flexible. Screens are usually available.

Bronze or steel cast portlights and deadlights are too heavy for most modern racing yachts. In addition, the great tumblehome of the sides allows water to collect in the spigot. This means the cushion or the unwary sleeper below gets a shower when the port is opened. I have seen no completely satisfactory method to cure this fault, but Figure 10-17 offers one possible solution.

Installation is no great problem if you have a powerful sabersaw or the larger reciprocating saw. If you have a number of openings to cut, take the time to make a router pattern (or use the side pattern discussed earlier). Use the spigot itself for marking locations, and exercise extreme care that both position and alignment are to the plans. Set the spigot in the hole with heavy epoxy glue under the flange and on the edges of the opening.

Some ports and deadlights are manufactured with spigots less than ½ inch deep. Also, you could saw off the spigot on a cast bronze port. Then, if the lower edge of the opening were beveled, it would drain. Another

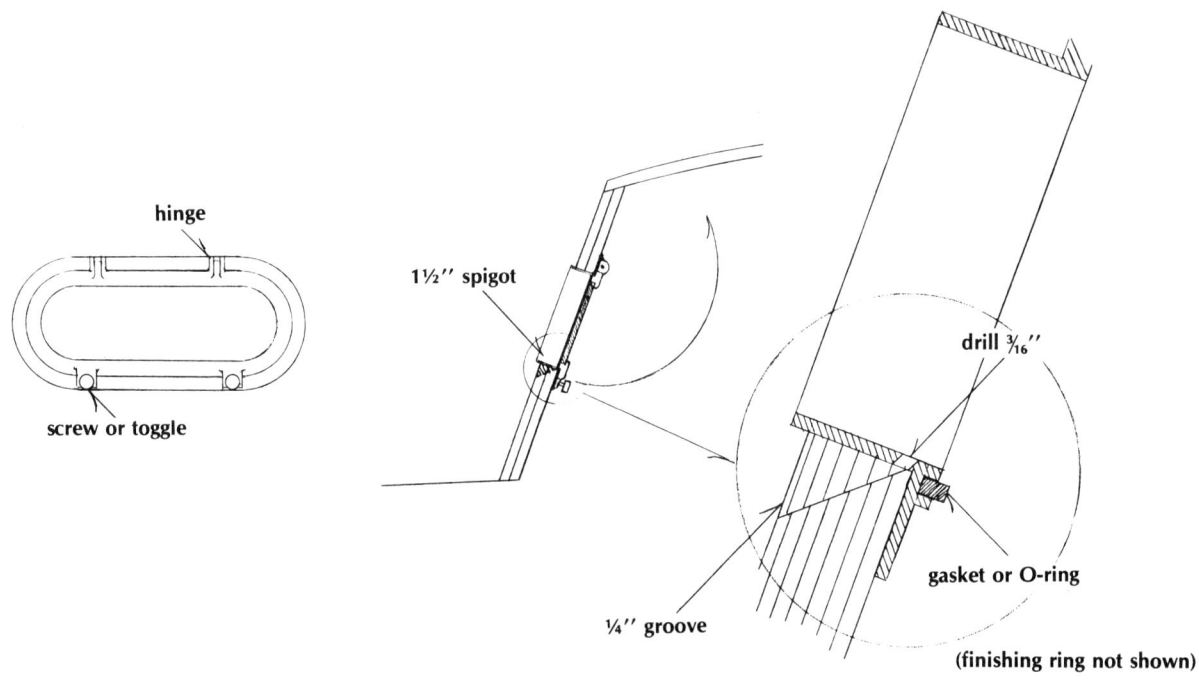

Figure 10-17. TYPICAL PORTLIGHT WITH SCUPPERED SPIGOT

possibility is hacksawing and filing a couple of little scuppers in the spigot to minimize water collection. The edge of the wood would have to be saturated with epoxy resin. I have not tried this, but I think it would look quite nice if done neatly. I show another scuppering method in Figure 10-17. Drill $3/16$- or $1/4$-inch holes at the ends of the spigot. Mark the spots, then saw out a groove $1/4$ inch wide to meet the holes. Sand this smooth and saturate with epoxy resin (use three applications). If you intend to install a bezel, the angle of the groove must be such that it will drain freely. Keep these scuppers clean.

DEADLIGHTS

Manufactured deadlights that match portlights are no problem, except for their weight and cost. If through-bolted, they probably are as strong as anything available. In large sizes, if they are screwed to the inside of the trunk, there is a hazard. The strength of the fitting is almost entirely dependent on screws threaded into wood. Bedding in epoxy glue would be inexpensive insurance, of course.

To achieve light weight and low cost, consider deadlights of plastic screwed directly to the cabin trunk side. See Figure 10-18. For maximum strength at the expense of appearance, these can be screwed or bolted directly to the exterior or interior surface, and bedded in a flexible compound to compensate for the different expansion and contraction rates of plastic and wood. The fastener holes should be drilled oversize for the same reason. I suggest that you not remove the paper that covers the plastic until your craft is completed. The paper in the area of contact should be removed, and the plastic surface should be sanded for satisfactory adhesion. Round-head screws or bolts with plastic washers allow the slight movement that will occur and seal out moisture.

Installation on the inside of the trunk side makes an attractive deadlight. The opening outside should be routed to a pleasing radius for drainage and the exposed surfaces saturated with epoxy resin. If you have trunk sides at least $7/8$ inch thick, the plastic may be fitted into a rabbet around the opening (Figure 10-19). The rabbets can be on the inside or the outside, the latter being the stronger of the two. The joint can be covered with a stock frame or bezel applied either inside or outside. Both the plastic and the bezel must be bedded in flexible compound.

An alternative to the stock frame, especially for larger openings of unusual shape, is a rabbeted frame of hardwood plywood or wood to retain the plastic (Figures 10-18 and 10-20). This can be sawed out of $3/4$-inch mahogany plywood and routed to a nice radius on the inner corners with a rabbet to receive the plastic. Of course, such a frame can be built up of solid wood with mitered corners — a much more laborious task. I see no good reason why such a frame could not be installed on the exterior, except that I feel it is unwise to emphasize such openings, regardless of size. Frames can be glued with epoxy to a cabin side without any other fastenings, or you can use just a few fasteners to hold the frame while the glue cures.

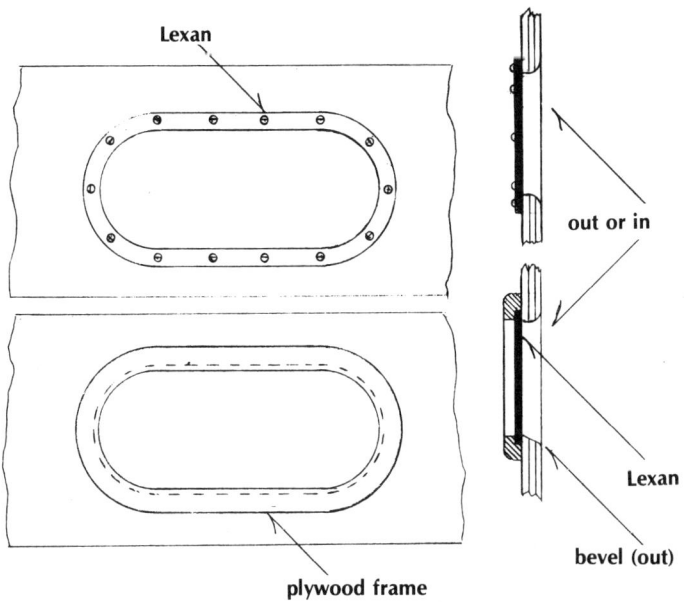

Figure 10-18. PLASTIC DEADLIGHTS DIRECT TO SIDE

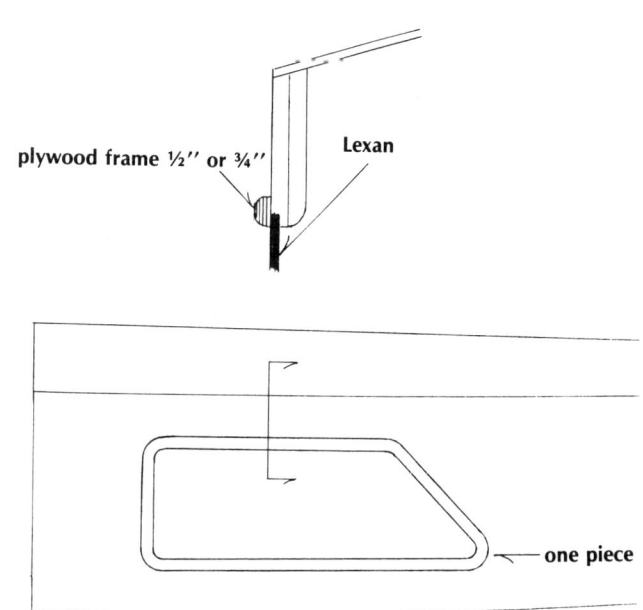

Figure 10-20. SHAPED "WINDOW" FRAME OR DEADLIGHT

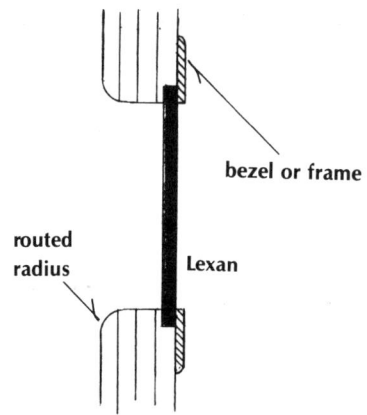

Figure 10-19. RABBETED TRUNK SIDE

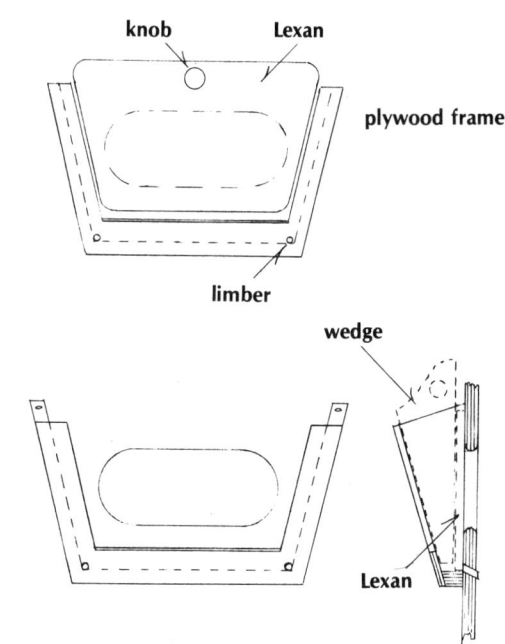

Figure 10-21. GOUGEON AND ROOT PORTLIGHTS

OPENING WINDOWS AND SHAPED PORTS

Figure 10-21 shows an idea borrowed from the book *The Gougeon Brothers on Boat Construction*. The frame should be routed from a piece of ¼-inch plywood to avoid joints and leaks. The scuppers should be fitted with copper tubing of about ¼-inch inside diameter. Brush epoxy glue in the holes with a pipe cleaner and smear it on the exterior of the tube. I would not expect this window to be impervious to driving rain or solid water. Better keep on hand a few little plugs to be inserted from outside.

This reminds me of the Root ports I once built for our sharpie. Invented by a famous yachtsman of the 1930s, their unique design allows them to be open at the top so that there is ventilation in a downpour, but not in a driving rain and wind storm. Wedges are needed to press the panes against the side in bad conditions. These ports always leak, but the water runs freely through the scuppers. Neither the Gougeon nor the Root port would be satisfactory for serious offshore cruising.

OUT OF THE PAST — A MODERN TRUNK

Before ending this chapter, I would like to mention an anachronism I saw recently on an extremely modern racing and cruising yacht. It's something I think should

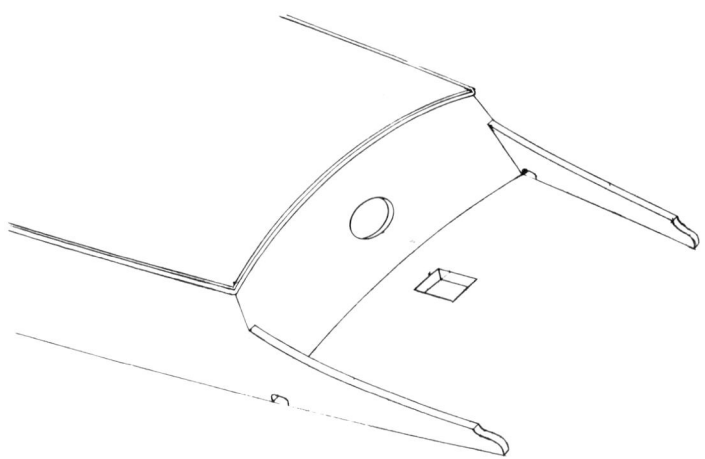

Figure 10-22. AN "OLD-FASHIONED" CABIN TRUNK

be reconsidered. The trunk sides continued forward for about 2½ feet and swept down into low coamings (Figure 10-22). This style was popular in the 1920s and 1940s, perhaps even a little later in smaller craft with open cockpits. This type of trunk eliminates all the difficult construction of corner posts; of course, the tumblehome was more moderate in those days. The extensions or coamings are handy for temporary stowage of a winch handle or a sail stop, and they provide safe footing on occasion. Unfortunately, they encroached somewhat on the foredeck. Structurally, however, they are sound and inexpensive. With the popular sharply raked forward end, this design could be very attractive if trimmed with a neat ogee or bullnose. Needless to say, there would have to be a good inside corner post and ample fastening with screws from beneath the deck.

ELEVEN

Building the Yacht Interior

Let's consider the interior fittings of a yacht as furniture, the things that make a barren hull a home. You'll want to furnish your yacht with settees, a companionway ladder, berths, bookshelves, a galley, hanging lockers, doors and drawers, dressers, and so on. In addition, you'll want to ceil your hull for warmth and protection against sweating, and for appearance. This chapter describes ways to provide these furnishings that almost any fair craftsman can follow.

SOME STANDARDS

There is convincing evidence that the human body is larger than it once was. There are certain space minimums we must provide so that the body will function efficiently. The standards indicated on page 180 come from reliable sources. Some may have to be expanded.

In his book *Ferro-Cement Design, Techniques and Application,* Bruce Bingham mentions how difficult it is to evaluate space by studying the accommodation plan. He recommends placing a figure of a man drawn to scale here and there. You might even make stick figures. It's amazing how rapidly some yachts shrink when this is done. "Ample seating" can turn out to be no larger than a phone booth for two. Or a quarter berth may be just wide enough for your shoulders, and the cockpit beams too close to the cushion for your feet.

I know I am encroaching on yacht design with these suggestions, but I hope you will do something similar before making a final design choice. On the other hand, if you are past that stage and already own a big, beautiful hull, I hope you will undertake another experiment — one that takes some time and money. Rough in the bare essentials of settees, sea berths, backrests, galley, and toilet enclosure. Even a mock-up engine made of plywood might expose an uncomfortable situation.

SOME BASIC DIMENSIONS

Item	Minimum	Comments
Berth width, at head	22 inches	28 inches in port, 22 inches at sea
Berth width, at foot	15 inches	18 inches is luxury
Berth length	6 feet 3 inches	from 3 inches to 4 inches over the sleeper's height
Settee width, if low	23 inches	22 inches if cushion is 14 inches wide
Settee width, if high	18 inches	19 to 20 inches if cushion is 16 or 17 inches
Settee clear, cushion to carling	36 inches	(more if decks are wide)
Berth clear, butt to shoulder	22 inches	(more if access is difficult)
Headroom, full	6 feet	6 feet 2 inches under beams
Hanging locker, rod length	9 inches	never enough
Hanging locker, depth	17½ inches	3 inches more than hanger length; additional for hooks
Hatch, escape and vent	18 by 18 inches	24 inches square, especially if used for sailhandling
Hatch, sliding	24 by 24 inches	larger, if over galley
Galley height	33 inches	36 inches with 3-inch kick space under
Passage width, forepeak	18 inches	OK if shaped for ease and ventilation
Passage with door	22 inches	OK (also double hinged, sliding, and accordion folding)
Clear above stove	30 inches	cover woodwork with asbestos and stainless steel or aluminum
Toilet, 15-inch height	headroom 36 inches above seat	learn to sit, regardless, for sanitation and safety
Portable toilet (build up to 15-inch height)	headroom 36 inches above seat	handy size may mean small capacity
Enclosed head, width	24 inches	allow 27 inches elbow room if possible, also foot room
Cockpit well, width	24 inches forward, 18 inches aft	just wide enough to brace feet against
Cockpit seats, cushioned	15 inches wide, 17 inches to cushion	helmsman must see over trunk comfortably
Side deck catwalks	12 inches	you can't get them too wide

ROUGHING IT IN

For example, knock together a plywood box 16 inches square and 15 inches high. That's a portable toilet. Set it on that stepped-up floor that's almost a shelf and try it for size. Elbow room OK? Do you have to unscrew your feet when you recline? Headroom OK? Or is this a "sitter" only? You have seen designs showing a quarter berth extending aft under and/or alongside the cockpit well. Many of these narrow down substantially at the foot. Raising a berth or settee only an inch can widen it considerably, depending on the hull section. This is especially true in the forepeak, where raising berths not only widens them but creates large storage spaces as well. Perhaps a double there instead of V-berths would permit building hanging lockers outboard of the pillow end. But perhaps your crew will hate climbing over the head of this berth.

Try it before you build it. Stretch out on the rough boards; don't rely on the blueprint entirely. If you're over 6 feet tall, you'll have to fudge here and there to work in a 6-foot 6-inch berth if the bulkheads are already in. Can you cut an aperture and extend the berth? Try it for size!

BERTHS IN GENERAL

Berths can vary greatly in otherwise similar yachts in terms of their usage. Think carefully before you act.

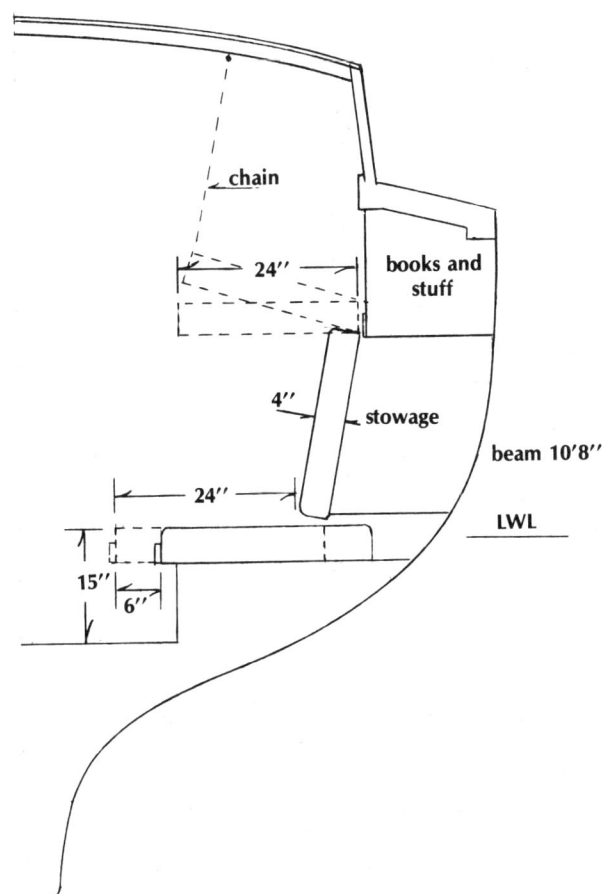

Figure 11-1. EXTENSION TRANSOM AND SEA BERTH

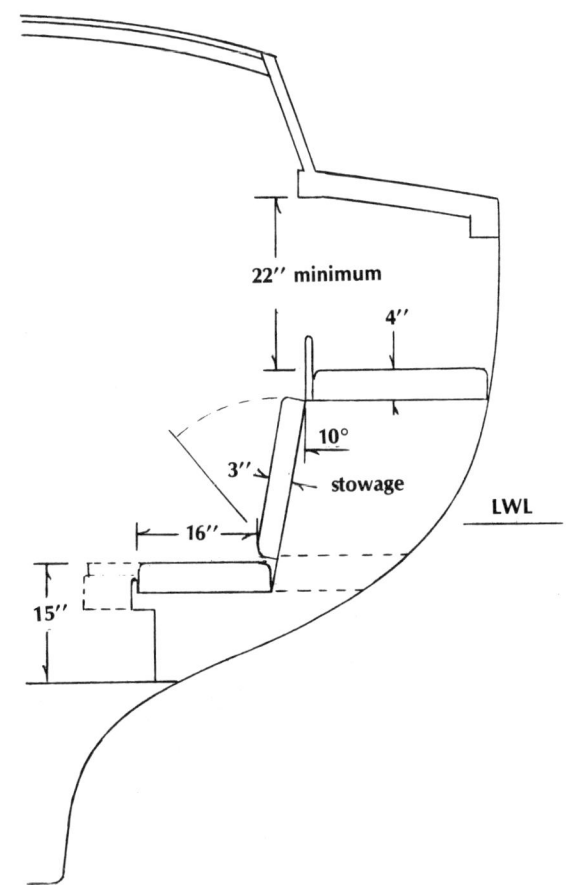

Figure 11-2. EXTENSION TRANSOM AND UPPER BERTH

Don't build broad, comfortable nests if you're likely to go bluewater cruising. And vice versa. In coastal cruising where 90 percent of the nights are spent in quiet anchorages, you'll probably want lots of roomy comfort. In a seaway, however, these berths would roll you back and forth — not the best setup for adequate rest. In such circumstances, you need narrower bunks you can chock yourself into with bunkboards or some other devices. Consider berths that can be tilted when the boat is on the same tack for many hours, days, or weeks. When the occasional guest or extra youngster comes aboard for a couple of nights, certain space-saver types can be used. More about these later.

It is customary for a sleeping berth to be built with a hardwood face and raised portions at head and foot to keep pillows and bedding in place. A section used for sitting has a raised side piece generally less thick than the mattress. A berth used exclusively for sleeping, however, should have side faces about 10 inches high, but with a somewhat lower center for ease in climbing in and out. Settees do not need more than about a 2-inch face or fiddle to keep the cushions in place.

Double berths are not for offshore cruising. I have used double berths (with a minimum of 48 inches at the head) and admit that they offer great comfort and other benefits. If you must have a double berth, you'd be wise to include a "bundling board" between the mattress pads, probably with pins fitted into sockets in the berth top. Otherwise, both sleepers end up in the lee. No further comment is required.

Dinette berths are definitely for quiet anchorages only. In rough conditions, they are too wide for one sleeper; two sleepers end up on the sole. Their construction has been described in dozens of books and articles.

TRANSOMS, SETTEES, AND BERTHS

A transom berth is a settee that is also used for sleeping. There is no way you can sit with comfort on a settee wide enough for sleeping. The wider it is, the more uncomfortable the sitting is. This discomfort is compounded if the backrest is vertical (10 degrees is recommended), and the seat is not likely to be angled as chairs are. Yet you need a width of 28 inches at the shoulders for sleeping while in port. Designers, of course, have come up with different ways to cope with this problem. I will describe a few of them here.

Extension berths are one answer, even in a yacht of modest beam, say, 8 feet. See Figures 11-1 and 11-2.

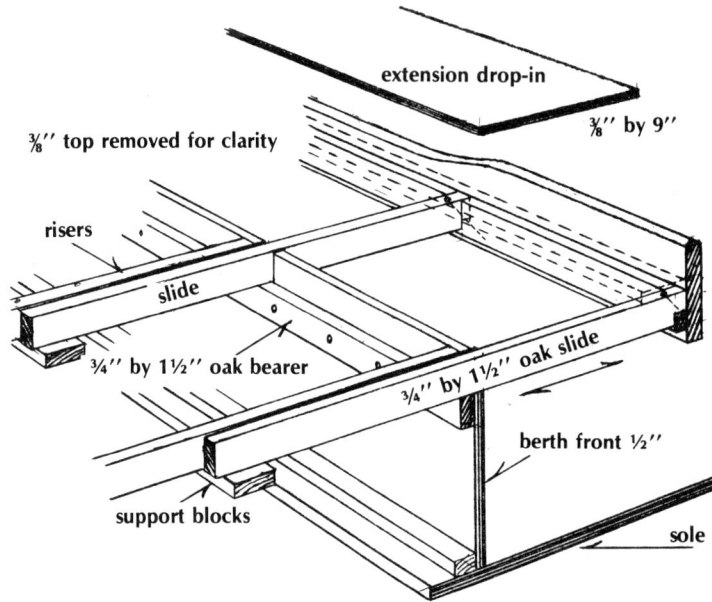

Figure 11-3. EXTENSION BERTH CONSTRUCTION

The sloping backrest can be hinged for access to the space behind it, and it can be upholstered, or you can use loose cushions or pillows. Blankets stuffed into attractive zippered covers make fine back padding. The berth top is built right back to the hull, extending into a recess beneath the storage compartment. This gives you a normal seat 16 inches wide, but more if the seat is more than 15 inches above the sole. The extension can extend to within 6 inches of the centerline of the sole and still leave a narrow space for passage. Some berths extend to join at the middle. This makes a huge playpen for a litter of cubs, or friendly folk.

A proven arrangement is the high fixed berth known as a pilot or sea berth, possibly because you can chock yourself in with generous boards for comfort and safety in any seaway. See Figure 11-1. Today each member of the crew has his own sleeping bag. Thus, when he's off watch, he tosses out the warm one and climbs into his own. A sea berth requires a pretty fair-sized vessel to get hip and shoulder room of 22 inches. Width, however, should not be more than 24 inches. I believe a beam of 10 feet 6 inches would be the minimum for a pilot berth. A pilot berth is ideal for the off-watch while the settee is being used by others.

Another possibility, where there is ample beam and height under the carlings, is to swing up the backrest, supporting it with chains hooked onto padeyes or eyebolts overhead. See Figure 11-2. This is good for temporary use, although I suppose one could learn to live with it. You must have a minimum of 22 inches between the berths and between the upper and the carling, so wide side decks might prohibit this. This upper needs little in the way of safety boards unless you are tacking frequently, for the chain may be adjusted to the angle of heel. Such a backrest berth could be a pipe berth with laced canvas, covered with perhaps a 2-inch foam pad.

The sliding framework of the extension transom is ¾- by 1½- to 2-inch stock, riding on an oak bearer, so there is no reduction of storage space below (Figure 11-3). The drop-in filler piece is ⅜-inch plywood. It stows under the mattress pad back out of sight.

Another extension that is quite easy to make, but adds weight, is shown in Figure 11-4. For this one, you set up the berth front in the usual way and secure it to cleats on the bulkheads. The outboard support board (A) may be 6 to 8 inches wide, fastened to cleats at each end and supported by a couple of ¾- by 2½-inch legs bonded or otherwise secured to the hull. This carries the weight of sitters and sleepers. For the slats, the lazy way is to have all 22 pieces of 3½-inch fir or spruce cut to one length. If there is a lot of taper or curvature, you'll want to cut overlength, fit each one against the hull, then nail the alternate ones in position properly spaced. Place the sliders in between, also to the hull. Clamp a straightedge end to end for a saw guide and cut them off. Now glue and screw the sliding slats to the berth face. This must be strong. Slide the whole thing back against the hull, clamp the batten (B) against the board (A) to locate it, and screw about six of the slider slats to the batten. Do not glue, for this must be disassembled if you should want to remove the extension. There is no access through the top, so be sure you cut nice, large doors or openings in the berth front. Be sure the batten (B) is in place before you fasten the fixed slats. This assembly is tricky.

The sea berth in Figure 11-1 has a hardwood face or coaming to keep you and the pad in place. In extreme weather, however, you'll need a bunkboard. The one

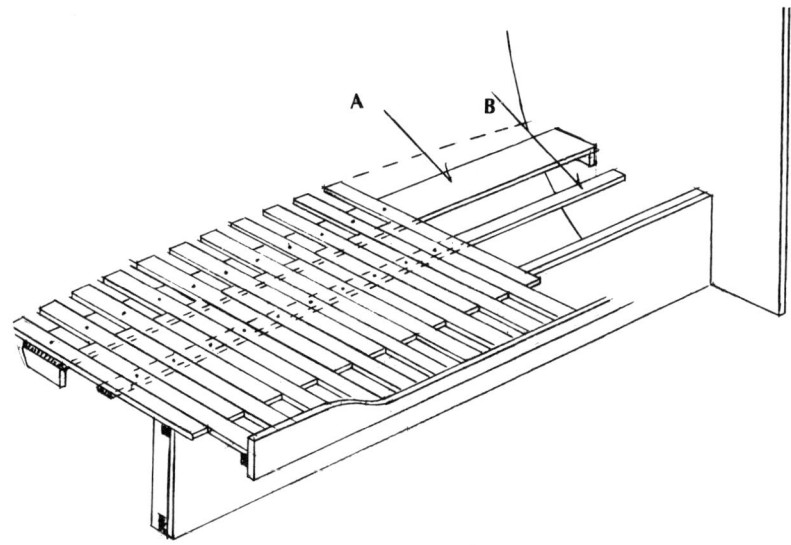

Figure 11-4. EXTENSION BERTH — SLAT CONSTRUCTION

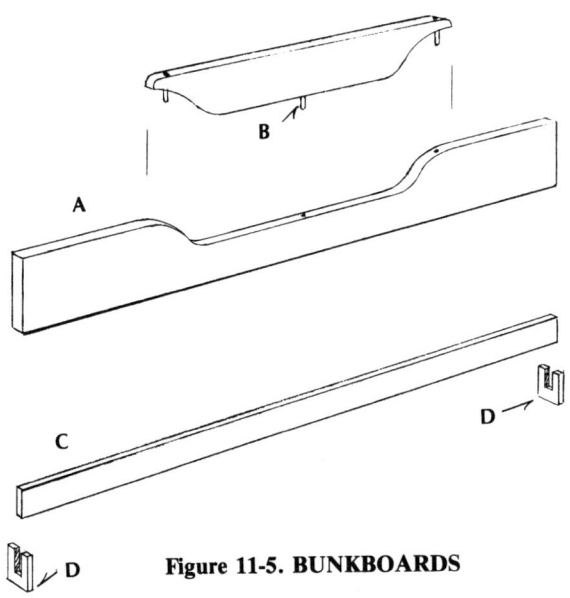

Figure 11-5. BUNKBOARDS

shown at the top in Figure 11-5 is exaggerated in thickness to clarify the detail of the brass pins. Use the berth face as a pattern for the addition (A), and make the board about 1 inch deeper than the opening to avoid feather edges. Bandsaw out and fit with care. C-clamp in place between pieces of scrap and bore two end holes down through the addition about 1¼ inches into the face. Drive the pins through, set in about ⅜ inch, and plug over. For the center pin (B), drive a small brad about halfway in and press the piece down to mark the center for the ⅜-inch hole. Pull the brad and bore. If your brass pins are not tight, put a few drops of epoxy glue in the three holes in the addition piece. Round the upper edges with a router to match the berth face. When the piece is not in use, stow it against the hull.

The simple bunkboard (C at the bottom in Figure 11-5) is self-explanatory. The chocks (D), of ¾-inch marine plywood or laminated wood, are glued and screwed to the bulkheads. Round the edges of the chocks and the board.

SPACE-SAVER BERTHS

One of the most practical, comfortable, and underrated berths is the pipe berth. This isn't joinery, but the discussion of berths would be incomplete if this equipment were omitted. See Figure 11-6. As I show it, it's not the handsomest addition to a fine yacht, but it can be improved by covering it with attractive material. With a 2-inch foam pad, it might make a fine backrest with bedding stowed behind. You don't need bunkboards of any kind, for the sag forms a natural nest for the body. In extreme angles of heel, the hanging chains can be adjusted. On the 18-day reach from Catalina to Diamond Head, I would choose this berth. The structure is 1-inch galvanized pipe. The inside dimensions of the pipe frame are 24 inches by 6 feet 6 inches. Grommets are placed all around on 4- to 6-inch centers, and, of course, the canvaswork must be strong. The brackets may be hook-shaped so the berth can be removed.

THE ROOT BERTH

The Root berth dates back to the 1930s. It is a stretcherlike arrangement that was dreamed up by Elihu Root, an imaginative cruising sailor. See Figure 11-7. I made a pair of these berths using 1½-inch aluminum tubing with 1⅜-inch fir dowels inside. Epoxy poured into the tubes and coated on the dowels would greatly increase

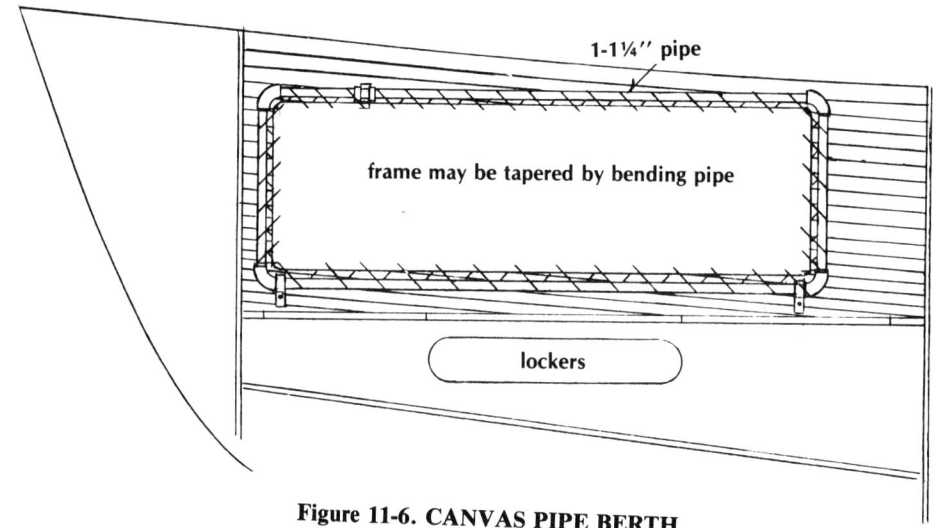

Figure 11-6. CANVAS PIPE BERTH

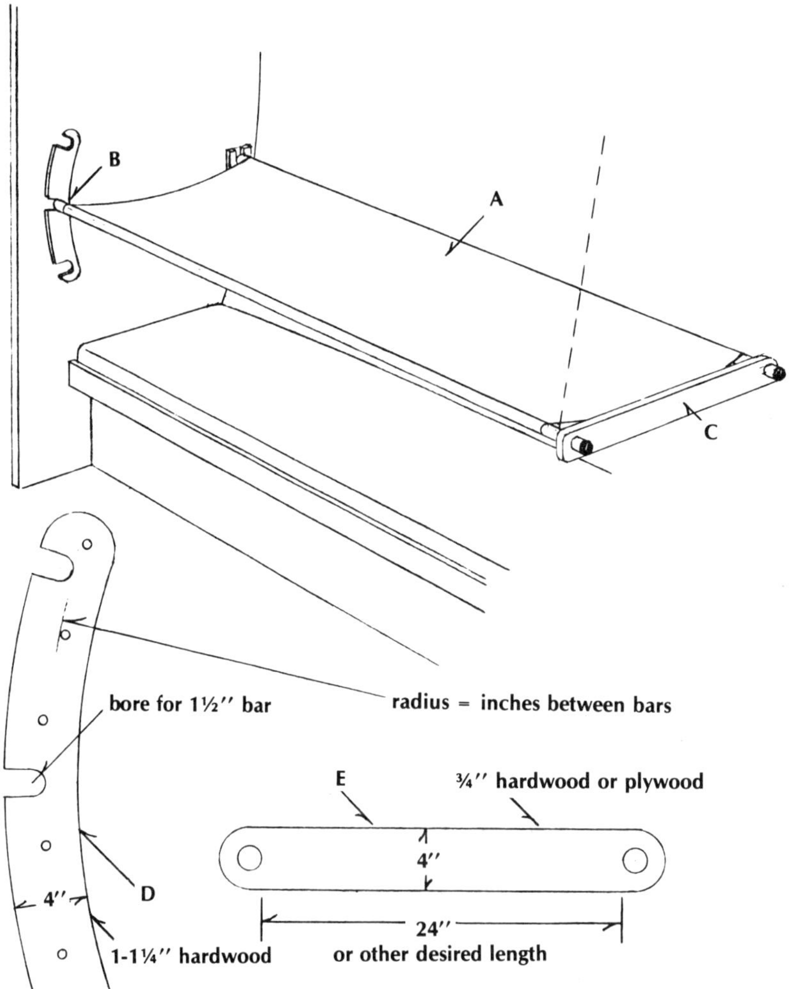

Figure 11-7. ROOT-TYPE STRETCHER BERTH

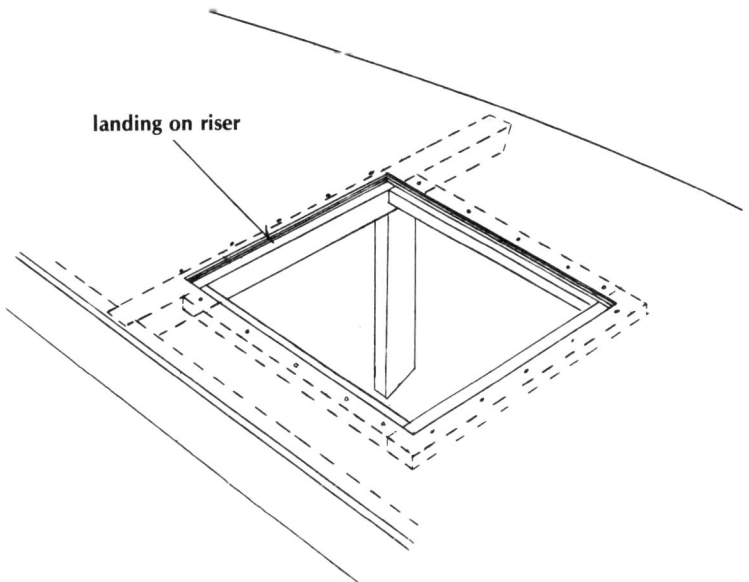

Figure 11-8. FRAMING BERTH TOP OPENING

stiffness. The canvas is a simple sleeve (A) strongly stitched and hemmed across the ends. This could be of striped awning cloth. Set the bars in chocks something like the one shown as D, and if you want to provide more sag for really bad weather, make a second set to go inside the first. This, however, may be a needless refinement. Clamp when boring so the expansion bit does not split the hardwood. Use 1- to 1¼-inch stock or doubled plywood to prevent the bars from coming out of the chocks. Glue and screw, then plug over. If there are no bulkheads, rig spreaders (E) supported by rope lanyards to padeyes. It takes five minutes to stow these. Or, when folded back and stuffed with blankets, they make passable backrests. Install a Root berth where it clears amply. In the forepeak, a Root berth makes a fair bin for sails when not being slept in. The cost and the weight of this contraption are minimal.

BERTH TOPS AND FRONTS

In all construction, try to keep the weight down. Every pound you add is a pound less ballast and less sail that the boat will carry. Berth tops never have to be heavier than ⅜-inch plywood — even ¼ inch will work if it is properly framed. Openings in settee or berth tops can be closed with the cutout if a circular saw is used to start the cuts and there are no bored holes. See Figure 11-8. The cuts to the corners can be done with a sabersaw, handsaw, or even a hacksaw blade. There must be a strong frame inside the opening to support the cutout. Make it about ¾ inch by 1½ inches, laid on the flat so there is a solid landing for the cutout and a full inch for screwing and gluing to the underside of the berth top. Berth tops take a beating from fat behinds and jumping juniors, so place screws on 4-inch centers with epoxy, Plastic Resin, or Aerolite glue. If your openings can be arranged to fall on the risers, the supports running from front to back, this is even better. To keep the structure light yet tremendously strong, place one or more legs under risers, and fasten them to the hull.

You should have generous access openings in the berth fronts also. These can be fitted with hinged or sliding ventilated doors, or you may elect to trim around the opening with hardwood. Berth fronts need not be over ½ inch thick if they are plywood. Even ⅜-inch plywood would be satisfactory. For this lighter construction, Figure 11-9 shows a method of trimming and reinforcing often used in superlight dinghies and racing craft. The frame can be of ¼- to ½-inch mahogany plywood, with edges routed or shaped and sanded, then glued to the plywood front. The plies will show, but this can be made very attractive when filled, stained, and varnished. Solid hardwood, too, can be used for the framing.

BACKRESTS

The simplest backrest is a plywood panel hinged along the lower edge for easy access to the storage space (Figure 11-3). Some backrests require considerable expense and work. The smooth surface with snap-on cushions, however, is most comfortable and easy to construct. For ultra-simplicity, use colorful pillows or zippered cases for folded blankets. Cloth or vinyl pads can be upholstered right on the panel or frame at low cost. Any visible frame should have an edging of mahogany or teak. Descriptions of doors and jambs follow.

Backrests can be built-in cabinets with three or four

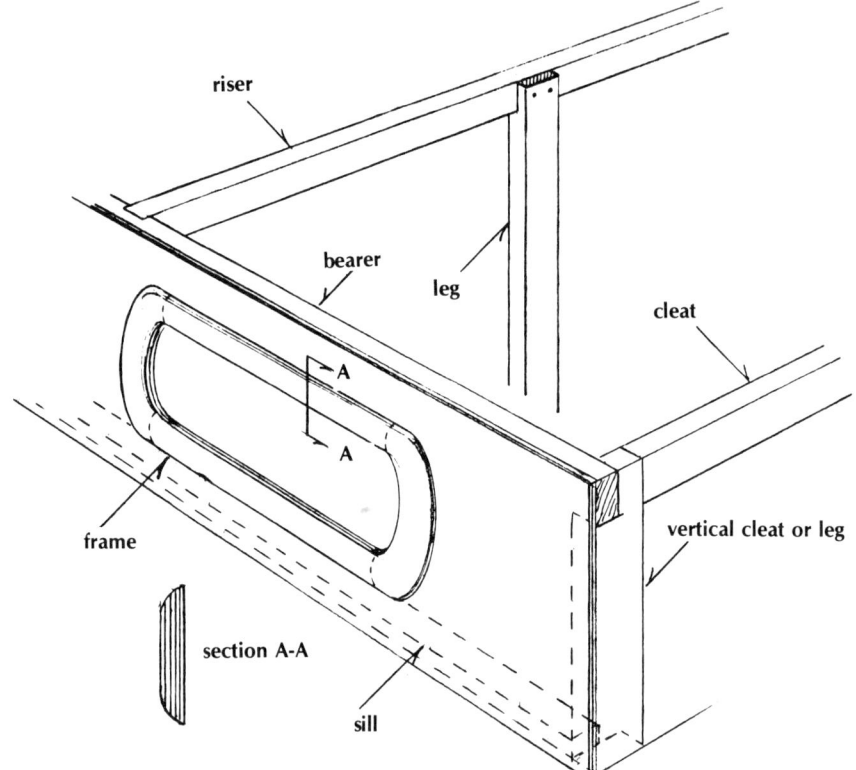

Figure 11-9. PLYWOOD FRAME

flush, paneled, or sliding doors. Remember, backs should slope about 10 degrees. The seat, too, should slope, but if it's to be used as a berth, this is not practical.

Half of the port backrest in my Allegra design does double duty as a dining and chart table. See Figure 11-10. This expedient saves space and is quite practical. It is ¾-inch plywood trimmed all around with ¼-inch mahogany. Fiddles are on the inside plastic-laminate surface. The table is held in place with loose-pin hinges and a turnbutton. To set it up, you screw the pipe leg into the 1-inch pipe flange. The pipe is then passed down through the plate in the sole and into a socket bonded to the hull or to a floor timber. The forward end of the table rests on a block. It is held there by a brass door bolt fitted into a brass plate. Another method is to mount two brass angles on the bulkhead with a pin passing through them and the plate. Or the table can be stood on two pipe legs independent of the bulkhead. A clever builder could devise a drop leaf for the hinge side to allow the diner on the starboard transom to eat in more comfort.

FRAMING BASICS

Whether you build a berth, dresser, galley, locker, or whatever, the principle is just about the same. If the structure is to rely on vertical supports (legs) to carry weight, the front can be very light indeed. It is common to screw and glue two vertical cleats or legs to the end bulkheads, and a sill lengthwise on the bottom (maybe on the sole). You then screw and glue the ⅜- or ½-inch front to these. Add a bearer or stiffener that carries the risers, if any, full length along the top — this may be set down the height of the risers so they sit on it. In this case, insert spacers between the risers so you have something solid to fasten the top to. If you use glue everywhere, very few screws are needed, for finish nails are ample to hold everything in position under pressure until the glue sets up. The framing material may be 1 by 2 clear pine, fir, Philippine mahogany, or oak. Watch the weight, however, and remember that oak does not take glue well. Rely on screws if you use oak.

THE GALLEY

Decide what equipment will be in your galley. You may have to juggle things around to make the best use of a small amount of space. If you go for simplicity, you'll choose a drop-in two-burner stove that needs only a cutout. A gimbaled range, however, must have a receptacle or recess built to order. You can settle for a plastic dishpan set into an opening, or select a double sink of stainless steel complete with pressure water. Will it be an ice chest or a mechanical refrigerator? Everything

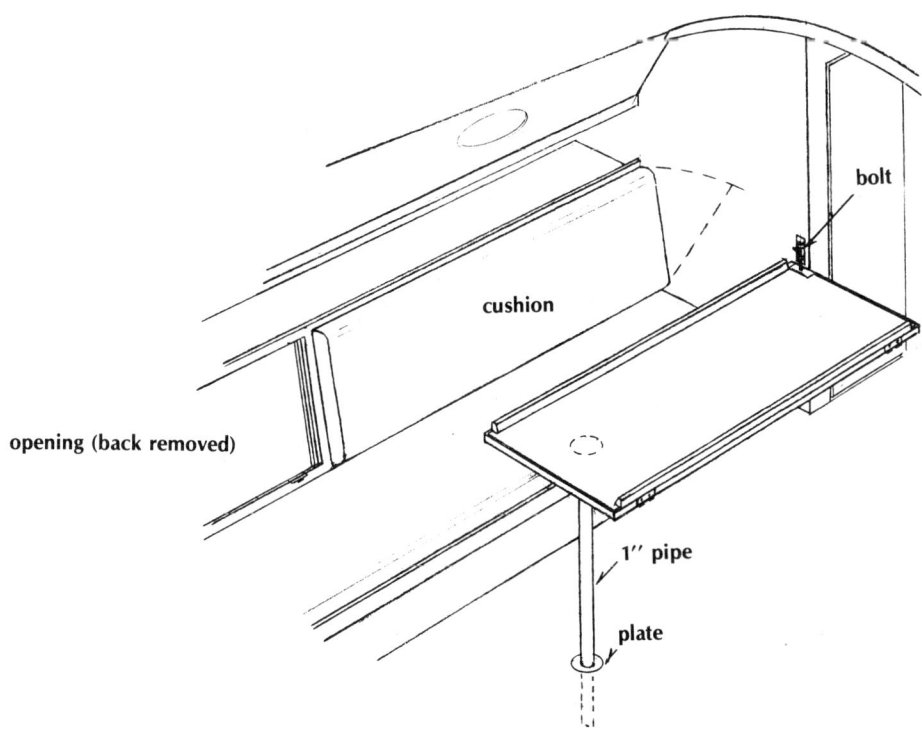

Figure 11-10. ALLEGRA'S BACKREST AS A TABLE

hinges on space available and your pocketbook, and perhaps the influence of the person using the galley most.

Figures 11-11 and 11-12 show the framing, front, and top of Allegra's galley. This is just about a minimum, being only 52 inches long. However, it does provide for a gimbaled range that takes up a lot of space. Study this quite complex framing. Little that you build will be more involved.

To start, fasten cleats (A and B) vertically and horizontally on bulkheads. Allow at least 4-inch clearance for the length of the range recess. This opening has to be deep enough so the range clears the base as it swings. Measure from the gimbal to the lower corner of the range; add 1 inch for clearance. This locates the height of the horizontal shown notched into the center vertical leg (E). Swing this dimension outboard to be sure the range also clears framing or any other obstruction (such as a bin). The frame from the sole to the underside of the top is 35¼ inches. Notice the kick space (D). This eases reaching into the ice chest, washing dishes, and getting up close when the boat is heeling. If this frame can't be nailed on top of the sole, it will have to be spiled to the hull and bonded. Make it 3 inches by 3 inches clear. Framing of ¾-by-1½-inch stock is typical.

Make allowances for the thicknesses of the front and top as well as the range enclosure, but leave the back of the recess open into the bin. The framing at C and E could be assembled on ¼-inch plywood, working on a floor. This would mean more material and more weight, but a rigid unit. Large lightening holes are advisable.

Clamp to a straightedge across the top and bond to the hull. Do not install the framing around the ice chest (*dotted lines*) until the chest is complete and chocked in place. There should be a light plywood bottom or floor to keep articles from becoming wet from occasional bilge water. The bin behind the stove also should have a bottom. Doorskins are fine for this because of their low cost and light weight.

The Galley Front and Top

The one-piece galley front is sawed out of ⅜- or ½-inch plywood to fit snugly between the bulkheads. The openings can be marked from the inside of the final framing so you have a clean saw cut on the exposed side. I prefer shelf space to drawers, for drawers are terrible space wasters. You can, however, install two drawers under the sink and one under the range. Details on drawer construction follow. For now, put the front aside until the ice chest has been installed.

The countertop should be ½- or ¾-inch plywood to which a laminate will be applied. Fit it by tacking thin plywood rippings or scrap into a template so it conforms to hull curvature. Apply a plastic laminate with a butcher-block or teak pattern, following instructions on the can of contact cement. Again, mark the openings on the underside. The cutout for the sink is 10 by 14 inches for the larger single sink. If you feel that a place to put dishes is more valuable, check out the smaller single size. Let the front edge project ½ to ¾ inch more than

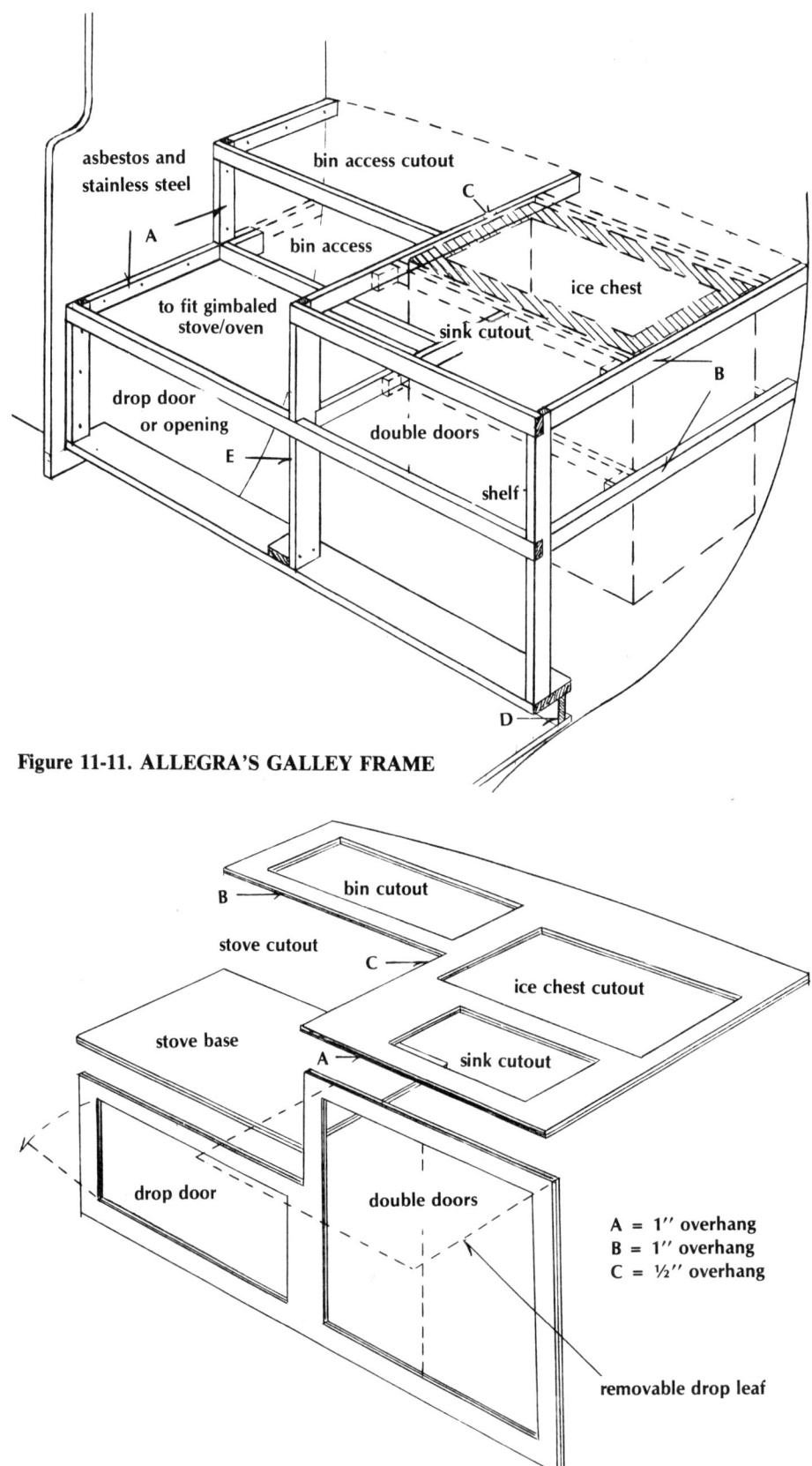

Figure 11-11. ALLEGRA'S GALLEY FRAME

Figure 11-12. ALLEGRA'S GALLEY FRONT AND COUNTERTOP

Figure 11-13. DRESSER FRONT (ONE PIECE)

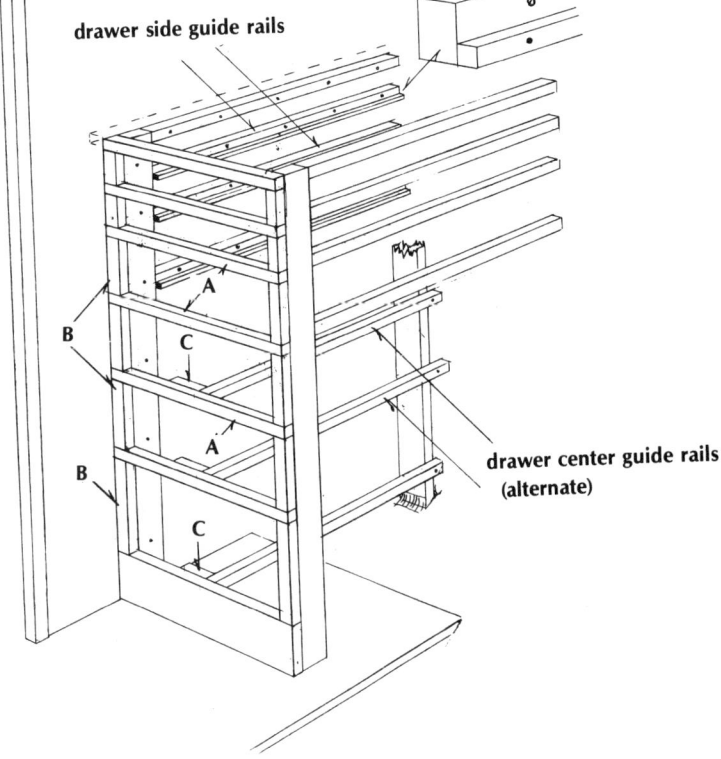

Figure 11-14. DRESSER FRAME

the plywood front. There should be allowances around the range recess, too.

Saw to the lines by clamping on a thick straightedge for a guide, except on the ice-chest opening. The remnants can be used for covers. Note the removable drop leaf in front of the sink. (There is also a drop leaf (not shown) on the aft side of the bulkhead in the foreground in the illustration.) Cover these with laminate and give them a nice hardwood edging of mahogany or teak. There must be generous fiddles around all sides of the galley counter.

I think it would be handy to make the galley top fairly easy to remove. You can fasten small angle brackets to the frame at four or five locations accessible from the front or through the openings. Be sure the screws do not reach the laminate. It would also be possible to have the top slide out by applying moldings at each side on the bulkheads. A removable top makes it easy to reach around the ice chest or to pull it out, if necessary.

Working surfaces are severely limited in small yachts. One possible solution (an expedient, really) is to make a cover for the galley in two sections. Fit these inside the fiddles. If there is no water pump, you have a large area suitable for a chart table. It might be possible to have half the cover in place with the range in use. Make the cover sections light enough so they can be stowed under a berth pad.

DRESSERS AND LOCKERS

Framing for dressers and lockers is similar to galley construction. Fronts may be very slim. There are many ways to construct a dresser front. Let's discuss these first, for they affect the framing procedure. The simplest front is of painted hardwood or hardwood $\frac{3}{8}$- or $\frac{1}{2}$-inch plywood. See Figure 11-13. Saw out as described above. The second front, shown in Figure 11-14, is assembled right on the vertical cleats or legs.

This will give you the look of solid mahogany or teak. The joints must be absolutely flush and the sanding done with extreme care to avoid unsightly scratches across the grain.

The rails (A) and stiles (B) must be cut very accurately with a fine-toothed blade, so clamp a stop on your table saw. Position it just this side of the blade to prevent jamming between the blade and the fence, or use the sliding auxiliary table described in Part One. The glue blocks (C) don't have to be cut accurately, but a similar setup is useful when the quantity makes it worthwhile.

A less conventional way to build a dresser front of hardwood is shown in detail from the reverse side in Figure 11-15. It's best to assemble this on a floor or bench on a sheet of light plastic. Tack blocks around three sides of the perimeter to the exact dimensions of the front. Make the stiles (B) full length, in conventional cabinetmaking style. Cut the rails (A) very accurately and cleanly to make a snug fit between the stiles. Now carefully mark the exact position of the rails on the stiles. Glue the mating surfaces of the stiles and rails. This is a good place to use Aerolite, for it is strong and sets up crystal clear. But put the resin on the end grain generously, and the liquid catalyst on the stile. Place all the parts in position, then tack down the holding blocks on the remaining side of the jig. Place the glue blocks as shown (the brads should have been driven in previously).

Clamp the whole thing with light pressure, using four or five bar or pipe clamps. Then drive the brads well in until the joints appear to be flush. Give the clamps a turn, but do not crush. If you don't have clamps, tap small wedges between the stiles and the jig blocks. In about four hours, if you handle the assembly very carefully, you can lay it on its back and wash off any glue that may have squeezed out. Water will dissolve Aerolite before it sets up permanently, but once it's hard, there's no hope. The only disadvantage to this kind of front is that it requires wider stiles than the other built-up front. Thus, it wastes a bit of space and you can't have side guide rails. You might try to assemble this front right on the framing verticals, but it would be difficult to apply pressure on the joints.

This assembly could be put together by doweling the joints, as previously described, using a boring jig (or by boring from the outside of the stiles). You could fasten with long screws, but screws do not hold as well in end grain.

There's still another method, one that is really yacht style. The rails are halved into the stiles (see Chapter Seven). This is picky work requiring fine, sharp tools, preferably a dado on the table saw. In ½-inch mahogany or teak it would be a real challenge. But where is it written that stiles can't be of ¾-inch material? I guarantee you would have an exceedingly strong front, and if you make fine, clean joints, you'll have something to enjoy as long as you own the boat.

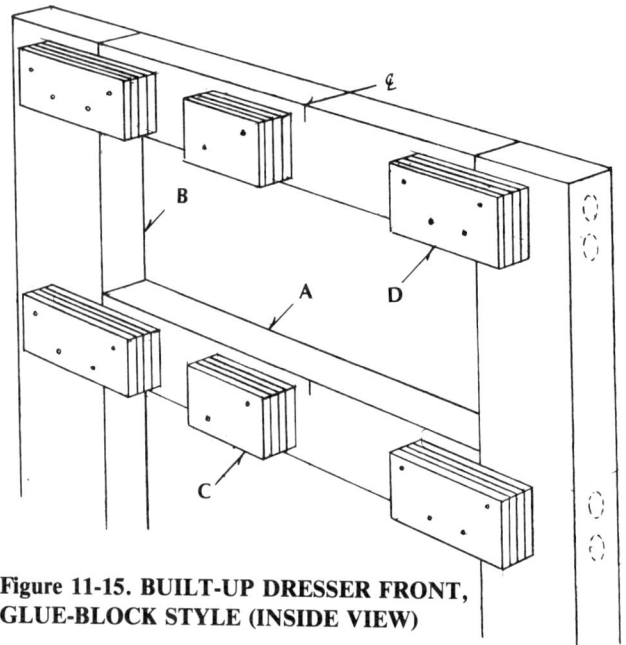

Figure 11-15. BUILT-UP DRESSER FRONT, GLUE-BLOCK STYLE (INSIDE VIEW)

Drawer Guide Rails

Which comes first, the framing or the drawers? You can't proceed with one unless you know how you are going to build the other. The trickiest part of this job is installation of the drawer guide rails (see Figure 11-14). These keep the drawers level, square to the front both ways, and prevent the drawers from swinging from side to side. In dry-land cabinetry this is accomplished efficiently by using roller devices or plastic glides that ride on grooved rails. You can use these, but often they require about 1½ inches between drawers. This is a lot of wasted space.

Your drawer rails don't need to be much larger than ¾ inch by ¾ inch because they support very little weight.

First, let's talk about the rails at the top half of the illustration. These are simply screwed and glued to the bulkheads. The configuration shown may be two-piece or rabbeted out of heavier stock. However, there's an important detail: drawers tend to slide out when the vessel heels, so they are often notched to lock onto the dresser front. Thus, in this case the guide rails must be located ⅛ to ³⁄₁₆ inch below the front pieces (A). (Also see the drawer construction shown in Figure 11-16.) The guide rails must also be dead level athwartships and across from one side to the other. You'll need a short torpedo level. While drawers may be of several lengths because of the shape of the hull, the rails don't have to reach full length.

The center guide rail may be mandatory because of the width of the dresser front stiles (B). It's com-

190

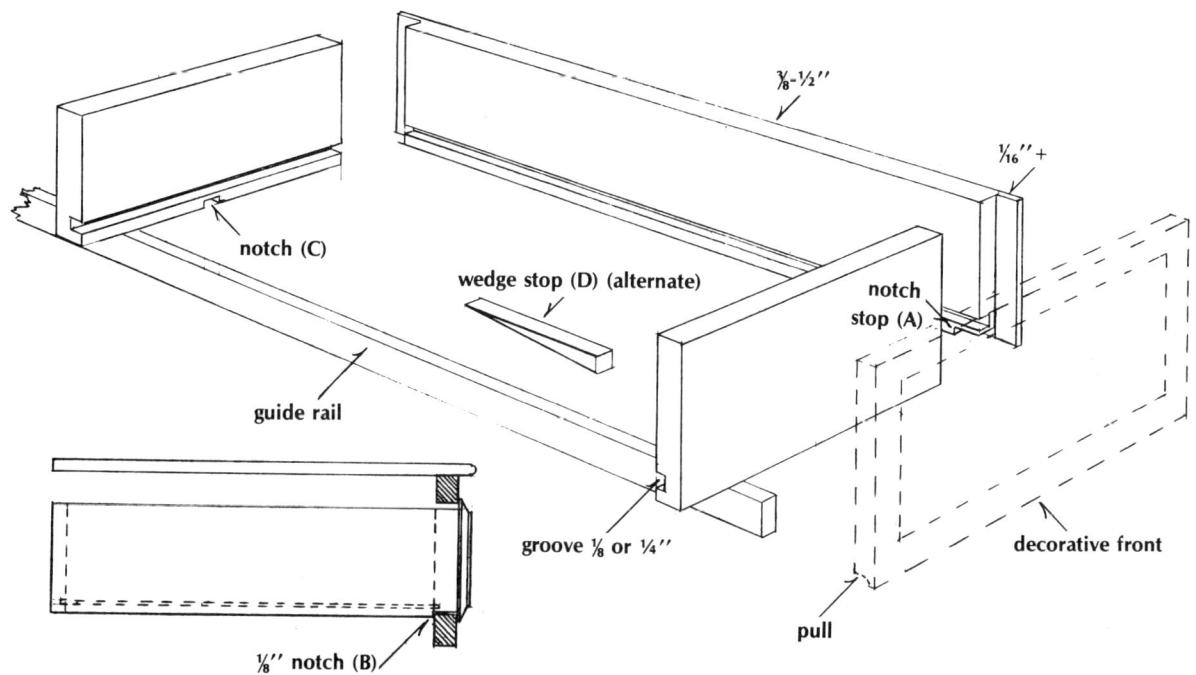

Figure 11-16. TYPICAL DRAWER CONSTRUCTION

plicated. This guide rail must level up with the front where it is attached to the glued block (C). It must also be dead center between the bulkheads so the drawer front matches the dresser front. Even a very small misalignment will be obvious. Prepare a vertical piece from 1 by 3 stock to take the outboard ends of the center rails. Clamp this for a moment to the dresser front and transfer the spacing to it. Now, when this vertical is erected in its final position and level from any front rail to any corresponding mark, all drawer guides will be level. The drawers will fit.

How to fasten this vertical depends on the type of boat. My guess would be that bonding with mat, cloth, and polyester resin would be the easiest, for this allows flexibility for adjustments side to side and up and down until the resin sets. Or it can be screwed and glued to horizontal pieces at the top and bottom of the cabinet. There may have to be two verticals because of different drawer lengths. Don't screw the rails in until the drawers are completed. Shimming or paring may be required if the vertical is not perfect. Rub a bit of paraffin on the upper surfaces of the guide rails for lubrication. I would use oak or ash for these rails.

Drawer Construction

There are many ways to build drawers. Start with the premise that every drawer, fully loaded, must withstand the shock of being slammed shut a thousand times. In addition, there are certain desirable features. Two examples are a double or rabbeted front that acts as a stop and a bottom fitted into grooved sides and ends. And I like the appearance of closely fitted flush fronts, but the alignment must be perfect and the spacing all around must be close and uniform for all drawers in a bank. Any of the overlapping or rabbeted fronts cover the opening completely, so your small errors are hidden. Figure 11-20 shows four ways to make the insides of drawer fronts.

The bottom panel fitted into grooves is the strongest possible drawer construction. It squares up the drawer assembly almost automatically. See Figure 11-16. Bottom panels may be of ¼-inch marine or exterior plywood or $\frac{3}{32}$-inch mahogany doorskins if you want space, appearance, economy, and adequate strength in a drawer less than 24 inches square. Don't store tools in such a drawer. Of course, bottom panels can be nailed and glued on the sides and ends to save space and time, but this is hardly yacht-style workmanship.

I prefer the deeply rabbeted corners shown in Figure 11-16. This structure creates more gluing surface than any other except the dadoed or dovetailed joint. And the appearance of sides and ends is good, although I'm assuming you will apply a decorative front. Dovetails are ideal, and they can be done quite easily with a dovetail router template. Another strong joint using a single dovetail is only a bit more difficult than the rabbeted corner. See Figure 11-17. Rather careful layout with a knife is recommended. Make up a couple of trial joints using scrap identical in thickness to the drawer sides and ends. Make the front first. Cut the dado as shown in Step 1, $\frac{7}{16}$ inch wide for a ½-inch side, ⅜ inch deep. Set the blade to 15 degrees when all rabbets are

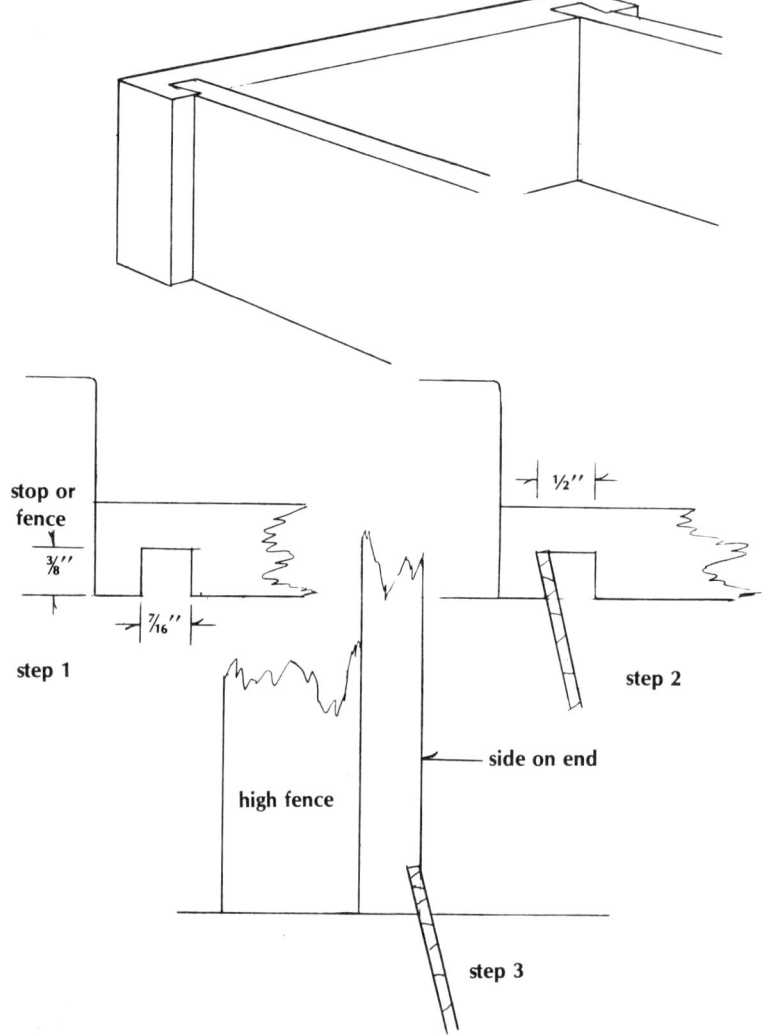

Figure 11-17. SINGLE DOVETAIL

cut, and make this single saw cut in all fronts. This is Step 2. For Step 3, clamp up a high fence to keep the pieces vertical. Form the corresponding angle in the side. Groove the parts for the bottom panel, as above. Assemble with Plastic Resin glue. No fastenings are required. Incidentally, use an ordinary rabbet joint for the back end. This drawer will take any type of added front over the single dovetailed front.

Drawer Fronts

I show only a few drawer front styles in Figure 11-18. You should read some of the fine cabinet and furniture construction books available in your public library. A great deal depends on your skill, tools, and patience. Number 1 in Figure 11-18 is just about self-explanatory. The fancy cutouts can be routed, sabersawed, or scroll sawed. If you want to repeat the design in other lockers, berth fronts, or what-have-you, make a template for a fine router bit. Keep the design simple. Sharp corners must be filed or sawed out. Use your imagination. Anchors and seagulls are a bit hackneyed. How about sharks, dolphins, swordfish, ducks, eagles, seals, whales, stars, burgees, and so on?

Number 2 is a raised panel, very handsome if made with a molding head so the surface is slightly concave. I use a single cutter head from Sears. I ground the bevel to the shape, an easy task, for there is but one blade. Another method is to set up a high fence and incline the saw blade. The edge is not quite as pretty and requires a lot of sanding, but I have made hundreds this way. A fine touch is to make the area to be molded of hardwood. It is then mitered and glued to the center panel. No nails should show, of course. Aerolite glue will do the job. Finish the molding bright against a painted center — beautiful!

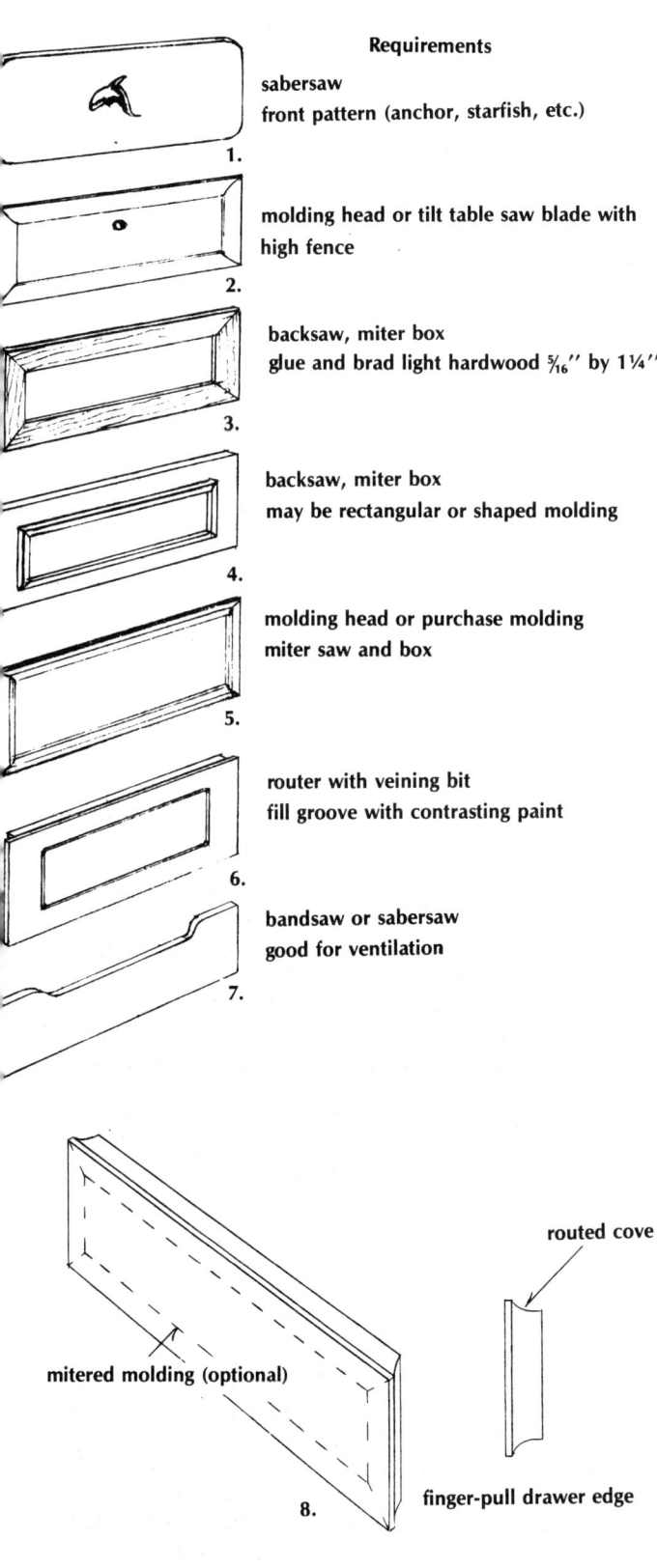

Figure 11-18. DRAWER FRONTS

Number 3 is a simulated panel effect. I call it a drop center. It looks best on drawers and doors if the mitered frame is rather delicate — say, ¼ inch by 1 to 1¼ inches. The center panel may be painted or bright if of the same material. Glue thoroughly and brad. This job requires a good miter box or a sliding auxiliary table. If you have confidence in your table-saw miter gauge, use it.

Number 4 also can be done with hardwood moldings, perhaps a tiny half round or a beaded molding. These are seldom found commercially in hardwood, so see what you can make with router bits, with the router mounted upside down in a little table. Even pine, painted a contrasting color or antiqued, looks great. All of this applies to Number 5 as well. In this drawer front, the edge might be molded with an applied molding added.

Number 6 shows a pattern routed in with a veining bit. This requires a guide template of ¼-inch plywood. Number 7 allows lots of ventilation and is easily made with a sabersaw or bandsaw. A router or shaper straight cutter can turn these out in minutes if you make a template. If made of plywood, this drawer front should be painted. In addition, it must be rabbeted, for it cannot be attached to an inside front.

Number 8 is a modern finger-pull front. The edge is undercut either by sawing the angle or by forming with a router, shaper, or molding head. A first-class job would be a hardwood mitered edge glued on, but it can be done in ¾-inch plywood, well sanded, and painted.

One drawer treatment I have not shown probably should have been Number 1, as it is pure yacht style and easy to make. See Figure 11-19. If you go for the one-piece plywood dresser front, the cutouts can be used as drawer fronts. Simply edge the front piece with hardwood about ¼ inch by ⅞ inch, miter the corners, and have the strips project ⅛ inch or less. Bullnose the corners and finish bright. This treatment is excellent for both cabinet and passage doors.

The inside views of drawer fronts need little comment. See Figure 11-20. The two rabbeted styles can be done with the table saw alone, or they can be dadoed. The third requires a dado set and great care to see that the bottom groove does not run out and ruin the appearance. The fourth is simple. You'll need only enough tools to make the light square molding. Rely on glue for strength.

Drawer Problems

One problem in any sailing yacht is drawer movement when the vessel heels. Designers, of course, are well aware of this problem. Steps can be taken to solve it. Look at Figure 11-16. You'll see notch stop A at the upper right-hand side, front. It is shown again in side elevation at the lower left (B). The notch should be just

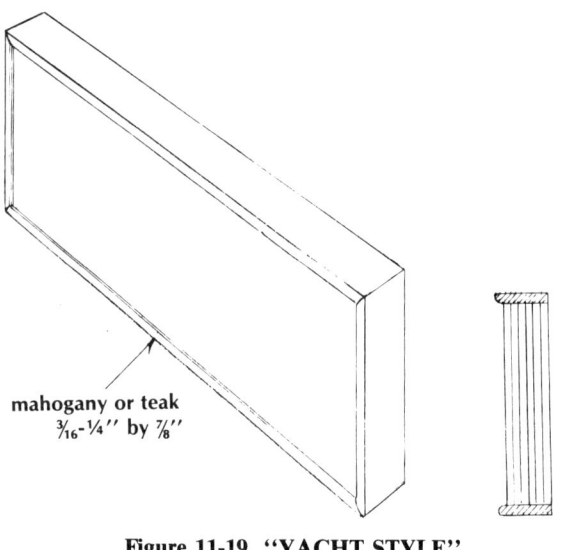

Figure 11-19. "YACHT STYLE" DOOR AND DRAWER TRIM

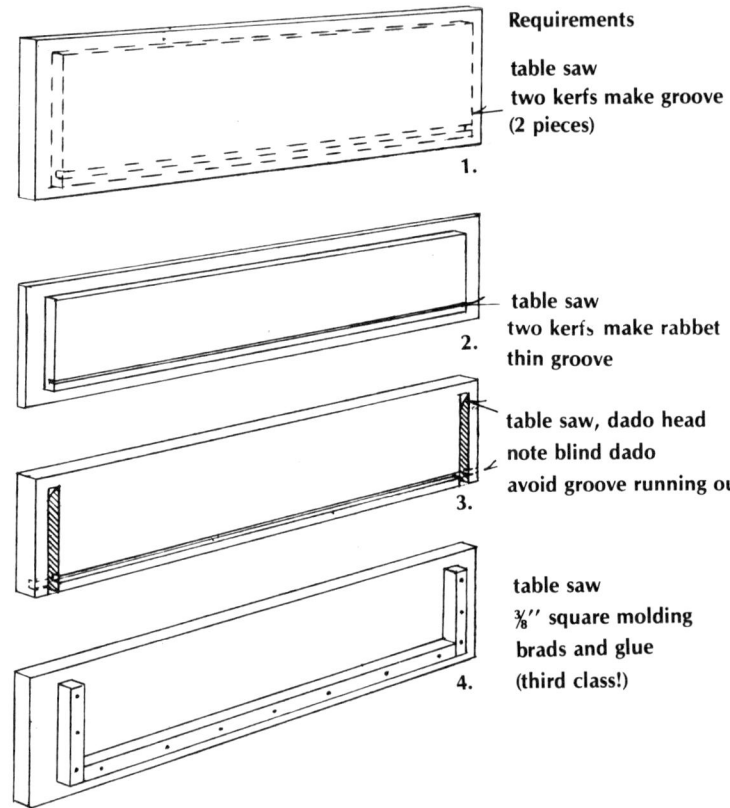

Figure 11-20. INSIDE DRAWER FRONTS

deep enough to let the drawer drop down over the rail of the front construction. Also note the clearance above the drawer side so it can be lifted up out of the notch. There is a difference. Notch A is cut out of the side only. Thus, it permits the drawer to slide forward ¾ inch, then it stops. Notch B requires the inner front to be reduced to the depth of the notch, perhaps by taking off a saw kerf before the decorative front goes on. Now go back a page or two to dresser framing. You will see that the side guide rails were located ⅛ inch lower than the front rails to accommodate the drawer dropdown. If you use the center guide rail, there must be a notch (C) in the back panel of the drawer. The alternative, the wedge stop (D), eliminates front-end notching. It automatically raises the drawer ⅛ inch, then allows it to drop down and lock. The back notch is not necessary if two guide blocks are glued on to ride on each side of the center rail.

If you use a center guide you must adjust the position of the vertical support for the guide rails. It's all right if you measure from a bulkhead at both ends to make sure the guide rail will be parallel. You'll have to shift the vertical support accordingly, or pare or shim it. If you install the drawer and then clamp or wedge it flush with the front of the dresser, you can mark the position of the guide rail at both ends. If they are not exactly alike, you'll have to move the vertical support as above.

The second problem is connected to the first. Guide rails must be square to the dresser front or an impossible jam will result. If you use the side guide rail construction, you merely have to see that the bulkheads either are absolutely parallel or allow so much slop on either side of the drawers that they square up when closed against the dresser front. This is not the best solution. Perhaps you could shim out the side rails from the bulkhead to line up the drawers.

There's still another way to line up a drawer square to the dresser front, regardless of the kind of guide rails used. Fashion quite long wedges to be glued to the bulkheads on each side. Place them in or out so they move the drawer sideways until it squares up. Brad and glue them in this position. The drawer will still be sloppy when it moves in and out, but perfect when fully closed. This is similar to the idea of shimming the side guide rails mentioned above.

A final word on drawers. Get used to shelves instead. With little fiddles on shelves, they are almost ideal because you get full use of the space, even if you have to pull everything out to find what's in back. Shelves save a lot of time and material.

SMALL DOORS

Let's cover cabinet and locker doors first, then get into passage doors. Some of the moldings for drawers already described would be attractive on small doors. See Figure 11-18. The last one described, a simple hardwood trim strip, would be practical and attractive for passage doors as well. Number 2, called the raised panel, gives a rich effect for a full overlapping door, that is, a door not rabbeted. Number 3, the fake panel drop center with mitered hardwood trim, also has a

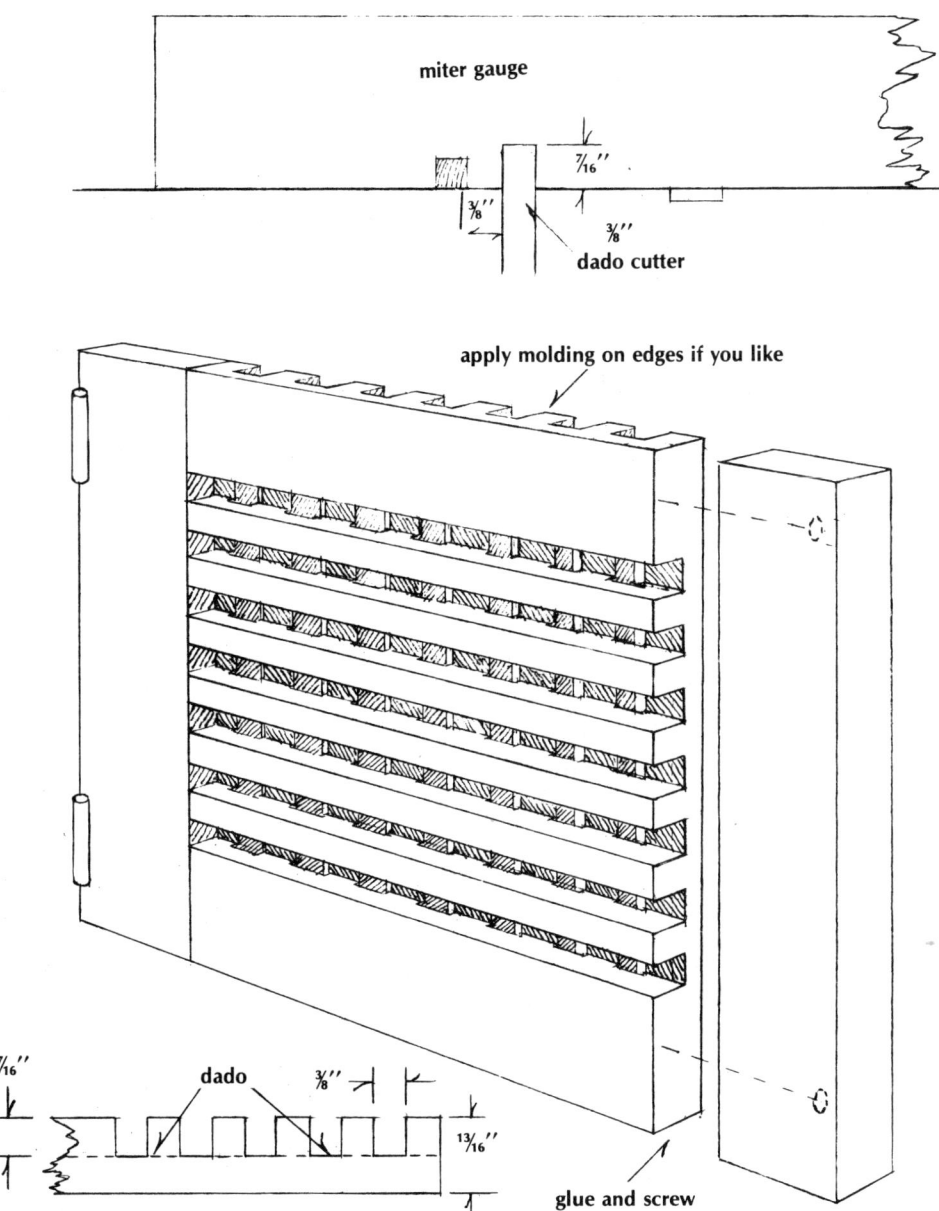

Figure 11-21. VENTED (DADOED) DOOR

traditional look about it. This would be good for stiffening a light door less than ¾ inch thick, but I would not recommend it for a passage door. Any door large enough to warp should be weighted down on a dead flat surface while being glued. The molding pattern, Number 4, could be used on any door, but Numbers 5 and 6 are suitable for cabinet doors only. The vent in Number 7 makes it good for a hanging locker, especially for storm gear. In this case, I would repeat the cutout at the bottom of the door. The more ventilation here, the better.

Most doors block air circulation, of course, so here are a couple of ideas for ventilating panels you can make (Figure 11-21). This job looks much more difficult and time-consuming than it really is because of the inadequacy of the drawing. All you do is set up your dado width, say, ⅜ to ½ inch, to cut to a depth slightly more than one-half the thickness of the material. The drawing shows ⁷⁄₁₆ inch for ¹³⁄₁₆-inch mahogany. Cut the dadoes on one side, then flip over and rotate the piece so the grooves intersect. This will leave a square of daylight where they cross. Screw and glue a substantial rail on the end-grain edge, assuming the grain runs horizontally. Use Aerolite or another good epoxy or Plastic Resin.

195

Figure 11-22. *These ash plywood doors were sawed out in one piece. Rabbeted in the back, they are strong enough to carry leaded glass.*

You may go all around with rails and stiles, or with a simple flat hardwood trim well fastened. Knock the sharp corners off the grooves with a sanding block.

How do you space the grooves and dadoes? In Chapter Five, I described a method of making box or finger corner joints. This is identical. Fashion a tiny block ⅜ inch wide, then glue this to your miter gauge. Place your piece against this block and cut your first dado. Now place that dado over the block, and run the second cut. Then just keep repeating to the width you want. If you like the heavier frame effect shown in the drawing, make the first cut, then fix the block in place. If this block is a nuisance, drive in a small brad, but remember to press the piece against it on each pass. If you have a sliding auxiliary table for your saw, the task will be easier and the result more accurate.

Plywood doors can be made more attractive by cutting out ventilation apertures. A series of slots is a simple design. Another design has holes bored in a pattern, using a template so all doors will be identical. Three-quarter-inch doors can be sawed out to leave stiles and rails for paneling, as in Figure 11-22. The openings were filled with leaded glass held in place by a rabbet in the back and small moldings. To avoid such unusual weight, use doorskins, ¼-inch plywood, or even molded plastic designs. Not yachty enough? Correct, but they are inexpensive, almost indestructible, light in weight, and no finish is required. Tempered Masonite is available in a variety of styles. This is true too for textured polystyrene and, of course, the ubiquitous wicker (preferably natural, brass, or aluminum, but not steel). If none of these will do, you can fashion very attractive panels by weaving thin strips of mahogany or teak ¹⁄₁₆ inch by ½ to ¾ inch. See Figure 11-23. This is quite a task, but appearance and practicality make it well worthwhile.

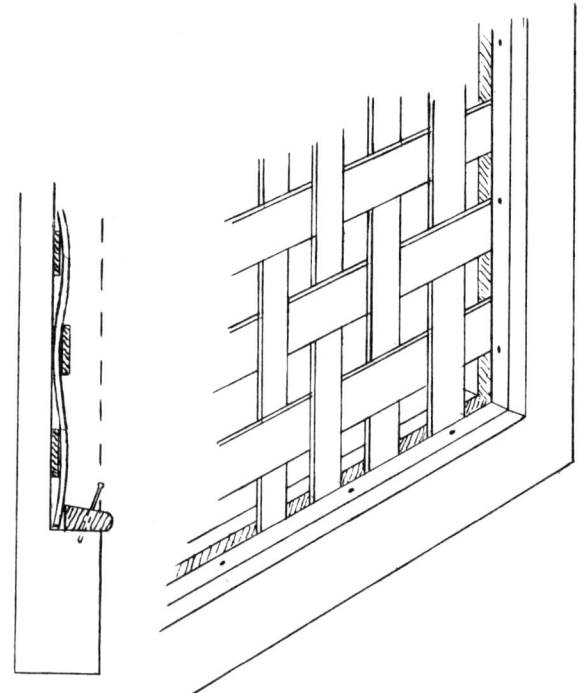

Figure 11-23. WOVEN DOOR PANEL

Woven Door Panels

Cut the strips to ¹⁄₁₆ inch or less, making them about ½ inch longer than the rabbeted opening dimensions. Sand well on a bench belt sander or portable belt sander. With the door frame rabbeted side up on a bench, square off the desired spacing, marking on the rabbets so they won't show later. Spacing equal to the width of the strips is about right. Your moldings have already been made and mitered. Weave the strips together on the bench to get started, then space them out over the marks on the rabbets. Excess lengths can be nipped off with a sharp chisel. Clamp a couple of battens over the strips so they won't move around and start bradding in the moldings. It's easy if the brads (#18 or #20) are driven well in beforehand and slightly canted. Press the moldings down hard with small C-clamps, being sure they are straight. Do the same on the opposite side, remove the temporary battens, and apply the third and fourth moldings. Glue under the moldings might help, but it's not vital. Hang this door either way. If it's hung molding side out, make the moldings wider so they project slightly, as in the sketch. A hardwood quarter round can be used.

SIMPLE PANEL DOORS

I have not mentioned traditional paneled doors because of space limitations. The procedure for building them is

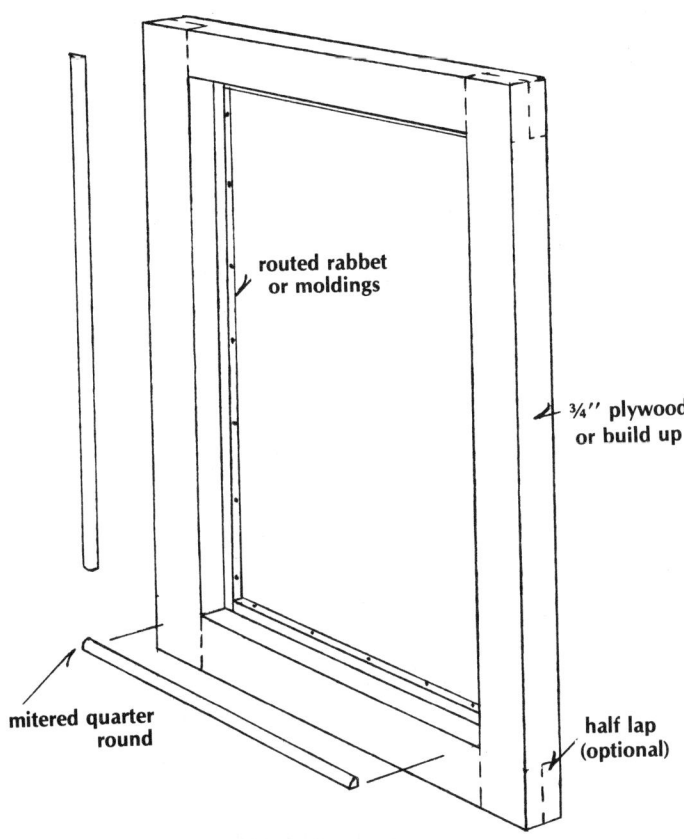
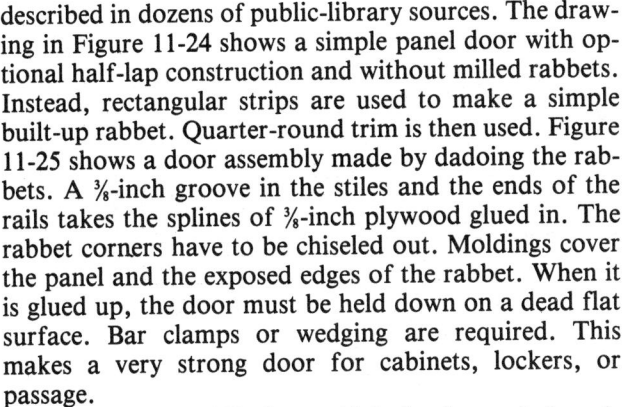

Figure 11-24. SIMPLE FRAME FOR PANELED DOOR

Figure 11-25. *A built-up door frame with splined corner joints and routed or dadoed rabbets. Assembly must be done on a flat surface and door must be weighted down while glue cures.*

described in dozens of public-library sources. The drawing in Figure 11-24 shows a simple panel door with optional half-lap construction and without milled rabbets. Instead, rectangular strips are used to make a simple built-up rabbet. Quarter-round trim is then used. Figure 11-25 shows a door assembly made by dadoing the rabbets. A ⅜-inch groove in the stiles and the ends of the rails takes the splines of ⅜-inch plywood glued in. The rabbet corners have to be chiseled out. Moldings cover the panel and the exposed edges of the rabbet. When it is glued up, the door must be held down on a dead flat surface. Bar clamps or wedging are required. This makes a very strong door for cabinets, lockers, or passage.

A method of stiffening a ¾-inch plywood door is shown in Figure 11-26. The frame is somewhat heavier than the plywood because it helps to counteract warping. It looks good, too. Like the door in Figure 11-25, this door depends on ¼-inch plywood-strip splines, but they run full length. This is a simple job with a dado set or with repeated saw kerfs. Set the fence back 1/16 to ⅛ inch when grooving the frame so it projects equally on both sides of the plywood. The mitered frame is like any other. The splines do not have to be mitered or even meet in the corners. Plastic Resin painted into the grooves would work well here.

PASSAGES AND DOORS

Every passage opening must be edge-trimmed. In addition, door jambs must provide a very solid stop. The one-piece construction shown in Figure 11-27(A) is best, for while it is light, it is also strong. Quite intricate jambs can be built up, as in Figures 11-27 (B) and (C), to minimize waste. The section in A is not difficult. It just requires time. Plan ahead. Jot down how much door jamb or simple strips will be required. Set up a dado for the groove in A or the rabbet in B, then run all pieces through. If you elect to make these with repeated saw kerfs, repeat the cut in all pieces, then reset the fence, and so on. Don't finish one piece, then set up all over again for the following pieces.

The drawings give suggested dimensions. For a ¾-inch bulkhead, you might want to make the piece in A from 1¼-inch mahogany or teak so the stop would be heavier. I suggest the following sequence. (1) Joint 1½-inch dressed mahogany plank edge. (2) Rip off ⅞ to 1 inch. (3) Joint this (plane) to ⅞ inch or more by 1¼ or 1⅜ inches. (4) Dado, shape, rout, or saw groove (bulkhead thickness). (5) Dado, rout, shape, or saw rabbet. The last pass takes out the dotted area. (6) Sand all surfaces except bulkhead groove, including the round-

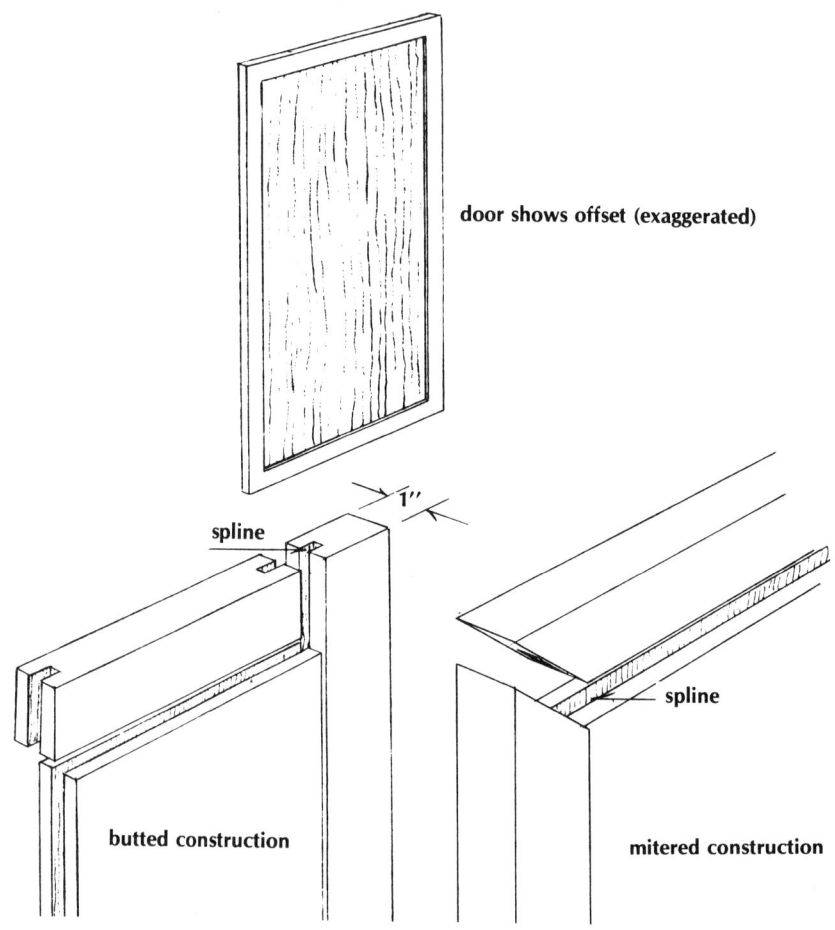

Figure 11-26. STIFFENING A ¾-INCH PLYWOOD DOOR

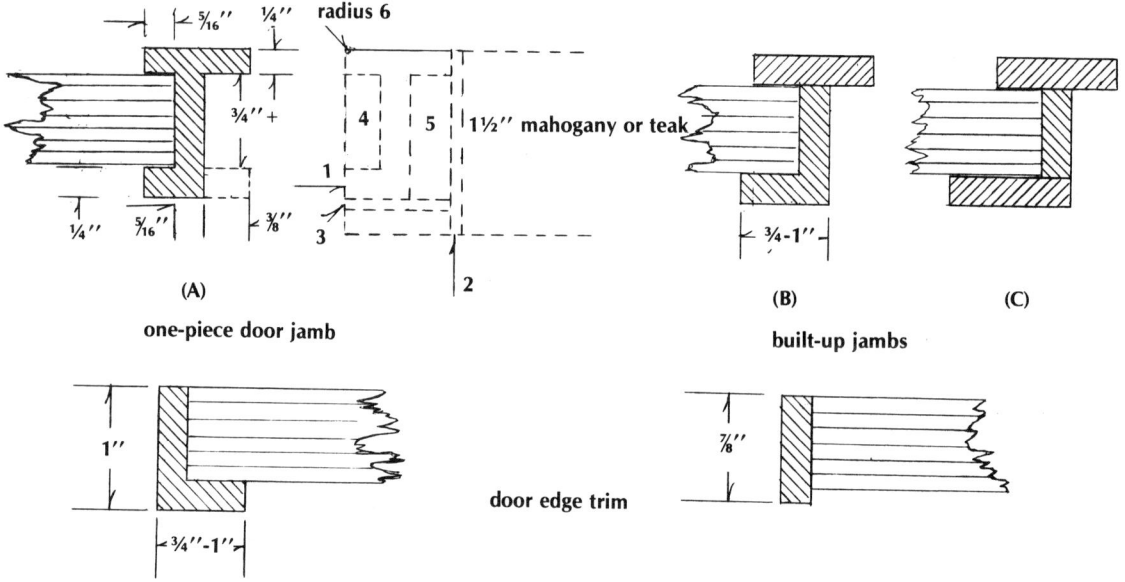

Figure 11-27. DOOR TRIM

198

Figure 11-28. "YACHT STYLE" PASSAGE

ing of corners. The form in B is similar but it comes out of full ¾-inch stock, so it saves a lot of material. The built-up form in C is all strips. You can get two ⁵⁄₁₆-inch dressed pieces from ¹³⁄₁₆-inch stock (the usual planed thickness of so-called ¾-inch mahogany when you buy from a lumberyard). This heavier thickness is desirable. Need I remind you that hold-downs are absolutely essential when working with small stuff like this? Safety as well as consistency are at stake. Use glue and 1-inch brass brads or galvanized finish nails to assemble. The corners are mitered, of course.

The door edge trim shown in Figure 11-27 is self-explanatory.

One of the most beautiful door designs has a 4- to 6-inch radius in the corners, both top and bottom (Figure 11-28). A passageway with a perfect arch top and bottom is even lovelier. These are a lot of work. They can be botched if you lack skill and patience, but they can add thousands of dollars to the value of your yacht if well done. If you follow the procedures below for the construction of corner trim for cutaway bulkheads as well as for passage doors, you will be halfway home. You'll create a beautiful interior. A word of warning. Don't start this involved work unless you are prepared to carry it from forepeak to aft bulkhead. The scheme must be coordinated and have integrity.

First of all, this work requires a shaper or a router set up as a shaper, with collars on the cutters for forming grooves in inside and outside curves. Second, some of this work is dangerous. You'll be handling small pieces up close to a cutter turning 28,000 r.p.m. Often you'll be cutting against the grain. To avoid having small pieces thrown about like missiles, always try to do the risky cutting while the piece is still in the plank. Don't bandsaw it out and then try to shape it. The plank's weight is your protection.

CORNER TRIM

First consider an outside corner trim for a door or bulkhead. For ¾-inch trim you need mahogany or teak dressed to 1¼ inches thick. For ½-inch trim you need ⅞ inch dressed. See section A-A in Figure 11-29. The width of the piece is 6 to 8 inches, depending on the desired radius. Let's do a 4-inch radius for doors and partial bulkheads. It is assumed that you have a shaper or router-shaper. Radius 1 in the drawing is 4 inches to the bottom of the groove to fit the bulkhead. Thus, radius 2 is the inside radius — 3¾ inches. Make your shaper pattern to cut that radius. Space out on your plank the number of pieces required, marking around the pattern for approximate location along both jointed edges. Allow plenty for the finished thickness of the piece to radius 3⅝ inches, plus some for dressing. This radius is 4⅜ inches plus. Make a pattern for later bandsawing of this outside curve.

The next step is bandsawing or sabersawing around the inside radius. Tack the shaper pattern in place. If you have a shaper cutter 1½ inches high, set it up with a collar to follow the pattern. If you are using a 1-inch cutter, make two passes. This should give you a surface that needs only a few strokes with sandpaper. Do the same for all parts.

Next, we need a groove ¼ inch by ¾ inch or ¼ inch by ½ inch, depending on bulkhead or door thickness. Cutters for rabbeting ¾ and ⅜ inch are available, the latter requiring two passes, of course. Set up with a collar ½ inch less than the cutter diameter, and adjust the height so the groove is dead center. Now run the radius against the collar. In making these shaper cuts, feed the work in very gingerly until you acquire the feel and control it needs. Remember, half of this pass will be against the grain and the shaper will try to fight you. One or two shallow freehand cuts are advisable until you see whether or not the reverse grain is going to split. Don't rush, but don't feed so slowly that the material scorches, for this will take the temper out of the tool. Always start the feed against the cutter rotation. Repeat this process for all the parts and the job is more than half done.

The next step is easy. Bandsaw outside of the radius mark, and use your bench disc sander to take the sawed surface down to the mark. After the corner has been connected to the straight trim, it will have to be sanded well with the grain to remove the cross-grain scratches.

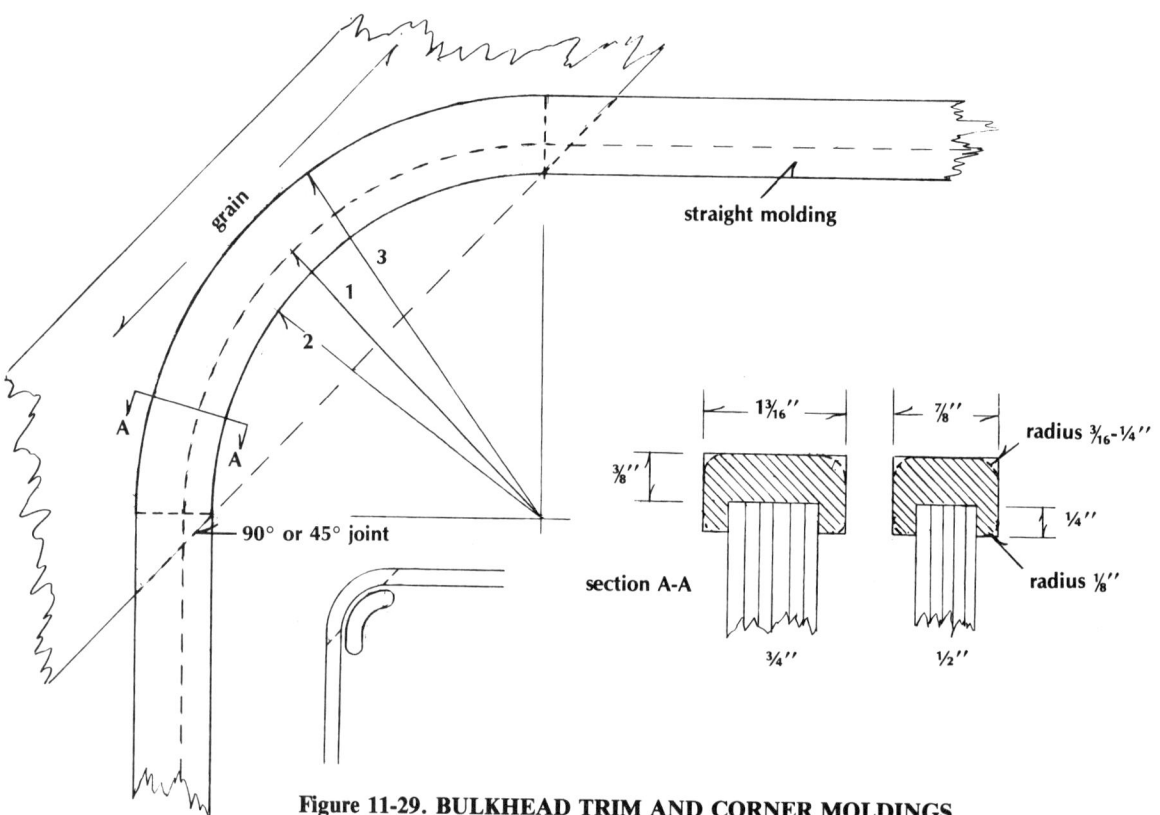

Figure 11-29. BULKHEAD TRIM AND CORNER MOLDINGS

Or the edge can be planed after the piece has been installed, and then sanded. This molding is a little scant for plugging over screws. I suggest 1-inch galvanized or brass finish nails, set in well and filled.

The joint with the straight trim is up to you. I feel that the 45-degree joint permits closer fitting. Use the 45-degree sawing jig shown in Figure 11-30. Whatever you do, however, tack all the moldings in place before gluing any. This way, precise pressure joints can be made. If you use the 90-degree joint and you cut a straight molding 1/32 inch too short, that piece will have to be used elsewhere. After fastening, take fine cuts on the sides with a block plane or a sanding block. The last step is to rout a radius all around on both inside and outside. This should be generous on the outside, possibly as much as 1/2 inch. On the inside, 1/8 inch is plenty. This means you will have to grind off a good part of the pilot on the bit. If you prefer the easy way, run the radii before assembly. Be careful, though. They look bad if they do not match up.

Figure 11-29 shows a hand grip just inside the molding. The hole should be about 1¼ inches in diameter. Sabersaw the hole out before moldings are installed.

Corner moldings of this type can be purchased in teak and mahogany for both ¾- and ½-inch bulkheads. Unfortunately, the only radius offered is 2½ inches. The manufacturer is H & L Marine Woodwork, Inc. The moldings are sold at most marine supply dealers.

MORE CORNER TRIM

The process of making inside corners by the method just described is about the same, but in reverse. There will be more waste because the pieces can't be nested together as well. There is a system for forming both inside and outside corner trim. See Figure 11-31. I know that this will draw snorts of derision from some because it is not difficult and few tools are required. You will need two jigs for inside and outside, for the radii are different by the thickness of the lamination. The bent segments are covered after installation by flat quadrants of whatever dimensions you choose. One definite advantage of this trim is that the flat quadrant can be dimensioned to make a stop for a door.

Make the forming jig of 1½- or 2-inch lumber or plywood. Make the strips 1/8 inch by about 1¾ inches. Lay down a piece of plastic and screw block A on top. Apply glue to the contacting surfaces, press block B against the strips, and clamp loosely. Tap the strips down against the plastic, make any necessary endwise adjustments, and clamp up snugly. When the glue has set, rip the lamination to the width wanted and cut the ends square or to a 45-degree angle, as you wish. Dress to match the bulkhead or door thickness. These can be fastened with glue and finish nails.

The flat quadrants are self-explanatory, except that the door jamb needs a stop. Lay out with a shorter inside radius so the door finds a rabbet to bear against.

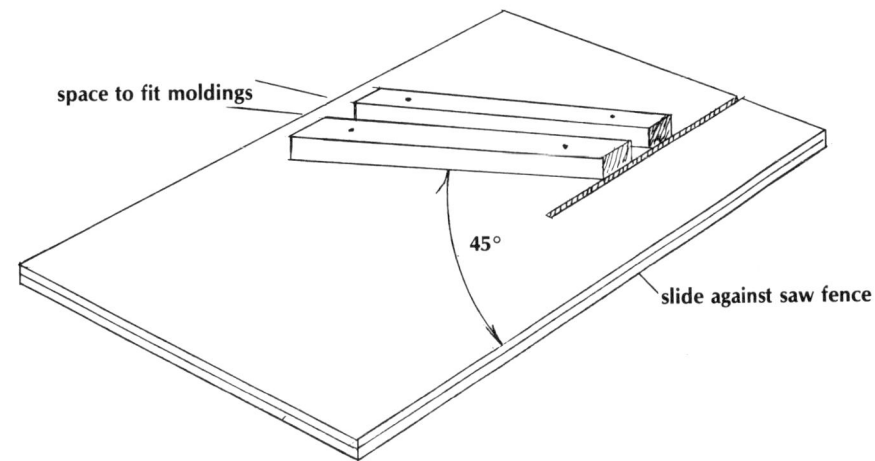

Figure 11-30. MOLDING MITERING JIG

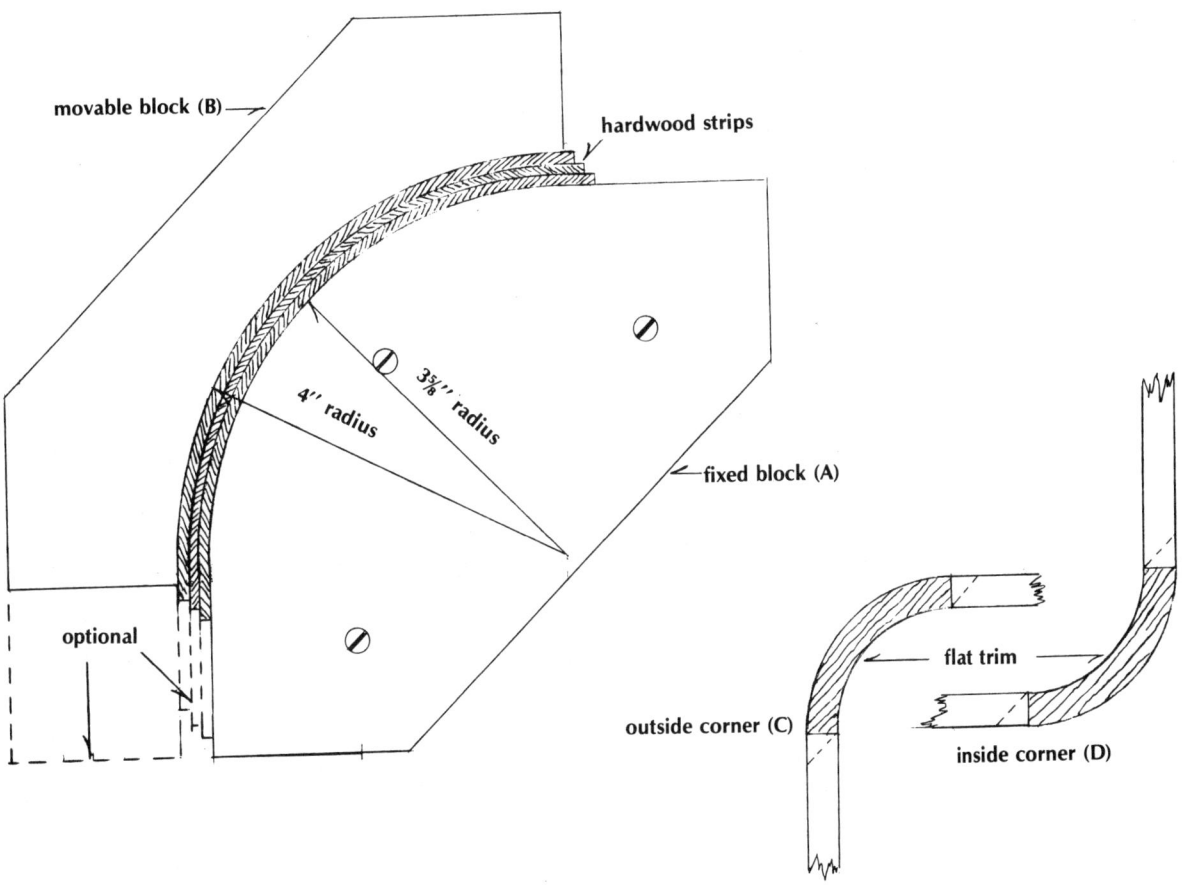

Figure 11-31. BENDING JIG FOR LAMINATED BULKHEAD AND DOOR TRIM

The straight trim can be shaped from one piece or built up as above. After all pieces match up, sand the surfaces of the laminate to a perfect blend. I think the door molding should be bullnosed, but it's optional for the door jamb and casing (as they are called ashore).

Some will think, "There's *got* to be an easier way!" There is, but it doesn't have as much class. It's a compromise using 45-degree angles instead of rounded corners (Figure 11-32). I've seen this a few times and it's not all that bad. If you go this way, all of the molding can be dadoed out in one step. The pieces all meet at 22½ degrees, so all you have to do is add two guide pieces to the 45-degree jig above. Round all the corners slightly to protect your ribs, and rout radii.

201

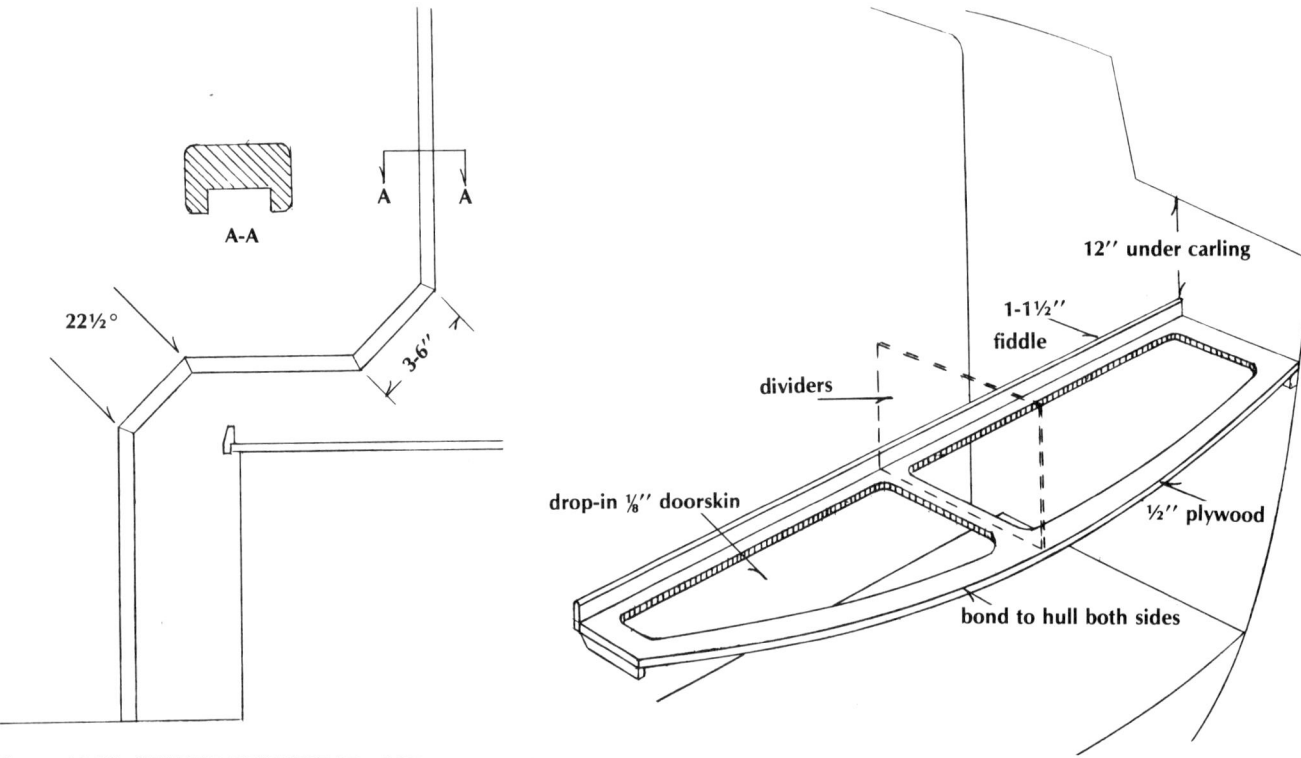

Figure 11-32. SIMPLE BULKHEAD CORNER MOLDINGS

Figure 11-33. LIGHTWEIGHT BOOKSHELF

SHELVES

Bookshelves are simple structures, and designers don't give them much attention. In a wooden hull, no one expects shelves to do anything but carry a little weight. In a fiberglass or ferrocement vessel, however, they sometimes act as light but important structural members. For example, they form a T girder when bonded to the hull. Thus, they must fit well and then be glassed in with mat and cloth tape over a fillet of Cab-O-Sil or chopped mat. This applies to berth tops against the hull as well. Weight, too, is important. Bruce Bingham reworked all the shelves in his commercially built Flicka with a sabersaw. He left flanges all around 1½ inches wide along the hull and 1 inch at the front. See Figure 11-33. Then he dropped in scraps of plastic laminate (I would use doorskin). This let him throw out about 50 pounds of plywood trash. If too many dividers interfere with this job in your older yacht, do it the hard way, on your back.

Plan your shelving so you have at least one good length with more than 12 inches of vertical space. Many marine books are being published in larger sizes. Width, too, must be adequate. Finally, fiddles that are too high make it awkward to get books in and out. I would go for 1-inch-high fiddles with a removable batten set in chocks about 6 to 8 inches above the shelf. A good trick is to stretch shockcord between the ends or dividers.

Shelves are frequently enclosed. See the medicine cabinet in Chapter Twelve for an example.

COMPANIONWAY LADDERS

Ladders are great space wasters. Thus, Figure 11-34(C) shows an attempt to make some small use of one. Likewise, we can't afford to make ladders comfortable to use, so my treads are much shallower than the standard, 6 to 8 inches. You can't use much more than the ball of your foot going up and your heel going down. The treads and rails (sides) should be full 1-inch stock. The rise must be 10 inches or more. Nonskid material must be cemented to the treads, bent under the front bullnose, and nailed underneath. All of this applies if space is at a premium. If your yacht is larger, the companionway ladder can be a stair, even a winding staircase.

Ladder A is straightforward. It has 1-inch treads dadoed ¼ inch into 1-inch rails. Bullnose the treads to ½-inch radius with a router or shaper. The plywood on the sole is one way to keep the ladder from slipping. It's a U-shaped chock that the foot of the ladder fits into. A wing bolt tapped into a plate holds the head.

Ladder B is curved to clear an engine. Notch the foot of this one to fit over a block or batten.

Ladder C has a back of ¼-inch plywood and little

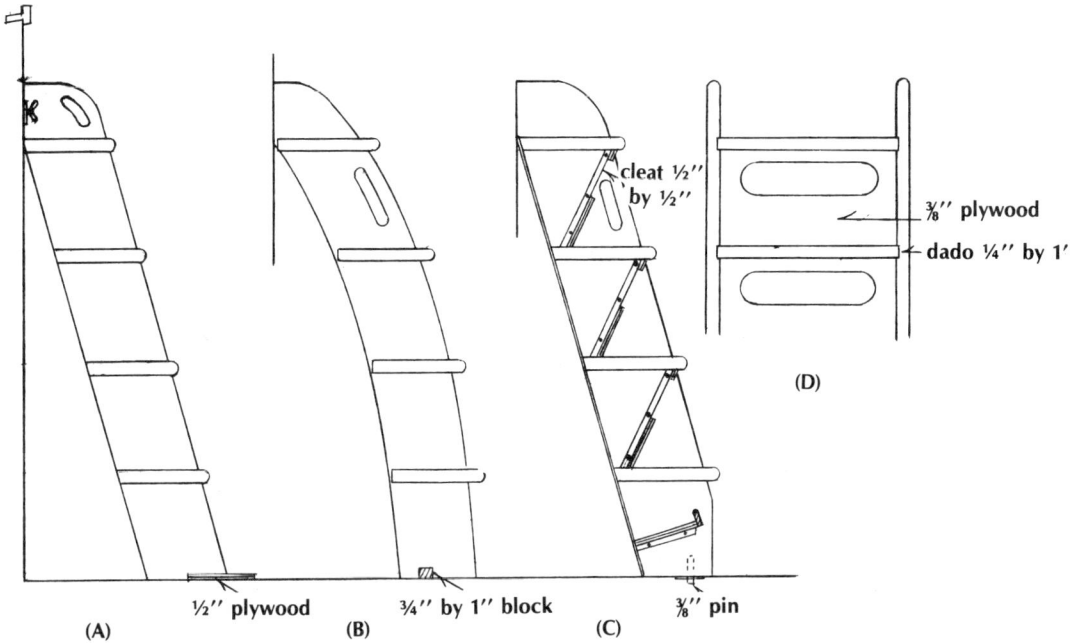

Figure 11-34. COMPANIONWAY LADDERS

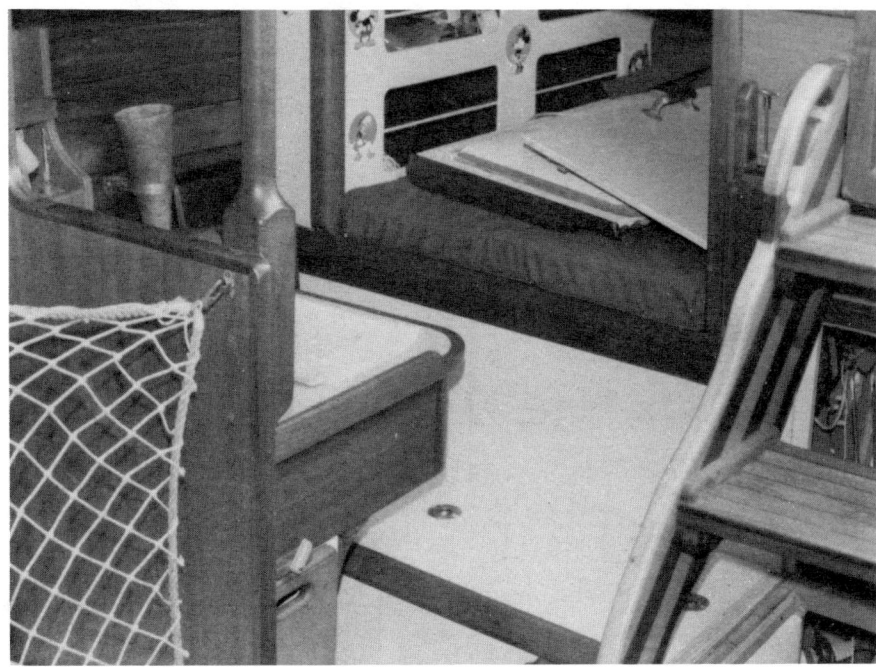

Figure 11-35. *Skilled amateur Steve Soltysik's beautiful and strong companionway ladder is laminated pine and mahogany scrap. Note exquisite desk and bulkhead molded trim.*

compartments under the treads. These are accessible through the apertures shown or through the back. Small as they may be, little compartments like these are valuable on a cruising yacht. They can store light tools, twine, wire, a first-aid kit, an extra winch handle — even a few drops of schnapps. The shelf under the bottom step is easier to build. Of oiled teak or mahogany filled and stained, and with five or six coats of varnish, any of these ladders would be a handsome piece of furniture. Figure 11-35 shows the companionway ladder in Steve Soltysik's *Anastasia*. The heavy rails are glued-up alternating pieces of mahogany and pine with routed hand grips.

ICE CHESTS

The costliest refrigerator is only as good as its insulation. This technology is changing so rapidly that my knowledge may already be obsolete. I will, however, describe an ice chest that will preserve food for two

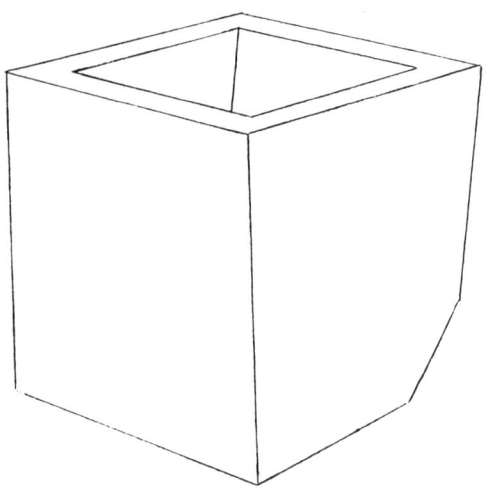

Figure 11-36. ICE CHEST SHAPED TO HULL

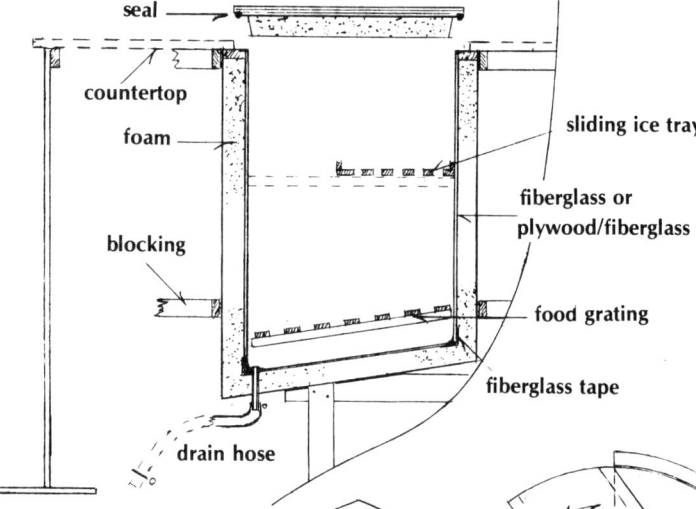

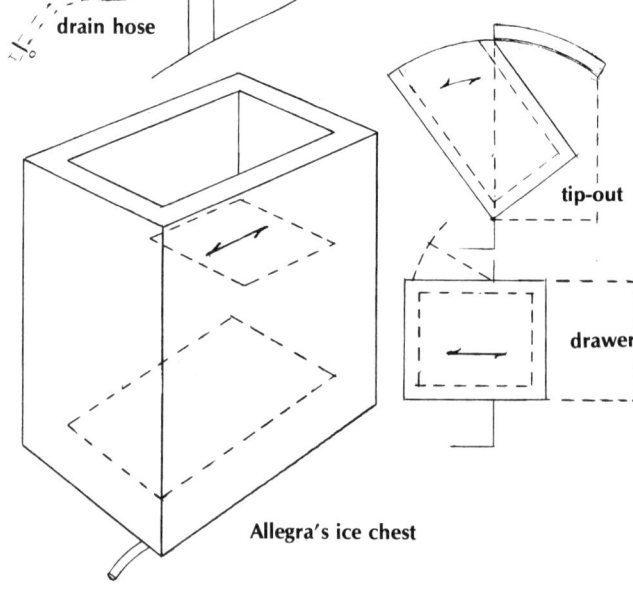

Figure 11-37. ICE CHEST IDEAS

weeks, less if you open it every hour for a drink. Boxes with side-opening doors should be avoided, for they spill out precious cold air at each opening. As for foam insulation, I suggest you check with your designer and local supplier for the latest information. Buy the best and the thickest one that you can crowd in.

Allegra's ice chest is too deep for total convenience — about 24 inches. It's 20 inches fore and aft by 17 inches across, inside dimensions. See Figures 11-36 and 11-37. To determine your size, deduct about 5 inches from each dimension of space available. This is ample allowance for insulation. There are a number of ways to build this box. It can be a plywood shell, lined with fiberglass and covered with foam. It can be a foam shell, lined with fiberglass. Or you can start with a plywood male mold and lay up a fiberglass shell. Foam on the outside completes this last job.

For the first chest, tack and epoxy glue together a box made of ⅜-inch exterior plywood. Build a frame outside around the opening, about the thickness of the foam. Form a ½-inch radius or fillet of Cab-O-Sil or microballoons in the corners. You'll need a lining that will stand up to years of hard knocks and scrubbing. That suggests to me Vectra or Versatex over 1-ounce mat, with epoxy resin. You can sand this smooth, gelcoat it, or paint it with AwlGrip. The foam is then cemented or epoxied to the outside and covered with a course of mat and polyester resin. Bore for a ⅜- or ½-inch galvanized drain pipe and epoxy it in. The sliding ice tray or shelf is made of teak or oak slats riding on battens screwed into the plywood box. The lower grating, also of hardwood, rests on battens at a reasonable height above the water. The drain hose is plastic. It is led to a point where it can be easily dumped into a jug — not into the bilge. The drain is closed with a laboratory-type tubing clamp.

The second ice chest is a foam shell taped together temporarily, or you can fiberglass-tape it. There is no plywood. Form a fillet in the corners and line with Vectra or Versatex cloth over mat, preferably with epoxy if compatible with your foam. Bend the mat and cloth over the top of the foam around the opening or build a wood frame. The top of the foam must be protected. Install the drain pipe with epoxy glue. Cover the exterior with mat and polyester resin (again, if compatible with the foam).

The third chest is not complicated. Build the plug like a box of Masonite with corner cleats to hold it together. Plane or rout a ⅜-inch radius all around, filling cracks and imperfections with microballoons or body putty. Sand and brush on a sealer or thinned varnish. Wax generously, and then spray on a mold-release preparation. Gelcoat, then lay up with cloth, mat and roving, and polyester resin. Glue the foam over this shell and cover with mat and resin. There should be a flange molded around the exterior of the opening. If tapered, the plug can be used again. If not, just rip it apart. The inside surface can be polished, if desired. Incidentally, the gelcoat may be skipped if you prefer to use AwlGrip, but the inside must be well sanded.

The ice chest, incidentally, should be built to conform to the hull so that every fraction of a cubic foot of space is used. This should be only a slight complication in construction.

The ice chest cover is the cutout from the countertop. See Figure 11-37. To locate this accurately, chock your box in position before building the frame around it. Mark the underside of the countertop around the exterior of the foam. Measure in about 1 inch for the actual saw cut. This can be a plunge cut with a power saw, finished with a sabersaw or hacksaw blade. Trim the edges of the opening and the lid with hardwood. Notice the piece of foam weatherstripping or tubing let into a small rabbet. This seals the lid and permits it to lie flush with the countertop.

The foam insulation under the lid is not mandatory, but it helps. To locate this, trim a piece of foam to an easy fit in the opening so it comes level with the flange. Smear this with glue and press the lid down over it. In about an hour, lift the lid carefully — it should bring the foam with it. Pare the foam down so the lid fits nicely, making allowance for the mat and cloth that will cover it. When you are satisfied with the fit, build the final framing around the box and under it. Install a lift ring in the lid.

The ice chest should be removable. To facilitate this, put the framing together with screws. Then, because the countertop, too, is screwed on from beneath, you can lift the chest up and out. Let's hope it will pass through the companionway hatch.

UNUSUAL ICE CHESTS

The tip-out and drawer ice chests in Figure 11-37 reveal a common fault. Heeling will cause these to either crash open or refuse to be pulled uphill, according to the tack. If they could be installed to open fore and aft, however, they might serve in a small vessel. The drawer type would fit under a bridge deck with the ice hatch outside. The great drawer suspension systems now available would work well, even though they might rust out in a few years. The tip-out is simply an idea, but I can hear a skipper yelling, "Hey, luff up 'til I get a beer!" Talk over these problems with your designer or a yachtbuilder.

CEILING

Ceiling adds a lot of class to any yacht, and it's always good insulation. It helps reduce the sweating common in fiberglass hulls, and it makes an attractive covering for insulating foam or other materials.

Wooden hulls pose no problem, for ceiling may be screwed lightly to the frames. There's precious little to screw into in a fiberglass hull, however, unless it is well over ½ inch thick. I'm haunted by a vision of hundreds of lead holes going right on through, of little points sticking out all over like five o'clock shadow. Let's see what can be done to avoid such problems. The drawing in Figure 11-38 is supposed to represent almost vertical battens sprung inside a hull. They lie naturally without forcing. The battens can be spruce, pine, fir, or strips of exterior plywood about ½ inch by 1½ inches. To get them to bend without cracking, kerf them about two-thirds of the thickness, spacing the cuts closer for sharper bends.

It's best to put in these strips with contact cement, plus an occasional self-tapping screw if your hull is heavy. Read the label on the cement can and follow instructions. Locate the battens about 12 inches apart. If you want to have foam insulation between the battens, rip the foam sheets into convenient widths and lengths, say, 12 by 30 inches. If these refuse to press to the hull, slash or dart where needed. Coat the foam and the hull with cement and allow it to set up. In about 10 minutes, when the cement is set enough to permit paper to just cling to it, but still pull away easily, cover the area with newspaper. Locate the foam sheet with one hand over the newspaper, raise the sheet at one end, and pull out part of the paper. Press the foam onto that area, lift the other end, pull out the rest of the paper, and let the foam fall back onto the cement. This stuff grabs instantly. There can be no second tries.

Go all over the foam with a small block and a hammer. Your next batten should locate against the foam you just cemented, and so on. I think ¼-inch foam should rectify any sweating problem. If, on the other hand, you want to live aboard through a Maine winter, you'll need much heavier foam. This means the battens, too, will have to be thicker, perhaps ¾ inch. My old friend Steve Soltysik ceiled his *Talofa* with ¾-inch battens of exterior fir ply, saw-kerfed for the bends. See Figure 11-39. He screwed these to the hull with self-tapping stainless steel screws. Then he placed fiberglass batts, insulation you can buy at any building supply store, between the frames. He tucked them in with the foil side against the hull. No cement was needed. His ceiling is Philippine mahogany $\frac{7}{16}$ inch by 2½ inches, fastened with oval-head brass screws. Each piece is rounded off slightly.

Spacing the ceiling looks good, but this probably reduces the insulation value of tight ceiling alone. The back of the ceiling should be sealed with Firzite, Rez, thinned varnish, or best of all, epoxy. Installation could be a two-man job. Use a couple of spacing blocks of ¼- or ⅜-inch plywood. Keep moving these along as you drive the screws, while your helper springs the ceiling to the sheer sweep.

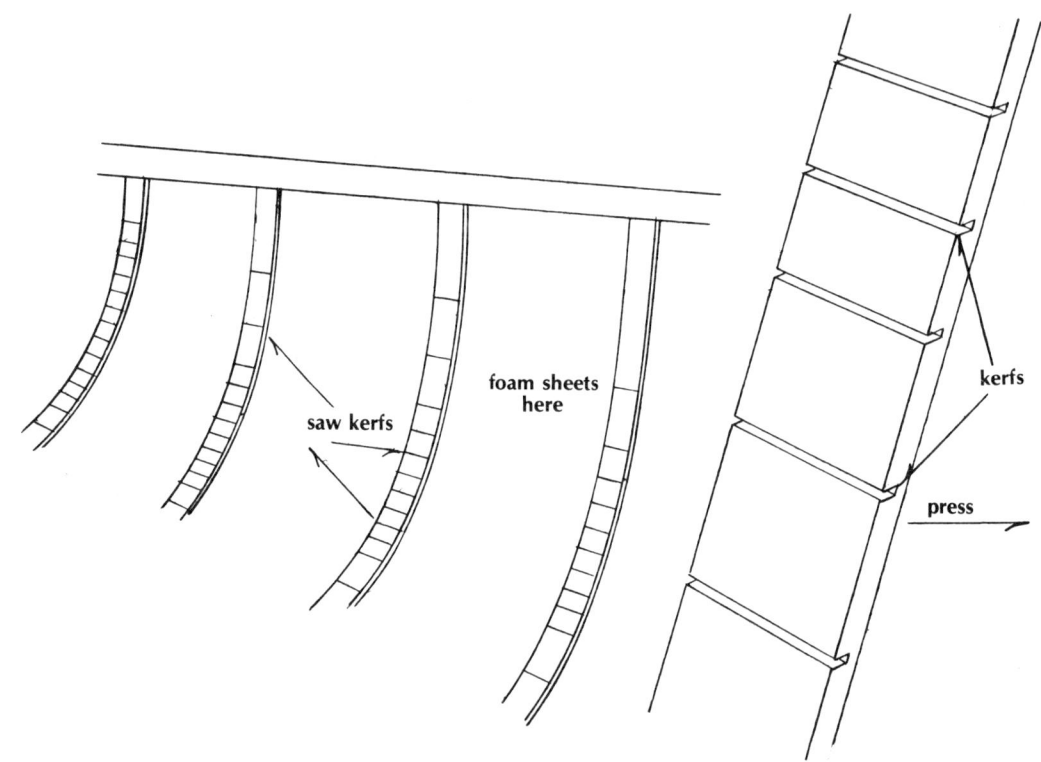

Figure 11-38. INSTALLING INSULATION IN HULL

Figure 11-39. *Steve Soltysik ceiled his hull with 7/16-inch mahogany on 3/4-inch bent plywood battens with fiberglass batts in between.*

Ceiling and foam can be installed in a ferrocement hull by the contact cement method. Even asbestos-filled mastics similar to auto undercoating are adequate insulation for these and metal hulls. Mastic with fiberglass batts stuck to it might be a good system for metal hulls, or for any hull material but wood. I don't know how you would fasten ceiling to a metal hull, unless you bolted wood cleats to the sides of the frames.

I have heard about insulating with two thicknesses of indoor-outdoor carpeting epoxy-glued with ceiling over. I once inspected a 24-foot production sailboat lined entirely with nylon loop carpeting. The pieces seemed to conform easily to the hull with little cementing. Apparently the panels had been cut accurately from a pattern to a rather snug fit, and the friction alone was almost enough to hold them. I did not see this boat after she put her rail under. I must say that the carpeting looked very neat, but it wasn't seamanlike. I'm sure, however, that it insulated and muted the noisiness of her hull.

Ceiling a hull is a lot of work. Materials are costly and you lose some space. Again, however, you just might add thousands to the value of your yacht. The next chapter deals with a few ideas that will add to your comfort and convenience and enhance the desirability of the vessel should it ever be placed on the market.

TWELVE

Niceties and Necessities Below Decks

To many, a toilet in an enclosed compartment is a necessity, not a nicety. This is probably the case when cruising with another couple or with children. Unfortunately, however, working such a facility into a small cruising sailboat almost always forces the designer to use some of the most desirable space in the yacht. This means at or near amidships. Thus, the enclosed head chops the accommodations into two parts, with two berths far forward and two far aft. As a result, the space needed to seat six or eight people is lost. The answer? An unobstructed cabin plan with a hidden marine pump toilet, the popular Porta-Potti, or even Herreshoff's wooden bucket. Hiding this can be accomplished in several ways that I will describe later. Let's talk about the head first.

THE ENCLOSED HEAD

The minimum space required between bulkheads is 24 inches. You'll need about 15 inches of floor space to compensate for the shape of the hull (in a normal vessel of 8-foot beam). To get that foot room, it may be necessary to raise the stool 4 to 8 inches in order to move it outboard. Place it on a low shelf, as shown in Figure 12-1. (The drawing includes dimensions at two stations to show the various relationships.) This means that one's feet either dangle or straddle the stool. It's a bit like sitting on a wide bicycle seat. If you move it too far out and up, you're coming close to the carling and deck where you must have 36 inches clear over the seat. Extending the bulkheads closer to the centerline would solve the problem, but what does that do to floor space and ease of passage? These are design problems, not joinery. But which comes first, the chicken or . . .? Please note in the drawing of Allegra's cubicle that I show the structures over and behind the pot to be padded. In my opinion, for sanitary reasons sitting is the best policy for both sexes.

A head under a seat between V-berths is a well-known solution. Such a head is often placed in the forepeak opposite a built-in or pipe berth. In Allegra's open plan Number Two, shown in Figure 12-2, the head is in an area least conducive to lounging, abaft the chain locker bulkhead. Yet it is easily reached and there is plenty of room. The hatch above provides needed ventilation. Also, building the hatch with a high coaming and pitching it somewhat slightly increases sitting headroom. The hanging space to starboard is adequate, but do install shockcord or ties to keep swaying clothing from rubbing. A few thousand rubs can reduce a good blazer to buttons.

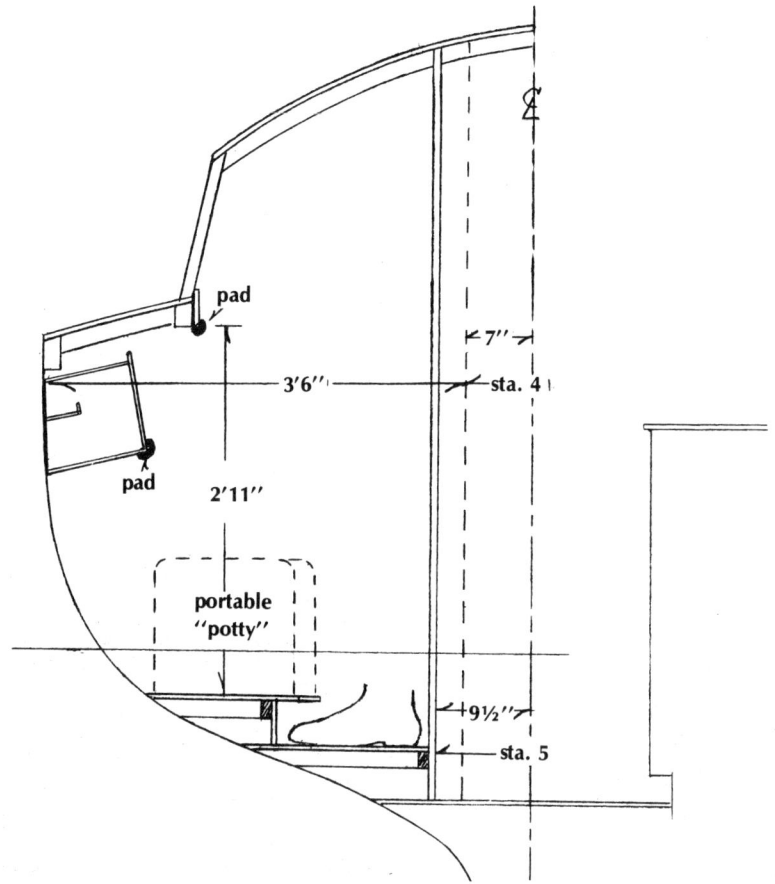

Figure 12-1. ALLEGRA'S "CUBICLE"

Sam Rabl's fine book for the amateur, *Boatbuilding in Your Own Backyard,* describes a toilet hidden under a dresser. The front door swings open, the dresser top swings up, and there it is! A curtain provides a semblance of privacy. Figure 12-3 is an attempt to show this arrangement without losing Sam's design ideas. He shows a head under a berth also, but to me this would be the height of inconvenience. Imagine waking everyone at four in the morning. In a situation such as that, I would recommend a portable toilet set out in the cockpit at bedtime (in an anchorage, of course). The thing can be hidden between the V-berths during the day.

WASH BASINS

In toilet rooms as small as those discussed here, a wash basin is usually dispensed with. In a beamier yacht, a small enclosed vanity can be mounted outboard of the head, perhaps with a small linen cabinet beneath. You could install a stainless steel basin with pump or pressure water, draining into a holding tank. But all of this is unnecessary if you just use the galley sink. If you must have privacy, it would be simple to rig up a shelf covered with plastic laminate and hinged on a bulkhead or against the hull. Saw a hole in the shelf for a round plastic basin. This eliminates plumbing, holding tanks, and holes in the hull. Look at Sam Rabl's Hidden Head in Figure 12-3. You'll see a basin installed in the dresser top. Fit a cover in the basin and hold it all together with small brass turnbuttons. Or simply stow the basin when it's not in use, and use the cutout to close the hole flush with the top.

A Folding Basin

At one time you could find folding wash basins in lovely hardwood cabinets, ready to be hooked up to the plumbing. Sam Rabl describes one very nearly as fine as those old-timers, but it lacks the china basin. See Figure 12-4. With a little patience, you might build this one in marine mahogany or teak plywood. The cabinet could be ⅜- or ½-inch plywood glued and finish-nailed together. No other dimensions are suggested, for much depends on the space available, the type of basin, and so on. For pressure water, a valve could be inserted in the

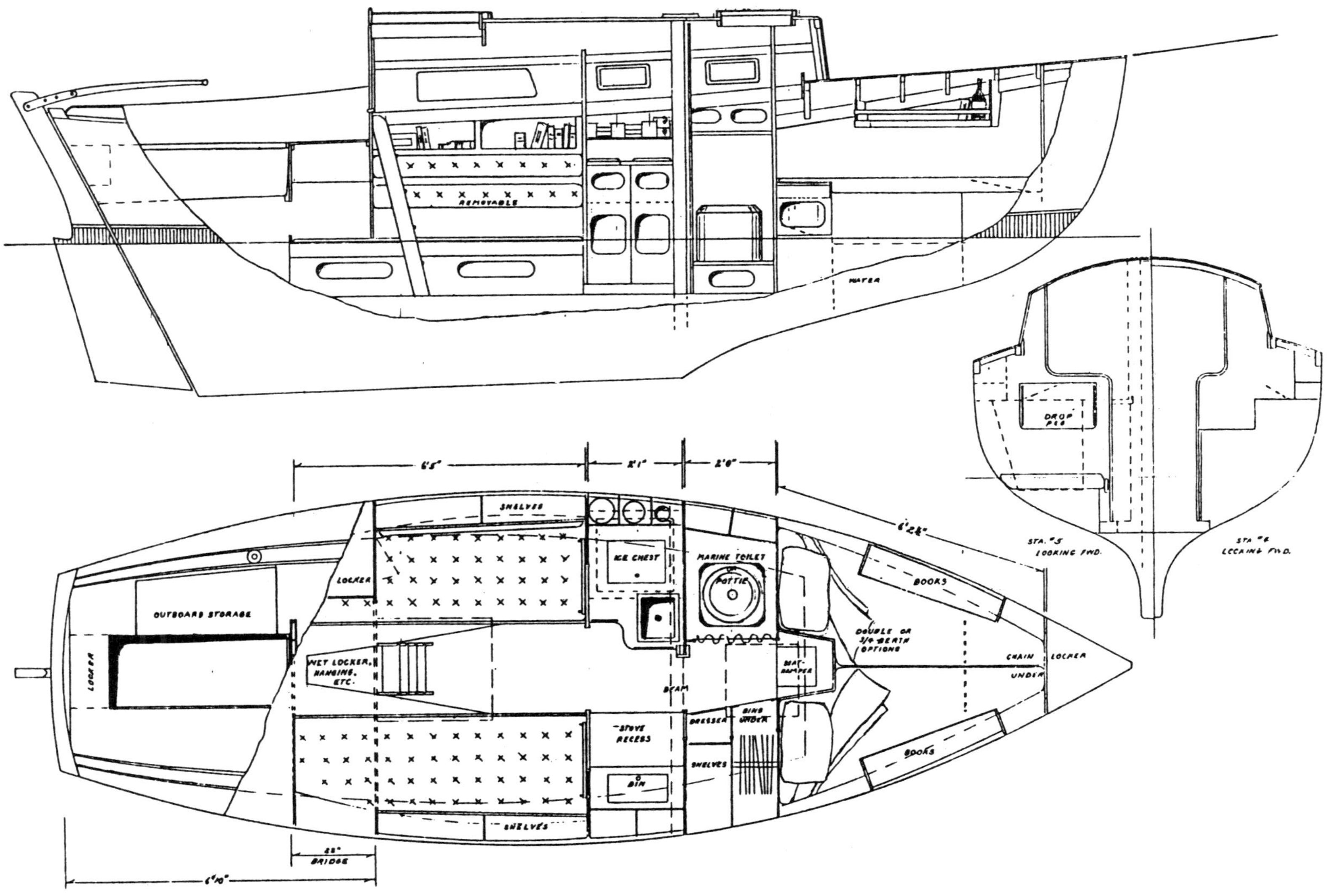

Figure 12-2. ALLEGRA'S ACCOMMODATIONS

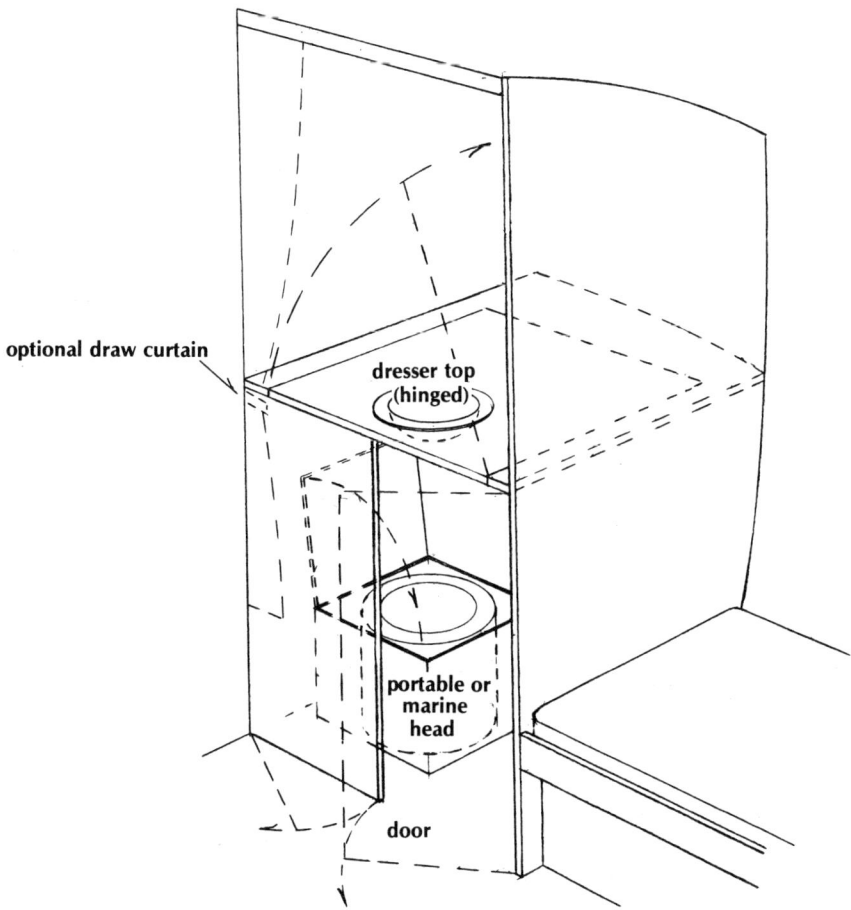

Figure 12-3. SAM RABL'S HIDDEN HEAD

½-inch brass pipe. The 90-degree bent pipe or L directs the flow into the basin.

The interior of the cabinet can be coated liberally with epoxy resin or fiberglassed. The stop block allows the top to recess so it rests vertically. There must be a brass hook, turnbutton, or pin to keep it closed. Be careful in locating the bolts or screws that pivot the cover. A brass chain supports the cover when it's open. If you have a marine head discharging overboard, you can lead the drain tube to it. Flatten the end of the tube so it fits under the seat. Otherwise, lead the drain tube to a holding tank or a large jug in the bilge or behind the head.

DISH RACK IDEAS

The china and utensil rack shown in Figure 12-5 can be built with ease if all parts are cut with precision from ⅜- to ½-inch plywood. Check the vertical space available. Allow for the rack to be at least 6 to 8 inches above the galley surface so there is minimum encroachment on that space. Be sure, however, that you can still get cutlery into its slot. First mark the divisions on the base board (A). Transfer the athwartships divisions to the back piece (B). Saw all dividers and ends (C) to exactly identical lengths with allowance for the front panels. Saw to their various heights. Measure fore-and-aft spacing — allow ¼ inch total clearance around the china — and mark square. Allow cup handles to protrude.

Now drive brads along lines through the base board so their points show. Pull these and drive from the underside. Glue and nail back, ends, and all dividers with Aerolite, T-88, or some other clear epoxy glue. Lay out the front panels of mahogany or teak plywood so slots are about 2 inches wide with corners and edges nicely rounded (not shown). Nail from the underside and front into dividers. Glue and use finish nails set in. The exposed edge of base A can be covered with a light molding. The rack can rest on cleats on each bulkhead or hang from the overhead on legs or the post (D).

TABLES

The problem with tables is that they are very difficult to stow when not in use. Earlier I showed Allegra's backrest/table, an expedient. If your vessel is large enough

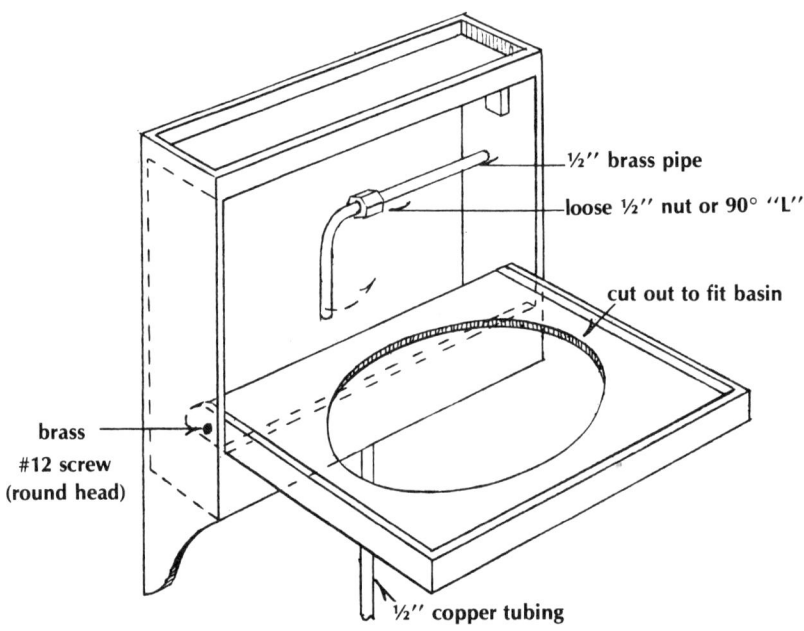

Figure 12-4. SAM RABL'S FOLDING WASH BASIN

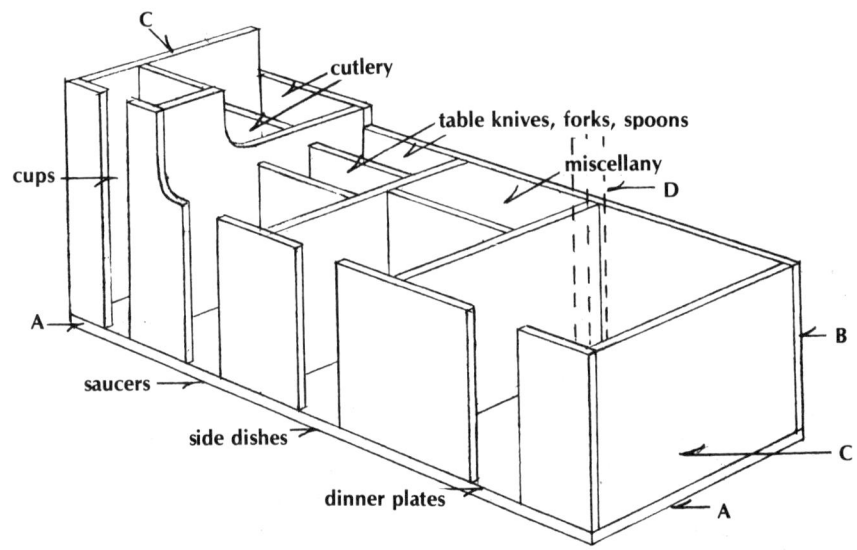

Figure 12-5. GALLEY DISH AND UTENSIL RACK

to allow a fixed table, there's no problem — unless you like to strip her for racing. The drop-leaf table shown in Figure 12-6 and the tubular-legged one shown in Figure 12-7 are impossible to stow, but they can be left ashore. A table mounted on the bulkhead is almost ideal if the bulkhead is wide enough (Figure 12-10).

The drop-leaf table is quite straightforward. It could be improved with a pair of matching drop-leaf router or shaper bits. A good piano hinge will work well. The swinging supports for the leaves could interfere with seating. One in the center, however, might do the job if the table is not too long. The trough marked "storage" would be great for books, bottles, condiments, and so on. Incidentally, the base can be much shorter than the top, perhaps 10 inches at each end. I have not indicated fiddles throughout the table drawings, but there defi-

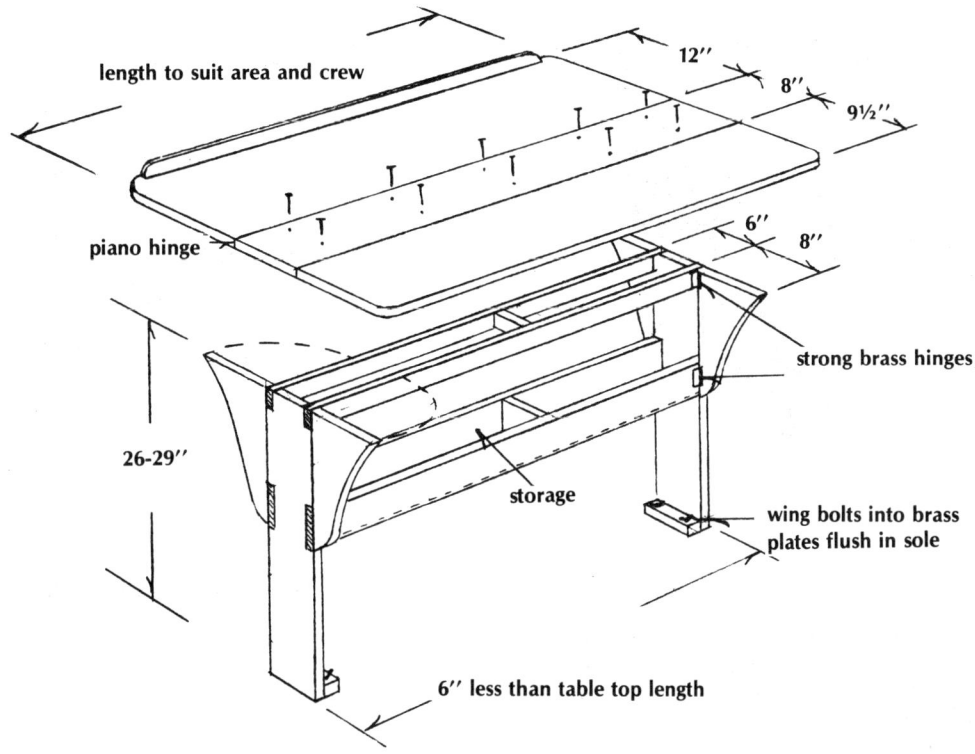

Figure 12-6. DROP-LEAF TABLE

nitely should be high fiddles around the center section. The base legs should be of 1-inch solid mahogany or teak. The top can be hardwood plywood with rounded edge trim or solid wood jointed up. Later I'll describe how such tables should be secured to the sole.

The tubular-legged table in Figure 12-7 is from *Prime Time,* Jim Burks's IOR yacht, where weight is a consideration. It straddles and is clamped to the mast. The whole thing can be removed in five minutes. The same design could use solid wood legs, of course. Steve's beautiful creation in Figure 12-8 is a permanent piece of furniture.

The gimbaled table shown in Figure 12-9 is rather spartan. With nicely rounded corners and gracefully shaped legs, it would be quite handsome. The pendulum trough marked "weighted" can be loaded with lead pigs or cement covered with ¼-inch plywood. If the latter, the trough can be used for storage. The pivot brackets may be of oak (two pieces each), bronze castings, or brass brazings bored to take ⅜- or ½-inch bronze bolts. They must be stout. I did not show a pin to lock the table at normal or other angles of heel. There must be generous fiddles all around. The drop leaves can be supported by sliding cleats. Again, piano hinges would be satisfactory.

The table folding up against a bulkhead shown in Figure 12-10 has possibilities. Try to find a long aircraft hinge with a removable wire-like pin. With this at the bulkhead end, the table can be removed at any time. The hinge in the center joint is under great tension, so it should be installed flat on the underside of the 3- to 4-inch oak cleats. This puts the screws in shear instead of the heads in tension. The two table halves must be closed up snug when the hinge is screwed down or the table will sag. As I show in the drawing, there could be another leg hinged near the center cleats. This one would lie alongside the leg shown. Note that the fiddles take quite a strain, so they must be well glued and screwed.

If your table tops are to be built up of solid hardwood, form joints as in Chapter Seven, and glue them up with bar clamps on both sides of the piece to prevent buckling and warping. Table tops should be about 11 to 12 inches above the seat cushion. This is one of the disadvantages of a gimbaled table.

Because of the many stresses a table sustains, it must be fastened down securely. You can't use less than ¾-inch plywood for the sole because less would be flexible. Locate the legs adjacent to a sole beam, if possible. Figure 12-11 shows an oak cleat or pad under the sole,

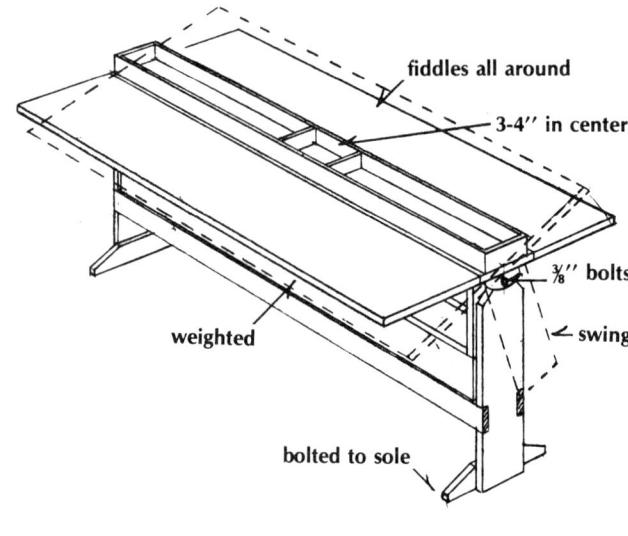

Figure 12-9. PLAIN GIMBALED TABLE

Figure 12-7. *Jim Burks's folding table is a fine production job. It is removable in moments. The tubular legs could be made of solid teak by an ambitious amateur builder. And the fiddles could be removable for harbor dining.*

Figure 12-8. *Steve Soltysik's huge table has a large drop leaf. Lift panels cover tableware storage. Note the precise fits and excellent fiddles.*

counterbored to hold the nuts. The best way is to bore down through the foot cleat, the sole, and the temporarily located oak cleat simultaneously. Just let the bit point come through, then remove the cleat and counterbore for the nut. Run the bolts into the nuts, then daub each counterbore with thick epoxy glue. Back off the bolts a bit so the threads have no glue, or take them out for cleaning. When the glue has set, tighten the bolts. I suggest 5/16-inch roundhead bronze stove bolts or machine screws. Although these nuts will never turn, you can do a nice job with a tapped brass plate let in flush or on the underside of the sole. This must be through-bolted, of course. You can also use brass angles instead of wood leg foot cleats.

A MEDICINE CABINET

To fit a cabinet between bulkheads — say, a galley rack or medicine cabinet — you must check measurements with care. If the bulkheads are already trimmed with overhanging moldings, you may have to spring them apart to slip the structure in. If the cabinet must fit the

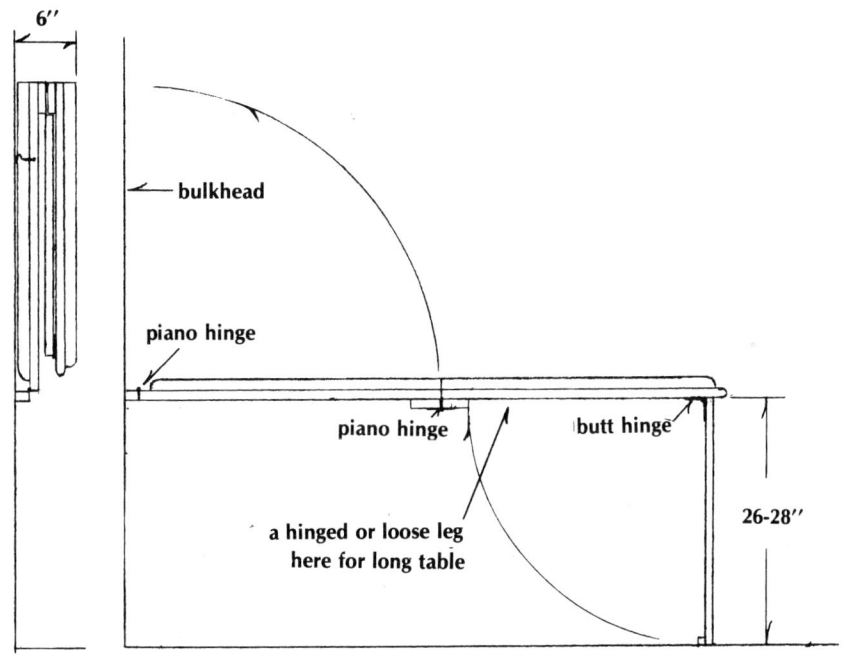

Figure 12-10. BRUCE BINGHAM'S FOLDING TABLE

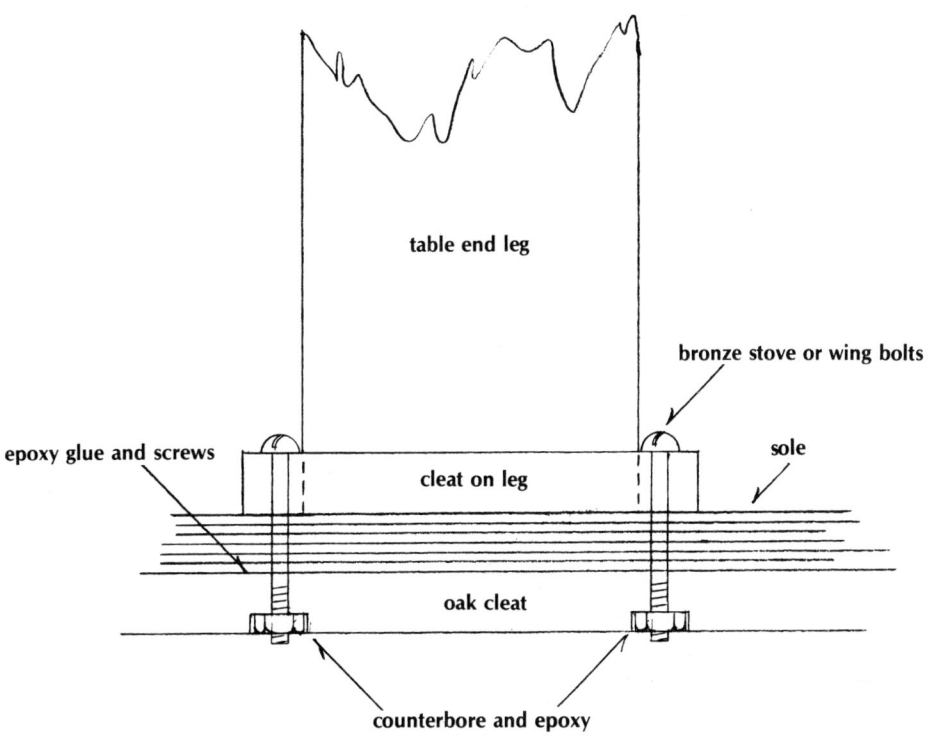

Figure 12-11. REMOVABLE TABLE LEG

215

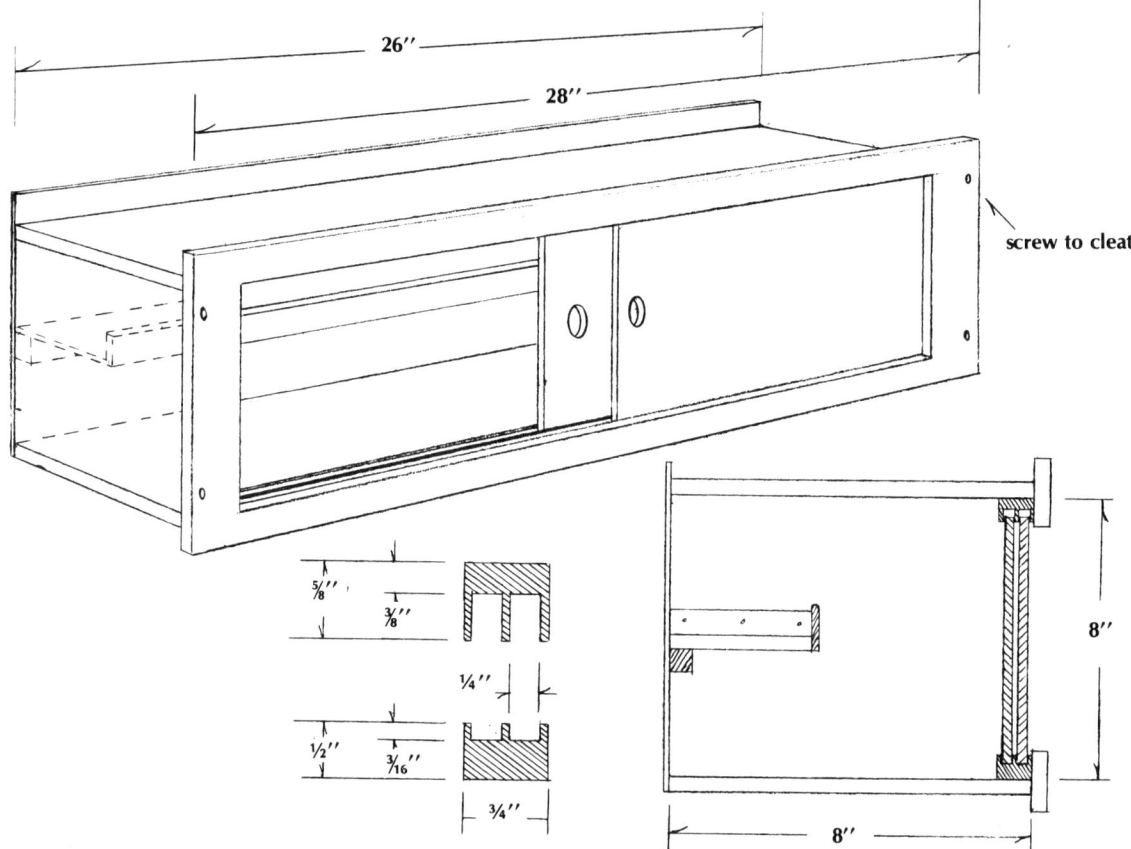

Figure 12-12. ALLEGRA'S MEDICINE CHEST

shape of the hull, however, you have a different problem. The cabinet front must be longer, for it is at an angle from bulkhead to bulkhead. Allegra's stations are 25 inches center to center. The head enclosure is designed to be 27 inches in between. Thus, this medicine cabinet's front (Figure 12-12) is 28 inches long. That's 2 inches longer than the box itself. Only a little trimming at the slight angle is needed to make a nice joint against the bulkheads. I suggest fastening to ¾- by 1-inch cleats set back at about 70 degrees so things can't dive out when the vessel is heeling. The cabinet should be far enough beneath the deck so its top can be used for small articles.

The front panel should be ⅜- or ½-inch mahogany or teak plywood. Mark on the inside and saw so all splintering occurs on the inside. Then trim with a fine ⅛-inch edging of hardwood (not shown). The ends are ½ inch by 8 inches by 8 inches, or whatever dimensions you choose. Brad and glue the small shelf cleats. Trim the shelf with a hardwood fiddle and attach it to a cleat on the doorskin back panel. Lay aside. The door tracks are quite delicate. They are best dadoed, but repeated saw cuts will work. Use hold-downs on your table saw for accuracy. Glue and brad these to the bottom and top on the bench, then assemble the ends, top, and bottom. Install the back, clamping and gluing the shelf to the side cleats previously fastened (you won't be able to drive brads). Finally, fasten the front to the box with glue and finish nails set in.

The sliding doors can be ¼-inch hardwood plywood, glass, or even mirrors. Carefully make the doors ⅛ inch higher than the distance from the bottom of the lower groove to the upper track. Paraffin rubbed on the edges of the doors makes them slide nicely. To install each door, pass it into the cabinet, insert the top edge well up into the groove, then drop the lower edge into its groove. A towel rack could be screwed to the bottom of the cabinet.

FIDDLES

A fiddle is a necessity that can be a decorative nicety. See Figure 12-13. Style A is strong enough to keep pots from sliding off the galley top, and it is good anywhere else. It looks best with the ends slanted back about 60 to 70 degrees, or ogeed, leaving the corners open for cleaning. Style B is popular with a graceful ogee in the ends and well rounded all over. To make it removable, insert ⁵⁄₁₆-inch brass pins or dowels. It's easy to locate these centers by clamping the fiddle in place, then boring up from beneath. It's advisable to have removable fiddles

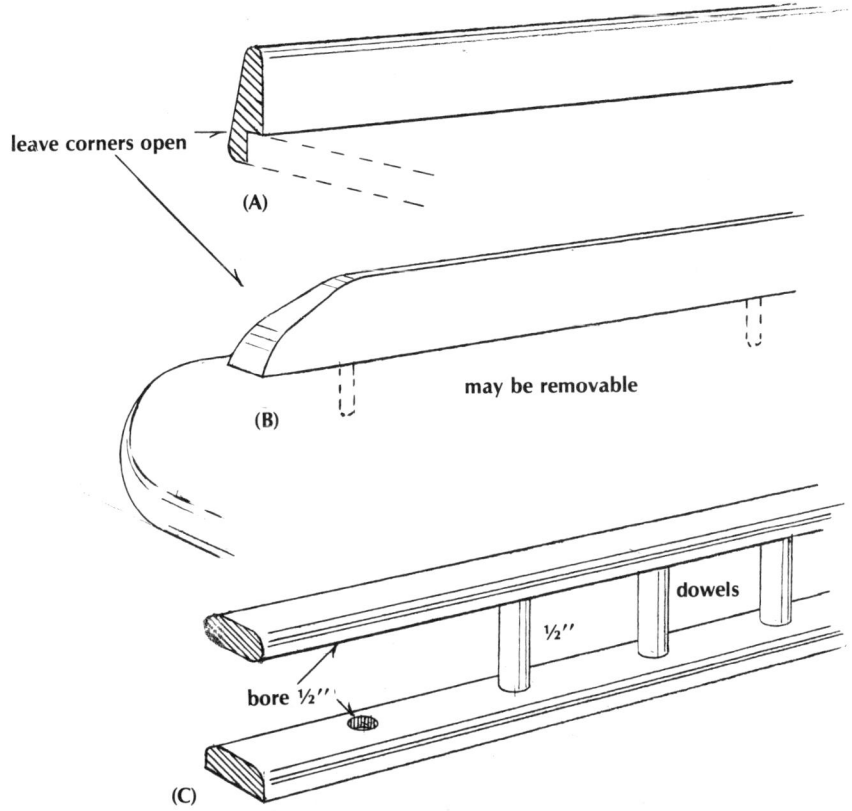

Figure 12-13. SOME FIDDLE STYLES

on the galley counter at several points to keep everything in its place. The front one, too, might be made removable if you use the countertop as a chart table. Style C is usually seen on shelves. The dowel holes can be bored accurately if you clamp upper and lower pieces together and bore simultaneously, being careful that the bit point does not emerge. Rout ¼-inch radii as shown. To install, glue and finish nail the lower rail, then glue and clamp the dowels and top rail. Use Aerolite, T-88, or another crystal-clear epoxy glue.

If you want precise spacing on many holes, build the boring jig shown in Figure 12-14. The dowel must be loose enough for easy insertion into each hole as it is bored. Set the drill press depth stop accurately. Use a Forstner bit rather than a twist drill bit. Your drill-press table should have a wooden cover for all woodwork. Incidentally, small wooden turnings can be found at most lumberyards if you like a more elaborate style of rail.

STOVE COVER

Galley space is at such a premium it's necessary to make double use of it. Figure 12-15 shows construction of a handsome cover for a four-burner range. The strips are from ¾ inch to 1⅛ inches in width by ¾ inch thick. Zebrawood, walnut, Honduras mahogany, teak, and maple are alternated. The glue can be any crystal-clear epoxy. Three pipe clamps were used to prevent distortion. The cover was dressed down with a belt sander. If it is to be used as a cutting board, it should be left bare and oiled periodically with mineral oil. Otherwise, four or five coats of polyurethane varnish make a beautiful and durable finish. The cover can be trimmed with light hardwood molding. A complete galley counter made this way would be an interesting and rewarding project.

BULKHEAD RACKS

The racks shown in Figures 12-16 and 12-17 can be made from scraps of teak or mahogany by resawing full 1-inch stock, then planing down to about ⅜ inch. The slats can be resawed from lighter material to about 3/16 inch or ¼ inch by 1 to 1¼ inches. I laid out the two ogees on a ¼-inch plywood pattern for router or shaper. From this I easily made matching racks for magazines, navigation books, instruments, first-aid kit, binoculars, and so on. Note that the shelf piece is dadoed in, and that a slot is left for cleaning. This lets

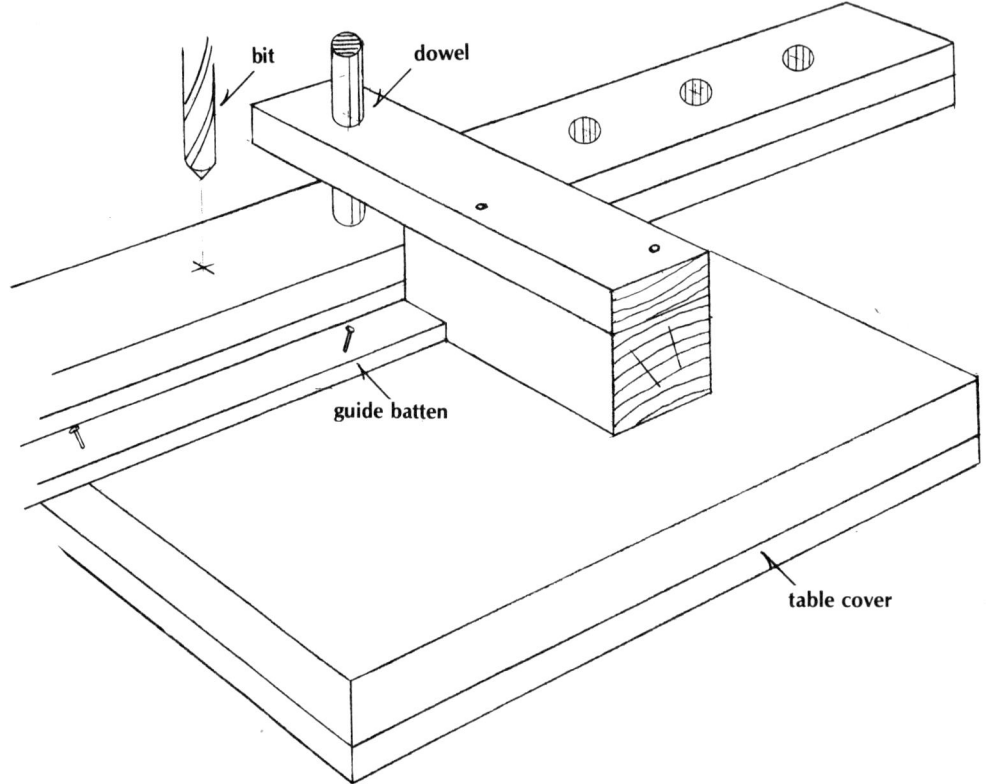

Figure 12-14. BORING AND SPACING JIG

Figure 12-15. *Mike Lafayurie's unfinished stove cover of exotic woods. This is a durable, easily cleaned, and handsome piece of work.*

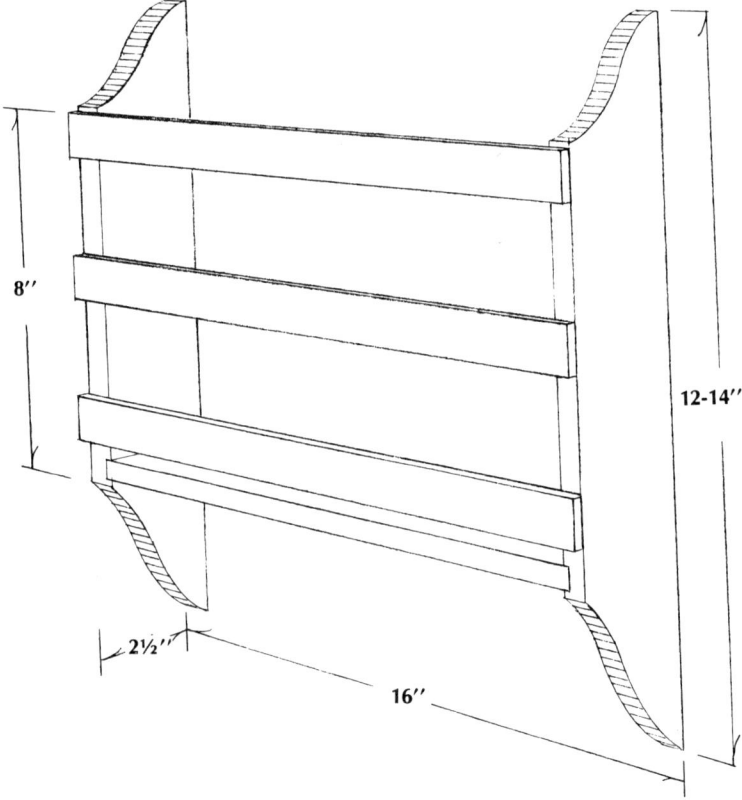

Figure 12-16. TYPICAL MAGAZINE RACK

Figure 12-17. *Finished bulkhead racks.*

you see pencils, but they can't fall out. Vary the dimensions and add vertical dividers to suit your needs. To mount, drill through the thin end of the ogees and drive roundhead screws at both top and bottom. I rubbed in a finish of varnish thinned with turpentine. If you use teak, rub in teak oil.

That's it for interior furnishings. Now let's go up on deck.

THIRTEEN

Things on Deck

It isn't possible to discuss everything on deck in a book of this type. Thus, what follows is a mixture of major projects and simple jobs. Let's start with the most involved task on deck, the main hatch.

COMPANIONWAY HATCHES

There must be as many varieties of hatch construction as there are builders. As I sketched the four shown in Figure 13-1, four others came to mind. I have yet to see the perfect hatch. This I define as one that never leaks, that you can walk on, is beautiful, and requires no maintenance. I should add that the perfect hatch will be easy to build also. With regard to leaks, the only sure way to keep a hatch from leaking under severe conditions is to leave it ashore. Wind-driven rain and spray invariably find the narrowest crevice, usually directly over the chef's neck. The forward end where the hatch beam meets the coaming is particularly vulnerable. I'm happy to see that this problem is solved on some modern boats with a cover husky enough to be walked on and carry the mainsheet track as well. See Figure 13-2. Let's look at the four hatch covers in Figure 13-1 before we get into hatch runners, which are called slide logs and coamings also.

Hatch A has a traditional feel, perhaps because it is straightforward, strong, and not too difficult to build. A rabbeted corner is used more often than the box or finger joint shown, but the latter looks good and would be very strong, especially if you put a dowel down through it. I do not show a separate side half round or other molding as the top extends past the runner and is nicely rounded to match the ends. If the camber is strong, the end moldings would have to be steamed or bandsawed to prevent splitting. Or you can rout a matching radius on the ends instead of fitting a molding. Or cover the end with a rabbeted external beam for a convenient hand grip. Any hatch would be improved with such a beam. Some are handsomely shaped, as in Figure 13-2. The best construction would be tongue and groove, splined (see Figure 13-1(B)), or doubled plywood. A brass strip $\frac{1}{8}$ inch by $1\frac{1}{2}$ inches running in a $\frac{3}{16}$- by $\frac{1}{2}$-inch groove is fairly successful at keeping water out, but watch out for sag in the cabin trunk top. The unseen beam in the forward end of the hatch top should be crowned to clear the cabin trunk. The after beam, too, can be crowned just for looks.

Style B is handsome. It permits easy installation and removal, for the flat brass is accessible. However, there is the tricky matter of fitting the split tube into a shallow rabbet. I suggest routing or sawing the rabbet before

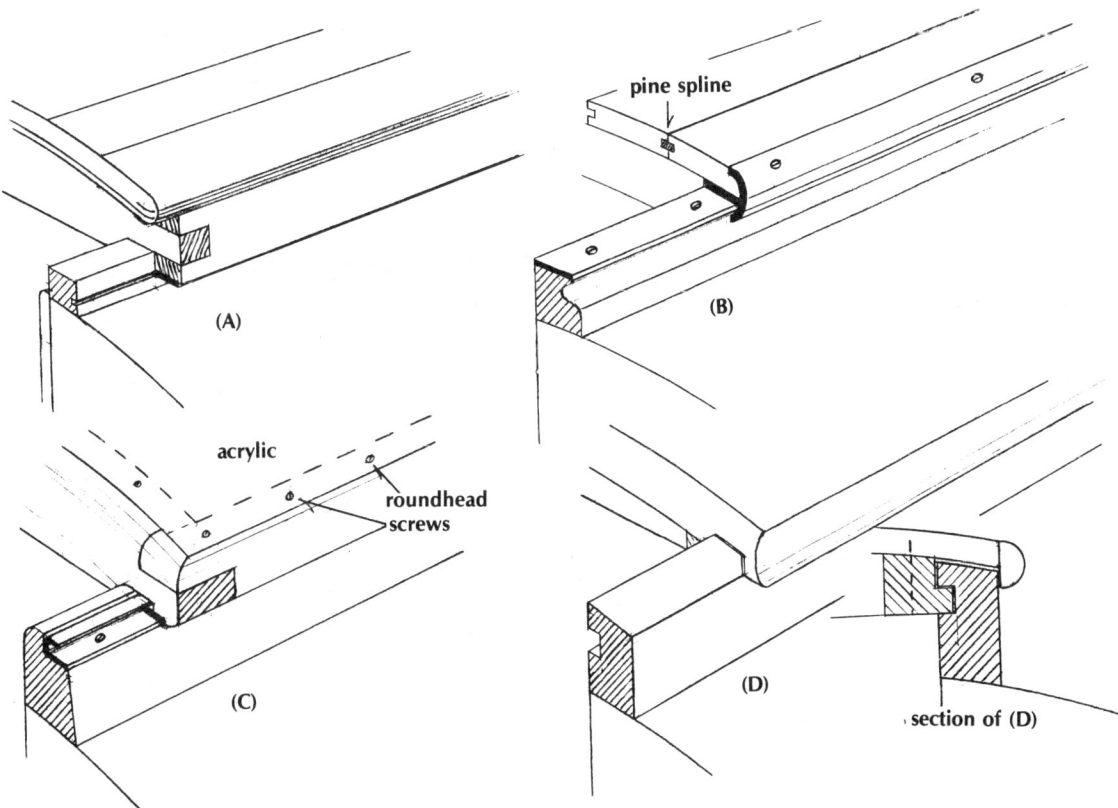

Figure 13-1. SLIDING HATCHES

Figure 13-2. *This hatch cover prevents leaks, avoids damage, and incorporates an efficient traveler. Note the external hatch beam molded into a hand grip.*

jointing the piece to width, then planing off the top corner to fit the tube. Make and fit this outside piece for both sides, dadoing the spline grooves as you go. Fasten the outsides first, then the next, and so on, until the final center piece closes in the top. The last splines can be tapped in from an end. The top material must be ¾ inch thick to take splines of ¼- by ¾-inch pine. Round the ends of the tubing by filing or grinding to match the rounded ends of the top planking. The draw-ing exaggerates the thickness of the split tube and the strip. These need not be over 1/16 inch. See How to Split a Brass Tube, page 222.

Style C is heavily constructed to allow rounding a large radius on all four sides — see Figure 13-3. The acrylic top panel could be fitted into any of the other hatches if they are heavy enough for a rabbet. Holes for the roundhead screws must be drilled oversize to allow for expansion and contraction of the acrylic. Because of

221

Figure 13-3. *The large radius on the hatch requires heavy material and looks great. The acrylic panel should be protected with hardwood strips.*

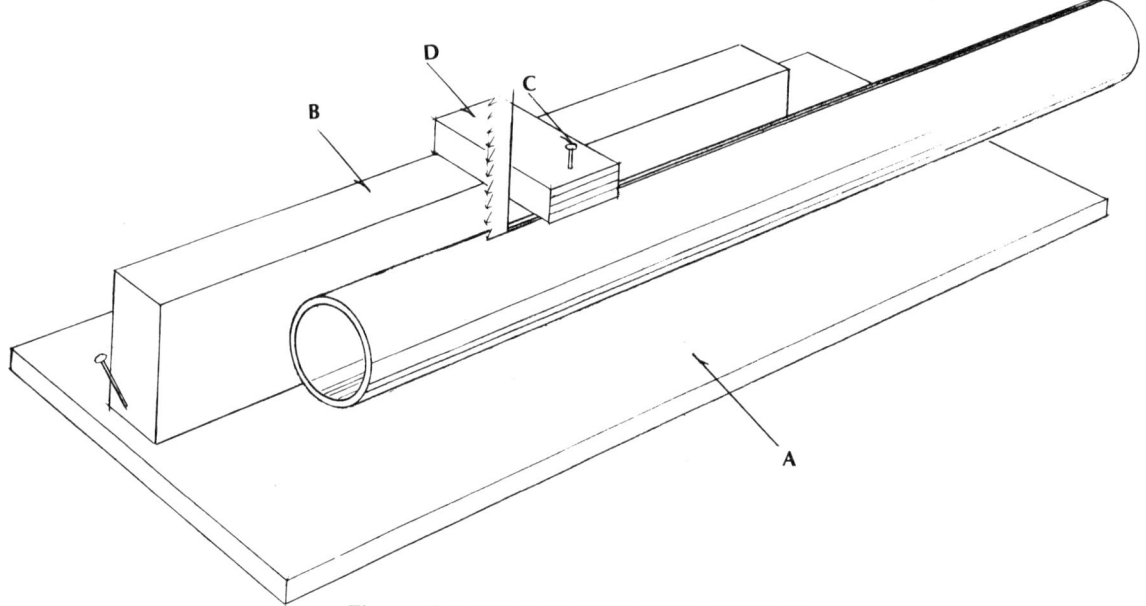

Figure 13-4. JIG FOR SPLITTING TUBING

this movement, the panel must be bedded in a flexible compound or rubber tape. The brass runner strip with the crimped edge could be quite difficult for an amateur metalworker. I think, however, that most sheet-metal shops could form it of 1/16-inch brass in a bending brake with no difficulty. The brass that rides in the crimp does not have to be full length. Pieces 3 inches long rabbeted into the four corners would be satisfactory as long as the wood frame also rides on the runner for a weatherproof contact. This hatch, too, can be installed easily, for the screws are accessible.

Style D needs no metalwork. The hatch framing must be heavy enough to permit formation of the 3/8- by 5/8-inch projection — although I guess this could be a batten thoroughly glued and screwed on. Don't use oak, however, for it does not take glue well. The beams are shown rabbeted into the sides. These could be half lapped, box jointed, or even mortised if set back a bit from the end. Also, you're not limited to half-round trim. A rectangular shape rounded over and covering the open joint would be acceptable.

HOW TO SPLIT A BRASS TUBE

Tubing has a tendency to rotate as it is being cut. The jig in Figure 13-4 is intended to prevent this. Pick a piece of plywood (A) large enough to clamp to your bandsaw. Rip it for half its length. From the split, mark off the outside radius of the tube to locate the fence (B). Clamp this assembly to the table. Carefully saw the tubing about 1 inch deep and check for centering. Drive a small nail (C) through block D, insert its point in the saw cut, and nail the block to the fence. The nail must be free in the kerf but not sloppy. It's best to use a new metal-cutting blade, for wandering may occur if the set of the teeth is off. Blade tension must be maximum. Do not rush. Belt-sand the rough edges after cutting.

HATCH RUNNERS, COAMINGS, OR SLIDE LOGS

The timbers on which the hatch slides must be substantial, although some think it looks sharp if both hatch and runners are very low. It is customary also to slope down slightly toward the forward end. Height depends entirely on style, as shown in Figure 13-1(A). The runner need not be more than 2 inches high, unless you need a bit more headroom. This allows the hatch side member to clear the cabintop by ½ to ¾ inch. The runner in B may be about the same dimensions. The groove can be simplified by shaping a simple rabbet and rounding off the lower corner with a plane. The tubing then rides against the brass strip alone, although I would prefer to see it ride the groove, too, for a better seal.

Style C could be simplified but not improved by eliminating the rabbet entirely. Looks would suffer, and the crimp could be damaged without the protection of the rabbet. Note the side taper here. This is optional on all runners.

Style D shows a rather tall runner, more properly a coaming about 1¾ by 2½ to 3 inches. The hatch slide, however, is very low, so the overall effect is excellent. Note that this hatch would be strengthened by doubling the after beam and fitting the end of the doubler into the groove. The best style is a top extending over and past the drop slides or doors.

Runners are fastened with long screws into the carlings. Avoid drilling into the slide grooves. The runners are usually a few inches longer than twice the hatch length. They terminate in a graceful ogee or bullnose. Forward, fasten into cabin trunk beams, if any, and from beneath at periodic intervals. In my designs, I extend the companionway carlings, if they are more than 24 inches apart, the full length of the trunk and eliminate all beams, except the strong beams at mast partners and mast-bearing bulkheads. It is vital that the runners fit the trunk top perfectly before fastening down, for the slightest distortion will cause your grooves to bind the brass strips. Spiling or scribing may be necessary. My limited experience with three-ply molded trunk tops indicates almost no flexing. I would rather feel confident that my heavy hatch runners were contributing to the needed rigidity.

LEAKPROOFING THE FORWARD COAMINGS

When it's blowing hard and rain and spray are beating against the hatches, you'll pray that the forward coaming is doing its job. The simplest construction is a hatch beam that just clears the deck crown and pulls back against the forward coaming. You can put weatherstripping on the beam and on the coaming, but it will still leak. If you make the coaming so high it just clears the inside of the hatch top, you won't be able to get the hatch on or off without removing some of the brass strip. That's all right with styles B and C in Figure 13-1.

You can compromise on styles A and B by making the after beam and the forward coaming shallow enough so they pass. Now you need external beams on the top to add the needed strength. An answer to this problem is a molded or laminated hatch cover. With this, you can do away with the after beam altogether, adding an external beam for strength insurance and for pulling the hatch closed. Your forward beam and coaming can now be full depth. This should give you a weathertight hatch.

A DOUBLE-COAMING/DOUBLE-BEAM HATCH

The hatch coaming shown in Figure 13-5 is one that I guarantee to be leakproof. It's a bit more work, however. The heart of this hatch is the double coaming matching double beams in the hatch cover (shown before the top is on). As you can see, water can be blasted through the joint, but it will run out through the second scupper. The stop piece (it would look better if it matched the deck camber, top and bottom) can be screwed on. This allows removal in case the trunk length does not permit pulling the hatch forward. Or remove the brass strip. If you make the side facings ⅞ to 1 inch thick, they may be well rounded to blend into the hatch top.

That's enough on sliding hatches, even though many questions might be left unanswered. When you build a hatch like the one shown in Figure 13-6, you'll have found the answers.

DROP BOARDS

Look at several yachts for variations in drop boards or slides. Vents are needed to keep your vessel dry and sweet smelling. Just be sure the vents drain aft so water cannot creep in. Holes bored in interesting patterns and slots are very common. Most boards are rabbeted into each other and into the sill. Or they are beveled to keep water out. Figure 13-7 shows a hatch cover overlapping the boards about 1½ inches. Or the hatch beam can meet them flush, but this is not water repellent. The drawing shows pieces let into the ends to prevent warping and to cover end grain. You can omit the 45-degree fitting. Straight end trim with glue and screws would be quite strong, but not as seamanlike in appearance. A rabbet or spline joint would be an improvement.

LOUVERED DOORS AND DROP BOARDS

Don't hesitate to tackle a louvered drop board or door. If you have a table saw and a dado set, it's easy. Build or saw out the frame as described previously. Then make two strips to fit each side of the opening. These

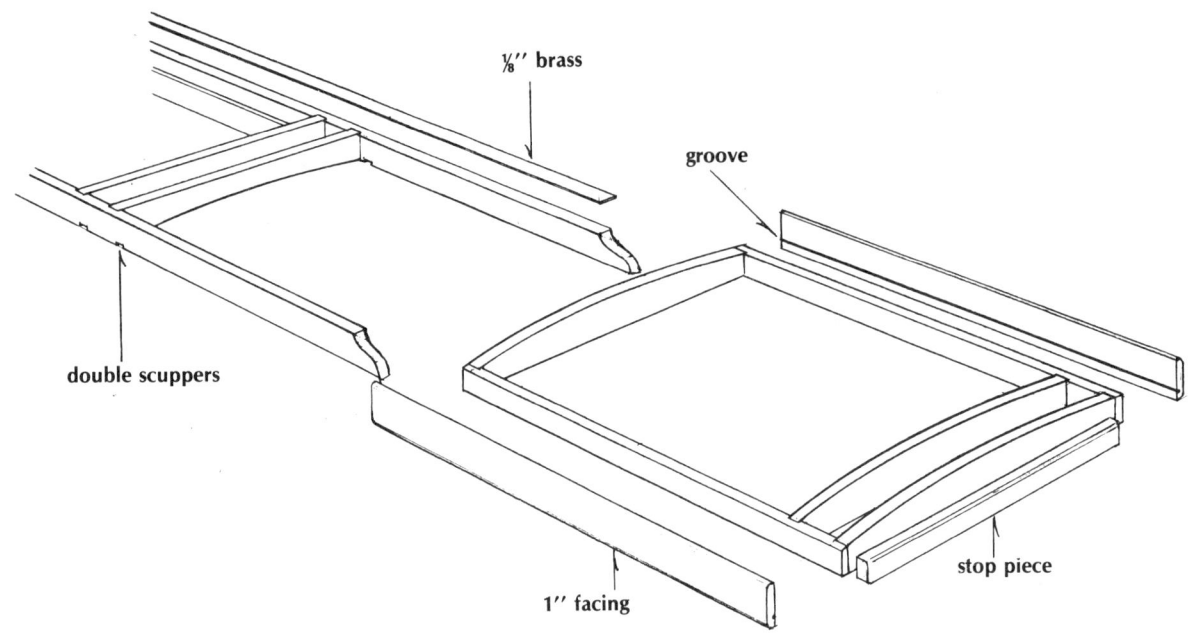

Figure 13-5. DOUBLE-COAMING SLIDING HATCH

Figure 13-6. *Note the contrasting plugs in this hatch. This fine workmanship helped transform the vessel into an outstanding yacht. (Bruce Bingham photo)*

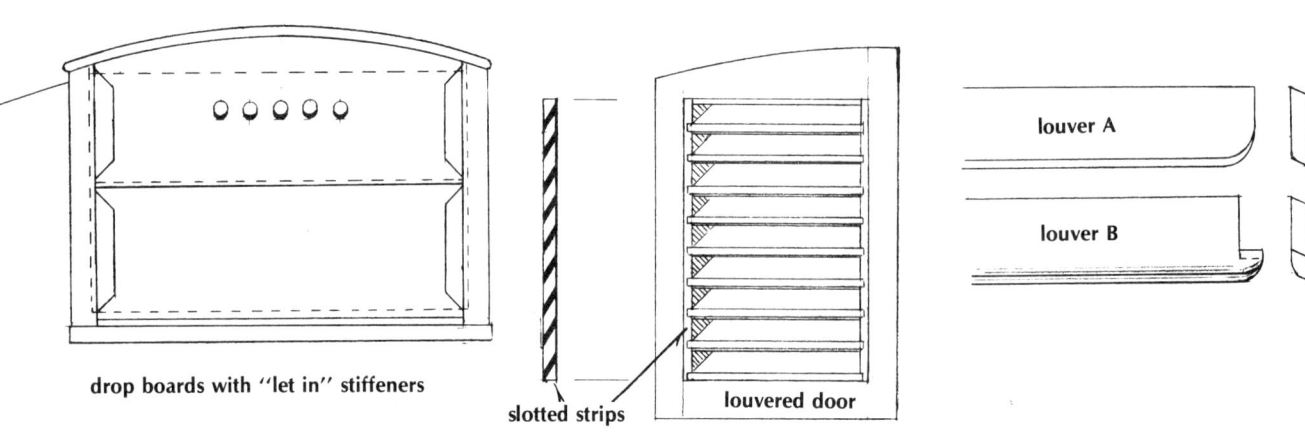

Figure 13-7. DROP BOARDS AND LOUVERED DOOR

Figure 13-8. *Traditional louvered companionway doors have hinges permitting instant unshipping. Note the modern plastic hatch top.*

should be about ¾ inch square. Divide the strips according to how many louvers you want. I show the louver slots at about 35 degrees from the perpendicular. A higher angle would be more watertight, but admit less air. The amount of overlapping of the louvers is more important.

Now go back to Chapter Five, where I described a jig for mitering moldings. The louver jig is similar except that you can't run against the fence of the table saw. Instead, just clamp a batten to the table for the base to slide along. Set your dado cutters to saw out the thickness of the louver material — ¼ to 5/16 inch. Don't go over 5/16 inch deep. Use a piece of scrap to adjust correctly. Place it between the guide pieces and cut a slot. Check for accuracy. Now find a bit of louver material from which to whittle a small batten the width and depth of the slot. Move the strip forward so the next slot will be at exactly the desired spacing. Make the cut, but hold the strip there while you insert the tiny batten into the first slot. Tack or glue it to the base. This makes a stop so that all spacing will be exactly even. If this takes more than 15 minutes, you don't understand the job. Another five minutes is needed to run each strip. Then glue and finish nail the strips in the opening just flush with the front.

Figure 13-7 shows two shapes for the louver ends. Louver A has a rounded corner. Louver B is cut to form a projection that covers the slot. Various shapes are common, and often the strips are covered by a small molding or frame all around. See Figure 13-8. The lower edges of the louvers should be left sharp so water will not cling. After the louvers are glued in with epoxy, plane off the inside edges flush to the door. Fit a piece of screen over the opening and cover the raw edges with a neat mitered frame. Incidentally, the bottom of the door should fit into a rabbet in the door sill, which itself should be covered with a formed brass or copper sheet (or at least a brass half oval where wear occurs).

Doors should swing on the type of hinge that permits lifting the door for removal. If you plan to use your yacht in cool weather, make plywood or doorskin inserts to fit inside the screen frames. Turnbuttons will hold them quite well.

LIFT HATCHES

There are almost as many options in lift hatches as there are in sliding hatches. The four shown in Figure 13-9 will be described in detail. Hatch A is as simple as they come, B is hinged to lie flat on deck, C is streamlined to match companionway hatch C, and D has a system of double coamings. Elements of any one could be combined with another.

Hatch A is a traditional hatch. There's no guarantee it will be completely watertight under all conditions. This is considered workboat style by some, but we had one like it on one of our boats and I don't remember that it ever leaked a drop. The top can be a single thickness of ½-inch plywood if flat, canvased or glassed. If there is a lot of camber, as in a cabin trunk, it would be advisable to build the hatch with a matching frame and a top of doubled ¼-inch plywood. It is customary to cover the canvas or fiberglass edge with a

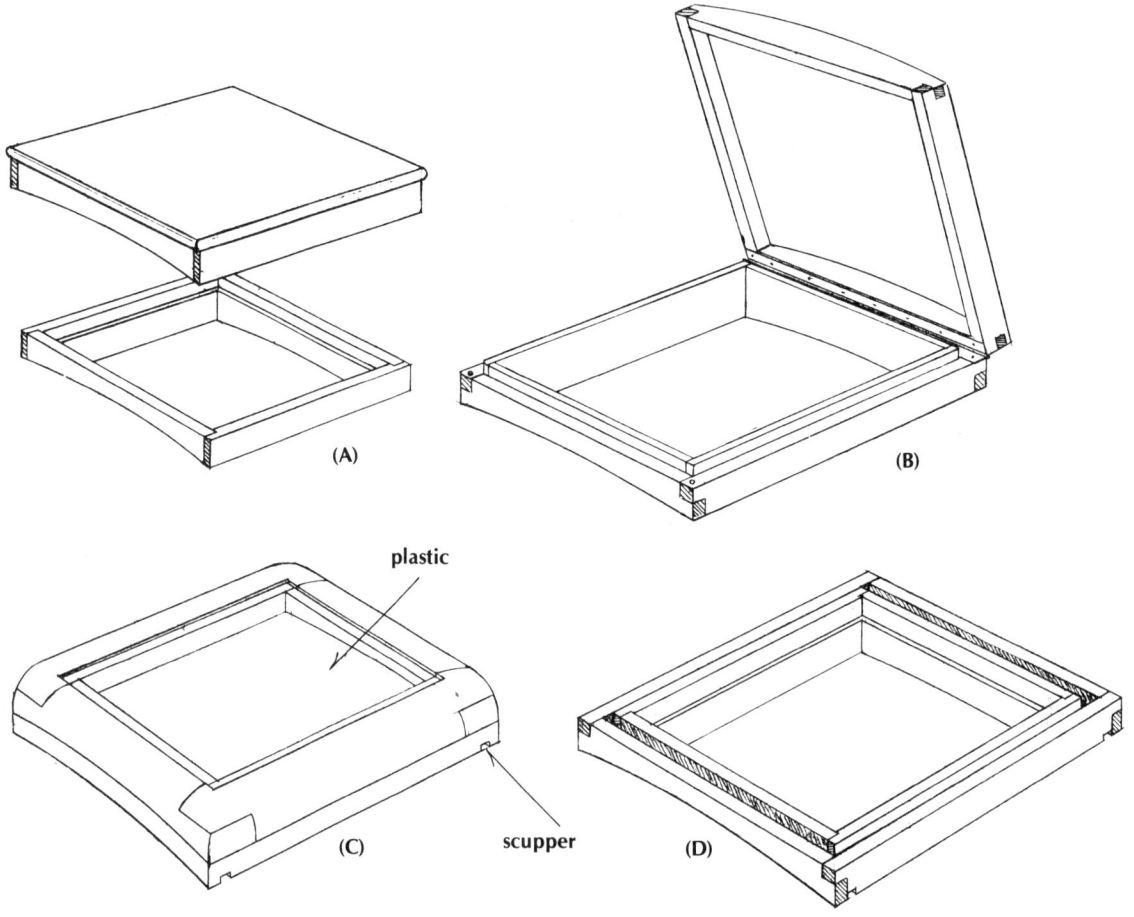

Figure 13-9. FOUR HATCHES — SIMPLE TO COMPLEX

half-round trim. The frame and coaming can be rabbeted. This isn't the best way to go, but it's quite simple and, with modern epoxy glues, should last a long time.

Scribe the ends of the coaming to the camber before assembly (then the upper crowned edges, if any, to match). Let the sides extend slightly above these so they can be planed off after installation. Do not build your hatch coamings inside the carlings and beams. This is an invitation to leaks and rot. The ones shown are all fastened down into the carlings and beams with long screws plugged over. Assuming the cover top and coaming have matching crowns, leave a 3/16-inch space between so you can apply weatherstripping inside the cover for insurance. A facing is mitered inside to cover the beams and carlings.

Hatch B has several interesting features. As shown, the facing just described extends to about ¾ inch above the coaming, forming a water stop. An improvement would be a heavier coaming with a rabbet sawed or dadoed in. This would make the half-lapped corners correspondingly heavier than indicated. Either way, such laps would be very strong if you put a dowel or a long screw down through the joint. Any hatch frame or coaming is a good candidate for the box or finger joint described in detail in Chapter Seven.

To hinge a cover so that it lies flat on the deck, the height of the hinge pin must be more than the thickness of the hatch cover at its center. This controls the dimensions of the coamings. Figure 13-9(B) shows a piano hinge, but marine stores carry hinges made for this purpose. See Figure 13-10. Butt hinges are also acceptable. Personally, I am not enthusiastic about hinged covers that lie flat, for there is always a temptation to step on them. My comments about weatherstripping apply here, too, if the facing or flange extends to a near contact with the hatch top.

Hatch C is shown beautifully in Figure 13-3. This one is fitted outside the coaming rather than on the coaming. Also, the plastic (evidently acrylic) is not rabbeted fully into the cover. The hinges are not the special type mentioned above; they force the hatch cover to stand upright. The construction is mitered or half-lapped and mitered (a very strong joint). This hatch looks massive — probably a 3- by 3-inch frame. Because of the generous radius, it does not take kindly to plywood or solid topping. These plastic panels should have a

Figure 13-10. *These hinges allow the hatch to lie flat on deck. The hinge pins are removable. (Bruce Bingham photo)*

number of teak battens or light beams extending across the opening to prevent scratching the surface. With such protection, they can be stepped on. Note that the screws are not countersunk. There may be fiber washers under the heads.

Hatch D shows the coaming I would suggest for C. Water blown through the joint runs out of the scuppers in the corners. It can't climb the inner coaming because the scuppers relieve the air pressure. I assumed this coaming would be used with a hinged cover. A lift cover, however, also would work well if you installed small blocks or molding inside the cover to line it up with the coaming. Better yet, you could rabbet the cover into the coaming as in hatch B.

The drawings show the hatches with sharp corners. Both covers and coamings, however, can be rounded generously on the vertical exterior corners. Take a look at the fine modern yachts in your harbor. The top corners of covers are all well rounded. All other corners carry a slight radius so varnish will last. Sharp corners wear fast.

DORADE VENTS

Back in the 1930s, the "Boy Genius" Olin Stephens designed *Dorade,* a yacht with real class. She cleaned up on everything in ocean racing and for years was famous for her speed. Then her star finally dimmed and died. But wait! It's not so dead after all. Stephens utilized several clever ideas. One is her ever-flowing ventilators that let nary a drop of water below. To this day, they are called Dorades. See Figures 13-11 and 13-12. The photograph shows the ventilator turned aft. Note that it carries a running light. Others have additions such as a built-in box for winch handles. Strong construction is mandatory, but the canted forward end is optional. Now look at the drawing. You'll see "dam optional"

dotted in. This could be easier for you than the plastic pipe glued into the cabintop. Be sure to screen the opening and provide a sliding door for controlling the ventilation. Flexible plastic ventilators are a fine idea, for they reduce the fouling of lines and sails and barked shins. Note the neat handrail in Figure 13-11. With a shaper, you could run this off quickly. It should be scuppered at several places along its length.

STORAGE BOXES

The beautiful mahogany box in Figure 13-13 was built by Frank Stapleman to enclose the LP gas tanks on his yacht, *Samurai.* The corner treatment is a fine example of what I call a box or finger joint. Frank ran a dowel down through the joints — a tremendously strong construction method. You might like to vary this design in an interesting and practical way by crowning or sloping the cover to shed spray and dew. The sides are spaced about ¾ inch above the deck, and there are vent holes bored in the back so air will circulate. Since LP gas should be kept cool, I suggest lining the box with foil, reflective side out, or fiberglass batts. Such a box also would be great for fenders, spare line, sail stops, or what-have-you.

A fine variation is Katy Burke's generator cover. See Figure 13-14. The box is mahogany marine plywood with rabbeted corners. Apparently it has an underlay cover of lighter plywood, with mitered frame of ⅜-inch mahogany. The V-grooved planking is being laid on a bed of epoxy glue. Because of this light construction, I suspect that the planking is weighted down without fastenings, with contrasting plugs put in later for looks. A small half-round molding covers the exposed edges of the cover. The generator gets its air supply through the open bottom.

Figure 13-11. *A typical Dorade ventilator doing double duty as a running-light screen.*

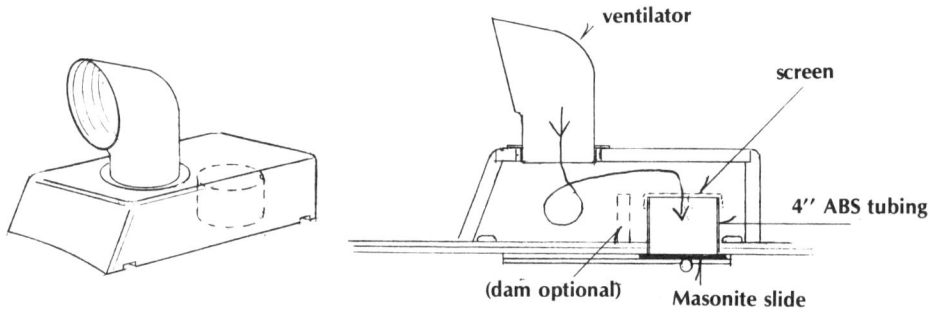

Figure 13-12. DORADE VENTILATOR

Figure 13-13. *Frank Stapleman covers his propane tanks on* Samurai *with this nicely jointed mahogany box. Note the box joints — a dowel runs down through for strength.*

Figure 13-14. *Katy Burke concentrates on fine workmanship in this generator cover. (Bruce Bingham photo)*

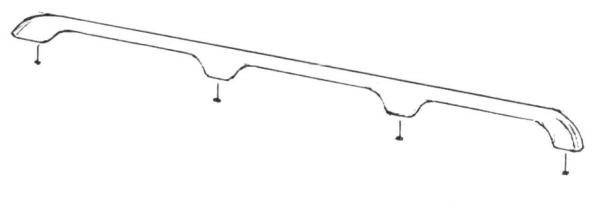

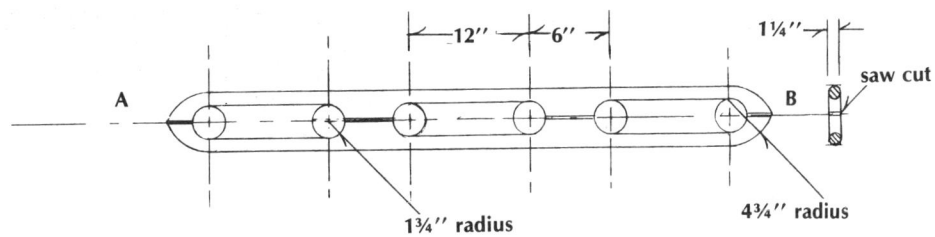

Figure 13-15. LAYOUT OF TYPICAL HAND GRIP (GRABRAIL) (not to scale)

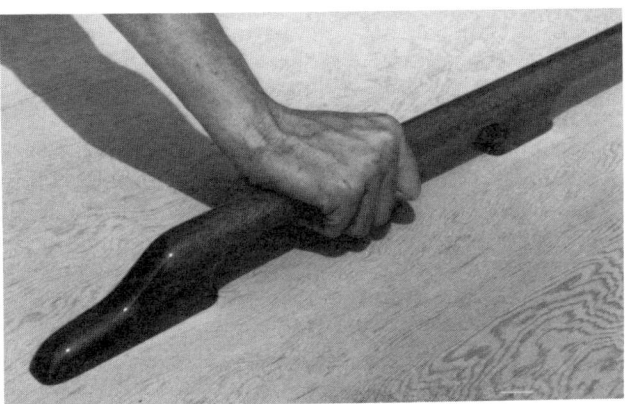

Figure 13-16. *A nicely shaped and finished mahogany handrail. (Bruce Bingham photo)*

MAKING HANDRAILS

Grabrails or handrails should not be thought of solely as deck features. You can be thrown about unmercifully in a cabin, or simply be unsteady on your feet, so it's worth putting in a hand grip here and there. There should be a short one near or over the head and on the galley bulkhead. Long ones running fore and aft under the cabin overhead are great. Spread these about 30 inches from the centerline so they do not interfere with headroom, even when heeling. On some yachts, they are on the facing covering the carlings. I have seen the facing itself formed into a grabrail.

Figure 13-15 shows a method of turning out grabrails of any length with a minimum of waste. Don't waste your time making them of ¾- or 13/16-inch stock, unless they are very short. They'll break just when you need them most. For short ones, 1 inch is all right. I would not consider less than 1¼-inch mahogany, teak, or oak on deck.

You can vary some of the dimensions specified in the drawing. The radius of the bored holes can be reduced from 1¾ inches if you wish a lower silhouette. Keeping in mind that you have to dress the sawed edges, however, don't go under 1¼ inches. Leave space for fat fingers. Spacing, of course, can be varied, perhaps to match beams.

The first step is to joint both edges, then lay out the centerline for locating borings. Place clamps across the piece when you bore it to prevent splitting. Use an expansion bit at low speed in a drill press or a solid ½-inch drill or a brace. Then rip end to end. To save material and heavy boring, bore at A and B, then bandsaw the rest to save the nice chunks of hardwood. Dress all surfaces and rout a ½-inch radius all around. When fitting any type of rail, whether to a highly crowned trunk or not, hollow the base by running the piece diagonally across a saw blade. Then bed it well. Use no. 12 bronze screws or through-bolts. Figure 13-16 shows a grabrail that terminates in a graceful ogee.

ANCHOR CHOCKS

The anchor chocks in Figure 13-17 were made by Katy Burke. Before bandsawing the pieces out of a full 1-inch plank, she drew in the shapes of the recesses, then routed them out freehand. (Of course, she practiced on scrap first.) You'll find that a straight ¼-inch bit can be maneuvered along a curved line reasonably easily. At such a slow feed, the bit will scorch, but that surface has to be pared down anyway. You might laminate two or three thicknesses of mahogany or teak with the grains

Figure 13-17. *Mahogany anchor brackets made by Katy Burke. To prevent splitting, these should be built up of two or three laminates. (Bruce Bingham photo)*

Figure 13-18. *A pair of running-light boards or screens for mounting on lower shrouds. (Bruce Bingham photo)*

running diagonally to keep these delicate forms from splitting during use. If you have several sets to make, use plywood router patterns.

LIGHT SCREENS

Figure 13-18 shows a nice pair of light screens. These are wired for electricity, but there is another set for oil lamps standing by (now illegal, incidentally). Both were made to be installed in the shrouds, but they could be mounted on the cabin trunk.

I'd like to describe a dozen other niceties and necessities for use on deck, but space is running short. I do, however, want to include a few remarks about cockpits.

COCKPIT COAMINGS

Many fine yachts of the past had cockpit coamings that were more or less continuations of the cabin trunk sides. If the inboard surface of the coaming was not doubled to provide a backrest, or the coaming canted back in a separate piece above the deck, the man at the helm sat in a virtual torture chamber. See Figure 13-19(A). I show several ways to avoid a kidney-killing coaming. Coamings are seldom high enough, or the seats low enough, to match the ease of a good old straight-back chair. Unfortunately, too, any canted coaming decreases the usable cockpit space and seat width. Slanted seats would add comfort, but they collect water unless drained by a rather involved system of channels and scuppers.

Sketch B shows what happens when the trunk sides tumble home drastically, as they do in most current fiberglass designs (*dotted line*). The only escape is to go far outboard, and never mind the loss of foot room on the catwalk, as in C. The only good thing in such a design is that you have the beginning of a fine winch base. If you build C, you get passable comfort but a more difficult woodworking job where the coaming meets the opposing angle of the trunk. If you go to D, you get more complicated construction but an easy and neat transition into the trunk side. Both B and D allow small storage spaces, but you should bore holes in the deck of D for ventilation. These coamings could be of plywood with a nice mahogany or teak cap, finished bright. I am not suggesting that you select one of these. I merely hope they stimulate your thinking.

COAMING BLOCKS

A discussion of cockpit coamings leads naturally to the joining of coamings and cabin trunks. I'm sure you have seen some of the awesome structures found on wooden yachts. There is no easy way. The three shown in Figure 13-20 are laminations. The block in A may be built up parallel to the coaming or to the side, or it may be built up starting flat on the deck. If there is no bridge deck, the block has to be installed forward so the joint with the coaming is over the deck. If there is curvature in the coaming, it will have to be steam-bent or built up of double plywood — this requires a carling separate from that of the trunk. Style B is fastened to a continuation of the trunk carling (from beneath). The angular block ought to be much easier to construct. Just round off the outside corner of the coaming piece to blend it in. Style C can't be done unless you bend light plywood (or doorskin) over a form, as has been done in Figure 13-21. Notice that the builders have worked a small half round along the top of the bent coaming — a nice touch. Too bad they forgot a scupper. Otherwise, this is a nice job. As shown in Figure 13-22, the aft corners of

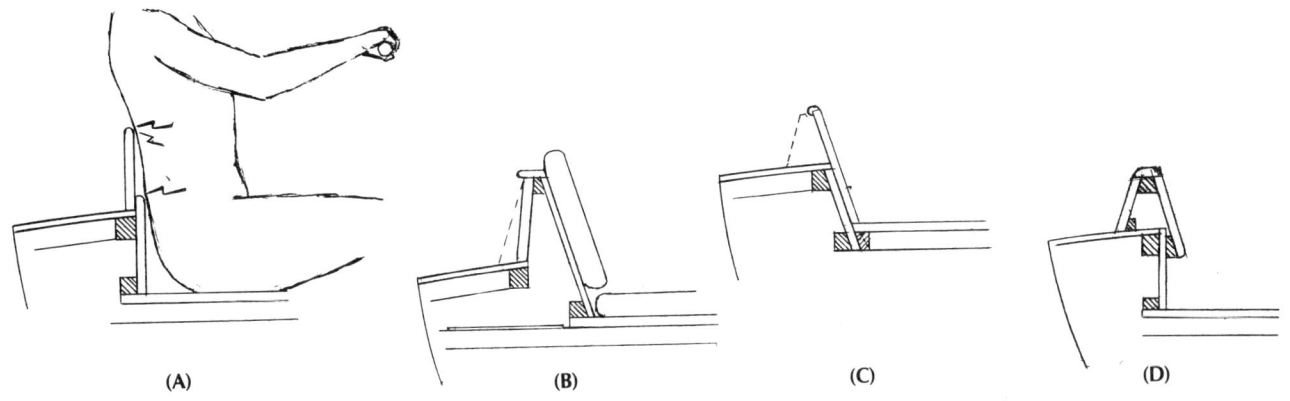

Figure 13-19. COCKPIT COAMING CONSTRUCTION

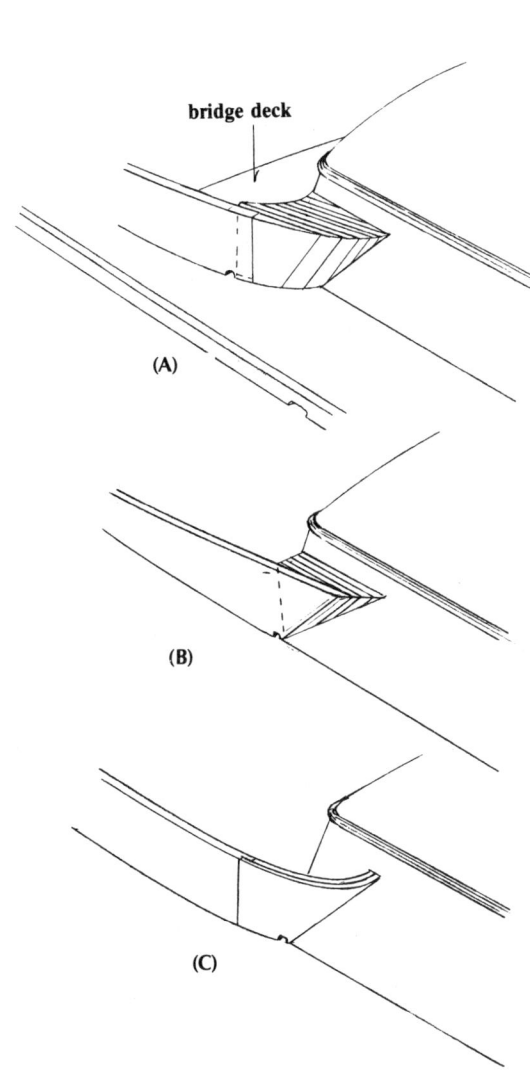

Figure 13-20. FAIRING COAMING TO TRUNK

Figure 13-21. *The beginning of rot can be seen in this nicely molded coaming block. It is formed of several laminations of teak plywood with a neat half-round cap.*

Figure 13-22. *This molded corner is rabbeted to receive the coaming side rabbet.*

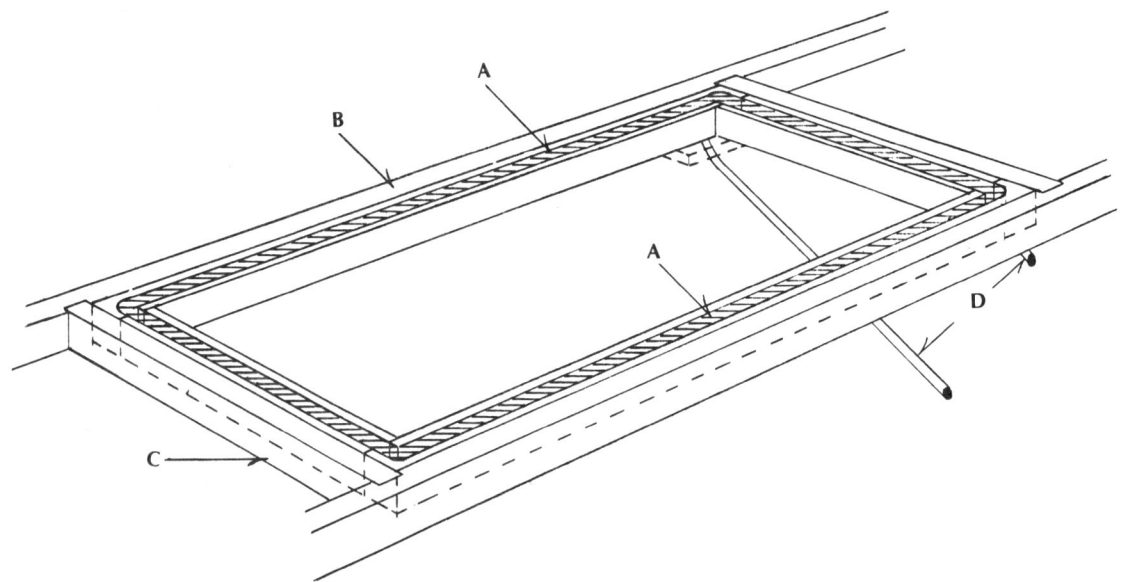

Figure 13-23. COCKPIT HATCH SCUPPERS

the cockpit coamings match this construction. Both corners are rabbeted to the coamings.

COCKPIT SEAT HATCH SCUPPERS

I could do a chapter on cockpit design, but let's concentrate here on watertightness. Typical hatch framing is shown in Figure 13-23. Inside the opening, the channels (A) are screwed and glued to the beam risers (B) and beams (C) with epoxy to make the connection strong and waterproof. These channels or scuppers can be routed out with a straight ¾-inch bit in two or three passes down to about ¾ inch deep. This will leave rounded corners, as I have tried to show. Or the channels can be run off with a dado or saw, if you miter the corners. Note, however, that some hatches are not rectangular, so mitering is a bit more difficult. A rabbet would be strong. These joints must be filled with epoxy glue. Bore for ½-inch copper tubing (D) near both the inboard and the outboard corners. Note that the lower corners when the vessel is at anchor may not be lower when she heels, so you may have to install three tubes. It would be wise to stabilize these tubes by gluing a block under the point where you bore. Bed the tubes in epoxy. Brush three penetrating coats in the channels. You might use short stubs and connect with plastic tubing. The scuppers should extend about ⅜ inch past the plywood front of the footwell.

COCKPIT SEAT HATCH COVERS

Figure 13-24 shows a handsome seat and hatches with natural teak decking and framing. Construction here is similar to that shown in Figure 13-25. It is basically ½- or ⅝-inch plywood to which ⅜- by 1¾-inch teak decking is glued by weighting down. No fastenings are used, but they could be if the decking were ½ inch thick. Since water travels along the underside of flat surfaces, you must encourage it to drip where you want it to — into the channels. The drip strip is 1/16-inch aluminum or brass set into a groove approximately ⅜ inch deep. Allow the metal to protrude ¼ inch (the drawing is somewhat exaggerated). You can make this fine groove with a veining bit or fine saw blade or continue the saw cuts right out and fill the kerfs with glue and sawdust. If you use a fine saw blade, some sharp knife work will be needed near the corners. Work epoxy glue into the groove and press the strips in. Don't worry about the groove being wider than the strip — the epoxy will fill it. Put a couple of drops in the corners also. You could make these strips of hardwood. They must be located so the water drips directly into the channels. The surrounding deck and/or frame should overhang the channels very slightly and the joint underneath must be watertight. I show a piano hinge because this helps to keep water out. Butt hinges would be satisfactory.

Figure 13-24. *The yacht shown in Figures 13-21 and 13-22 has handsome teak hatch covers built over a plywood underlay. Scuppers (if any) under joints are not visible.*

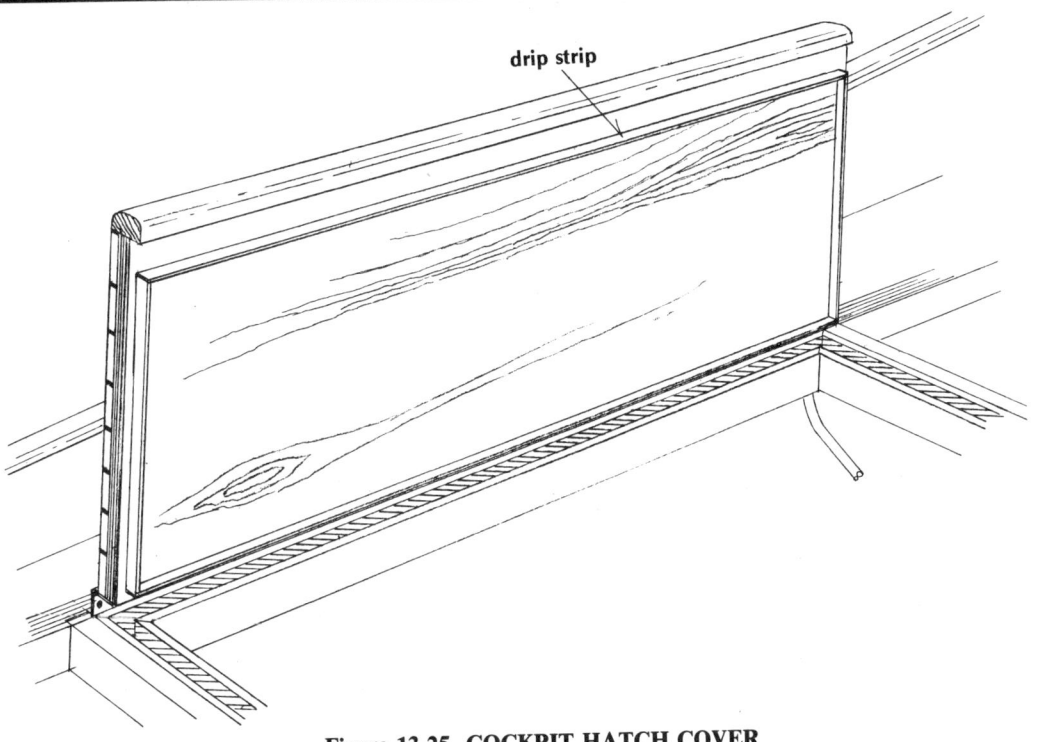

Figure 13-25. COCKPIT HATCH COVER

SKYLIGHTS

Skylights are closely linked to hatches, because that's what they are. Part of the construction of the one shown in Figures 13-26 and 13-27 is similar to that of the cockpit seat hatch just discussed. Like most hatches, skylights are prone to leaking, only more so, primarily because of the two hinged joints running down the ridge. The outer edges are also subject to leaking. You can apply moldings and hope to cover some joints, and you can fill some joints with weatherstripping, which, of course, deteriorates. After these fail, just direct the water into a scupper and forget about it being watertight. Let the moldings and weatherstripping be insurance. Use them to slow down the entrance of water and driven air.

The upper portion of the corners (B) in Figure 13-26 can be extended to act as a spout. Or you could bore for

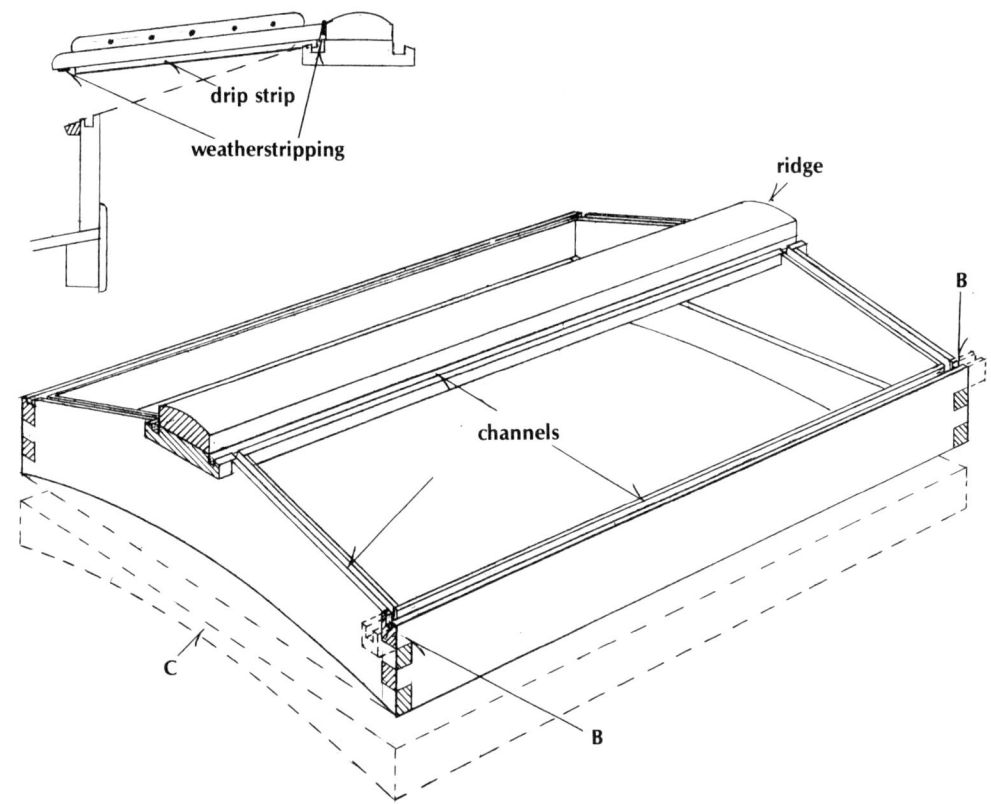

Figure 13-26. SKYLIGHT FRAME CONSTRUCTION

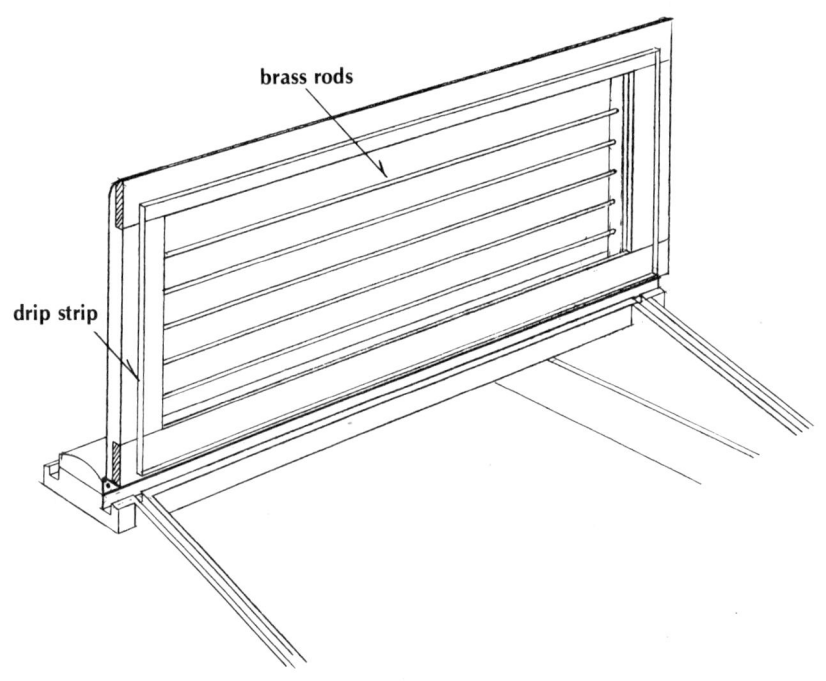

Figure 13-27. SKYLIGHT COVER

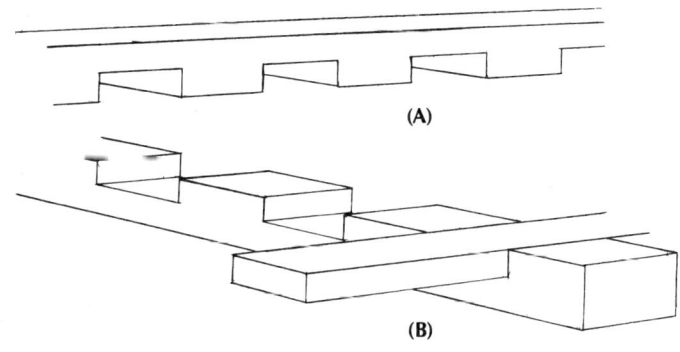

Figure 13-28. GRATINGS

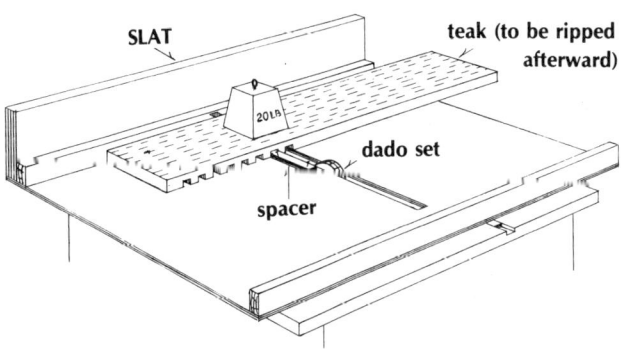

Figure 13-29. DADO SETUP FOR MAKING GRATINGS

a small drain tube to keep water from running down the frame. The ridge extension of about 1 inch shows this clearly. Note the weatherstrip inside the piano hinge. Do not put this hinge on flat. The dotted lines (C) indicate an optional separate coaming if you want a removable skylight. If you build this perfectly square, you have a skylight that you can turn to catch the best breeze. Of course, you must have hatch hold-downs to secure the coaming, and the skylight covers must have dependable locking devices and lifting mechanisms.

Next to a dovetail joint, the corner construction on this project is the best possible. This is the box joint described earlier. To simplify matters, the ridge is constructed from two pieces. The lower part carries the grooves, channels, or scuppers that carry off the water. I suggest you dado or saw these out, then saw the bevel. This applies to the outboard frame member also. Of course, the frame is bedded to the trunk, and fastened with long screws from beneath through the carlings and strong beams. The cover should be half-lapped, and of material not less than 1 inch finished. When gluing this up, be sure it is held down with weights or clamps to a dead-flat surface. Aerolite glue would be ideal. There is about a 1-inch overhang of the cover so that moldings could be included.

You could use acrylic plastic or wire glass or you could build the cover solid with two or three large deadlights. The latter would be good for serious offshore cruising. The rods should have an additional support. Moreover, an opening this long would need another cross member in the center.

Again, for other ideas, look at yachts in your marina and take photographs or make sketches — with permission, of course. Ask about performance under extreme conditions, then go build the perfect skylight.

GRATINGS

To make a grating my way, you must have a sharp dado cutter, preferably the single-blade adjustable type with carbide teeth. And a fine-toothed carbide blade on your table saw, too. Again, I urge you to equip your saw with the sliding auxiliary table (SLAT) described in Part One.

There are at least two good ways to make your grating. The first is slightly better, being all ¾-inch teak. See Figure 13-28(A). The second, (B), uses the heavier teak only in the cross members, the longer pieces being strips ⅜ inch thick. There is no difference in strength or utility if the grating is fully supported. Making uniform dadoes is no trick. Spacing them precisely is. Go back to the principle of the box or finger joint jig. But this time let's use the SLAT instead of the less rigid miter gauge. See Figure 13-29.

Make a 2- or 3-inch batten the exact dimensions of the desired dado — say, ¼ inch wide by ¼ inch thick. Select enough wide pieces of ¾-inch teak to produce all the cross members (21 in Figure 13-30). Joint one edge. Practice on scrap. Hold this firmly (a 20-pound weight leaves both hands free) on the SLAT while you run a dado. Check to see that the little piece is a snug fit. Again place the trial piece against the dado blade, using the batten as a gauge. Cut a dado and check the spacing against the batten. They must be identical. When you feel confident, tack the batten in place as in Figure 13-29. Run three or four dadoes across your scrap, placing each dado, as it is cut, over the batten. Then do the same with three or four narrow pieces about like your grating will be, say, ¼ inch wide. These should press together into a small grating.

If the spaces are too wide or too narrow, adjust your dado cutter carefully. Get it right! Check depth, too. When you're finally satisfied, weight your teak down on the SLAT, run a dado, jump over to the spacing batten, run a dado, and so on. For a check, try one of the narrow scrap pieces in the first three new dadoes. Glue that batten and brad it down. Now you can run all the dadoes in that piece of teak, cut a length or two for the longer pieces, joint the edges, and dado these.

What do you have now? Three or four pieces of teak with grooves running across them, right? Now these

Figure 13-30. *A teak cockpit grating before construction of its frame.*

Figure 13-32. *This rounded helmsman's seat on* Hoku Kea *offers slightly more comfort as the yacht heels. It doubles as a lazarette hatch cover.*

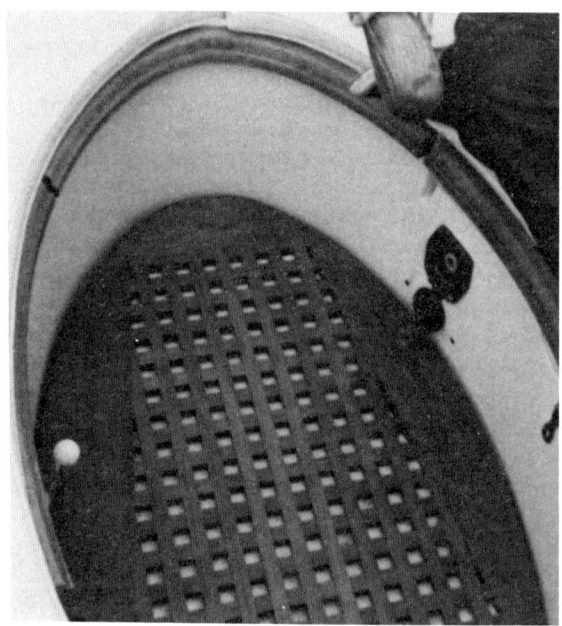

Figure 13-31. *A neat oval cockpit grating. A fine production job a skilled amateur can match.*

have to be ripped into pieces that will fit into the grooves. Start with a piece of scrap, set the table saw fence to the proper width, and rip off a couple of pieces. Try these, adjust, and try again until you produce a piece that is a squeaky fit. Once you achieve this, rip all your teak. Clamp on hold-downs both ways for precision. These parts should press together snugly. If some are too snug, a pass or two over your belt sander should take off enough. Don't worry about dressing over the saw cuts — if you used a fine-toothed blade, the surface is all right. Put a dab of epoxy glue in each intersection, then press it all together with weights.

You'll need a frame all around the grating. Take the dimensions of the cockpit sole, allowing ¼ to ½ inch total clearance. If you have a rudderport in the cockpit, the grating must be in two sections. Also, if you like to rig up bunks in the cockpit, two sections are handy. To simplify, however, my instructions are for a single grating.

Lay out the dimensions on a piece of junk plywood, cut to the lines, and try for size. If you want a 2½-inch frame all around, come in 1¾ inches and mark that on all four sides. Center the grating on the plywood and the lines and brad it securely with the upper surface against the plywood. Set the table saw fence to take out 1¾ inches with the depth at about ⅛ inch deeper than the grating thickness. If you now run the plywood pattern edge along the fence, you will trim off the grating right on the marks. Do this on sides and ends.

Next, you need a rabbet ¾ inch wide around the upper surface of the grating. This is to fit into a similar rabbet in the frame. So remove the pattern and set your dado for ⅜ inch deep and ¾ inch wide (use a wooden face on the saw fence). Run four sides of the grating over the dado, pressing down well or using a hold-down so the depth is uniform. Don't rush it.

Here are a few suggestions on frame joints. Half laps would be the strongest. You could also run the rabbet full length on the side pieces, make the ends 1½ inches longer, and rabbet these into the sides. Or you could miter the corners, strengthening them with a spline. If the grating needs fitting into the frame, trim with a belt sander. Do not try to plane. Glue it all up with pipe clamps across and with C-clamps over battens. If you can stand a tedious job, and your material is at least $^{13}/_{16}$ inch thick, drive brass brads at the intersections and/or along the rabbet. When completed, your grating should look something like the one in Figure 13-31. If you intend to use the grating for cockpit bunks, saw a couple of removable legs to length, and have these ready to jam under the grating.

The simpler grating in Figure 13-28(B) is self-explanatory. The strips are ripped to width from heavy stock with your table saw set for the cross pieces. Thus, they are identical. Then rip to the desired thickness, dress down on a jointer or planer, and glue and brad.

Before we go on to spars, here's one more interesting project. See Figure 13-32. This helmsman's seat is also the cover to the lazarette hatch. As the vessel heels, the helmsman always has a more-or-less-comfortable seat that is far better than a sloping flat seat. I'll leave the seat's construction to your imagination and skill.

FOURTEEN

Bulwarks, Log-rails, and Toerails

The following comments about bulwarks may interest only those who have a hull or want to build a vessel over 40 feet on deck that requires bulwarks a minimum of 8 inches high. Some very exceptional smaller yachts, too, might require such bulwarks. See Figure 14-1.

First, I assume you have a lofting of the hull lines. If you don't, I'll try to explain another method later. I hope your designer included the bulwark in his offsets so there's no guesswork. A bulwark can't just be stuck on any hull. The stem and transom construction, for example, must include this significant increase in height. You should be a fair draftsman if you lack these offsets, because it will be necessary to make a 1-inch scale drawing of the vessel's sheer.

LOFTING BULWARKS

Remember that a rail or bulwark properly decreases from its greatest height at the stemhead in the elevation (side view or profile). The amount of decrease is a matter of design, and you can find that in books on the subject. Use your good eye, too. Try ¼ inch lower at each station, so an 8-inch bulwark comes down to about 5 inches at the transom. Using a ⅜-inch reduction for a 12-inch bulwark, you have 12 inches directly over the waterline forward and 8¼ inches at the waterline aft. All this is by Bingham's Rule. It has no authority. Once you have drawn a bulwark sheer that blends well with the original sheer and bow and stern, take off the heights above the sheer with care. Lay these heights on your lofting of the side elevation, and drive 1-inch brads through these points. Then spring a batten along the brads and make the adjustments until your batten lies fair.

The new sheer, as I want to call it, is the exact height of the bulwark stanchion heads. Locate these midway between frames, possibly three or four between the lofted stations. Indicate by a single vertical line. Now go to the lofted cross sections and draw short lines at these sheer heights. Follow this with the original sections extended fairly but by eye somewhat past the new sheerline. If your vessel is rather straight sided, you have no problem. Where there is flare or tumblehome, however, these guesswork half-breadths should be transferred to the plan view and faired with a batten. Check back and forth until the lofted lines have corrected one another. If the topsides look fair, that's enough until you get the stanchions in. Additional corrections can then be made, if needed. Usually, however, the better the lofting, the less woodwork required.

Now is a good time to loft the rail cap around the stanchion heads in the plan view. You will need a pat-

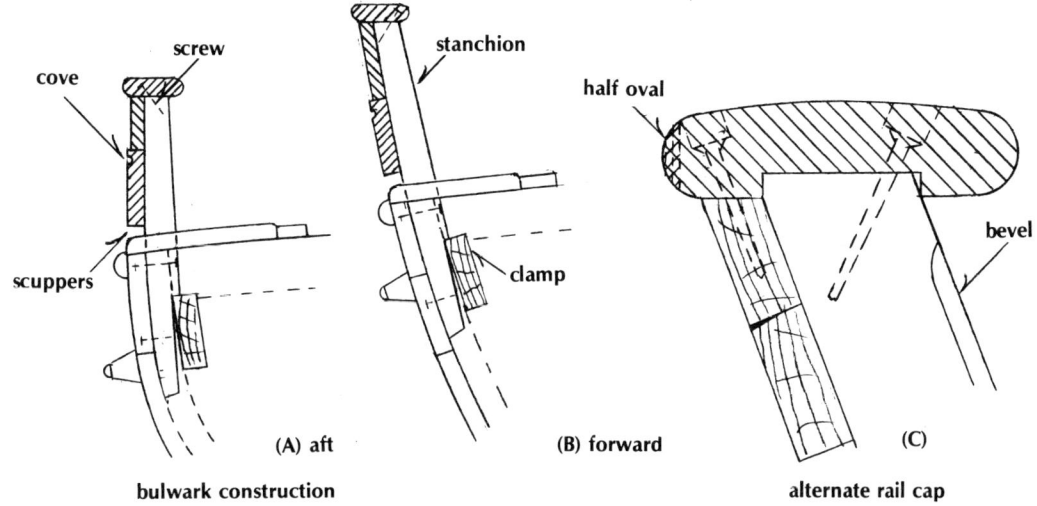

Figure 14-1. BULWARKS

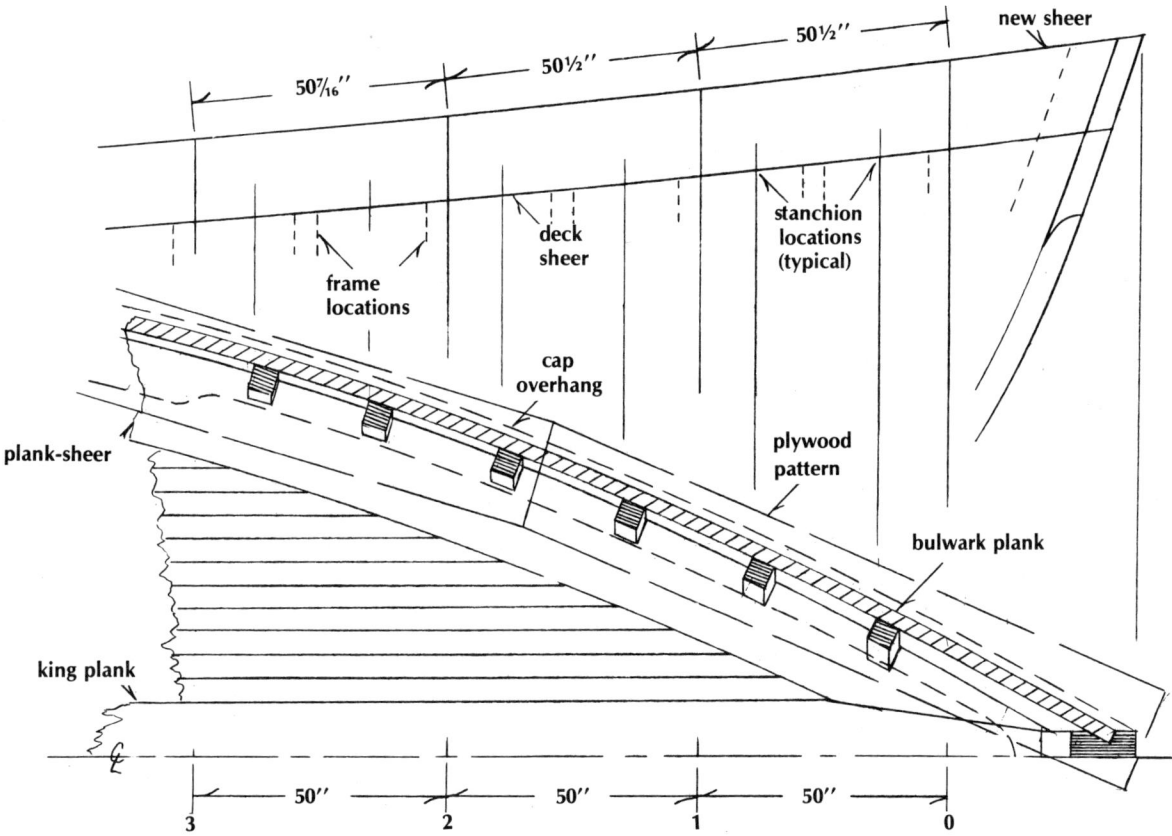

Figure 14-2. LOFTING STANCHIONS AND BULWARK CAP

tern of the cap that considers the bulwark planking thickness, the slight outboard overhang, the greater inboard overhang, and the scarf or butt joints. Later, this pattern will be useful to help line up the stanchion heads. It may have to be made of several lengths of plywood or lumber butt-blocked together for the necessary length. See Figure 14-2. To get a true development of the sweep of the cap, take measurements from centerline to outboard edge of the new sheer at each station. Then go to the sheer profile and take off measurements following the curve from station to station. Lay your plywood or butted lumber on the floor, on top of the deckline. Draw in these expanded station lines square to the centerline. Now mark the half-breadths (above) from the centerline. If your original hull lofting was to the inside of the planking, add that thickness and the amount of the overhang to the outboard edge of the pattern layout. Spring a batten, mark, and saw out. Scribe the desired width of the cap. Increase the cap width at the chainplates, possibly for a pinrail. Saw out and dress to lines. Put aside.

BULWARK STANCHIONS

In Chapter Nine, I described how to lay out and install a covering board or plank-sheer. Some authorities recommend lowering the plank-sheer over the stanchion heads, which is mandatory if the stanchions are also the bent or sawed frame heads. This is a system that causes problems, for there are the spring of the sheer to fight and super-accurate hole locations to find and fits to make. In Figure 14-1 you'll note that the lower ends of the stanchions are tapered. In addition, make the holes in the plank-sheer slightly larger than the stanchions at the deck. If you can pass the stanchions down through the holes, you eliminate the problems, right?

Lay the plank-sheer in position and clamp it to the deck beams. Put in a couple of screws so it can be relocated accurately. Mark the underside along the sheerstrake and at each stanchion-beam location. Remove the plank-sheer after you have provided for scarfs. Draw in the rectangles for the stanchion holes and bore these out, leaving a little for trimming. You can saw them out with a good sabersaw or keyhole saw, following with a sharp chisel to smooth up. Make these a practical fit, right to the line of the sheerstrake, but leave $\frac{1}{16}$ to $\frac{1}{8}$ inch open on the other three sides. Wedges will close these later. The plank-sheer can now be installed and screw-fastened, with luting in the joint, and the scarf is all taken care of.

Drop the stanchions through the holes, fit the notches to the clamp, and tack temporarily but securely in a vertical position. With them all standing up neatly, spring a heavy batten around them. You'll want to trim a bit below or take off a shaving above the deck. The same batten will show you where to saw them off level athwartships. When they are all back in again, place the cap template on the heads for a double-check and a few more shavings. If there's anything that gets me, it's a lumpy sheer or rail cap! And port *and* starboard must match!

Now daub epoxy in the holes and replace each stanchion. Screw from the planking if you can keep the screws from being covered by fenders or trim to allow for easy repairs. Or fasten from the inside, two or three in each stanchion. You can even go through the clamp if there's no space between. In the meantime, your helper should have been cutting a bushel of thin cedar wedges. Make these the exact width of the stanchions at the sides and inner face, with the thin ends $\frac{1}{16}$ to $\frac{1}{8}$ inch, depending on your workmanship. Smear them with a little epoxy glue and slip them into the gaps, but not hard enough to strain the fastenings. Put none in the outboard joint. You should now have a permanent watertight joint. In large vessels, these joints are sometimes caulked. I think, however, that you can depend on your skill and good old epoxy.

BULWARK CAP

The bulwark cap can be installed next, after its lower corners have been rounded with a shaper or router. The cap meets other sections in a scarf joint, so it is preferable to round the upper corners after final installation. I think, however, that it makes some sense to plank up the bulwark, then cap it. The lower strake should be heavier, as shown, and it should have a cove routed in to be filled later with gold or contrasting bright paint.

You may elect to put generous scuppers in this plank as well as openings for docking cleats and chocks. Three to five scuppers 1 inch by 5 or 6 inches should work, although I must say that I like to see this plank about ¾ inch above the plank-sheer nearly the full length. It clears fast and tends to prevent rot. If there is a lot of flare, this lower plank will have to be spiled. The uppers, however, are usually light enough to spring to the sheer. Plane these flush with the stanchion heads and screw the cap down to them. The cap should be fastened to the heads also, but never drive a screw straight into end grain. Instead, screw at about a 60-degree angle, alternating the direction every second frame. (See Figure 14-1.) To avoid getting the cap chewed up, I suggest a galvanized or bronze half oval for the vessel's middle third and a good length up forward.

These flaring topsides are often subjected to an awful beating against a piling, so Figure 14-1(C) shows an alternate cap construction worth considering. Old-timers tenoned the heads into mortises in the cap. I would settle for a groove fitting over the heads, thus keeping the cap from being knocked loose or split. Notice the slight crown that adds style and helps to shed dew. The bevel, chamfer, or radius on the inner corners looks neat and prevents wear.

If you don't have a lofting to help you do this major job, here's a somewhat dubious way to go about it. Cut your stanchions an inch or so above the probable heights, according to location. Clamp about four in position, with notches on the clamp in, say, a 16- to 20-foot length of the vessel. Spring a light batten vertically like a continuation of the topsides so you can pencil this on the side of the stanchion. Saw or plane these down and clamp in position again. Then spring a stiff batten around them. If and when it looks good, move the batten along to take in another two or three stanchions, trimming them as you go. Or you can leave the batten as is and add another one under or over it to get the necessary reach to another three stanchions. You treat these as you did the first. Eventually, you'll have a line of stanchions more or less fair. If it looks pretty, and there are no lumps, you are in luck. Now just go back and fit all the missing stanchions to the battens.

Getting a fair sheer is something else! And the problem is compounded if the vessel is in a small building. You can measure up from the sheer perpendicularly with a level across, marking about every third or fourth stanchion. Assume you are reducing the height as you work aft. Again clamp the battens on these marks, for the full length of the vessel. To sight properly, you'll have to stand off at a good distance. You may have to climb up on a tall stepladder to bring your eye level with the sheer. Move the battens up or down a smidgen here and there until you get the lumps out. Call for another opinion. Go away for a day or two, and then take another squint. Sighting from off the bow and stern helps, and a look directly on the bow is sometimes revealing. If your vessel is in a crowded shed, however, you are licked. Leave the sheer heights until you get the hull outside. If your original sheer is fair, your bulwarks should come out fair.

BULWARKS ON AN EXISTING YACHT

You must be prepared to compromise if you wish to add bulwarks to a yacht not designed for them. Any considerable increase in freeboard can do harm aesthetically, and no one can calculate the effect of the additional windage on the vessel's performance. Bulwarks should not be considered for anything but a short-ended or plumb-stemmed yacht; if the latter has a long counter, forget it. The only remotely possible expedient is to terminate the bulwarks quite short of the bow and stern, perhaps with a decorative ending, ogee, bullnose, or whatever. No matter what you do, you will not have a handsome yacht, because the designer knew what he was doing. Afterthoughts rarely do anything but hurt. If, however, the vessel has low freeboard, high houses (trunks), very short ends, and a lot of sail power, follow the procedures just described (with a few variations).

Mark the locations of the stanchions on the planksheer, using special care to find the inside of the planking. Lay out the rectangles, bore out and square up, then fit the stanchions as above. If the yacht has a bowsprit, the bulwark caps join over the spar with a form of knee. If there is no bowsprit, the knee may be laminated to the rail height and crowned slightly. The same applies at the stern. The rail cap usually meets a wider cap over the transom, joined by a knee. See Figure 14-3. Sometimes called a fashion piece, this cap is supported by long knees extending forward on the deck.

LOG-RAILS AND TOERAILS

Unless they are specifically designed for extensive offshore cruising, most modern yachts do not require bulwarks. Instead, metal stanchions and lifelines or liferails that, theoretically, prevent crews from falling or being swept overboard, are added. Owners and designers are reluctant to increase windage, of course, but there is a mysterious feeling of security that comes from the sight of a generous rail. Part of this is pure illusion, however, for a 4- or 5-inch rail will do little to prevent a body from being washed overboard. A 2-inch toerail will keep you from skidding off the deck and save the life of many a tool, but that's it.

The distinction between a log-rail and a toerail is not precise. A log-rail generally follows the contour of the topsides (flared, straight, or tumblehome), may be made of two or more pieces of lumber on edge, and usually has a cap. Log-rails taper down to the stern also. Toerails are always one piece of lumber (or they are laminated to look like one). The outboard faces are 90 degrees to the plank-sheer, while the inboard faces always cant outboard at a uniform angle. Toerails may be tapered or of uniform height and they may be as low as ¾ inch on small boats. All rails must be set back a minimum of ⅛ inch from the edge of the plank-sheer.

Figure 14-4(A) shows a log-rail about 6 inches high. The lower log is drifted (rods driven down) into the deck beams or the sheer batten (if the hull is fiberglass or ferrocement), as in C. The second rail can be screwed or drifted or nailed into the log. The cap should be grooved to prevent movement and to ensure a fair line. On Chesapeake Bay they once used an open log-rail consisting of a heavy cap resting on short pipe stanchions. Drifts went through the cap and the pipes into the lower log. This is a practical workboat style that could be adapted to some so-called character boats, replacing expensive turned wooden stanchions. A cap can be screwed to a narrower single log-rail also (B), with the latter drifted, spiked, or screwed into the sheerstrake or sheer batten.

The forward ends of lower logs and of toerails are always wider for a foot or more from the stem to provide for bow chocks, which must be screwed securely through the rail and preferably let in so the screws are relieved of shear stresses. See Figure 14-5. The screws should be long enough to hold in the plank-sheer. Chocks can also be fitted into a mortise in the rail if you can find the right dimensions. The greater width can be carried aft, tapering down at about a fourth of the total length. Where chainplates penetrate the rail, it is customary to swell the rail out to double its thickness elsewhere.

Toerails may be of one timber scarfed to make the length or strip-built of two or three laminations. In the latter, it's all right to use plain horizontal scarfs. If the scarfed lengths can be handled, make them up on a bench. But if the length is such that it might break of its

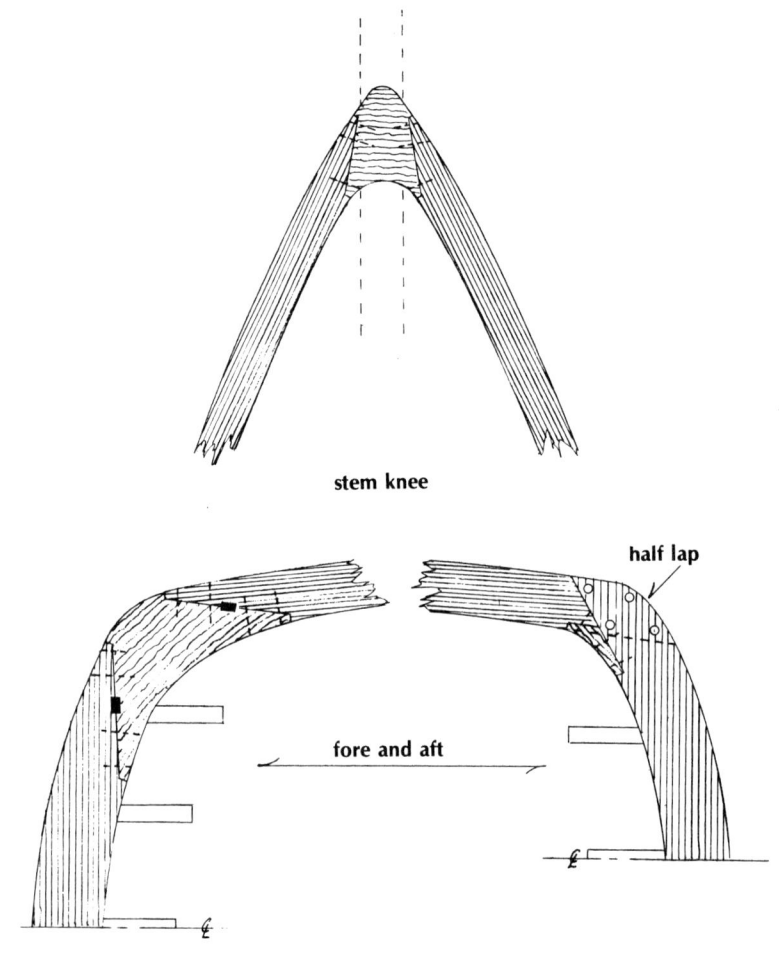

Figure 14-3. JOINING CAPS AT BOW AND STERN

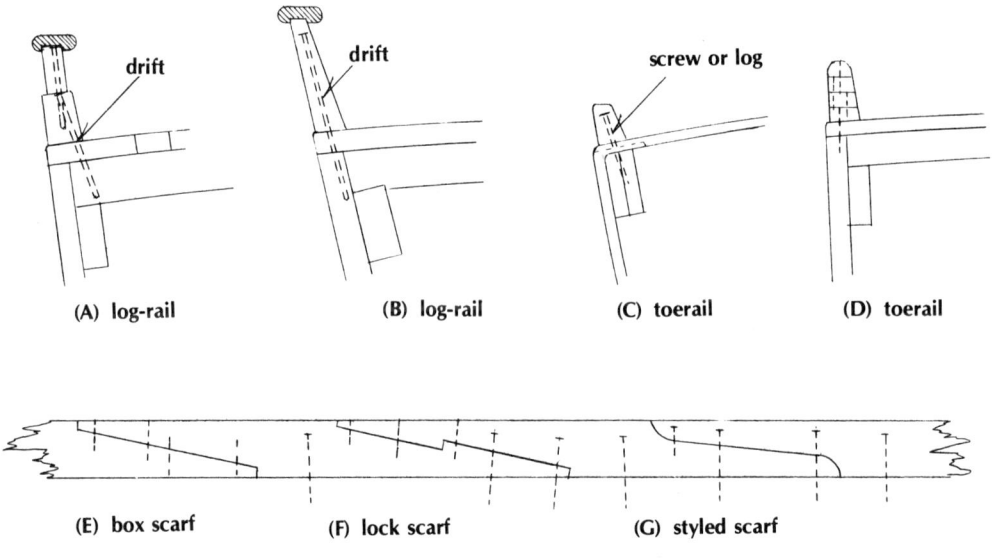

Figure 14-4. RAILS AND RAIL SCARFS

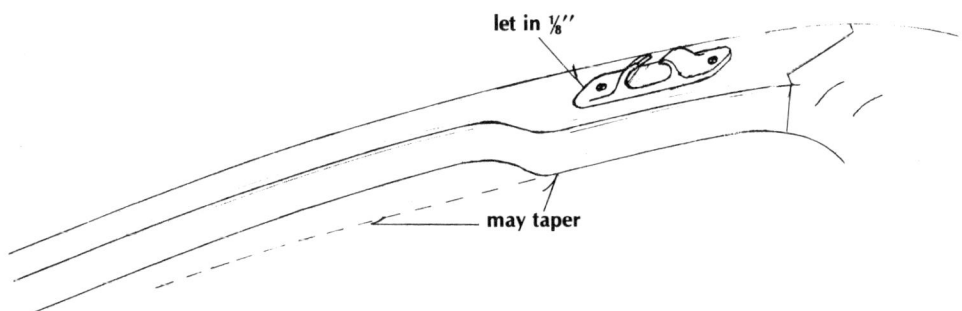

Figure 14-5. TOERAIL AT BOW

own weight in handling, the scarfs can be made on the plank-sheer or a lower lamination. Care must be taken to make the joint so fair that it is invisible from above.

The safest way is to do the fitting on a bench (see the scarfing jig in Chapter Five) and tack in a couple of small finish nails so the relationship is easy to repeat. Lay the two on the plank-sheer, fasten one, apply glue, tap the nails into the original holes, and clamp the sides of the joint between two long pieces of scrap. This will hold the scarf so that it will bend fair while you screw down the rest of the rail or lamination. Fasten down through the scarf with screws and finish nails. Let it set for at least 24 hours before releasing the clamps. Scatter such lamination joints as far apart as possible.

If the toerail is higher than wide, don't use a common scarf, especially if it is 3 or 4 inches tall. Use a box, locked, or styled scarf, as shown in Figure 14-4(E), (F), and (G). Side clamping is even more important here, and it should be predrilled for long screws. If you can get several in from below while the assembly is on a bench, do so.

All rails must be set in bedding or epoxy glue. Scarfs are glued, of course.

The toerail shown in Figure 14-4(D) has four laminations. This rail, if one piece, would be difficult to bend and fasten. I suggest sawing all the bevels (the inboard surface) and dressing carefully so they need only sanding after installation. The outboard edges can be sawed to the decreasing widths as the rail is built up, planed as accurately as possible before installation, then planed and sanded after the rail is completed. This convex surface is easy to work, whereas the inner concave side would be very difficult. Where scuppers are cut through the lower piece, a hard spot is likely to show when the piece is bent to the curve. Clamp a two- or three-foot length of stiff scrap inside the piece so that the hard spot is faired out, then glue and screw to the deck. Use your eye.

The types of scarf in Figure 14-4(E), (F), and (G) are the same for caps. Strong rails such as in A should be able to take a cap sprung around the curve. This is preferable to cutting it out of a wide plank. However, if B has any deflection because of its height, its cap will have to be sawed from a pattern. Scarfing from a router pattern is described in Chapter Nine.

FIFTEEN

Spars

I have enough material on the design, layout, and construction of wooden spars to fill a fair-sized book. On the other hand, what I know about aluminum spars can be written on my cuff. I'm attempting to steer you toward wooden spars because the amateur boatbuilder can't build an aluminum spar. In most instances, however, a properly engineered aluminum mast is an excellent replacement for a wooden mast. Thus, you should go to a recognized company for a metal mast if you can afford one.

Unfortunately, the best wood — Sitka spruce — is so costly that you will come out only slightly ahead if you count your labor at zero dollars. One major reason for this is that the metal mast comes with tangs and other attachments neatly and strongly built on, and with a groove for the sail. The chances are good that the whole rig will be significantly lighter, too, which will pay off in sail-carrying ability.

Am I trying to talk you out of building your spars? Yes, if you have the least doubt about your capabilities. Because this is where careless workmanship, or less-than-perfect material, or faulty assembly will almost always result in a dismasting, an injury, or worse!

But hold on. There are good reasons why you should choose wooden spars. Yes, aluminum spars work and they have their own functional beauty — meaning that they are ugly. Only the costliest tapered aluminum spar even remotely approaches the beauty of a gracefully shaped spruce mast gleaming like pale gold under many coats of varnish. I think the ugliest rig in aluminum is the gaff rig, unless it is viewed from a half-mile away. Look at the massive 9-inch mast on a Cape Cod catboat. Note how it fights the thrust of a mighty gaff yet slims down rapidly to its head, topped off with a neat truck. And remember that wooden spars still stand up to their work, just as they have for thousands of years throughout the world.

In keeping with the purpose of this book, I will show you a few simple ways to construct spars. Note that much of what follows has already been covered by giants such as L. Francis Herreshoff, Howard I. Chapelle, Robert M. Steward, and others. I have used most of these methods in my small shops with inadequate tools under conditions quite similar to yours — if you are the average amateur boatbuilder. I have never hewn a mast from a sapling or tree — from a timber, yes. However, what I pass on to you comes from men who spent years turning rough logs into beautiful spars.

HOLLOW BOX SPARS

Round solid or hollow marconi masts are now completely obsolete except on small boats and traditional rigs such as sprit rigs. In these cases you build exactly to the spar plans provided by the designer. Of course, round solid masts are required for gaff rig, for the sails need rings or lacing, except in rare cases when a recessed sail track is used. Not that a round or oval spar is not occasionally built with a hollow core. If you are concerned only with round spars, you can skip much of what follows.

The familiar box mast is the only way to go for an amateur builder, except for the mast of a dinghy or very small boat. The box is stronger than a solid timber of the same section, and uses less material. Thus, it costs less. A box mast requires a lot of work, but not really hard work. The layout must be precise and the workmanship equally accurate. The assembly must be held rigidly in a jig or bench of some sort. You'll need many clamps, as well as a pair of assembly (gluing) hands about every eight or 10 feet of length. Other than that, the job is simple.

HOLLOW-SPAR LUMBER

Spruce is the most desirable lumber for any spar because of its stiffness and strength combined with light weight. Spruce weighs in at 26 to 28 pounds per cubic foot. Its appearance, a light creamy tan, is beautiful. Try to find the type of Sitka spruce known as aircraft quality. Inspect this or any other lumber for spars before buying it. Look for almost perfectly straight vertical grain, which should not run out of the board at more than a 1-degree angle, if at all. If the grain is straight, but runs at a greater angle across the board without bending, you may have to settle for a much wider board. The waste can be used later to make small sticks, tillers, and so on. Do not accept lumber with knots, pitch pockets, checks, or other blemishes. But do expect short checking at the ends.

Sitka spruce is difficult to locate and extremely costly. Because it comes from the Northwest, you can only inspect it personally if you live up that way. If you need a fair quantity of it, try contacting a lumberyard near the coast for a recommendation. It's possible your small order (100 board feet and up) can be shipped into your area with a large load of other lumber. I am confident you can trust a reputable yard to supply your exact needs — if the material is available to them. Sometimes they, too, have to wait. And there may be others in line before you. Perhaps a boatbuilder in your area could take care of these details as your agent — for a small fee, of course.

Your local lumberyard could be very useful in seeking out this special grade of spruce. Some have lumber specialists who handle rare, exotic, and boatbuilding woods. Be sure to state in writing what you need, and for what purpose. Last but not least, be sure to consult a local boatshop operator about woods from your part of the world that might serve nearly as well as Sitka spruce.

If you are unable to acquire the right kind of spruce, go to Douglas fir vertical-grain lumber, available in lengths to 30 feet. Its weight runs as high as 40 pounds per cubic foot, but it is stronger. Most designers say you can reduce the thickness of the staves proportionately. Usually the outside dimensions of the box remain the same, with only the wall thicknesses being reduced from, say, ¾ to ⅝ inch. The desirability of Douglas fir, also called Oregon pine, is well established, for it was used almost exclusively by L. Francis Herreshoff. See Figure 15-1(D). His spar for the R-boat Yankee had a section 5½ by 7 inches (his standard proportions), with side staves only ½ inch thick and ends ⅝ inch thick. Don't just copy this design. The boat had an intricate double-spreader rig that kept the stick in place. The mast scantlings did not do the job alone.

MAST AND SPAR SECTIONS

Figure 15-1 shows mast sections designed to a ratio of about 5 inches in width to 7 inches in length (fore and aft). Herreshoff used 5½ to 7, but note that today's modern foretriangles, tremendous headsails, and adjustable backstays place stresses on spars that he never dreamed of. Many modern masts are occasionally under loads that equal or exceed the vessel's total displacement.

Figure 15-1(A) shows a simple box section. This is suitable for small boats with under 250 square feet of working sail area. The dotted line indicates an optional thickening of the aft stave if there is any question about the holding power of the sail-track screws. This applies also to the boxes in B and C. The construction in A would be suitable for large hollow booms. The corner in B is stronger because of the much-increased gluing area. The rabbet makes it easier to glue up the spar, for it aligns the sides to the ends and prevents the sides from being pressed in too far. This is a major problem with configuration A.

I like the style in Figure 15-1(C), for it can be made easily with a table saw. The battens can be lined up precisely with a little spacing jig and fastened quickly with glue and small nails. Even style B can be rabbeted on a table saw if you are careful with the blade settings. None of these corners need sanding if you use a cabinetmaker's combination or planer blade, for glues such as Aerolite and T-88 need a slightly toothy surface and very little pressure. Style C makes a slightly heavier spar, of course. You can refine it by making the battens triangular instead of square or rectangular.

SPAR LAYOUT

Spar dimensions are shown in the designs of all responsible naval architects and designers. You must not trifle

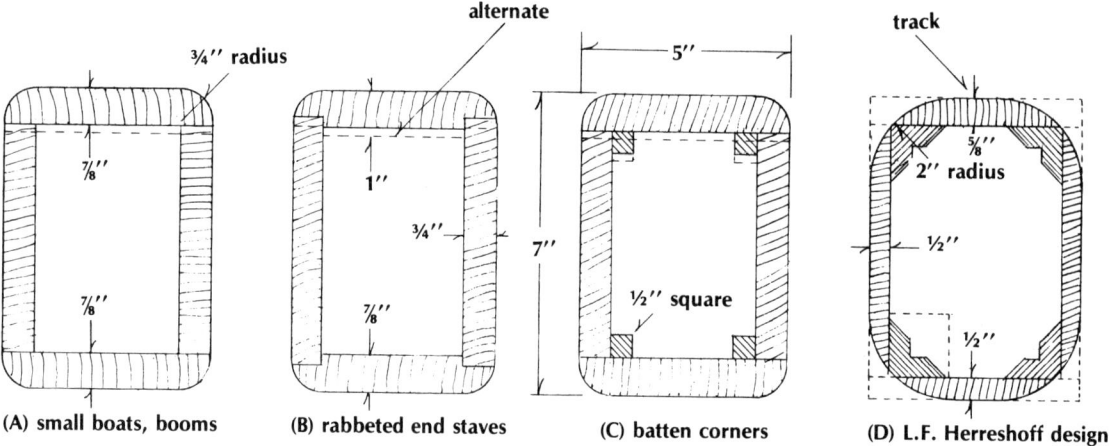

Figure 15-1. HOLLOW SPAR SECTIONS

with these. However, I have seen designs showing mast tapers as a series of straight lines, some with a straight taper from about midpoint to head. It is up to you to see that these deficiencies are corrected, either by going to a qualified designer or sparbuilder, who will charge you for his time, or by doing the necessary design work yourself. This task is simply a matter of accurate drafting, assuming that the original basic spar sections are adequate. Ask a designer or builder for his opinion on that, but don't expect him to give you a written guarantee. Sections and walls proportional to those I have included here would not be far off, but rigs do vary.

The drawing in Figure 15-2 is of the mast of Allegra, a 24-foot heavy-displacement cruising cutter design. Note the two scales in the drawing. If your drawing board is large, draw the cross section of the spar full size. (I drew it to a scale of ⅜ inch equals 1 inch for better reproduction in this book.) The longitudinal scale, however, is best if shortened, for the curves are more easily faired in a short bend. My scale is ½ inch equals 1 foot. (My working drawings for amateur builders have a longitudinal scale of ¾ inch equals 1 foot.) The only real difference between the two drawings is that my job of dimensioning sections, stave widths, and so on, is easier and more accurate with the larger cross section.

TAPERING SPARS

I use a tapering system that has been employed by sparbuilders since the invention of the so-called marconi mast. Herreshoff, Steward, Chapelle, and others have described this style. I believe you can rely on it. First, let's assume that your dimensions at the masthead are one-half the greatest fore-and-aft dimension, or slightly more. Note that, technically, a spar should be heaviest at the point of greatest stress. Thus, a mast should taper from the deck toward its foot (the bury). You'll see this in all fine spar designs. However, the saving in weight is trivial and the extra work is considerable, so Allegra's mast is straight from its tabernacle up to the spreader and lower shroud area.

The graceful taper to the head is then achieved with a compass. At the right-hand side of the drawing, I swung an arc equal to the 6-inch spar dimension, a 3-inch radius. From the forward intersection of the head and the predetermined length (3¾ inches), I projected to the arc and erected a vertical there. I then divided the dimension between that vertical and the center of the radius into the number of ordinates from the spreader to the head. In this case it was five. It could be more, or less, depending on the length of the spar. Erected verticals from these points intersect the arc. These are numbered the same as the ordinates, and project each point accurately back to its ordinate. I connected these points with a fair line around a batten. This is the forward shape of the mast.

To get the side stave width, use a compass or dividers set to the material thickness. Measure ⅝ inch to the inside tangent of the rabbet (or a full ⅞ inch if there is no rabbet). Some designers give only the outside dimensions of their spars, so you have to lay out the spar full size and deduct for the thicknesses. I save you this step. You will still have to use your eye on the batten, however, for discrepancies are always possible because you are picking up from a small pencil line drawing.

The athwartships taper layout is the same. It requires great accuracy in projecting from the arc points back to the ordinates, for there is much less bend in this side view. I have made Allegra's mast a little heavier than the ideal, perhaps. Study a great many spar plans by recognized designers. If your yacht's sail area and displacement are similar to the examples you study, and the rigging is equal, you can assume the proportions will

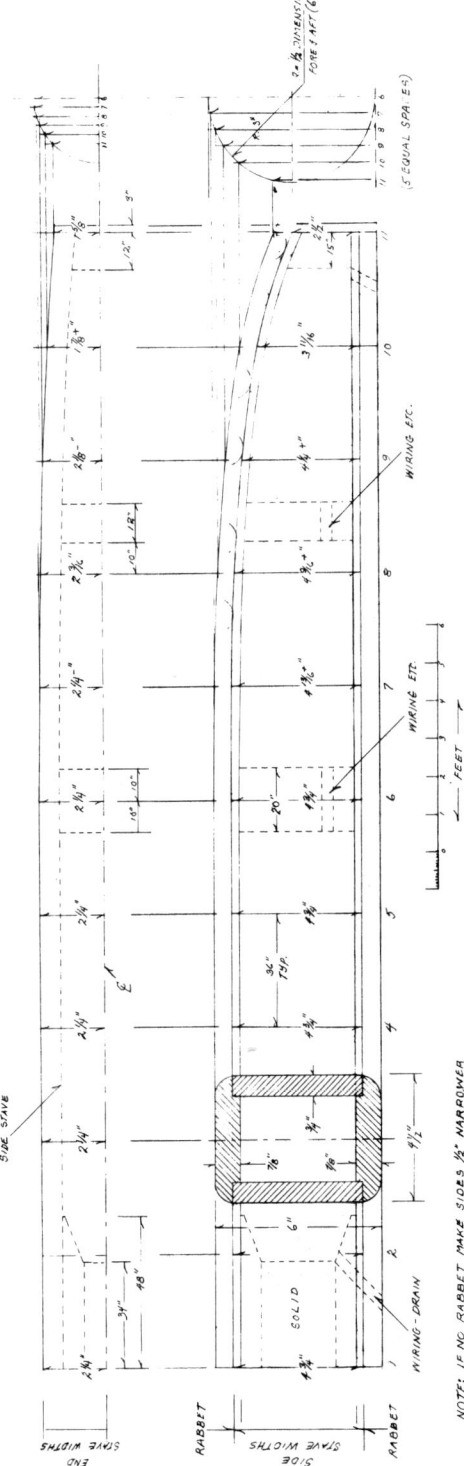

Figure 15-2. ALLEGRA'S MAST SHOWING TAPER LAYOUT SYSTEM

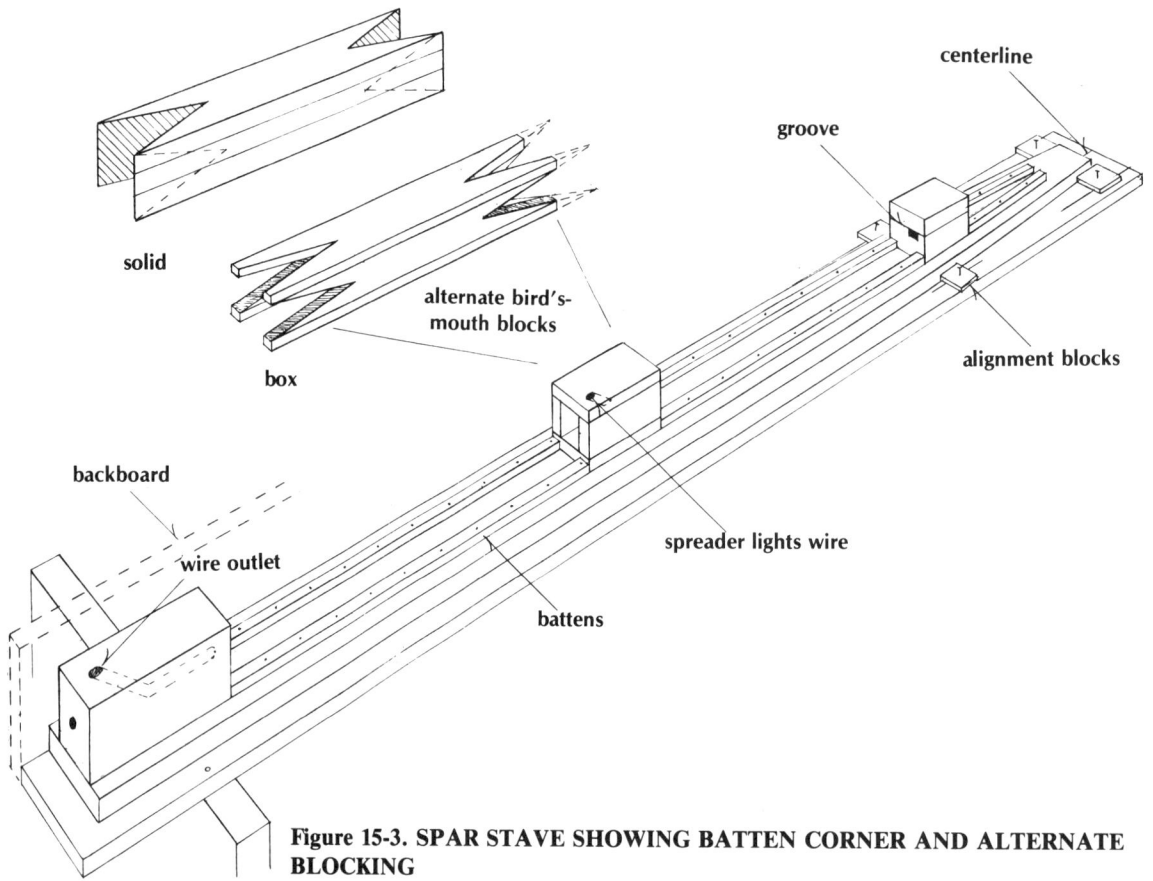

Figure 15-3. SPAR STAVE SHOWING BATTEN CORNER AND ALTERNATE BLOCKING

be appropriate for your rig. Again, however, get advice or professional consultation if you can.

The same intersected-arc projection system is used for solid spars such as booms, gaffs, clubs, sprits, and so on. Booms and gaffs are tapered to both ends, with a straight edge on the side to which the sail is attached. A jibboom or club for a loose-footed staysail is usually mounted on a pedestal. This spar is under pure compression so it tapers equally all ways, just like an elongated barrel. Sprits are the same. An unsupported mast, such as for a sailing dinghy or sharpie, involves a different kind of design — a taper from above the bury. See Howard Chapelle's *Yacht Designing and Planning* (W.W. Norton) for traditional spar design.

LAYOUT OF FORE-AND-AFT SPARS

Later I'll describe briefly how to construct solid round spars for use with gaff rig, so here are the essential proportions that Chapelle specifies for such masts.

Catboats with an unsupported mast. Diameters: at deck, .02 of total length, heel to truck; at gaff jaws, .90 of deck diameter (a gentle curve on forward side); a fast taper to peak halyard block, .65 of deck diameter.

Sloops and cutters, normally rigged. Diameters: at deck, .02 of overall mast length; at head or peak halyard eye, .70 of deck diameter; at butt or step, .50 of deck diameter. If heavily rigged, deduct about 10 percent of diameters.

Schooners. Mainmast diameters: at deck, .023 to .029 of the length from deck to hounds; at hounds, .85 of diameter at deck; at masthead, .80 of diameter at hounds. The foremast should be larger than the mainmast by about 10 percent. *Gaffs:* Greatest diameter .015 to .018 of total length; diameter at jaws, .90 of greatest diameter; at head, .72 of greatest diameter. *Solid booms, round:* Diameter at mainsheet blocks, .015 of total length; at jaws, .80 of greatest diameter; at aft end, .70 of greatest diameter. *Schooner fore boom:* At sheet blocks, .022 to .026 of its length; at jaws, .90 of greatest diameter; outer end, .80 of greatest diameter.

This is only a portion of the information Chapelle provides in his famous book. I have tried to boil it down to essentials. I used these proportions and others for unsupported masts in designing the rig for *Bay Bird*, known as a three-sail bateau in Marylandese. We called it a modified sharpie with a modern bugeye rig. Her 36-foot sticks whipping in a breeze gave many a midlander heart attacks.

SPAR BENCHES AND ALIGNMENT

Let's talk about ways to keep spars aligned properly during construction and gluing. They must be aligned

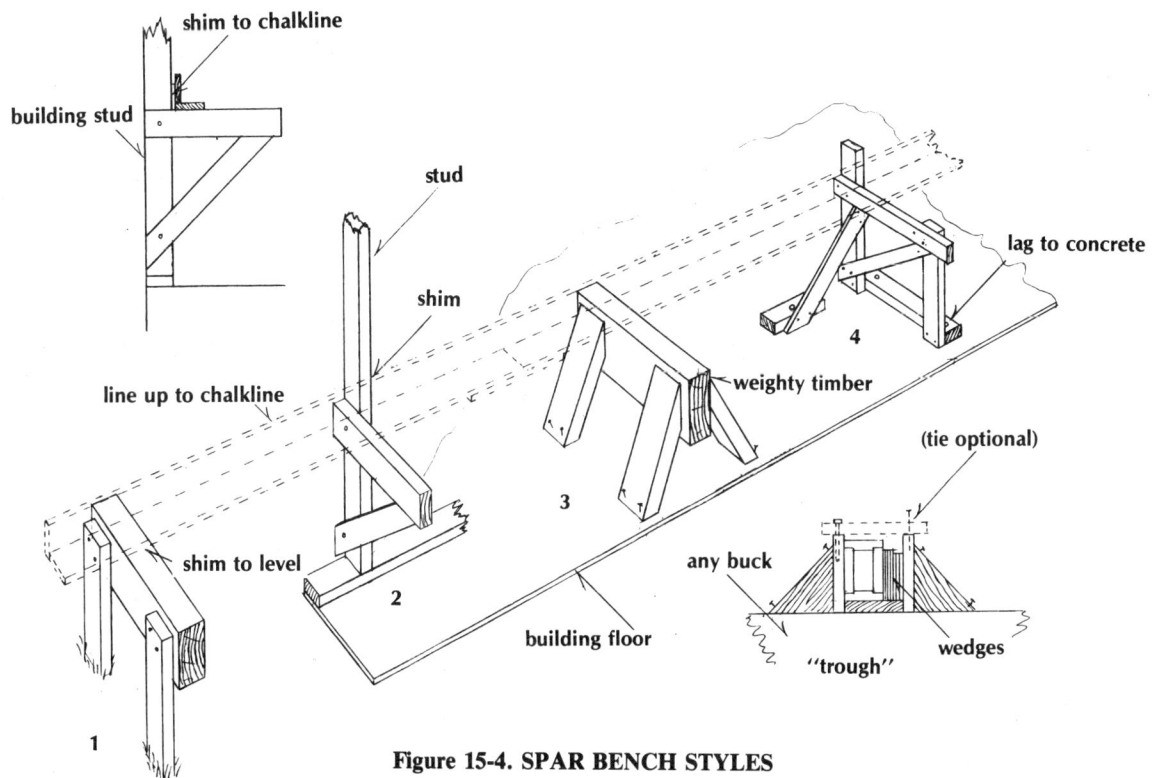

Figure 15-4. SPAR BENCH STYLES

precisely whether they are hollow-box (most common) construction or worked out of a massive timber or log. Most of you will be building box spars (Figures 15-1 and 15-2), so we'll postpone solid-spar support systems until later.

On all spars, masts, booms, and gaffs, the side to which the sail is attached must always be dead straight. No sailmaker can construct a proper sail for a crooked stick. Thus, some means of holding the spar components in alignment must be incorporated in the spar bench. The mast consists of four staves. The two side staves are identical, each being tapered toward the head on their forward edges only. The forward and aft staves taper in toward their centerlines, so they are identical in shape, but they may vary somewhat in thickness, as shown. The other components are blocking at points where stresses occur, such as at the bury from deck to step, the gooseneck, the area of the spreaders and lower shroud attachment, the forestay intersection, and the head. See Figure 15-3.

The supports for your spar bench must be solidly immovable or so heavy that movement will be unlikely. Figure 15-4 shows four types of bucks for a spar bench. Many others could be devised. If you are working outside or in a rough building with an earthen floor, No. 1 would do fine. No. 2 shows the bench frame attached to building studs (which are never in alignment). No. 3 represents a series of sawhorses built of very heavy timbers to resist movement. Note that these are toe-nailed to a wooden floor. If the floor is concrete, you'll count on the weight of the timber to be sufficient. No. 4 has a built-up frame nailed to a wooden floor, ideally, or lagged down to a concrete floor, less than ideal.

Make each buck not less than two feet long and space them from four to eight feet apart (the latter for large masts). See Figure 15-5. Set up the end bucks level, then stretch a wire or 50-pound nylon monofilament as tight as you can. A line level would help to level these approximately. Tack ¼-inch blocks under each end of the line so it is spaced ¼ inch above the actual top of the bucks. Now the bucks in between may be shimmed or raised or lowered by using a ¼-inch block as a gauge. If your spacing is so long that sag is visible in the line, you can work from a center buck out to the ends. Failing this, you may have to use a long level or a level on a long straightedge. Being truly level is not critical, but having a dead straight line from end to end is.

The principal bench-top board should be of straight ¾-inch stock, carefully butt-blocked with glue and screws. Its width should be such that it cannot interfere with clamping. Make up the backboard width less than the spar's greatest dimension, joining with butts. Nail the backboard to the bench-top board to form a continuous girder. Then this entire assembly must be lined up with a chalkline and fastened. The backboard must be vertical, so shims or blocks behind it may be necessary. If the bucks are not perfectly level, glue shims under the board. Check the top with a level and straightedge. You can't have any humps or valleys.

An alternate bench called a trough is shown in Figure

Figure 15-5. *Sixty-two-foot rectangular mainmast built by skilled amateur Leland Cass. Note the perfect scarf and threaded rod clamps on glued-up mizzenmast. These were Cass's first spars.*

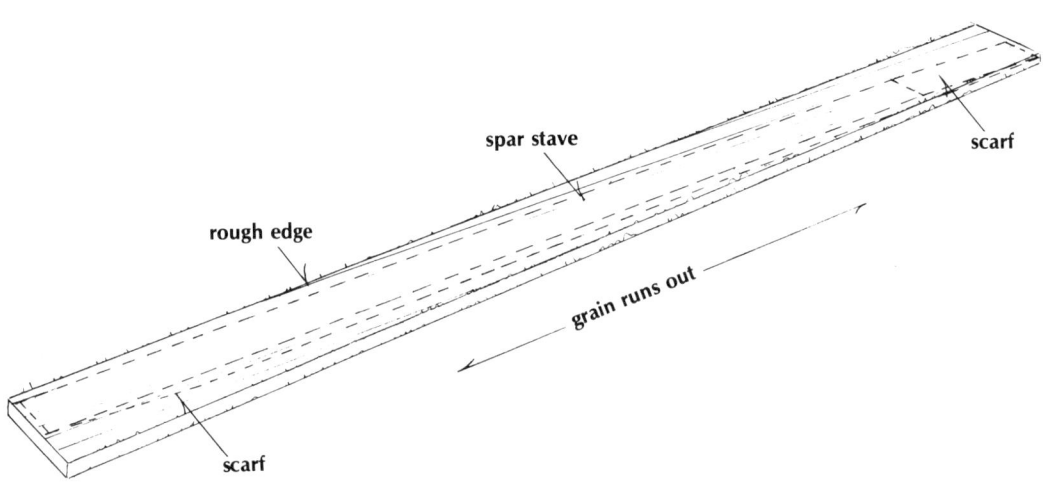

Figure 15-6. STAVE SHIFTED TO FOLLOW GRAIN

15-4. It, too, can be built with the opening in the side, but either way the sides must be rigid. The trough could eliminate the need for clamps entirely if the ties were to be nailed securely with wedges under them as well as inside the trough itself. This device is often built on the wall studs or on a wooden floor.

SCARFING AND ASSEMBLY OF STAVES

You may have to use spar lumber wider than the principal width of the staves because of grain run-out. In this case, the grain will not be perfectly parallel to the edge of the boards, although the grain itself should run perfectly straight. See Figure 15-6. Unfortunately, this creates some scrap. You may have to piece together three or four short lengths to get a complete stave. This involves considerable work, of course, but do not be nervous about the strength of a properly constructed 12-to-1 scarf. (A scarfing jig was described in Chapter Five. Its use was then discussed in Chapter Seven.) Plan to join continuous lengths before assembly of the box. Do not expect to join the scarfs during the box glue-up. Also, unless you have been lucky enough to find spruce or fir in which the grain runs dead straight in the boards, you can't just scarf them together willy-nilly, then lay out the widths and tapers.

Your first step is to snap a chalkline on each board parallel to the grain. Then tack a stiff, straight batten or board on the scrap side of the line so that this straightedge can guide the saw, whether you use a table saw or a power handsaw. All your pieces now have a

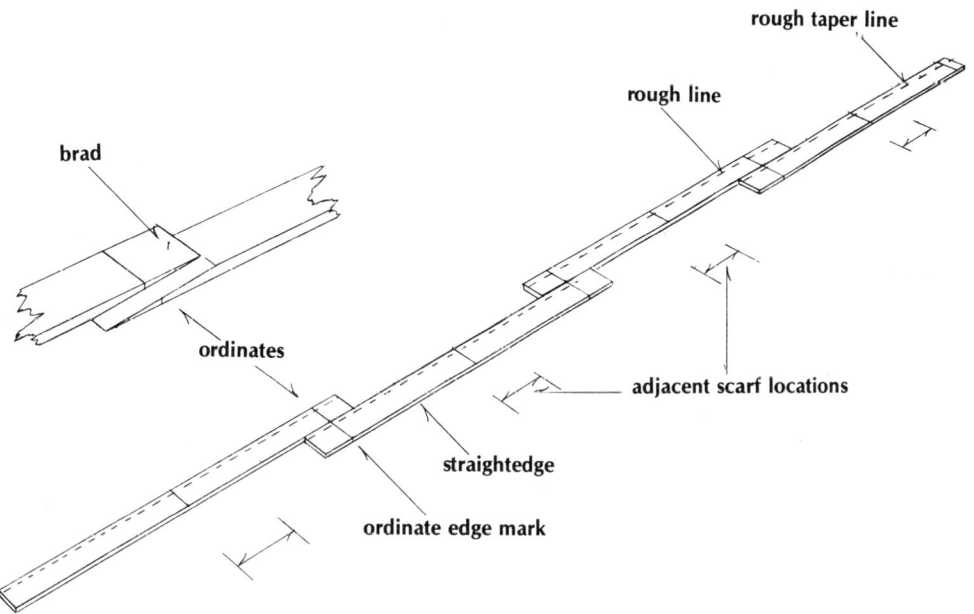

Figure 15-7. LAYOUT OF JOINTS AND ORDINATES

sawed straight edge, but two will need a considerable taper on the opposite edge, and two will taper on both edges. Remember that the scarfs must be scattered, that is, no joints opposite or close together. Take the lengths, allowing for the checking areas at the ends, and lay these out in pencil on a sketch of the spar plan. Number the pieces of lumber accordingly. Lay these out on the spar bench in their relative positions, allowing for the scarf overlaps, and mark off locations of the ordinates. See Figure 15-7. At these points lay out the approximate widths of the tapers and the general widths of the lower spar.

Let's see why this is done. First of all, consider these questions. Do you rabbet the pieces (1) before scarfing, (2) after the scarfs are fashioned but before gluing, or (3) after the full-length assembly is glued up?

Let's go through these step by step so you can make your choice intelligently. Let's agree that rabbeting, dressing, or any operation is easier to do when the components are short and easily handled. The rabbeting can be done with a router, with a table saw, with a router-shaper, or with a shaper. The steps for No. 1 are to lay out excess widths on the temporary ordinates so you can leave at least $\frac{3}{8}$ inch more than the final width. The reason for this is that some lumber takes a set or spring when a portion is ripped off. The excess must be enough to allow corrections, to go back to a straightedge or chalkline and still have enough stock for the final opposite edge. Once this edge is sawed straight to your satisfaction — and it might be from the first cut — dress it accurately to the line. Mark the widths on the ordinates, connect with a batten, and saw close to that line. Plane down, then form the rabbet on both edges with the best tools you have. Now you can go ahead with machining the scarfs, being careful to locate them so the ordinates marked on the edges match up perfectly.

No. 2 is just the opposite. The scarfs are located by the ordinates — the marks on the edges — then fitted, and the pieces are bradded to prevent shifting. Now take them apart and plane the straight edges, from which you mark the stave widths on the ordinates. Saw to these lines, dress, and rabbet both edges.

Whether you followed No. 1 or No. 2, the pieces are ready to be glued into full-length staves. If you have one or two helpers, you can follow No. 3. When the pieces have satisfactory straight edges, form the scarfs, glue all together (details follow), and let cure. Lay off the dimension on the ordinates and dress to the line. It would be easy now to rout the rabbets without help. If you want to form the rabbets on a saw or shaper, you'll need help to handle the stave's long, limp weight. Be sure you set up ample hold-downs on the saw or shaper table. In addition, you'll need a high fence on your table saw so the rabbet comes out precisely square to its matching part.

GLUING THE SCARFS

Butt-block several good pieces of lumber to make a gluing surface on your spar bench. Cover this with vinyl or waxed paper. I prefer Aerolite or T-88 adhesive, but Plastic Resin has stood up for many years, and it does cost less. Lay the scarfs in position dry against a line of blocks tacked on a chalkline. Drive in a brad or small nail to prevent shifting and let the head be available for pulling later. Take apart a joint at a time, apply the

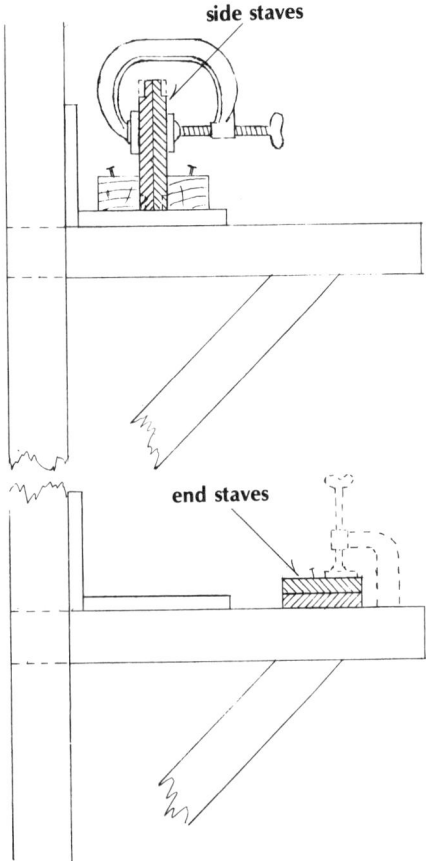

Figure 15-8. MATCHING STAVES ON SPAR BENCH

glue, get the nail back in the same hole, and line up against the blocks (or the bench backboard) with a few C-clamps so nothing can slide around. Cover the area with plastic sheet or waxed paper, place blocks, and clamp up firmly but do not crush.

Observe whether the joint appears to be closed uniformly. Plastic Resin requires pressure, the others do not. Wipe away the glue that extrudes from the joint for several hours, more or less. When all the scarfs in each stave are glued, let the assembly cure for not less than 24 hours. Then plane and sand the joint surfaces for appearance and a fair surface. Be sure there are no globs or runs of glue in the rabbets. Of course, if you have decided to build with corner battens instead of rabbets, this will be a future step. My only advice on this is to use galvanized 3d nails or brads. And make a little gauge for locating the battens uniformly so the outer surfaces meet smoothly everywhere. But first, match the staves for width.

Obviously, both pairs of staves must be exactly alike when finished. Even if the rabbets were made in the two side staves before you scarfed them to full length, try to make them match perfectly. Set these two up on their straight back edges between blocks on the spar bench (see Figure 15-8) or against the backboard. Press them down against the bench and clamp here and there. Be sure the ordinate marks coincide. Now run your hand along the top edge of the pair. If you feel or see the slightest difference, shave this off. Replace the pencil marks that were planed off. Now go back and rework the rabbets accordingly. If you elected to rout the rabbets after scarfing, or if you plan to use the batten glue system, you have no problem. Just dress the staves to match.

The fore-and-aft staves may not be so easy to match. Lay one on top of the other to check and clamp together here and there. Now turn the pair on edge on the open part of the bench and shave one edge. Then turn and shave the other edge. You may have to shift the clamps one at a time if they interfere. Replace any ordinate marks planed off.

I show C-clamps for this matching job in Figure 15-8. If your mast is to be painted, it would be easier and quite all right to use small nails, especially the bright nails that are available in 18 and 16 gauge. If you are in such a hurry that you decide to skip this matching operation, your spar will probably hold together, but don't expect perfect or almost invisible joints.

GLUING UP THE BOX

I have glued up several conventional box spars without help, using Plastic Resin. But I had many sleepless nights afterward. Did I get the 40 or 50 clamps on before the glue started to set? Were the joints fully closed and under proper pressure everywhere? Was the sun too hot that day? You can avoid these problems by getting four or five people to help for an hour or so.

First of all, there's the clamp problem. You should have C-clamps of ample span, and enough of them to place them 12 inches apart. It's unlikely that the average amateur builder will have that many clamps on hand. Borrow or rent. If you plan the assembly for a weekend, you might be able to rent clamps from a couple of local cabinet shops. Or a welder might have some. Professional boatbuilders, of course, will have plenty.

If you can't round up enough clamps, you'll have to build your own. The most common type of make-do clamp does an excellent job. See Figure 15-9. The length of the bolts could be a problem if your mast is large. Ask a hardware dealer if he will let you use 100 of his longest carriage bolts (size is unimportant) and washers for a couple of days. Return them in good condition and pay a rental fee much smaller than their selling price. Or buy them and share with another sparbuilder. Threaded rod works just fine, too. The two-bolt clamp shown can be made from any 2 by 2 stock, or use lighter stock for smaller masts. Allow for the bench-top board beneath and long scrap and/or wedges on top. The slots can be bored and then bandsawed or table sawed.

One-bolt clamps may not be required closer than every two or three feet. These are set up in advance of the hold-downs just tight enough to press the sides

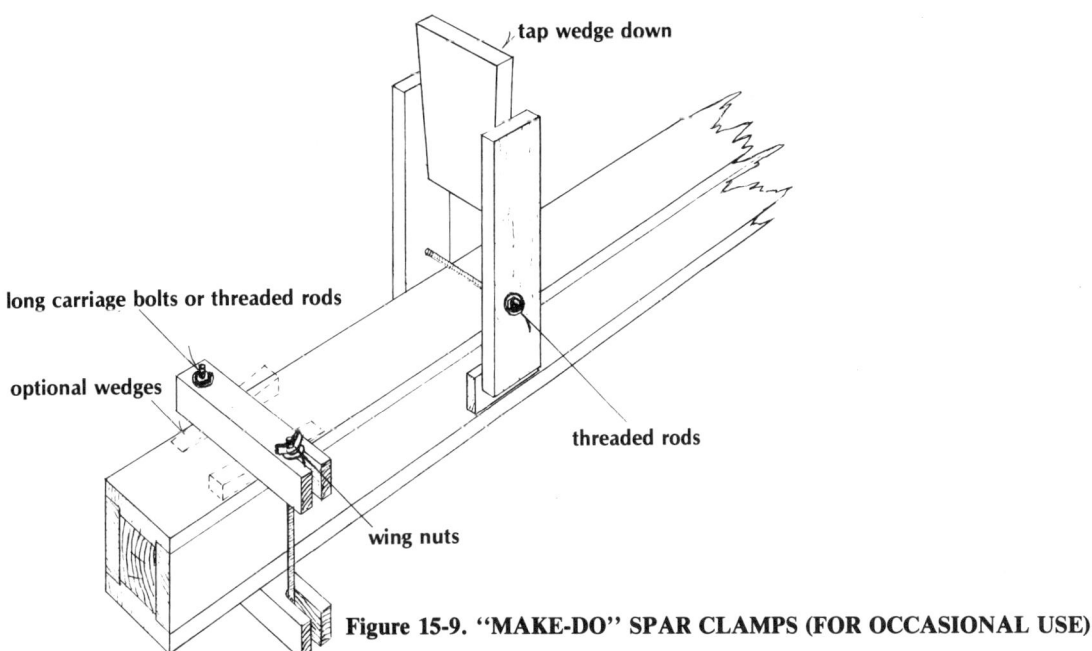

Figure 15-9. "MAKE-DO" SPAR CLAMPS (FOR OCCASIONAL USE)

against the back of the rabbet (or batten) gently, and especially against the blocking. After the end staves are seated well in the rabbets, these one-bolt clamps can be given a couple of taps and then all clamps are pulled down. If you see only a small amount of glue oozing out, tighten down. This assumes that you spread the glue evenly.

A fast crew could probably glue your spar in one step, after the locating and gluing of blocking as shown in Figure 15-3. That is, you apply glue to all four corners and staves simultaneously. This enables the box to rest on its back, with one side against the bench backboard and taper blocks as shown. There's no reason to move anything. Experience here would be very valuable. Two stages might be easier for you. The only real problem is that often the sides have a tendency to go out of square when under pressure. The solution is to cut a dozen spacers to fit temporarily between the side staves. The spacers must be accurately cut — exactly the same size as the blocking and varied to take care of the side tapers. Wrap plastic around them to prevent bonding. Also, don't forget that the side against the backboard can be clamped square.

Another way to guarantee squareness is to include the front stave as a spacer only, without glue. Then, when this three-sided box has cured at least 24 hours, remove the front stave, spacers, and so on. Paint the interior with at least two coats of epoxy resin to prevent rot caused by sweating. (Of course, hollow blocking should have been so treated before assembly.) Any bored holes should be stopped at one end while resin is poured into the holes or applied with a soaked pipe cleaner. Finally, the necessary wiring should be installed for lights, coaxial cable, conduit, or what-have-you.

The front stave must be given two coats of epoxy resin. You can unclamp your spar in 24 to 36 hours. Then plane and sand it clean.

Plane the masthead crane (see below). Rout the radius if your bit is large enough, but skip the head area. Small 1 to 1¼ h.p. routers usually handle no more than a ½-inch radius. You may be able to rent a model that takes a ¾-inch radius bit. A moderately heavy shaper could do this job, but you would need a helper or two, several strong hold-downs, and some skill. Other than these possibilities, you'll have to plane or saw a 45-degree angle, then knock off the 22½-degree flats with a plane, then the high spots, and end up with a hand scraper blade or pieces of broken glass.

The major job, planing the 45-degree angle, can be made easier by sawing it off using your power handsaw — if the guard permits close adjustments. The sketches in Figure 15-10 show radii of ¾ inch, 1 inch, and 1¼ inches and the saw setting required to leave just a smidgen for planing. If you use a table saw, you'll need a temporary wooden face screwed to the fence or clamped to the table. And a helper. Luckily, in this job a slight movement takes off less material, so no damage results. When you get ready to sand these rounded corners, remember that uniformity is a must. Irregularities will mark it as a backyard job. Make your sanding blocks of tooling foam or plaster of paris formed on a board to fit the radius.

Figure 15-11 summarizes spar construction in simplified form.

MASTHEADS

Almost every marconi mast of any size has an enlargement at its head. This is usually called the crane (Figure

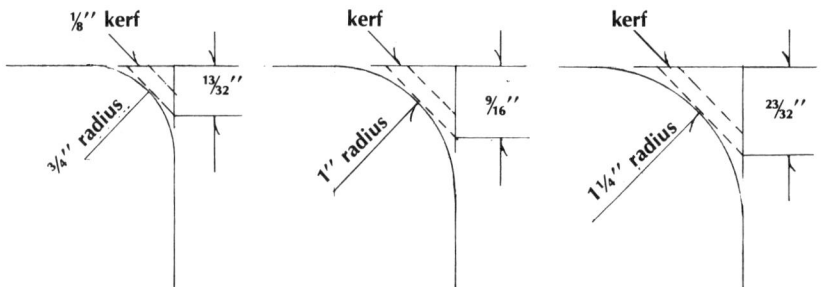

Figure 15-10. SAW SETTINGS TO PRODUCE SPAR RADII

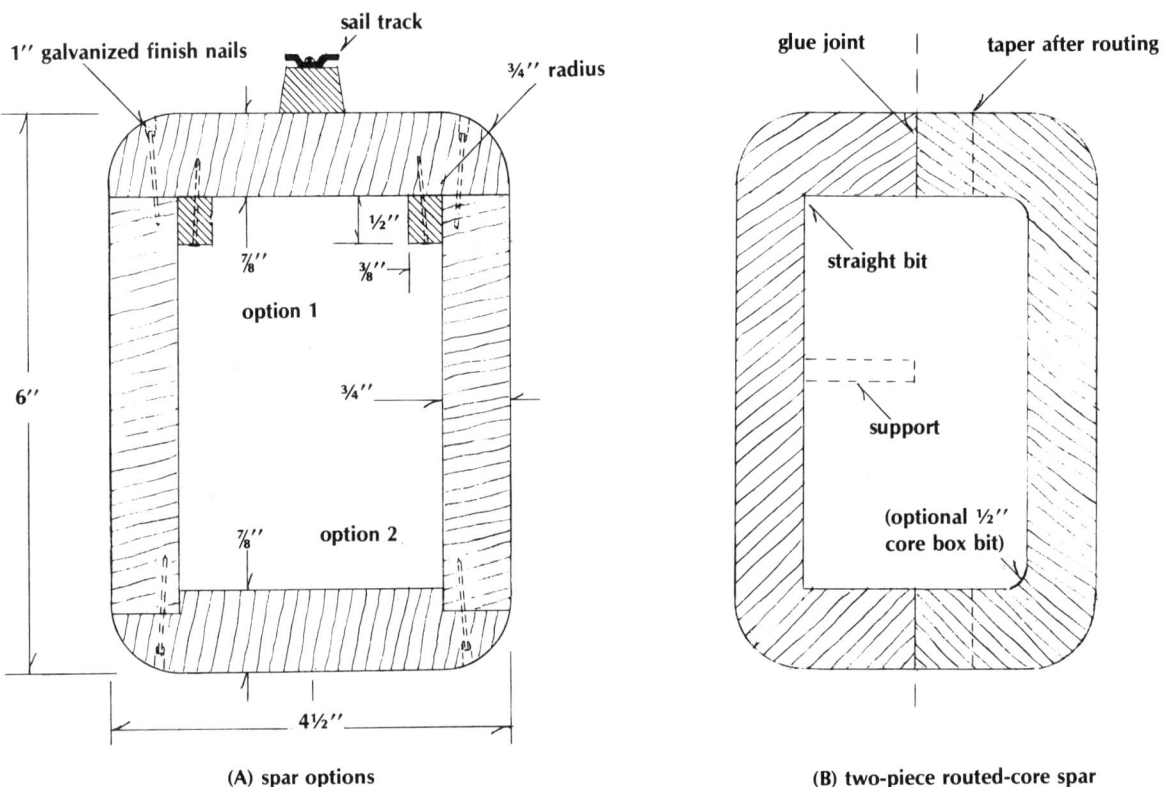

(A) spar options

(B) two-piece routed-core spar

Figure 15-11. SPAR CONSTRUCTION SIMPLIFIED

15-12). The masthead crane is formed from spruce blocks bandsawed to the desired profile the full width of the masthead. These are then glued and faired in before the mast radii are routed. The radius is formed all the way around the new profile, leaving a flat for the tangs bent over the head. The halyard sheave (or sheaves) is also covered with spruce blocks to prevent a wire halyard from jumping over the score in the sheave. These, too, are formed along with the radii, to match.

The slot for the sheave(s) is usually bored out undersized, then cleaned up with a sharp chisel to form a deep mortise. A copper lining in the mortise is no longer considered good practice, for it wears and fouls the halyard. I have seen several light stainless steel boxes, bored for the sheave pins, installed neatly in this slot. To get the bolt (or pin) holes to line up, clamp the box to the side and use it as a guide for the bit. Insert the box, line it up with a pin, then bore clear through. Incidentally, you can save significant weight in rigging by using hollow bolts of bronze or Monel, or threaded stainless steel tubing or pipe.

Figure 15-12, a hypothetical masthead, shows a long diagonal bolt. This is a Herreshoff system designed to resist the stresses of large headsails. I think this would have to be a special bolt. I suggest instead a rod of steel or bronze, threaded at both ends to take eye nuts and

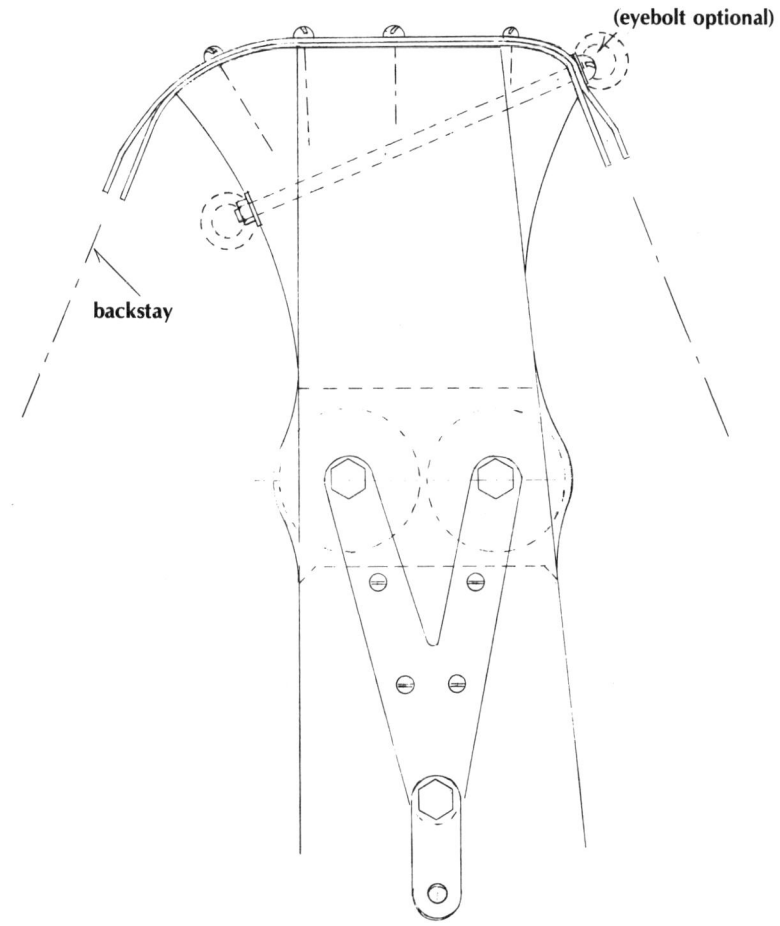

Figure 15-12. MASTHEAD CRANE AND APPROXIMATE TANGS

washers. These may still be available from good hardware manufacturers. If not, they could be fabricated by a clever welder. Or use stainless steel threaded rod from a marine supply house. The forward eye could be used for the spinnaker halyard block. The one aft would be perfect for the topping lift.

The tangs in the drawing are only approximations of what your designer may specify. All screws should be roundheaded. There are several good reasons to avoid flathead countersunk screws. First, working of the tangs has been known to wedge screw heads out of the countersinks. Also, the knife edge of hard, thin tangs can act like a shear, literally slicing off screw heads. Bolts running through tangs and the spar should be encased in compression tubes to prevent crushing the staves and loosening up. Do not scale the drawing in Figure 15-12 — it is just a sketch.

GAFFS AND BOOMS

Gaffs in large sizes should be hollow, if possible. Saving weight in this big spar is extremely important. It makes the difference between a stiff vessel able to carry her sail and a miserably tender tub never up to showing its inherent speed. In addition, because the gaff is under severe bending strains, these loads should be spread by the use of proper bridles and many blocks. Avoid eyebolts except at the ends. Study the sail plans of fine large yachts and old fishing vessels for workable rigging schemes.

There is usually little advantage in trying to save weight in a boom. Weight here acts something like a vang, helping to keep the sail down flat, and it often reduces slatting around in light air. Have a member of the crew stand on the cabin trunk and sit on the boom. This is much faster and safer than a bothersome preventer. I designed a T-boom for Allegra because it is the lowest-cost rigid spar and the easiest for an amateur builder to put together, but I recommend staves of full 1-inch Douglas fir to add weight. Clear stock called stair treads comes up to $1\frac{1}{8}$ inches thick and is ideal for this purpose. Warning: The mainsheet bail on a T-boom exerts a great twisting strain that can damage the gooseneck or split the boom. Provide some sort of

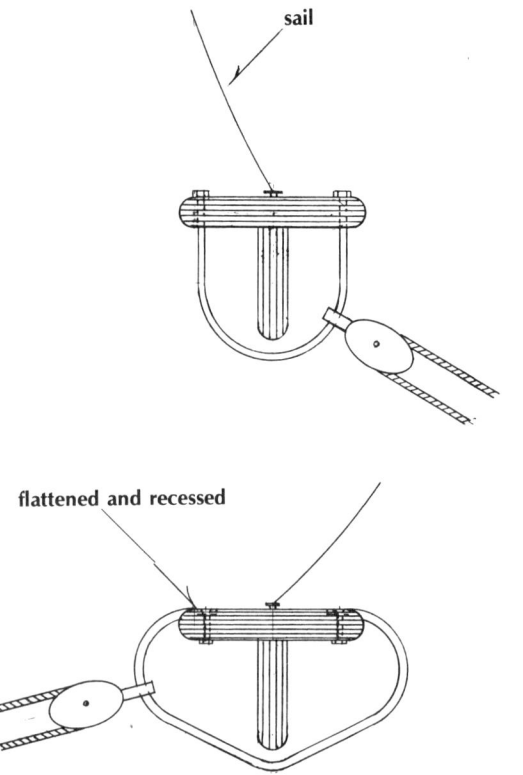

Figure 15-13. T-BOOM MAINSHEET BAILS

swivel or lots of play in the gooseneck, and install a bail that permits the sheet blocks to travel. See Figure 15-13.

SIMPLIFIED MAST ASSEMBLY

For years I have been an admirer of yacht designers, boatbuilders, and sailors from New Zealand and Australia. In the 1960s these folks had the guts to risk all by diving headlong into ferrocement construction. They had the intelligence, skill, and perseverance needed to turn out a large number of successful ferrocement yachts while we belatedly and sloppily overbuilt ours, creating revolting failures or mere disappointments. A better reason for my admiration is that sailors Down Under are so accustomed to their awesome weather that they often sally forth for a casual sail or a race in gales that would send many of us into hiding. They design and build their yachts accordingly.

R.T. Hartley, one of their designers who is little known in the United States, came to my attention in 1972 when Bruce and I were memorizing every word we could find on ferrocement. His book, *Hartley's Ferro-Cement Boat Building,* introduced me to a dozen new ideas and to cruising yachts and motorsailers that look like they're flying even when at anchor. When they're turned loose, they really fly! Consequently, when Hartley described a method of nailing spars instead of clamping, I listened and learned.

The use of nails has long been taboo because of added weight. The effect of a pound of nails distributed over the length of a mast, however, cannot be measured by any instrument I know of. On the other hand, pressure is not distributed as equally as required by glues such as Resorcinol and Plastic Resin. Because of this latter argument, I never used or advocated the use of nails instead of clamps. I did not have the courage. But now we have powerful adhesives with crack-filling qualities that give even a tyro's $\frac{1}{16}$-inch gaps 100 percent strength. That's why I am including a description of how to secure with nails until the glue cures.

Here's the procedure. (See Figure 15-11.) Locate the blocking very accurately on the aft stave, and nail and glue, using 1- to 1½-inch galvanized finish nails according to the thickness of the material. If you have helpers, go right ahead, but if you are shorthanded, let the assembly cure for 24 hours. Next, lay old lumber or blocks on the bench and drive the same nails the full length of the forward and aft staves on about 6-inch centers. Let the points come through about ⅛ inch, and note that the nails are at an angle. This angle will tend to pull the side staves tightly into the rabbet or batten gluing corner, assuming that you have by now nailed and glued the battens accurately.

You'll need several small blocks on the bench to elevate the tapered ends of the side staves so their centerlines are level. Set the two staves on edge, apply the glue, match the aft stave with the various pencil marks, and start driving. Have someone follow immediately to set the heads in about ¼ inch or enough to clear the finished radius. Flip the three-sided box onto the bench, remove the elevating blocks, and weight down or clamp the box. Wipe off the oozing glue. Paint the interior with two coats of epoxy resin and let the assembly stand for 24 hours. If there is any indication that a side is not standing square at any point, press or clamp in a small spacer, to be removed later. Install the wiring, conduit, or whatever.

In the meantime, coat the forward stave inside surface with epoxy resin. Drive nails as described, and weight and clamp to the bench to maintain alignment. Complete as for a clamped-up mast.

I expect critics to ask, "Ain't them one-inch nails a leetle small?" No, because even if you could pull all them nails, the spar would still be full strength. After all, do the clamps hold the conventional spar together? Hardly. Now, I would not use nails with Resorcinol or Plastic Resin, for they require high pressure evenly distributed to produce hairline joints. The new adhesives only have to be held together immovably during curing.

There is one fault with nailing. The final surface is probably unsatisfactory for varnished spars. When they are filled for painting, however, you wouldn't know that nails were under the lovely contours.

A TWO-PIECE MAST

The routed-core spar construction method is suitable for small masts. I built a 36-foot stick about 3⅞ by 5½ inches by routing out the centers of two full 2-inch-thick vertical-grain spruce planks. Of course, this method wastes material, but it is fast and produces a good spar while eliminating most gluing problems. Today the planks would have to be scarfed.

Once you have a straight edge on each, the tapered curvature on the leading edges must be laid out, sawed, and dressed. Match the two pieces by planing simultaneously with the pieces clamped together. Don't be concerned about the side tapers at this point. Tack pieces of scrap to the planks or staves in the areas to be left solid so there will be a neat termination of the routed core. If you don't have a manufactured router guide, screw a guide piece to the router base. This is to follow the outer contour of the spar. If the hollow works out to be wider than the router base, leave a ridge near the center for support, then chisel it out later. Rout in two or three passes. In some cases you may have to deepen the cut by pulling the bit out of the collet slightly. Be sure the collet is locked tightly! Any diameter of bit from ⅜ to ¾ inch will do. The latter will create a load on the motor if you do not take shallow cuts.

Now for the side tapers. The material must be removed from the *open* side, so lay out the curvature on ordinates in the usual way. This is an easy freehand resawing job for a power handsaw, but not a table saw. If the kerfs do not reach from each side, the remaining bit can be sawed with a bandsaw or even a hand ripsaw. If you do the resawing entirely with a bandsaw, play safe on the line. When the two are dressed down to the line, rout out generous grooves through the solid areas for wiring, or whatever, and provide a scupper in the butt. Also rout the slot for the halyard sheave or sheaves. Now, when you glue up on your straight bench, the sides will be sprung in so there is no run-out of grain. It's best to lay out blocks on the bench to locate the tapers equally about the centerline. Then glue and clamp in the usual way. Complete the mast as described above.

SPAR TERMS

Stick length is measured from the tenon in the heel to the truck. The tenon is that reduced square that fits in the mast step or socket. *Bury* is measured from the bottom of the socket to the top of the deck. *Hounded length* is measured from deck to the hounds, the point where the shrouds join the mast, eyesplices resting on a hardwood bolster or shoulder or shackled to an eye band or wye. *Deck to pin* is from the deck to the pin in the peak halyard sheave or block. There is usually a shoulder at this point to support an eye band or the splices of the upper shrouds. The *head* is the rapidly tapering portion from that shoulder to the tip or truck, which is also confusingly called the head. The *truck* is a circular hardwood disc mortised over the tip of the head and containing sheaves or slots for the flag halyards. The *pole* is the length from the hounds to the shoulder at pin height. Some of these terms are included in Figure 15-14.

SOLID SPARS FROM A TIMBER OR BAULK

A timber or baulk is a rough-sawed squared piece of lumber, not a sapling or tree. Solid masts are used today only in gaff rig. Again, Sitka spruce is the best, but being soft, it does not take the chafing of gaff and boom jaws well. Douglas fir makes excellent spars, even though it is heavier. Other good woods are white or Norway pine and a spruce in the Northeast that is quite knotty. This makes good large spars if the knots are quite small — the size of a dime and, of course, tight. I don't know whether any is available at this time.

Try to pick a straight timber in which the heart is near the center at both ends. You can check the solidity of the heart clear through by having a pal rap with a hammer on the heart while you place your ear at the other end. A solid heart will conduct this sound readily. A bad heart will transmit a mushy sound. If a good timber otherwise has a slight bend, you may be able to take out the bend by blocking up the timber and placing heavy weights on it for six months or a year. Look out for cross grain (run-out), exposed heart, sap pockets and sapwood, checks anywhere but near the ends, and so on. A spiral grain is very strong. However, you will need three or four feet more timber than the total length of your spar (its stick length) because of the tendency to check at the ends. If a good timber shows some wind (twist), you may have to purchase a larger size and work it into shape. This is extra work, but perhaps you can buy such a timber at lower cost. As mentioned, the West Coast is the most likely place to find large timbers.

If your solid spar can come out of a 6 by 6, the rough shaping can be done with a big power saw. Four or five ordinary sawhorses would make a satisfactory temporary bench. If the timber is an 8 by 8 or larger, you may have to shape it with a broadaxe and adze, which means it will have to be supported on heavy blocks or timbers at just above knee height. If you are an expert with a chain saw and wouldn't recognize an adze if it crept up and bit you, that's your answer. But be sure you can saw right on the vertical. Suffice it to say that your horses or blocks must be level across, and long enough to permit rolling the timber 360 degrees.

Your first move is to decide which is to be the straight aft side. If the timber has a slight bend (1 inch in 30 feet) that could be pulled out by the head or springstay, pick this hollow side to face aft. There must be no bend sideways. Lay the timber with the hollow side up. Use a couple of weights to pull it down to the blocks and a

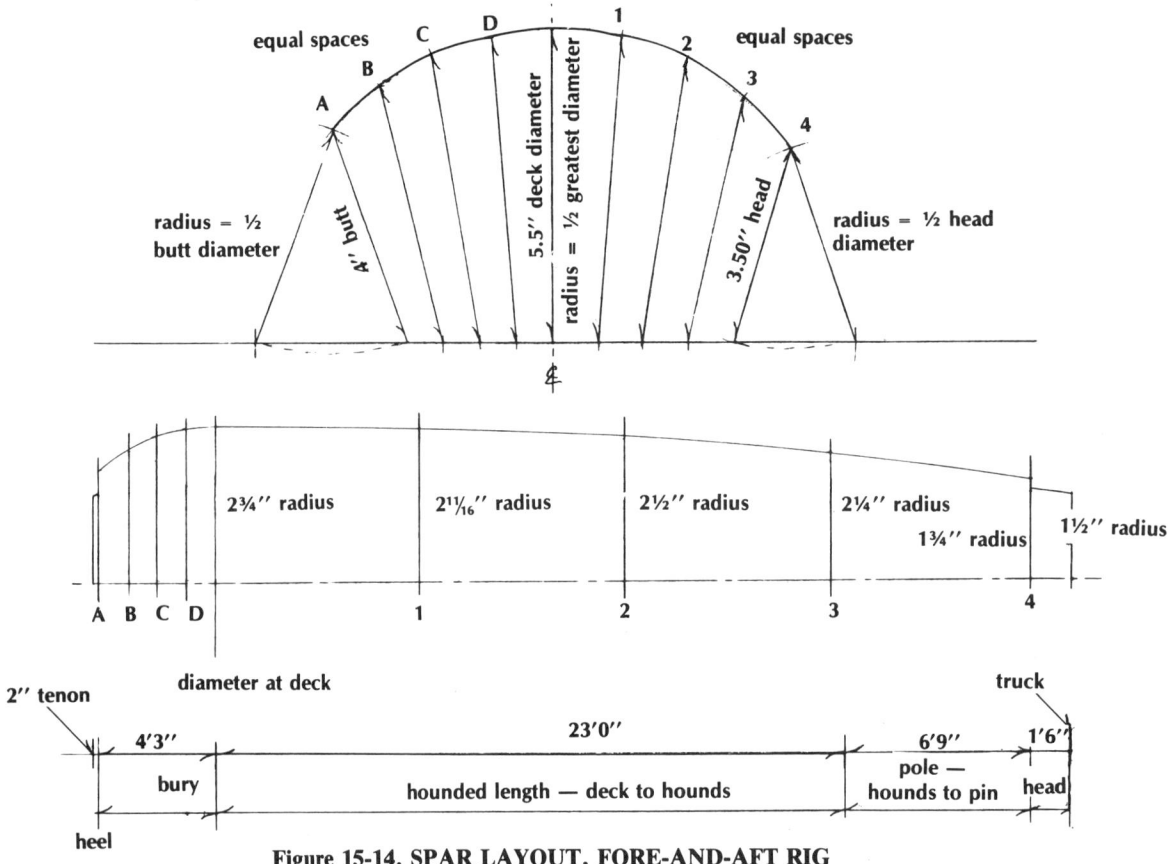

Figure 15-14. SPAR LAYOUT, FORE-AND-AFT RIG

long wooden jointer or jack or an electric plane to take off the sawed surface. Check for fairness with a chalked 1 by 3 on the flat and level across if there is wind in the timber. The other sides must be squared to this first surface.

The next step is to snap a chalkline down the center. Is the timber actually relaxed? You'll see that you can shift an end slightly without moving the opposite end. To relax the stick, lift an end so the sag clears all the blocks or horses. Prop it there, then level down to the blocks and mark each location. A series of blocks tacked in these spots will fix the timber while you find the centerline. It doesn't matter if the stick now shows a slight bend. It is relaxed, and your shaping will produce a straight spar. You can see why the rough timber must be somewhat larger than the finished diameter of the mast.

Locate the center of the heart in each end. Plumb a line top to bottom. Hook your chalkline around a nail in the marks and stretch it taut. Stand near the center of the stick and press a thumb firmly on the line. Carefully lift the line far to the right and let it snap, then lift far to the left and snap. You now have a perfect centerline from which all diameters will be laid out. Go over the chalkline with a pencil and straightedge so you don't lose it.

LAYING OUT A SPAR

There are different, slightly contradictory methods for laying out spars for the fore-and-aft rig. You can use the proportions from Chapelle given earlier, or you can use a geometrical projection system (see Figure 15-14). I have used both without complaints. I have also arbitrarily picked a diameter at the gaff of 90 percent of the deck diameter, picked two-thirds for the head, sprung a batten from the hounds to head, and — voilà — a mast layout! But this was for my own spar. So don't do as I do, do as I say. Also, there is a nice shape to the geometrical design, and the masts might be nearly identical if one were superimposed on the other.

Start the projection method by swinging an arc equal to the 5½-inch deck diameter on a piece of plywood or paper — a 2¾-inch radius in Figure 15-14. Take 3½ inches (approximately .65) as a rugged masthead (where the peak halyard goes), and step off the radius of 1¼ inches along the arc to point 4 in the drawing. Then swing from there to the baseline. Divide the arc geometrically from the vertical centerline to point 4 into four equal parts (or as many as you choose). Do the same along the baseline. Connect as shown. These are the radii at four equally spaced ordinates on the mast

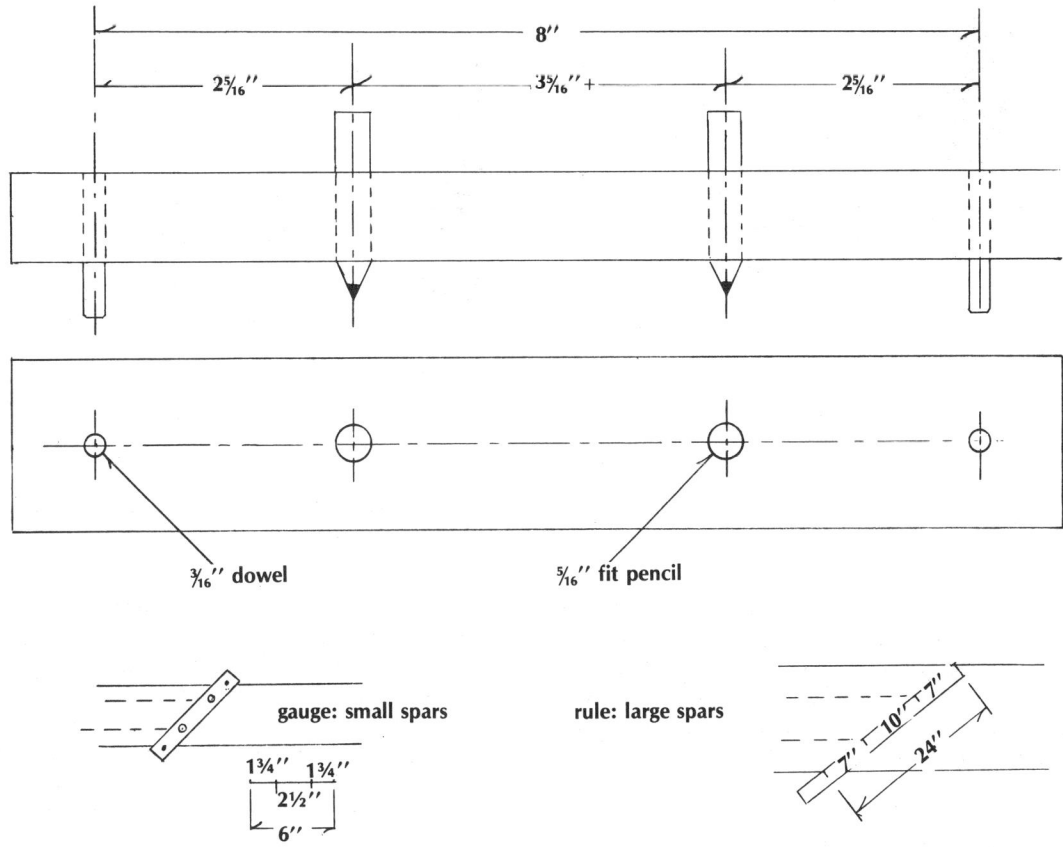

Figure 15-15. DEVICES FOR EIGHT-SIDING SPARS

from deck to head. Divide the left half of the arc similarly to find the diameters of the bury.

Lay out the ordinates and radii on the timber surface and all other points of your spar length. Drive brads at these points and spring a batten fair to correct small errors. Sawing close to this line will be little problem if you have access to a bandsaw large enough to carry the weight and accommodate the thickness. Perhaps a steady helper can aid by pulling moderately as you guide and push the stick. Or it can be sawed with a big power saw by duplicating the layout of the opposite side. If the kerfs don't meet (unlikely), the material in between must be sawed out with a ripsaw. Of course, you could do this in one pass of a chain saw, but please allow plenty of room for error.

Now you have both sides rough tapered. Plane these surfaces close to the lines, preferably with a wooden jack. Mark the ordinates square to the aft face, then swing the same diameters or merely pick up the measurements from the face. Again saw fairly close to the lines and dress down nice and fair. You now have a clean square timber tapering gracefully to head and butt. There may be just a slight curvature in the aft straight side, with the head bending aft a smidgen.

AN EIGHT-SIDE GAUGE

Now we come to an intriguing part of spar shaping — the octagon. The spar must be eight-sided in the same proportions from butt to head, unless it is to remain square in the bury. Figure 15-15 shows several methods, using gauges and rules, to accomplish the lining off rapidly and accurately. The upper detail is a gauge laid out for spars from just under 8 inches in diameter down to as small as 3 or 4 inches. The lower left-hand sketch dimensions a gauge for 6-inch and smaller spars. It is easier to use. These gauges are simply dragged along with their dowels against the side of the stick, leaving pencil lines in their wakes. At the lower right, I show the use of a rule, making marks at the 7-inch and 17-inch points all along the spar, to give you a series of dots as close as you have time for. Or you could make a gauge on the 24-, 17-, and 7-inch marks.

Set your power handsaw to an accurate 45 degrees and rip off the corners. Stay safely away from the lines and roll the stick if the kerfs do not meet. To rotate a heavy timber, clamp a four-foot 2 by 4 to the butt and heave. The last time I built a solid spar, I knocked off the rough with an electric plane. I must admit that this

Figure 15-16. *Simple hand-made spar calipers.*

Figure 15-17. *Sanding boards of plaster, paper tubing, and shaped wood.*

saved hours and sweat. Then I took a couple of passes on the corners to 16-side the spar to just above the gooseneck. If there had been jaws on the boom, the mast would have been rounded to below the jaw's lowest position and an oak ring would have been fitted to support the boom.

SHAPING A SOLID SPAR

I discussed a drawknife in Chapter Two, but large sizes are needed for spar work. This is the traditional tool for knocking off to 8 and 16 sides, but it is designed for rough work. It is very easy, if you pull the drawknife straight along the stick, to catch in the grain and rip off a splinter as long as your arm. This is wrong. The proper draw is a spiraling motion at about 60 degrees across the stick. Find a drawknife with a blade well over 2 inches deep and about 24 to 26 inches between the handles. See the sharpening notes in Part One. If you let the knife bite too deep, mark the area with a crayon so you can avoid planing there and creating a low spot. I made the simple calipers shown in Figure 15-16 many years ago. Set yours to the diameter of the original planed 8 sides, then you can gauge the high spots. I prefer to work on a quarter for the full length, rather than rotating the spar. By the time you have worked all four quarters, you will be amazed at the improvement in the fourth quarter. No matter. Go back and shave the high spots until your eye and your calipers tell you that you have a fair spar. You can't get perfection with a drawknife. Thus, it's time to plane.

I have planed several good-sized spars with small planes. I hope you can buy or borrow a wooden jack plane about 16 inches long. Work end to end, a quarter at a time, then repeat, then rotate for the next quarter, and so on. When you think the spar is perfect, go over it again with a 24-inch jointer set fine. It will find high spots you won't believe are there. Never plane at the slightest angle to the grain. Your chances of finding a hollow wooden smooth plane of the right hollow are remote. So use ordinary window glass broken up so the fragments have a concave sharp edge. Even though these may not match the spar's actual radii, glass is great for taking off fine shavings like fuzz.

Follow with a coarse 50- to 60-grit open-coat garnet sandpaper or aluminum oxide production paper. Do not waste your money with white flint paper. You may prefer to double over the sheet, holding it under your entire palm. The hollow sanding block in Figure 15-17 was made with plaster on a board. You may want several to fit the spar reasonably. In general, stroke around the spar at about a 45-degree angle. Next, use about 100- or 120-grit paper and go with the grain on the last half-dozen strokes if you intend to paint. If varnish is your thing, finish with 200-grit folded sheets, but no blocks. If your spars show checks, do not panic. These have no effect on strength as long as they follow the grain. Use an oil can to squirt clear Cuprinol generously into the checks. Most checks will open and close with the weather and humidity. Never fill them with anything, because moisture will then get in and stay there, forming a natural feeding ground for fungi.

I wish I could tell you that epoxy is the perfect sealer for solid spars, but no one seems to be sure of that. I would, however, cheerfully settle for a couple of coats of boiled linseed oil thinned with one-third turpentine (some swear by thinning with kerosene). After this is well dried, scuff-sand lightly and varnish with four coats. Or don't varnish, but give the spar a couple of coats of the oil during the season. I have had good results by soaking the spar with two thinned coats of varnish, followed by three or four of full strength. Sand lightly between coats, of course. Polyurethane varnish sounds good and looks great on some things I have built, but these were things that were not out in the

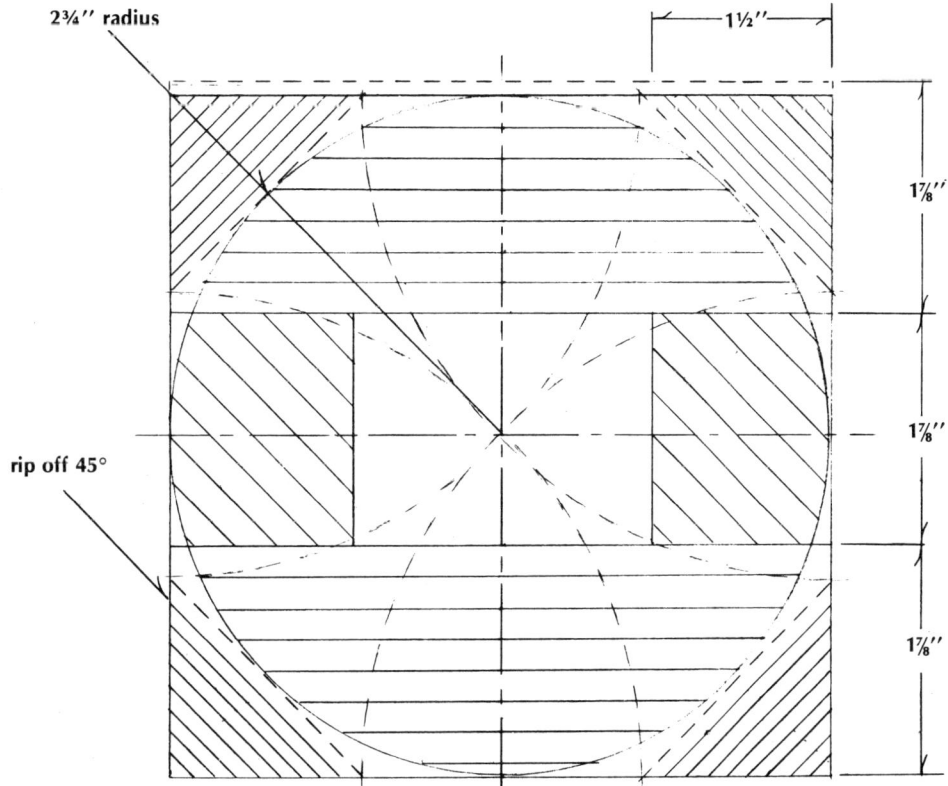

Figure 15-18. HOLLOW-CORE FORE-AND-AFT MAST PLAN

weather. Get competent advice on modern finishes before you use any of them.

LAMINATED HOLLOW-CORE SPARS

The answer to the lack of long spar lumber is to scarf and laminate. The example diagrammed in Figure 15-18 is a 5½-inch-diameter mast built up of three layers or laminations of Douglas fir or Sitka spruce. Most yards handle 2-inch rough spruce stock. Such boards can be planed to 1⅞ inches. The few remaining saw marks, if any, are of little concern. The mill may be able to plane only one side if the dimensions are close. Epoxy glue will fill these minute depressions and hold securely. The mill may have to resaw a fir timber to get the 1⅞ inches when planed, for rough fir boards are not stock items. Use only vertical-grain lumber. The two internal laminations measuring 1½ by 1⅞ inches may be ripped out of a standard 2 by 6. The side tapers can be laid out on this plank from the layout instructions above. It's best not to take all the taper off one side, for the grain would then run out. Lay it out about a centerline. The example would taper down to only ½ inch at its tip. Scarf into full-length staves and dress to lines, then put aside.

Next, lay out the tapers on the two side staves exactly as described for the solid stick (above) and dress nearly to size. Scarf into perfect full-length staves with the scarfs well scattered.

Gluing is the next step. You should nail straight boards to your horses or blocks, or build a precision bench, so the tapered end of the spar can be elevated by a series of small blocks to compensate for the taper. Snap a straight line on the bench board to align the aft edge of the spar, remembering that this fore-and-aft spar tapers above the hounds and may have a slight curvature from deck to hounds. Lay a side stave on the bench, make a dry run with the internal laminations in place, and fit the solid blocking at the bury, hounds to head, and at any other required areas. Disassemble, spread glue, and reassemble. Clamp well and let cure for at least 24 hours. Then glue on the remaining stave. You can make this in one step if you nail enough blocks on the bench to spring the internal staves correctly. In this case, the entire side of the spar would be outlined in quite high blocks between which all the parts would be pressed down, then clamped. This calls for fast action and several good helpers. Clean up all excess glue as it oozes out. When the rough is cured, plane all over to a good working surface, then proceed as described above for the solid stick.

This cored spar will be just as strong as a solid of the same dimensions and significantly lighter, and it will save lumber. A larger spar could be built with more laminations, perhaps from 1½-inch stock fir lumber, or

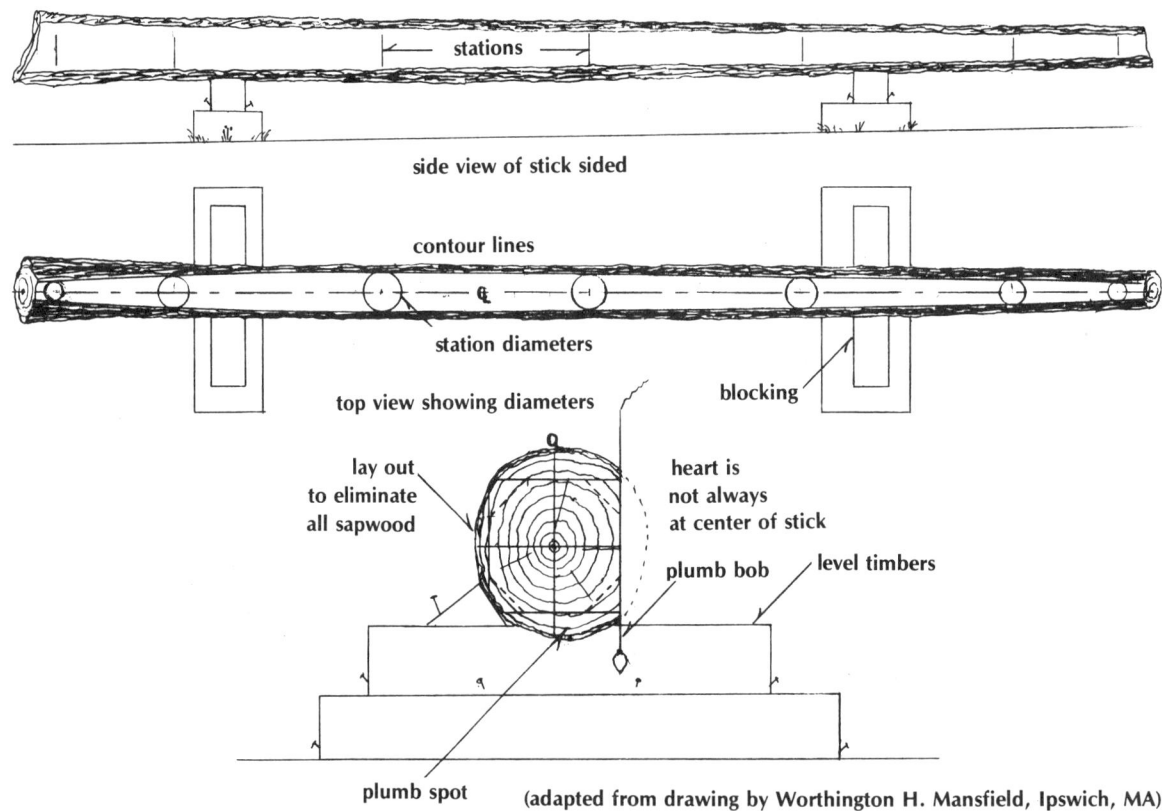

Figure 15-19. HEWING A SOLID SPAR

you could use many more laminations of thinner material. The more glue joints, the stiffer the spar.

MASTS HEWN FROM TREES OR SAPLINGS

I promised to describe briefly the construction of a mast from a tree trunk or log. As I said at the beginning, I have no such experience, so I am going to summarize an article called "Sparmaking," by Worthington H. Mansfield, that appeared in the July-August 1943 issue of *The Rudder* magazine. Many of the details in the article have been covered in this chapter, but Mansfield included instructions regarding the use of the broadaxe and adze. However, no written instruction can make a skilled craftsman. Only working alongside an expert and then years of using these tools can do that. Maybe some modern power tools will be more suitable to a worker with less skill but lots of will.

Here is what Mansfield has to say about materials (remember, this was in 1943). Woods he suggests are:

White pine, lowland growth; Canadian black spruce (his first choice); red spruce; Norway pine; western fir (presumably Douglas fir); Riga fir (excellent but tough to work; no source known today).

Mansfield suggests removing bark while the wood is still green, and floating it in salt water for six months or longer. Then nail on a 4-foot cleat so the log can be turned over every month. Place the log on two timbers about one-quarter of its total length from each end so weight distribution eliminates sag. Blocks should be at knee height, level, and long enough so the spar can be rolled. Secure with blocking, wedges, and cleats. Remove all protruding knots, loose bark, and so on. At each supporting block, hew a plumb spot. Could this be done with a chain saw by shifting the block temporarily? It must be accurate. Roll the stick so it rests on these flats. Plumb a line through the heart at each end, and snap a chalkline from these. From your spar plan, take measurements of lengths, such as bury, deck to hounds, hounds to head, and so on, and divide length as in my solid spar layout in Figure 15-19.

Here is Mansfield's description of chalklining the rounded side: "Leave one-quarter inch more wood at each station than called for by any of the dimensions. Lay off on both sides of centerline, and with chalkline (and preferably natural white chalk), line from spot or station to station on both sides of stick. You will now be snapping a line on a rounded surface, and this procedure is much different from snapping a line on a flat surface and requires quite some practice and skill to obtain a good fair line. The line must not be pulled too taut, neither must it be too slack. The right amount of tension must be learned by practice. When ready to snap the line, raise it gently, all the while rolling between index finger and thumb toward you, standing on the opposite side of the stick from which you are lining, and let fly or drop. After a little practice, a beautiful fair line can be struck on the round side of a stick."

With a sharp chopping axe, stand on the timber and notch within ½ inch of the line, about 10 to 12 inches apart for the full length, both sides. Mansfield says, "Take a broadaxe and proceed to beat off surplus wood between scores, taking care not to cross the line. After all surplus wood has been beaten off both sides of the stick, start tracing the line for the entire length of the stick on both sides." (Does he mean a pencil mark?) "Then with plumb bob at hand, hew an accurate plumb spot at each station mark, and make a mark with heavy black crayon at each plumb spot across entire plumb spot perpendicularly." Start hewing with the broadaxe at the end of the stick, keeping an eye on the plumb spot ahead of you. Surely, if you practice on an old post or telephone pole, you could do this with a chain saw. But keep it vertical! That's the trick. After the sides are plumb, turn the log on its side and snap another centerline. Remember, one side must be straight — the aft side. Line off again as above with chalkline between stations, leaving ¼ inch extra wood. "Score, beat off, trace, spot, and hew. In spotting at each station this time, instead of using the plumb bob, use a steel square at all stations and be accurate in squaring."

Mansfield at this point goes into the 8-siding procedure I have described above. He must be right, but to me the spar seems a bit rough for accurate dividing. Wouldn't it be better to fair up this square somewhat with a jack plane, then mark the octagon? Mansfield takes off the eighths with a drawknife, then the sixteenths. Finally, he planes. The remaining procedure is as I have covered it a few pages back.

The second part of Mansfield's article includes a lot on his tools, making hafts for adze and broadaxe, grinding an axe, and other information useful if you wish to build your spars in a strictly traditional way. It's good to know how these things were done by those skilled craftsmen, even if you never intend to hew a mast from a tree trunk.

If you have remained alert to this point, you already have the essential ingredient (perseverance) of a respected joinerman. If you show that same splendid characteristic in the performance of your work, you will not merely succeed, you will excel. And I shall take pride in having contributed something to that excellence.

Appendix

The Allegra 24 is a stout little cruising cutter that was developed from Bruce Bingham's well-known Flicka, a 20-foot sloop. The new design by Fred P. Bingham, Sr., and Nelson Zimmer provides an alternative for those admirers of Flicka who found her just a trifle too small. Size, of course, is a relative thing, but the addition of an enclosed head will make the extra expense worthwhile for more modest sailors.

Several yards on the East Coast and West Coast, and Mestiza Yachts in the Philippines are now licensed to build Allegra. She may be had in either cold-molded wood or fiberglass. The former construction specifications call for three layers of mahogany planking sealed with epoxy. External iron or lead ballast is also specified.

The interior layout is straightforward, with V-berths forward and head and hanging locker amidships. Just aft of the partitioning bulkhead is the galley with ice chest and sink to port and stove, counter space, and storage racks to starboard. Main cabin transom berths measure 6 feet 5 inches. Headroom is 6 feet 3 inches. A bridge deck cockpit 6 feet 7 inches long adds space below decks and will be a secure and comfy place to lie in the cockpit. This important feature also minimizes the amount of water that can collect in the cockpit if pooped and will prevent it from washing through into the cabin below.

A small diesel can be fitted, or, alternatively, a 7½ h.p. outboard may be used on a transom bracket and stowed under the port cockpit seat. The designer favors a sweep as auxiliary power, as he believes Allegra's rig will move her well in light airs.

A cutter rig of 348 square feet and a waterline of 20 feet 10 inches should indeed move this husky little brute and, with roller furling on the jib, reducing sail should be an easy task when the wind picks up. The staysail is fitted to a club and traveler, so the rig is self-tending with the exception of the jib. She should be easy and fun to sail. Four persons could cruise her coastwise and two would find her adequate for more extended passagemaking, including a ride over the mountains, because her 8-foot beam and shallow draft make trailering a possibility as well.

For more information contact Fred P. Bingham, Yacht Design and Construction, 249 Montana Way, Los Osos, California 93402. (805) 528-8017.

(Reprinted courtesy of *Cruising World*)

ALLEGRA 24

LOA	24′ 0″ (7.3 m)
LWL	20′ 10″ (6.3 m)
Beam	8′ 0″ (2.7 m)
Draft	3′ 5½″ (1.1 m)
Sail Area	348 sq. ft. (32.3 sq m)
Ballast	2,400 lb. (1,225 kg)
Displacement	6,500 lb. (2,812 kg)
Spars	Wood or aluminum
Hull	Wood or fiberglass
Auxiliary	Outboard or optional marine diesel
Berths	4
Designers	Fred P. Bingham and Nelson Zimmer

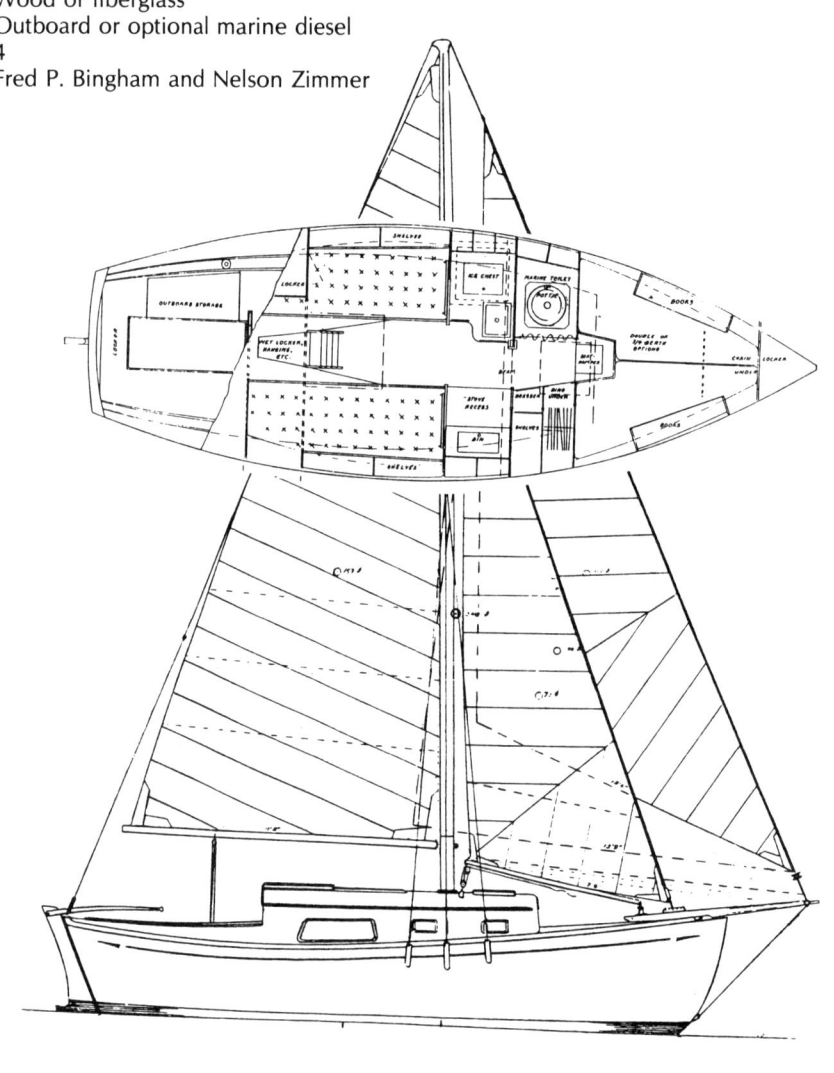

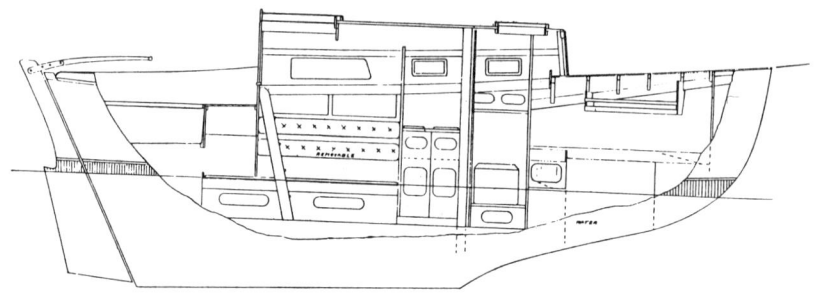

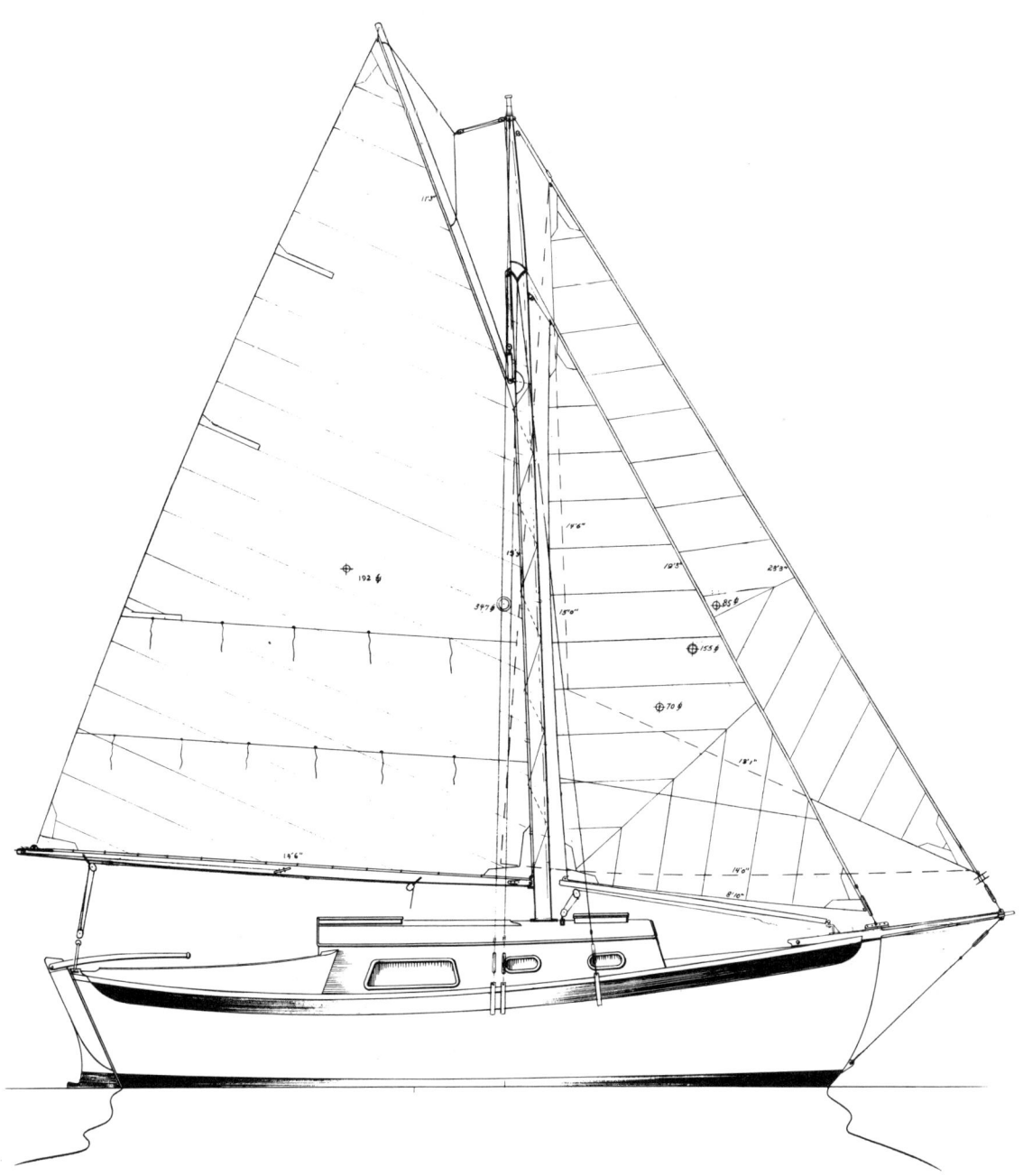

ALLEGRA SAIL PLAN — GAFF RIG

Index

A

Access opening, 8
Accessories: radial-arm saw, 76, 79; router, 50, 51, 53
Adhesives, for boatbuilders, 110, 111, 112
Adhesives: Aerolite, 96, 97, 99, 110, 111, 112, 121, 123, 128, 136, 137, 168, 172-175, 195, 212, 217, 245, 251, 252, 256; Arabol, 115; contact, 205, 206, 207; lagging, 115; Plastic Resin, 96, 97, 99, 108, 110, 111, 112, 121, 136, 137, 174, 251, 252, 256; T-88, 110, 111, 112, 156, 173, 212, 217, 245, 251; Thiokol, 110, 173
Adjustable counterbores, 28
Adjustable dado cutter, 73, 74
Adjusting plane, 20
Aerolite. *See* Adhesives
Alignment: hinges, 28, 29; table-saw, 69
Allegra, 210; mast, 247, 254
Alterations, effects of, 9
Amateur woodwork, 5-7
Anchor chocks, 229, 230
Anchorfast nails, 13, 175
Angle, plane iron: grinding, 22
Appliance motor, jointer, 58
Arabol ("Airball") adhesive, 115
Assembly, plane, 23
Auger bits, 24, 25, 61; ship's, 26
Awl, brad, 28, 29

B

Backrests, 185, 186
Bandsaws, 62, 63-67; adjustment, 64, 65; kit-built, 82
Bar clamps, 30, 32
Basic tools, list, 11
Basin, wash, 209, 211
Batten, sheer, 151, 152

Beam, hatch, 220, 221; laminated, 8, 146-149, 173; sawn, 146, 147; setting, 150, 151; sole, 141, 142, 143
Beam pattern (mold), 146, 147, 150
Belt, sanding, 48, 49
Belt sander, bench, 55, 56; portable, 48, 49
Bench, spar, 248, 249, 251, 252
Bench hook, 16, 97, 98
Bench sanders: belt, 48, 49, 55, 56; disc, 55
Bench stops, 97, 98
Bench vises, 32, 33
Bending, saw kerf, 108
Berths, 180-184
Bevel edge tool, 22
Bevel gauge, 15
Bits: drill, 25-26, 27; rabbet, router, 87; rounding, 86; router, pilot, 52, 53; spade, 61
Blades: bandsaw, 65; carbide-tipped saw, 70; hacksaw, 34, 35; planer, 49, 50; saw, 43-45, 69, 70; table-saw, 69, 70
Blind groove, 128, 129
Blocking, deck, 152, 153
Block plane, 17; assembly, 23
Block sanding, 47
Board, shooting. *See* Shooting board
Bonding, bulkheads to hulls, 139
Books: boatbuilding, 4; tool information, 11
Booms, 248, 255, 256. *See also* Spars
Boring, edge, 79
Boring: guides, 123, 124, 217, 218; jigs, 92, 123, 124, 217, 218; plug counterbore, 25
Bowsprit, traditional, 6
Box, deck storage, 227
Box, miter, 15, 16, 17
Box, tool, 11, 40-42
Box joint, 96, 97, 131, 227; jig, 96, 97
Brace and bit, 24, 25
Brad awl, 28, 29
Breast drill, 24, 46

Breasthook, 145
Brookstone Company, 20
Buffing: tool edge, 22; wheel, 22, 54
Bulkhead racks, 217, 218, 219
Bulkheads, 135-138, 139, 169, 199, 200-202; bonding, 139; installation, 133, 134, 135, 139; moldings and trim, 199, 200-202
Bullnose plane, 19
Bulwarks and rails, 239-243
Bungs, 37, 109, 110. *See also* Plugs
Bunkboards, 182, 183
Bunks. *See* Berths
Burnishing, 39
Butt joint, dovetailed, 122

C

Cabinet, medicine, 209, 214-216
Cabinetmaker's blade, 44, 45
Cabinet scraper, 37, 38
Cabin side, systems, 169-173; tumblehome, 150
Cabin sole, 135, 136, 138-145
Cabin trunk, 165-178
Camber, 103, 104, 146, 147, 165, 166; cabin, 165, 166; layout, 103, 104; scribers, 103, 104, 165, 166
Canvas decks, 156, 157, 160, 161
Caps, rail, 242
Carbide-tipped blade, 45, 70
Carlings, 142, 143, 144, 149, 150, 170, 171; alignment, 149, 150; canted, 170, 171
Carpet insulation, 207
Catalogs, tool, 12
C-clamps, 30, 31
C-clamp buttons, 31
Ceiling: carpet, 207; wood, 205, 206-207
Centers, dowel, 123
Chemicals, rot-treating, 116, 117
Chem-Tech, 110, 111, 112, 157
Chisel, mortising jig, 62, 63
Chisels, 33, 34, 35, 37, 62, 63; techniques, 34, 35, 37
Chocks, bow, 241, 243
Chromated copper arsenate, 116, 117
Chuck: collet, 61; Jacobs, 61
Clamps: bar, 30, 32; C-clamps, 30, 31; Jorgensen, 32; laminating, 171; pipe, 32; sheer, 151; spar, 249, 250, 252; spring, 32; quick-acting, 30
Cleat, wooden, 110
Coamings, 230, 231; hatch, 221, 222, 223
Cockpit bunks, 236
Cockpits, 230, 231-232
Cold-molded trunk top, 174, 175
Collet chuck, 61
Comb hold-down, 71, 72
Combination saw blade, 44, 45
Companionway, 7
Compass, scribing and spiling, 39, 40
Compass saw, 15, 17
Concave surface, sanding, 56
Concentric sawing, 67
Copper naphthanate, 116
Corner: joint, 125; moldings, 199, 200-202; rounding, 88
Corner post, cabin, 167-169

Corrugations, planer, 37, 38, 55
Counterbores, 25, 28
Countersinks, 25, 28
Cove: bulwarks/rail, 239, 240
Cover, stove, 217, 218
Covering boards, 157, 158, 159, 160
Cradle, receiving/turning, 133, 134
Crane, masthead, 254, 255
Crosscut blade, 44, 45
Crosscut handsaw, 15
Crosscutting, precision, 83
Cut-off blade, 44, 45
Cut, plunge. *See* Plunge cut
Cutters, plug. *See* Plug cutters
Cutters, shaper, 58, 59, 60

D

Dado: plane, 17; set, 17, 73, 74; techniques, 16, 17, 50, 52, 53, 73, 74, 85, 96, 97, 121, 122, 195, 196, 235, 236
Dadoed butt joint, 121, 122
Dadoed door, vented, 195, 196
Dadoing, with router, 50, 52, 53; with saw, 16
Deadlights, 175, 176, 177
Deck, painting, 163
Deck coverings, 156, 157, 160, 161-163, 164. *See also* Canvas deck; Teak strip deck
Deck fastenings, 110
Deck fittings, 220-237
Deck flange, 156
Decking, 114
Deck oil, 115
Decks, 154-163
Decorative effects, 51
Deep-C clamps, 30
Deep-hole bits, 26
Deks Olje deck oil, 115
Depth stops, drill bit, 93
Design, cabin trunk, 165
Design, importance of, 5
Designer approval, alterations requiring, 9
Disc sander, 79; bench, 55, 87, 88
Dishracks, 211, 212
Doors, 74, 194, 195, 216; passage, 197, 198; raised-panel, 74; simple plywood, 196, 197; sliding, 216; vented, 195, 196
Doorskin laminate, 175
Dorade vents, 114, 227, 228
Double-iron plane, 23
Dovetail fixture, 50, 51, 191
Dovetail joints: blind, 130; butt, 122; corner, 130; dado, 122
Dowel centers, 123
Doweled butt joint, 123, 124
Drawers, 189-194
Drawknife, 36
Drifts, in rail, 241, 242
Drill bits, 25, 26, 27; breast, 24, 46; depth stops, 93; extended, 26, 27; Forstner, 25, 61; grinding, 27
Drilling metals, 62
Drill jigs, 92, 93
Drill press: accessories, 61, 62; stand, 46

Drills: electric, 46, 47; hand, 24, 25; push, 24; variable-speed, 46
Drop boards, 223, 224, 225
Drop-leaf table, 213, 214
Drum sanding, 79
Drying lumber, 112, 113
Dry rot, 115-117
Dynel fabric, 157

E

Edge molding, 52, 53, 55, 58, 59, 60, 72, 73, 74
Edges, decorative, 51
Electric tools: drills, 46, 47; handsaws, 43, 44; hand tools, 43-79; planes, 49, 50; sanders, 47-48, 49
"English pattern" screwdriver, 24
Epoxy, 110, 111, 112, 164
Expansion bits, 26
Extended twist drill bits, 26, 27

F

Fashion piece, 160
Fastenings, 108, 109, 110
Feather hold-down, 71, 72 (see also Comb hold-down); jointer, 57, 95
Fence: extension, 95; jointer, 57; rip, 94; shaper, 57, 58, 62
Ferrocement, 5
Fiberglass insulation, 205, 206
Fiddles, 9, 216, 217, 218
Files, 27; rat-tail, 27
Finger joint jig, 96, 97. See also Box joint
Finish sander, 47, 48
Firzite. See Sealers
Fittings, deck, 220-237
Fixture, dovetail, 50, 51, 130, 191
Flicka: spars, 6, 7; workmanship, 5
Foam: ice chest, 204, 205; insulation, 205, 206, 207; sanding blocks, 107, 108
Foam sandwich, 153
Folding table, 215
Fore-and-aft spars, 248, 257-263
Fore plane, 17
Forstner drill bits, 25, 61
Framing: deck, 149, 150-155; extension berth, 182, 183, 185; interior, 186-190, 191
Fun With a Saw (book), 76

G

Gaff jaws, 6
Gaffs, 6, 248, 255
Galleys, 186, 187-189
Gallows frame, 6
Gauges: beam socket, 151, 152; bevel, 15; hidden edge, 174; marking, 36; miter, 70, 71; spar, 259
Gilliom Manufacturing Co., power tool kits, 81, 82, 83
Gimbaled table, 213, 214
Glass, plastic window, 175, 176, 177
Glass scrapers, 38, 260

Glue block corner, 128
Glues, 73, 110, 111, 112. *See also* Adhesives; Epoxy
Gluing shelf, 53
Gougeon Brothers, 164
Grabrails, 7, 229
Gratings, teak, 8, 235-237
Grinders: bench, 54, 57; tool, 50, 54; wet, 54, 55
Grinding: jig, 97, 98, 99; plane iron, 21; twist drills, 27
Groove, blind, 128, 129
Guide: boring, 123, 124; honing, 22; square and rip, 91; square used as, 14
Guide bushings, router, 51

H

Hacksaw, 34, 35
Half-lap joint, 125, 126
Hammer, 12, 13
Hand drill, 24, 25
Handhold, 7 (*see also* grabrail); layout, 229
Handsaws, 15, 16, 17; electric, 43, 44
Hatch: double coaming, 7; lift, 225, 226, 227; seat, 232, 233; sliding, 8
Hatches, 220-227
Head, molding, 55, 74, 75
Head. See Toilets
Herringbone deck, 159, 163
Hewn mast, 262, 263
High-speed steel drill bits, 26, 62
Hinge gain, jig, 101, 102
Hinges, alignment of, 28, 29
Hold-downs: belt sander, 96; jointer, 95; table-saw, 71, 72. *See also* Comb; Feather
Hollow box spars, 245-257
Hollow-core masts, 261
Hollowing plane, 19
Holly strip sole, 145
Honing: guide, 22; plane iron, 22; power plane knives, 50
Hook, bench, 16, 97, 98

I

Ice chests, 203, 204, 205
Indentations, surface, 28
Instant vise, 100, 101
Insulation: carpet, 207; fiberglass, 205, 206; hull, 205, 206-207
Interior furnishings, 208-219
Interiors, 179-195
Irons, plane, 19, 70

J

Jack plane, 17, 19
Jaws, gaff, 6
Jennings bits, 25
Jigs: beam laminating, 148, 149; belt sander, 96; boring, 92; boring and spacing, 217, 218; box joint, 96, 97; camber, 103; dado spacing, 235, 236; dowel grooving, 124; drill guide, shelves, 92, 93; drill bit guide, 60; grinding, tool, 97, 98, 99; hinge gain, 101, 102; joint, half-lap, 102, 103;

271

laminated molding, 200, 201; mitered molding, 90; molding holding, 86; scarfing, 99, 100
Jigsaw, 45, 46
Joinery, amateur, 5-7
Jointer, 17, 56-57, 58
Jointer hold-down, 57, 95
Joints: box, 131, 196, 226, 228; box, jig, 96, 97; butt, 121; corner, 128, 129, 130; covering board, 158, 159, 160; deck beam, 151, 152; dovetail, 191; finger, 96, 97, 196 (*see also* Box joint); glued, 110, 111, 112; halved, 73, 102, 103; mitered, 124, 125; mortise, 73, 122, 123; plywood deck, 154, 155; rabbet, 19, 59, 245; scarf, 99, 100, 131, 132; spline, 127, 128, 172, 197, 198; tenon, 73, 122
Joint techniques, 120-132, 151, 152, 158, 159, 160, 172, 197, 198
Jointing: edge, 17; saw and dado set, 74
Jorgensen clamps, 32

K

Kerf, saw, 44
Keyhole saw, 15, 17
King plank, 162, 163
Kits, home-built tools, 69, 81-82, 83
Kitty, tool, 10, 11
Knees, 8; hanging and lodging, 154, 155; quarter, 242; stem, 242
Knives: molding head, 74; planer, 48, 49; shaper, 58, 59, 60

L

Ladder, companionway, 202, 203
Laid decks, 163, 164
Laminate, doorskin, 175
Laminated: beams, 173; knees, 154, 155; rail, 242, 243; spars, 261
Laminating, 148-149; bulkheads, 135, 136, 137; clamp, 171; epoxy, 80; mold, 104
Lap corner, 131
Lap joint, 125, 126
Layout, camber, 103, 104
Level, torpedo, 14
Lexan, 175. *See also* Windows
Lifting hull, 133, 134
Light screens, 230
Line level, 14
Lockers, 189, 190
Lofting bulwarks, 238-239, 240
Log-rail, 241, 242, 243
Louvers, 224, 225
Lumber: boat, 112, 113, 114; spar, 243, 244

M

Machine bits, 26
Magazines, boating, 4
Magnetic screwdriver, 24
Manufacturers, tool, 12
Marking gauge, 36
Marks, surface, 28

Masthead crane, 254, 255
Masts: hewn, 262, 263; hollow, 245-247, 254, 256, 257, 261. *See also* Spars
Medicine cabinet, 209, 214-216
Metals, drilling, 62
Miniature table saw, 41
Miter: box, 15, 16, 17; joints, 124, 125
Miter gauges, 70, 71, 87; shaper, 87
Mitering, 83, 85; jigs, 90, 95; moldings, 90, 91, 124
Mold: beam, 103, 104; laminating, 104
Molder-planer, 79, 80
Molding: deck, 162, 163; edge, 52, 53, 58, 59, 60; fastening, 109; head, 71, 74, 75; jig, 75, 86; mitering, 90, 91, 124; panel edge, 55; sawing, 16; techniques, 16, 52, 53, 58, 59, 60, 75, 86, 90, 91, 124, 196, 202, 220
Mortise-and-tenon joint, 122, 123
Mortise, cutting, 34, 35
Mortising, on drill press, 62, 63
Motors: appliance, 54, 68, 87, 89, 90; building mount, 89, 90; direct-drive, 68
Motors: speeds, 106, 107; pulleys, 106, 107

N

Nails: Anchorfast, 13, 109, 110, 175; bronze, 13; finish, 13; pulling, 13; ringed, 13; serrated, 13, 108, 109, 110
Nail set, 27, 28; using, 13
Nibbing, 157, 159

O

Ogee, shaping, 36
Oil, deck, 115
Oilstone, using, 21, 22
Opening, access, 8; trim, 186
Open-side planer-molder, 79, 80
Orbital sander, 47, 48

P

Painting deck, 163
Panels: wicker, 196; woven, 196
Panel saw, 44
Passage doors, 197, 198
Patterns: beam, 103, 104; bulwarks, 239, 240; cutting plywood, 45, 46; trunk side, 166, 167
Pentachlorophenol, 116
Phillips-head screwdriver, 23
Pilot berth, 181, 182
Pipe clamps, 32
Plane irons: grinding bevel, 22; honing, 21
Planer, with jointer, 56-57
Planer-molder, 79-80
Planers, 79-80; blades, 44, 45, 49, 50; blade sharpening, 50; corrugations, 37, 38, 55; double iron, 23; Emmerich Wood, 17; knives, 48, 49; rotary, 61, 62, 79; thickness, 79, 80
Planes: assembly of, 23; block, 17; bullnose, 19; care of, 20; dado, 19; electric, 49, 50; fore, 17; hollowing, 19; jack, 17, 19; jointer, 17, 18; power, 49, 50; rabbet, 17; scrub, 17, 19; smooth, 17; using, 20, 21; wooden, 17, 20, 104, 105
Planing, with jointer, 56-57, 58

Plans, choosing, 4
Plastic Resin. *See* Adhesives
Plexiglas, 175, 176
Plug boring bit, 25
Plug cutters, 37, 62
Plugs, 109, 110. *See also* Bungs
Plunge cut, 45
Plywood: cabin trunk, 169, 170, 171; deck, 154-156; doors, 196, 197; square, 44, 52, 53
Polishing: tool bevel edge, 22
Polypropylene fabric, 157. *See also* Vectra; Versatex
Portable tools: sanders, 47-48, 49; table saw, 93, 94, 95; vise, 32. *See also* Tools; Skilsaw
Ports, 175, 177
Power planes, 49, 50
Power tools: hand, 43-49; stationary, 54-80
Preservatives, wood, 116
Prick punch, 28, 29
Pulleys, 61, 107
Punch, prick, 28, 29
Push drill, 24
Pushers, 57, 58, 71, 72

R

Rabbet joint, 245
Rabbet plane, 17, 105
Rabbets, 19
Racks: bulkhead, 217, 218, 219; dish/utensil, 211, 212
Radial-arm saws, 75-79
Radial drill presses, 61
Rail: grab, 229; laminated, 242, 243
Rails, 238-243; caps, 242
Rail scarf, 131, 132, 242
Raised-panel door, 74
Rasp, 27
Rat-tail file, 27
Reciprocating sander, 47, 48
Rez. *See* Sealers
Roughing plane, 19
Router guide bushings, 51
Router-shaper, 50, 51, 85, 86, 87
Router techniques, 50, 53, 85, 86, 87, 99, 100, 102, 232, 254, 257
Routing: on drill press, 61; spars, 51, 52
Runners, hatch, 223, 224

S

Sabersaws, 45, 46
Sailing magazines, 4
Sanders, 47-48, 49, 55, 56, 79; belt, 48, 49; bench, 55, 56; disc, 55, 79. *See also* Finish sander; Orbital sander; Reciprocating sander; Straight-line sander
Sanding: belts, 48; block, 47; drum, 79
Sanding board, bench, 88
Sanding techniques, 48, 49, 56, 79, 88, 107, 108, 164
Sandpaper, 47
Sawing: concentric, 67; precision crosscut, 83; stack, 63, 67

Saws: hand, 15, 16, 17; panel, 44; radial-arm, 75-79; saber, 45, 46; scroll, 45. *See also* Skilsaw; Table saws
Scaffold, in-hull, 133, 134
Scarf, rail, 131, 132, 242
Scarffer, The, 146
Scarfing: jig, 99, 100, 250; techniques, 99, 100, 146, 250, 251, 252
Scrapers, 37-39; glass, 38, 260; sharpening, 38, 39
Screens, running light, 230
Screw-Mate bits, 28
Screwdriver attachment for drill, 47
Screwdrivers: "English pattern," 24; magnetic, 24; Phillips-head, 23; spiral, Yankee, 36
Scriber, camber, 103, 104, 165, 166
Scribing compass, 39, 40
Scroll saw, 45
Scrub plane, 17, 19
Sea berths, 181-182
Sealers (Firzite, Rez), 160, 205
Seat, helmsman's, 236, 237
Serrated nails, 13, 108, 109, 110
Shaper-router table, 50, 51, 85, 86, 87
Shapers, 58-59, 60; fence, 62; kit-built, 82, 83; techniques, 58-59, 60, 61, 127, 199
Shaping, drill press, 60, 61
Sharpening: blades, 50; plane, 21; saw, 16; scraper, 38, 39; tool, 50, 51, 54
Sheer batten, 145, 146
Sheer clamps, 151
Shelf, adjustable, 92, 93
Shelf routing and gluing, 52, 53
Shelves, 202
Ship's auger bits, 26
Shooting board, 97, 98
Skilsaw, 43
Skylights, 233, 234, 235
SLAT (Sliding Auxiliary Table), 83, 84, 85, 94, 95, 121, 124
Slick, 12, 33; trimming plugs, 37
Sliding Auxiliary Table. *See* SLAT
Slots, screwdriver, 24
Smooth plane, 17
Sole, cabin, 135, 136, 138-145; holly-strip, 144, 145
Solid spars, 257-263
Spade bits, 27, 61
Spar bench, 248, 252
Spars, 244-263; building, 69, 80; clamps, 249, 250, 252; lumber, 243, 244; sections, 245-247; taper layout, 246, 247; terms, 257, 258
Speeds, tool, 106, 107
Spiling compass, 39, 40
Spline joint, 124, 125, 127, 128, 197, 198
Splines, deck, 163
Spokeshave, 36
Spring clamps, 32
Sprung deck, 160
Squares: carpenter's, 14; cut-off guide, 91; try, 13, 14; plywood, 52, 53
Stability, 9
Stack sawing, 63, 67
Stanchions, bulwarks, 238, 240, 241
Stand, drill press, 46, 47
Standards, 106, 107, 179-182
Stanley Surform plane, 27, 28

Stationary power tools, 54-80
Sticking. *See* Drying lumber
Stop: bench, 97, 98; radial-arm saw, 101
Stop blocks, radial-arm saw, 77
Stop blocks and rods, table saw, 71
Stove cover, 217, 218
Straight-line sander, 47
Strip cabin trunk, 169, 172, 173
Strongback: beam, 150; cabin top, 165, 166, 167; deck, 152, 153
Strop, leather, 22
Surface marks, 28
Surform planes, 27, 28
Systems: cabin trunk, 169-173; stringer/beam, 174

T

T-88. *See* Adhesives
Tables, 212, 213-215; drop-leaf, 213, 214; folding, 215; gimbaled, 213, 214
Table saws, 67-75; alignment of, 69; blades, 69, 70; inexpensive, 93, 94, 95; kit-built, 69, 81, 82; miniature, 41; movable, 75
Taffrails, 242
Tape, pocket, 15
Teak strip deck, 164
Techniques: bandsaw, 66, 67, 221, 222; bending, 108; bunging, 109, 110; dado, 96, 97, 196, 235, 236; disc sander, 87, 88; dowel, 124; drawer, 194; gluing, 174, 175; jigsaw, 45, 46; jointer, 56-57, 58; mitering, 124; molding, 75, 127, 196, 201, 220; plugging, 109, 110; rabbet, 128; radial-arm saw, 76-79; router, 50, 53, 99, 100, 102, 122, 123, 132, 199, 254, 257; router-shaper, 158, 159; sander, 48, 49; sanding, 107, 108, 164; scarf, 158, 159, 250, 251, 252; shaper, 127, 199; wood, 112, 113
Templates, 45, 46
Terms, spar, 257, 258
Thiokol. *See* Adhesives
Tick stick, bulkhead, 135, 136
Toerails, 241-243

Toilets: forepeak, 208, 210; hidden, 209, 211; portable, 209, 210, 211
Tongue-and-groove joint, 126
Tool box, author's, 41
Tool catalogs, 12
Tools, basic hand, 10-29; list of, 11, 12; kit-built, 81-82, 83
Tools, hand: grinding, 50, 54; kitty, 10, 11; reversing, 107; selecting, 10-29; operating speeds, 106, 107; using, 12-29
Tools, power. *See* Electric tools
Transom berth, 180, 181, 185, 186
Trunk, cabin, 165-178; systems, 169-173
Tube, splitting, 220, 221, 223
Tumblehome, 50, 165, 166, 167
Turning hull, 133, 134
Twist drill bits, 26, 27

V

Variable-speed drills, 46
Vectra (cloth), 157, 174
Vents, Dorade, 114, 227, 228
Versatex (cloth), 157, 174
Vises: bench, 32, 33; instant, 100, 101; portable, 32; wedge-action, 41, 42

W

Wash basin, 209, 211
Weight, excessive, effects of, 9
WEST System, deck, 164
Whetting plane iron, 22
Wicker panel, 196
Windows, 175-177. *See also* Ports
Woodcraft Supply Co., 20
Wooden boatbuilding: publications on, 4, 5; lumber, 112, 113
Wooden planes, 20, 104, 105
Woodwork, amateur, 5-7
Woven panel, 196

SHOP NOTES

SHOP NOTES

SHOP NOTES

SHOP NOTES

SHOP NOTES

SHOP NOTES

SHOP NOTES

SHOP NOTES